CLYMER®
INDMAR
INBOARD SHOP MANUAL
GM V-8 ENGINES • 1983-2003

The World's Finest Publisher of Mechanical How-to Manuals

PRIMEDIA
Information Data Products

P.O. Box 12901, Overland Park, KS 66282-2901

Copyright ©2005 PRIMEDIA Business Magazines & Media Inc.

FIRST EDITION
First Printing September, 2005

Printed in U.S.A.

CLYMER and colophon are registered trademarks of PRIMEDIA Business Magazines & Media Inc.

ISBN: 0-89287-976-9

Library of Congress: 2005906130

AUTHOR: Mark Rolling.

TECHNICAL PHOTOGRAPY: Mark Rolling.

TECHNICAL ILLUSTRATIONS: Steve Amos.

WIRING DIAGRAMS: Bob Meyer, Lee Buell and Mark Rolling.

EDITORS: Clymer Staff.

PRODUCTION: Justin Marciniak.

CLYMER®

Publisher Shawn Etheridge

EDITORIAL

Managing Editor
James Grooms

Associate Editor
Lee Buell

Technical Writers
Jay Bogart
Jon Engleman
Michael Morlan
George Parise
Mark Rolling
Ed Scott
Ron Wright

Editorial Production Manager
Dylan Goodwin

Senior Production Editor
Greg Araujo

Production Editors
Holly Messinger
Darin Watson

Associate Production Editors
Susan Hartington
Julie Jantzer-Ward
Justin Marciniak

Technical Illustrators
Steve Amos
Errol McCarthy
Mitzi McCarthy
Bob Meyer

MARKETING/SALES AND ADMINISTRATION

Marketing Director
Rod Cain

Trade Show & Retention Marketing Manager
Elda Starke

Sales Channel & Brand Marketing Coordinator
Melissa Abbott Mudd

New Business Marketing Manager
Gabriele Udell

Art Directors
Jennifer Knight
Chris Paxton

Sales Managers
Justin Henton
Dutch Sadler
Matt Tusken

Business Manager
Ron Rogers

Customer Service Manager
Terri Cannon

Customer Service Representatives
Shawna Davis
Courtney Hollars
Susan Kohlmeyer
Jennifer Lassiter
April LeBlond

Warehouse & Inventory Manager
Leah Hicks

PRIMEDIA
Business Magazines & Media

P.O. Box 12901, Overland Park, KS 66282-2901 • 800-262-1954 • 913-967-1719

The following books and guides are published by PRIMEDIA Information Data Products.

More information available at *primediabooks.com*

Contents

Quick Reference Data

MODEL:_____ YEAR:_____

VIN NUMBER:_____

ENGINE SERIAL NUMBER:_____

CARBURETOR SERIAL NUMBER OR IDENTIFICATION MARK:_____

GENERAL ENGINE SPECIFICATIONS

Item	Specification
Firing order	
5.0L, 5.7L, 7.4L and 8.2L models	
Standard-rotation models	1-8-4-3-6-5-7-2
Counter-rotation models	1-2-7-5-6-3-4-8
8.1L models	1-8-7-2-6-5-4-3
Idle speed (NEUTRAL)	600-650 rpm
Ignition timing adjustment	10° BTDC
Minimum battery capacity	
Carburetor-equipped models	650 cold cranking amps (CCA)
Electronic fuel injection (EFI) models	750 cold cranking amps (CCA)
Breaker point gap	0.015 in. (0.38 mm)
Breaker point dwell	24-30°

SPARK PLUG RECOMMENDATIONS

Model	Spark plug No.	Spark plug gap
5.0L and 5.7L models		
With 12-bolt intake manifold		
AC plug	MR43T	0.035 in. (0.9 mm)
Champion plug	RV12YC	0.035 in. (0.9 mm)
NGK plug		
1983-1987	UR5	0.035 in. (0.9 mm)
1988-1997	BR6FS	0.035 in. (0.9 mm)
With 8-bolt intake manifold		
1998-2001		
AC plug	MR43LTS	0.045 in. (1.1 mm)
Champion plug	RS12YC	0.045 in. (1.1 mm)
NGK plug	BPR6EFS	0.045 in. (1.1 mm)
2002-2003		
AC plug	41-932	0.060 in. (1.5 mm)

(continued)

SPARK PLUG RECOMMENDATIONS (continued)

Model	Spark plug No.	Spark plug gap
7.4L and 8.2L models		
1983-1997		
AC plug	MR43T	0.035 in. (0.9 mm)
Champion plug	RV8C	0.035 in. (0.9 mm)
NGK plug	BR6FS	0.035 in. (0.9 mm)
1998-2000		
AC plug	MR43LTS	0.045 in. (1.1 mm)
NGK plug	BPR6EFS	0.045 in. (1.1 mm)
Champion plug	RS12YC	0.045 in. (1.1 mm)
8.1L models		
Nippon Denso plug	TJ14R-P15	0.060 in. (1.5 mm)

DIAGNOSTIC TROUBLE CODES (ALL EFI MODELS)

Code	Fault
12	Normal condition (diagnostic system is operational)
14	
MEFI 1 or MEFI 2 ECU	Engine temperature sensor (ECT) out of range
MEFI 3 or MEFI 4 ECU	Engine temperature sensor (ECT) reading too low
15	Engine temperature sensor (ECT) reading too high
21	
MEFI 1 or MEFI 2 ECU	Throttle position sensor (TPS) out of range
MEFI 3 or MEFI 4 ECU	Throttle position sensor (TPS) reading too high
22	Throttle position sensor (TPS) reading too low
23	Intake air temperature sensor (IAT) reading too low
25	Intake air temperature sensor (IAT) reading too high
33	
MEFI 1 or MEFI 2 ECU	Manifold air pressure (MAP) sensor out of range
MEFI 3 or MEFI 4 ECU	Manifold air pressure sensor (MAP) reading too high
34	Manifold air pressure sensor (MAP) reading too low
41	Open ignition control circuit
42	Shorted ignition control or bypass circuit
43	Incorrect knock sensor module voltage
44	Knock sensor not operating
51	Engine control unit (ECU) calibration failure
81	Fuel pump driver circuit failure
81	Injector driver circuit failure
81	Sensor reference voltage out of range

MAINTENANCE INTERVALS

Before each use	Check engine oil level
	Check transmission fluid level
	Check power steering fluid level*
	Check propeller for damage
	Check propeller shaft for bending
	Inspect steering system
	Check coolant level (closed cooling system)*
	Check emergency stop (lanyard) switch operation
After each use	Flush the cooling system
	Clean the engine
	Inspect the propeller for damage
	(continued)

MAINTENANCE INTERVALS (continued)

First 20 hours of operation	Change the engine oil and oil filter
	Change the transmission fluid
	Check power steering fluid level*
	Clean or replace primary fuel filter
	Adjust shift cable (refer to Chapter Five)
	Lubricate steering cable ram*
	Check drive belt tension (refer to Chapter Nine)
	Tighten hose clamps and engine mounts
Every 50 hours of operation	Check drive belt tension (refer to Chapter Nine)
	Clean flame arrestor
	Check rubber hoses for deterioration
Every 60 days or 50 hours of operation	Lubricate the steering cable ram*
Once a year or every 100 hours of operation	Change the engine oil and oil filter
	Change the transmission fluild
	Clean or replace primary fuel filter
	Check shift cable adjustment (refer to Chapter Five)
	Check engine alignment (refer to Chapter Six)
	Clean PCV valve*
	Clean and inspect spark plugs
	Replace breaker points and condenser*
Every two years or 200 hours of operation	Replace water pump impeller (refer to Chapter Eight)
	Change closed cooling system coolant*

*This maintenance item does not apply to all models.

ENGINE OIL CAPACITIES

Model	Approximate capacity	
5.0L and 5.7L models	5 qt. (4.7 L)	
7.4L and 8.2L models	7 qt. (6.6 L)	
8.1L models	9 qt. (8.5 L)	

TRANSMISSION FLUID CAPACITIES

Model	Approximate capacity	
Borg-Warner or Regal Beloit		
71C (inline transmission)	64 oz. (1.4 L)	
72C (V-drive transmission)	3.0 qt. (2.8 L)	
5000A series	2.5 qt. (2.4 L)	
5000V series	3.0 qt. (2.8 L)	
ZF Hurth		
360	47 oz. (1.4 L)	
450	2.0 qt. (1.8 L)	
630V	4.5 qt. (4.3 L)	
630A	3.25 qt. (3.1 L)	
800A	5.75 qt. (5.4 L)	
Walters V-drive		
RV-36	32 oz. (0.95 L)	

GENERAL TORQUE SPECIFICATIONS

Screw or nut size	in.-lb.	ft.-lb.	N•m
U.S. Standard			
6-32	9	–	1.0
8-32	20	–	2.3
10-24	30	–	3.4
10-32	35	–	4.0
12-24	45	–	5.1
1/4-20	70	–	7.9
1/4-28	84	–	9.5
5/16-18	160	13	18
5/16-24	168	14	19
3/8-16	–	23	31
3/8-24	–	25	34
7/16-14	–	36	49
7/16-20	–	40	54
1/2-13	–	50	68
1/2-20	–	60	81
Metric			
M5	36	–	4.0
M6	70	–	8.0
M8	156	13	18
M10	–	26	35
M12	–	35	48
M14	–	60	81

Chapter One

General Information

This detailed and comprehensive manual covers Indmar GM V-8 engines from 1983-2003.

This manual can be used by anyone from first-time do-it-yourselfers to professional mechanics. The manual provides step-by-step information on maintenance, tune-up, repair and overhaul. Hundreds of photos and drawings guide the reader through every job.

A shop manual is a reference that should be used to find information quickly. Clymer manuals are designed with this in mind. All chapters are thumb-tabbed, and important items are indexed at the end of the manual. All procedures, tables, photos and instructions in this manual are designed for the reader working on the machine or using the manual for the first time.

Keep the manual in a handy place such as a toolbox or in the boat. It will increase understanding of how the boat runs, lower repair and maintenance costs and generally increase enjoyment of the boat.

Frequently used specifications and capacities from individual chapters are summarized in *Quick Reference Data* at the front of the manual. Specifications concerning a specific system are included in the tables at the end of each chapter. **Tables 1-4** in this chapter list technical ab-

breviations, conversion tables, U.S. standard tap and drill sizes and metric tap and drill sizes. **Table 5** lists general torque specifications. **Tables 1-5** are at the end of this chapter.

MANUAL ORGANIZATION

All dimensions and capacities are expressed in U.S. standard and metric units of measure.

This chapter provides general information on shop safety, tool use, service fundamentals and shop supplies.

Chapter Two presents methods and suggestions for quick and accurate diagnoses of engine trouble. The troubleshooting procedures describe typical symptoms and provide logical troubleshooting methods.

Chapter Three explains all periodic lubrication and routine maintenance necessary to keep the inboard marine engine operating at peak efficiency. Chapter Three also includes all recommended tune-up procedures, which eliminate the need to refer to other chapters on the various systems.

Chapter Four describes preparing the inboard marine engine for storage. Preparation for operation after the lay-up period is also described in this chapter.

Chapter Five describes adjustments for the fuel, ignition and shifting systems.

Subsequent chapters describe specific systems and provide disassembly, repair and assembly procedures in step-by-step form.

Some of the procedures in this manual require special tools. When possible, the tool is illustrated in use. Well-equipped mechanics may substitute similar tools or fabricate a suitable replacement. However, in some cases, the specialized equipment or expertise may make it impractical for the home mechanic to attempt the procedure. When necessary, such operations are identified in the text with the recommendation to have a dealership or specialist perform the task. It may be less expensive to have a professional perform these jobs, especially when considering the cost of the equipment. This is true regarding machine work for engine rebuilds because machinists spend years perfecting their trade, and even professional mechanics often rely upon their services.

WARNINGS, CAUTIONS AND NOTES

The terms WARNING, CAUTION, and NOTE have specific meanings in this manual.

A WARNING emphasizes areas where personal injury or even death could result from negligence. Mechanical damage may also occur. WARNINGS *are to be taken seriously*.

A CAUTION emphasizes areas where equipment damage could occur. Disregarding a CAUTION could cause permanent mechanical damage; however, personal injury is unlikely.

A NOTE provides additional information to make a step or procedure easier or clearer. Disregarding a NOTE could cause inconvenience or misdiagnosis but would not cause damage or injury.

SAFETY

Professional mechanics can work for years and never sustain a serious injury. Follow these guidelines and practice common sense to safely service the inboard marine engine.

1. Do not operate the inboard marine engine in an enclosed area. The exhaust gasses contain carbon monoxide, an odorless, colorless, tasteless and poisonous gas. Carbon monoxide levels build quickly in small enclosed areas and can cause unconsciousness and death in a short time. Make sure to properly ventilate the work area or operate the inboard marine engine outside.

2. *Never* use gasoline or any extremely flammable liquid to clean parts. Refer to *Cleaning Parts* and *Handling Gasoline Safely* in this chapter.

3. *Never* smoke or use a torch in the vicinity of flammable liquids such as gasoline or cleaning solvent.

4. After removing the engine cover, allow the engine to air out before performing any service work.

5. Use the correct type and size of tools to avoid damaging fasteners.

6. Keep tools clean and in good condition. Replace or repair worn or damaged equipment.

7. When loosening a tight or stuck fastener, always consider what would happen if the wrench should slip. In most cases, it is safer to pull on a wrench or ratchet than it is to push on it. Be careful; protect yourself accordingly.

8. When replacing a fastener, make sure to use one with the same measurements, material and strength as the old one. Refer to *Fasteners* in this chapter for additional information.

9. Keep the work area clean and uncluttered. Keep all hand and power tools in good condition. Clean grease or oil from tools after using them. Unkept tools are difficult to hold and cause injury. Replace or repair worn or damaged tools. Do not leave tools, shop rags or anything that does not belong in the hull.

10. Wear safety goggles during all operations involving drilling, grinding or the use of a cold chisel or *anytime* eye safety is in question (when debris may spray or scatter). *Always* wear safety goggles when using solvent or compressed air.

11. Do not carry sharp tools in clothing pockets.

12. Always have an approved fire extinguisher available. Make sure it is rated for gasoline (Class B) and electric (Class C) fires. Read and fully understand the operating instructions for the fire extinguisher before beginning the work.

13. Do not use compressed air to clean clothes, the boat/engine or the work area. Debris might blow into eyes or skin. *Never* direct compressed air at anyone. Do not allow children to use or play with any compressed air equipment.

14. When using compressed air to dry rotating parts, hold the part so that it cannot rotate. The air jet is capable or rotating the parts at extremely high speed. The part can become damaged or disintegrate and cause serious injury.

Handling Gasoline Safely

Gasoline is a volatile flammable liquid and is one of the most dangerous items in the shop.

Because gasoline is used so often, many people forget that it is hazardous. Only use gasoline as fuel for gasoline internal combustion engines. Do not use it as a cleaner or degreaser. When working, keep in mind gasoline is always present in the fuel tank, fuel lines and carburetor or fuel rail. To avoid a disastrous accident when working around the fuel system, carefully observe the following precautions.

1. *Never* use gasoline to clean parts. Refer to *Cleaning Parts* in this chapter.

2. When working on the fuel system, work outside or in a well-ventilated area.

3. Do not add fuel to the tank or service the fuel system while near open flames, sparks or where someone is smoking. Gasoline vapor is heavier than air. It collects in low areas and is more easily ignitable than liquid gasoline.

4. Allow the engine to cool completely before working on any fuel system component.

5. When draining the carburetor, fuel rail or fuel lines, catch the fuel in a suitable plastic container. Then pour it into an approved gasoline storage device.

6. Do not store gasoline in a glass container. If the glass breaks, a serious explosion or fire can occur.

7. Immediately wipe up spilled gasoline with suitable shop towels. Store the towels in a metal container with a lid until they can be properly disposed of, or place them outside in a safe place so the fuel can evaporate.

8. Do not pour water onto a gasoline fire. Water spreads the fire and makes it more difficult to extinguish. Use a class B, BC or ABC fire extinguisher to extinguish the fire.

9. Always turn off the engine before refueling. Do not spill fuel onto the engine components. Do not overfill the fuel tank. Leave an air space at the top of the tank to allow for expansion should the temperature of the fuel increase.

Cleaning Parts

Cleaning parts is one the more tedious and difficult service jobs performed in the home garage. There are many types of chemical cleaners and solvents available for shop use. Most are poisonous and extremely flammable. To prevent chemical exposure, vapor buildup, fire and serious injury, observe each product warning label and note the following:

1. Read the entire product label before using any chemical. Always know what type of chemical is being used and whether it is poisonous and/or flammable.

2. Do not use more than one type of cleaning solvent at a time. If mixing chemicals is necessary, measure the proper amounts according to the manufacturer.

3. Work in a well-ventilated area.

4. Wear chemical-resistant gloves.

5. Wear safety glasses.

6. Wear a vapor respirator if the instructions call for it.

7. Wash hands and arms thoroughly after cleaning parts.

8. Keep chemical products away from children and pets.

9. Thoroughly clean all oil, grease and cleaner residue from any parts that must be heated.

10. Use a nylon brush when cleaning parts. Metal brushes can cause a spark.

11. When using a parts washer, use only the solvent recommended by the equipment manufacturer. Make sure the parts washer is equipped with a metal lid that lowers if a fire occurs.

MODEL IDENTIFICATION

Before servicing or troubleshooting the engine, verify the model name and serial number of the engine and transmission. It is absolutely essential that the unit be correctly identified before performing any service on the engine. In many cases, service specifications vary by model, type of fuel system and type of transmission.

The engine serial number is located in one of three locations. On most models, the serial number is stamped (**Figure 1**) into the flat surface of the engine near the flywheel housing mating surface. On other models, the serial number is stamped into the flat surface of the block near the mechanical fuel pump mounting surface. On late models, the serial number and model name are printed on a decal (**Figure 2**) affixed to the side of the oil pan. On early models, the model name is printed on a decal affixed to the flame arrestor cover. On models using an inline transmission (**Figure 3**), the serial number is located on the starboard side of the engine. On models with a V-drive transmission (**Figure 4**), the engine faces the stern or rear of the boat so the serial number is located on the port side

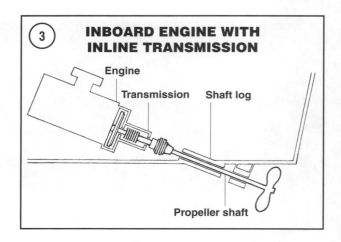

of the engine. The transmission identification tag (**Figure 5**) is affixed to the transmission housing.

NOTE
The manufacturer might make changes during a model year; therfore, when ordering parts, always order by boat manufacturer and model name, engine model name and engine serial number. For reference, record the serial number in the Quick Reference Data (QRD) section at the front of the manual. Compare new parts with old before purchasing them. If the parts are not alike, have the parts manager explain the difference and verify compatibility before installing the part.

ENGINE OPERATION

All marine engines, whether two- or four-stroke, gasoline or diesel, operate on the Otto cycle of intake, compression, power and exhaust phases. The models covered in this manual are a four-stroke design. **Figure 6** shows typical four-stroke gasoline engine operation.

FASTENERS

Proper fastener selection and installation is important to make sure that the engine operates as designed. The choice of original equipment fasteners is not arrived at by chance. Make sure replacement fasteners meet all of the same requirements as the originals.

CAUTION
Inboard marine engines commonly use fasteners made of stainless steel or other corrosion-resistant material. Never install a common steel fastener in a water-exposed location. The fastener will corrode and fail

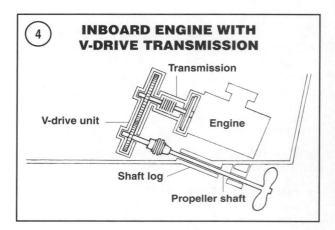

and cause damage or loss of engine components.

Threaded Fasteners

Threaded fasteners secure most of the components on the boat and engine. Most are tightened by turning them

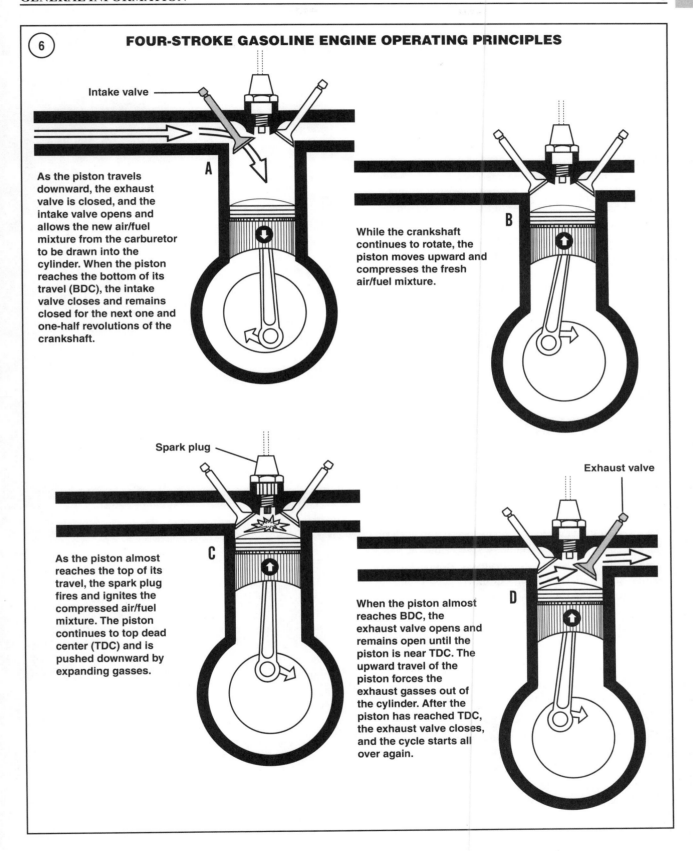

FOUR-STROKE GASOLINE ENGINE OPERATING PRINCIPLES

Intake valve

As the piston travels downward, the exhaust valve is closed, and the intake valve opens and allows the new air/fuel mixture from the carburetor to be drawn into the cylinder. When the piston reaches the bottom of its travel (BDC), the intake valve closes and remains closed for the next one and one-half revolutions of the crankshaft.

While the crankshaft continues to rotate, the piston moves upward and compresses the fresh air/fuel mixture.

Spark plug

Exhaust valve

As the piston almost reaches the top of its travel, the spark plug fires and ignites the compressed air/fuel mixture. The piston continues to top dead center (TDC) and is pushed downward by expanding gasses.

When the piston almost reaches BDC, the exhaust valve opens and remains open until the piston is near TDC. The upward travel of the piston forces the exhaust gasses out of the cylinder. After the piston has reached TDC, the exhaust valve closes, and the cycle starts all over again.

clockwise (meaning they have right-hand threads). If the normal rotation of a particular component would tend to loosen a normal right-hand threaded fastener, a fastener with left-hand threads may be used to secure the component. Then, the normal rotation of the component would tend to tighten the fastener, thereby preventing it from loosening. Fasteners with left-hand threads must be turned counterclockwise to tighten. When a fastener with left-hand threads is used, it is noted in the manual.

Nuts, bolts and screws are manufactured in a wide range of thread patterns. To join a nut and bolt, the diameter of the bolt and the diameter of the hole in the nut must be the same, and the threads must match.

The best way to determine whether the threads of two fasteners match is to turn the nut on the bolt (or the bolt into the threaded hole in a piece of equipment) with fingers only. Make sure both pieces are clean; remove Loctite or other sealant from the threads if present. If force is required, check the thread condition on each fastener. If the thread condition is good but the fasteners jam, the threads are not compatible. A thread pitch gauge (**Figure 7**) can also be used to determine pitch.

> *NOTE*
> *To make sure the fastener threads are not mismatched or cross-threaded, start all fasteners by hand. If a fastener is hard to start or turn, determine the cause before tightening it with a wrench.*

Two dimensions are required to match the thread size of the fastener: the number of threads in a given distance and the outside diameter of the threads.

Two systems are currently used to specify threaded fastener dimensions: the U.S. standard system and the metric system. Although fasteners might appear similar, close inspection shows that the thread designs are not the same (**Figure 8**). Pay particular attention when working with unidentified fasteners; mismatching thread types can damage threads.

> *NOTE*
> *Indmar marine engines use both U.S. standard and International Organization for Standardization (ISO) metric fasteners.*

U.S. standard fasteners are sorted by grades (hardness/strength). Bolt heads are marked to represent different grades; no marks mean the bolt is grade zero, two marks equal grade two, three marks equal grade five, four marks equal grade six, five marks equal grade seven, and six marks equal grade eight. It is important when replacing fasteners to make sure the replacements are of equal or greater strength than the original.

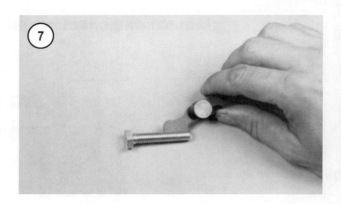

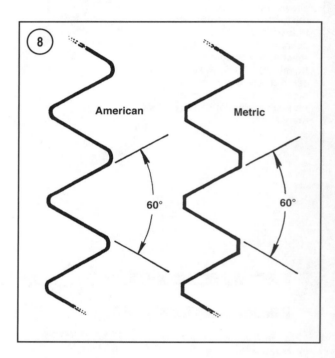

U.S. standard fasteners are generally available in two pitches: coarse and fine. Coarsely threaded fasteners have fewer threads per inch than finely threaded fasteners. They are normally referred to by size such as 1/2-16 or 3/8-24. In these examples, the first number, 1/2 or 3/8, represents the bolt diameter. The second number represents the number of threads per inch (16 or 24 in this example).

International Organization for Standardization (ISO) metric threads are available in three standard thread sizes: coarse, fine and constant pitch. The ISO coarse pitch is used for most common fastener applications. The fine-pitch thread is used on certain precision tools and instruments. The constant pitch thread is used mainly on machine parts and not for fasteners. The constant pitch thread, however, is used on all metric-thread spark plugs.

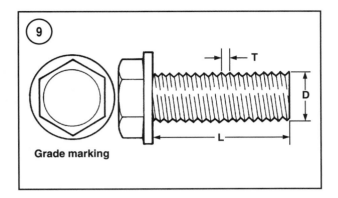

Grade marking

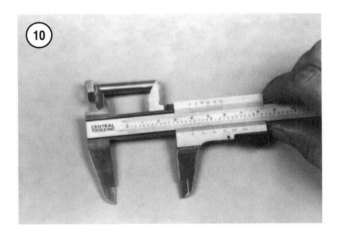

The measurement across two flats on a nut or bolt indicates the wrench size necessary to turn the fastener.

> *CAUTION*
> *Do not install fasteners with a strength classification lower than what was originally installed by the manufacturer. Doing so may cause equipment failure and/or damage.*

Torque Specification

The material used during the manufacturing of the engine might be subjected to uneven stresses if the fasteners of the various subassemblies are not installed and tightened correctly. Fasteners that are improperly installed or work loose can cause extensive damage. It is essential to use an accurate torque wrench, described in this chapter, with the torque specifications in this manual. If a torque is not listed, use the general torque specification in **Table 5** of this chapter.

Specifications for torque are provided in foot-pounds (ft.-lb.), inch-pounds (in.-lb.) and Newton-meters (N•m). Torque specifications for specific components (including all critical torque figures) are at the ends of the appropriate chapters. Torque wrenches are covered in the *Basic Tools* section.

Self-Locking Fasteners

Several types of bolts, screws and nuts incorporate a system that creates interference to prevent loosening. Interference is achieved in various ways. The most common type is the nylon insert nut and a dry adhesive coating on the threads of a bolt.

Compared to standard fasteners, self-locking fasteners offer greater holding strength, which improves their resistance to vibration. Most self-locking fasteners cannot be reused because the material used to form the lock becomes distorted after the initial installation and removal. It is a good practice to discard and replace self-locking fasteners after removal. Do not replace self-locking fasteners with standard fasteners.

Washers

There are two basic types of washers: flat washers and lockwashers. Flat washers are simple discs with a hole to fit a screw or bolt. Lockwashers prevent a fastener from working loose. Washers can be used as spacers and seals or to help distribute fastener load and to prevent the fastener from damaging the component.

The length (L, **Figure 9**), diameter (D) and distance between thread crests (pitch) (T) is used to classify metric fasteners. The numbers 8—1.25 × 130 typically identify a bolt with a diameter of 8 mm, 1.25 mm between thread crests and a length of 130 mm.

> *NOTE*
> *When purchasing a bolt, it is important to know how to specify bolt length. The correct way to determine bolt length is to measure the length, starting underneath the bolt head to the end of the bolt (Figure 10). Always measure bolt length in this manner to avoid purchasing or installing bolts that are too long.*

The grade mark located on the top of the fastener (**Figure 9**) indicates the strength of metric screws and bolts. The higher the number, the stronger the fastener. Unnumbered fasteners are the weakest.

Many screws, bolts and studs are combined with nuts to secure particular components. To indicate the size of a nut, manufacturers specify the internal diameter and the thread pitch.

As with fasteners, when replacing washers, make sure the replacement washers are the same design and quality as those originally installed by the manufacturer.

NOTE
Give as much care to the selection and purchase of washers as given to other fasteners. Avoid washers that are made of thin and weak material. These will deform and crush the first time they are used in a high torque application and allow the nut or bolt to loosen.

Cotter Pins

A cotter pin is a split metal pin inserted into a hole or slot to prevent a fastener from loosening. In certain applications, the fastener must be secured in this way. For these applications, a cotter pin and castellated (slotted) nut are used.

To use a cotter pin, first make sure the diameter is correct for the hole in the fastener. After correctly tightening the fastener and aligning the holes, insert the cotter pin through the hole and bend the ends over the fastener (**Figure 11**). Cut the ends to a suitable length to prevent them from snagging on clothing or, worse, skin; remember that exposed ends of the pin cut flesh easily. When the cotter pin is bent and the ends are cut to length, it must be tight. If it can be wiggled, it is improperly installed.

Unless instructed to do so, never loosen a fastener to align the holes. If the holes do not align, tighten the fastener just enough to achieve alignment.

Cotter pins are available in various diameters and lengths. Measure length from the bottom of the head to the tip of the shorter end.

Do not reuse cotter pins because the ends can break and cause the pin to fall out and allow the fastener to loosen.

Snap Rings

Snap rings (**Figure 12**) are circular metal retaining clips. They help secure in place parts such as shafts, pins, gears or rods. In some applications, in addition to securing components, snap rings of varying thicknesses determine end play. These are usually called selective snap rings.

There are two basic types of snap rings: machined and stamped snap rings. Machined snap rings (**Figure 13**) can be installed in either direction because both faces have sharp edges. Stamped snap rings (**Figure 14**) have a sharp and a round edge. When installing a stamped snap ring in

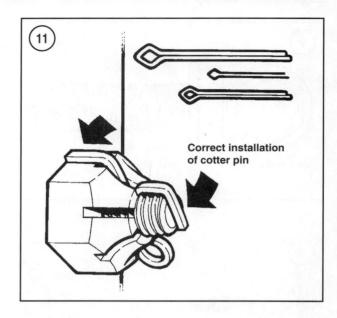

Correct installation of cotter pin

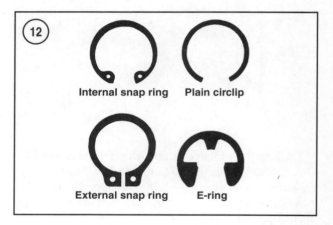

Internal snap ring   Plain circlip

External snap ring   E-ring

a thrust application, install the sharp edge facing away from the part producing the thrust.

Observe the following when installing snap rings:

1. Remove and install snap rings using snap ring pliers. Refer to *Snap Ring Pliers* in this chapter.

2. In some applications, it might be necessary to replace snap rings after removing them.

3. Compress or expand snap rings only enough to install them. If overly expanded or compressed, they lose their retaining ability.

4. After installing a snap ring, make sure it seats completely.

5. Wear eye protection when removing or installing snap rings.

E-rings and circlips (**Figure 12**) are used when it is not practical to use a snap ring. Remove E-rings by prying be-

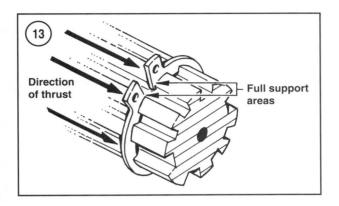

Direction of thrust — Full support areas

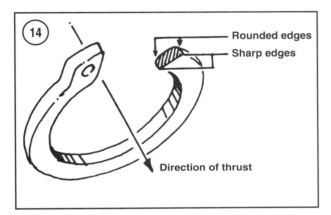

Rounded edges — Sharp edges — Direction of thrust

tween the shaft and E-ring. To install an E-ring, center it over the shaft groove and push or tap it into place.

SHOP SUPPLIES

Lubricants and Fluids

Periodic lubrication helps ensure long life for any type of equipment. The *type* of lubricant used is just as important as the lubrication service itself, though in an emer-gency, the wrong type of lubricant is usually better than no lubricant at all. The following information describes the types of lubricants most often used on marine equipment. Be sure to follow the manufacturer's recommendation for lubricant types.

Generally, all liquid lubricants are called *oil*. They may be mineral-based (including petroleum bases), natural-based (vegetable and animal bases), synthetic-based or emulsions (mixtures). *Grease* is oil to which a thickening base was added so that the end product is semi-solid. Grease is often classified by the type of thickener added; lithium soap is commonly used.

Four-Stroke Engine Oil

Four-stroke oil for motorcycle, marine and automotive engines is classified by the American Petroleum Institute (API) and the Society of Automotive Engineers (SAE) in several categories. Oil containers display these classifications on the top or label (**Figure 15**).

The API oil classification is indicated by letters; oils for gasoline engines are identified by an *S*.

Viscosity is an indication of the oil thickness. The SAE uses numbers to indicate viscosity. Thin oils have low numbers, and thick oils have high numbers. A *W* after the number indicates that the viscosity testing was done at low temperature to simulate cold-weather operation. Four-stroke engine oils typically fall into the 5W-30 and 20W-50 range.

Multigrade oils (for example 10W-40) are less viscous (thinner) and flow well at low temperatures. This allows the oil to perform efficiently across at wide range of engine operating conditions. The lower the number, the better the engine will start in cold climates. Higher numbers are usually recommended for engine operation in hot weather conditions. To help ensure the best performance and durability, use only the recommended oil grade and viscosity as described in Chapter Three.

Transmission Lubricant

Transmission fluid is a specialized lubricant that provides protection against wear of moving or sliding components and serves as the operating fluid for the transmission's hydraulic control systems. Transmission fluid is available in two types; Type A (Dexron III) and Type F. These fluids contain different ingredients and are not generally compatible. However, some transmissions can use either type of fluid. Transmission fluid recommendations are described in Chapter Three.

Grease

Grease is lubricating oil with thickening agents added to it. The National Lubricating Grease Institute (NLGI) grades grease. Grades range from No. 000 to No. 6, with No. 6 being the thickest. Typical multipurpose grease is NLGI No. 2. For specific applications, manufacturers might recommend water-resistant grease or one with an additive such as molybdenum disulfide (MoS_2).

Cleaners, Degreasers and Solvents

Many chemicals are available to remove oil, grease and other residue.

Before using cleaning solvents, consider how they will be used and disposed of, particularly if they are not water-soluble. Local ordinances might require special procedures for disposal of many types of cleaning chemicals. Refer to *Safety* and *Cleaning Parts* in this chapter for more information on solvent use.

Use electrical contact cleaner to clean wiring connections and components without leaving any residue. Carburetor cleaner is a powerful solvent used to remove fuel deposits and varnish from fuel system components. Use this cleaner carefully because it can damage finishes.

Generally, degreasers are strong cleaners used to remove heavy accumulations of grease from engine and drive components.

Most solvents are used in a parts-washing cabinet for individual component cleaning. For safety, use only non-flammable or high-flash point solvents.

Gasket Sealant

Sealants are used with a gasket or seal and are occasionally used alone. Follow the manufacturer's recommendation when using sealants. Use extreme care when choosing a sealant different from the type originally recommended. Choose sealants based on resistance to heat and various fluids as well as sealing capabilities.

One of the most common sealants is RTV, or room-temperature vulcanizing sealant. This sealant cures at room temperature over a specific time period. This allows the repositioning of components without damaging gaskets.

Moisture in the air causes RTV sealant to cure. Always install the tube cap as soon as possible after applying RTV sealant. RTV sealant has a limited shelf life and does not cure properly if the shelf life has expired. Keep partial tubes sealed and discard them if they have surpassed the expiration date.

Applying RTV sealant

Clean all old gasket residue from the mating surfaces. Remove all gasket material from blind threaded holes; it can cause inaccurate bolt torque. Spray the mating surfaces with aerosol parts cleaner and then wipe dry with a lint-free cloth. The area must be clean and dry for the sealant to adhere.

Apply RTV sealant in a continuous bead 0.08-0.12 in. (2-3 mm) thick. Circle the fastener holes unless otherwise specified. Do not allow any sealant to enter these holes. Assemble and tighten the fasteners to the specified torque within the time frame recommended by the RTV manufacturer (usually within 10-15 minutes).

Gasket Remover

Aerosol gasket remover can help remove stubborn gasket material and prevent damage to the mating surfaces that can be caused by using a scraping tool. Most of these products are very caustic. Follow the manufacturer's instructions.

Threadlocking Compound

Threadlocking compound is a fluid applied to the threads of fasteners. After tightening the fastener, the fluid dries and hardens to become a solid filler between the threads. This makes it difficult for the fastener to work loose from vibration or heat expansion and contraction. Some threadlocking compounds also provide a seal against fluid leaks.

Before applying threadlocking compound, remove any old compound from both thread areas and clean them with aerosol parts cleaner. Use the compound sparingly. Excess fluid can run into adjoining parts.

Threadlocking compounds come in different strengths. Follow the manufacturer's recommendations regarding compound selection. Two manufacturers of threadlocking compound are ThreeBond and Loctite, which offer a wide range of compounds for various strength, temperature and repair applications.

Applying threadlocking compound

Make sure all surfaces are clean. If threadlocking compound was previously applied to the component, remove this residue.

Shake the container thoroughly and apply the compound to both parts. Then assemble the parts and tighten the fasteners.

GALVANIC CORROSION

A chemical reaction occurs whenever two different types of metal are joined by an electrical conductor and immersed in an electrolytic solution such as water. Electrons transfer from one component to the other through the electrolyte and return to the conductor.

The hardware on a boat is made of many different types of metal. The boat hull acts as a conductor between the metals. Even if the hull is wooden or fiberglass, the slightest film of water on the hull provides conductivity by acting as the electrolyte. This combination creates a good environment for electron flow. Unfortunately, this electron flow results in galvanic corrosion of the metal involved and causes one of the metals to be corroded or eroded. The amount of electron flow and, therefore, the amount of corrosion depend on several factors:

1. The types of metal involved.
2. The efficiency of the conductor.
3. The strength of the electrolyte.

Metals

The chemical composition of the metal used in marine equipment has a significant effect on the amount and speed of galvanic corrosion. Certain metals are more resistant to corrosion than others. These electrically negative metals are commonly called *noble*; they act as the cathode in any reaction. Metals that are more subject to corrosion are electrically positive; they act as the anode in a reaction. The more noble metals include titanium, 18-8 stainless steel and nickel. Less noble metals include zinc, aluminum and magnesium. Galvanic corrosion becomes more excessive as the difference in electrical potential between the two metals increases.

In some cases, galvanic corrosion can occur within a single piece of metal. For example, brass is a mixture of zinc and copper, and when immersed in an electrolyte, the zinc portion of the mixture will corrode away as a galvanic reaction occurs between the zinc and copper particles.

Conductors

The hull of the boat often acts as the conductor between different types of metal. Marine equipment such as the propeller shaft and shaft strut are also efficient conductors. Large masses of metal, firmly connected together, are more efficient conductors than water. Rubber mountings and vinyl-based paint can act as insulators between pieces of metal.

Electrolyte

The water in which a boat operates acts as the electrolyte for the corrosion process. The more efficient the conductor is, the more excessive and rapid the corrosion will be.

Cold, clean freshwater is the poorest conductor. Pollutants increase conductivity; therefore, brackish or saltwater is a more efficient electrolyte. This is one of the reasons that most manufacturers recommend a freshwater flush after operating in polluted, brackish or saltwater.

Protection from Galvanic Corrosion

Because of the environment in which marine equipment must operate, it is practically impossible to totally prevent galvanic corrosion. However, there are several ways by which the process can be slowed. After taking the precautions, the next step is to cause the process to occur only in certain places. This is the role of sacrificial anodes and impressed current systems.

Slowing corrosion

Some simple precautions can help reduce the amount of corrosion taking place outside the hull. These precautions are not substitutes for the corrosion protection methods discussed in *Sacrificial Anodes* and *Impressed Current Systems* in this chapter, but they can help these methods reduce corrosion.

Use fasteners made of a material more noble than the parts they secure. If corrosion occurs, the parts they secure may suffer but the fasteners are protected. The larger secured parts are better able to withstand the loss of material. Also, major problems could arise if the fasteners corrode to the point of failure.

Keep all painted surfaces in good condition. If paint is scraped off and bare metal is exposed, corrosion rapidly increases. Use vinyl- or plastic-based paint, which acts as an electrical insulator.

Be careful when applying metal-based antifouling paint to the boat. Do not apply antifouling paint to metal parts of the propeller shaft and support strut. If applied to metal surfaces, this type of paint reacts with the metal and results in corrosion between the metal and the layer of paint. Maintain a minimum of 1.0 in. (25.0 mm) border between the painted surfaces and any metal parts. Organic-based paints are available for use on metal surfaces.

Where a corrosion protection device is used, remember that it must be immersed in the electrolyte along with the boat to provide any protection. Never paint or apply any coating to anodes or other protection devices. Paint or other coatings insulate them from the corrosion process.

Any change in boat equipment, such as the installation of a new stainless steel propeller, changes the electrical potential and may cause increased corrosion. Always consider this fact when adding equipment or changing exposed materials. Install additional anodes or other protection equipment as required to make sure the corrosion protection system is up to the task. The expense to repair corrosion damage usually far exceeds that of additional corrosion protection.

Sacrificial anodes

Sacrificial anodes are specially designed to do nothing but corrode. Properly fastening such pieces to the boat causes them to act as an anode in any galvanic reaction that occurs; any other metal in the reaction acts as a cathode and is not damaged.

Anodes are usually made of zinc or with an aluminum and indium alloy. This alloy is less noble than the aluminum alloy in the drive system components and provides the desired sacrificial properties. In addition, the aluminum and indium alloy is more resistant to oxide coating than zinc anodes. Oxide coating occurs as the anode material reacts with oxygen in the water. An oxide coating insulates the anode and dramatically reduces corrosion protection.

Anodes must be used properly to be effective. Simply fastening anodes to the boat in random locations does not do the job.

First determine how much anode surface is required to adequately protect the equipment surface area. A good starting point is provided by the military specification MIL-A-818001, which states that 1 sq. in. of new anode protects:

1. 800 sq. in. of freshly painted stainless steel.
2. 250 sq. in. of bare steel or bare aluminum alloy.
3. 100 sq. in. of copper or copper alloy.

This rule is valid for a boat at rest. When underway, additional anode area is required to protect the same surface area.

The anode must be in good electrical contact with the metal that it protects.

Quality anodes have inserts located around fastener holes that are made of a more noble material. Otherwise, the anode can erode away around the fastener hole and allow the anode to loosen or possibly fall off, thereby losing needed protection.

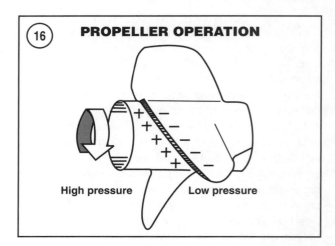

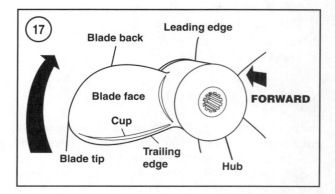

Impressed current systems

An impressed current system can be added to any boat. The system generally consists of an anode, controller and reference electrode. The anode in this system is coated with a very noble material, such as platinum, so that it is very corrosion-resistant and can last almost indefinitely. Under the boat waterline, the reference electrode allows the controller to monitor the current in the water for any indication of galvanic corrosion. If the controller senses current associated with galvanic corrosion, it applies positive battery voltage to the anode. Current then flows from the anode to all other metal components, regardless of how noble these components may be. Essentially, the electrical current from the battery counteracts the galvanic reaction to dramatically reduce corrosion damage.

Only a small amount of current is needed to counteract corrosion. Using input from the reference electrode, the controller provides only the amount of current needed to suppress galvanic corrosion. Most systems consume a maximum of 0.2 A•h at full demand. Under normal conditions, these systems can provide protection for 8-12

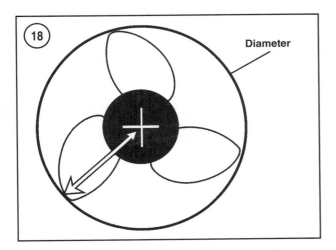

weeks without recharging the battery. Remember that this system must have a constant connection to the battery. Often, the battery supply to the system is connected to a battery switching device causing the operator to inadvertently shut off the system while docked.

An impressed current system is more expensive to install than sacrificial anodes, but considering the low maintenance requirements and the superior protection it provides, the long-term cost might be lower.

PROPELLERS

The propeller is the final link between the boat drive system and the water. A perfectly maintained engine and hull are useless if the propeller is the wrong type, worn or damaged. Although propeller selection for a specific application is beyond the scope of this manual, the following provides the basic information needed to make an informed decision. A professional at a reputable marine dealership is the best source for a propeller recommendation.

How a Propeller Works

As the curved blades of a propeller rotate through the water, a high-pressure area forms on one side of the blade, and a low-pressure area forms on the other side of the blade (**Figure 16**). The propeller moves toward the low-pressure area and carries the boat with it.

Propeller Parts

Although a propeller is usually a one-piece unit, it is made of several different parts (**Figure 17**). Variations in

the design of these parts make different propellers suitable for different applications.

The blade tip is the point of the blade farthest from the center of the propeller shaft bore. The blade tip separates the leading edge from the trailing edge.

The leading edge is the edge of the blade closest to the front of the boat. During forward operation, this is the area of the blade that first cuts through the water.

The trailing edge is the surface of the blade farthest from the boat. In reverse, this is the area of the blade that first cuts through the water.

The blade face is the surface of the blade that faces away from the boat. During forward operation, high-pressure forms on this side of the blade.

The blade back is the surface of the blade that faces toward the boat. During forward gear operation, low-pressure forms on this side of the blade.

The cup is a small curve or lip on the trailing edge of the blade. Cupped propeller blades generally perform better than noncupped propeller blades.

The hub is the center portion of the propeller. It connects the blades to the propeller shaft.

Propeller Design

Changes in length, angle, thickness and the material the propeller is made of make different propellers suitable for different applications.

Diameter

Propeller diameter is the distance from the center of the hub or propeller shaft to the blade tip multiplied by two. Essentially, it is the diameter of a circle formed by the blade tips during propeller rotation (**Figure 18**).

Pitch and rake

Propeller pitch and rake describe the placement of the blades in relation to the propeller hub (**Figure 19**). Pitch describes the theoretical distance the propeller would travel in one revolution. In A, **Figure 20**, the propeller would travel 10 in. (25.4 cm) in one revolution. In B, **Figure 20**, the propeller would travel 20 in. (50.8 cm) in one revolution. This distance is only theoretical during typical operation because the propeller achieves only 75-85 percent of the pitch. Slip rate describes the difference in actual travel relative to the pitch. Lighter, faster boats typically achieve a lower slip rate than heavier, slower boats.

Propeller blades can be constructed with constant pitch (**Figure 21**) or progressive pitch (**Figure 22**). On a progressive pitch propeller, the pitch starts low at the leading edge and increases toward the trailing edge. The propeller pitch specification is the average of the pitch across the entire blade. Propellers with progressive pitch usually provide better overall performance than constant pitch propellers. Constant pitch propellers are generally better suited for heavier, slower boats.

Blade rake is specified in degrees and is measured along a line from the center of the hub to the blade tip. A blade that is perpendicular to the hub (A, **Figure 23**) has 0° rake. A blade that is angled from perpendicular (B, **Figure 23**) has a rake expressed by its difference from perpendicular. Most propellers have rakes ranging from 0-20°. Lighter, faster boats generally perform better using a propeller with a greater amount of rake. Heavier, slower boats generally perform better using a propeller with less rake.

Blade thickness

Blade thickness is not uniform at all points along the blade. For efficiency, blades are as thin as possible at all points while retaining enough strength to move the boat. Blades are thicker where they meet the hub and thinner at the blade tips. This construction is necessary to support the heavier loads at the hub section of the blade. Overall blade thickness depends on the strength of the material used. When cut along a line from the leading edge to the trailing edge in the central portion of the blade, the propeller blade resembles an airplane wing. The blade face, where high pressure exists during forward rotation, is almost flat. The blade back, where low pressure exists during forward rotation, is curved with the thinner portions at the edges and the thickest portion at the center.

Number of blades

The number of blades on a propeller is a compromise between efficiency and vibration. A one-bladed propeller would be the most efficient, but it would create an unacceptable amount of vibration. As blades are added, efficiency decreases, but so does vibration. Most propellers have three or four blades, representing the most practical compromise between efficiency and vibration.

Material

Propeller materials are chosen for strength, corrosion resistance and economy. Stainless steel, aluminum, plastic

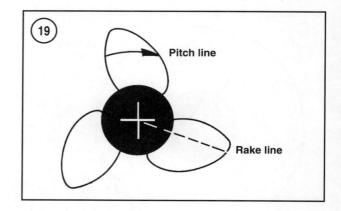

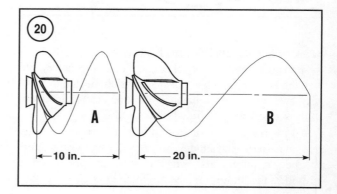

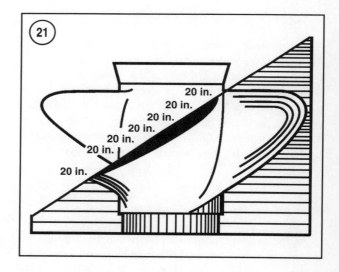

and bronze are the most commonly used materials. Bronze is quite strong but rather expensive. Stainless steel is more common than bronze because of the combination of strength and a lower cost. Aluminum alloy and plastic materials are the least expensive but lack the strength of stainless steel. Plastic propellers are more suited for lower-horsepower applications.

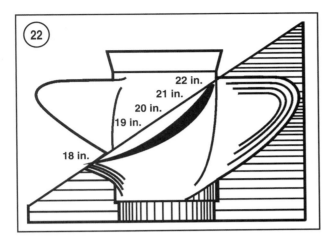

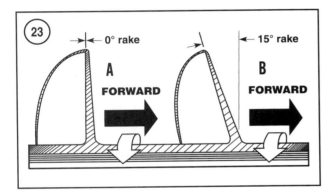

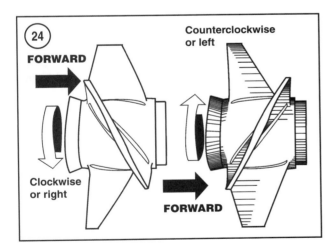

Direction of rotation

Propellers are made for both right-hand and left-hand rotations, though right-hand is the most commonly used. As viewed from the rear of the boat while in forward gear, a right-hand propeller turns clockwise, and a left-hand

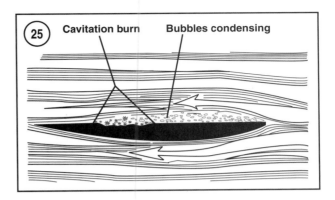

propeller turns counterclockwise. The direction of rotation is determined by observing the angle of the blades (**Figure 24**). Right-handed propeller blades slant from the upper left to the lower right; left-handed propeller blades are opposite.

Cavitation and Ventilation

Cavitation and ventilation are *not* interchangeable terms; they refer to two distinct problems encountered during propeller operation.

To help understand cavitation, consider the relationship between pressure and the boiling point of water. At sea level, water boils at 212° F (100° C). As pressure increases, the boiling point of the water increases. It boils at a temperature higher than 212° F (100° C). The opposite is also true. As pressure decreases, water boils at a temperature lower than 212° F (100° C). If the pressure drops low enough, water will boil at room temperature.

During normal propeller operation, low pressure forms on the blade back. Normally, the pressure does not drop low enough for boiling to occur. However, poor propeller design, damaged blades or using the wrong propeller can cause unusually low pressure on the blade back (**Figure 25**). If the pressure drops low enough, boiling occurs, and bubbles form on the blade surfaces. As the boiling water moves to a higher-pressure area of the blade, the boiling ceases, and the bubbles collapse. The collapsing bubbles release energy that erodes the surface of the propeller blade.

This entire process of pressure drop, boiling and bubble collapse is called *cavitation*. The ensuing damage is called *cavitation burn*. Cavitation is caused by a decrease in pressure, not an increase in temperature.

Corroded surfaces, physical damage or even marine growth combined with high-speed operation can cause cavitation on the propeller shaft support strut and other exposed drive system surfaces. In such cases, low pressure forms as water flows over a protrusion or rough sur-face. The boiling water forms bubbles that collapse as they move to the higher-pressure area toward the rear of the surface imperfection.

Ventilation is not as complex a process as cavitation. Ventilation refers to air entering the blade area from above the water surface. On inboard engines, ventilation is com-monly caused by operation in rough water where the bot-tom of the boat momentarily leaves the water surface. As the blades meet the air, the propeller momentarily loses contact with the water and subsequently loses most of its thrust. During ventilation, cavitation can occur as the en-gine overrevs and creates very low pressure on the back of the propeller blade.

BASIC TOOLS

Most of the procedures in this manual can be accom-plished using simple hand tools and test equipment famil-iar to the home mechanic. Always use the correct tools for the job at hand. Keep tools organized and clean. Store them in a tool chest with related tools organized together.

After using a tool, wipe off dirt and grease with a clean cloth. Wiping off tools is especially important when ser-vicing the craft in areas where they can come in contact with sand. Sand is very abrasive and causes premature wear to engine parts.

Quality tools are essential. The best are constructed of high-strength alloy steel. These tools are light, easy to use and resistant to wear. Working surfaces are devoid of sharp edges, and the tools are carefully polished. They have an easy-to-clean finish and are comfortable to use. Quality tools are a good investment.

When purchasing tools, consider the potential fre-quency of use. If starting a tool kit, consider purchasing a basic tool set (**Figure 26**) from a large tool supplier. These sets are available in many combinations and offer a sub-stantial savings when compared to individually purchased tools. As work experience grows and tasks become more complicated, specialized tools may be added.

Screwdrivers

Screwdrivers of various lengths and types are manda-tory for the simplest tool kit. The two basic types are the slotted tip (flat blade) and Phillips tip. These are available in sets that often include an assortment of tip sizes and shaft lengths.

As with all tools, use a screwdriver designed for the job. Make sure the size of the tip conforms to the size and shape of the fastener. Use them only for driving screws.

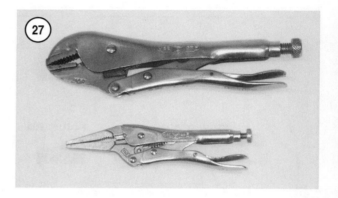

Never use a screwdriver for prying or chiseling metal. Re-pair or replace worn or damaged screwdrivers. A worn tip may damage the fastener and make it difficult to remove.

Phillips screwdrivers are sized according to point size. They are numbered one, two, three and four. The degree of taper determines the point size; the No. 1 Phillips screwdriver is the most pointed. The points are more blunt as the number increases.

Pliers

Pliers come in a wide range of types and sizes. Al-though pliers are useful for holding, cutting, bending and crimping, they should never be used to turn bolts and nuts.

Each design has a specialized function. Slip-joint pliers are general-purpose pliers used for gripping and bending. Diagonal cutting pliers are needed to cut wire and may be used to remove cotter pins. Needlenose pliers are used to hold or bend small objects. Locking pliers (**Figure 27**), sometimes called Vise-Grips, are used to hold objects very tightly. They have many uses ranging from holding two parts together to gripping the end of a broken stud. Use caution when using locking pliers because the sharp jaws can damage the objects they hold.

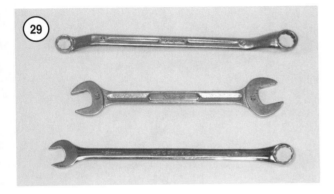

Snap Ring Pliers

Snap ring pliers (**Figure 28**) are specialized pliers with tips that fit into the ends of snap rings to remove and install them.

Snap ring pliers are available with fixed action (either internal or external) or with convertible action (one tool works on both internal and external snap rings). They may have fixed tips or interchangeable ones of various sizes and angles. For general use, select convertible pliers with interchangeable tips.

> *WARNING*
> *Snap rings can slip and fly off during removal and installation. Also, the snap ring pliers tips can break. Always wear eye protection when using snap ring pliers.*

Hammers

Various types of hammers are available to perform a number of tasks. A ball-peen hammer is used to strike another tool, such as a punch or chisel. Soft-faced hammers are required when a metal object must be struck without damaging it. *Never* use a metal-faced hammer on engine components because damage will occur in most cases.

Always wear eye protection when using a hammer. Make sure the hammer face is in good condition and the handle is not cracked. Select the correct hammer for the job and make sure to strike the object squarely. Do not use the handle or side of the hammer to strike an object.

When striking a hammer against a punch, cold chisel or similar tool, the face of the hammer should be at least 1/2 in. (12.7 mm) larger than the head of the tool. If it is necessary to strike hard against a steel part without damaging it, use a brass hammer. Brass will give when used on a harder object.

Wrenches

Box-end, open-end and combination wrenches (**Figure 29**) are available in a variety of types and sizes.

The number stamped on the wrench refers to the distance between the work areas. This size must match the size of the fastener head.

The box-end wrench is an excellent tool because it grips the fastener on all sides. This factor reduces the chance of the tool slipping. The box-end is designed with either a six- or 12-point opening. For stubborn or damaged fasteners, the six-point opening provides superior holding ability by contacting the fastener across a wider area at all six edges. For general use, the 12-point opening works well because it allows the wrench to be used without moving the handle over such a wide arc.

An open-end wrench is fast and works best in areas with limited overhead access. It contacts the fastener at only two points and can slip under heavy force or if the tool or fastener is worn. A box-end wrench is preferred in most instances, especially when breaking loose and applying the final tightening to a fastener.

The combination wrench has a box end on one end and an open end on the other. This combination makes it a very convenient tool.

Adjustable Wrenches

An adjustable wrench can fit nearly any nut or bolt head that has clear access around the entire perimeter. Adjustable wrenches are best used as a backup wrench to keep a large nut or bolt from turning while the other end is loosened or tightened with a box-end or socket wrench.

Adjustable wrenches contact the fastener at only two points, which makes them more subject to slipping off the fastener. The fact that one jaw is adjustable and can loosen only aggravates this shortcoming. Make certain the solid jaw is the one transmitting the force.

Socket Wrenches, Ratchets and Handles

Sockets that attach to a ratchet handle (**Figure 30**) are available in six-point or 12-point openings and different drive sizes. The drive size (1/4, 3/8, 1/2 and 3/4 in.) indicates the size of the square opening that accepts the ratchet handle. The number stamped on the socket is the size of the work area and must match the fastener head.

As with wrenches, a six-point socket provides superior holding ability, though a 12-point socket needs to be moved only half as far to reposition on the fastener.

Sockets are designated for either hand or impact use. Impact sockets are made of thicker material for more durability.

> *WARNING*
> *Do not use hand sockets with air or impact tools because they can shatter and cause injury. Always wear eye protection when using impact or air tools.*

Various handles are available for sockets. The speed handle is used for fast operation. Flexible ratchet heads in various lengths allow the socket to be turned with varying force and at odd angles. Extension bars allow socket setup to reach difficult areas. The ratchet is the most versatile. It allows the user to install or remove the nut without removing the socket.

Sockets combined with any number of drivers undoubtedly make the fastest, safest and most convenient tools for fastener removal and installation.

Impact Driver

An impact driver provides extra force for removing fasteners by converting the impact of a hammer into a turning motion. This makes it possible to remove stubborn fasteners without damaging them. Impact drivers and interchangeable bits (**Figure 31**) are available from most tool suppliers. When using a socket with an impact driver, make sure the socket is designed for impact use. Refer to *Socket Wrenches, Ratchets and Handles* in this section.

> *WARNING*
> *Do not use hand sockets with air or impact tools because they can shatter and cause injury. Always wear eye protection when using impact or air tools.*

Impact drivers are great for the home mechanic because they offer many of the advantages of air tools without the need for a costly air compressor to operate them.

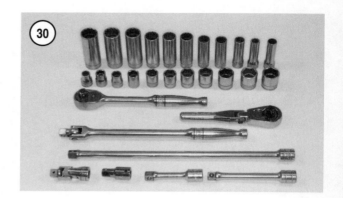

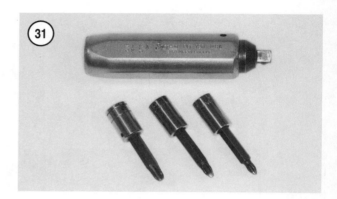

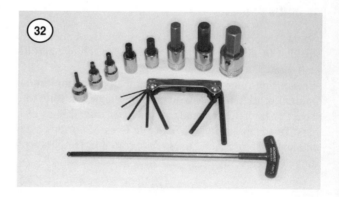

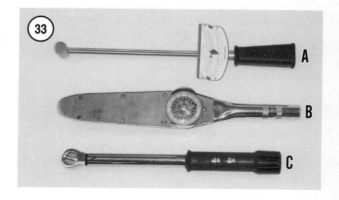

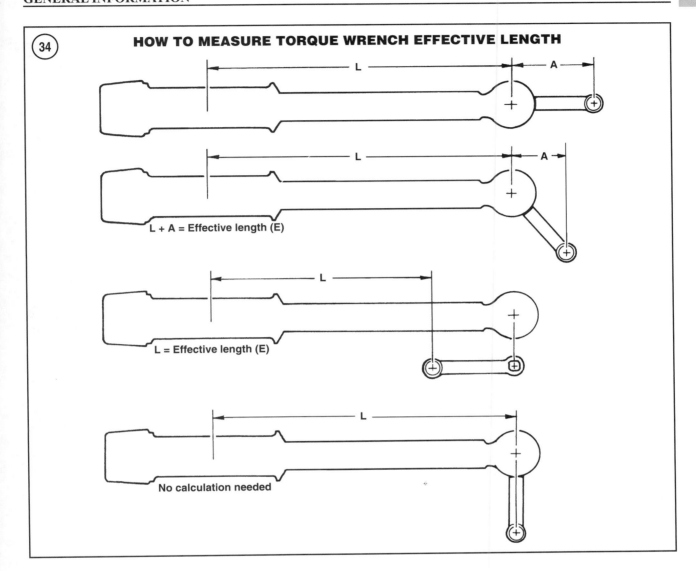

HOW TO MEASURE TORQUE WRENCH EFFECTIVE LENGTH

(34)

L + A = Effective length (E)

L = Effective length (E)

No calculation needed

Allen Wrenches

Allen or setscrew wrenches (**Figure 32**) are used on fasteners with hexagonal recesses in the fastener heads. These wrenches come in L-shaped bar, socket and T-handle forms. Allen bolts are sometimes called socket bolts.

Torque Wrenches

A torque wrench is used with a socket, torque adapter or similar extension to measure torque while tightening a fastener. Torque wrenches are available in several drive sizes (1/4, 3/8, 1/2 and 3/4 in.) and have various methods of reading the torque value. The drive size is the size of the square drive that accepts the socket, adapter or extension. Common types of torque wrenches include the de-

flecting beam (A, **Figure 33**), the dial indicator (B) and audible click (C).

When choosing a torque wrench, consider the torque range, drive size and accuracy. The torque specifications in this manual indicate the range required.

A torque wrench is a precision tool that must be properly cared for to remain accurate. Store torque wrenches in cases or separate padded drawers within a toolbox. Follow the manufacturer's care and calibration instructions.

Torque Adapters

Torque adapters or extensions extend or reduce the reach of a torque wrench. The torque adapter shown on the top of **Figure 34** is used to tighten a fastener that cannot be reached because of the size of the torque wrench head, drive and socket. If a torque adapter changes the effective lever length, the torque reading on the wrench will not equal the actual torque applied to the fastener. It is necessary to recalibrate the torque setting on the wrench to compensate for the change of lever length. When using a torque adapter at a right angle to the drive head, calibration is not required because since the effective length has not changed.

To recalibrate a torque reading when using a torque adapter, use the following formula, and refer to **Figure 34**.

$$TW = \frac{TA \times L}{L + A}$$

TW is the torque setting or dial reading on the wrench.

TA is the torque specification (the actual amount of torque that should be applied to the fastener).

A is the amount that the adapter increases (or in some cases reduces) the effective lever length as measured along the centerline of the torque wrench (**Figure 34**).

L is the lever length of the wrench as measured from the center of the drive to the center of the grip.

The effective length of the torque wrench measured along the centerline or the torque wrench is the sum of L and A (**Figure 34**).

Example:

TA = 20 ft.-lb.
A = 3 in.
L = 14 in.
$$TW = \frac{20 \times 14}{14 + 3} = \frac{280}{17} = 16.5 \text{ ft.-lb.}$$

In this example, the torque wrench would be set to the recalculated torque value (TW = 16.5 ft.-lb.). When using a beam wrench, tighten the fastener until the pointer aligns with 16.5 ft.-lb. In this example, although the torque wrench is preset to 16.5 ft.-lb., the actual torque applied is 20 ft.-lb.

SPECIAL TOOLS

Some of the procedures in this manual require special tools. These are described in the appropriate chapters and are available from either the engine manufacturer or a tool supplier.

In many cases, an acceptable substitute may be found in an existing tool kit. Another alternative is to make the tool. Many schools with a machine shop curriculum welcome outside work that can be used as practical shop applications for students.

PRECISION MEASURING TOOLS

The ability to accurately measure components is essential to successfully rebuilding an engine. Equipment is manufactured to close tolerances, and obtaining consistently accurate measurements is necessary to determine which components require replacement or further service.

Each type of measuring instrument is designed to measure a dimension with a certain degree of accuracy and within a certain range. When selecting the measuring tool, make sure it is applicable to the task.

As with all tools, measuring tools provide the best results if cared for properly. Improper use can damage the tool and result in inaccurate results. If any measurement is questionable, verify the measurement using another tool. A standard gauge is usually provided with measuring tools to check accuracy and calibrate the tool if necessary.

Precision measurements can vary according to the experience of the person performing the procedure. Accurate results are only possible if the mechanic possesses a feel for using the tool. Heavy-handed use of measuring tools produces less accurate measurements than if the fingertips grasp the tool gently so the point at which the tool contacts the object is easily felt. This feel for the equipment produces more accurate measurements and reduces the risk of damaging the tool or component. Refer to the following sections for specific measuring tools.

Feeler Gauges

The feeler or thickness gauge (**Figure 35**) is used for measuring the distance between two surfaces.

A feeler gauge set consists of an assortment of steel strips of graduated thicknesses. Blades can be of various lengths and angles for different procedures.

A common use for a feeler gauge is to measure valve clearance. Wire (round) gauges are used to measure spark plug gap.

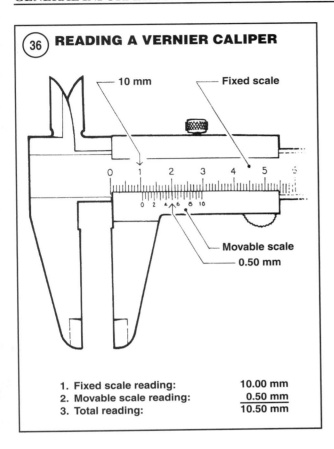

36 READING A VERNIER CALIPER

10 mm — Fixed scale

Movable scale
0.50 mm

1. Fixed scale reading:	10.00 mm
2. Movable scale reading:	0.50 mm
3. Total reading:	10.50 mm

To obtain a proper measurement using a feeler gauge, make sure the properly sized blade passes through the gap with a slight drag. The blade should not need to be forced through and should not have any up-and-down play between the surfaces being measured.

Calipers

Calipers are excellent tools for obtaining inside, outside and depth measurements. Although not as precise as a micrometer, they allow reasonable precision, typically to within 0.001 in. (0.05 mm). Most calipers have a range up to 6 in. (150 mm).

Calipers are available in dial, vernier or digital versions. Dial calipers have a dial gauge readout that provides convenient reading. Vernier calipers have marked scales that are compared to determine the measurement. Most convenient of all, the digital caliper uses an LCD to show the measurement.

To help ensure accurate readings, properly maintain the measuring surfaces of the caliper. There must not be any dirt or burrs between the tool and the object being measured. Never force the caliper closed around an object;

close the caliper around the highest point so it can be removed with a slight drag. Some calipers require calibration. Always refer to the manufacturer's instructions when using a new or unfamiliar caliper.

To read a metric vernier caliper, refer to **Figure 36**. The fixed scale is marked in 1.0 mm increments. Ten individual lines on the fixed scale equal 1.0 cm. The movable scale is marked in 0.05 mm (five-hundredth) increments. To obtain a reading, establish the first number by location of the 0 line on the movable scale in relation to the first line to the left on the fixed scale. In this example, the number is 10.0 mm. To determine the next number, note which of the lines on the movable scale align with a mark on the fixed scale. A number of lines will seem close, but only one aligns exactly. In this case, 0.50 mm is the reading to add to the first number. The result of adding 10.0 mm and 0.50 mm is a measurement of 10.50 mm.

Micrometers

A micrometer is an instrument designed for linear measurement using the decimal division of the inch or meter (**Figure 37**). Although there are many types and styles of micrometers, most of the procedures in this manual require an outside micrometer. Use an outside micrometer to measure the outside diameters of cylindrical forms and the thicknesses of materials.

Micrometer size indicates the minimum and maximum size of a part that it can measure. The usual sizes are 0-1 in. (0.25 mm), 1-2 in. (25-50 mm), 2-3 in. (50-75 mm) and 3-4 in. (75-100 mm).

Micrometers covering a wider range of measurement are available and use a large frame with interchangeable anvils of various lengths. This type of micrometer offers cost savings; however, the overall size makes it less convenient.

When reading a micrometer, numbers are taken from different scales and added together. The following sections describe how to take measurements with various types of outside micrometers.

For accurate results, properly maintain the measuring surfaces of the micrometer. There cannot be any dirt or burrs between the tool and the measured object. Never force the micrometer closed around an object. Close the micrometer around the highest point so it can be removed with a slight drag. **Figure 38** shows the markings and parts of a standard inch micrometer. Be familiar with these terms before using a micrometer in the following sections.

DECIMAL PLACE VALUES*

0.1	Indicates 1/10 (one tenth of an inch or millimeter)
0.01	Indicates 1/100 (one one-hundreth of an inch or millimeter)
0.001	Indicates 1/1000 (one one-thousandth of an inch or millimeter)

*This chart represents the values of figures placed to the right of the decimal point. Use it when reading decimals from one-tenth to one one-thousandth of an inch or millimeter. It is not a conversion chart (for example: 0.001 in. is not equal to 0.001 mm).

③⑦

Reading a standard inch micrometer

The standard inch micrometer is accurate to one thousandth of an inch or 0.001 in. The sleeve is marked in 0.025 in. increments. Every fourth sleeve mark is numbered 1, 2, 3, 4, 5, 6, 7, 8 and 9. These numbers indicate 0.100 in., 0.200 in., 0.300 in. and so on.

The tapered end of the thimble has 25 lines marked around it. Each mark equals 0.001 in. One complete turn of the thimble will align the 0 mark with the first mark on the sleeve or 0.025 in.

When reading a standard inch micrometer, perform the following steps while referring to **Figure 39**.

1. Read the sleeve and find the largest number visible. Each sleeve number equals 0.100 in.

2. Count the number of lines between the numbered sleeve mark and the edge of the thimble. Each sleeve mark equals 0.025 in.

3. Read the thimble mark that aligns with the sleeve line. Each thimble mark equals 0.001 in.

NOTE
If a thimble mark does not align exactly with the sleeve line, estimate the amount between the lines. For accurate readings in ten-thousandths of an inch (0.0001 in.), use a vernier inch micrometer.

4. Add the readings from Steps 1-3.

Reading a vernier inch micrometer

A vernier inch micrometer is accurate to one ten-thousandth of an inch or 0.0001 in. It has the same markings as a standard inch micrometer with an additional vernier scale on the sleeve (**Figure 40**).

The vernier scale consists of 11 lines marked 1-9 with a 0 on each end. These lines run parallel to the thimble lines and represent 0.0001 in. increments.

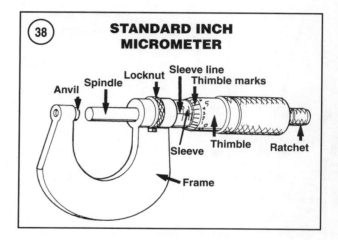

③⑧ **STANDARD INCH MICROMETER**

Anvil · Spindle · Locknut · Sleeve line · Thimble marks · Sleeve · Thimble · Ratchet · Frame

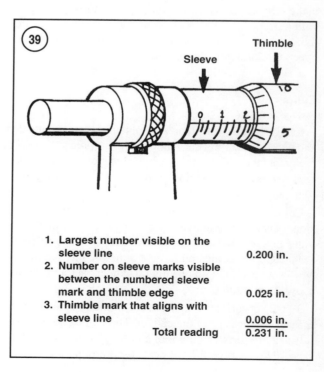

③⑨ Sleeve · Thimble

1. Largest number visible on the sleeve line	0.200 in.
2. Number on sleeve marks visible between the numbered sleeve mark and thimble edge	0.025 in.
3. Thimble mark that aligns with sleeve line	0.006 in.
Total reading	0.231 in.

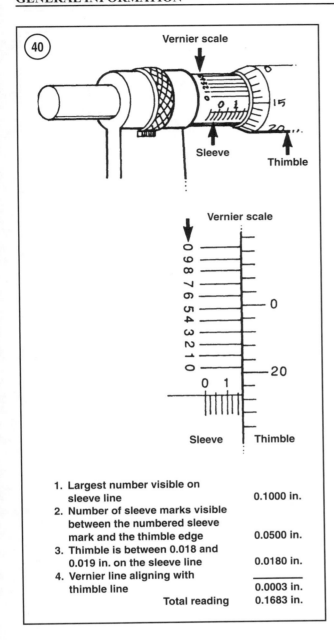

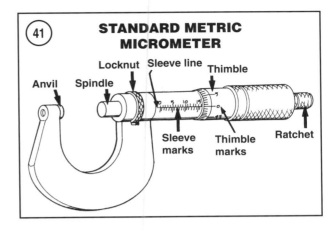

1. Largest number visible on sleeve line	0.1000 in.
2. Number of sleeve marks visible between the numbered sleeve mark and the thimble edge	0.0500 in.
3. Thimble is between 0.018 and 0.019 in. on the sleeve line	0.0180 in.
4. Vernier line aligning with thimble line	0.0003 in.
Total reading	0.1683 in.

When reading a vernier inch micrometer, perform the following steps while referring to **Figure 40**.

1. Read the micrometer in the same way as a standard inch micrometer. This is the initial reading.

2. If a thimble mark aligns exactly with the sleeve line, reading the vernier scale is not necessary. If it does not, read the vernier scale as described in Step 3.

3. Determine which vernier scale mark aligns with one thimble mark. The vernier scale number is the amount in ten-thousandths of an inch to add to the initial reading from Step 1.

Reading a standard metric micrometer

The standard metric micrometer (**Figure 41**) is accurate to one hundredth of a millimeter (0.01 mm). The sleeve line is graduated in millimeter and half-millimeter increments. The marks on the upper half of the sleeve line equal 1.00 mm. Every fifth mark above the sleeve line is identified with a number. The number sequence depends on the size of the micrometer. For example, a 0-25 mm micrometer has sleeve marks numbered 0 through 25 in 5 mm increments. This numbering sequence continues with larger micrometers. On all metric micrometers, each mark on the lower half of the sleeve line equals 0.50 mm.

The tapered end of the thimble has fifty lines marked around it. Each mark equals 0.01 mm.

One complete turn of the thimble aligns the 0 mark with the first line on the lower half of the sleeve line or 0.50 mm.

When reading a standard metric micrometer, add the number of millimeters and half millimeters on the sleeve line to the number of hundredth millimeters on the thimble. Perform the following steps while referring to **Figure 42**.

1. Read the upper half of the sleeve line and count the number of lines visible. Each upper line equals 1.00 mm.

2. See whether the half-millimeter line is visible on the lower sleeve line. If so, add 0.50 mm to the reading in Step 1.

3. Read the thimble mark that aligns with the sleeve line. Each thimble mark equals 0.01 mm.

> *NOTE*
> *If a thimble mark does not align exactly with the sleeve line, estimate the amount between the lines. For accurate readings in two thousandths of a millimeter (0.002 mm), use a metric vernier micrometer.*

4. Add the readings from Steps 1-3.

Reading a metric vernier micrometer

A metric vernier micrometer (**Figure 43**) is accurate to two thousandths of a millimeter (0.002 mm). It has the same markings as a standard metric micrometer with the addition of a vernier scale on the sleeve. The vernier scale consists of five lines marked 0, 2, 4, 6 and 8. These lines run parallel to the thimble lines and represent 0.002-mm increments.

When reading a metric vernier micrometer, refer to **Figure 43** and perform the following steps.

1. Read the micrometer in the same way as a standard metric micrometer. This is the initial reading.

2. If a thimble mark aligns exactly with the sleeve line, reading the vernier scale is not necessary. If it does not align, read the vernier scale as described in Step 3.

3. Determine which vernier scale mark aligns exactly with one thimble mark. The vernier scale number is the amount in two thousandths of a millimeter to add to the initial reading from Step 1.

Micrometer Calibration

Before using a micrometer, check the calibration as follows.

1. Clean the anvil and spindle faces.

2A. To check a 0-1 in. or 0-25 mm micrometer:

   a. Turn the thimble until the spindle contacts the anvil. If the micrometer has a ratchet stop, use it to make sure the proper amount of pressure is applied.

   b. If the adjustment is correct, the 0 mark on the thimble will align exactly with the 0 mark on the sleeve line. If the marks do not align, the micrometer requires adjustment.

   c. Follow the manufacturer's instructions to adjust the micrometer.

2B. To check a micrometer larger than 1 in. or 25 mm, use the standard gauge supplied by the manufacturer. A standard gauge is a steel block, disc or rod that is machined to an exact size.

   a. Place the standard gauge between the spindle and anvil and measure the outside diameter or length. If the micrometer has a ratchet stop, use it to make sure the proper amount of pressure is applied.

   b. If the adjustment is correct, the 0 mark on the thimble will align exactly with the sleeve line. If the marks do not align, the micrometer requires adjustment.

   c. Follow the manufacturer's instructions to adjust the micrometer.

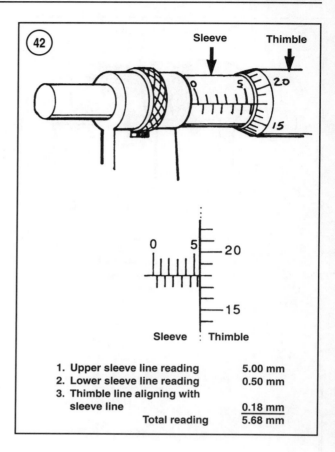

1. Upper sleeve line reading	5.00 mm
2. Lower sleeve line reading	0.50 mm
3. Thimble line aligning with sleeve line	0.18 mm
Total reading	5.68 mm

Micrometer care

Micrometers are precision instruments. Use and maintain them with great care.

Note the following:

1. Store micrometers in protective cases or separate padded drawers in a toolbox.

2. When in storage, make sure the spindle and anvil faces do not contact each other or another object. If they do, temperature changes and corrosion may damage the contact faces.

3. Do not clean a micrometer with compressed air. Dirt forced into the tool causes wear.

4. Lubricate micrometers with light oil to prevent corrosion.

Telescoping and Small-Bore Gauges

Use telescoping gauges (**Figure 44**) and small-bore gauges to measure bores. Neither gauge has a scale for direct reading. Use an outside micrometer to determine the reading.

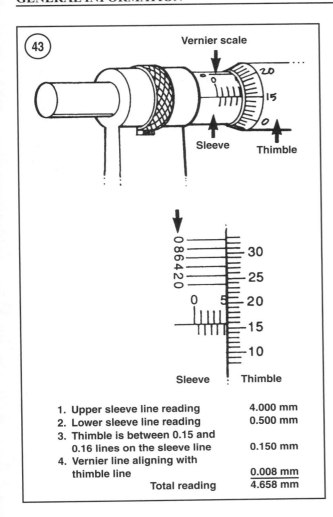

43

Vernier scale

Sleeve

Thimble

1.	Upper sleeve line reading	4.000 mm
2.	Lower sleeve line reading	0.500 mm
3.	Thimble is between 0.15 and	
	0.16 lines on the sleeve line	0.150 mm
4.	Vernier line aligning with	
	thimble line	0.008 mm
	Total reading	4.658 mm

44

MADE IN U.S.A.

To use a telescoping gauge, select the correctly sized gauge for the bore. Loosen the knurled end of the gauge to allow the post to extend. Compress the movable post and carefully insert the gauge into the bore. Carefully move the gauge in the bore to make sure it is centered. Tighten the knurled end of the gauge to hold the movable post in

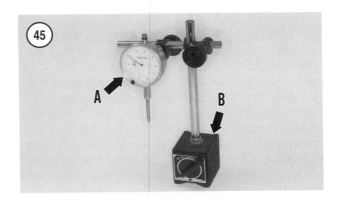

45

A

B

position. Carefully remove the gauge and measure the length of the post. Telescoping gauges are typically used to measure cylinder bores.

To use a small-bore gauge, select the correctly sized gauge for the bore. Carefully insert the gauge into the bore. Tighten the knurled end of the gauge to carefully expand the gauge fingers to the limit within the bore. Do not overtighten the gauge because there is no built-in release. Excessive tightening can damage the bore surface and the tool. Remove the gauge and measure the outside dimension. Small-bore gauges are typically used to measure valve guides.

Dial Indicator

A dial indicator (**Figure 45**) is a gauge with a dial face and needle used to measure dimensional variations and movements, such as crankshaft and gearshaft runout and end play.

Dial indicators are available in various ranges and graduations and with three basic types of mounting bases: magnetic, clamp or screw-in stud. When purchasing a dial indicator, select the magnetic stand type (B, **Figure 45**) with a continuous dial (A).

Cylinder Bore Gauge

The cylinder-bore gauge is a very specialized precision tool that is only needed for major engine repairs or rebuilds. The gauge set shown in **Figure 46** comprises a dial indicator, handle and a number of different length adapters (anvils) used to fit the gauge to various bore sizes. The bore gauge can be used to measure bore size, taper and out-of-round. When using a bore gauge, follow the manufacturer's instructions.

Compression Gauge

A compression gauge (**Figure 47**) measures the combustion chamber (cylinder) pressure usually in psi or kg/cm^2. An engine is capable of mechanically generating pressure on the compression stroke. The gauge adapter is either inserted or screwed into the spark plug hole to obtain the reading. Disable the ignition or fuel control system so the engine does not start, and hold the throttle in the wide-open position when performing a compression test. An engine that does not have adequate compression cannot be properly tuned.

Multimeter

A multimeter (**Figure 48**) is an essential tool for electrical system diagnosis. The voltage function indicates the voltage applied or available to various electrical components. The ohmmeter function test circuits for continuity or lack of continuity and measures the resistance of a circuit.

Some less-expensive models contain a needle gauge and are known as analog meters. Most high-quality (but not necessarily expensive) meters available today contain digital readout screens. Digital multimeters are often know as DVOMs. When using an analog ohmmeter, the needle must be zeroed or calibrated according to the meter manufacture's instructions. Some analog and almost all digital meters are self-zeroing, and no manual adjustment is necessary.

Some manufacturers' specifications for electrical components are based on results using a specific test meter. Results may vary if using a meter not recommended by the manufacturer.

ELECTRICAL SYSTEM FUNDAMENTALS

A thorough study of the many types of electrical systems used in engines today is beyond the scope of this manual. However, a basic understanding of electrical basics is necessary to perform simple diagnostic tests.

Voltage

Voltage is the electrical potential or pressure in an electrical circuit and is expressed in volts. The more pressure (voltage) in a circuit, the more work that can be performed.

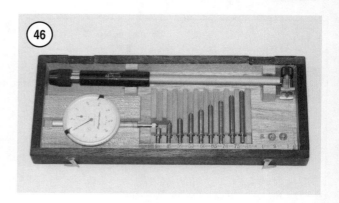

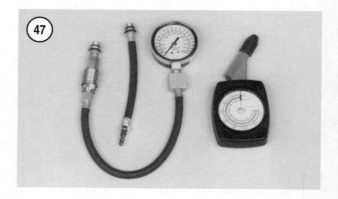

Direct current (DC) voltage means the electricity flows in one direction. All circuits powered by a battery are DC circuits.

Alternating current (AC) means the electricity flows in one direction momentarily and then switches to the opposite direction. Alternator output is an example of AC voltage. The voltage must be changed or rectified to direct current to operate in a 12-volt battery powered system.

Measuring voltage

Unless otherwise specified, perform all voltage tests with the electrical connectors attached.

When measuring voltage, select a meter range one scale higher than the expected voltage of the circuit to prevent damage to the meter. To determine actual voltage in a circuit, use a voltmeter. To simply check if voltage is present, use a test light.

NOTE
When using a test light, either lead can be attached to ground.

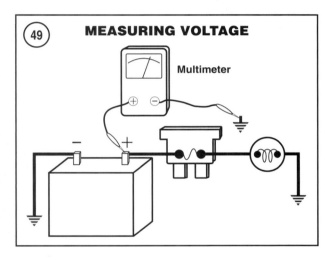

MEASURING VOLTAGE

Multimeter

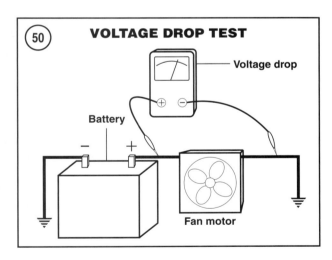

VOLTAGE DROP TEST

Voltage drop

Battery

Fan motor

1. Attach the negative meter test lead to a good ground (bare metal). Make sure the ground is not insulated with a rubber gasket or grommet.

2. Attach the positive meter test lead to the point being checked for voltage (**Figure 49**).

3. If necessary for the circuit being tested, turn on the ignition switch. This is necessary if the point being tested only has power applied when the ignition switch is turned on, but the example in **Figure 49** shows a measurement at the positive battery terminal, which should always have voltage if the battery is charged. The test light should light, or the meter should display a reading. The reading should be within 1 volt of battery voltage. If the voltage is less, there is likely a problem in the circuit.

Voltage drop test

Resistance causes voltage to drop. This resistance can be measured in an active circuit by using a voltmeter to perform a voltage drop test. A voltage drop test compares the difference between the voltage available at the start of a circuit to the voltage at the end of the circuit. But it does so while the circuit is operational. If the circuit has no resistance, there will be no voltage drop. The greater the resistance, the greater the voltage drop will be. A voltage drop of 1 volt or more usually indicates excessive resistance in the circuit.

1. Connect the positive meter test lead to the electrical source (where the electricity is coming from).

2. Connect the negative meter test lead to the electrical load (where the electricity is going. See **Figure 50**.

3. If necessary, activate the component(s) in the circuit.

4. A voltage reading of 1 volt or more indicates excessive resistance in the circuit. A reading equal to battery voltage indicates an open circuit.

Resistance

Resistance is the opposition to flow of electricity within a circuit or component and is measured in ohms. Resistance causes a reduction in available current and voltage.

Resistance is measured in an inactive circuit using an ohmmeter. The ohmmeter sends a small amount of current into the circuit and measures how difficult it is to push the current through the circuit.

An ohmmeter, though useful, is not always a good indicator of the actual ability of the circuit under operating conditions. This fact is due to the low voltage (6-9 volts) that the meter uses to test the circuit. The voltage in an ignition coil secondary winding can be several thousand volts. Such high voltage can cause the coil to malfunction, even though it appears to be acceptable during a resistance test.

Resistance generally increases with temperature. Unless specified otherwise, perform all testing with the component or circuit at room temperature. Resistance tests performed at high temperatures might indicate high resistance readings and result in unnecessary replacement of a component.

Resistance and continuity test

> *CAUTION*
> *Only use an ohmmeter on a circuit that has no voltage present. The meter will be damaged if it is connected to a live circuit. Remember, if using an analog meter, it must be calibrated each time it is used or the scale is changed.*

A continuity test can determine whether a circuit is complete. Perform this type of test using an ohmmeter or a self-powered test lamp.

1. Disconnect the negative battery cable.
2. Attach one test lead (ohmmeter or test light) to one end of the component or circuit.
3. Attach the other test lead to the opposite end of the component or circuit. See **Figure 51**.
4. A self-powered test lamp will light if the circuit has continuity or is complete. An ohmmeter will indicate either low or no resistance if the circuit has continuity. An open circuit is indicated if the meter displays infinite resistance.

Amperage

Amperage is the unit of measure for the amount of current within a circuit. Current is the actual flow of electricity. The higher the current, the more work that can be performed up to a given point. If the current flow exceeds the circuit or component capacity, the system will be damaged.

Measuring amperage

An ammeter measures the current flow or amps of a circuit (**Figure 52**). Amperage measurement requires that the circuit be disconnected and the ammeter be connected in series in the circuit. Always use an ammeter that can read higher than the anticipated current flow to prevent damage to the meter. Connect the red test lead to the electrical source and the black test lead to the electrical load.

BASIC MECHANICAL SKILLS

Most of the service procedures covered in this manual are straightforward and can be performed by anyone reasonably handy with tools. It is suggested, however, to con-

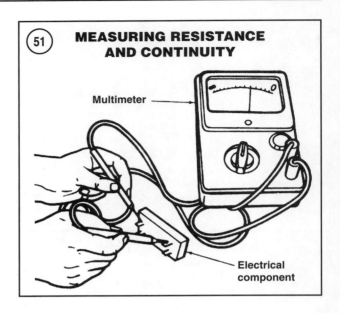

51   MEASURING RESISTANCE AND CONTINUITY

Multimeter

Electrical component

sider your own capabilities carefully before attempting any operation involving major disassembly.

1. *Front*, as used for models with an inline transmission, refers to the front of the engine or the side of the engine facing the front or *bow* of the boat. On V-drive models, the front of the engine faces toward the rear or *stern* of the boat and the flywheel faces toward the bow of the boat. The left side is referred to as the *port* side. Likewise, the right side is referred to as the *starboard* side. These terms are simple, but confusion can cause a major inconvenience during service.

2. When disassembling engine components, mark the parts for location and mark all parts that mate together. Placing them in plastic bags can identify small parts, such as bolts. Seal the bags and label them with masking tape and a marking pen. Because many types of ink fade when applied to tape, use a permanent ink pen. If reassembly will take place immediately, place nuts and bolts in a cupcake tin or egg carton in the order of disassembly.

3. Protect finished surfaces from physical damage or corrosion. Keep gasoline off painted surfaces.

4. Use penetrating oil to free frozen or tight bolts. Then strike the bolt head a few times with a hammer and punch. (Use a screwdriver on screws.) Avoid the use of heat where possible because it can warp, melt or affect the temper of parts. Heat also ruins finishes, especially paint, decals and plastics.

5. Unless otherwise noted, no parts removed or installed (other than bushings and bearings) in the procedures given in this manual should require unusual force during disassembly or assembly. If a part is difficult to remove or install, find out why before proceeding.

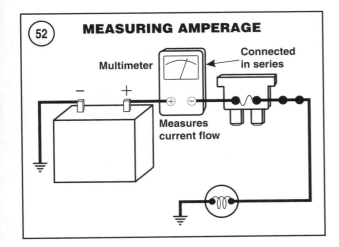

MEASURING AMPERAGE

Multimeter

Connected in series

Measures current flow

6. Cover all openings after removing parts or components to prevent such things as dirt or small tools from falling in.

7. Read each procedure *completely* while looking at the actual parts before starting a job. Make sure to *thoroughly* understand what is to be done, and then carefully follow the procedures step by step.

8. For the do-it-yourselfer, recommendations are occasionally made to refer service or maintenance to a dealership or specialist in a particular field. In these cases, the work will be done more quickly and economically than performing the job alone.

9. In procedural steps, the term *replace* means to discard a defective part and replace it with a new or exchange unit. *Overhaul* means to remove, disassemble, inspect, measure, repair or replace defective parts, reassemble and install major systems or parts.

10. Some operations require the use of a hydraulic press. If a suitable press is not available, it is wiser to have these operations performed at a shop equipped for such work rather than to try to do the job alone with makeshift equipment that can damage the engine.

11. Repairs go much faster and easier if the machine is clean before beginning work.

12. If special tools are required, make arrangements to get them before starting. It is frustrating and time-consuming to start a job and then be unable to complete it.

13. Make diagrams or take a picture wherever similar-appearing parts are found. For instance, intake manifold bolts often are not the same length. Do not try to remember where everything came from because mistakes are costly. It is also possible to get sidetracked and not return to work for days or even weeks, in which time, carefully arranged parts might have been disturbed.

14. When assembling parts, be sure all bolts and washers are reinstalled in their original locations.

15. Use new gaskets if there is any doubt about the condition of the used ones. A thin coating of silicone sealant on nonpressure gaskets may help them seal more effectively.

16. If it becomes necessary to purchase gasket material to make a gasket for the engine, measure the thickness of the used gasket (at an uncompressed point) and purchase the same type of gasket material with the same approximate thickness.

17. Heavy grease can be used to hold small parts in place if they tend to fall out during assembly. However, keep grease and oil away from electrical components unless otherwise directed.

18. Never use wire to clean out jets and air passages. They are easily damaged. First remove the diaphragm before using compressed air when cleaning the carburetor or other fuel system components.

19. Take the time and do the job right. Do not forget that a newly rebuilt engine must be broken in just like a new one.

Removing Frozen Fasteners

If a fastener cannot be removed, several methods may be used to loosen it. First, apply penetrating oil such as Liquid Wrench, WD-40 or PB Blaster. Apply it liberally and let it penetrate for 10-15 minutes. Rap the fastener several times with a small hammer. Do not hit it hard enough to cause damage. Reapply the penetrating oil if necessary.

For frozen screws, apply penetrating oil as described previously. Then insert a screwdriver into the slot and rap the top of the screwdriver with a hammer. This method loosens the corrosion so the screw can be removed in the normal fashion. If the screw head is too damaged to use this method, grip the head with locking pliers and twist the screw out.

Avoid applying heat unless specifically instructed because it can melt, warp or remove the temper from parts.

Removing Broken Fasteners

If the head breaks off a screw or bolt, several methods are available for removing the remaining portion. If a large portion of the remainder projects out, try gripping it with locking pliers. If the projecting portion is too small, or a sufficient grip cannot be obtained on the protruding piece, file it to fit a wrench or cut a slot in it to fit a screwdriver (**Figure 53**).

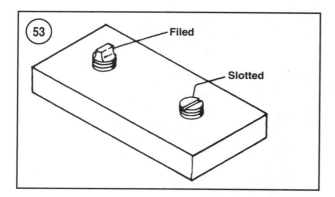

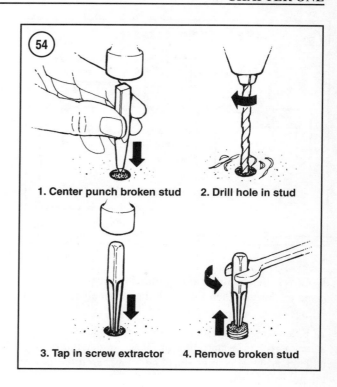

1. Center punch broken stud   2. Drill hole in stud

3. Tap in screw extractor   4. Remove broken stud

If the head breaks off flush, use a screw extractor. To do this, center punch the exact center of the remaining portion of the screw or bolt. Drill a small hole in the screw and tap the extractor into the hole. Back the screw out using a wrench on the extractor (**Figure 54**).

> *NOTE*
> *Broken screw extraction sometimes fails to remove the fastener from the bore. If this occurs, or if the screw is drilled off-center, and the threads are damaged, use a threaded insert to repair the bore. Check for one at a local dealership or supply store and follow the manufacturer's instructions for installation.*

Repairing Damaged Threads

Occasionally, threads are stripped through carelessness or impact damage. Often, the threads can be repaired by running a tap (for internal threads on nuts) or die (for external threads on bolts) through the threads (**Figure 55**). Use only a specially designed spark plug tap to clean or repair spark plug threads.

If an internal thread is damaged, it may be necessary to install a Heli-Coil or other type of thread insert. Follow the manufacturer's instructions when installing the insert.

If it is necessary to drill and tap a hole, refer to **Table 3** or **Table 4** for tap drill sizes.

Stud Removal/Installation

A stud removal tool that makes the removal and installation of studs easier is available from most tool suppliers. If one is not available, thread two nuts onto the stud and tighten them against each other to lock them in place. Then remove the stud by turning the lower nut (**Figure 56**).

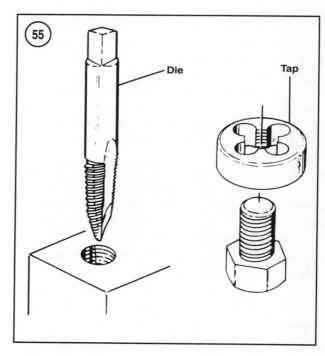

> *NOTE*
> *If the threads on the damaged stud do not allow installation of the two nuts, remove the stud using a pair of locking pliers or a stud remover.*

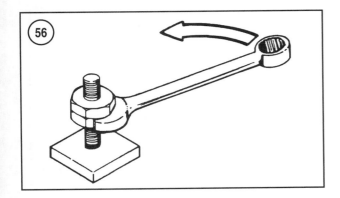

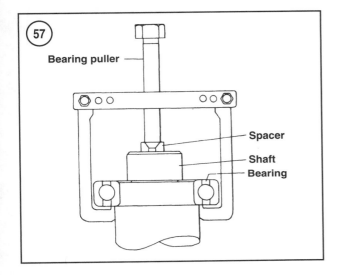

Bearing puller

Spacer
Shaft
Bearing

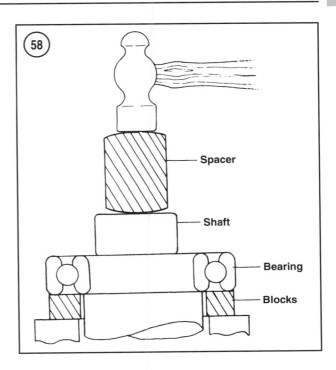

Spacer

Shaft

Bearing

Blocks

replacement procedures are included in the individual chapter where applicable; however, use the following sections as a guideline.

NOTE
Unless otherwise specified, install bearings with the manufacturer's marking, symbol or number facing outward.

Removing Hoses

When removing stubborn hoses, do not apply excessive force to the hose or fitting. Remove the hose clamp and carefully insert a small screwdriver or pick tool between the fitting and hose. Apply a spray lubricant under the hose and carefully twist the hose from the fitting. Clean the fitting of any corrosion or rubber hose material using a wire brush. Thoroughly clean the inside of the hose. Do not use any lubricant when installing the hose (new or used). The lubricant might allow the hose to come off the fitting, even with the clamp secure.

Bearings

Bearings are used in engine-mounted components to reduce power loss, heat and noise resulting from friction. Because bearings are precision parts, it is necessary to maintain them with proper lubrication and maintenance. If a bearing is damaged, replace it immediately. Bearing

Removal

Although bearings are normally removed only when damaged, there might be times when it is necessary to remove and reuse a bearing that is in good condition. However, improper removal will damage the bearing, shaft, and/or case half. Note the following when removing bearings:

1. When using a puller (**Figure 57**) to remove a bearing from a shaft, take care not to damage the shaft. Always place a piece of metal between the end of the shaft and the puller bolt. In addition, place the puller arms next to the inner bearing race.

2. When using a hammer to remove a bearing from a shaft, do not strike the hammer directly against the shaft. Instead, use a brass or aluminum spacer between the hammer and shaft (**Figure 58**) and make sure to support both bearing races with wooden blocks as shown.

3. The ideal method for bearing removal is using a hydraulic press. To prevent damage to the bearing and shaft or case, note the following when using a press:

    a. Always support the inner and outer bearing races with a suitably sized wooden or aluminum spacer ring (**Figure 59**). If only the outer race is supported, pressure applied against the bearing rollers and/or the inner race will damage them.

    b. Always make sure the press ram (**Figure 59**) aligns with the center of the shaft. If the ram is not centered, it can damage the bearing and/or shaft.

    c. The moment the shaft is free from the bearing, it will drop to the floor. Secure the shaft to prevent it from falling.

Installation

1. When installing a bearing into a housing, apply pressure to the *outer* bearing race (**Figure 60**). When installing a bearing onto a shaft, apply pressure to the *inner* bearing race (**Figure 61**).

2. When installing a bearing as described in Step 1, use some type of driver. Never strike the bearing directly with a hammer, or the bearing will be damaged. Use a section of pipe or driver with a diameter that matches the bearing race. **Figure 62** shows the correct way to use a driver and hammer to install a bearing onto a shaft.

3. Step 1 describes how to install a bearing into a case half or over a shaft. However, when installing a bearing over a shaft *and* into a housing at the same time, a tight fit is required for both outer and inner bearing races. In this situation, install a spacer under the driver tool so that pressure is applied evenly across both races. See **Figure 63**. If the outer race is not supported as shown, the balls or rollers will push against the outer bearing race and damage it.

Installing an interference fit bearing over a shaft

When a tight fit is required, the bearing inside diameter will be slightly smaller than the shaft. In this case, simply driving the bearing onto the shaft might cause bearing damage. Instead, heat the bearing before installation. Note the following:

1. Secure the shaft so that it is ready for bearing installation. While the parts are still cold, determine the proper size and gather all necessary spacers and drivers for installation.

2. Clean the bearing surface on the shaft of all residue. Remove burrs with a file or sandpaper.

3. Fill a suitable pot or beaker with clean mineral oil. Place a thermometer rated higher than 248° F (120° C)

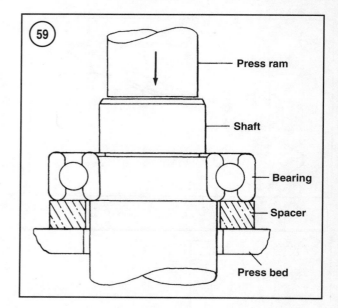

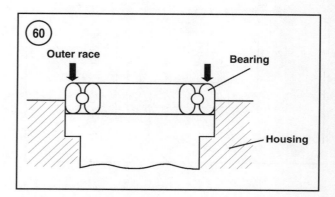

into the oil. Support the thermometer so it does not rest on the bottom or side of the container.

4. Secure the bearing using a piece of heavy wire bent to hold it in the container. Hang the bearing so it does not touch the bottom or sides of the container.

5. Turn the heat on and monitor the thermometer. When the oil temperature rises to approximately 248° F (120° C), remove the bearing from the container and quickly install it. If necessary, place a driver against the inner bearing race and tap the bearing into place. As the bearing cools, it will tighten on the shaft so work quickly when installing it. Make sure the bearing is installed completely.

Replacing an interference fit bearing in a housing

Bearings are generally installed into a housing with a slight interference fit. Driving the bearing into the housing can damage the housing or bearing. Instead, heat the

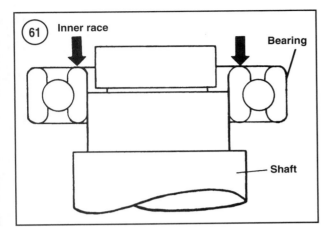

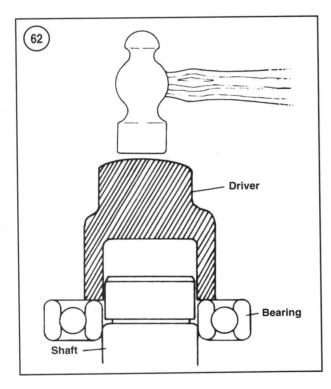

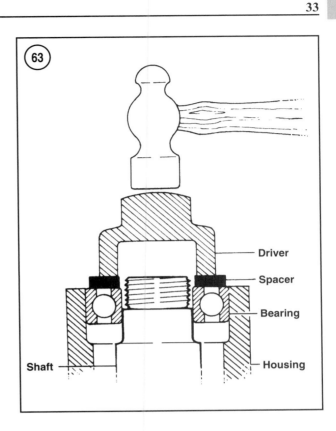

housing (to make the inner diameter of the bore larger) and chill the bearing (to make the outer diameter slightly smaller) before installation. This makes bearing installation much easier.

CAUTION
Before heating the housing in this procedure to remove the bearing(s), wash the housing thoroughly with detergent and clean water. To prevent a possible fire hazard, rinse and rewash the housing as required to remove all traces of oil and other chemical deposits.

1. While the parts are still cool, determine the proper size and gather all necessary spacers and drivers for installation.

2. Place the new bearing into a freezer to chill it and slightly reduce its outside diameter.

3. While the bearing is chilling, heat the housing to a temperature of about 212° F (100° C) in an oven or on a hot plate. An easy way to check if the housing is hot enough is to place tiny droplets of water onto the case; if they sizzle and evaporate immediately, the temperature is correct. Heat only one housing at a time.

CAUTION
Do not heat the housing with a propane or acetylene torch. Never bring a flame into contact with the bearing or housing. The direct heat will destroy the case hardening of the bearing and will likely warp the housing.

4. Remove the housing from the oven or hot plate using heavy protective gloves or heavy shop cloths.

NOTE
A suitably sized socket and extension works well for removing and installing bearings.

5. Hold the housing with the bearing side down and tap the used bearing out. Repeat the process for all bearings in the housing.

NOTE
Always install bearings with the manufacturer's marking, symbol or number facing outward.

6. While the housing is still hot, install the chilled new bearing(s) into the housing. Install the bearing(s) by hand, if possible. If necessary, lightly tap the bearing(s) into the bore(s) using a driver placed against the outer bearing race. *Do not* install the bearings by driving against the inner bearing race. Drive each bearing into the bore until it seats completely.

Seal Replacement

Seals (**Figure 64**) are used to contain oil, water, grease or combustion gasses in a housing or shaft. Improper removal of a seal can damage components. Improper installation can damage the seal and/or other components. Note the following:

1. Prying is generally the easiest and most effective method to remove a seal from a housing. However, always place a shop towel under the pry tool to prevent damage to the housing.
2. Pack water-resistant grease into the seal lips before installing the seal.
3. In most cases, install seals with the manufacturer's markings or numbers facing outward.
4. Install seals with a driver placed against the outside of the seal as shown in **Figure 65**. Drive the seal squarely into the housing. Never install a seal by hitting directly against the top of the seal with a hammer.

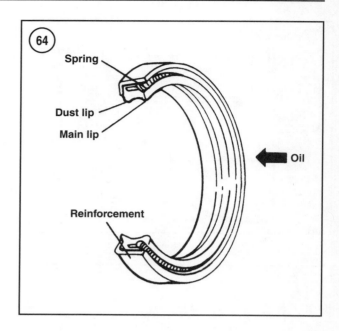

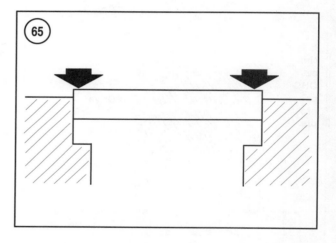

Table 1 TECHNICAL ABBREVIATIONS

ABDC	After bottom dead center
ATDC	After top dead center
BBDC	Before bottom dead center
BDC	Bottom dead center
BIA	Boating Industry Association
BID	Breakerless ignition distributor
BTDC	Before top dead center
C	Centigrade
cc	Cubic centimeters
CDI	Capacitor discharge ignition
CKP	Crankshaft position
CMP	Camshaft position
CT	Cylinder temperature
CTP	Closed throttle position
	(continued)

Table 1 TECHNICAL ABBREVIATIONS (continued)

cu.-in.	Cubic inches
DOHC	Dual overhead camshafts
ECU	Electronic control unit
EFI	Electronic fuel injection
EI	Electronic ignition
EM	Exhaust manifold
EST	Electronic spark timing
ETS	Engine temperature sensor
F	Fahrenheit
ft.-lb.	Foot-pounds
g	Gram
gal.	Gallons
hp	Horsepower
HPDI	High-pressure direct injection
IAC	Idle air control motor
IAT	Intake air temperature
in.	Inches
kg	Kilogram
kg/cm^2	Kilograms per square centimeter
kgm	Kilogram meters
km	Kilometer
L	Liter
M	Meter
MAG	Magneto
MAP	Manifold absolute pressure
mm	Millimeter
MPI	Multiport fuel injection
N.A.	Not available
N•m	Newton-meters
oz.	Ounce
OHC	Overhead camshaft
psi	Pounds per square inch
pto	Power take off
pts.	Pints
qt.	Quarts
RFI	Radio frequency interference
rpm	Revolutions per minute
TBI	Throttle body injection
TPS	Throttle position sensor
WOT	Wide open throttle

Table 2 CONVERSION TABLES

Multiply	By	To get equivalent of
Length		
Inches	25.4	Millimeter
Inches	2.54	Centimeter
Miles	1.609	Kilometer
Feet	0.3048	Meter
Millimeter	0.03937	Inches
Centimeter	0.3937	Inches
Kilometer	0.6214	Mile
Meter	3.281	Foot
Fluid volume		
U.S. quarts	0.9463	Liters
U.S. gallons	3.785	Liters
U.S. ounces	29.573529	Milliliters
Imperial gallons	4.54609	Liters

(continued)

Table 2 CONVERSION TABLES (continued)

Multiply	By	To get equivalent of
Fluid volume (continued)		
Imperial quarts	1.1365	Liters
Liters	0.2641721	U.S. gallons
Liters	1.0566882	U.S. quarts
Liters	33.814023	U.S. ounces
Liters	0.21997	Imperial gallons
Liters	0.8799	Imperial quarts
Milliliters	0.033814	U.S. ounces
Milliliters	1.0	Cubic centimeters
Milliliters	0.001	Liters
Torque		
Foot-pounds	1.3558	Newton-meters
Foot-pounds	0.138255	Meter-kilograms
Inch-pounds	0.11299	Newton-meters
Newton-meters	0.7375622	Foot-pounds
Newton-meters	8.8507	Inch-pounds
Meter-kilograms	7.2330139	Foot-pounds
Volume		
Cubic inches	16.387064	Cubic centimeters
Cubic centimeters	0.0610237	Cubic inches
Temperature		
Fahrenheit	(F−32°) × 0.556	Centigrade
Centigrade	(C × 1.8) + 32°	Fahrenheit
Weight		
Ounces	28.3495	Grams
Pounds	0.4535924	Kilograms
Grams	0.035274	Ounces
Kilograms	2.2046224	Pounds
Pressure		
Pounds per square inch	0.070307	Kilograms per square centimeter
Kilograms per square centimeter	14.223343	Pounds per square inch
Kilopascals	0.1450	Pounds per square inch
Pounds per square inch	6.895	Kilopascals
Speed		
Miles per hour	1.609344	Kilometers per hour
Kilometers per hour	0.6213712	Miles per hour

Table 3 U.S. STANDARD TAP AND DRILL SIZES

Tap size	Drill size	Decimal equivalent
#0-80	3/64	0.047
#1-64	No. 53	0.059
#1-72	No. 53	0.059
#2-56	No. 50	0.070
#2-64	No. 50	0.070
#3-48	5/64	0.078
#3-56	No. 46	0.081
#4-40	No. 43	0.890
#4-48	No. 42	0.935
#5-40	No. 39	0.938
#5-44	No. 37	0.104
#6-32	No. 36	0.107
#6-40	No. 33	0.113
#8-32	No. 29	0.136
#8-36	No. 29	0.136
#10-24	No. 25	0.150

(continued)

Table 3 U.S. STANDARD TAP AND DRILL SIZES (continued)

Tap size	Drill size	Decimal equivalent
#10-32	No. 21	0.159
#12-24	No. 16	0.177
#12-28	No. 14	0.182
1/4-20	No. 7	0.201
1/4-28	No. 3	0.213
5/16-18	F	0.257
5/16-24	I	0.272
3/8-16	5/16	0.3125
3/8-24	Q	0.332
7/16-14	U	0.368
7/16-20	25/64	0.390
1/2-13	27/64	0.422
1/2-20	29/64	0.453
9/16-12	31/64	0.484
9/16-18	33/64	0.516
5/8-11	17/32	0.531
5/8-18	37/64	0.578
3/4-10	21/32	0.656
3/4-16	11/16	0.688
7/8-9	49/64	0.766
7/8-14	13/16	0.813
1-8	7/8	0.875
1-14	15/16	0.938

Table 4 METRIC TAP AND DRILL SIZES

Metric tap (mm)	Drill size	Decimal equivalent	Nearest fraction (in.)
3 × 0.50	No. 39	0.0995	3/32
3 × 0.60	3/32	0.0937	3/32
4 × 0.70	No. 30	0.1285	1/8
4 × 0.75	1/8	0.125	1/8
5 × 0.80	No. 19	0.166	11/64
5 × 0.90	No. 20	0.161	5/32
6 × 1.00	No. 9	0.196	13/64
7 × 1.00	16/64	0.234	15/64
8 × 1.00	J	0.277	9/32
8 × 1.25	17/64	0.265	17/64
9 × 1.00	5/16	0.3125	5/16
9 × 1.25	5/16	0.3125	5/16
10 × 1.25	11/32	0.3437	11/32
10 × 1.50	R	0.339	11/32
11 × 1.50	3/8	0.375	3/8
12 × 1.50	13/32	0.406	13/32
12 × 1.75	13/32	0.406	13/32

Table 5 GENERAL TORQUE SPECIFICATIONS

Screw or nut size	in.-lb.	ft.-lb.	N•m
U.S. Standard			
6-32	9	–	1.0
8-32	20	–	2.3
10-24	30	–	3.4

(continued)

Table 5 GENERAL TORQUE SPECIFICATIONS (continued)

Screw or nut size	in.-lb.	ft.-lb.	N•m
U.S. Standard (continued)			
10-32	35	–	4.0
12-24	45	–	5.1
1/4-20	70	–	7.9
1/4-28	84	–	9.5
5/16-18	160	13	18
5/16-24	168	14	19
3/8-16	–	23	31
3/8-24	–	25	34
7/16-14	–	36	49
7/16-20	–	40	54
1/2-13	–	50	68
1/2-20	–	60	81
Metric			
M5	36	–	4.0
M6	70	–	8.0
M8	156	13	18
M10	–	26	35
M12	–	35	48
M14	–	60	81

Chapter Two

Troubleshooting

This chapter describes troubleshooting and test procedures for all engine systems. An Indmar inboard marine engine comprises two basic assemblies: the engine and the transmission. Engine systems include the starting system, charging system, fuel system and ignition system. Troubleshooting is a relatively simple matter if done logically. Taking a haphazard approach might eventually solve the problem, but it can be very costly in terms of wasted time and unnecessary parts replacement.

The first step is to determine which system is malfunctioning. Subsequent steps help determine which part of the system is malfunctioning. Further testing determines which component(s) of the system need adjustment or repair.

Most problems are very simple in nature and are easily corrected. Become familiar with the engine compartment. Notice wire and hose connection points. Note the normal full throttle speed, idle speed, sound of the engine and any peculiarities. A rough idle, reduced power output, unusual sounds or strange odors usually indicate trouble. Perform a quick visual inspection at the first sign of trouble. Look for fluid leakage and loose wires, hoses or belts. If a quick inspection does not identify the cause of a problem, refer to *Preliminary Inspection* for a list of additional items to check. **Tables 1-3** list starting, ignition and fuel system troubleshooting items. **Tables 4-7** list charging system, power steering system, cooling system and warning system troubleshooting recommendations. **Tables 8-13** list ignition, fuel and warning system test specifications. **Table 14** lists tightening specifications for fasteners that must be tightened during troubleshooting procedures. Use the General Torque Specifications listed in Chapter One for fasteners not listed in **Table 14**. **Tables 1-14** are located at the end of this chapter.

Proper lubrication, maintenance and periodic tune-up reduces the need to troubleshoot the engine. Lubrication, maintenance and tune-up are described in Chapter Three. Even with the best of care, however, problems can and eventually do occur.

PRELIMINARY INSPECTION

Every internal combustion engine requires three things to run (**Figure 1**): an uninterrupted supply of fuel and air in the proper proportion, adequate compression and a

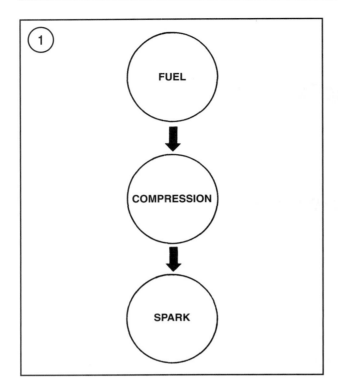

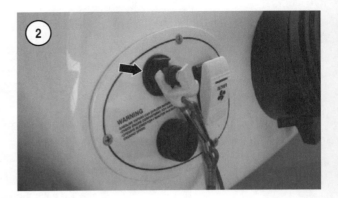

source of ignition at the proper time. If any are inadequate the engine will not run properly. If any are missing, the engine will not run.

Perform the following if the engine fails to start, runs rough, does not reach the maximum operating speed or hesitates during rapid acceleration. The maximum engine operating speed is listed in the owner's manual.

1. If so equipped, check the position of the emergency stop (lanyard) switch (**Figure 2**).

2. Check for loose, dirty or damaged wire connections (**Figure 3**).

3. Check the fuses (**Figure 4**) and circuit breakers (**Figure 5**).

4. Supply the engine with fresh fuel.

5. Check and fully charge the battery as described in Chapter Nine.

6. Clean the flame arrestor. Refer to *Cleaning the Flame Arrestor* in Chapter Three.

7. Check for spark at the spark plugs as described in this chapter.

8. Clean, inspect or replace the spark plugs as described in Chapter Three.

9. Check for damaged or improperly adjusted throttle or shift cables.

10. If checking or correcting all of the previous items fails to identify or correct the malfunction, refer to **Tables 1-3** for additional items to check. Refer to the causes listed

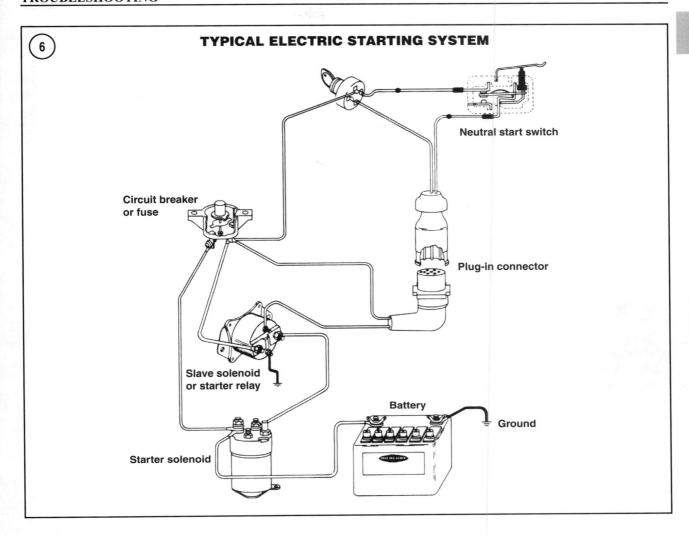

⑥ **TYPICAL ELECTRIC STARTING SYSTEM**

Neutral start switch

Circuit breaker
or fuse

Plug-in connector

Slave solenoid
or starter relay

Battery

Ground

Starter solenoid

next to the symptom that best describes the malfunction. Perform the test or adjustment suggested as a corrective action. Other useful information and tips are described with specific test instructions.

11. It can be difficult to determine whether a starting problem is related to fuel, ignition or other causes. It is usually easiest to first verify that the ignition system is operating. Check the fuel and fuel system if the ignition system is operating but the engine will not start or starting is difficult. Refer to *Checking for spark at the coil and spark plugs* in this chapter to determine whether spark is present at the spark plugs.

ELECTRIC STARTING SYSTEM

This section provides a brief description of how the electric starting system operates followed by testing instructions for the individual components.

The starting system consists of the battery, starter motor, starter relay or slave solenoid, ignition key switch, neutral start switch and wiring.

Electric Starting System Operation

Refer to **Figure 6** for a typical starting system circuit. Battery current is supplied to the ignition switch from a circuit breaker or fuse. When the ignition switch is turned to START, battery current flows to the neutral start switch in the remote control or mounted onto the transmission. Current flows through the switch to energize the slave solenoid or starter relay, provided the control is in NEUTRAL. When energized, the slave solenoid or starter relay supplies current to the starter solenoid. The solenoid then mechanically engages the starter pinion gear with the flywheel ring gear and supplies the current to operate the starter motor.

Due to the voltage drop associated with the long wires connecting the key switch to the engine, Indmar inboard marine engines must use either a slave solenoid or starter relay to activate the starter solenoid. These components perform the same function but are not interchangeable. The slave solenoid mounts to the engine and uses eyelet or push-on connectors to connect to the engine wire harness. The starter relay plugs directly into the engine harness connector and is secured to the mounting bracket with a hook and loop band or a slide-on tab.

Once the engine is started and the key switch is released, the slave solenoid or starter relay de-energizes, thereby deactivating the starter solenoid. At this point, the solenoid disengages the starter pinion gear from the fly-wheel and discontinues supplying current to the starter motor.

Neutral Start Switch

The neutral start switch is incorporated into the remote control or mounted on the transmission on all Indmar inboard marine engines. The neutral start switch is designed to prevent starting system operation if the shift control is in FORWARD or REVERSE. The switch should allow starter operation only if the remote control is in NEUTRAL. A faulty switch can prevent the starter from operating with the control in NEUTRAL or allow the starter to operate with the engine in gear. Some engines use both a remote control and transmission-mounted switch. This does not present a problem provided both switches are operating correctly. If so equipped, test both switches as described in this section.

Remote control-mounted switch

1. Disconnect the battery cables.
2. Locate the pair of yellow or yellow/red wires leading to the remote control housing (**Figure 7**). One of the wires connects to the key switch. The other wire connects to the instrument harness yellow/red wire that leads to the engine. Mark the wires to identify the connection points. Then disconnect the wires. In most cases the wires are connected with crimp connectors. If necessary, cut the wiring and install new connectors after testing.
3. Calibrate an ohmmeter to the R × 1 scale. Connect the meter test leads to the disconnected yellow/red wires leading to the remote control.
4. Observe the meter while repeatedly shifting the remote control into FORWARD, NEUTRAL and REVERSE. Repeating the shifting cycles will often identify an intermittent switch malfunction.

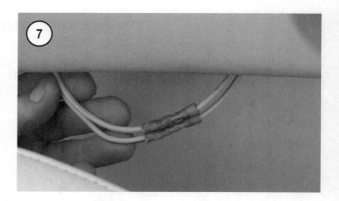

5. The meter must indicate full continuity each time the remote control reaches NEUTRAL and no continuity each time the remote control reaches FORWARD or REVERSE. Disassemble the remote control and replace the neutral start switch if it fails to perform as specified.
6. Reconnect one of the yellow/red neutral switch wires to the wire leading to the key switch. Reconnect the other yellow/red neutral switch wire to the yellow/red instrument harness wire leading to the engine. Do not inadvertently connect the switch wires together or connect the key switch directly to the instrument harness wiring.
7. Connect the battery cables.
8. Pull the cord to activate the emergency stop (lanyard) switch (**Figure 2**). This prevents the ignition system from operating, though the lanyard switch does not prevent starter motor operation. If the engine is not equipped with a lanyard switch, disconnect and ground the ignition coil secondary wire to prevent accidental starting.
9. Verify proper neutral start switch operation as follows:
    a. Shift the remote control into FORWARD. Then attempt to start the engine. Repeat this step with the remote control in REVERSE. The starter must not operate with the remote control in FORWARD and REVERSE. Check for faulty wiring or replace the switch if the switch fails to perform as specified.
    b. Shift the remote control into NEUTRAL. Then momentarily attempt to start the engine. Check for faulty wiring, a faulty switch, faulty transmission-mounted neutral start switch or other faulty starting system components if the starter fails to operate as specified.
10. Reattach the lanyard switch or reconnect the ignition coil secondary lead.

Transmission-mounted switch

1. Disconnect the battery cables.

2. Locate the pair of yellow or yellow/red wires leading to the transmission-mounted neutral start switch (**Figure 8**). Do not confuse the transmission temperature switch wires with the neutral start switch. Identify the wires by color. The wire terminals are exposed on some models and covered by an insulating boot on others. Mark the wires to identify the connection points. Then disconnect the wires. In most cases, the wires are connected with ring terminals. On models so equipped, pull the rubber insulating boot back on the wiring to access the terminals. Work carefully to avoid tearing the boot.

3. Calibrate an ohmmeter to the R × 1 scale. Connect the meter test leads to the disconnected yellow/red wires leading to the remote control.

4. Observe the meter while repeatedly shifting the remote control into FORWARD, NEUTRAL and REVERSE. Repeating the shifting cycles will often identify an intermittent switch malfunction.

5. The meter must indicate full continuity each time the remote control reaches NEUTRAL and no continuity each time the remote control reaches FORWARD or REVERSE. Replace the neutral start switch as described in Chapter Nine if it fails to perform as specified.

6. Reconnect the yellow or yellow/red wires to the neutral start switch terminals. If so equipped, carefully slide the rubber boot over the switch terminals and position it fully over the switch.

7. Connect the battery cables.

8. Pull the cord to activate the emergency stop (lanyard) switch (**Figure 2**). This prevents the ignition system from operating but does not prevent starter motor operation. If the engine is not equipped with a lanyard switch, disconnect and ground the ignition coil secondary wire to prevent accidental starting.

9. Verify proper neutral start switch operation as follows:

   a. Shift the remote control into FORWARD. Then attempt to start the engine. Repeat this step with the remote control in REVERSE. The starter must not operate with the remote control in FORWARD and REVERSE. Check for faulty wiring or a faulty switch if the switch fails to perform as specified.

   b. Shift the remote control into NEUTRAL. Then momentarily attempt to start the engine. Check for faulty wiring, a faulty switch, faulty transmission-mounted neutral start switch or other faulty starting system components if the starter fails to operate as specified.

10. Reattach the lanyard switch or reconnect the ignition coil secondary lead.

Key Switch

The key switch is secured to the dash with a decorative nut on the exposed side and a larger nut on the underside of the dash. On most switches, the wires are connected to the terminals with small screws. Other switches use push-on terminals. With either type, wire identification marks are molded into the housing next to each terminal. The test procedure in this section covers the standard three-terminal switch. Some switches have a fourth and fifth terminal for use on many brands of outboard motors. If the switch has more than three terminals, perform the test using only the three indicated terminals.

The first test sequence measures the voltage at the key switch terminals. The second sequence tests the internal switch circuits.

Voltage test

1. Pull the cord to activate the emergency stop (lanyard) switch (**Figure 2**) to prevent the ignition system from operating. The lanyard switch does not prevent starter motor operation. If the engine is not equipped with a lanyard switch, disconnect and ground the ignition coil secondary wire to prevent accidental starting.

2. Disconnect the white or purple and yellow or yellow/red wires from the switch terminals. Do not disconnect the red or red/purple wire from the terminal.

3. Calibrate a voltmeter on the 20 or 40 VDC scale. Connect the meter negative test lead to the black wire at tachometer or other suitable ground wire under the dash.

4. Touch the positive test lead to the red or red/purple wire terminal on the switch. The meter must indicate within 0.5 volt of battery voltage. If not, refer to the following:

   a. If the meter shows 0 volt, check for a blown fuse or tripped circuit breaker on the engine. Faulty wiring or connection is indicated if *all* of the fuses and circuit breakers are good.

b. If the meter shows low voltage, check for loose or corroded wire terminals on the engine-mounted starter, starter solenoid or starter relay and at the dash-mounted instruments and switches. Make sure that no accessories (radios, pumps, fans) are wired to the key switch. The accessory load may cause a starting system or ignition system malfunction.

5. Place the key switch in OFF or STOP. Observe the meter while touching the meter positive test lead to the *S* and *I* terminals on the switch. The meter must indicate 0 volt at each connection point. If any voltage is indicated, the switch is shorted internally and must be replaced.

6. Connect the meter positive lead to the *I* terminal of the key switch. Observe the meter while repeatedly turning the switch to ON or RUN and START. The switch must show within 0.5 volt of battery voltage with the key switch in ON or RUN and START. Replace the switch if it fails to perform as specified.

7. Connect the positive meter lead to the *S* terminal on the key switch. Observe the meter while repeatedly turning the switch to ON or RUN and START. The switch must show within 0.5 volt of battery voltage with the key switch in START and 0 volt with the switch in ON or RUN. Replace the switch if it fails to perform as specified.

8. Connect the white or purple wire terminal to the *I* terminal on the key switch. Connect the yellow or yellow/red wire terminal to the *S* terminal on the switch. Route the wiring to prevent interference with moving components. Secure the wiring with clamps as needed.

9. Reattach the lanyard cord to the emergency stop (lanyard) switch to allow engine starting.

Internal circuit test

1. Disconnect the battery cables.

2. Disconnect the red or red/purple, white or purple, and yellow or yellow/red wires from the key switch. If other wires are attached to the switch, note the wire routing and connection points. Then disconnect the wires.

3. Remove the key. Then remove the decorative outer nut. Pull the key switch out of the dash. Insert the key into the switch. Remove the lockwasher from the switch.

4. Calibrate an ohmmeter on the R × 1 scale.

5. Connect the positive test lead to the *B* or *Batt* terminal on the key switch. Connect the negative test lead to the *I* terminal on the switch. Note the meter reading while cycling the switch to OFF or STOP, ON or RUN and START. The meter must indicate no continuity with the key switch in OFF or STOP and full continuity with the key switch in the ON or RUN and START positions. Replace the key switch if it fails to perform as specified.

6. Connect the positive test lead to the *B* or *Batt* terminal on the key switch. Connect the negative test lead to the *S* terminal on the switch. Note the meter reading while cycling the switch to OFf or STOP, ON or RUN and START. The meter must indicate no continuity with the key switch in OFF or STOP and ON or RUN and full continuity with the key switch in START. Replace the key switch if it fails to perform as specified.

7. Install the lockwasher onto the key switch and seat it against the internal nut.

8. Remove the key from the switch. Install the key switch into the dash opening and secure with the decorative nut. If necessary, tighten the internal nut to secure the switch in the opening. Insert the key into the switch.

9. Connect the red or red/purple wire terminal onto the *B* or *Batt* switch terminal. Connect the white or purple wire terminal onto the *I* switch terminal. Connect the yellow or yellow/red wire terminal onto the *S* switch terminal. Route the wiring to prevent interference with moving components. Secure the wiring with clamps as needed.

10. Connect the battery cables.

Starter Motor Cranking Voltage

This test measures the voltage at the starter battery cable during cranking. The battery must be fully charged, and the spark plugs must be installed for accurate testing.

> **WARNING**
> *The engine may unexpectedly start or motor over during testing. Keep all persons, clothing, tools or loose objects away from the drive belts and other moving components on the engine.*

> **CAUTION**
> *Use a flush device to supply the engine with cooling water if testing the starter motor with the boat out of the water. Operation of the starter motor results in operation of the seawater pump. The seawater pump is quickly damaged if operated without adequate cooling water.*

1. Place the key switch in OFF or STOP and the remote control in NEUTRAL.

2. Pull the cord to activate the emergency stop (lanyard) switch (**Figure 2**). This prevents the ignition system from operating but does not prevent starter motor operation. If the engine is not equipped with a lanyard switch, disconnect and ground the ignition coil secondary wire to prevent accidental starting.

3. Carefully move the insulator boot away from the battery cable terminal on the starter solenoid.

4. Set a voltmeter on the 20 or 40 VDC scale. Touch the negative lead to an engine ground. Touch the positive lead to the battery cable-to-starter solenoid terminal (A, **Figure 9**). The meter must show battery voltage. If otherwise, test the battery as described in Chapter Nine and check for dirty terminals or a faulty battery cable.

5. Touch the positive test lead to the starter solenoid cable terminal (A, **Figure 9**). Touch the negative lead to an engine ground.

6. Observe the meter while an assistant cycles the key switch to START. The meter must indicate 9.5-11.5 volts while the starter cranks the engine at an adequate speed for starting. Refer to the following:

   a. If the voltage is less than 9.5 volts and the starter rotates slowly, fully charge and test the battery as described in Chapter Nine. Test the starter solenoid if the battery is in acceptable condition.

   b. If the voltage exceeds 11.5 volts but the starter does not operate or turns slowly, test the starter solenoid as described in this chapter. Repair the starter motor as described in Chapter Nine if the solenoid tests satisfactorily.

7. Touch the positive test lead to the braided wire terminal on the starter solenoid. If the starter does not have a braided wire, touch the test lead to the large solenoid terminal opposite the battery terminal. Touch the negative meter lead to an engine ground.

8. Observe the meter while an assistant cycles the key switch to START. The meter must indicate 9.5-11.5 volts while the starter cranks the engine at an adequate speed for starting. Refer to the following:

   a. If the voltage is less than 9.5 volts, and the starter rotates slowly, fully charge and test the battery as described in Chapter Nine.

   b. If the voltage exceeds 11.5 volts, but the starter does not operate or operates slowly, repair the starter motor as describe in Chapter Nine.

   c. If the voltage is within 9.5-11.5 volts and the starter rotates slowly or does not operate, check for a seized engine or transmission. Repair the starter as described in Chapter Nine if no fault is found with the engine or transmission.

9. Make sure all terminal nuts are securely tightened and the wire terminals are not contacting other terminals. Reposition the wiring as necessary. To prevent terminal corrosion and starting system malfunction, thoroughly coat the terminals with Black Neoprene Dip. Purchase the neoprene dip (OMC part No. 909570) from an OMC dealership or automotive parts store.

10. Reposition the insulator over the battery cable terminal on the starter solenoid.

11. Reattach the lanyard cord to the emergency stop (lanyard) switch. If the engine is not equipped with a lanyard switch, reconnect the ignition coil secondary wire.

Starter Solenoid

The starter solenoid mounts to the starter motor. The first test sequence measures the voltage supplied to the starter solenoid and checks for proper switching while mounted on the engine. The second test checks for proper operation of the solenoid. The functional test is useful to test the solenoid if removed from the starter motor.

Voltage test

WARNING
The engine may unexpectedly start or motor over during testing. Keep all persons, clothing, tools or loose objects away from the drive belts and other moving components on the engine.

CAUTION
Use a flush device to supply the engine with cooling water if testing the starter solenoid with the boat out of the water. Operation of the starter motor results in operation of the seawater pump. The seawater pump is quickly damaged if operated without adequate cooling water.

This test requires a voltmeter and clear access to the starter solenoid terminals. The starter and solenoid are mounted on the lower rear and starboard side of the engine. Correct test results are only possible if the test leads make good contact to the correct terminals.

The starter motor may operate during testing. Avoid entrapment in belts or other moving components on the engine. This procedure also tests the bypass circuit function of the solenoid. While the starter motor is operating, the bypass circuit uses the *R* terminal on the solenoid to supply voltage to the ignition coil on models with a standard point ignition system or electric fuel pump. The circuit is used only on carburetor-equipped models.

1. Place the key switch in OFF or STOP and the remote control in NEUTRAL.

2. Pull the cord to activate the lanyard switch (**Figure 2**). This prevents the ignition system from operating but does not prevent starter motor operation. If the engine is not equipped with a lanyard switch, disconnect and ground the ignition coil secondary wire to prevent accidental starting.

3. Set the voltmeter to the 20 or 40 VDC scale.

4. Check for battery voltage at the solenoid as follows:

   a. Carefully pull the insulator boot away from the battery cable terminal (A, **Figure 9**).

   b. Touch the positive meter lead to the battery cable terminal.

   c. Observe the meter while touching the negative meter lead to an engine ground. The meter must indicate battery voltage. If not, test the battery as described in Chapter Nine and check for loose or dirty connections or a faulty battery switch.

5. Disconnect the battery cables.

6. Remove the brass nut (B, **Figure 9**). Then disconnect the large wire that connects the starter solenoid to the starter end cap. Completely cover the wire and terminal with electrical tape and position it away from all starter solenoid terminals.

7. Reconnect the battery cables.

8. Check for voltage from the slave solenoid or starter relay as follows:

   a. Touch the positive meter lead to the yellow or yellow/red wire terminal on the starter solenoid (C, **Figure 9**). Touch the negative meter lead to an engine ground. The meter must indicate 0 volt. If any voltage is indicated, disconnect the yellow or yellow/red wire from the terminal and repeat the test. If any voltage is indicated with the wire disconnected, the solenoid is shorted internally and must be replaced. If the meter indicates 0 volt *only* with the yellow/red wire disconnected, test the slave solenoid or starter relay as described in this section. Reconnect the yellow/red wire.

   b. Connect the test leads as described in Step 8a. Observe the meter while an assistant cycles the key switch to the ON or RUN. The meter must indicate

0 volt. If any voltage is indicated, test the slave solenoid or starter relay as described in this section.

   c. Connect test leads as described in Step 8a. Observe the meter while an assistant cycles the key switch to START. The meter must indicate battery voltage each time the switch is placed in START. If the meter indicates less than battery voltage, perform the starter solenoid functional test as described in this section.

9. Check the solenoid switching function as follows:

   a. Touch the positive meter lead to the large solenoid terminal (B, **Figure 9**) for the braided wire or wire opposite the battery cable wire terminal. The braided or large-gauge wire must be disconnected from the terminal for this test. Touch the negative meter lead to an engine ground. Place the key switch in OFF or STOP. The meter must indicate 0 volt. If any voltage is indicated, the solenoid is shorted internally and must be replaced.

   b. Connect the meter leads as described in Step 9a. Observe the meter while an assistant cycles the key switch to START. The meter must indicate battery voltage, and the solenoid must make a clicking sound each time the switch is placed in START. Perform the functional test, as described in this section, if the solenoid fails to perform as specified.

10. Test the bypass circuit as follows:

   a. Touch the positive meter lead to the purple or purple/yellow wire terminal (D, **Figure 9**) on the solenoid. Touch the negative meter lead to an engine ground.

   b. Observe the meter while an assistant cycles the key switch to OFF or STOP, ON or RUN, and START. The meter must indicate 0 volt each time the key switch is placed in OFF or STOP and ON or RUN and battery voltage each time the switch is placed in START. Replace the starter solenoid if the switching circuit fails to perform as specified.

11. Disconnect the negative battery cable.

12. Remove the protective tape. Connect the braided cable or large-gauge wire to the starter solenoid terminal (B, **Figure 9**) and secure with the brass nut.

13. Make sure all terminal nuts are securely tightened and the wire terminals are not contacting other terminals. Reposition the wiring as necessary. To prevent terminal corrosion and starting system malfunction, thoroughly coat the terminals with Black Neoprene Dip. Purchase the neoprene dip (OMC part No. 909570) from an OMC dealership or automotive parts store.

14. Reposition the insulator over the battery cable terminal on the starter solenoid.

15. Connect the battery cable.

16. Reattach the lanyard cord to the emergency stop (lanyard) switch. If the engine is not equipped with a lanyard switch, reconnect the ignition coil secondary wire.

Functional test

This test requires a fully charged battery, ohmmeter and jumper wires.

1. Disconnect the battery cables.
2. Remove the starter motor and then starter solenoid as described in Chapter Nine.
3. Calibrate an ohmmeter on the R × 1 scale.
4. Connect the positive meter lead to one of the large terminals on the solenoid. Connect the negative meter lead to the other large terminal. The meter must indicate no continuity. If continuity is present, the solenoid is shorted internally and must be replaced.
5. Test the solenoid plunger operation and starter switching circuits as follows:
   a. Connect a jumper wire to the positive battery terminal and the S terminal on the starter solenoid. Do not inadvertently connect the jumper to the R terminal.
   b. Connect a second jumper lead to the negative battery terminal.
   c. Observe the meter while repeatedly touching the second jumper lead to a clean metal surface on the solenoid housing. The meter must indicate full continuity and the solenoid must make a clicking sound as the plunger retracts each time the jumper touches the housing. Replace the solenoid if it fails to perform as specified.
6. Test the bypass circuit in the solenoid as follows:
   a. Move the positive meter lead to the R terminal on the starter solenoid. Do not disconnect the meter lead from the other large terminal. Do not disconnect the jumper lead from the battery and solenoid.
   b. Observe the meter while repeatedly touching the second jumper lead to a clean metal surface on the solenoid housing. The meter must indicate full continuity each time the jumper touches the housing. Replace the solenoid if it fails to perform as specified.
7. Remove the jumper and meter leads.
8. Install the starter solenoid and starter motor as described in Chapter Nine.
9. Connect the battery cables.

Slave Solenoid

Two types of slave solenoids are used. On some models equipped with a breaker-point ignition system, a switch type solenoid is used. On these models, the solenoid supplies battery voltage to the ignition coil during starter motor operation. This bypasses the ignition resistor circuit to provide battery voltage to the ignition coil for more efficient starting. Later models equipped with breaker-point ignition use a standard solenoid, and the starter solenoid provides the bypass circuit. A cranking bypass circuit is not required on late models equipped with transistorized ignition.

The switch-type and standard solenoids are very similar in appearance and usually use the same number and size of terminals. The easiest way to determine if a switch-type solenoid is used is to look at the wiring colors. On a switch-type solenoid, a yellow or yellow/red wire connects to one of the smaller terminals, and a tan or purple/yellow wire connects to the other smaller terminal. The switch-type solenoid grounds through the mounting plate, and this can be verified by checking for continuity between the S terminal used by the yellow or yellow/red wire and the mounting plate.

On a standard solenoid, a yellow or yellow/red wire connects to one of the smaller terminals, and a black wire connects to the other smaller terminal. The solenoid grounds through the black wire connected to the smaller terminal, and this can be verified by checking for continuity between the smaller terminal used for the yellow or yellow/red wire and the smaller terminal used for the black wire.

Use a 12-volt test lamp for this procedure.

1. Place the key switch in OFF or STOP and the remote control in NEUTRAL.
2. Pull the cord to activate the emergency stop (lanyard) switch (**Figure 2**). This prevents the ignition system from operating but does not prevent starter motor operation. If the engine is not equipped with a lanyard switch, disconnect and ground the ignition coil secondary wire to prevent accidental starting.
3. Connect the cord of the test lamp to an engine ground. Touch the test lamp probe to a positive battery voltage source to verify the ground and test lamp operation. Locate a proven ground or repair the test lamp as needed.
4. Touch the test lamp probe to the red or red/purple wire terminal on the slave solenoid (A, **Figure 10**, typical). The lamp must illuminate. If not, check for a blown fuse along the wire connecting the solenoid to the starter motor terminal. Repair the faulty wiring or connections if the fuses are good.
5. Test the voltage from the key switch and neutral start switch to the solenoid as follows:
   a. Disconnect the yellow or yellow/red wire from the smaller solenoid terminal (B, **Figure 10**, typical).

b. Connect the test lamp to an engine ground as described in Step 3.

c. Touch the test probe to the disconnected yellow or yellow/red wire terminal.

d. Observe the lamp while an assistant repeatedly turns the key switch to OFF or STOP, ON or RUN, and START. The lamp must illuminate each time the key switch is in START must not illuminate with the switch in OFF or STOP and ON or RUN. Test the key switch and neutral start switch as described in this section if the circuit fails to perform as specified. Repair the yellow or yellow/red wire leading to the instruments and switches if the key switch and neutral start switch are in acceptable condition.

e. Reconnect the yellow or yellow/red wire onto the smaller solenoid terminal.

6A. On models with a switch-type solenoid, test the solenoid ground as follows:

a. Connect the test lamp between a positive battery source and an engine ground to verify the voltage source. Check for faulty engine ground cables, wiring or connections if the lamp fails to illuminate.

b. Touch the test probe to the metallic solenoid mounting plate. The test lamp must illuminate. If not, correct the loose fasteners, dirty mating surfaces or damaged ground wires to restore the ground.

6B. On models with a standard solenoid, test the solenoid ground as follows:

a. Connect the test lamp between a positive battery source and an engine ground to verify the voltage source. Check for faulty engine ground cables, wiring or connections if the lamp fails to illuminate.

b. Touch the test probe to the terminal for the small black wire (D, **Figure 10**, typical). The test lamp must illuminate. If not, repair the black wire or connecting terminals to restore the ground.

7. Test the solenoid operation as follows:

a. Connect the test lamp between an engine ground and a positive battery source to verify the ground and lamp operation.

b. Touch the test probe to the larger yellow or yellow/red terminal (C, **Figure 10**, typical) on the solenoid. Observe the lamp while an assistant repeatedly turns the key switch to OFF or STOP, ON or RUN, and START. The lamp must illuminate, and the solenoid must click each time the key switch is in START and must not illuminate with the key switch in OFF or STOP and ON or RUN positions. Replace the slave solenoid if it fails to perform as specified.

8. On models with a switch-type solenoid, test the bypass circuit as follows:

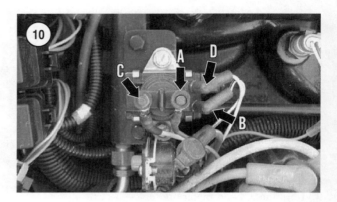

a. Disconnect the tan or purple/yellow wire from the smaller solenoid terminal.

b. Connect the test lamp between an engine ground and a positive battery source to verify the ground and lamp operation.

c. Touch the test probe to the small terminal on the solenoid for the tan or purple/yellow wire (D, **Figure 10**, typical). Observe the lamp while an assistant repeatedly turns the key switch to OFF or STOP, ON or RUN, and START. The lamp must illuminate each time the key switch is in START and must not illuminate with the key switch in OFF or STOP and ON or RUN. Replace the slave solenoid if it fails to perform as specified.

d. Reconnect the tan or purple/yellow wire to the smaller solenoid terminal.

Starter Relay

The starter relay (**Figure 11**) has a common five-terminal design. This procedure tests for proper current delivery to the relay and checks for proper relay switching. Relays are relatively inexpensive. Replace the relay if it is in questionable condition.

Use a 12-volt test lamp for this procedure.

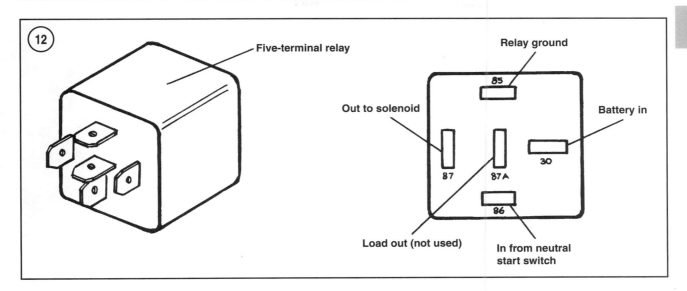

1. Place the key switch in OFF or STOP and the remote control in NEUTRAL.

2. Pull the cord to activate the emergency stop (lanyard) switch (**Figure 2**). This prevents the ignition system from operating but does not prevent starter motor operation. If the engine is not equipped with a lanyard switch, disconnect and ground the ignition coil secondary wire to prevent accidental starting.

3. Disconnect the battery cables. Remove the starter relay as described in Chapter Nine. Reconnect the battery cables.

4. Refer to **Figure 12** and the terminals in the wire harness or relay mounting bracket to identify the relay terminals. The relay will only fit one way into the plug or bracket. Compare the orientation of the No. 30 and No. 87 terminal blades for reference.

5. Test the relay ground circuit as follows:
   a. Connect the test lamp between the positive battery terminal and a good engine ground to verify the battery source and lamp operation.
   b. Touch the test probe to the No. 85 terminal in the harness connector that aligns with the black engine wire leading to the connector. If the No. 85 terminal does not align with the black wire, touch the test probe to the No. 86 terminal in the harness connector. The lamp must illuminate. If not, check for a faulty terminal connection or fault in the black relay ground wire.

6. Test the battery current supply to the relay as follows:
   a. Connect the test lamp between the negative battery terminal or good engine ground and the positive battery terminal to verify the ground connection and lamp operation.
   b. Touch the test probe to the No. 30 terminal in the harness connector that aligns with the red or red/purple wire leading to the connector. If the No. 30 terminal does not align with the red or red/purple wire, touch the test probe to the No. 87 terminal in the connector. The lamp must illuminate. If not, check for a blown fuse or circuit breaker, faulty terminal or battery supply wire to the terminal.

7. Test the start circuit as follows:
   a. Connect the test lamp between the negative battery terminal and positive battery terminal to verify the ground connection and lamp operation.
   b. Touch the test probe to the No. 86 terminal in the harness connector that aligns with the yellow or yellow/red wire leading to the connector. If the No. 86 terminal does not align with the yellow or yellow/red wire, touch the test probe to the No. 85 terminal in the connector. The lamp must not illuminate with the key switch in OFF or STOP. If the lamp illuminates, check the key switch as described in this section. Check for a shorted instrument or engine wire harness if the key switch is in good condition.
   c. Observe the lamp while an assistant cycles the key switch to ON or RUN and START. The lamp must not illuminate with the key switch in ON or RUN, and the lamp must illuminate with the switch in START. If otherwise, check for a faulty key switch, faulty instrument or engine wire harness.

8. Replace the relay if no faults are found with the wiring and connecting circuits but the relay fails to supply current to the starter solenoid.

9. Install the starter relay as described in Chapter Nine.

10. Reattach the lanyard switch cord (**Figure 2**).

CHARGING SYSTEM

All models use an internally regulated belt-driven alternator (**Figure 13**). The major components of the alternator (**Figure 14**, typical) are the rotor, stator, brushes, rectifier bridge and the voltage regulator.

The drive belt spins the rotor (3, **Figure 14**, typical) at approximately twice the crankshaft speed. The brushes (7, **Figure 14**, typical) maintain contact with the slip rings on the rotor.

When the key switch is turned on, battery voltage is supplied to the alternator by the white or purple wire. This voltage passes through the voltage regulator to the positive brush lead. The voltage flows through the rotor winding and back to ground through the negative brush lead and the voltage regulator. Current flowing through the winding creates a magnetic field.

Alternating current forms as the spinning magnetic field passes through the stator windings. This alternating current is directed to the rectifier bridge where diodes convert it to direct current. The direct current flows from the alternator output terminal through a fuse or circuit breaker and finally to the positive battery terminal.

The voltage regulator (6, **Figure 14**, typical) controls alternator output by controlling the amount of current flowing through the rotor winding. The regulator senses battery voltage via the small red wire connecting the regulator to the engine wire harness. If the voltage drops below a predetermined value, the regulator allows additional current flow through the rotor. This increases the strength of the magnetic field and thereby increases alternator output. If the voltage exceeds a predetermined value, the regulator restricts current flow through the rotor. This decreases the strength of the magnetic field and thereby decreases alternator output.

A series of three diodes, referred to as the diode trio, in the rectifier bridge directs some of the output current back to the rotor to sustain the magnetic field. The current delivered from the diode trio is not strong enough to fully energize the field until the engine reaches approximately 1000 rpm. Once the alternator energizes it does not require current from the white or purple wire and will provide output at all engine speeds. If not energized, the alternator essentially discharges the battery.

A charging system malfunction generally causes the battery to be undercharged. Modern boats are equipped with numerous electric accessories such as depth finders, radios and lighting. Frequently, the current required to operate these accessories exceeds the output of the charging system.

Monitor the voltmeter with the accessories switched ON and OFF. A voltage reading of 12.3 volts or less with the accessories ON indicates the electrical load exceeds the output of the charging system. In such instances, install an auxiliary battery and switch device (**Figure 15**) to prevent a discharged cranking battery. Wire the accessories to draw from the auxiliary battery.

Charging system malfunction is generally caused by a defective alternator, battery, fuse or circuit breaker. The malfunction may also be caused by something as simple as incorrect drive belt tension. Always check these items before beginning the troubleshooting procedure. Refer to **Table 4** for troubleshooting recommendations if the battery loses its charge at rest or if the dash-mounted voltmeter indicates discharging (less than 12.3 volts) or overcharging (greater than 13.8 volts) with the engine running at normal cruising speed. The recommended test procedures are described in this section.

Indmar inboard marine engines use alternators produced by several different manufacturers, and many of them are interchangeable. The general alternator test procedures in this section apply to all alternators that may be installed on the engine. Some of the alternators have additional terminals on the rear of the alternator that may be used on other types of equipment or applications. The additional terminals are usually covered with an insulating cap. Perform all tests using only the specified wire colors to ensure accurate test results.

WARNING
Use extreme caution when working around batteries. Batteries produce hydrogen gas that can explode and result in severe injury or death. Never make the final connection of a circuit to the battery because an arc can occur and lead to fire or explosion.

2

⑭ BELT-DRIVEN ALTERNATOR (TYPICAL)

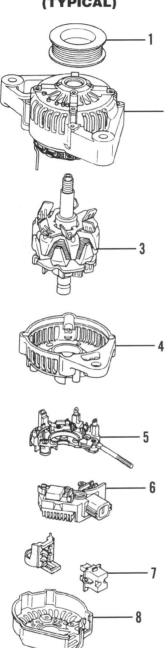

1. Pulley
2. Stator and front housing
3. Rotor
4. Rear housing
5. Rectifier bridge
6. Voltage regulator
7. Brushes
8. Shield

⑮

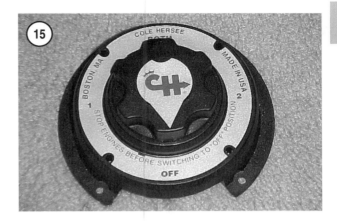

CAUTION
Charging system damage will occur if the battery cable(s) or any charging system output wires are disconnected while the engine is running. Make sure any battery-switching device does not break the circuit when switching from one battery to the next. Otherwise, operate the switch only with the engine not running.

CAUTION
Never operate the engine without first providing cooling water. Use a flush device or operate the engine with the boat in the water. Operating the engine without providing adequate cooling water will quickly damage the seawater pump and can result in serious engine damage.

Alternator Output

This test requires an ammeter and a load tester (such as Stevens LB-85 Load Bank) or other suitable carbon pile load set. This test measures the alternator output at various engine speeds to determine alternator efficiency.

1. Disconnect the battery cables.
2. Disconnect the larger-gauge red, red/white or orange lead from the POS terminal stud (A, **Figure 16**, typical) on the rear of the alternator.
3. Connect the ammeter (B, **Figure 16**, typical) in series between the POS terminal stud (A) and the red, red/white or orange wire terminal (C). Make sure the positive terminal on the ammeter connects to the POS and the negative terminal connects to the output lead. Otherwise, the ammeter will read the opposite of the actual output.
4. Connect the battery cable.
5. Attach the load tester to the battery terminals.
6. Start the engine and operate at fast idle (1200-1500 rpm) until it reaches normal operating temperature.

7. Return the engine to idle speed and switch off all accessories. Switch on the load tester and note the alternator output on the ammeter. The ammeter must indicate a minimum of 20 amps for either the 51-amp or 65-amp alternator. The alternator output rating is stamped or printed on the alternator housing. Switch off the load tester.

8. Raise the engine speed to 1500 rpm. Switch on the load tester and note the alternator output on the ammeter. The ammeter must indicate a minimum of 47 amps for the 51-amp alternator and 53 amps for the 65-amp alternator. Switch off the load tester. If the engine is using an alternator with a higher amp rating, the output must be proportional to the rating when compared to the 56- and 65-amp models.

9. Raise the engine speed to 2000 rpm. Switch on the load tester and note the alternator output on the ammeter. The ammeter must indicate a minimum of 51 amps for the 51 amp alternator and 56 amp for the 65 amp alternator. If the engine is using an alternator with a higher amp rating, the output must be proportional to the rating when compared to the 56 and 65 amp models. Switch off the load tester.

10. Stop the engine.

11. Disconnect the negative battery cables.

12. Disconnect the ammeter and reconnect the red/red/white or orange wire to the POS terminal stud on the rear of the alternator. Make sure to position the rubber insulating boot (**Figure 17**) fully over the terminal.

13. Connect the battery cable.

14. Test the excitation circuit, sensing circuit, alternator ground, output wire circuit and diode trio if no output or low output was measured in Steps 7-9. Replace the alternator with a new or rebuilt unit if the excitation circuit, sensing circuit, alternator ground and output wire circuit are in acceptable condition.

Excitation Circuit Test

The transistorized voltage regulator, mounted inside the alternator housing or attached to the rear of the alternator, contains excitation and sensing circuits. The excitation circuit, which is connected to the ignition switch circuit, sends a small amount of current to the alternator rotor field winding to build a magnetic field and initiate charging output. This allows the alternator to generate output more quickly after startup than relying solely on residual magnetism in the rotor.

This test requires an accurate voltmeter.

1. Place the key switch in OFF or STOP.

2. Set the voltmeter to the 20 or 40 VDC scale.

3. Unplug the white or purple alternator wire (B, **Figure 18**, typical) from the engine harness connector. On some later model engines, the red wire is also incorporated into

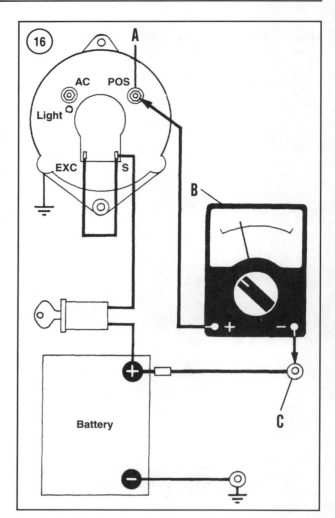

the connector. Disconnecting the red wire along with the purple wire does not affect the test results. Connect the positive meter lead to the red/purple alternator wire terminal. Connect the negative meter lead to an engine ground. The meter must indicate 0 volt. Observe the meter while

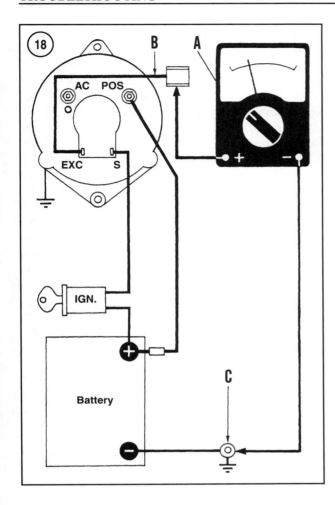

an assistant turns the key switch to ON or RUN. The meter must indicate 0 volt with the ignition switch in OFF or STOP and within 1 volt of actual battery voltage with the key switch in ON or RUN. If otherwise, test the key switch as described in this chapter. If no fault is found with the key switch, check all connecting wiring for corroded or dirty terminals and damaged wiring.

4. Disconnect the meter leads. Reconnect the white or red alternator wire to the engine harness connector.

Sensing Circuit

The transistorized voltage regulator contains excitation and sensing circuits. The sensing circuit allows the regulator to sense resistance inside the alternator and outside the alternator by comparing the voltage on the sense and output terminal leads.

This test requires an accurate voltmeter and 12-volt test lamp.

1. Place the key switch in OFF or STOP.

2. Set the voltmeter to the 20 or 40 VDC scale.

3. Unplug the smaller-gauge red alternator wire from the engine harness connector. On some later model engines, the purple wire is also incorporated into the connector. Disconnecting the purple wire along with the red wire does not affect the test results. Connect the positive meter lead to the red alternator wire terminal. Connect the negative meter lead to an engine ground. The meter must indicate within 1 volt of actual battery voltage. If the voltage is less than specified, check for faulty wiring, a blown fuse, tripped circuit breaker or faulty terminal along the red wire leading to the starter solenoid battery terminal.

4. Connect the test lamp between the disconnected red wire and an engine ground to verify lamp operation.

5. Touch the test probe to the alternator terminal or red sensing circuit wire. If the sensing circuit in the voltage regulator is operating properly, the test lamp will light dimly for 1-2 seconds and then fade, or it will not light at all. However, depending on the type of test lamp used, the sensing circuit could allow sufficient current flow to maintain dim illumination of the test lamp.

   a. If the lamp does not illuminate or is very dim, the sense circuit is not shorted to ground. Any draw on the battery with the engine not running is from another source. If in question, have the alternator tested by a reputable alternator and starter repair shop.

   c. If the lamp illuminates brightly, the regulator or other internal alternator components are shorted to ground. Replace the alternator with a new or rebuilt unit.

6. Reconnect the red wire to the alternator.

Alternator Ground

The alternator must have a good ground connection to operate at full efficiency. A poor ground can cause no output, low output and repeat alternator failures. A digital multimeter is required for the procedure.

1. Disconnect the battery cables.

2. Connect the meter test leads together. Select the ohms setting on the meter and note the internal resistance reading.

3. Touch the negative test lead to the negative battery terminal. Touch the positive test lead to an unpainted surface of the alternator housing and note the meter reading.

4. Subtract the internal resistance reading noted in Step 2 from the reading noted in Step 3. This is the actual resistance in the alternator ground circuit. A typical reading is 1-5 ohms. The resistance reading is affected by battery cable length and the length of the wires in the engine wire harness. Check for faulty wiring and loose or dirty wire

connections along the entire ground circuit if the resistance reading is significantly higher than 5 ohms.

5. Connect the battery cables.

Output Circuit

This test checks for an open or shorted alternator output circuit. An open or shorted output circuit will cause insufficient alternator output and can cause an excessive drain on the battery while the engine is off. A voltmeter and 12-volt test lamp are required to perform this test.

1. Disconnect the battery cables.

2. Disconnect the larger-gauge red, red/white or orange lead from the POS terminal stud (A, **Figure 16**, typical) on the rear of the alternator. Then disconnect the smaller-gauge red wire from the alternator.

3. Select the ohms setting on the meter. Touch the positive test lead to the disconnected red or orange wire. Touch the negative test lead to an unpainted surface of the alternator case or other engine ground surface. The meter must indicate no continuity.

   a. If the meter indicates continuity or very low resistance (less than 5 ohms), inspect the large-gauge red or orange wire for faulty terminals.

   b. If no problems are found with the wiring or terminals, disconnect the instrument harness from the engine harness plug and note the meter reading. The instrument harness is shorted, or one or more of the electrical accessories is shorted if the reading changes to no continuity or the resistance increases significantly with the plug disconnected. Inspect the harness. If no fault is found with the harness, reconnect the harness to the engine. Then note the meter reading while disconnecting each accessory connected to the red instrument wiring harness to isolate the fault.

   c. If no fault is found with the instrument harness or connected accessories, note the meter reading while disconnecting the engine control unit (EFI models), circuit breaker, slave solenoid, starter relay and starter solenoid. A short is indicated in the component if the meter switches to no continuity or the resistance reading increases significantly with that component disconnected.

4. Reconnect the smaller-gauge red wire to the alternator. If disconnected, reconnect the instrument harness to the engine harness plug.

5. Route the disconnected larger-gauge red or orange alternator output wire so the terminal cannot contact an engine ground or other component. Reconnect the battery cables.

6. Connect the test lamp to the terminal of the disconnected red or orange output lead. Touch the test lamp probe to an engine ground. The lamp must illuminate. If not, connect the test lamp to the positive battery terminal to verify the light is operational. Check for a blown fuse, tripped circuit breaker or faulty terminal in the red or orange wire if the lamp illuminates only when touching the battery terminal.

7. With the test lamp connected to the red or orange output wire, touch the test light probe to the POS terminal stud (A, **Figure 16**, typical) on the rear of the alternator. Refer to the following:

   a. If the lamp illuminates brightly, the rectifier bridge has one or more failed diodes, the output terminal is shorted to ground, the output terminal is corroded, or the output terminal insulator is damaged. Replace the alternator with a new or rebuilt unit.

   b. If the lamp does not illuminate, is very dim or glows orange, any current draw on the battery with the engine off is from a different source. If necessary, have the alternator tested at a reputable starter and alternator repair shop. Depending on the type of test lamp used, normal operation of the rectifier bridge can cause enough current flow to dimly illuminate the test lamp.

8. Disconnect the battery cables.

9. Reconnect the red or orange output lead to the alternator output terminal. Position the rubber insulating boot (**Figure 17**) fully over the terminal.

10. Reconnect the battery cables.

Diode Trio Test

The diode trio is located inside the alternator. This component supplies stator output to the voltage regulator after startup to energize the rotor field. This prevents the regulator from relying solely on the excitation circuit for current to energize the rotor field.

This test requires an accurate voltmeter.

CAUTION
Never operate the engine without first providing cooling water. Use a flush device or operate the engine with the boat in the water. Operating the engine without providing adequate cooling water will quickly damage the seawater pump and can result is serious engine damage.

1. Locate the white or purple wire on the alternator. Remove boat structure as necessary to provide access to the purple wire with the engine running. If the red wire and purple wire are enclosed in a single connector that does

not provide a means to disconnect only one wire, cut the purple wire in a location that will allow a proper and permanent repair after testing. Temporarily install crimp-on connectors in series on the red wire to allow testing.

2. Connect a voltmeter to the battery terminals.

3. Start the engine and raise the speed to 1500 rpm to energize the alternator. The alternator must energize to test the diode trio. The dash-mounted gauge will indicate 12.3-13.8 volts when the alternator energizes. Return the engine to idle speed.

4. Note the voltmeter reading. Normal charging voltage is 12.3-13.8 volts. With the engine running at idle speed, note the voltmeter reading while disconnecting the purple wire from the alternator. Do not allow any tools or terminals to contact the alternator housing or other engine components. Refer to the following:

    a. If the voltage does not change or changes only slightly (0.3 volts or less) with the wire disconnected, the diode trio is operating properly.

    b. If the voltage reading decreases significantly (0.4 volt or more) when the lead is disconnected, observe the meter while reconnecting the lead. The diode trio has failed if the voltage increases significantly with the purple lead connected. Replace the alternator with a new or rebuilt unit.

5. Stop the engine. Then disconnect the battery cables. Reconnect the purple wire to the alternator. If the purple and red wire share a common connector, repair the cut purple wire with a soldered connection. Cover the connection with a shrink tube and coat with Black Neoprene Dip to make sure the repair is waterproof and well-insulated. Purchase the neoprene dip from an OMC dealership (OMC part No. 909570) or automotive parts store.

IGNITION SYSTEM

Five different types of ignition systems are used on the models covered in this manual. This section provides a brief description of each system followed by troubleshooting procedures for the various components and systems. Refer to **Table 2** for a list of items to check if the engine will not start or if the ignition system is suspected of causing an engine malfunction. Refer to the causes listed next to the symptom that best describes the malfunction. Perform the test or adjustment suggested as a corrective action. Other useful information and tips are described with the specific test instructions.

Basic Ignition System Troubleshooting

Early Indmar marine engines covered in this manual use a conventional breaker-point ignition system. All late models use a fully transistorized ignition system that offers higher spark output than the breaker-point system, provides excellent reliability and requires low maintenance.

Failure of the breaker-point ignition system is usually caused by dirty, maladjusted or burned contact points, a faulty condenser, or loose or dirty wire terminals. Failure of the transistorized ignition system is rare and is usually caused by corroded, loose or dirty wire terminals. This section describes troubleshooting procedures that apply to all of the ignition systems covered in this manual. Procedures that apply only to the individual ignition systems are described after the system description.

Ignition system trouble may be roughly divided between trouble affecting a single cylinder and trouble affecting all cylinders. A malfunction that affects all cylinders is almost always caused by dirty or maladjusted breaker points, a failed condenser, a failed ignition module, defective distributor rotor, shorted tachometer or low operating voltage. Refer to *Checking for spark at the ignition coil and spark plugs* in this section to determine whether an ignition system malfunction is affecting one or more cylinders.

Spark plug inspection

No single component affects engine operation more than the spark plugs. Spark plugs operate in a harsh environment that includes high heat, high pressure and the corrosive effects of the combustion process. Because of these conditions, spark plug failure is inevitable. Marine engines operate for extended periods of time under high throttle loads, and the spark plugs are subjected to much harsher conditions than the plugs used in most internal combustion engines.

Remove the spark plugs as described in Chapter Three. Arrange the plugs to identify the cylinder in which they were installed. Compare the plugs to those shown in **Figure 19**. Spark plug condition is an important indicator of engine performance and condition. Spark plugs in a properly operating engine will have slightly pitted electrodes and a light tan insulator tip. **Figure 19** shows a normal plug and a number of others indicating trouble in the respective cylinders. All of the spark plugs should be nearly alike. If one or more of the spark plugs appear different from the rest, it is an important clue that the cylinder is somehow different from the others. The difference could be a faulty plug, spark plug wire, distributor cap (where

SPARK PLUG CONDITION

NORMAL

- Identified by light tan or gray deposits on the firing tip.
- Can be cleaned.

GAP BRIDGED

- Identified by deposit buildup closing gap between electrodes.

OIL FOULED

- Identified by wet black deposits on the insulator shell bore and electrodes.
- Caused by too much oil entering combustion chamber through worn rings and pistons, excessive clearance between valve guides and stems, or worn or loose bearings. Can be cleaned. If engine is not repaired, use a hotter plug.

CARBON FOULED

- Identified by dry, fluffy black carbon deposits on insulator tips, exposed shell surfaces and electrodes.
- Caused by a too-cold plug, weak ignition, dirty air cleaner, too-rich fuel mixture or excessive idling. Can be cleaned.

LEAD FOULED

- Identified by dark gray, yellow, tan or black deposits or a fused glazed coating on the insulator tip.
- Caused by highly leaded gasoline.

WORN

- Identified by severely eroded or worn electrodes.
- Caused by normal wear. Should be replaced.

FUSED SPOT DEPOSIT

- Identified by melted or spotty deposits resembling bubbles or blisters.
- Caused by sudden acceleration. Can be cleaned.

OVERHEATING

- Identified by a white or light gray insulator with small black or gray-brown spots with bluish-burnt appearance of electrodes.
- Caused by engine overheating, wrong type of fuel, loose spark plugs, a too-hot plug or incorrect ignition timing. Replace the plug.

PREIGNITION

- Identified by melted electrodes and possibly blistered insulator. Metallic deposits on insulator indicate engine damage.
- Caused by wrong type of fuel, incorrect ignition timing or advance, a too-hot plug, burned valves or engine overheating. Replace the plug.

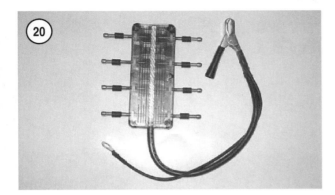

diagrams at the end of the manual to identify fuses, circuit breakers and wire connection points. After the inspection, clean, regap and install the spark plugs as described in Chapter Three. For future reference, note which cylinders are in questionable condition.

Checking for spark at the ignition coil and spark plugs

The most basic ignition system test is checking for spark at the plugs and ignition coil(s). If a strong blue spark is present at the plugs and coil, the voltage supply, ignition coil, and ignition module or engine control unit are operating the ignition system. A faulty spark plug wire or distributor rotor is indicated if good spark is present at the coil(s) but not at the plugs.

Test the fuel system if the engine will not start or runs improperly but good spark is present at the plugs. This test requires a spark gap tester (**Figure 20**). Purchase the spark gap tester from a tool supplier or an automotive parts store.

> *WARNING*
> *High voltage is present in the ignition system. Never touch any wires or electrical components while running the engine or operating the electric starter. Never perform ignition system tests in wet conditions.*

> *WARNING*
> *The engine might unexpectedly start during testing. Keep all persons, clothing, tools or loose objects away from the drive belts and other moving components on the engine.*

> *CAUTION*
> *Use a flush device to supply the engine with cooling water if testing the ignition system with the boat out of the water. Operation of the starter motor results in operation of the seawater pump. Also, the engine might start during the troubleshooting procedure. The seawater pump is quickly damaged if operated without adequate cooling water.*

applicable), ignition coil (8.1L models), fuel injector (multiport injection [MPI] models) or internal engine damage that affects only that cylinder.

If the spark plugs reveal a problem that affects all of the cylinders, then the trouble is most likely caused by a faulty ignition module (where applicable), faulty rotor (where applicable), low operating voltage (battery-supplied) or faulty wiring. Do not forget to check all wiring connectors, fuses and circuit breakers. Refer to the wiring

1. Shift the engine into NEUTRAL.

2. On electronic fuel injection (EFI) models, disconnect the engine harness connectors from the electric fuel pump harness. Refer to *Electronic Fuel Injection* in Chapter Seven.

3A. On all 5.0L, 5.7L, 7.4L and 8.2L models with a distributor (**Figure 21**, typical), disconnect the ignition coil secondary wire from the ignition coil tower. See **Figure 22** for earlier models with a breaker-point or Prestolite

BID ignition system. See **Figure 23** for later models with a Delco EST ignition system.

3B. On 5.7L LT-1 models with distributorless ignition, disconnect the spark plug wire from one of the ignition coils (9-16, **Figure 24**).

3C. On 8.1L models with distributorless ignition, disconnect the spark plug wire from one of the ignition coils (**Figure 25**). The coils are located on the rocker arm cover directly above the corresponding cylinders.

4. Connect the ground lead of the spark gap tester to a suitable engine ground.

5. Connect the spark gap tester to the coil tower. Adjust the gap to approximately 1/4 in. (6.3 mm).

6. Observe the spark gap tester while an assistant cranks the engine. The engine may momentarily start on 5.7L LT-1 and 8.1L models but will stop when residual fuel rail pressure dissipates. The presence of a strong blue spark indicates the ignition system is producing output at the coil. If the spark is weak or absent, test the ignition system as described in this section.

7A. On all 5.0L, 5.7L, 7.4L and 8.2L models with a distributor (**Figure 21**, typical), remove the spark gap tester and reconnect the ignition coil secondary wire to the coil tower. See **Figure 22** or **Figure 23**.

7B. On 5.7L LT-1 models, reconnect the spark plug wire to the coil. Repeat Steps 3-6 for the remaining ignition coils. Record the test results for each cylinder. Refer to **Figure 24** to determine which cylinders correspond to the ignition coils. Remove the spark gap tester and reconnect the spark plug wire to the corresponding coil tower after testing all coils.

7C. On 8.1L models, reconnect the spark plug wire to the coil. Repeat Steps 3-6 for the remaining ignition coils. Record the test results for each cylinder. The coil is mounted over the corresponding cylinder. Remove the spark gap tester and connect the spark plug wire to the coil tower after testing all coils.

8. Connect the ground lead of the spark gap tester to a suitable engine ground.

9. Note the cylinder number. Then disconnect the spark plug wire from one of the spark plugs. Connect the spark plug wires to the spark gap tester. Adjust the gap to approximately 1/4 in. (6.3 mm).

10. Observe the spark gap tester while an assistant cranks the engine. The presence of a strong blue spark at the tester indicates the ignition system is producing spark to that cylinder. Record the test results for each cylinder.

11. Remove the spark gap tester and reconnect the spark plug wire.

12. Repeat Steps 8-11 for the remaining cylinders.

13A. On 5.0L, 5.7L, 7.4L and 8.2L models with a distributor, note the test results and refer to the following:

a. If spark is missing at all cylinders but the spark is good at the ignition coil, the fault is with the distributor rotor or coil wire. Replace the rotor and retest. Replace the coil wire if spark is not restored with the replacement rotor.

b. If spark is good on some cylinders and weak or missing on others, the fault is with the spark plug wire(s) or distributor cap. Replace the distributor cap and retest. Replace the suspect spark plug wires if spark is not restored with the replacement cap.

13B. On 5.7L LT-1 models, note the test results in Step 6 and Step 10 and refer to the following:

a. If spark is missing on all cylinders, test the ignition system as described in this chapter.

b. If spark is missing on a cylinder that has spark at the corresponding ignition coil, the spark plug wire is shorting to ground or open. Replace the spark plug wire.

c. If spark is missing on a pair of cylinders that share an ignition coil, switch the mounting locations and wiring of the suspect coil with a coil that is producing spark for a different pair of cylinders and repeat the test. If spark is restored with the known good coil, replace the suspect ignition coil and return the test coil to the original location as described in Chapter Nine. If spark is not restored by switching the coils, test the ignition system as described in this chapter.

13C. On 8.1L models, note the test results in Step 6 and Step 10. Then refer to the following:

a. If spark is good at the coil but is weak or missing at the corresponding spark plug wire, the spark plug wire is shorted or open. Replace the spark plug wire.

b. If spark is weak or missing at one coil but is good on other coils, the fault is probably with the coil. Switch the mounting location and wire connections

2

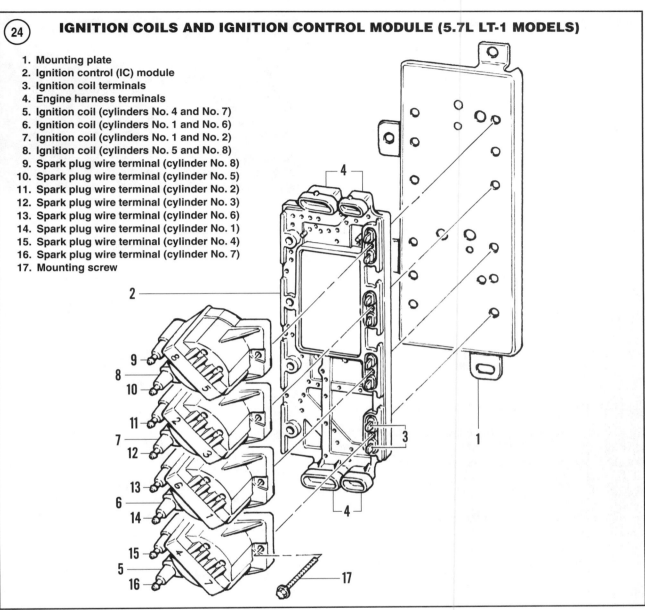

(24) IGNITION COILS AND IGNITION CONTROL MODULE (5.7L LT-1 MODELS)

1. Mounting plate
2. Ignition control (IC) module
3. Ignition coil terminals
4. Engine harness terminals
5. Ignition coil (cylinders No. 4 and No. 7)
6. Ignition coil (cylinders No. 1 and No. 6)
7. Ignition coil (cylinders No. 1 and No. 2)
8. Ignition coil (cylinders No. 5 and No. 8)
9. Spark plug wire terminal (cylinder No. 8)
10. Spark plug wire terminal (cylinder No. 5)
11. Spark plug wire terminal (cylinder No. 2)
12. Spark plug wire terminal (cylinder No. 3)
13. Spark plug wire terminal (cylinder No. 6)
14. Spark plug wire terminal (cylinder No. 1)
15. Spark plug wire terminal (cylinder No. 4)
16. Spark plug wire terminal (cylinder No. 7)
17. Mounting screw

with a coil that delivers good spark and repeat the test. Replace the coil if the fault follows the coil. If spark is not restored by switching the coils, test the ignition system as described in this chapter.

14. Remove the spark gap tester and reconnect the spark plug lead.

15. On electronic fuel injection models, connect the engine harness connectors to the electric fuel pump harnesses. Refer to *Electronic Fuel Injection* in Chapter Seven.

Checking for a shorted tachometer

On all models except 5.7L LT-1 and 8.1L, the gray tachometer wire connects to the primary coil winding. The pulsating signal developed in the winding that occurs during normal ignition system operation provides the input to operate the tachometer. Any short along the wire from the coil to the tachometer terminal or an internally shorted tachometer will cause no spark or weak spark at the coil. A common complaint is misfiring at higher throttle settings.

On 5.7L LT-1 and 8.1L models, the gray tachometer wire connects to the engine control unit (ECU). The ECU generates the signal to operate the tachometer. On 5.7L LT-1 and 8.1L models, a shorted tachometer or gray wire should not affect ignition system operation.

> *WARNING*
> *High voltage is present in the ignition system. Never touch any wires or electrical components while running the engine or performing a test. Never perform ignition system tests in wet conditions.*

1. Check for spark at the coil as described in this chapter.

2. If spark is weak or missing on all cylinders, first inspect the gray wire for damaged insulation and the wire connection on the tachometer for shorting to ground or other terminals. Repair as necessary and recheck for spark at the coil.

3. If no faults are found with the wiring, disconnect the gray wire from the tachometer. Tape the terminal to prevent a short circuit during testing. Check for spark as described in this chapter. Replace the tachometer if good spark is restored with the gray tachometer wire disconnected.

4. If spark is not restored with the gray tachometer lead disconnected, disconnect the purple wire from the tachometer. Tape the wire to prevent a short circuit during testing. Check for spark as described in this chapter or operate the engine at the throttle setting where the misfire is occurring. Replace the tachometer if good spark is restored or the misfire is absent with the purple tachometer wire disconnected.

5. Reconnect the gray and purple tachometer wires. Orient the terminals and route the wiring to prevent shorting at the terminals or interference with moving components such as steering components and control cables. Secure the wiring with plastic locking clamps as needed.

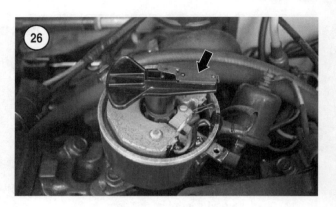

Checking for distributor rotation
(except 5.7L LT-1 and 8.1L models)

The rotor on the distributor shaft directs the coil output to the individual cylinders, and a shaft-mounted device is used to initiate spark at the coil. The distributor shaft must rotate to operate the ignition system.

> *WARNING*
> *The engine might unexpectedly start during testing. Keep all persons, clothing, tools or loose objects away from the drive belts and other moving components on the engine.*

> *CAUTION*
> *Use a flush device to supply the engine with cooling water if testing the ignition system with the boat out of the water. Operation of the starter motor results in operation of the seawater pump. The seawater pump is quickly damaged if operated without adequate cooling water.*

1. Remove the distributor cap as described in Chapter Nine. *Do not* remove the rotor for this test.

2. Pull the cord to activate the emergency stop (lanyard) switch (**Figure 2**). This prevents the ignition system from operating. If the control does not incorporate an emergency stop (lanyard) switch, disconnect the coil wire from the distributor cap and connect to an engine ground to disable the ignition system.

3. Observe the distributor rotor (**Figure 26**) while an assistant cranks the engine. The rotor must rotate while cranking the engine. If it does not, remove the distributor (refer to Chapter Nine) and inspect the distributor drive gear for missing teeth or other damage. If the drive gear is good, the camshaft, timing chain or sprockets have failed. Refer to Chapter Six to inspect the timing components.

4. Install the distributor cap as described in Chapter Nine.

5. Reattach the lanyard to the emergency stop (lanyard) switch or reconnect the coil wire to the distributor cap.

Testing the emergency stop (lanyard) switch

The emergency stop (lanyard) switch (**Figure 2**) is wired in series with the purple lead that connects the key switch *I* terminal to the instrument harness. The purple wire supplies voltage to operate the ignition system (carburetor-equipped models) or the system relay (fuel injection models). A defective switch can cause no spark or weak spark at the coil on carburetor-equipped models or no activation of the system relay on fuel injection models.

An ohmmeter is required for this procedure.

1. Disconnect the negative battery cable.

2. Locate the purple wires leading to the emergency stop (lanyard) switch. One of the wires connects to the key switch. The other wire connects to the purple instrument harness wire that leads to the engine. Mark the wires to identify the connection points. Then disconnect the wires. In most cases, the wires are connected with crimp connectors. If necessary, cut the wiring and install new connectors after testing.

3. Calibrate an ohmmeter on the R × 1 scale. Connect the meter test leads to the disconnected purple wires leading to the switch. With the lanyard cord connected to the switch and the plunger depressed, the meter must indicate continuity. If not, the switch has failed open or has corroded internal contacts and must be replaced.

4. With the meter leads attached as described in Step 3, observe the meter while pulling the cord to dislodge the connector and allow the plunger to extend. The meter must now indicate no continuity. If not, the switch is shorted internally and must be replaced.

5. Repeat Step 3 and Step 4 several times to verify a possible intermittent switch failure.

6. Reconnect one of the purple switch wires to the wire leading to the *I* terminal on the key switch. Reconnect the other purple wire to the purple instrument harness wire leading to the engine. Do not inadvertently connect the switch wires or connect the key switch directly to the instrument harness wiring.

7. Connect the battery cable.

8. Start the engine. Pull the cord to dislodge the connector and allow the plunger to extend. The engine must stop immediately. If it does not, the switch, wiring or system relay (EFI models) is faulty. Repair the wiring or replace faulty components as needed. Do not operate the engine until proper switch operation is restored.

Breaker-Point Ignition System

A breaker-point ignition system is used on early 5.0L, 5.7L and 7.4L models. The breaker-point ignition system consists of the distributor (with breaker points and condenser), ignition coil, key switch, ballast resistor, battery, spark plugs and connecting wiring.

Operation

When the ignition is switched ON, battery voltage is applied to the white or purple wire connecting the switch *I* terminal to the ignition coil positive terminal. A second wire connects the ignition coil negative terminal to the breaker points in the distributor (**Figure 27**). The rotor in the distributor rotates at one-half crankshaft speed. As it rotates, the lobes on the shaft open and close the breaker points.

When closed, the breaker points complete the circuit between the ignition coil negative terminal and distributor. This allows battery current to flow through the coil primary winding creating a strong magnetic field in the winding.

Rotation of the distributor shaft causes the lobes to open the breaker points. This opens the ground path and prevents battery current from flowing through the coil primary winding. This causes the magnetic field in the coil to collapse. The collapsing field passes through the ignition coil secondary winding inducing very high voltage current in this winding. The current flows from the coil tower (coil wire terminal) to the distributor rotor. The rotor directs the current to the distributor cap terminal for the individual spark plug. High-tension wires connect the cap terminals to the spark plugs. Further distributor shaft rotation closes the points and repeats the sequence.

A ballast resistor (**Figure 28**) or resistor wire is integrated into the circuit supplying battery voltage to the ignition coil. The resistor lowers the voltage delivered to the ignition coil to prevent the ignition coil from overheating and breaker-point damage.

The condenser is designed to absorb excess voltage as the breaker points open to prevent arcing and breaker-point damage. The condenser also helps the primary winding collapse quicker to produce higher secondary voltage.

The fuel/air mixture in the cylinder must ignite and burn at a precise time to push the piston down on the power stroke. Because fuel burns at a relatively constant rate, spark must occur earlier with increased engine speed. Ideally, the pressure from the burning fuel should peak as the piston starts moving down on the power stroke. This provides the maximum pressure on the piston

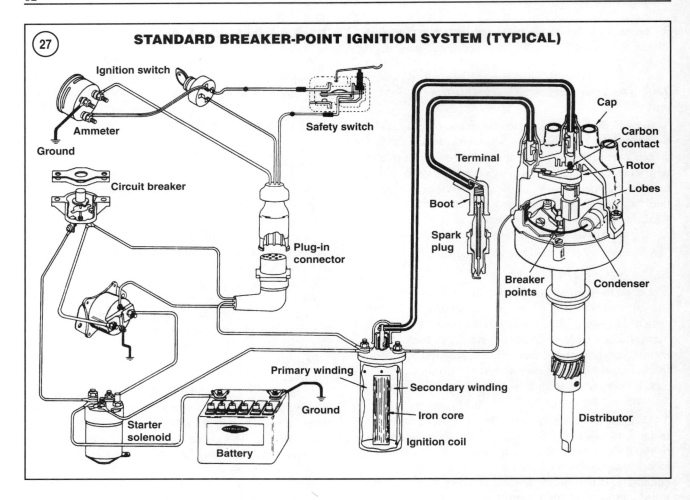

STANDARD BREAKER-POINT IGNITION SYSTEM (TYPICAL)

and maximum power output. If the spark timing is not advanced, the pressure peaks well after the piston starts moving down, and power output decreases. As the distributor rotates, centrifugal force applied to the weights in the distributor cause them to swing out and exert force against springs and cams that drive against the advance mechanism in the distributor. This causes the advance mechanism to advance the lobes relative to the distributor shaft and results in earlier opening of the points. This provides automatic timing advance for the given engine speed.

The bypass circuit consists of the slave solenoid or starter solenoid and a wire connecting the solenoid to the positive terminal of the ignition coil. During starter motor operation, the slave or starter solenoid delivers battery voltage to the bypass wire (purple or purple/yellow) using a dedicated terminal. This bypasses the ballast resistor to provide higher voltage and a stronger spark during starting.

The breaker-point ignition system does not provide engine overspeed protection.

WARNING
High voltage is present in the ignition system. Never touch any wires or electrical components while running the engine or operating the electric starter. Never perform ignition system tests in wet conditions.

WARNING
The engine might unexpectedly start during testing. Keep all persons, clothing, tools or loose objects away from the drive belts and other moving components on the engine.

CAUTION
Use a flush device to supply the engine with cooling water if testing the ignition system with the boat out of the water. Operation of the starter motor results in operation of the seawater pump. Also, the engine might start during the troubleshooting procedure. The seawater pump is quickly damaged if operated without adequate cooling water.

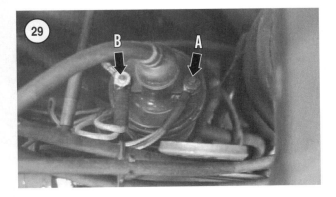

Voltage test

Perform this procedure if the ignition system fails to generate spark at the coil, the spark is weak, or the ignition system is misfiring. This procedure tests the voltage available at various points in the ignition system. A multimeter is required for this procedure.

1. Disconnect the ignition coil secondary wire from the ignition coil tower (**Figure 22**). Connect the secondary wire to an engine ground to prevent arcing or accidental starting.

2. If so equipped, make sure the lanyard (**Figure 2**) is fully attached onto the switch and is fully depressing the plunger. If not, the switch will open the circuit that supplies current to the ignition system.

3. Set the multimeter on the 20 or 40 VDC scale.

4. Touch the positive meter lead to the positive battery terminal and the negative lead to the negative battery terminal. Charge the battery if the voltage is not above 12.0 volts. Record the battery voltage for reference during the test procedure.

5. Turn the key switch to ON or RUN. The dash gauges must turn on. If not, check for a blown fuse, tripped circuit breaker or loose wire connection. Correct faulty wiring, replace the fuse, or reset the circuit breaker to restore

gauge operation. If this does not restore gauge operation, test the key switch as described in this chapter.

6. Disconnect the tachometer and distributor leads from the negative coil terminal (A, **Figure 29**).

7. Connect the negative test lead to an engine ground. With the key switch in ON or RUN, touch the positive test lead to the positive terminal of the ignition coil (B, **Figure 29**). The meter must indicate 9.5 volts or greater. Repeat the test with the positive test lead touching the negative terminal of the ignition coil. The meter must indicate 8.5 volts or greater. Refer to the following:

   a. If the meter indicates 9.5 volts or more on the positive coil terminal and 8.5 volts or more on the negative terminal, the ignition ON circuit and the ignition coil primary circuit are operating properly. Proceed to Step 8.

   b. If the meter indicates 0 volts on the positive and negative ignition coil terminals, test the emergency stop (lanyard) switch as described in this section. If the switch is good, test the ballast resistor or resistor wire as described in this section. An open circuit or short to ground along the white or purple wire in the instrument or engine harness is evident if the ballast resistor or resistor is good. Repair faulty wiring or terminals before proceeding.

   c. If the meter indicates 9.5 volts or more on the positive terminal and 0 volt on the negative terminal, the primary winding in the ignition coil is open. Replace the ignition coil as described in Chapter Nine.

   d. If the meter indicates 9.5 volts or more on the positive terminal and 0.1-8.4 volts on the negative terminal, the ignition coil probably is partially shorted in the primary circuit. Test the ignition coil resistance as described in this section.

   e. If the meter reads 0.1-9.4 volts on the positive terminal, disconnect the white or purple wire from the positive coil terminal (B, **Figure 29**). Repeat the test with the positive test lead contacting the disconnected wire. If the voltage is 9.5 volts or more *only* with the wire disconnected from the coil, the coil probably is likely shorted internally and must be replaced as described in Chapter Nine. If the meter reads less than 9.5 volts with the lead disconnected from the coil, inspect the wiring for a dirty, loose or corroded terminal along the white or purple wire. If no fault is found with the wiring, check for a shorted electric choke heater, if so equipped, or shorted alternator excitation circuit. Disconnect the white or purple wires from the choke heater (**Figure 30**, typical) and then the alternator (**Figure 31**, typical) while monitoring the voltage. Replace the choke heater or test the alternator excitation circuit if the voltage is within the specification *only* with the wire disconnected from the heater or alternator. Faulty wiring or connections in the instrument or engine harnesses are evident if the voltage on the white or purple wire remains low with the indicated wires disconnected.

8. Remove the distributor cap as described in Chapter Nine. Rotate the crankshaft pulley in the normal direction of rotation until the ignition points are fully open. Refer to Chapter Six to determine the correct engine rotation. Reconnect the white or purple leads to the positive ignition coil terminal and the distributor and gray tachometer lead to the negative coil terminal.

9. Connect the positive test lead to the positive battery terminal. Observe the meter while touching the negative test lead to an unpainted metallic portion of the distributor body. Repeat the test with the test lead touching the breaker point mounting plate. Refer to the following:

    a. If the meter indicates 0 volt when touching the distributor body, remove the distributor clamp bolt (A, **Figure 32**) and the clamp (B). Do not remove or rotate the distributor. Clean any paint, corrosion or other material from the bolt, bolt threads in the intake manifold and the surfaces of the clamp that contact the bolt and distributor. Reinstall the clamp and bolt. Make sure the arms of the clamp fit fully over the flange of the distributor. Tighten the bolt to 30 ft.-lb. (41 N•m).

    b. If the meter indicates within 1 volt of battery voltage at the distributor and low voltage (exceeding 1 volt below battery voltage) at the breaker point mounting plate, inspect the mounting plate for looseness or heavy corrosion. Tighten screws, clean corrosion, or replace the distributor (Chapter Nine) to provide the ground needed to restore ignition system operation.

10. Connect the negative test lead to an engine ground. Observe the meter while touching the positive test lead to the positive contact of the ignition points. The distributor wire and condenser connect to the positive contact. Refer to the following:

    a. If the voltage is 9.3 volts or more, sufficient ignition voltage is supplied to the ignition points. Proceed to Step 11.

    b. If no voltage is noted, the distributor wire is open. Replace the wire connecting the distributor to the negative terminal of the ignition coil.

    c. If the voltage is 0.1-9.2 volts, disconnect the gray tachometer lead from the negative ignition coil terminal and repeat the test. A shorted tachometer or gray wire is evident if the voltage is satisfactory *only* with the wire disconnected. Test for a shorted

tachometer or replace or repair the wiring as necessary. If the voltage is not satisfactory with the lead disconnected, the ignition points are shorted to ground and must be replaced as described in Chapter Three. Refer to *Tune-up*.

11. Turn the key switch to OFF or STOP. Reconnect all wires. Clean the ignition points and adjust the gap as described in Chapter Three. Install the rotor and distributor cap as described in Chapter Nine. Check for spark at the ignition coil and spark plugs as described in this chapter. Refer to the following:

    a. If spark is now present at the ignition coil and plugs, the ignition system is operating. Adjust the dwell and ignition timing as described in Chapter Five.

    b. If spark is present at the ignition coil but not at the spark plugs, replace the distributor rotor as described in Chapter Nine to restore ignition system operation.

    c. If no spark is present at the ignition coil, check for distributor rotation as described in this chapter. If the distributor is rotating, replace the breaker points and condenser as described in Chapter Three and check for spark. If there is still no spark, disconnect the gray tachometer lead from the ignition coil and check for spark. If spark is present *only* with the

gray lead disconnected, check for a short to ground on the gray lead between the tachometer and coil. Replace the coil if no short is found. If no spark is present with the gray lead disconnected, replace the ignition coil as described in Chapter Nine.

12. Disconnect and ground the ignition coil secondary lead to prevent spark at the plugs. Connect the negative test lead to an engine ground. Touch the positive test lead to the positive coil terminal (B, **Figure 29**). Observe the meter while an assistant turns the key switch to START. The meter must indicate 9.5 volts or higher. Refer to the following:

   a. If no voltage is noted, test the starter solenoid or slave solenoid as described in this chapter. Refer to *Starting System*. An open circuit is evident in the tan or purple/yellow ballast- or resistor-bypass wire connecting the slave solenoid or starter solenoid. Repair the wiring as required.

   b. If the meter indicates 0.1-9.4 volts, the contacts in the slave solenoid or starter solenoid are dirty or corroded. Replace the solenoid.

   c. If the meter indicates 9.5 volts or higher, the ballast or resistor wire bypass circuit is operational. Proceed to Step 14.

13. Reconnect the ignition coil to the ignition coil and distributor cap.

14. After starting the engine, adjust the ignition timing as described in Chapter Five.

Ballast resistor test

> *WARNING*
> *Allow the engine to rest for at least 30 minutes with the ignition OFF before touching the ballast resistor. Current flowing through the resistor creates significant heat anytime the engine is running or if the breaker points are closed with the ignition ON.*

The ballast resistor (**Figure 28**) is used on early models with a breaker-point ignition system. A multimeter is required for this procedure.

1. Disconnect and ground the ignition coil secondary lead to prevent starting.

2. Measure the ballast resistor resistance as follows:

   a. Disconnect the two white or tan leads from the resistor.

   b. Calibrate the multimeter on the R × 10 scale.

   c. Touch the meter test leads to each of the two resistor terminals. The meter should indicate 1.8-5.0 ohms. Replace the ballast resistor if the meter indicates fewer than 1.8 ohms resistance or reading is significantly more than 5 ohms.

   d. Do not reconnect the resistor wires at this time.

3. Check for voltage at the ignition circuit to the resistor as follows:

   a. Set the multimeter on the 20 or 40 VDC scale. Connect the negative test lead to an engine ground. Turn the key switch to OFF or STOP.

   b. Touch the positive test lead to the tan or purple lead connecting the main engine harness to the resistor. The other tan or purple lead connects the resistor to the ignition coil.

   c. Note the meter reading while an assistant turns the key switch to ON or RUN. The meter must indicate within 1 volt of battery voltage. If not, the instrument wire harness, engine wire harness or instrument harness to engine wire harness plug is damaged.

4. Check the ballast resistor-to-ignition coil circuit as follows:

   a. Calibrate the multimeter on the R × 1 scale.

   b. Disconnect the leads from the positive ignition coil terminal (B, **Figure 29**). Connect one of the test leads to the disconnected wire at the coil that leads to the ballast resistor.

   c. Observe the meter while touching the other test lead to the disconnected wire that leads to the ignition coil. The meter must indicate continuity. Replace the wire connecting the resistor to the coil to restore ignition system operation.

   d. Connect one of the test leads to one end of the resistor-to-coil wire. Touch the other test lead to an engine ground. The meter must indicate no continuity. If continuity is noted, the wire is shorted to ground and must be replaced to restore ignition system operation.

   e. Reconnect the wires to the ignition coil.

5. Reconnect the two white or tan leads to the resistor. Route the wires to prevent contact with the resistor body.

6. Connect the ignition coil secondary wire to the coil and distributor cap.

Resistor wire test

This test requires an accurate digital multimeter.

1. Disconnect and ground the ignition coil wire to prevent accidental starting.

2. Disconnect the white or purple wires from the positive coil terminal (B, **Figure 29**).

3. Calibrate an ohmmeter on the R × 10 scale.

4A. On models with an electric choke heater, measure the resistor wire resistance as follows:

    a. Disconnect the white or purple wire from the positive terminal of the choke heater (**Figure 30**).

    b. Connect one of the test leads to the disconnected choke heater wire (white or purple).

    c. Connect the other test lead to the white or purple ignition coil wire. The meter must indicate 1.8-6.0 ohms. Replace the wire harness or individual wire (if available for the model) if the resistance exceeds 6 ohms.

    d. Connect the white or purple wire to the positive terminal of the choke heater.

4B. On models without an electric choke heater, measure the resistor wire resistance as follows:

    a. Disconnect the white or purple exciter circuit wire from the rear of the alternator (**Figure 31**).

    b. Connect one of the test leads to the disconnected exciter wire (white or purple).

    c. Connect the other test lead to the white or purple ignition coil wire. The meter must indicate 1.8-6.0 ohms. Replace the wire harness or individual wire (if available for the model) if the resistance exceeds 6 ohms.

    d. Connect the white or purple exciter circuit wire to the alternator.

5. Connect the white or purple wire to the positive coil terminal (B, **Figure 29**).

6. Reconnect the ignition coil secondary wire to the ignition coil and distributor cap terminals.

Ignition coil test

This section describes the resistance test for the primary and secondary ignition coil windings. Although the test can reveal an open or shorted circuit, it should not be considered a benchmark test for the coil. Due to the high voltage generated in the secondary winding, internal arcing can occur in partially shorted circuits or near windings with damaged insulation and can cause an ignition misfire at any engine speed. This is usually not detected with a resistance test. However, when internal arcing is occurring, a clicking noise is often heard emanating from the coil. Replace the coil if it fails either of the resistance tests, internal arcing is suspected or no spark, weak spark or an ignition misfire is present, and all other ignition system components are operating properly.

> *NOTE*
> *For accurate testing, perform a resistance test on the ignition coil with the coil and air temperature in the work area at approximately 68° F (20° C). The windings will have higher resistance at higher temperatures and lower resistance at lower temperatures.*

An accurate digital ohmmeter is required for this procedure.

1. Remove the ignition coil as described in Chapter Nine.

2. Calibrate an ohmmeter on the 2-ohm or 10-ohm scale. Touch one of the meter leads to the positive coil terminal. Touch the other meter lead to the negative coil terminal. The meter must indicate 0.9-1.5 ohms. If not, replace the coil.

3. Calibrate the ohmmeter on the 20k scale. Touch one of the meter leads to the coil tower (high-tension) terminal. Touch the other lead to either the positive or negative coil terminal. The meter must indicate 7500-15,000 ohms. If not, repleace the coil.

4. Install the ignition coil as described in Chapter Nine.

Prestolite BID (Breakerless Integral Distributor) Ignition System

The Prestolite BID (breakerless integral distributor) ignition system is used on early carburetor-equipped models and uses the type of distributor and ignition coil shown in **Figure 33**. The distributor houses the ignition module with integrated impulse sensor, the rotor, the distributor shaft and the integrated impulse sender.

Operation

When the ignition is switched ON, battery voltage is applied to the purple wire connected to the positive ignition coil terminal. The purple ignition module wire also connects to the positive ignition coil terminal to supply the current needed to operate the ignition module. A black wire connects the module to the negative coil terminal.

Current supplied by the module flows through a winding in the integrated impulse sensor where it creates a

2

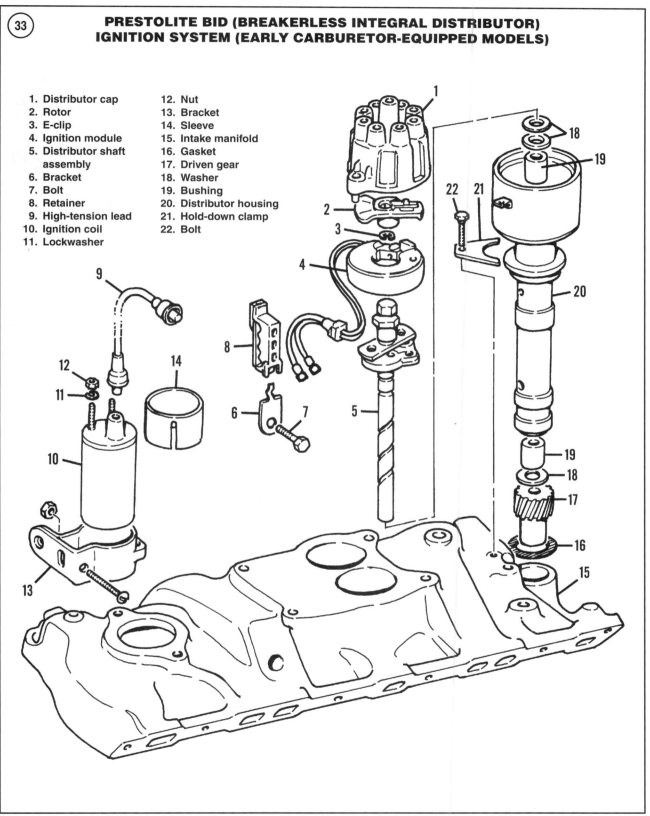

(33) **PRESTOLITE BID (BREAKERLESS INTEGRAL DISTRIBUTOR) IGNITION SYSTEM (EARLY CARBURETOR-EQUIPPED MODELS)**

1. Distributor cap
2. Rotor
3. E-clip
4. Ignition module
5. Distributor shaft assembly
6. Bracket
7. Bolt
8. Retainer
9. High-tension lead
10. Ignition coil
11. Lockwasher
12. Nut
13. Bracket
14. Sleeve
15. Intake manifold
16. Gasket
17. Driven gear
18. Washer
19. Bushing
20. Distributor housing
21. Hold-down clamp
22. Bolt

small magnetic field. The rotor in the distributor rotates at one-half crankshaft speed. As it rotates, the fingers of the impulse sender (**Figure 34**) pass by the impulse sensor integrated into the module.

When one of the fingers aligns with the sensor, it disturbs the magnetic field and causes the sensor to switch on the module. The module then completes the ground circuit for the ignition coil. This allows battery current to flow through the ignition coil primary winding and to create a strong magnetic field.

With further rotation, the finger moves out of alignment with the sensor, the magnetic field is restored, and the sensor switches off the module.

When switched off, the module interrupts the ground circuit, which prevents battery current from flowing and causes the magnetic field to collapse. The collapsing field passes through the ignition coil secondary winding inducing very high-voltage current in this winding. The current flows from the coil tower (coil wire terminal) to the distributor rotor. The rotor directs the current to the distributor cap terminal for each individual spark plug. High-tension wires connect the cap terminals to the spark plugs.

The fuel/air mixture in the cylinder must ignite and burn at a precise time to push the piston down on the power stroke. Because fuel burns at a relatively constant rate, spark must occur earlier with increased engine speed. Ideally, the pressure from the burning fuel should peak as the piston starts moving down on the power stroke. This provides the maximum pressure on the piston and maximum power output. If the spark timing is not advanced, the pressure peaks well after the piston starts moving down, and power output decreases.

Advance weights in the distributor automatically advance the ignition timing in proportion to engine speed. The ignition system does not provide engine overspeed protection. The system may be equipped with a tachometer amplifier to provide the stronger ignition system pulse required with some types of tachometers. The amplifier is wired in series in the gray wire connecting the negative coil terminal to the engine wire harness. The amplifier receives operating current from the primary coil winding via the gray wire connection. A separate black wire provides a ground circuit for the amplifier.

CAUTION
The air gap between the impulse sensor and impulse sender fingers must be correctly adjusted for proper ignition system operation. An improper gap can cause no spark, weak spark or incorrect ignition timing. Incorrect ignition timing can cause poor performance or serious engine damage.

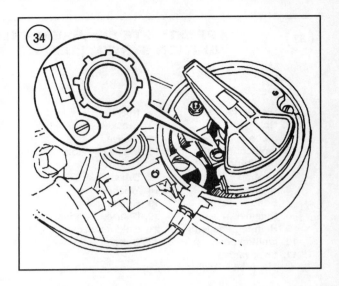

Voltage test

Perform this procedure if the ignition system fails to deliver spark at the coil, the spark is weak, or the ignition system is misfiring. This test checks for battery voltage at the ignition coil and ignition module. A voltmeter is required for this procedure.

WARNING
High voltage is present in the ignition system. Never touch any wires or electrical components while running the engine or performing a test. Never perform ignition system tests in wet conditions.

1. Make sure the lanyard cord (**Figure 2**) is fully attached to the switch. If not, the switch will open the circuit that supplies current to the ignition system.

2. Set the voltmeter on the 20 or 40 VDC scale.

3. Touch the positive meter lead to the positive battery terminal and the negative lead to the negative battery terminal. Charge the battery if the voltage is not above 12.0 volts. Record the battery voltage for reference during the test procedures.

4. Turn the key switch to ON or RUN. The dash gauges must turn on. If not, check for a blown fuse, tripped circuit breaker or loose connections. Correct faulty wiring, replace the fuse, or reset the circuit breaker to restore gauge operation. If this does not restore gauge operation, test the key switch as described in this chapter.

5. Connect the negative meter lead to an engine ground. Touch the positive meter lead to the positive ignition coil terminal. The purple wire connects to the positive coil terminal. The voltage must be within 1 volt of the battery

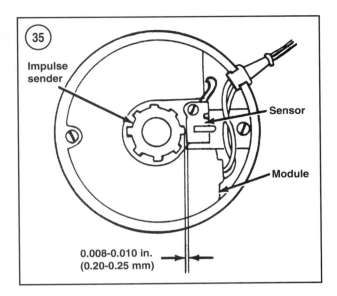

Impulse sender

Sensor

Module

**0.008-0.010 in.
(0.20-0.25 mm)**

10. Connect the meter leads and measure the voltage as described in Step 5. Note the meter while inserting a feeler gauge between the impulse sender finger and the impulse sensor at the point indicated in **Figure 35**. If the voltage changes from 4.0-8.0 volts to near the battery voltage recorded in Step 3 when the feeler gauge passes through the gap, measure the ignition coil primary and secondary resistance as described in this section. If the voltage does not change, and the system does not produce a spark, replace the ignition module as described in Chapter Nine.

11. Turn the key switch to OFF or STOP. Disconnect the test leads.

12. Disconnect the negative battery cable.

13. Install the rotor and distributor cap as described in Chapter Nine.

14. Connect the battery cable.

15. Adjust the ignition timing as described in Chapter Five.

voltage recorded in Step 3. If not, check for corroded, dirty or loose wire connections and damaged wiring.

6. Connect the negative meter lead to an engine ground. Touch the positive meter lead to the negative ignition coil terminal. The black wire connects to the negative coil terminal. With the key switch in ON or RUN, the meter must indicate 4.0-8.0 volts. If not, refer to the following:

    a. If the voltage exceeds 8.0 volts, the distributor is not properly grounded to the engine, or the ignition module is not properly grounded to the distributor. Clean the mating surfaces and tighten loose fasteners to correct the ground and repeat the test.

    b. If the voltage is less than 4.0 volts, disconnect the black wire from the negative ignition coil terminal. Touch the positive meter lead to the coil terminal. Connect the negative meter lead to an engine ground. Turn the key switch to ON or RUN and note the meter. If the voltage is now near the battery voltage recorded in Step 3, the ignition module is faulty and must be replaced. If the voltage remains less than 4.0 volts, the ignition coil primary winding is open and the coil must be replaced.

7. Disconnect the negative battery cable.

8. Remove the distributor cap and rotor as described in Chapter Nine. Adjust the air gap between the impulse sender fingers and the impulse sensor (**Figure 35**) as described in the module installation instructions. Refer to *Ignition Module Replacement*. Do not disconnect the module wiring or install the rotor or distributor cap at this time.

9. Connect the battery cable. Turn the key switch to ON or RUN.

Ignition coil test

    This section describes the resistance test for the primary and secondary ignition coil windings. Although the test can reveal an open or shorted circuit, it should not be considered a conclusive test for the coil. Due to the high voltage generated in the secondary winding, internal arcing can occur in partially shorted circuits or near windings with damaged insulation and can cause an ignition misfire at any engine speed. This is usually not detected with a resistance test. However, when internal arcing is occurring, a clicking noise is often heard emanating from the coil. Replace the coil if it fails either of the resistance tests, internal arcing is suspected and no spark, weak spark or an ignition misfire is present, and all other ignition system components are operating properly.

NOTE
For accurate testing, perform a resistance test on the ignition coil with the coil and air temperature in the work area at approximately 68° F (20° C). The windings will have higher resistance at higher temperatures and lower resistance at lower temperatures.

    An accurate digital ohmmeter is required for this procedure.

1. Remove the ignition coil as described in Chapter Nine.

2. Calibrate an ohmmeter on the 2-ohm or 10-ohm scale. Touch one of the meter leads to the positive coil terminal. Touch the other meter lead to the negative coil terminal. The meter must indicate 1.25-1.40 ohm. If not, replace the coil.

**DELCO EST (ELECTRONIC SPARK TIMING) IGNITION SYSTEM
(LATER CARBURETOR-EQUIPPED AND ALL ELECTRONIC FUEL INJECTION
[EFI] MODELS [EXCEPT LT-1 AND 8.1L MODELS])**

1. Ignition coil
2. Distributor shaft
3. Rotor
4. Distributor cap
5. Ignition module
6. Retainer
7. Washer
8. Pickup coil
9. Pole piece
10. Locating pin
11. Housing
12. Bolt
13. Hold-down clamp
14. Washer
15. Washer
16. Driven gear
17. Gasket
18. Intake manifold

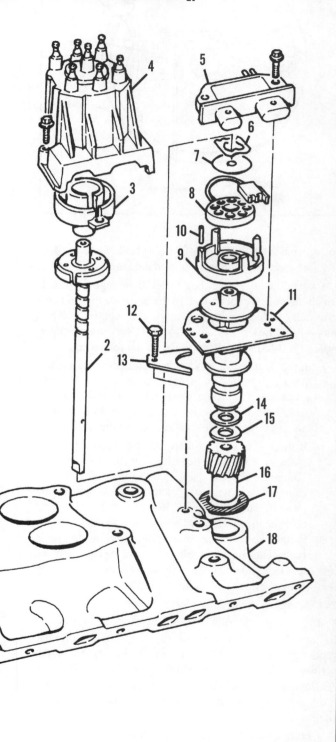

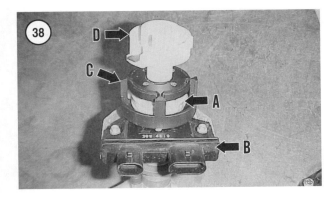

3. Calibrate the ohmmeter on the 20k scale. Touch one of the meter leads to the coil tower (high-tension) lead terminal. Touch the other lead to either the positive or negative coil terminal. The meter must indicate 9400-11,700 ohms. If not, replace the coil.

4. Install the ignition coil as described in Chapter Nine.

Tachometer amplifier

A faulty tachometer can result in improper tachometer reading, a no-start condition or ignition misfiring at any engine speed.

1. Check the gray wire connections at the tachometer amplifier for corroded, dirty or loose terminals and damaged wiring. Correct faulty terminals or wiring as needed. Make sure the black ground wire for the amplifier has a secure, clean connection to the engine ground.

2A. If the engine runs properly but the tachometer is not operating, test the amplifier as follows:

    a. Note the connection points and routing. Then disconnect all of the wires from the tachometer.

    b. Temporarily connect a known good, compatible tachometer to the tachometer leads. It is not necessary to mount the tachometer in the dash for this test.

    c. Start the engine. If the substitute tachometer operates, replace the original tachometer. If the substitute tachometer does not operate, replace the tachometer amplifier.

    d. Reconnect the tachometer wiring. Make sure the wire terminals are oriented to prevent contact with other tachometer terminals or wiring. Securely tighten the wire terminal nuts. They tend to work loose during boat operation.

2B. If the engine will not start or misfires, check for a shorted tachometer amplifier as follows:

    a. Disconnect the two gray wire connectors from the amplifier. Plug the gray wire leading to the ignition coil directly onto the gray engine harness wire to bypass the amplifier.

    b. Start the engine and operate at the engine speed and under the conditions in which the misfire is usually evident. Replace the amplifier if the engine operates properly with the amplifier bypassed. Check for a shorted tachometer as described in this chapter if the engine misfires with the amplifier bypassed.

    c. Reconnect the gray coil wire and engine harness gray wire to the amplifier connectors.

Delco Electronic Spark Timing (EST) Ignition System

The Delco EST (electronic spark timing) ignition system is used on late carburetor-equipped models and all electronic fuel injection (EFI) models except 5.7L LT-1 and 8.1L models.

Major components of the system include the distributor (**Figure 36**), ignition coil (**Figure 37**), spark plugs and wires. The ignition coil is a very robust design, and failure is extremely rare. Coil failure is almost always caused by corroded or dirty terminals.

The EST distributor houses the pickup coil (A, **Figure 38**), ignition module (B), poles (C), rotor (D) and distributor shaft.

EST Operation

On carbureted models, battery voltage is supplied to the ignition coil when the ignition is switched ON. On models equipped with electronic fuel injection (EFI), battery voltage is supplied to the EFI relay. The relay then switches on and supplies battery voltage to the ignition coil. On all models, a circuit inside the ignition coil provides voltage to operate the ignition module.

The rotor in the distributor rotates at one-half crankshaft speed. As it rotates, magnetic poles on the rotor shaft and pickup coil align and misalign. When they are aligned, a magnetic field passes through the pickup coil winding and creates an electric pulse. This pulse is directed to the timing circuits inside the ignition module.

The timing circuit modifies the pulse and directs it to a transistor in the module. The transistor functions as a switch to control current flow through the ignition coil primary winding.

The transistor switches on when the pulse flows from the timing circuit and switches off when the pulse ceases. When switched on, the transistor provides a connection to ground for the ignition coil primary winding; this allows battery current to flow through the primary winding and creates a strong magnetic field.

When switched off, the transistor interrupts the ground, which prevents battery current from flowing and causes the magnetic field to collapse. The collapsing field passes through the ignition coil secondary winding inducing very high-voltage current in this winding. The current flows from the coil tower (coil wire terminal) to the distributor rotor. The rotor directs the current to the distributor cap terminal for each individual spark plug. High-tension wires connect the cap terminals to the spark plugs.

The timing circuits in the ignition module automatically advance the ignition timing in proportion to engine speed. The ignition system does not provide engine overspeed protection; however, the engine control unit (ECU) used on fuel injection (EFI) models limits engine speed by shutting off the fuel injectors at a predetermined rpm.

On fuel injection (EFI) models, the engine control unit (ECU) computes the optimum amount of spark advance for the given operating conditions and adjusts the timing accordingly. The ECU timing circuit essentially overrides the timing circuit in the ignition module. The timing circuit in the module assumes control of the ignition timing if a fault in the ECU circuitry or connecting wiring should occur.

Voltage test

Perform this procedure if the ignition system fails to generate spark at the coil, the spark is weak, or the ignition system is misfiring. This test checks for battery voltage at the ignition coil and ignition module. A 12-volt test lamp is required for this procedure.

WARNING
High voltage is present in the ignition system. Never touch any wires or electrical components while running the engine or

performing a test. Never perform ignition system tests in wet conditions.

WARNING
The engine might unexpectedly start during testing. Keep all persons, clothing, tools or loose objects away from the drive belts and other moving components on the engine.

CAUTION
Use a flush device to supply the engine with cooling water if testing the ignition system with the boat out of the water. Operation of the starter motor results in operation of the seawater pump. The seawater pump is quickly damaged if operated without adequate cooling water.

1. Make sure the emergency stop (lanyard) switch cord (**Figure 2**) is fully attached to the switch and is fully depressing the plunger. If not, the activated switch will open the circuit that supplies current to the ignition system.
2. Turn the ignition key switch to ON or RUN. The dash gauges must turn on. If not, check for a blown fuse, tripped circuit breaker or loose wire connection. If this does not restore gauge operation, test the key switch as described in this chapter.

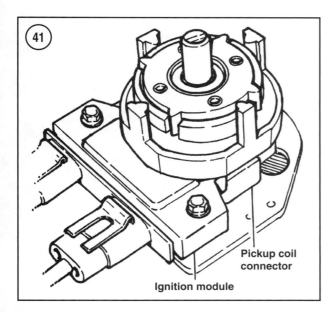

(41)

Pickup coil
connector

Ignition module

3. Disconnect the wire harness connectors (A and B, **Figure 39**) from the ignition coil. Connect the ground lead of the test lamp to an engine ground.

4A. On carburetor-equipped models, touch the test probe to the purple wire in the gray connector. With the key switch in ON or RUN, the lamp must illuminate. If not, test the lanyard switch as described in this chapter. A defective instrument harness or engine harness wiring is indicated if no fault is found with the lanyard switch.

4B. On electronic fuel injection (EFI) models, touch the test probe to the purple wire in the gray connector. With the key switch in ON or RUN, the lamp must illuminate. If not, test the EFI system relay as described in this chapter. Refer to *Electronic Fuel Injection System*.

5. Reconnect the gray connector to the ignition coil. Do not connect the black connector to the coil for this test. Touch the test lamp probe to each of the two open terminals in the ignition coil. With the key switch in ON or RUN, the lamp must illuminate when touched to each terminal. If not, replace the coil.

6. Reconnect the gray and black connectors to the ignition coil. Disconnect the two-wire terminal (**Figure 40**) from the distributor-mounted ignition module. The harness contains a pink and brown wire. Touch the test probe to each of the two open terminals in the harness connector. With the key switch in ON or RUN, the lamp must illuminate when touched to each terminal. Otherwise, the two-wire harness connecting the coil to the module has failed open and must be replaced.

7. Turn the key switch to OFF or STOP. Reconnect the two-wire harness connector to the ignition module.

Pickup coil test

The pickup coil (A, **Figure 38**) is located inside the distributor housing. The coil can be tested without removing the coil from the distributor.

An ohmmeter is required for this procedure.

1. Disconnect the negative battery cable.

2. Remove the distributor cap as described in Chapter Nine.

3. Pull up on the locking tab. Then disconnect the pickup coil connector (**Figure 41**) from the module.

4. Calibrate an ohmmeter on the R × 100 scale.

5. Touch one of the meter leads to the white coil wire. Touch the other meter lead to the green coil wire. The meter must indicate 500-1500 ohms. If not, replace the pickup coil as described in Chapter Nine.

6. Plug the pickup coil connector (**Figure 41**) onto the module. The locking tab must engage the tab on the module.

7. Install the rotor and distributor cap as described in Chapter Nine.

8. Connect the battery cable.

Ignition module

Failure of the ignition module is relatively rare, and most problems are caused by corroded, dirty or defective wiring or terminals. Although test equipment is available, the cost far exceeds the cost of the module. Unless the equipment is available, test the module by a process of elimination.

Perform the following procedure.

1. Check for spark at the coil and spark plugs as described in this section.

2. Check for a shorted tachometer as described in this section.

3. Check the battery voltage to the ignition system as described in this section.

4. Test the pickup coil as described in this section.

5. Check for distributor rotation as described in this section.

6. Observe the tachometer while cranking the engine. A 200 rpm or higher reading indicates the pickup coil and ignition module are operating correctly. Check for a defective ignition coil or connecting wiring.

7. Replace the ignition module as described in Chapter Nine and check for spark at the coil and spark plugs. If no spark is present with the replacement module, replace the ignition coil to restore ignition system operation.

Ignition coil

This section describes the resistance test for the primary and secondary ignition coil windings. Although the test can reveal an open or shorted circuit, it should not be considered a conclusive test for the coil. Due to the high voltage generated in the secondary winding, internal arcing can occur in partially shorted circuits or near windings with damaged insulation and can cause an ignition misfire at any engine speed. This is usually not detected with a resistance test. However, when internal arcing is occurring, a clicking noise is often heard emanating from the coil. If not, repair or replace the two-wire harness that connects the ignition coil to the module.

> *NOTE*
> *For accurate testing, perform a resistance test on the ignition coil with the coil at approximately 68° F (20° C). The windings will have higher resistance measurement at higher temperatures and lower resistance at lower temperatures.*

An accurate digital ohmmeter is required for this procedure. The test leads must have probes with a diameter small enough to fit fully into the terminal openings in the coil yet be long enough to reach the contacts. If necessary, insert straightened paper clips into the openings and connect the test probes to the ends.

1. Remove the ignition coil as described in Chapter Nine.

2. Carefully scrape the paint down to bare metal on a small surface of the mounting bracket (A, **Figure 42**).

3. Touch one of the test leads to the cleaned surface of the mounting bracket (A, **Figure 42**) and the other test lead to the terminal in the plug opening (B). The meter must indicate no continuity. If not, replace the ignition coil as described in Chapter Nine.

4. Touch one of the test leads to the terminal in the plug opening (B, **Figure 42**) and the other test lead to the terminal in the plug opening (C). The meter must indicate continuity. If not, replace the ignition coil as described in Chapter Nine.

5. Touch one of the test leads to the terminal in the plug opening (D, **Figure 42**) and the other test lead to the coil wire terminal (E). The meter must indicate continuity. A high resistance reading is also acceptable. Replace the ignition coil as described in Chapter Nine if the meter indicates no continuity.

6. Apply paint to the bare spot on the mounting bracket to prevent corrosion.

7. Install the ignition coil as described in Chapter Nine.

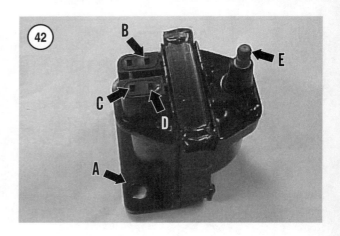

Distributorless Electronic Ignition (EI) System (5.7L LT-1 Models)

A distributorless ignition system is used on all 5.7L LT-1 models. The system consists of two crankshaft position sensors, the reluctor wheel, engine control unit and four ignition coil units.

The crankshaft position sensors (4 and 5, **Figure 43**) are located on the mounting bracket at the front of the engine. The reluctor wheel (8, **Figure 43**) mounts on the crankshaft pulley so the edge of the wheel is in close proximity to the crankshaft position sensors. The ignition coils (5-8, **Figure 24**) mount on the ignition control (IC) module (2) and mounting bracket (1) on the front of the engine.

System operation (5.7L LT-1 models)

When the ignition is switched ON, battery voltage is applied to the EFI system relay, which switches on and supplies battery voltage to the injector and ECU fuses. From the fuses, battery voltage is supplied to the ECU, fuel injectors and ignition control module (3, **Figure 24**). The ignition control module in turn supplies battery current to each of the four ignition coils. Each ignition coil contains a primary and secondary winding. The secondary winding contains two output terminals. Current flowing through the primary winding creates a strong magnetic field.

The reluctor ring (8, **Figure 43**) has 32 unevenly spaced notches along the outer edge. The notches passing next to the sensors create small electrical pulses that are directed to the ignition control module and then to the engine control unit (ECU). The ECU decodes the pulses to determine the exact position of each piston relative to the top of the stroke (TDC). This input allows the ECU to compute

2

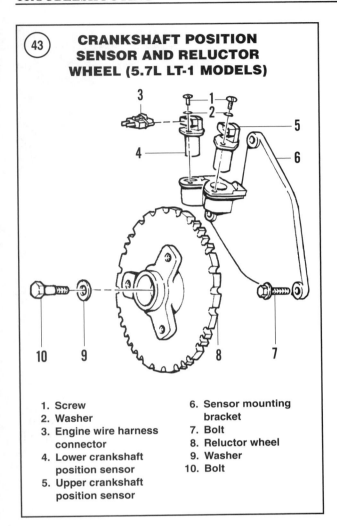

CRANKSHAFT POSITION SENSOR AND RELUCTOR WHEEL (5.7L LT-1 MODELS)

1. Screw
2. Washer
3. Engine wire harness connector
4. Lower crankshaft position sensor
5. Upper crankshaft position sensor
6. Sensor mounting bracket
7. Bolt
8. Reluctor wheel
9. Washer
10. Bolt

which cylinders are in the firing position and when to fire the plug.

When the No. 1 cylinder reaches the firing position, the ECU electronically opens the ground circuit for the ignition coil for cylinders No. 1 and No. 6. This prevents battery current from flowing and causes the magnetic field in the coil primary winding to collapse. The collapsing field passes through the ignition coil secondary winding inducing very high voltage in this winding. The current flows from the coil tower and directly to the spark plugs for cylinders No. 1 and No. 6 through the high-tension wires. Both plugs fire simultaneously. When the No. 1 cylinder is on the compression stroke, the No. 6 cylinder is on the exhaust stroke. This does not create a backfire because no fuel is left in the combustion chamber during the exhaust stroke. This arrangement is commonly referred to as a wasted-spark system. In exactly one revolution of the crankshaft, the No. 6 cylinder is on the compression

stroke, and the No. 1 cylinder is on the exhaust stroke. The remaining cylinders operate in the same manner. Cylinders 5 and 8 share the top ignition coil. Cylinders 2 and 3 share the second ignition coil. Cylinders 4 and 7 share the bottom ignition coil.

The fuel/air mixture in the cylinder must ignite and burn at a precise time to push the piston down on the power stroke. Because fuel burns at a relatively constant rate, spark must occur earlier with increased engine speed. Ideally, the pressure from the burning fuel should peak as the piston starts moving down on the power stroke. This provides the maximum pressure on the piston and maximum power output. If the spark timing is not advanced, the pressure peaks well after the piston starts moving down, and power output decreases. The ECU computes the optimum ignition timing advance for the given operating conditions and adjusts the timing accordingly. The ignition system in itself does not provide engine overspeed protection; however, the ECU limits engine speed by shutting off the fuel injectors at a predetermined speed.

Troubleshooting the electronic ignition (EI) system (5.7L LT-1 models)

The ignition system is controlled by the ECU (engine control unit), which also controls the fuel injection system and warning system. Effective troubleshooting relies heavily on knowing which inputs are reaching the ECU. The ECU stores a diagnostic trouble code if the crankshaft position sensor(s) or ignition module inputs exceed predetermined limits. The trouble might not be detected if the crankshaft position sensor(s) fail open because the ECU does not detect rotation and assumes the crankshaft is not rotating. In this case, the ECU does not store a trouble code. Keep in mind that each coil provides spark to two designated cylinders; therefore, if a single cylinder is misfiring, the fault must be with the spark plug wire or plug. Misfiring affecting only the designated pair of cylinders probably is due to a faulty ignition coil or coil connections.

> *WARNING*
> *High voltage is present in the ignition system. Never touch any wires or electrical components while running the engine or performing a test. Never perform ignition system tests in wet conditions.*

> *WARNING*
> *The engine might unexpectedly start during testing. Keep all persons, clothing, tools or*

loose objects away from the drive belts and other moving components on the engine.

CAUTION
Use a flush device to supply the engine with cooling water if testing the ignition system with the boat out of the water. Operation of the starter motor results in operation of the seawater pump. The seawater pump is quickly damaged if operated without adequate cooling water.

Test the EI system as follows:

1. Check all fuses and circuit breakers for blown fuses and a tripped circuit breaker. Refer to the wiring diagrams at the end of the manual to identify fuses, circuit breakers and connecting wiring.

2. Check for spark at the coil and spark plugs as described in this section. Weak spark indicates a faulty coil or wiring. Even weak spark indicates the crankshaft position sensors and ECU ignition control circuits are operational. Refer to the following:

   a. If spark is missing or weak on a pair of cylinders that share an ignition coil, temporarily switch the coil with one from a pair of cylinders that is firing. Replace the coil if the fault follows the coil.

   b. If spark is missing on a single cylinder, replace the spark plug wire for the suspect cylinder. If spark is not restored with the replacement wire, replace the ignition coil as described in Chapter Nine.

   c. If spark is missing on all cylinders, proceed to Step 3.

3. Turn the key switch to ON or RUN. The electric fuel pump(s) should operate, and the warning horn should sound for a few seconds and then cease. Test the EFI system relay if the warning horn does not sound and the fuel pump(s) do not operate as specified.

NOTE
If no spark is present at the coils, the tachometer does not indicate cranking speed and the fuel pumps do not operate while cranking, yet the horn sounds and the fuel pumps operate for a few seconds after turning the ignition ON, then a no-spark condition is almost always caused by a faulty crankshaft position sensor. The sensors are relatively inexpensive and easy to replace. Replacing the sensors probably will restore spark at the coils.

4. Attempt to start the engine while noting the tachometer and operation of the electric fuel pumps. Refer to the following:

   a. If the tachometer indicates 200 rpm or greater and fuel pump(s) start operating, the crankshaft position

sensors and engine control unit (ECU) are operational. Check for faulty wiring and corroded, dirty or loose connections at the coils and ignition control module. If no faults are found with the wiring, replace the ignition control module and check for spark at the coil. Faulty wiring or connections between the ignition control module and ECU are likely if spark is not restored with the replacement ignition control module.

   b. If the tachometer is not indicating cranking speed yet the fuel pump(s) operate while cranking, check for a shorted tachometer as described in this section.

   c. If the tachometer is not indicating cranking speed and the fuel pump(s) are not operating, check for faulty wiring and corroded, dirty or loose terminals at the crankshaft position sensors. If the connections are good, test the voltage at the ignition control (IC) module as described in this section. If the voltage at the ignition control module is as specified, replace the crankshaft position sensors as described in Chapter Nine and check for spark. If spark is not restored with the replacement crankshaft position sensors, replace the ignition control module as described in Chapter Nine. If spark is not restored with the replacement sensors and module, check for and repair faulty wiring or connections between the ignition control module and ECU.

5. If spark is not restored by this point, check for diagnostic trouble codes as described in this chapter. Refer to *Electronic Fuel Injection System*. If no codes are stored, have an Indmar dealership attach scanning equipment to the engine harness and check for abnormal sensor input. Replace components with abnormal readings.

Ignition control (IC) module voltage test

A multimeter and 12-volt test lamp are required for this procedure.

1. Remove the four ignition coils from the IC module as described in Chapter Nine.

2. Calibrate the meter to the 20 or 40 VDC scale.

3. Connect the negative test lead to an engine ground.

4. Lift the locking tab. Then unplug the three-wire connector from the ignition module (2, **Figure 24**). Locate the terminal in the connector that aligns with the red wire.

5. Turn the key switch to ON or RUN. Touch the positive test lead to the red engine harness wire. The meter must indicate within 1 volt of battery voltage. If not, test the EFI system relay as described in this chapter. Refer to *Electronic Fuel Injection System*. Replace the faulty EFI/ECU fuse or repair the wiring between the relay and ignition control module if the relay tests correctly.

6. Connect the test lamp to the positive battery terminal. Locate the terminal in the disconnected three-wire connector that aligns with the black wire. Touch the test lamp probe to the terminal for the black wire. The lamp must illuminate. If not, repair the black wire or connection from the three-wire connector to the engine ground stud on the flywheel housing.

7. Lift the locking tab. Then carefully plug the three-wire connector onto the ignition control (IC) module.

8. Lift the locking tabs. Then carefully unplug both of the six-wire connectors from the ignition control (IC) module. This step is necessary to isolate the internal circuitry from the crankshaft position sensors and ECU.

9. With the negative meter test lead connected to an engine ground, touch the positive test lead to the ignition coil contacts (3, **Figure 24**) projecting from the ignition control (IC) module. The meter must indicate within 1 volt of battery voltage on one of the terminals and 0 volts on the other terminal for each coil. Replace the ignition control (IC) module if the battery voltage is incorrect on any pair of terminals.

10. Turn the ignition key switch to OFF or STOP.

11. Lift the locking tabs. Then carefully plug both six-wire connectors onto the ignition control (IC) module. Tug on the harness to verify a secure connection.

Distributorless Ignition System

A distributorless ignition system is used on all 8.1L models. The system consist of the crankshaft position sensor, camshaft position sensor, engine control unit and eight individual ignition coils.

The crankshaft position sensor is located on the upper rear of the cylinder block. The sensor extends vertically into an opening adjacent to the crankshaft. The camshaft position sensor (**Figure 44**) is located on the front of the timing chain cover. The eight individual coils (**Figure 45**) are mounted on the rocker arm covers (four on each side). The coils are positioned directly over the corresponding cylinders.

Operation

When the ignition is switched ON, battery voltage is applied to the EFI system relay. The relay switches on when it receives the voltage and supplies voltage to the pink/white wire that supplies voltage to the eight ignition coils. The system relay also activates the engine control unit (ECU).

The crankshaft position sensor creates electrical pulses as fingers on the crankshaft-mounted sensor ring pass near the sensor tip. The pulses are directed to the ECU. Different spacing between the fingers produces a different length of time between the pulses that allows the ECU to determine the position of each piston relative to the top of the compression stroke.

The camshaft position sensor creates electrical pulses as raised bosses on the camshaft gear wheel pass near the sensor tip. The pulses are directed to the ECU where they are used to determine which cylinder is on the compression stroke. Without the camshaft position sensor signal, the ECU could not determine whether the piston is on the compression or exhaust stroke.

The combined input from the crankshaft and camshaft position sensors allow the ECU to determine which cylinder requires spark and when to fire the plug.

Each ignition coil contains a primary winding, secondary winding and a solid-state switch that controls the ground circuit for the primary winding.

The solid-state switch in each ignition coil is controlled by the ECU. At the predetermined time, the ECU activates the switch, which completes the primary winding ground circuit. This allows battery voltage to flow through the primary winding and to create a strong magnetic field. At the predetermined time, the ECU deactivates the solid-state switch, which interrupts the primary winding ground circuit and causes the magnetic field to collapse. The collapsing field passes through the ignition coil secondary winding and induces very high-voltage current in this winding. The current flows from the coil tower directly to the spark plug through the high-tension wire.

The fuel/air mixture in the cylinder must ignite at a precise time to push the piston down on the power stroke. Because fuel burns at a relatively constant rate, spark must occur earlier with increased engine speed. Ideally, the pressure from the burning fuel should peak as the piston starts moving down on the power stroke. This provides the maximum pressure on the piston and maximum power output. If the spark timing is not advanced, the pressure peaks well after the piston starts moving down, and power output decreases. The ECU computes the optimum ignition timing advance for the given operating conditions and adjusts the timing accordingly. The ignition system in itself does not provide engine overspeed protection; however, the ECU limits engine speed by shutting off the fuel injectors at a predetermined speed.

Troubleshooting

The ignition system is controlled by the engine control unit (ECU), which also controls the fuel injection and warning systems. Effective troubleshooting relies heavily on knowing which inputs are reaching the ECU. The ECU stores a diagnostic trouble code if the crankshaft position sensor or camshaft position sensor inputs exceed predetermined values. The trouble might not be detected if the crankshaft position fails open because the ECU does not detect rotation and assumes the crankshaft is not rotating. In this case, the ECU does not store a trouble code.

If good spark is present on some cylinders and not on others, the fault probably is with the ignition coil from the suspect cylinder(s). The easiest way to determine whether the coil is faulty is to switch the coil with coil from another cylinder. Replace the coil if no spark or weak spark follows the coil.

If spark is present on any of the cylinders, the crankshaft position sensor and camshaft position sensor are operating.

WARNING
High voltage is present in the ignition system. Never touch any wires or electrical components while running the engine or performing a test. Never perform ignition system tests in wet conditions.

WARNING
The engine might unexpectedly start during testing. Keep all persons, clothing, tools or loose objects away from the drive belts and other moving components on the engine.

CAUTION
Use a flush device to supply the engine with cooling water if testing the ignition system with the boat out of the water. Operation of the starter motor results in operation of the seawater pump. The seawater pump is quickly damaged if operated without adequate cooling water.

Test the distributorless ignition system as follows:
1. Check all fuses and circuit breakers for blown fuses and a tripped circuit breaker. Refer to the wiring diagrams at the end of the manual to identify fuses, circuit breakers and wiring.
2. Check for spark at the coil and spark plugs as described in this section. Weak spark indicates a faulty coil or wiring. Even weak spark indicates the crankshaft position sensor, camshaft position sensor and ECU ignition control circuits are operational.
3. Turn the key switch to ON or RUN. The electric fuel pumps should operate, and the warning horn should sound for a few seconds and then cease. Test the EFI system relay if the warning horn does not sound or the fuel pumps do not operate as specified.

NOTE
If no spark is present at any of the ignition coils, the tachometer does not indicate cranking speed, and the fuel pumps do not operate while cranking, yet the horn sounds and the fuel pumps operate for a few seconds after turning the ignition ON, then a no-spark condition is almost always caused by a faulty crankshaft position sensor. The sensor is relatively inexpensive and easy to replace. Replacing the sensor probably will restore spark at the coils.

4. Attempt to start the engine while noting the tachometer reading and operation of the electric fuel pumps. Refer to the following:
   a. If the tachometer indicates 200 rpm or greater and the fuel pump(s) start operating, the crankshaft and camshaft position sensors and ignition control circuits in the ECU are operational. Check for corroded, dirty or loose wire connections on the wiring connecting the ignition coils to the EFI system relay and engine control unit. Faulty wiring can affect all cylinders or only some of the cylinders.

b. If the tachometer does not indicate cranking speed yet the fuel pump(s) operate while cranking, check for a shorted tachometer as described in this section.

c. If the tachometer does not indicate cranking speed and the fuel pump(s) are not operating, check for faulty wiring and corroded, dirty or loose connections at the crankshaft and camshaft position sensors. If no faults are found with the wiring, replace the crankshaft position sensor as described in Chapter Nine and check for spark. If spark is not restored, replace the camshaft position sensor as described in Chapter Nine. If spark is still not restored, check for stored diagnostic trouble codes as described in this chapter. Refer to *Electronic Fuel Injection System*. If no codes are stored, have an Indmar dealership attach scanning equipment to the engine and check for abnormal sensor inputs. Replace components with abnormal readings.

BASIC FUEL SYSTEM TROUBLESHOOTING

Refer to **Table 3** for a list of items to check if the engine will not start or if the fuel system is causing an engine malfunction. Other useful information and tips are described with the specific test instructions. Refer to *Carburetor Fuel System* or *Electronic Fuel Injection System*, in this section, for specific troubleshooting procedures.

Most fuel system malfunctions (both carburetor and electronic fuel injection) are caused by the fuel used. Using the proper type of fresh, quality fuel and storing it properly, along with regular maintenance of the fuel filters, will reduce fuel system problems. Fuel storage recommendations and filter maintenance are described in Chapter Three.

Fuel/Air Mixture

A gasoline engine must receive fuel and air mixed in precise proportions to operate efficiently at various loads and engine speeds. Determining whether a fuel system malfunction is causing an excessively rich or lean condition can help determine the cause of the malfunction and identify the corrective action.

An engine that is receiving too much fuel for the amount of air flowing into the engine is operating too rich. Symptoms of an excessively rich condition include rough operation (particularly at idle speed), excessive exhaust smoke (soot near the exhaust outlet), hesitation during acceleration, dark black fluffy deposits on the spark plugs and stalling while idling (commonly called loading up).

Operating an engine that is too rich will result in increased fuel usage, increased exhaust emissions, premature fouling of the spark plugs, increased combustion chamber deposits and dilution of the crankcase oil. To identify an excessively rich condition, remove and inspect the spark plugs as described in Chapter Three. Compare the spark plugs to those shown in **Figure 19**.

On carburetor-equipped models, an excessively rich condition is usually caused by one or more of the following:

a. An improperly adjusted carburetor.
b. A dirty or damaged flame arrestor.
c. Improper choke valve operation.
d. A fuel-saturated or improperly adjusted float.
e. A worn or leaking fuel inlet valve.
f. Damaged or stuck power valve.
g. Inadequate ventilation of the engine compartment.

On electronic fuel injection (EFI) models, an excessively rich condition is usually caused by one of more of the following:

a. A dirty or damaged flame arrestor.
b. Leaking fuel injector.
c. Too-high fuel pressure.
d. Malfunction of a fuel injection system sensor.
e. Internal leak in fuel pressure regulator.
f. Inadequate ventilation of the engine compartment.

An engine that is receiving too little fuel for the amount of air flowing into the engine is operating too lean. Symptoms of an excessively lean mixture include hard starting, hesitation or backfiring during rapid acceleration, poor high speed performance, overheating (particularly at higher throttle settings) and overheating of the spark plug insulator tip. Operating an engine that is too lean will result in poor performance and promotes preignition and detonation that damages the pistons and valves. To positively identify an excessively lean condition, remove and inspect the spark plugs as described in Chapter Three. Compare the spark plugs to those shown in **Figure 19**.

On carburetor-equipped models, an excessively lean condition is usually caused by one or more of the following:

a. A restriction in the fuel supply line.
b. Air leakage in the fuel supply line.
c. Blockage or air leakage in the fuel filters.
d. Faulty fuel pump.
e. An improperly adjusted carburetor.
f. Plugged carburetor fuel jet or passage.
g. Improperly adjusted float.
h. A sticking fuel inlet valve.
i. Damaged or stuck power valve.

On electronic fuel injection (EFI) models, an excessively lean condition is usually caused by one of more of the following:

    a. A restriction in the fuel supply line.
    b. Air leakage in the fuel supply line.
    c. Blockage or air leak in the fuel filters.
    d. Too-low fuel pressure.
    e. Malfunction of a fuel injection system sensor.
    f. Faulty or blocked fuel injector(s).

Fuel inspection

Fuel-related problems are common with most marine engines. Gasoline has a relatively short shelf life and becomes stale within a few weeks under some conditions. This gasoline works fine in an automobile because the fuel is consumed in a week or so. Because marine engines might set idly for several weeks at a time, the gasoline often becomes stale.

As fuel evaporates, a gummy deposit usually forms in the carburetor or other fuel system components. These deposits can restrict fuel filters, fuel lines, fuel pumps and small passages in the carburetor or fuel injection system.

Fuel stored in the fuel tank tends to absorb water vapor from the air. Over time, this water separates from the fuel and then settles to the bottom of the fuel tank. Water in the fuel tank can lead to the formation of rust and other contaminants in the fuel tank. These contaminants block fuel filters and other fuel system passages. Inspect the fuel when the engine refuses to start and the ignition system is not at fault. An unpleasant odor usually indicates the fuel has exceeded the shelf life.

> *WARNING*
> *Use extreme caution when working with the fuel system. Fuel is extremely flammable and, if ignited, can result in injury or death. Never smoke or allow sparks to occur around fuel or fuel vapor. Wipe up any spilled fuel at once with a shop towel and dispose of the shop towel in an appropriate manner. Check all fuel hoses, connections and fittings for leakage after any fuel system repair.*

Most models covered in this manual are equipped with a spin-on water-separating fuel filter (**Figure 46**, typical) mounted on or near the engine. To inspect the fuel, place a suitable container under the filter. Then remove the filter as described in Chapter Four. Refer to *Servicing the Water-Separating Fuel Filter*. Empty the fuel into a container. Then reinstall the filter as described in Chapter Seven. Promptly clean up any spilled fuel. On models

without a spin-on fuel filter, place the container under the mechanical or electric fuel pump. Then loosen the fuel inlet fitting at the pump (**Figure 47**, typical) to drain a sample of the fuel from the fuel supply hose or outlet line. Securely tighten the fitting and promptly wipe up any spilled fuel.

Inspect and carefully smell the fuel. An unusual odor, debris, cloudy appearance or the presence of water indicates a problem with the fuel. If any of these conditions are noted, dispose of all the fuel in an environmentally responsible manner. Contact a local marine dealership or automotive repair facility for information on the proper disposal of the fuel. Clean and inspect the entire fuel system if water or other contamination is in the fuel.

Checking for a restriction in the fuel supply hose

> *WARNING*
> *Safely performing on-water testing or adjustments requires two people: one person to operate the boat and the other to monitor the gauges or test equipment and make necessary adjustments. All personnel must remain seated inside the boat at all times. Do not lean over the transom while the boat is underway. Use extensions to allow all gauges and test equipment to be located in normal seating areas.*

Perform this test if the engine will not start or runs too lean at higher engine speeds. This test cannot be performed on electronic fuel injection (EFI) models using an in-tank electric fuel pump.

1. Remove the spin-on water-separating fuel filter (**Figure 46**, typical) as described in Chapter Four. Refer to *Servicing the Water-Separating Fuel Filter*. If the engine is not equipped with this filter, place the container under the mechanical or electric fuel pump. Then loosen the fuel inlet fitting at the pump (**Figure 47**, typical) to drain a

sample of the fuel from the fuel supply hose. Check for the presence of fuel. If no or very little fuel is found in the filter or fuel supply hose, perform the following:

a. Check the fuel tank for fuel and check all hoses and connections for broken or loose clamps and loose or damaged fittings.

b. Inspect the fuel line for cut, broken, cracked or weathered surfaces. If it is not in excellent condition, replace the hose with a *new* U.S Coast Guard-approved fuel hose.

c. Locate the antisiphon valve threaded into the fuel supply hose fitting on the boat fuel tank. Remove and inspect the antisiphon valve for blockage, a loose fit in the fuel line fitting, cracking of the valve housing and damaged threads. Replace the valve with a new suitable replacement if any defects are evident.

WARNING
Never install a simple fitting in place of the antisiphon valve, modify the antisiphon valve, or bypass the antisiphon valve. The valve provides an important safety feature by preventing fuel in the tank from siphoning into the engine compartment if a fuel hose, fuel line or other fuel system component develops a leak.

2. Disconnect the fuel supply hose from the inlet fitting on the spin-on fuel filter housing (**Figure 46**) or the mechanical fuel pump inlet fitting (**Figure 47**). Drain residual fuel from the hose into a suitable container. If not contaminated, pour the fuel back into the boat fuel tank. Clean up any spilled fuel.

3. Temporarily connect a common outboard fuel supply hose with a primer bulb to the fuel inlet fitting. The arrow on the primer bulb must face the fuel inlet fitting.

4. Connect the other end of the fuel supply hose to a compatible outboard fuel tank filled with fresh fuel. Make sure the hose and portable tank fittings have at least a 1/4

in. (6.1 mm) inside diameter. Open the vent on the portable fuel tank.

5. Pump the primer bulb to prime the system and check for leakage at the fuel supply hose, hose fittings and fuel lines. Correct any leaks before proceeding.

WARNING
Safely performing on-water testing or adjustments requires two people: one person to operate the boat and the other to monitor the gauges or test equipment and make necessary adjustments. All personnel must remain seated inside the boat at all times. Do not lean over the transom while the boat is underway. Use extensions to allow all gauges and test equipment to be located in normal seating areas.

6. Operate the engine at the speed and conditions that the malfunction occurs. Refer to the following.

a. If the engine performs properly using a portable tank, the malfunction is caused by a blocked fuel tank pickup, damaged fittings, faulty antisiphon valve, loose or leaking fuel tank pickup, improper fuel tank venting, air leakage at fittings or faulty fuel hose. Inspect, repair or replace these components to restore proper engine operation. Proceed to Step 8.

b. If the malfunction is still present, proceed to Step 7.

7. Have an assistant operate the engine at the speed and conditions that the malfunction occurs. As soon as the symptoms occur, *vigorously* pump the primer bulb and note the reaction. Wait a few minutes for symptoms to reappear and then repeat the pumping action. Refer to the following:

a. If the motor operates properly only after pumping the primer bulb, the fault probably is with the mechanical or electric low-pressure fuel pump. Replace the mechanical fuel pump as described in Chapter Seven. Test the low-pressure electric fuel pump as described in this chapter.

b. If the malfunction is still present (carburetor-equipped models), check the fuel pump fittings and all filters for blockage. If no blockage is found, disassemble, clean and assemble the carburetor as described in Chapter Nine.

c. If the malfunction is still present (electronic fuel injection [EFI] models), check the fuel pressure as described in this chapter. If the fuel pressure is correct, check for a diagnostic code as described in this chapter. If no codes are stored, check the fuel injectors.

8. Stop the engine. Disconnect the portable tank from the inlet fitting. Drain residual fuel from the hose. Reconnect the boat fuel tank supply hose. Securely tighten the clamp(s). Clean up any spilled fuel.

9. Operate the engine at the speed and conditions that the malfunction occurs to verify the fault. Often, the fault is corrected by securely tightening the supply hose clamp.

Fuel tank vent inspection

A defective fuel tank vent can cause a no-start condition or restrict fuel flow at any engine speed. Typically, the symptom worsens the longer the engine operates. This occurs because as fuel is drawn from the tank, improper venting will cause a vacuum to form in the area above the fuel. The more fuel withdrawn, the stronger the vacuum becomes. In time, the vacuum will overcome the pumping ability of the fuel pump and fuel starvation will occur. To verify a venting problem, simply open the fuel fill cap when the symptoms occur. Improper venting is evident if the symptoms quickly improve. Improper venting is usually caused by insects, insect nests or webs, or other debris in the vent fitting (on the boat) or in the vent hose connecting the vent fitting to the fuel tank.

Carburetor Fuel System

Refer to **Table 3** for a list of items to check if the engine will not start or if the fuel system is suspected of causing an engine malfunction.

Carburetor operation

The carburetor (**Figure 48**, typical) is designed to maintain the fuel/air proportions while providing for sudden acceleration and varying loads.

The choke valve (A, **Figure 48**) and electric choke heater (B) in the carburetor provide a richer-than-normal fuel/air mixture until the engine warms up. When cooled by surrounding air, the coil in the electric choke partially closes the choke valve to restrict air flow into the throttle openings. This decreases air pressure in the opening and causes the metering circuits to deliver more fuel. After starting the engine, current supplied by the alternator causes a heating element in the electric choke to heat the choke coil. This causes the coil to gradually open as the engine warms.

The accelerator pump provides the additional fuel required during rapid acceleration. The sudden manifold pressure change that occurs during rapid acceleration can momentarily disrupt fuel flow from the low-speed meter-

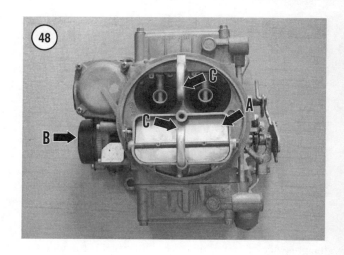

ing circuits at a time when more fuel is required. The accelerator pump provides an instantaneous spray of fuel into the carburetor opening to bridge the gap between the low-speed and high-speed fuel metering circuits.

The power valve provides additional fuel during heavy load conditions. Manifold pressure is applied to the diaphragm on the power valve. At idle and when the engine is lightly loaded, manifold pressure is low (high vacuum), and the power valve remains closed. While accelerating, when the engine is heavily loaded or when operating at higher throttle settings, the manifold pressure is higher (low vacuum), and the power valve opens. The open power valve allows additional fuel to bypass the normal metering circuits to provide the additional fuel required for heavy loads.

> *CAUTION*
> *Various jets, passages and adjustment screws meter fuel to provide the precise amount of fuel for the engine model. Never use a carburetor or carburetor components from a different model on the engine. This can adversely affect the fuel metering and cause an excessively rich or excessively lean operating condition. Operating too rich or too lean can cause poor running quality and serious engine damage.*

Checking for a flooding carburetor

A flooding carburetor can cause hard starting, stalling, rough idle, hesitation during acceleration, excessive exhaust smoke and fouled spark plugs.

> *WARNING*
> *Safely performing on-water testing or adjustments requires two people: one person*

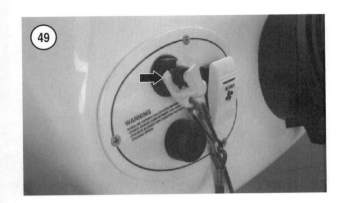

to operate the boat and the other to monitor the gauges or test equipment and make necessary adjustments. All personnel must remain seated inside the boat at all times. Do not lean over the transom while the boat is underway. Use extensions to allow all gauges and test equipment to be located in normal seating areas.

WARNING
The engine might unexpectedly start during testing. Keep all persons, clothing, tools or loose objects away from the drive belts and other moving components on the engine.

CAUTION
Use a flush device to supply the engine with cooling water if testing the fuel system with the boat out of the water. Operation of the starter motor results in operation of the seawater pump. The seawater pump is quickly damaged if operated without adequate cooling water.

1. Remove and clean the flame arrestor as described in Chapter Three.
2. Pull the cord to activate the lanyard switch (**Figure 49**). This prevents the ignition system from operating but does not prevent starter motor or fuel pump operation. If the control does not incorporate an emergency stop (lanyard) switch, disconnect the coil wire from the distributor cap and connect it to an engine ground to disable the ignition system. The wire must make a secure connection to prevent arcing.
3. Observe the carburetor bowl overflow/vent tube(s) (C, **Figure 48**) for fuel flowing from the tubes while an assistant attempts to start the engine. A single tube is used on a two-barrel carburetor, and two tubes are used on four-barrel carburetors. Stop cranking the engine *immediately* if fuel begins flowing from the tube(s). This indicates the carburetor is flooding due to a faulty needle and seat, im-

properly adjusted or damaged float, or excessive fuel pressure. Disassemble, clean and assemble the carburetor as described in Chapter Seven. Replace the mechanical or electric low-pressure fuel pump if flooding is evident and no fault is found with the carburetor.
4. Stop the engine. Install the flame arrestor and plastic cover as described in Chapter Three.
5. Reattach the lanyard cord to the emergency stop (lanyard) switch or reconnect the coil wire to the distributor cap to allow engine starting.

Choke operation

Improper choke valve operation can cause hard starting, a rich running condition, rough idle, hesitation during rapid acceleration or poor overall performance.

WARNING
Safely performing on-water testing or adjustments requires two people: one person to operate the boat and the other to monitor the gauges or test equipment and make necessary adjustments. All personnel must remain seated inside the boat at all times. Do not lean over the transom while the boat is underway. Use extensions to allow all gauges and test equipment to be located in normal seating areas.

CAUTION
Use a flush device to supply the engine with cooling water if testing the fuel system with the boat out of the water. Operation of the starter motor results in operation of the seawater pump. The seawater pump is quickly damaged if operated without adequate cooling water.

1. Remove and clean the flame arrestor as described in Chapter Three.
2. Note the position of the choke valve (A, **Figure 48**). The choke valve should almost be closing off the air horn opening if the engine and surrounding air are at normal room temperature or cooler. If the valve is almost closed, proceed to Step 3. If not, refer to the carburetor disassembly procedure in Chapter Seven and remove the electric choke and coil. Do not remove the choke housing from the carburetor. Reinstall the choke as described in the assembly procedure. Replace the electric choke and coil if the choke does not perform as specified after proper installation.
3. Observe the choke valve while an assistant starts the engine. The choke valve should open a little more as soon as the engine starts. If the valve performs as specified,

proceed to Step 4. If the valve does not open as specified, the choke piston and lever in the choke housing are sticking or damaged. Refer to the carburetor disassembly procedure in Chapter Seven. Then remove, clean and inspect the piston, lever and related components. Replace worn or damaged components. Reinstall the piston and related components as described in the assembly procedure.

4. Observe the choke valve as the engine warms to normal operating temperature while running at idle speed. The choke should gradually open as the engine warms and should be completely open when the engine reaches normal operating temperature. If the choke valve opens as specified, proceed to Step 8. If not, proceed to Step 5.

5. Cautiously touch a finger to the side of the electric choke (B, **Figure 48**). The electric choke should feel warm to the touch. If not, proceed to Step 6. The choke valve, piston, or connecting lever or linkages are sticking if the electric choke is warm yet the choke valve is not opening as specified. Refer to the carburetor disassembly procedure in Chapter Seven. Then remove, clean and inspect the piston, choke valve, lever and related linkage. Replace worn or damaged components. Reinstall the piston and related components as described in the assembly procedure.

6. Disconnect the purple or purple/white (A, **Figure 50**) and black (B) wires from the electric choke terminals. Set a voltmeter to the 10 or 20 VDC scale.

7. Connect a voltmeter positive lead to the purple/white wire (A, **Figure 50**) and the negative meter lead to the black wire (B). With the engine running at idle speed, the meter should indicate 6.5 volts or more. Refer to the following:

   a. If the voltage is within the specification and the choke did not become warm in Step 5, replace the electric choke as described in the carburetor disassembly and assembly instructions in Chapter Seven.

   b. If the voltage is below the specification, repeat the test with the negative test lead connected to a known good engine ground. Repair or replace the ground wire if the voltage is now correct. If the voltage is below the specification while using the alternate ground, repeat the test with the positive meter lead connected to the white or purple terminal leading to the alternator. If the voltage is now within the specification, repair the faulty connection or open circuits in the purple or purple/white wire. If the voltage is below the specification with the lead touching the alternator terminal. Test the alternator excitation circuit as described in this chapter.

8. Stop the engine. Reconnect the purple or purple/white and black wire to the choke. The terminals must fit se-

curely. If necessary, disconnect the terminal(s) and pinch the wire or choke terminal to achieve a secure fit. Route the wiring to prevent interference with moving components or contact with hot engine surfaces. Secure the wiring with plastic locking clamps as needed.

9. Install the flame arrestor and plastic cover as described in Chapter Three.

Mechanical Fuel Pump Pressure

A defective mechanical fuel pump can cause an inability to start the engine, carburetor flooding due to excessive fuel pressure (rare event), stalling at idle or misfiring, and poor performance at higher throttle settings.

> *WARNING*
> *The engine might unexpectedly start during testing. Keep all persons, clothing, tools or loose objects away from the drive belts and other moving components on the engine.*

> *WARNING*
> *Safely performing on-water testing or adjustments requires two people: one person to operate the boat and the other to monitor the gauges or test equipment and make necessary adjustments. All personnel must remain seated inside the boat at all times. Do not lean over the transom while the boat is underway. Use extensions to allow all gauges and test equipment to be located in normal seating areas.*

> *CAUTION*
> *Use a flush device to supply the engine with cooling water if testing the fuel system with the boat out of the water. Operation of the starter motor results in operation of the seawater pump. The seawater pump is quickly damaged if operated without adequate cooling water.*

This procedure requires a fuel pressure test gauge capable of accurately measuring 3-7 psi (20.7-48.3 kPa) and a suitable T-fitting for attaching the gauge between the fuel pump outlet and carburetor.

1. Inspect the fuel and check for a restriction in the fuel supply hose as described in this section. Refer to *Basic Fuel System Troubleshooting*.

2. Check for fuel in the sight tube (A, **Figure 51**, typical). Any fuel in the tube indicates the diaphragm in the pump is leaking, and the mechanical pump must be replaced as described in Chapter Seven.

3. Place a suitable container under the fitting to capture spilled fuel and disconnect the fuel line from the outlet fitting (B, **Figure 51**, typical) on the fuel pump. Drain residual fuel from the hose. If the fuel is not contaminated, empty the fuel into the boat fuel tank.

4. Connect a suitable barbed T-fitting to the fuel line between the fuel pump and carburetor. Attach the fuel pressure gauge to the T-fitting. Secure all connections with clamps to prevent leakage.

5. Pull the cord to activate the emergency stop (lanyard) switch (**Figure 49**). This prevents the ignition system from operating but does not prevent starter motor or fuel

pump operation. If the control does not incorporate an emergency stop (lanyard) switch, disconnect the coil wire from the distributor cap and connect it to an engine ground to disable the ignition system. The wire must make a secure connection to prevent arcing.

6. Observe the fuel gauge and connections for leakage while an assistant cranks the engine. Stop cranking the engine *immediately* if fuel leakage is detected. Correct fuel leaks before proceeding.

7. Observe the gauge while an assistant cranks the engine for approximately 20 seconds. The gauge must indicate 3-7 psi (20.7-48.3 kPa). Refer to the following:

   a. If the fuel pressure is 3-7 psi (20.7-48.3 kPa), the fuel pressure is correct at cranking speed. Proceed to Step 8.

   b. If the pressure exceeds 7 psi (48.3 kPa), replace the fuel pump as described in Chapter Seven.

   c. If the pressure is less than 3 psi (20.7 kPa), check for a flooding carburetor as described in this section. If the carburetor is not flooding, replace the fuel pump as described in Chapter Seven.

8. Reattach the lanyard cord to the emergency stop (lanyard) switch or reconnect the coil wire to the distributor cap. Prepare the boat and engine for operating under normal operating conditions.

9. Observe the gauge while an assistant operates the engine under load at different speeds from idle to full-throttle. The gauge must indicate 3-7 psi (20.7-48.3 kPa) at all engine speeds. If not, refer to the following:

   a. If the pressure exceeds 7 psi (48.3 kPa), replace the fuel pump as described in Chapter Seven.

   b. If the pressure drops to less than 3 psi (20.7 kPa) with increased engine speed, check for a restriction in the fuel supply hose as described in this section. Refer to *Basic Fuel System Troubleshooting*. If no restriction is evident, replace the mechanical fuel pump as described in Chapter Seven.

10. Stop the engine. Remove the pressure gauge and T-fitting from the fuel pump and fuel line. Reconnect the fuel line and tighten the fittings to 177-212 in.-lb. (20-24 N•m).

Run the engine and check for leakage as described in Chapter Seven. Refer to *Mechanical fuel pump replacement*.

Low-Pressure Electric Fuel Pump

A defective low-pressure electric fuel pump can cause an inability to start the engine, carburetor flooding due to excessive fuel pressure, stalling at idle or misfiring, and poor performance at higher throttle settings.

Two types of electric fuel pumps are used on carburetor-equipped models. The larger and more common Carter pump (**Figure 52**) mounts on the starboard side of the engine next to the engine mount. The smaller and less common Delco pump (**Figure 53**) mounts on the front starboard side of the engine. To prevent premature failure of the pump, replace the water-separating fuel filter (**Figure 46**) when replacing the pump and at the specified maintenance intervals. Water-separating fuel filter replacement and maintenance intervals are described in Chapter Three.

The first test in this section tests the electrical circuit for the pump. The second test checks the fuel pump pressure.

Electrical circuit test

Voltage to operate the pump is provided by the battery and is controlled by the fuel pump oil pressure switch and the starting system bypass circuit. The oil pressure switch (**Figure 54**) threads into an oil passage on the top of the engine and near the distributor.

With the key switch ON, battery voltage is supplied to the oil pressure switch and from the oil pressure switch to the electric fuel pump. A dedicated wire provides a ground circuit for the fuel pump. The oil pressure switch closes and provides voltage for the electric fuel pump only once engine oil pressure reaches approximately 4 psi (27.6 kPa). Therefore, the fuel pump will not operate simply with the key switch ON. During cranking, voltage is supplied to the electric fuel pump by a circuit that bypasses the oil pressure switch through the *I* terminal on the starter solenoid (**Figure 55**). When the engine starts and the starter circuit is deactivated, the bypass circuit opens. Voltage for the fuel pump is then provided through the oil pressure switch, which closes when engine oil pressure is sufficient to close the switch. If the engine should stall or lose oil pressure, the oil pressure switch will open and stop fuel pump operation.

Faulty electric fuel pump circuitry will prevent the fuel pump from operating during starting, prevent the fuel pump from operating while running or allow the fuel pump to operate with the engine off and the key switch in ON or RUN.

> *WARNING*
> *Safely performing on-water testing or adjustments requires two people: one person to operate the boat and the other to monitor the gauges or test equipment and make necessary adjustments. All personnel must remain seated inside the boat at all times. Do not lean over the transom while the boat is underway. Use extensions to allow all gauges and test equipment to be located in normal seating areas.*

> *WARNING*
> *The engine might unexpectedly start during testing. Keep all persons, clothing, tools or loose objects away from the drive belts and other moving components on the engine.*

> *CAUTION*
> *Use a flush device to supply the engine with cooling water if testing the fuel system with the boat out of the water. Operation of the starter motor results in operation of the seawater pump. The seawater pump is quickly damaged if operated without adequate cooling water.*

Use a 12-volt test lamp and mechanic's stethoscope for this procedure.

1. Disconnect the coil wire from the distributor cap and connect it to an engine ground to disable the ignition system.

2A. On models using a Carter electric fuel pump, slide the rubber insulator off the terminal nuts. Then remove the nuts that secure the wires to the terminals (A, **Figure 52**).

2B. On models using a Delco electric fuel pump, push on the locking clip. Then carefully unplug the connector (A, **Figure 53**) from the fuel pump.

3. Connect the cord of the test lamp to the positive battery cable. Touch the test lamp probe to an engine ground to verify the light and a good engine ground.

4A. On models using a Carter electric fuel pump, touch the test lamp probe to the black wire in the fuel pump connector.

4B. On models using a Delco electric pump, touch the test lamp probe to the black wire in the fuel pump connector.

5. The lamp must illuminate. If not, repair the wiring or connections.

6. Connect the cord of the test lamp to an engine ground. Touch the test lamp probe to the positive battery terminal to verify the lamp and the engine ground. Touch the test lamp probe to the other fuel pump wire (not the black ground wire). The lamp must not illuminate. If the lamp illuminates, disconnect the wire from the starter solenoid (**Figure 55**). If the lamp extinguishes with the wire disconnected, the starter solenoid is shorted internally. Replace the starter solenoid as described in Chapter Nine. Reconnect the bypass wire to the starter solenoid.

7. Connect the test lamp to the fuel pump connection as described in Step 6. Observe the lamp while an assistant turns the key switch to ON or RUN. The lamp must not illuminate. If the lamp illuminates, test the fuel pump oil pressure switch as described in this section. If the switch functions correctly, the wire connecting the switch to the fuel pump is shorted to a battery voltage source. Repair the wiring before proceeding.

8. Connect the test lamp to the fuel pump connector as described in Step 6. Observe the lamp while an assistant turns the key switch to START. The lamp must illuminate. If the lamp illuminates with the key switch in START, the fuel pump circuit is operational. Record the test result and proceed to Step 10. If the lamp does not illuminate, touch the test lamp to the bypass circuit terminal on the starter solenoid (**Figure 55**) and repeat the test.

a. If the lamp illuminates, repair the wire connecting the bypass terminal to the fuel pump wire.

b. If the lamp does not illuminate, test the starter solenoid as described in this chapter.

9A. On models using a Carter fuel pump, reconnect the fuel pump (A, **Figure 52**). Position the rubber insulating boots fully over the wire terminals.

9B. On models using a Delco fuel pump, push on the locking clip and carefully plug the connector (A, **Figure 53**) onto the electric fuel pump.

10. Touch a mechanic's stethoscope to the body of the fuel pump (B, **Figure 52** or B, **Figure 53**). Listen carefully for fuel pump operation while an assistant turns the key switch to START and back to ON or RUN. The fuel pump must operate, and the starter must activate each time with the switch in START. Replace the electric fuel pump if the starter operates as specified but the fuel pump does not operate.

11. Place the key switch in OFF or STOP. Disconnect the battery terminals.

12. Make sure all terminal nuts are securely tightened and the wire terminals are not contacting other terminals. Reposition the wiring as necessary. To prevent terminal corrosion and starting system malfunction, thoroughly coat the starter solenoid bypass, fuel pump oil pressure switch and fuel pump terminals (Carter fuel pump only) with Black Neoprene Dip. Purchase the neoprene dip (OMC part No. 909570) from an OMC dealership.

13. Connect the battery cable.

14. Start the engine and operate at idle speed. Touch a mechanic's stethscope to the body of the fuel pump (B, **Figure 52** or B, **Figure 53**). Listen carefully for fuel pump operation. Listen to the pump while the assistant stops the engine. The pump should operate continuously while the engine runs and stop when the engine stops. Test the fuel pump oil pressure switch if the pump fails to operate as specified. Test the engine oil pressure as described in this chapter if the switch operates correctly.

Oil pressure switch test

This test requires a multimeter and a vacuum/pressure pump. Purchase the vacuum/pressure pump from a local automotive parts or tool supply store. Test the switch as follows:

1. Remove the oil pressure switch as described in Chapter Nine.

2. Carefully slide an appropriately sized hose over the threaded fitting of the oil pressure switch (**Figure 56**). Install a clamp to ensure an airtight connection. Do not apply pressure at this time.

3. Connect the meter leads to the two switch terminals. The meter must indicate no continuity. If continuity is noted, the switch is shorted internally and must be replaced.

4. Observe the meter and the pressure gauge while *slowly* applying pressure to the switch. Note the pressure gauge reading when the ohmmeter reading changes to continuity.

5. Observe the meter and pressure gauge while *slowly* relieving the pressure. Note the pressure gauge reading when the ohmmeter reading changes to no continuity.

6. Repeat Step 4 and Step 5 several times to check for an intermittent switch failure. The meter must change to continuity each time the pressure reaches approximately 5 psi (34.4 kPa) and no continuity each time the pressure drops below 5 psi (34.4 kPa). Replace the switch if it fails to perform as specified.

7. Remove the test leads and pressure/vacuum pump from the oil pressure switch. Clean all hose material from the threaded section of the switch.

8. Install the oil pressure switch as described in Chapter Nine.

Electric fuel pump pressure test

> *WARNING*
> *Safely performing on-water testing or adjustments requires two people: one person to operate the boat and the other to monitor the gauges or test equipment and make necessary adjustments. All personnel must remain seated inside the boat at all times. Do not lean over the transom while the boat is underway. Use extensions to allow all gauges and test equipment to be located in normal seating areas.*

> *WARNING*
> *The engine might unexpectedly start during testing. Keep all persons, clothing, tools or loose objects away from the drive belts and other moving components on the engine.*

> *CAUTION*
> *Use a flush device to supply the engine with cooling water if testing the fuel system with the boat out of the water. Operation of the starter motor results in operation of the seawater pump. The seawater pump is quickly damaged if operated without adequate cooling water.*

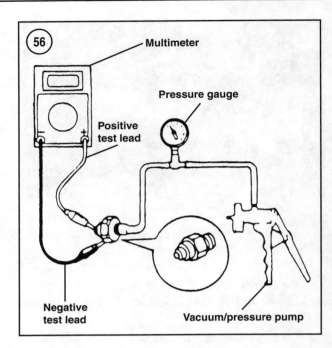

This procedure requires a fuel pressure test gauge capable of accurately measuring 3.5-8.5 psi (24.1-58.6 kPa) and a suitable T-fitting to attach the gauge to the fuel line.

1. Inspect the fuel and check for a restriction in the fuel supply hose as described in this section. Refer to *Basic Fuel System Troubleshooting*.

2. Disconnect the ignition coil secondary wire and connect it to ground to disable the ignition system. The secondary wire must make a secure connection to prevent arcing.

3. Touch a mechanic's stethoscope to the body of the fuel pump (B, **Figure 52** or B, **Figure 53**). Listen carefully for fuel pump operation while an assistant turns the key switch to START and back to ON or RUN. The fuel pump must operate each time the starter activates and stop running within a few seconds after placing the key switch in ON or RUN. If the pump fails to operate as specified, test the low-pressure electric fuel pump circuit as described in this section.

4. Place a suitable container under the fitting to capture spilled fuel. Then disconnect the fuel line from the outlet fitting (C, **Figure 52** or C, **Figure 53**) on the fuel pump. Drain residual fuel from the line. If the fuel is not contaminated, empty the fuel into the boat fuel tank.

5. Connect a suitable barbed T-fitting in the fuel pump outlet fitting and fuel line. Connect the hose of a fuel pressure gauge to the barbed fitting. Secure the pressure gauge hose with a suitable clamp. Secure the fuel gauge and hose to prevent contact with moving or hot engine components. Clean up any spilled fuel before proceeding.

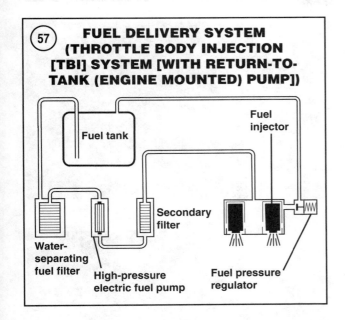

FUEL DELIVERY SYSTEM (THROTTLE BODY INJECTION [TBI] SYSTEM [WITH RETURN-TO-TANK (ENGINE MOUNTED) PUMP])

Fuel tank

Fuel injector

Secondary filter

Water-separating fuel filter

High-pressure electric fuel pump

Fuel pressure regulator

6. Observe the fuel gauge and the fuel fittings for leakage while an assistant cranks the engine. Stop cranking the engine *immediately* if fuel leakage is detected. Correct fuel leaks before proceeding.

7. Observe the gauge while an assistant operates the starter for approximately 20 seconds. The gauge must indicate 4.9-8.5 psi. (33.8-58.6 kPa) while cranking. Refer to the following:

   a. If the pressure is 4.9-8.5 psi. (33.8-58.6 kPa), the fuel pressure is correct at cranking speed. Proceed to Step 8.

   b. If the pressure exceeds 8.5 psi (58.6 kPa), the relief valve in the pump has seized. Replace the electric fuel pump as described in Chapter Seven.

   c. If the pressure is less than 4.9 psi (33.8 kPa), the fuel pressure is too low. Check for a flooding carburetor as described in this section. If the carburetor is not flooding, replace the fuel pump as described in Chapter Seven.

8. Reconnect the coil wire to the distributor cap.

9. Prepare the boat and engine for operating under normal operating conditions.

10. Observe the gauge while an assistant operates the engine under normal load at all speeds from idle to wide-open throttle. The fuel pressure may vary but must remain within 4.9-8.5 psi. (33.8-58.6 kPa) at any operating speed.

   a. If the pressure exceeds the specification at any speed, replace the electric fuel pump as described in Chapter Seven.

   b. If the pressure is less than the specification at any speed (particularly at higher engine speeds), check for a restriction in the fuel supply hose as described in this section. Refer to *Basic Fuel System Troubleshooting*. If no restriction is evident, replace the electric fuel pump as described in Chapter Seven.

11. Remove the pressure gauge and T-fitting from the fuel pump and fuel line. Reconnect the fuel line and tighten the fittings to 177-212 in.-lb. (20-24 N•m).

Run the engine and check for fuel leakage as described in Chapter Seven.

ELECTRONIC FUEL INJECTION (EFI) SYSTEM

Refer to **Table 3** for a list of items to check if the engine will not start or if the fuel system is suspected of causing an engine malfunction. Refer to the causes listed next to the symptom that best describes the malfunction. Perform the test or adjustment suggested under corrective action. Other useful information and tips are described with the specific test instructions.

Fuel Delivery System

Four different types of fuel injection systems are used on the models covered in this manual. The differences are the mounting location of fuel injectors, location of the electric (high-pressure) fuel pump and location of the fuel pressure regulator. Refer to the following descriptions and physically identify the components and hose routing to determine the fuel delivery system used on the engine.

Throttle body injection (TBI) (fuel return to tank [with engine-mounted pump])

Refer to **Figure 57**.

On this TBI system, the two injectors (**Figure 58**) are located in the throttle body assembly along with the throttle position sensor (TPS) (A, **Figure 59**) and idle air control (IAC) motor (B). Pressurized fuel is delivered to the fuel injectors through internal passages in the throttle body assembly.

The high-pressure electric fuel pump (**Figure 60**) is mounted on the engine and is controlled by the engine control unit (ECU) and the fuel pump relay. When operating, the high-pressure fuel pump draws fuel from the fuel tank and then through the water-separating fuel filter. The fuel passes through the fuel pump and then the secondary fuel filter. The fuel is then delivered to the fuel pocket in the throttle body assembly for use by the fuel injectors.

The throttle body-mounted fuel pressure regulator opens when the fuel pressure reaches approximately 30 psi (207 kPa) and allows fuel to exit the fuel pocket and return to the fuel tank through the fuel return line. This arrangement allows fuel that is not used by the engine to circulate back to the fuel tank for purging of air or fuel vapor and eventual return to the throttle body. This system requires a special return line to the fuel tank.

Throttle body injection (TBI) (fuel return to filter [with engine-mounted pump])

Refer to **Figure 61** for this description.

On this TBI system, the two injectors (**Figure 58**) are located in the throttle body assembly along with the throttle position sensor (A, **Figure 59**) and idle air control motor (B). Pressurized fuel is delivered to the fuel injectors through internal passages in the throttle body assembly.

The high-pressure electric fuel pump (**Figure 60**) is mounted on the engine and is controlled by the ECU and the fuel pump relay. When operating, the high-pressure fuel pump draws fuel from the fuel tank and then through the water-separating fuel filter. The fuel passaes through the fuel pump and then through the secondary fuel filter. The fuel is then delivered through the pressure line to the fuel pocket in the throttle body assembly for use by the fuel injectors. The throttle body-mounted fuel pressure regulator opens when the fuel pressure reaches approximately 30 psi (207 kPa) and allows fuel to exit the fuel pocket and return to the water-separating fuel filter housing through the fuel return hose. This arrangement allows fuel that is not used by the engine to circulate back to the filter for purging of air or fuel vapor and eventual return to the throttle body. This system does not require a return line to the fuel tank.

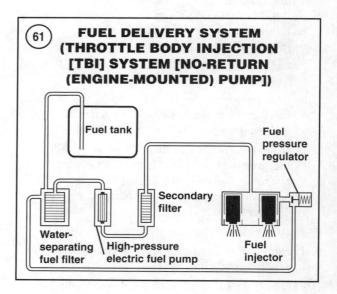

FUEL DELIVERY SYSTEM (THROTTLE BODY INJECTION [TBI] SYSTEM [NO-RETURN (ENGINE-MOUNTED) PUMP])

Throttle body injection (TBI) (fuel return to tank [with tank-mounted pump])

Refer to **Figure 62** for this description.

On this TBI system, the two injectors (**Figure 58**) are located in the throttle body assembly along with the

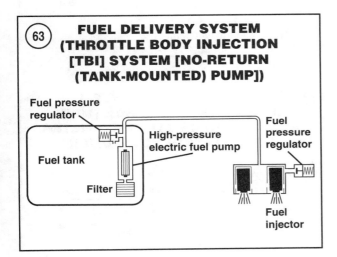

62 FUEL DELIVERY SYSTEM (THROTTLE BODY INJECTION [TBI] SYSTEM [WITH RETURN-TO-TANK (TANK-MOUNTED) PUMP])

Fuel tank

High-pressure electric fuel pump

Filter

Fuel injector

Fuel-pressure regulator

63 FUEL DELIVERY SYSTEM (THROTTLE BODY INJECTION [TBI] SYSTEM [NO-RETURN (TANK-MOUNTED) PUMP])

Fuel pressure regulator

Fuel pressure regulator

High-pressure electric fuel pump

Fuel tank

Filter

Fuel injector

throttle position sensor (A, **Figure 59**) and idle air control motor (B). Pressurized fuel is delivered to the fuel injectors through internal passages in the throttle body assembly.

The high-pressure electric fuel pump is mounted inside the boat fuel tank and is controlled by the ECU and the fuel pump relay. When operating, the high-pressure fuel pump draws fuel through the pump-mounted filter and then directs the fuel through the pressure line to the fuel pocket in the throttle body assembly for use by the fuel injectors. The throttle body-mounted fuel pressure regulator opens when the fuel pressure reaches approximately 30 psi (207 kPa) and allows fuel to exit the fuel pocket and return to the fuel tank through the fuel return hose. This arrangement allows fuel that is not used by the engine to circulate back to the fuel tank for purging of air or fuel vapor and eventual return to the throttle body. This system requires a special return line to the fuel tank.

Throttle body injection (TBI)
(no-return [with tank-mounted pump])

Refer to **Figure 63** for this description.

On this TBI system, the two injectors (**Figure 58**) are located in the throttle body assembly along with the throttle position sensor (A, **Figure 59**) and idle air control motor (B). Pressurized fuel is delivered to the fuel injectors through internal passages in the throttle body assembly.

The high-pressure electric fuel pump is mounted inside the boat fuel tank and is controlled by the ECU and the fuel pump relay. When operating, the high-pressure fuel pump draws fuel through the pump-mounted filter and then directs the fuel through the pressure line to the fuel pocket in the throttle body assembly for use by the fuel injectors. On models with a no-return fuel system, the fuel pressure regulator is integrated into the fuel tank-mounted electric fuel pump. The fuel pressure regulator opens when the pressure delivered by the fuel pump reaches approximately 30 psi (207 kPa). The excess fuel is directed back into the fuel tank through internal passages. A fuel pressure regulator is also incorporated into the throttle body unit. The return line fitting on the throttle body unit is blocked because the fuel pressure is regulated by the in-tank fuel pump. However, the diaphragm in the fuel pressure regulator is able to move the housing and dampen pressure fluctuation that can occur during normal fuel injector operation. This feature offers smoother operation, improved fuel economy and reduced exhaust emissions. On this system, any air or vapor in the fuel hoses or lines must purge through the fuel injectors. This system does not requires a return line to the fuel tank.

Multiport injection (MPI) (fuel return to
tank [with engine-mounted pump])

Refer to **Figure 64** for this description.

On this MPI system, the eight fuel injectors are secured in individual openings in the intake manifold by the fuel rail. A fuel injector is provided for each cylinder. Pressurized fuel is delivered to the injectors by the fuel rail, and the pressure is regulated by the rail-mounted fuel pressure regulator. The throttle body used on MPI models houses the TPS and IAC. The fuel injectors spray fuel into the individual cylinder intake ports just above the intake valve.

The high-pressure electric fuel pump (**Figure 60**) is mounted on the engine and is controlled by the ECU and the fuel pump relay. When operating, the high-pressure fuel pump draws fuel from the fuel tank and then through the water-separating fuel filter. The fuel passes through the fuel pump and then through the secondary fuel filter. The fuel is then delivered to the fuel rail for use by the fuel injectors. The fuel rail-mounted fuel pressure regulator opens when the fuel pressure reaches 40-50 psi (276-345 kPa) and allows fuel to exit the fuel rail and return to the fuel tank through the fuel return line. This arrangement allows fuel that is not used by the engine to circulate back to the fuel tank for purging of air or fuel vapor and eventual return to the fuel rail.

Some high-output models are equipped with a boost pump mounted on the engine and connected to the line connecting the fuel tank to the water-separating fuel filter. The boost pump assists with drawing fuel from the fuel tank to deliver the additional fuel delivery required by high-output models. The boost pump is controlled by the ECU using the same fuel pump relay that supplies current to the high-pressure electric pump.

A dedicated hose applies manifold pressure (vacuum) to the diaphragm chamber in the fuel pressure regulator. This allows the regulator to change the fuel pressure to compensate for varying operating conditions. This feature provides a consistent pressure differential between fuel pressure delivered to the injectors and intake manifold pressure where the injector sprays fuel. This control feature is needed to prevent variable manifold pressure from adversely affecting fuel delivery.

This system requires a special return line to the fuel tank.

Multiport injection (MPI) (fuel return to filter [with engine-mounted pump])

Refer to **Figure 65** for this description.

On this MPI system, the eight fuel injectors are secured to individual openings in the intake manifold by the fuel rail. A fuel injector is provided for each cylinder. Pressurized fuel is delivered to the injectors by the fuel rail and the pressure is regulated by the rail-mounted fuel pressure regulator. The throttle body used on MPI models houses the TPS and IAC. The fuel injectors spray fuel into the individual cylinder intake ports just above the intake valve.

The high-pressure electric fuel pump (**Figure 60**) is mounted on the engine and is controlled by the ECU and the fuel pump relay. When operating, the high-pressure fuel pump draws fuel from the fuel tank and then through the water-separating fuel filter. The fuel passes through the fuel pump and then through the secondary fuel filter. The fuel is then delivered to the fuel rail and fuel injectors. The fuel rail-mounted fuel pressure regulator opens when the fuel pressure reaches 40-50 psi (276-345 kPa) and allows fuel to exit the fuel rail and return to the water-separating fuel filter housing through the fuel return line. This arrangement allows fuel that is not used by the engine to

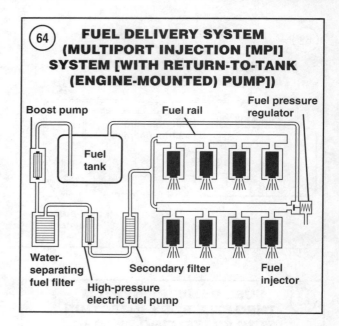

64 FUEL DELIVERY SYSTEM (MULTIPORT INJECTION [MPI] SYSTEM [WITH RETURN-TO-TANK (ENGINE-MOUNTED) PUMP])

Boost pump — Fuel rail — Fuel pressure regulator — Fuel tank — Water-separating fuel filter — High-pressure electric fuel pump — Secondary filter — Fuel injector

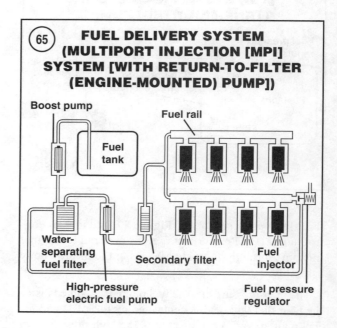

65 FUEL DELIVERY SYSTEM (MULTIPORT INJECTION [MPI] SYSTEM [WITH RETURN-TO-FILTER (ENGINE-MOUNTED) PUMP])

Boost pump — Fuel rail — Fuel tank — Water-separating fuel filter — High-pressure electric fuel pump — Secondary filter — Fuel injector — Fuel pressure regulator

circulate back to the filter for purging of air or fuel vapor and eventual return to the fuel rail.

Some high-output models are equipped with a boost pump mounted on the engine and connected to the line between the fuel tank and the water-separating fuel filter. The boost pump assists with drawing fuel from the fuel tank to deliver the additional fuel required by high-output models. The boost pump is controlled by the ECU using the same fuel pump relay that supplies current to the high-pressure electric pump.

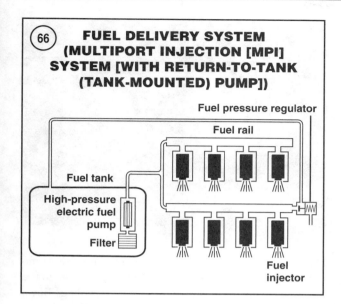

66 FUEL DELIVERY SYSTEM (MULTIPORT INJECTION [MPI] SYSTEM [WITH RETURN-TO-TANK (TANK-MOUNTED) PUMP])

Fuel pressure regulator

Fuel rail

Fuel tank

High-pressure electric fuel pump

Filter

Fuel injector

67

A dedicated hose applies manifold pressure (vacuum) to the diaphragm chamber in the fuel pressure regulator. This allows the regulator to change the fuel pressure to compensate for varying operating conditions. This feature provides a consistent pressure differential between fuel pressure delivered to the injectors and intake manifold pressure where the injector sprays fuel. This control feature is needed to prevent variable manifold pressure from adversely affecting fuel delivery.

This system does not require a return line to the fuel tank.

Multiport injection (MPI) (fuel return to tank [with tank-mounted pump])

Refer to **Figure 66** for this description.

On this MPI system, the eight fuel injectors are secured into individual openings in the intake manifold by the fuel

rail. A fuel injector is provided for each cylinder. Pressurized fuel is delivered to the injectors by the fuel rail, and the pressure is regulated by the rail-mounted fuel pressure regulator. The throttle body used on MPI models houses the TPS and IAC. The fuel injectors spray fuel into the individual cylinder intake ports just above the intake valve.

The high-pressure electric fuel pump is mounted inside the boat fuel tank and is controlled by the ECU and the fuel pump relay. When operating, the high-pressure fuel pump draws fuel through the pump-mounted filter and then directs the fuel through the pressure line to the fuel rail and fuel injectors. The fuel rail-mounted fuel pressure regulator opens when the fuel pressure reaches 40-50 psi (276-345 kPa) and allows fuel to exit the fuel rail and return to the fuel tank through the fuel return line. This arrangement allows fuel that is not used by the engine to circulate back to the tank for purging of air or fuel vapor and eventual return to the fuel rail.

A dedicated hose applies manifold pressure (vacuum) to the diaphragm chamber in the fuel pressure regulator. This allows the regulator to change the fuel pressure to compensate for varying operating conditions. This feature provides a consistent pressure differential between fuel pressure delivered to the injectors and intake manifold pressure where the injector sprays fuel. This control feature is needed to prevent variable manifold pressure from adversely affecting fuel delivery.

This system requires a special return line to the fuel tank.

Fuel Injection Control System

The fuel injection control system consists of the ECU, manifold air pressure sensor (MAP), intake air temperature sensor (IAT), engine temperature sensor (ETS), TPS and IAC.

The ECU (**Figure 67**, typical) controls operation of the fuel injection system, ignition timing and warning system. There are four different versions of electronic control units used on the models covered in this manual.

The earliest models used the marine electronic fuel injection (MEFI 1) ECU. The MEFI 1 ECU can be identified by the harness plug connectors located on each end of the unit and the gray finish.

The MEFI 2 ECU is used on models produced from 1995-1998 and can be identified by the harness plug connectors on the ends of the unit. However, the MEFI 2 unit is slightly shorter than the MEFI 1 unit and has a black finish. The internal circuitry of the MEFI 2 unit is very similar to the MEFI 1 version, and on some models, the MEFI 2 can be used in place of the MEFI 1.

The MEFI 3 ECU is used on models produced from 1999-2001 and can be identified by the harness plug connections on the same side of the ECU (**Figure 68**, typical). The MEFI 3 ECU uses different internal circuitry than the MEFI 1 and MEFI 2 units and cannot be used to replace them.

The MEFI 4 ECU is used on models produced from 2002-2004 and can be identified by the harness plug connections on the same side of the ECU (**Figure 68**, typical). The MEFI 3 and MEFI 4 ECU are physically identical. Identify the ECU by the MEFI 3 or MEFI 4 stamping on the rear of the unit. The MEFI 4 ECU contains different internal circuitry and cannot be used to replace MEFI 3 units.

Battery voltage is continually supplied to the ECU using the fuse-protected red/purple and then orange wire. This wire provides the operating voltage when the ECU is switched on. Battery voltage is also continuously supplied to the No. 30 terminal on the EFI system relay. A black wire connects the No. 85 relay terminal to an engine ground terminal. When the key switch is turned to ON or RUN, battery voltage is supplied to the No. 86 terminal on the EFI system relay using the purple wire. This energizes the system relay. When energized, the relay supplies battery voltage to the fuel injectors, ignition coil(s) and fuel pump relay. The relay also supplies voltage to the No. 11 terminal on the J1 ECU connector plug on models using an MEFI 1 or MEFI 2 ECU. The relay supplies voltage to the No. 32 terminal on the J2 ECU connector plug on models using an MEFI 3 ECU. The relay supplies voltage to the No. 19 terminal on the J2 ECU connector plug on models using an MEFI 4 ECU.

The voltage from the relay powers the ECU and causes it to supply a 5-volt power source to the TPS, MAP, IAT and ETS. Each sensor sends input back to the ECU, which determines the throttle position, air pressure (elevation), air temperature and engine temperature. The IAC is not a sensor. The idle air control valve is simply an air valve used by the ECU to control the amount of air entering the intake manifold at lower engine speeds (particularly at idle speeds). The ECU sends pulsating signals to the motor winding to open or close the air opening. The ECU uses input from the sensors to compute the amount of IAC opening required to start the engine under the given conditions (primarily temperature and elevation).

On models using an MEFI 1 or MEFI 2 ECU, battery voltage is supplied by the system relay to the No. 30 fuel pump relay terminal by the pink/black wire. A dark green/white wire connects the No. 85 fuel pump relay terminal to the No. 9 terminal on the J2 ECU connector plug. A black/white wire connects the No. 86 fuel pump relay terminal to an engine ground. A gray wire connects the

No. 87 fuel pump relay terminal to the electric fuel pump terminal. When powered, the ECU applies voltage to the No. 85 terminal of the fuel pump relay. The voltage flows through a coil and then to ground using the No. 86 relay terminal. This causes the relay to energize and complete the internal circuit that connects the No. 30 terminal to the No. 87 terminal and supplies battery voltage to the electric fuel pump. The fuel pump will operate for 2 seconds to prime the fuel system for starting and then shut off when the ECU removes the voltage on the No. 85 relay terminal to de-energize the relay.

On models using an MEFI 3 or MEFI 4 ECU, battery voltage is supplied by the system relay to the No. 30 and No. 86 fuel pump relay terminals by the pink wires. On models using an MEFI 3 ECU, a dark green/white wire connects the No. 85 fuel pump relay terminal to the No. 23 terminal on the J1 ECU connector plug. On models using an MEFI 4 ECU, a dark green/white wire connects the No. 85 fuel pump relay terminal to the No. 6 terminal on the J1 ECU connector plug. A gray wire connects the No. 87 fuel pump relay terminal to the electric fuel pump. When powered, the ECU connects the No. 23 or No. 6 terminal to engine ground for approximately 2 seconds by using internal circuitry. This completes the ground circuit for the fuel pump relay and causes it to energize and complete the internal circuit that connects the No. 30 terminal to the No. 87 terminal and supplies battery voltage to the electric fuel pump. The fuel pump will operate for 2 seconds to prime the fuel system for starting and then shut off when the ECU removes the ground path on the No. 23 or No. 6 terminal to de-energize the relay.

The ECU controls fuel delivery by completing or interrupting the ground circuit for the fuel injectors. The injectors (**Figure 69**) are solenoid-activated fuel valves that spray fuel in a very fine pattern when activated. Because battery voltage is supplied to the injectors by the system relay, the injectors operate when the ECU provides the

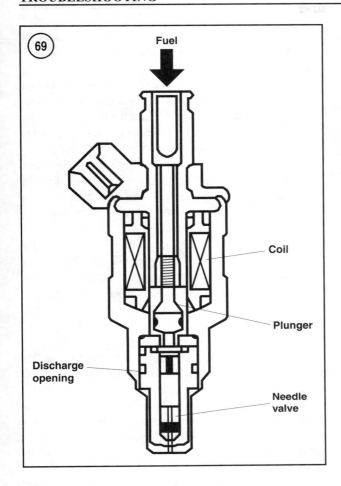

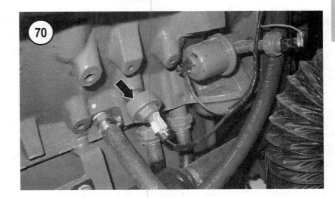

ground circuit by using internal driver circuits. Input from the ignition system allows the ECU to determine engine speed and compute the number of times to open the injectors for the given engine speed. This is often referred to as the injector frequency. A greater frequency delivers more fuel, and a lesser frequency delivers less fuel. Input from the sensors allows the ECU to determine the amount of fuel required for the given operating conditions. The ECU adjusts the fuel delivery by controlling the length of time the injectors are activated. This is often referred to as the duration or on-time. A longer duration or on-time delivers more fuel, and a shorter duration or on-time delivers less fuel.

While the engine starts, the ECU receives input from the ignition system and starts activating the injectors to provide fuel for starting.

After starting, the ECU maintains the fuel pump relay ground to keep the pump operating as long as it receives input from the ignition system. The ECU continuously monitors input from the sensors to determine the precise amount of fuel needed and adjusts the injector frequency

and on-time accordingly. This allows the ECU to quickly change the fuel delivery to compensate for any change in throttle position, manifold vacuum, engine temperature and air temperature. Using input from the sensors, the ECU determines the optimum ignition timing for the given conditions and adjusts the timing accordingly.

The ECU controls idle speed by opening or closing the IAC and changing the ignition timing to provide the optimum idle speed and smoothest operation for the given operating conditions. This allows the fuel injection system to compensate for sudden loading and unloading that occur when shifting into and out of gear. The IAC is opened more when the engine is cold, and the engine will idle considerably faster. The idle speed will drop gradually as the engine reaches normal operating temperature. The ECU uses input from the TPS to determine whether the throttle is closed. The ECU will open the IAC with increased throttle opening to allow more air into the system. This increases power slightly and helps prevent stalling if the throttle quickly returns to idle speed. This will cause the engine to gradually return to normal idle speed if the throttle is closed abruptly.

All EFI models are equipped with a detonation (knock) sensor threaded into the side(s) of the cylinder block (**Figure 70**, typical). The knock sensor creates a pulsating voltage signal when subjected to noise resonating in the cylinder block cooling passages. On 8.1L models, two knock sensors (one on each side) are used. On models using an MEFI 1 or MEFI 2 ECU, this signal is directed to circuits in the knock sensor module. The knock sensor module amplifies the signal and determines whether the noise frequency is within the normal range for the engine. Provided that the signal indicates normal engine noise, the knock sensor module applies 8 volts to the brown/orange wire leading to the ECU. If detonation develops, the knock sensor signal exceeds the normal range, and the knock sensor removes the 8-volt signal from the brown/orange wire. This causes the ECU to retard the ignition timing and increase fuel delivery until the detonation ceases. On models using an MEFI 3 or MEFI 4 ECU, the knock sensor signal is directed to the ECU by the dark blue or light blue sensor wires. The ECU uses the sensor signal to determine whether detonation is occurring and to adjust the ignition timing and fuel delivery accordingly.

The ECU continuously monitors the sensor and various operating system voltages. If any of the sensor inputs and some of the operating system voltages exceed a predetermined range, the ECU substitutes a limp-home value for the suspect sensor or operating system voltage. This allows continued operation; however, the engine might operate with reduced power or with less than desirable running quality. In this event, the ECU stores a diagnostic trouble code that is used to troubleshoot the fuel injection control system. If the sensor input or operating system voltages return to the predetermined range, the ECU will return to using the input or voltage. However, the diagnostic trouble code remains stored in the ECU. Unlike some systems, disconnecting the battery does not erase the code from the ECU memory.

Operation of the warning horn is controlled by the ECU. The ECU controls operation of the horn by grounding the horn circuit wire using internal circuitry. The oil pressure switch grounds the tan/blue wire if the oil level drops below a preset value. The transmission overheat switch grounds the tan/blue wire if the transmission fluid temperature exceeds a preset limit. The ECU monitors the engine temperature sensor to determine whether the engine is overheating. The ECU will complete the ground circuit and turn on the warning horn if it determines that the engine is overheating. The horn will continue sounding until the engine or transmission temperature drops to an acceptable level, the oil pressure rises above the preset limit or the engine is shut off.

When powered, the ECU sounds the horn to test the horn operation and indicate that the ECU is operational. This can be an important troubleshooting tool because it indicates that the EFI system relay is operating properly and the ECU and the warning horn are operational. Keep this in mind if trouble should occur.

EFI system relay test

The EFI system relay provides voltage to operate the fuel injectors and ignition coil(s) and powers the engine control unit. A defective EFI system relay will prevent the engine from starting or cause the engine to stall at any speed.

A 12-volt test lamp is required for this procedure.

1. Make sure the lanyard switch is in RUN position.

2. Turn the key to ON or RUN. The dash instruments must turn on, and the warning horn must sound for 2 seconds. Refer to the following:
   a. If the instruments did not turn on, check for a blown fuse, tripped circuit breaker or loose wire connection. Repair the wiring, replace the fuse, or reset the circuit breaker. If this does not restore gauge operation, test the switch as described in this chapter.
   b. If the instruments are on but the warning horn does not sound, test the lanyard switch as described in this chapter. Refer to *Basic Ignition System Troubleshooting*. If the lanyard switch operates correctly, proceed to Step 3.
   c. If the instruments are on and the warning horn did sound, the system relay is operational. Proceed to Step 11 to check the injector wire circuit.

3. Remove the EFI system relay as described in Chapter Nine.

4. To identify the relay terminals, refer to **Figure 71**, which shows the relay terminals and the terminals in the relay mounting bracket. The relay will only fit into the bracket one way. Compare the orientation of the No. 30 and No. 87 terminal for reference.

5. Connect the cord of the test lamp to the positive battery terminal. Touch the test lamp probe to the No. 85 terminal in the mounting bracket or harness plug. The lamp must illuminate. If not, check for a faulty connection or an open in the black relay ground wire.

6. Connect the cord of the test lamp to the negative battery terminal. Touch the test probe to the No. 30 terminal in the mounting bracket or harness plug. The lamp must illuminate. If not, check for a blown fuse or circuit breaker. Refer to the wiring diagrams at the end of the manual to identify any fuses or circuit breakers in the circuit. Check for a faulty terminal or battery supply wire to the terminal if the fuses and circuit breaker are good.

7. Place the key switch in OFF or STOP. Connect the cord of the test lamp to the negative battery terminal. Touch the test probe to the No. 86 terminal in the mounting bracket or harness plug. The lamp must not illuminate. If the lamp illuminates, test the key switch as described in this chapter. If the switch is good, the purple wire leading to the relay mounting bracket is shorted to a battery positive source. Repair the wiring before proceeding.

8. Connect the cord of the test lamp to the negative battery terminal. Touch the test probe to the No. 86 terminal in the mounting bracket or harness plug. Observe the lamp while an assistant turns the key switch to ON or RUN. The lamp must illuminate. If not, test the key switch and lanyard switch as described in this chapter. If both switches operate correctly, an open circuit or short to ground is

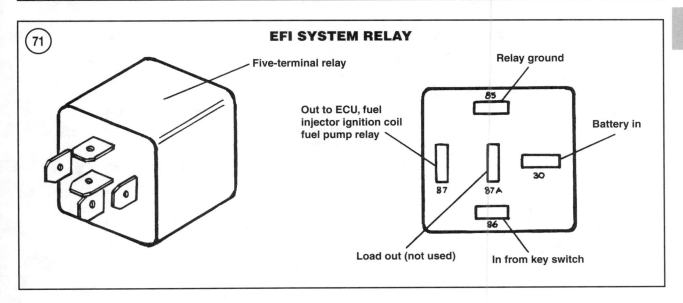

⑦①

EFI SYSTEM RELAY

Five-terminal relay

Relay ground

Out to ECU, fuel injector ignition coil fuel pump relay

Battery in

85

87   87A   30

86

Load out (not used)

In from key switch

present in the purple wire of the instrument or engine wire harness. Repair the wiring or terminal before proceeding.

9. Install the system relay as described in Chapter Nine.

10. Turn the key switch to OFF or STOP. Disconnect the plug from one of the fuel injectors. Connect the cord of the test lamp to the negative battery terminal. Touch the test probe to the red, pink or pink/white wire in the injector connector. The test lamp must not illuminate. If the lamp illuminates, the relay is shorted internally or stuck in the energized position and must be replaced.

11. Connect the cord of the test lamp to the negative battery terminal. Touch the test probe to the red, pink or pink/white wire in the connector. Observe the lamp while an assistant turns the key switch to ON or RUN. The lamp must illuminate. If not, the relay is open or stuck in the de-energized position. Replace the relay and repeat the test. The pink/white wire is open or shorted to ground if the lamp does not illuminate with the replacement relay.

12. Turn the key switch to OFF or STOP.

Fuel pump relay test (MEFI 1 or MEFI 2 ECU)

WARNING
The engine might unexpectedly start during testing. Keep all persons, clothing, tools or loose objects away from the drive belts and other moving components on the engine.

CAUTION
Use a flush device to supply the engine with cooling water if testing the ignition system with the boat out of the water. Operation of the starter motor results in operation of the

seawater pump. The seawater pump is quickly damaged if operated without adequate cooling water.

The fuel pump relay provides battery voltage to operate the high-pressure electric fuel pump. The relay also provides voltage to operate the low-pressure boost pump (on models so equipped). This procedure tests the complete fuel pump circuit. A 12-volt test lamp and ohmmeter are required for this procedure.

1. Make sure the lanyard switch is in RUN.

2. Turn the key to ON or RUN. The dash instruments must turn on, the warning horn must sound for 2 seconds, and the high-pressure fuel pump must operate for 2 seconds. On models with an engine-mounted pump, touch the tip of a mechanic's stethoscope to the pump body to hear the pump operation as needed. On models with a tank-mounted fuel pump, remove seating or floor panels for access to the pump harness and to hear the pump operation better. Refer to the following:

   a. If the instruments did not turn on, check for a blown fuse, tripped circuit breaker or loose wire connection. Repair the wiring, replace the fuse, or reset the circuit breaker. If this does not restore gauge operation, test the key switch as described in this chapter.

   b. If the instruments are on but the warning horn did not sound, test the emergency lanyard switch as described in this chapter. Refer to *Basic Ignition System Troubleshooting*. If the lanyard switch operates correctly, test the EFI system relay as described in this section.

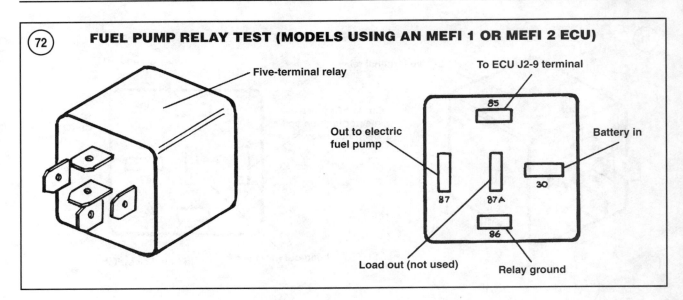

(72) FUEL PUMP RELAY TEST (MODELS USING AN MEFI 1 OR MEFI 2 ECU)

Five-terminal relay

To ECU J2-9 terminal

85

Out to electric
fuel pump

Battery in

87   87A   30

Load out (not used)   Relay ground   86

c. If the instruments are on and the warning horn did sound but the fuel pump did not operate, the system relay and ECU are operational. Proceed to Step 3.

d. If the instruments are on, the warning horn did sound and the fuel pump operates, the fuel pump relay is operational. Remove the fuel pump relay as described in Chapter Nine. Then proceed to Step 16.

3. Disconnect the engine harness connector from the high-pressure electric fuel pump. Refer to Chapter Seven to locate the high-pressure electric fuel pump. Refer to *Electric Fuel Pump Replacement (Electronic Fuel Injection [EFI] Models)*.

4. Connect the cord of the test lamp to the positive battery cable. Touch the test probe to an engine ground to verify the lamp and a good engine ground. Touch the test probe to the black wire in the fuel pump connector. The lamp must illuminate. If not, repair the black wire from the fuel pump connector to the engine ground terminal.

5. Turn the key switch to OFF or STOP. Connect the cord of the test lamp to the negative battery cable. Touch the test probe to the gray wire in the fuel pump connector. The test lamp must not illuminate. If the lamp illuminates, the fuel pump relay is shorted internally, the relay is stuck in the energized position, the gray wire is shorted to ground, or the ECU is faulty. Proceed with testing to isolate the fault.

6. Connect the cord of the test lamp to the negative battery cable. Touch the test probe to the gray wire in the fuel pump connector. Observe the test lamp while an assistant turns the key switch to ON or RUN. The lamp must illuminate for 2 seconds and then extinguish.

a. If the lamp illuminates as described, the fuel pump relay is operational, and wire connections to the pump are good. If the pump *did not* operate as noted in Step 2, check the high-pressure fuel pump pressure as described in this chapter.

b. If the lamp did not illuminate, the fuel pump relay, power supply to the relay, related wiring or ECU is faulty. Proceed with testing to isolate the fault.

7. Remove the fuel pump relay as described in Chapter Nine.

8. To identify the relay terminals, refer to **Figure 72**, which shows the relay terminals and the terminals in the relay mounting bracket or harness plug. The relay will only fit into the bracket one way. Compare the orientation of the No. 30 and No. 87 terminal blades for reference.

9. Connect the cord of the test lamp to the negative battery terminal. Touch the test probe to the No. 30 terminal in the mounting bracket or harness plug. The lamp must illuminate. If not, check for a blown fuse or circuit breaker. Refer to the wiring diagrams at the end of the manual to identify any fuses or circuit breakers in the circuit. Check for a faulty terminal or battery supply wire to the terminal if the fuses and circuit breaker are good.

10. Connect the cord of the test lamp to the positive battery terminal. Touch the test probe to the No. 86 terminal in the relay mounting bracket or harness plug. The lamp must illuminate. If not, repair the wire or terminal connecting the No. 86 terminal to the engine ground.

11. Calibrate the ohmmeter on the R × 1 scale. Touch one of the ohmmeter test leads to the No. 87 terminal in the relay bracket or harness plug. Note the meter reading while touching the other meter lead to the gray wire in the fuel

pump connector. The meter must indicate continuity. If not, repair the open circuit in the gray wire.

12. Touch one of the ohmmeter test leads to the No. 87 terminal in the relay bracket or harness plug. Touch the other lead to an engine ground. The meter must indicate no continuity. If the meter shows continuity, the gray wire in the fuel pump harness is shorted to ground, and the harness must be repaired or replaced.

13. Reconnect the harness connector to the high-pressure electric fuel pump. Route the wiring to prevent interference with drive belts or other moving components. Secure the wiring with plastic locking clamps as needed.

14. Turn the key switch to OFF or STOP. Connect the cord of the 12-volt test lamp to an engine ground. Touch the test probe to the No. 85 terminal in the relay mounting bracket or harness plug. The lamp must not illuminate. If the lamp illuminates, the dark green/white wire connecting the No. 85 relay terminal to the ECU is shorted to ground, or the ECU is faulty. Either condition will cause the fuel pump relay to remain in the energized position, and the pump will operate anytime the system relay is energized. Check the wiring and terminals for shorting. Replace the ECU only if all other components and wiring on the circuit test correctly. Failure of the ECU is extremely rare.

15. Touch the test lamp probe to the No. 85 terminal in the relay mounting bracket or harness plug. Observe the test lamp while an assistant turns the key switch to ON or RUN. The lamp must illuminate for 2 seconds and then extinguish. If not, test the EFI system relay as described in this section. If the system relay is good, the dark green/white wire connecting the No. 85 relay terminal to the ECU is open, or the ECU is faulty. Check the wiring and terminals and correct as needed. Replace the ECU only if all other components and wiring on the circuit are good. Failure of the ECU is extremely rare.

16. Disconnect and ground the spark plug leads to prevent the engine from starting during the following procedure.

17. Touch the test lamp probe to the No. 85 terminal in the relay mounting bracket or harness plug. Observe the test lamp while an assistant turns the key switch to START position. The lamp must illuminate continuously while cranking the engine and extinguish within a few seconds after stopping cranking. If not, test the ignition system as described in this section. If the ignition operates correctly and spark is present at the plugs, the wiring connecting the ignition system to the ECU is open, or the ECU is faulty. Check the wiring and correct as needed. Replace the ECU only if all other components and wiring on the circuit test correctly. Failure of the ECU is extremely rare. Turn the key switch to OFF.

18. Replace the fuel pump relay if the fuel pump does not operate as described in Step 2 and all circuits operate correctly in Steps 3-17.

19. Install the fuel pump relay as described in Chapter Nine.

20. On models with a tank-mounted high-pressure electric fuel pump, reinstall any seating or floor panels removed to access the fuel pump.

21. Reconnect the spark plug leads.

Fuel pump relay test (MEFI 3 or MEFI 4 ECU)

> *WARNING*
> *The engine might unexpectedly start during testing. Keep all persons, clothing, tools or loose objects away from the drive belts and other moving components on the engine.*

> *CAUTION*
> *Use a flush device to supply the engine with cooling water if testing the ignition system with the boat out of the water. Operation of the starter motor results in operation of the seawater pump. The seawater pump is quickly damaged if operated without adequate cooling water.*

The fuel pump relay provides battery voltage to operate the high-pressure electric fuel pump. The relay also provides voltage to operate the low-pressure boost pump on models so equipped. This procedure tests the complete fuel pump circuit. A 12-volt test lamp and ohmmeter are required for this procedure.

1. Make sure the lanyard switch is in RUN.

2. Turn the key to ON or RUN. The dash instruments must turn on, the warning horn must sound for 2 seconds, and the high-pressure fuel pump must operate for 2 seconds. On models with an engine-mounted pump, touch the tip of a mechanic's stethoscope to the pump body to hear the pump operation as needed. On models with a tank-mounted fuel pump, remove seating or floor panels for access to the pump harness and to hear the pump operation better. Refer to the following:

   a. If the instruments did not turn on, check for a blown fuse, tripped circuit breaker or loose wire connection. Repair the wiring, replace the fuse, or reset the circuit breaker. If this does not restore gauge operation, test the key switch as described in this chapter.

   b. If the instruments are on but the warning horn did not sound, test the emergency lanyard switch as described in this chapter. Refer to *Basic Ignition System Troubleshooting*. If the lanyard switch operates

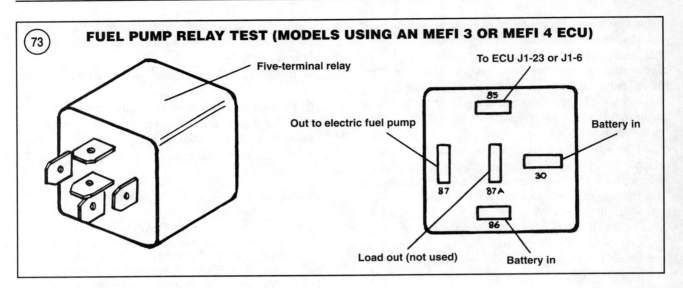

FUEL PUMP RELAY TEST (MODELS USING AN MEFI 3 OR MEFI 4 ECU)

Five-terminal relay

To ECU J1-23 or J1-6

Out to electric fuel pump

Battery in

85

87 *87A* *30*

86

Load out (not used)

Battery in

correctly, test the EFI system relay as described in this section.

c. If the instruments are on and the warning horn did sound but the fuel pump did not operate, the system relay and ECU are operational. Proceed to Step 3.

d. If the instruments are on, the warning horn did sound and the fuel pump operates, the fuel pump relay is operational. Remove the fuel pump relay as described in Chapter Nine. Then proceed to Step 15.

3. Disconnect the engine harness from the high-pressure electric fuel pump. Refer to Chapter Seven to locate the high-pressure electric fuel pump. Refer to *Electric Fuel Pump Replacement (Electronic Fuel Injection [EFI] Models)*.

4. Connect the cord of the test lamp to the positive battery cable. Touch the test probe to an engine ground to verify the lamp and ground. Touch the test probe to the black wire in the fuel pump connector. The lamp must illuminate. If not, repair the wiring or black wire from the fuel pump connector to the engine ground terminal.

5. Turn the key switch to OFF or STOP. Connect the cord of the test lamp to the negative battery cable. Touch the test probe to the gray wire in the fuel pump connector. The test lamp must not illuminate. If the lamp illuminates, the fuel pump relay is shorted internally, the relay is stuck in the energized position, the gray wire is shorted to ground, or the ECU is faulty. Proceed with testing to isolate the fault.

6. Connect the cord of the test lamp to the negative battery cable. Touch the test probe to the gray wire in the fuel pump connector. Observe the test lamp while an assistant

turns the key switch to ON or RUN. The lamp must illuminate for 2 seconds and then extinguish.

a. If the lamp illuminates as described, the fuel pump relay is operational, and wire connections to the pump are good. If the pump *did not* operate as noted in Step 2, check the high-pressure fuel pump pressure as described in this chapter.

b. If the lamp did not illuminate, the fuel pump relay, power supply to the relay, related wiring or ECU is faulty. Proceed with testing to isolate the fault.

7. Remove the fuel pump relay as described in Chapter Nine.

8. To identify the relay terminals, refer to **Figure 73**, which shows the relay terminals and the terminals in the relay mounting bracket or harness plug. The relay will only fit into the bracket one way. Compare the orientation of the No. 30 and No. 87 terminals for reference.

9. Connect the cord of the test lamp to the negative battery terminal. Touch the test probe to the No. 30 terminal and then the No. 86 terminal in the relay mounting bracket or harness plug. The lamp must illuminate at both connection points. If not, check for a blown fuse or circuit breaker. Refer to the wiring diagrams at the end of the manual to identify any fuses or circuit breakers in the circuit. If the fuses and circuit breakers are good, check the battery supply wire for an open circuit or loose connection.

10. Calibrate the ohmmeter on the R × 1 scale. Touch one of the meter leads to the No. 87 terminal in the relay mounting bracket or harness plug. Note the meter reading while touching the other meter test lead to the gray wire in the fuel pump connector. The meter must indicate continuity. If not, repair the open circuit in the gray wire.

11. Touch one of the meter leads to the No. 87 terminal in the relay bracket or harness plug. Touch the other lead to an engine ground. The meter must indicate no continuity. If the meter shows continuity, the gray wire in the fuel pump harness is shorted to ground, and the harness must be repaired or replaced.

12. Reconnect the harness connector to the high-pressure electric fuel pump. Route the wiring to prevent interference with drive belts or other moving components. Secure the wiring with plastic locking clamps as needed.

13. Turn the key switch to OFF or STOP. Connect the cord of the test lamp to the positive battery terminal. Touch the test probe to the No. 85 terminal in the relay mounting bracket or harness plug. The lamp must not illuminate. If the lamp illuminates, the dark green/white wire connecting the No. 85 relay terminal to the ECU is shorted to ground, or the ECU is faulty. Either condition will cause the fuel pump relay to remain in the energized position, and the pumps will operate anytime the system relay is energized. Check the wiring and terminals for shorts. Replace the ECU only if all other components and wiring on the circuit are good. Failure of the ECU is extremely rare.

14. Touch the test lamp probe to the No. 85 terminal in the relay mounting bracket or harness plug. Observe the test lamp while an assistant turns the key switch to ON or RUN. The lamp must illuminate for 2 seconds and then extinguish. If not, test the EFI system relay as described in this section. If the system relay operates correctly, the dark green/white wire connecting the No. 85 relay terminal to the ECU is open, or the ECU is faulty. Check the wiring and terminals and correct as needed. Replace the ECU only if all other components and wiring on the circuit are good. Failure of the ECU is extremely rare.

15. Disconnect and ground the spark plug leads to prevent the engine from starting during this following procedure.

16. Touch the test lamp probe to the No. 85 terminal in the relay mounting bracket or harness plug. Observe the test lamp while an assistant turns the key switch to START. The lamp must illuminate continuously while cranking the engine and extinguish within a few seconds after stopping cranking. If not, test the ignition system as described in this section. If the ignition operates correctly and spark is present at the plugs, the wiring connecting the ignition system to the ECU is open, or the ECU is faulty. Check the wiring and terminals and correct as needed. Replace the ECU only if all other components and wiring in the circuit are good. Failure of the ECU is extremely rare. Turn the key switch to OFF.

17. Replace the fuel pump relay if the fuel pump did not operate as described in Step 2 and all circuits test correctly in Steps 3-16.

18. Install the fuel pump relay as described in Chapter Nine.

19. On models with a tank-mounted high-pressure electric fuel pump. Reinstall any seating or floor panels removed to access the fuel pump.

20. Reconnect the spark plug leads.

Electric Boost Pump (EFI Models)

The electric boost pump is used on high-output MPI models.

Two types of electric boost pumps are used. The larger and more common Carter pump (**Figure 52**) mounts on the side of the engine next to the side engine mount. The smaller and less common Delco pump (**Figure 53**) mounts on the side of the engine near the high-pressure electric fuel pump.

> *WARNING*
> *Safely performing on-water testing or adjustments requires two people: one person to operate the boat and the other to monitor the gauges or test equipment and make necessary adjustments. All personnel must remain seated inside the boat at all times. Do not lean over the transom while the boat is underway. Use extensions to allow all gauges and test equipment to be located in normal seating areas.*

> *WARNING*
> *The engine might unexpectedly start during testing. Keep all persons, clothing, tools or loose objects away from the drive belts and other moving components on the engine.*

> *CAUTION*
> *Use a flush device to supply the engine with cooling water if testing the fuel system with the boat out of the water. Operation of the starter motor results in operation of the seawater pump. The seawater pump is quickly damaged if operated without adequate cooling water.*

Circuit test

Use a 12-volt test lamp and mechanic's stethscope for this procedure.

1. Make sure the lanyard switch is in RUN.

2. Turn the key to ON or RUN. The dash instruments must turn on, the warning horn must sound for 2 seconds, and both the high-pressure and boost fuel pump must operate for 2 seconds. Touch the tip of a mechanic's stethscope to the body of the pumps to hear the pump operation as needed. Refer to the following:

a. If the instruments did not turn on, check for a blown fuse, tripped circuit breaker or loose wire connection. Correct the wiring, replace the fuse, or reset the circuit breaker. If this does not restore gauge operation, test the key switch as described in this chapter.

b. If the instruments are on but the warning horn did not sound, test the emergency lanyard switch as described in this chapter. Refer to *Basic Ignition System Troubleshooting*. If the lanyard switch operates correctly, test the EFI system relay as described in this section.

c. If the instruments are on and the warning horn did sound but neither fuel pump operated, test the fuel pump relay as described in this section.

d. If the instruments are on, the warning horn did sound and only the high-pressure fuel pump operates, the fuel pump relay is operational. Proceed to Step 3.

e. If the instruments are on, the warning horn did sound and only the electric boost pump operates, perform the fuel pump relay test as described in this section.

3. Disconnect the coil wire from the distributor cap and connect it to an engine ground to disable the ignition system. On 5.7L LT-1 and 8.1L models, disconnect each of the spark plug leads and connect them to ground to disable the ignition system.

4A. On models using a Carter electric boost pump, slide the rubber insulator off the terminal nuts. Then remove the nuts that secure the wires to the terminals (A, **Figure 52**).

4B. On models using a Delco electric boost pump, push on the locking clip. Then carefully unplug the connector (A, **Figure 53**) from the fuel pump.

5. Connect the cord of the test lamp to the positive battery cable. Touch the test probe to an engine ground to verify the lamp and ground.

6A. On models using a Carter electric fuel pump, touch the test probe to the black wire.

6B. On models using a Delco electric pump, touch the test probe to the black wire in the harness connector.

7. The test lamp must illuminate. If not, repair the wiring or connections between the pump and engine ground.

8. Connect the cord of the test lamp to an engine ground. Touch the test probe to the positive battery terminal to verify the lamp and the ground. Touch the test probe to the

gray wire terminal. The lamp must not illuminate. If the lamp illuminates, test the fuel pump relay as described in this section.

9. Touch the test lamp probe to the gray wire terminal. Observe the lamp while an assistant turns the key switch to START. The lamp must illuminate for 2 seconds and then extinguish. Refer to the following:

a. If the lamp illuminates as described but the electric boost pump did not operate in Step 2, replace the electric boost pump as described in Chapter Seven.

b. If the lamp did not illuminate, repair the wiring or connection in the gray wire connecting the electric boost pump to the fuel pump relay.

c. If the lamp did not extinguish after 2 seconds, test the fuel pump relay as described in this section.

10. Place the key switch in OFF or STOP. Disconnect the battery cables from the battery.

11. Make sure all terminal nuts are securely tightened and the wires are not contacting other terminals. Reposition the wiring as necessary. To prevent corrosion on models using a Carter electric boost pump, thoroughly coat the fuel pump terminals with Black Neoprene Dip. Purchase the neoprene dip (OMC part No. 909570) from an OMC dealership.

12. Reconnect the secondary wire to the distributor cap or spark plug leads.

13. Connect the battery cables.

14. Start the engine and operate at idle speed. Touch a mechanic's stethscope to the body of the electric boost pump (B, **Figure 52** or B, **Figure 53**). Listen carefully for fuel pump operation. Listen to the pump while an assistant stops the engine. The pump should operate continuously while the engine runs and stop when the engine stops. If the pump fails to operate as described, test the fuel pump relay as described in this chapter.

Pressure test

This procedure requires a fuel pressure test gauge capable of accurately measuring 3.5-8.5 psi (24.1-58.6 kPa) and a suitable T-fitting for attaching the gauge to the hose connecting the electric boost pump to the water-separating fuel filter inlet fitting.

1. Inspect the fuel and check for a restriction in the fuel supply hose as described in this section. Refer to *Basic Fuel System Troubleshooting*.

2. Disconnect the ignition coil secondary wire and connect it to ground to disable the ignition system. The secondary wire must make a secure connection to prevent arcing. On 5.7L LT-1 and 8.1L models, disconnect each of the spark plug leads and connect them to ground to disable the ignition system.

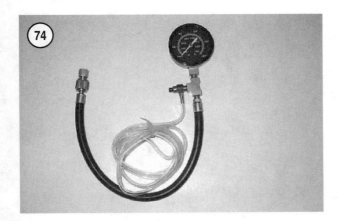

3. Touch a mechanic's stethscope to the body of the boost pump (B, **Figure 52** or B, **Figure 53**). Listen carefully for pump operation while an assistant turns the key switch to ON or RUN. The fuel pump must operate for 2 seconds and then stop. Test the electric boost pump circuit if the pump fails to operate as described.

4. Place a suitable container under the fitting to capture spilled fuel. Then disconnect the fuel line from the outlet fitting (C, **Figure 52** or C, **Figure 53**) on the pump. Drain residual fuel from the line. If the fuel is not contaminated, empty the fuel into the boat fuel tank.

5. Connect a suitable T-fitting, to the fuel line. Connect the fuel pressure gauge to the fitting. Secure the pressure gauge hose with a suitable clamp. Securely tighten the fittings to prevent fuel leakage. Secure the fuel gauge and hose to prevent contact with moving or hot engine components. Clean up any spilled fuel before proceeding.

6. Observe the fuel gauge and the connections for leakage while an assistant cranks the engine. Stop cranking the engine *immediately* if fuel leakage is detected. Correct fuel leakage before proceeding.

7. Observe the gauge while an assistant operates the starter for approximately 20 seconds. The gauge must indicate 4.9-8.5 psi. (33.8-58.6 kPa) while cranking. Refer to the following:

    a. If the pressure is 4.9-8.5 psi (33.8-58.6 kPa), the fuel pressure is correct at cranking speed. Proceed to Step 8.

    b. If the pressure exceeds 8.5 psi (58.6 kPa), the relief valve in the pump is seized. Replace the electric boost pump as described in Chapter Seven.

    c. If the pressure is less than 4.9 psi (33.8 kPa), replace the electric boost pump as described in Chapter Seven.

8. Reconnect the coil wire to the distributor cap or spark plugs.

9. Prepare the boat and engine for operation under normal operating conditions.

10. Observe the gauge while an assistant operates the engine under normal load and at all speeds from idle to wide-open throttle. The fuel pressure may vary but must remain within 4.9-8.5 psi (33.8-58.6 kPa) at any normal operating speed.

    a. If the pressure exceeds the specification at any speed, replace the electric boost pump as described in Chapter Seven.

    b. If the pressure is less than the specification at any speed (particularly at higher engine speeds, check for a restriction in the fuel supply hose as described in this section. Refer to *Basic Fuel System Troubleshooting*. If no restriction is evident, replace the electric boost pump as described in Chapter Seven.

11. Stop the engine and disconnect the battery cables.

12. Remove the pressure gauge and T-fitting from the fuel pump and fuel line. Reconnect the fuel line and tighten the fittings to 177-212 in.-lb. (20-24 N•m).

13. Connect the battery cables.

14. Start the engine and immediately check for fuel leaks. Correct any leaks before operating the engine.

Fuel Pressure Test (EFI models)

Check the fuel pressure to verify that fuel is supplied to the fuel injectors at the required pressure.

A suitable pressure gauge with a bleed hose and the necessary adapters are required for this procedure. Refer to **Figure 74**. Use Kent-Moore part No. J-29658-D for TBI models or part No. J-34730-1A for MPI models.

WARNING
Safely performing on-water testing or adjustments requires two people: one person to operate the boat and the other to monitor the gauges or test equipment and make necessary adjustments. All personnel must remain seated inside the boat at all times. Do not lean over the transom while the boat is underway. Use extensions to allow all gauges and test equipment to be located in normal seating areas.

WARNING
The engine might unexpectedly start during testing. Keep all persons, clothing, tools or loose objects away from the drive belts and other moving components on the engine.

CAUTION
Use a flush device to supply the engine with cooling water if testing the ignition system

with the boat out of the water. Operation of the starter motor results in operation of the seawater pump. The seawater pump is quickly damaged if operated without adequate cooling water.

1. Inspect the fuel and check for a restriction in the fuel supply hose as described in this section. Refer to *Basic Fuel System Troubleshooting*.

2. Make sure the lanyard switch is in RUN.

3. Turn the key to ON or RUN. The dash instruments must turn on, the warning horn must sound for 2 seconds and the high-pressure electric fuel pump must operate for 2 seconds. Touch the tip of a mechanic's stethoscope to the pump body or fuel tank (on models with a tank-mounted pump) to check for pump operation as needed. If the instruments turn on, warning horn sounds and high-pressure fuel pump operates as specified, proceed to Step 4. If not, test the fuel pump relay as described in this section.

4. Turn the key switch to OFF.

5. Disconnect the battery cables.

6A. On TBI models, connect the fuel pressure gauge as follows:

    a. Unthread the screw (A, **Figure 75**) and then lift the plastic cover (B) off the flame arrestor.

    b. Locate the fuel delivery line (**Figure 76**) at the rear of the throttle body assembly. Use compressed air to remove debris from around the fittings.

    c. Wrap a suitable shop towel around the fitting to capture spilled fuel.

    d. Hold the throttle body fitting with a suitable wrench to prevent rotation. Then use a flare-nut wrench to loosen the fuel line fitting.

    e. Slowly loosen the fuel line fitting by hand until fuel just starts dripping from the connection. Wait until the fuel stops dripping and then unthread the fitting.

    f. Drain residual fuel in the line into a suitable container. Clean up any spilled fuel at once.

    g. Remove the O-ring from the groove at the end of the fuel line fitting. Discard the O-ring.

    h. Attach the gauge hose to the throttle body and disconnected fuel delivery line. Make sure the gauge hose fits the line and throttle body fittings and has the fuel pressure gauge connector in the middle of the hose. Securely tighten the gauge hose fittings.

    i. Connect the pressure gauge to the gauge hose.

6B. On MPI models, connect the fuel pressure gauge as follows:

    a. Refer to *Relieving the Fuel System Pressure* in Chapter Seven to locate the fuel pressure test port.

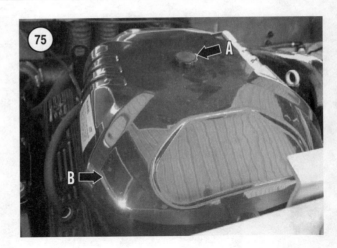

    b. Remove the cap from the fitting. Wrap a suitable shop towel around the test point to capture spilled fuel.

    c. If the test gauge uses a lever to lock the hose fitting on the test port, pull up the locking lever and then *quickly* push the connector onto the test port and release the locking lever.

    d. If the test gauge threads onto the test port, hold the hose fitting in firm contact with the test port fitting. Then *quickly* thread the hose fitting onto the test port.

7. Observe the pressure gauge while an assistant turns the key switch to ON or RUN. Note the pressure reading. Then have the assistant turn the key switch to OFF or STOP. Wait approximately 30 seconds for the ECU to reset. Repeat this step several times to purge any air from the system. The pressure gauge must indicate the specified pressure as follows:

    a. On TBI models, the gauge must indicate 27-31 psi (186-214 kPa).

    b. On MPI models, the gauge must indicate 35-47 psi (241-324 kPa).

8. If the pressure indicated in Step 7 is less than the minimum specification, replace the fuel pressure regulator as described in Chapter Seven and repeat the test. The high-pressure electric fuel pump is faulty, or blockage is present in a hose, line or filter if the pressure remains below the specification after replacing the regulator. Replace the high-pressure electric fuel pump if no fault is found with the hoses, lines or filters.

9. If the pressure indicated in Step 7 exceeds the maximum specification, replace the fuel pressure regulator as described in Chapter Seven and repeat the test. The fuel return hose or related fitting is blocked if the pressure remains above the specification with the new regulator. Re-

move the blockage or replace the hose as needed to correct the fuel pressure.

10. Prepare the boat and engine for operation under actual running conditions. Do not disconnect the fuel pressure gauge at this time, however. Route the gauge hose to prevent contact with drive belts, pulleys and other moving components. Secure the hose with clamps as needed.

11. Observe the gauge while an assistant operates the engine under normal load and at speeds from idle to wide-open throttle. The gauge must indicate the pressure range specified in Step 7 at all engine speeds. Refer to the following:

a. If the fuel pressure is correct at all engine speeds, the fuel delivery system is operating properly. Any engine malfunction is related to old or contaminated fuel, faulty spark plugs or other ignition system components, a faulty fuel injection control system or a mechanical problem with the engine. Check these items as described in the appropriate section of this chapter. Proceed to Step 12.

b. If the fuel pressure exceeds the specification at any engine speed, replace the fuel pressure regulator as described in Chapter Seven and repeat the test. The fuel return hose or related fitting is blocked if the pressure remains above the specification with the replacement regulator. Remove the blockage or replace the hose as needed to correct the fuel pressure.

c. If the fuel pressure is less than the specification at any engine speed (particularly at higher engine speed), test the electric boost pump (if so equipped) and check for a restriction in the fuel supply hose as described in this section. Refer to *Basic Fuel System Troubleshooting*. If no fault is found with the boost pump and no restriction is evident, replace the fuel pressure regulator as described in Chapter Seven and repeat the test. If the pressure remains below the specification with the replacement regulator, re-

place the high-pressure electric fuel pump as described in Chapter Seven.

12. Stop the engine.

13A. On TBI models, disconnect the fuel pressure gauge as follows:

a. Direct the bleed hose into the fuel tank fill opening.

b. Open the valve and allow all fuel to drain from the hose.

c. Wrap a suitable shop towel around the fitting to capture spilled fuel.

d. Hold the throttle body fitting with a suitable wrench to prevent rotation. Then use a flare nut wrench to loosen the test gauge hose fitting.

e. *Slowly* loosen the fuel line fitting by hand until fuel just starts dripping from the connection. Wait until fuel stops dripping and then unthread the fitting.

f. Drain residual fuel in the line into a suitable container. Clean up any spilled fuel at once.

g. Install a *new* O-ring into the fuel delivery line fitting groove. Then thread the delivery line fitting into the throttle body fitting by hand.

h. Hold the throttle body fitting with a suitable wrench to prevent rotation. Then tighten the fuel line fitting to 204 in.-lb. (23 N•m). Do not allow the fuel line to twist during tightening. Twisting damages the line.

i. Close the fuel tank fill cap.

13B. On MPI models, disconnect the fuel pressure gauge as follows:

a. Direct the bleed hose into the fuel tank fill opening.

b. Open the valve and allow all fuel to drain from the hose.

c. Lift the locking lever and *quickly* pull the connector off the test port.

d. Thread the cap onto the fuel pressure test port.

e. Close the fuel tank fill cap.

14. Clean up any spilled fuel.

15. Start the engine and immediately check for fuel leakage at all fuel line or hose connections. Correct any fuel leakage before operating the engine.

16. On TBI models, install the plastic cover (B, **Figure 75**) onto the flame arrestor. Guide the screw (A, **Figure 75**) into the cover, flame arrestor and throttle body openings. Lift the cover and flame arrestor slightly to assist with aligning the screw with the threaded opening.

Fuel Injector Test

One of more defective injectors can cause either an excessively rich or lean condition on one or more cylinders. On models with TBI using two injectors, a defective injector will tend to affect only one bank of cylinders. On models with MPI, a defective injector will affect only the cylinder to which it supplies fuel.

A leaking fuel injector will result in an excessively rich condition, especially at slow speed. At higher engine speed, however, the engine is able to consume excessive fuel and may perform properly.

A fuel injector with a poor spray pattern due to debris or deposits in the valve will usually cause a poor idle because the poor spray pattern can prevent the fuel from atomizing before it reaches the combustion chamber. Poor idle occurs because the fuel droplets will not burn efficiently at lower engine speeds. The engine will usually operate properly at mid-range and higher throttle settings because the higher velocity of the air entering the intake will promote better atomization. A lean condition might occur at higher throttle settings because the condition causing the poor spray pattern usually restricts fuel flow to some degree.

Blockage in the fuel injector will cause a lean condition because the injector will not spray the proper amount of fuel for the given operating conditions. The engine might perform properly at lower engine speeds if the blockage is not overly restrictive. The resulting lean condition will worsen as the engine speed and fuel demand increase.

Throttle body injection (TBI) models

The TBI system allows easy visual inspection of the fuel injector spray pattern. Remove the flame arrestor and observe the fuel injectors while an assistant operates the engine under normal operating conditions and at various engine speeds and throttle settings. Observe the injectors after stopping the engine to identify a leaking fuel injector.

Multiport injection (MPI) models

The design of the MPI system prevents visual inspection of the fuel injector spray pattern. An easy way to identify injector trouble is to remove and inspect the spark plugs as described in Chapter Three. All spark plugs should appear the same. A suspect injector is one in which the spark plug from the corresponding cylinder appears markedly different from the others.

Operational test

WARNING
The engine might unexpectedly start during testing. Keep all persons, clothing, tools or loose objects away from the drive belts and other moving components on the engine.

CAUTION
Use a flush device to supply the engine with cooling water if testing the ignition system with the boat out of the water. Operation of the starter motor results in operation of the seawater pump. The seawater pump is quickly damaged if operated without adequate cooling water.

CAUTION
Safely performing on-water testing or adjustments requires two people: one person to operate the boat and the other to monitor the gauges or test equipment and make necessary adjustments. All personnel must remain seated inside the boat at all times. Do not lean over the transom while the boat is underway. Use extensions to allow all gauges and test equipment to be located in normal seating areas.

Perform this procedure if the engine will not start or if failure of one or more of the injectors is suspected. Use a mechanic's stethscope for this procedure.

1A. On models using a throttle body fuel injection (TBI) system, unthread the screw (A, **Figure 75**) and then lift the plastic cover (B) off the flame arrestor.

1B. On models using a multiport fuel injection (MPI) system, remove the plastic engine cover to access the fuel injectors.

2. Start the engine. Touch the tip of the stethoscope to the body of one of the fuel injectors. Listen for the distinct clicking noise. Touch the stethoscope to the body of each fuel injector on the engine and note the clicking noise. Stop the engine and refer to the following:

   a. If all injectors make the same clicking noise, the injectors are operating. Low fuel pressure, an ignition malfunction or mechanical problem in one or more cylinders is the likely cause of the engine malfunction.

   b. If one or more of the injectors sound markedly different from others, check for voltage at the injector as described in this section. If the injector voltage is correct, remove and inspect the spark plugs to check for an excessively rich or lean condition as described in this chapter. Refer to *Basic Fuel System Troubleshooting*. Replace the injector if the spark plug to which it delivers fuel (MPI models) or the spark plugs on the cylinder bank in which it delivers fuel (TBI models) show an excessively rich or lean condition.

3A. On models using a throttle body fuel injection (TBI) system, install the plastic cover (B, **Figure 75**) onto the flame arrestor. Guide the screw (A, **Figure 75**) into the cover, flame arrestor and throttle body openings. Lift the cover and flame arrestor slightly to assist with aligning the screw with the threaded opening.

3B. On models using a multiport fuel injection (MPI) system, install the plastic engine cover.

Voltage test

> **WARNING**
> *The engine might unexpectedly start during testing. Keep all persons, clothing, tools or loose objects away from the drive belts and other moving components on the engine.*

> **CAUTION**
> *Use a flush device to supply the engine with cooling water if testing the ignition system with the boat out of the water. Operation of the starter motor results in operation of the seawater pump. The seawater pump is quickly damaged if operated without adequate cooling water.*

> **CAUTION**
> *Do not use a high-capacity test lamp to check the injector voltage. A high-capacity lamp might draw excessive amperage and damage the injector driver circuit in the engine control unit (ECU).*

This procedure checks for voltage at the injectors and checks for proper switching from the engine control unit (ECU).

Use a 12-volt lamp for this procedure. *Do not* use a high-capacity test lamp. The test lamp must consume less than 0.3 amp when connected to a 12-volt source. To determine the amperage draw, connect the negative terminal of a digital multimeter to the negative terminal of the battery. Touch the test lamp probe to the positive terminal of the battery. Connect the positive terminal of the multimeter to the cord of the test lamp and read the amperage draw. For accurate test results, the lamp must draw 0.1-0.3 amps.

1. Disconnect the high-tension coil lead from the distributor cap. Connect the coil lead securely to an engine ground to prevent engine starting. On 5.7L LT-1 and 8.1L models, disconnect each of the spark plug leads and connect them to ground to disable the ignition system.

2A. On models using a TBI system, unthread the screw (A, **Figure 75**) and then lift the plastic cover (B) off the flame arrestor.

2B. On models using an MPI system, remove the plastic engine cover to access the fuel injectors.

3. Note the wire routing. Then disconnect the connectors from each fuel injector.

4. Connect the cord of the test lamp to an engine ground. Touch the test probe to the positive battery cable to verify the test lamp and ground connections.

5. With the key switch in OFF or STOP, touch the test probe to the pink, pink/white or red wire in each of the injector connectors. The lamp must not illuminate at any of the test points. If the lamp illuminates, the EFI system relay or relay circuit is faulty. Test the relay as described in this section. If the relay and related circuits operate correctly, the pink, pink/white or red wire in the connector is shorted to a battery power source. Repair the wiring before proceeding.

6. Turn the key switch to ON or RUN. Touch the test probe to the pink, pink/white or red wire in each of the injector connectors. The lamp must illuminate at each of the test points. If not, the EFI system relay or relay circuit is faulty. Test the relay as described in this section. If the relay and related circuits operate correctly, the pink, pink/white or red wire in the suspect connector is open or shorted to engine ground. Repair the wiring before proceeding.

7. Touch the test probe to the other wire terminal (not the pink, pink/white or red wire) in one of the injector connectors. Observe the test lamp while an assistant cranks the engine. The test lamp must flash repeatedly while cranking. Repeat this step for the remaining injector connector(s). Refer to the following:

  a. If the test lamp flashes at each connector, the injector voltage is correct, and the ECU is switching the injectors. Proceed to Step 8.

  b. If the test lamp does not flash at any connection, test the ignition system as described in this chapter. If the ignition system operates properly, check for damaged wiring between the ignition system, ECU and fuel injectors. Repair or replace the wiring as required. Replace the ECU only if all other components are in acceptable condition. ECU failure is extremely rare.

  c. If the test lamp flashes at some connections but not at others, the wiring to the nonfunctional injector(s) is open or shorted to ground. If the wiring is in good condition, ECU failure is likely. Replace the ECU only if all other components are in acceptable condition. ECU failure is extremely rare.

8. Turn the key switch to OFF or STOP.

9. Reconnect each of the connectors onto the injectors. Route the wiring to prevent contact with moving or hot engine components.

10A. On models using a TBI system, install the plastic cover (B, **Figure 75**) onto the flame arrestor. Guide the screw (A, **Figure 75**) into the cover, flame arrestor and throttle body openings. Lift the cover and flame arrestor slightly to assist with aligning the screw with the threaded opening.

10B. On models using an MPI system, install the plastic engine cover.

DIAGNOSTIC TROUBLE CODES

The engine control unit (ECU) continuously monitors input voltage from various sensors. The ECU stores a diagnostic trouble code if voltage from one or more of the sensors exceeds the predetermined value. Unlike many other electronic fuel injection (EFI) systems, the code remains stored if the battery is disconnected.

Two available tools for reading the stored codes are the diagnostic code tool (**Figure 77**) and the scan tool (**Figure 78**, typical).

Contact an Indmar dealership for information about purchasing either tool.

Reading Codes Using a Diagnostic Code Tool

Identify trouble codes by reading the flashing lamp on the diagnostic code tool. Refer to the following example to understand how to identify codes.

A short-duration flash followed by a pause and then another flash indicates a code 2. See **Figure 79**. The second part of the trouble code is displayed after a slightly longer pause. In this example (**Figure 79**), the second code is a 1; therefore, the trouble code is a 21. The trouble code flashes three times. Then a longer pause separates the individual trouble codes. If the first code repeats, no additional codes are stored in the ECU. To make sure all codes are identified, record them until they repeat.

1. Place the control in NEUTRAL. Turn the key switch to OFF or STOP.

2. Connect the code tool as follows:

   a. Remove the protective cap from the diagnostic link connector (DLC). See **Figure 80**.

   b. Carefully connect the tool to the DLC.

   c. Move the tool switch (**Figure 81**) to OFF.

3. Turn the key switch to ON or RUN. The code lamp must illuminate steadily.

   a. If the lamp does not illuminate, check for a blown fuse, faulty wire connector or faulty throttle position sensor. Temporarily unplug the throttle position sensor connector to check the sensor. The sensor is faulty if the light illuminates with the sen-

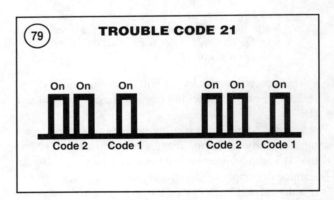

TROUBLE CODE 21

On On   On   On On   On

Code 2   Code 1   Code 2   Code 1

sor disconnected. Test the EFI system relay as described in this section if the wiring and throttle position sensor are good.

   b. If the lamp is flashing, the white/black wire connecting the DLC to the ECU is shorted to ground.

4. Move the tool switch (**Figure 81**) to ON. The lamp should display code 12. This code indicates the diagnostic system is functioning properly. If not, check for damaged wiring between the DLC and ECU.

5. Read the flashing light to identify trouble codes as described earlier in this procedure. Record all trouble codes.

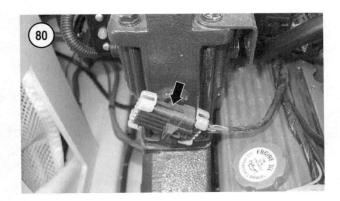

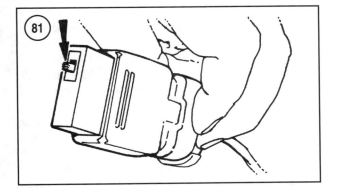

6. Move the tool switch (**Figure 81**) to OFF. Turn the key switch to the OFF or STOP.

7. Refer to **Table 10** to match the code(s) to the system or sensor. Refer to the information (in this section) for the stored trouble codes. Perform the suggested repair or test.

8. Clear the trouble code(s) as described in this section.

9. Remove the diagnostic code tool and install the cap onto the DLC (**Figure 80**).

Clearing codes

The engine must be started to clear the codes.

CAUTION
Use a flush device to supply the engine with cooling water if testing the ignition system with the boat out of the water. Operation of the starter motor results in operation of the seawater pump. The seawater pump is quickly damaged if operated without adequate cooling water.

1. Place the control in NEUTRAL. Turn the key switch to OFF or STOP.

2. Connect the code tool as follows:
   a. Remove the protective cap from the DLC.

b. Carefully plug the tool onto the DLC.
   c. Move the tool switch (**Figure 81**) to ON.

3. Turn the key switch to ON or RUN.

4. Advance the throttle to wide-open and then back to idle.

5. Move the tool switch (**Figure 81**) to OFF. Do not turn the key switch to OFF or STOP before starting the engine in the next step.

6. Start the engine and run for approximately 15 seconds. Turn the key switch to OFF or STOP.

7. Check for stored trouble codes as described in this section. Check for a discharged or defective battery if the codes did not clear.

8. Remove the diagnostic code tool and install the cap onto the DLC (**Figure 80**).

Reading Codes Using a Scan Tool

1. Place the control in NEUTRAL. Turn the key switch to OFF or STOP.

2. Connect the scan tool as follows:
   a. Remove the protective cap from the DLC. See **Figure 80**.
   b. Carefully connect the tool onto the DLC.

3. Turn the key switch to ON. Follow the instruction booklet and the on-screen instructions and retrieve the stored trouble codes.

4. Turn the key switch to OFF or STOP.

5. Refer to **Table 10** to match the code(s) to the system or sensor. Refer to the information (in this section) for the stored trouble codes. Perform the suggested repair or test.

6. Clear the trouble code(s) as described in this section.

7. Disconnect the scan tool and install the cap onto the DLC (**Figure 80**).

Clearing codes

CAUTION
Use a flush device to supply the engine with cooling water if testing the ignition system with the boat out of the water. Operation of the starter motor results in operation of the seawater pump. The seawater pump is quickly damaged if operated without adequate cooling water.

The codes must be cleared with the engine running.

1. Place the control in NEUTRAL. Turn the key switch to OFF or STOP.

2. Connect the scan tool as follows:
   a. Remove the protective cap from the diagnostic link connector (DLC).

b. Carefully connect the tool onto the DLC plug.

3. Start the engine and operate at idle speed. Follow the instruction booklet and the on-screen instructions to clear the trouble codes.

4. Stop the engine. Check for stored trouble codes as described in this section. Repeat the code clearing procedure if the code(s) did not clear.

5. Disconnect the scan tool and install the cap onto the DLC (**Figure 80**).

Code 14 (MEFI 1 or MEFI 2 ECU)

This code sets if the ECU detects the engine coolant temperature (ECT) sensor voltage is below or above the preset value.

A sensor producing low output voltage will cause the ECU to deliver too much fuel for the actual engine temperature. The excess fuel will cause symptoms consistent with an excessively rich condition.

A sensor producing high output voltage will cause the ECU to deliver too little fuel for the actual engine temperature. The excess fuel will cause symptoms consistent with a lean condition. Refer to *Basic Fuel System Troubleshooting* in this chapter. If a fault is detected, the ECU will calculate the fuel and timing for an engine operating at approximately 32° F (0° C). The substitute temperature will cause the ECU to increase the engine idle speed above the normal speed (600 rpm) with the engine at normal operating temperature.

If code 14 is stored, test the engine temperature sensor resistance as described in this section. If the sensor resistance is as specified, check for an open or short circuit in the wiring between the sensor and ECU. Refer to the wiring diagrams at the end of the manual to identify the sensor wiring and connections. Clear the trouble code as described in this section.

Code 14 (MEFI 3 or MEFI 4 ECU)

This code sets if the ECU detects the ECT sensor voltage is below the preset value.

A sensor producing low output voltage will cause the ECU to deliver too much fuel for the actual engine temperature. The excess fuel will cause symptoms consistent with a rich condition. Refer to *Basic Fuel System Troubleshooting* in this chapter. If a fault is detected, the ECU will calculate the fuel and timing for an engine operating at approximately 32° F (0° C). The substitute temperature will cause the ECU to increase the engine idle speed above the normal speed (600 rpm) with the engine at normal operating temperature.

If code 14 is stored, test the engine temperature sensor resistance as described in this section. If the sensor resistance is as specified, check for an open circuit in the wiring between the sensor and ECU. Refer to the wiring diagrams at the end of the manual to identify the sensor wiring and connections. Clear the trouble code as described in this section.

Code 15 (MEFI 3 or MEFI 4 ECU)

This code sets if the ECU detects excessive ECT output voltage.

Excessive ECT output voltage will cause the ECU to deliver too little fuel for the actual engine temperature. Running the engine with too little fuel will cause symptoms consistent with a lean condition. Refer to *Basic Fuel System Troubleshooting* in this chapter. Also, the excessive voltage will cause the ECU to set the engine idle speed to the normal speed (600 rpm) with the engine well below the normal operating temperature. In some instances, the sensor will incorrectly indicate engine overheating and cause the ECU to sound the warning horn when the engine is actually not overheating.

If code 15 is stored, test the engine temperature sensor resistance as described in this section. If sensor resistance is as specified, check for a short circuit in the wiring between the sensor and ECU. Refer to the wiring diagrams at the end of the manual to identify the sensor wiring and connections. Clear the trouble code as described in this section.

Code 21 (MEFI 1 or MEFI 2 ECU)

This code sets if the ECU detects a throttle position sensor (TPS) voltage that is above or below the preset value.

If the TPS is producing excessive voltage, the ECU will determine that the throttle is open wider than it actually is. Reacting to this, the ECU will cause excessive fuel delivery and open the idle air control (IAC) motor as part of the programmed follower function. This will result in a high idle speed and symptoms consistent with an excessively rich fuel mixture.

If the TPS voltage is low, the ECU will conclude that the throttle opening is less than the actual opening. This will prevent the ECU from opening the IAC motor and result in stalling at idle speed.

A faulty TPS can also prevent the ECU from detecting and reacting to rapid throttle opening and cause the engine to hesitate during acceleration.

If code 21 is stored, check for a short or open circuit in the wiring between the sensor and ECU. Refer to the wiring diagrams at the end of the manual to identify the sensor wiring and connections. Replace the throttle position sensor as described in Chapter Nine if the wiring and connections are good. Clear the trouble code as described in this section.

Code 21 (MEFI 3 or MEFI 4 ECU)

This code sets if the ECU detects excessive TPS voltage.

If the TPS output voltage is excessive, the ECU will establish that the throttle opening is wider than it actually is and cause excessive fuel delivery and IAC motor opening. This will result in excessive idle speed and symptoms consistent with a rich condition. Excessive TPS output voltage can also prevent the ECU from reacting to rapid throttle opening causing the engine to hesitate during acceleration.

If a code 21 is stored, check for an open or short circuit in the wiring connecting the sensor to the ECU and repair the wiring as required. Refer to the wiring diagrams at the end of the manual to identify the wiring and connections. Replace the TPS (Chapter Nine) if the wiring is in good condition. After repair, clear the trouble code as described in this chapter.

Code 22 (MEFI 3 or MEFI 4 ECU)

This code sets if the TPS voltage is less than the preset value.

Low TPS voltage will cause the ECU to establish that the throttle opening is less than the actual opening.

A sensor producing a low output voltage will cause the ECU to determine a lower-than-actual throttle opening. This will prevent the ECU from opening the IAC motor as part of the programmed follower function and cause stalling when the throttle is returned to idle. This can also prevent the ECU from reacting to rapid throttle opening and cause the engine to hesitate during acceleration.

If code 22 is stored, check for a short or open circuit in the wiring connecting the sensor to the ECU. Refer to the wiring diagrams at the end of the manual to identify the sensor wiring and connections. If no fault is found with the wiring, replace the throttle position sensor as described in Chapter Nine. Clear the trouble code as described in this section.

Code 23 (MEFI 1 or MEFI 2 ECU)

This code sets if the ECU detects the intake air temperature (IAT) sensor voltage is above or below the preset limit.

An IAT sensor producing a low output voltage will cause the ECU to deliver too much fuel for the actual temperature of air entering the engine. The excess fuel will cause symptoms consistent with a rich condition. Refer to *Basic Fuel System Troubleshooting* in this chapter.

A sensor producing a high output voltage will cause the ECU to deliver too little fuel for the actual temperature of air entering the engine. Running the engine with too little fuel will cause symptoms consistent with a lean condition. Refer to *Basic Fuel System Troubleshooting* in this chapter.

If code 23 is stored, test the intake air temperature sensor resistance as described in this section. If the sensor resistance is good, check for an open or shorted circuit in the wiring connecting the sensor to the ECU. Refer to the wiring diagrams at the end of the manual to identify the sensor wiring and connections. Clear the trouble code as described in this section.

Code 23 (MEFI 3 or MEFI 4 ECU)

This code sets if the ECU detects the IAT sensor voltage is below the preset limit.

A sensor producing a low output voltage will cause the ECU to deliver too much fuel for the actual temperature of air entering the engine. The excess fuel will cause symptoms consistent with a rich condition. Refer to *Basic Fuel System Troubleshooting* in this chapter.

If code 23 is stored, test the intake air temperature sensor resistance as described in this section. If the resistance is within specification, check for an open or shorted circuit in the wiring connecting the sensor to the ECU. Refer to the wiring diagrams at the end of the manual to identify the sensor wiring and connections. Clear the trouble code as described in this section.

Code 25 (MEFI 3 or MEFI 4 ECU)

This code sets if the ECU detects the IAT sensor voltage is exceeding the preset limit.

A sensor producing a high output voltage will cause the ECU to deliver too little fuel for the actual temperature of air entering the engine. Running the engine with too little fuel will cause symptoms consistent with a lean condition. Refer to *Basic Fuel System Troubleshooting* in this chapter.

If code 25 is stored, test the intake air temperature sensor resistance as described in this section. If the sensor resistance is as specified, check for an open or shorted circuit in the wiring connecting the sensor to the ECU. Refer to the wiring diagrams at the end of the manual to identify the sensor wiring and connections. Clear the trouble code as described in this section.

Code 33 (MEFI 1 or MEFI 2 ECU)

This code sets if the ECU detects the manifold air pressure (MAP) sensor voltage is above or below the preset limit.

A sensor producing a high output voltage will cause the ECU to deliver too much fuel for the actual air pressure in the intake manifold. The excess fuel will cause symptoms consistent with a rich condition. Refer to *Basic Fuel System Troubleshooting* in this chapter.

A sensor producing a low output voltage will cause the ECU to deliver too little fuel for the actual air pressure in the intake manifold. Running the engine with too little fuel will cause symptoms consistent with a lean condition. Refer to *Basic Fuel System Troubleshooting* in this chapter.

If code 33 is stored, check for an open or shorted circuit in the wiring connecting the sensor to the ECU. Refer to the wiring diagrams at the end of the manual to identify the sensor wiring and connections. If no fault is found with the wiring, replace the sensor as described in Chapter Nine. Clear the trouble code as described in this section.

Code 33 (MEFI 3 or MEFI 4 ECU)

This code sets if the ECU detects the MAP sensor voltage is exceeding the preset limit.

A sensor producing a high output voltage will cause the ECU to deliver too much fuel for the actual air pressure in the intake manifold. The excess fuel will cause operational symptoms consistent with a rich condition. Refer to *Basic Fuel System Troubleshooting* in this chapter.

If code 33 is stored, check for an open or shorted circuit in the wiring connecting the sensor to the ECU. Refer to the wiring diagrams at the end of the manual to identify the sensor wiring and connections. If the wiring is good, replace the sensor as described in Chapter Nine. Clear the trouble code as described in this section.

Code 34 (MEFI 3 or MEFI 4 ECU)

This code sets if the ECU detects the sensor voltage is below the preset limit.

A sensor producing a low little output voltage will cause the ECU to deliver too little fuel for the actual air pressure in the intake manifold. Running the engine with too little fuel will cause symptoms consistent with a lean

condition. Refer to *Basic Fuel System Troubleshooting* in this chapter.

If code 34 is stored, check for an open or shorted circuit in the wiring connecting the sensor to the ECU. Refer to the wiring diagrams at the end of the manual to identify the sensor wiring and connections. If the wiring is good, replace the sensor as described in Chapter Nine. Clear the trouble code as described in this section.

Code 41 (MEFI 3 or MEFI 4 ECU)

This code sets if the ECU detects an open circuit in the green/white wire connecting the ECU to the distributor-mounted ignition module. On models without a distributor (5.7L LT-1 and 8.1L models), this code will set if the ECU detects an open circuit in the wiring connecting the ECU to the ignition control module (5.7L LT-1) or ignition coils (8.1L models). The open circuit will prevent the ECU from controlling the ignition timing. The ECU will then relinquish control, and the timing advance will be controlled by the ignition module. The engine will start and run with noticeably reduced power and efficiency, starting difficulty and noticeably rougher idle characteristics.

If code 41 is stored, check for an open circuit in the green/white wire and connections. Refer to the wiring diagrams at the end of the manual to identify the wire connections. If the wiring is good, replace the ignition module as described in Chapter Nine. Clear the trouble code as described in this section.

Code 42 (MEFI 1 or MEFI 2 ECU)

This code sets if the ECU detects a fault in the green/white wire connecting the ECU to the distributor-mounted ignition module. The open or shorted circuit will prevent the ECU from controlling the ignition timing. The ECU will then relinquish control, and the timing advance will be controlled by the ignition module. The engine will start and run with noticeably reduced power and efficiency, starting difficulty and noticeably rougher idle characteristics.

If code 42 is stored, check for an open or shorted circuit in the green/white or loose connections. Refer to the wiring diagrams at the end of the manual to identify the wire connections. If the wiring is good, replace the ignition module as described in Chapter Nine. Clear the trouble code as described in this section.

Code 42 (MEFI 3 or MEFI 4 ECU)

This code sets if the ECU detects a fault in the white/tan wire connecting the ECU to the ignition module. The open or shorted circuit will prevent the ECU from activating the switching circuits in the ignition module. This prevents the ECU from controlling the ignition timing. The ECU will then relinquish control and the timing advance will be controlled by the ignition module. The engine will start and run with noticeably reduced power and efficiency, starting difficulty and noticeably rougher idle characteristics.

If code 42 is stored, check for an open or shorted circuit in the white/tan wire or faulty connections. Refer to the wiring diagrams at the end of the manual to identify the wire connections. If the wiring is good, replace the ignition module as described in Chapter Nine. Clear the trouble code as described in this section.

Code 43 (MEFI 1 or MEFI 2 ECU)

This code sets if the ECU fails to receive a signal from the knock control module. If code 43 is stored, check for an open or shorted wire connecting the knock sensor(s) to the knock control module and the knock control module to ECU. If the wiring is good, replace the knock control module as described in Chapter Nine.

Code 44 (MEFI 3 or MEFI 4 ECU)

During operation, the ECU continuously monitors the voltage and frequency produced by the knock sensor(s). If the voltage or frequency indicates detonation (knocking), the ECU adjusts ignition timing and fuel delivery in an attempt to stop detonation. The ECU stores code 44 if the ECU detects a voltage or frequency that indicates a faulty sensor, knock sensor wiring or connections (open circuit, high resistance or short to ground).

If code 44 is stored, inspect the wiring connecting the knock sensor(s) to the ECU. Refer to the wiring diagrams at the end of the manual to identify the wire connections. If the wiring is good, replace the knock sensor as described in Chapter Nine. Clear the trouble code as described in this section. If the engine uses two knock sensors, run the engine with the replacement sensor. Check for stored diagnostic trouble codes as described in this chapter. If code 44 is stored, reinstall the original sensor and replace the remaining sensor. Again, clear the trouble code, run the engine and check for codes. The system is operating properly if the trouble code does not replicate.

Code 51 or code 52

The ECU sets these codes if it detects a failure of the calibration circuits. The calibration circuits control the fuel delivery, ignition, engine overspeed, idle speed and other values unique to the engine in which the unit is used. This failure can cause a no-start condition, hard starting, poor performance or poor operating characteristics. If code 51 or 52 is stored, clear the trouble code as described in this section. Run or attempt to start the engine. Stop the engine and check for stored trouble codes as described in this section. If code 51 or 52 is stored, replace the ECU as described in Chapter Nine.

Code 81 (MEFI 3 or MEFI 4 ECU)

The ECU sets code 81 if it detects unusual voltage from the fuel pump driver circuit, injector driver circuit or sensor reference voltage. If code 81 is stored, perform the following procedure.

1. Check for voltage at the injectors as described in this section. Refer to the following:
   a. If the injector voltage is correct, the injector driver circuit is functioning properly. Proceed to Step 2.
   b. If the injector voltage is correct, check for damaged wiring connecting the injectors to the ECU and repair as needed. Clear the code as described in the chapter. Run the engine. If code 81 resets, proceed to Step 6.
2. Test the fuel pump relay as described in this section. Refer to the following:
   a. If the relay and related circuitry test correctly, the fuel pump driver circuit is operating properly. Proceed to Step 3.
   b. Correct any problems with the relay or related circuitry. Then clear the code as described in the chapter. Run the engine. Stop the engine and check for stored trouble codes as described in this section. If code 81 resets, proceed to Step 6.
3. Set a digital voltmeter to the 10 or 20 VDC scale.
4. Carefully unplug the connector from the engine temperature sensor. Refer to Chapter Nine to locate the sensor. Refer to *Engine Temperature Sensor Replacement*.
5. Touch the positive meter lead to the blue/orange wire in the harness. Touch the negative meter test lead to an engine ground. Turn the key switch to ON or RUN. The meter must indicate 4.9-5.1 volts. Refer to the following:
   a. If the meter indicates 0 volt, test the EFI system relay as described in this chapter.
   b. If the voltage is significantly lower (10 percent or more) than the specification, monitor the voltage while unplugging (one at a time) the connectors

from the manifold air pressure sensor, intake air temperature sensor and throttle position sensor. Refer to Chapter Nine to locate the sensors. Replace the sensor if the voltage returns to the normal range when the corresponding sensor is unplugged. Clear the code as described in this chapter. Run the engine. Stop the engine and check for stored trouble codes as described in this section. If code 81 resets, proceed to Step 6.

  c. If the voltage is significantly higher (10 percent or more) than the specification, one of the sensor wires is shorted to a battery voltage source, or the ECU is faulty. Inspect all wiring connecting the ECU to the sensors. Refer to the wiring diagrams at the end of the manual to identify the wire connections. Replace the ECU only if wiring is good. Failure of the ECU is extremely rare.

  d. If the voltage is within the specification, code 81 is set due to another sensor or associated wiring. Proceed to Step 6.

6. Inspect the wiring connecting the ECU to the various sensors for shorts or open circuits. After verifying the wiring, clear the code as described in the chapter. Attempt to start or run the engine. Stop the engine and check for stored trouble codes as described in this section. If code 81 resets, a faulty replacement sensor, wiring or ECU is evident. Replace the ECU only if no problems are found in the wiring or replacement sensor(s). ECU failure is extremely rare.

Engine Temperature Sensor (ETS) Resistance

A defective ETS can cause poor cold-engine operating characteristics, excessive idle speed on a fully warmed engine or improper activation of the overheat warning system.

This test requires an accurate digital or analog multimeter, a liquid thermometer and a container of water that can be heated.

1. Remove the ETS as described in Chapter Nine.
2. Calibrate the meter to the appropriate scale for the resistance specification in **Table 11**. Connect the meter leads between the two sensor terminals. Test lead polarity is not important for this test.
3. Suspend the sensor in a container of water that can be heated (**Figure 82**, typical). Make sure the sensor does not touch the bottom or sides of the container and the tip of the sensor is completely below the water surface.
4. Add ice or heat the container until the water temperature reaches the temperatures specified in **Table 11**. Record the resistance at each temperature.

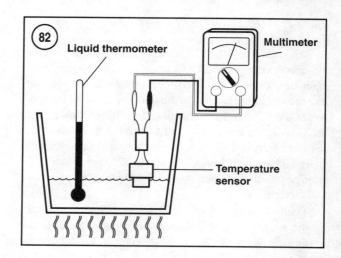

5. Compare the resistance readings with the specifications in **Table 11**. A slight variance is resistance (less than 10 percent) is common and does not indicate a defective sensor. Replace the ETS if the resistance is significantly different from the specification at any of the specified temperatures.

6. Install the ETS as described in Chapter Nine.

Intake Air Temperature (IAT) Sensor Resistance

The IAT sensor is used only on multiport injection (MPI) models. A defective intake air temperature sensor can cause poor cold-engine operating characteristics and symptoms consistent with a lean or rich operating condition. Refer to *Basic Fuel System Troubleshooting* in this chapter.

This test requires an accurate ohmmeter and a thermometer suitable for accurately measuring air temperature.

1. Remove the IAT sensor as described in Chapter Nine.
2. Calibrate the meter to the appropriate scale for the resistance specification in **Table 12**. Connect the meter leads between the two sensor terminals. Test lead polarity is not important for this test.
3. Wait a few minutes for the sensor to react to the temperature of the air in the work area. Compare the resistance reading on the meter and the surrounding air temperature with the specification in **Table 12**.
4. The resistance at the actual air temperature should be within the range for the nearest temperature listed in **Table 12**. Heat or cool the work area or move to a different area to test the sensor at various temperatures. A slight variance in resistance (less than 10 percent) is common and does not indicate a defective sensor. Replace the IAT

sensor if the resistance is significantly different from the specification at any of the specified temperatures.

5. Install the IAT sensor as described in Chapter Nine.

Idle Air Control Motor (IAC)

CAUTION
Use a flush device to supply the engine with cooling water if testing the ignition system with the boat out of the water. Operation of the starter motor results in operation of the seawater pump. The seawater pump is quickly damaged if operated without adequate cooling water.

A defective IAC can cause stalling at idle, excessive idle speed or stalling during deceleration. A defective IAC will not cause operational problems at higher engine speeds. A diagnostic code tool (**Figure 77**) or a scan tool (**Figure 78**, typical) is required for this procedure.

1. Start the engine and run at idle speed until the engine reaches normal operating temperature.

2. Stop the engine. Remove the protective cap from the DLC (**Figure 80**). Carefully plug the tool onto the DLC. If using a diagnostic code tool, move the tool switch (**Figure 81**) to OFF.

3A. On models using an MEFI 1 or MEFI 2 ECU, start the engine and raise the idle speed to approximately 1500 rpm in NEUTRAL. Then use the tool to place the engine in service mode. If using a diagnostic code tool, place the engine in service mode by moving the tool switch (**Figure 81**) to ON. If using a scan tool, follow the instruction booklet and the on-screen instructions to put the engine in service mode.

3B. On models using an MEFI 3 or MEFI 4 ECU, start the engine and run at idle speed in NEUTRAL. Then use the tool to place the engine in service mode. If using a diagnostic code tool, place the engine in service mode by moving the tool switch (**Figure 81**) to ON. If using a scan tool, follow the instruction booklet and the on-screen instructions to put the engine in service mode.

4A. On models using an MEFI 1 or MEFI 2 ECU, the engine speed must drop by 200 rpm or more while in service mode.

4B. On models using an MEFI 3 or MEFI 4 ECU, the engine speed must automatically increase while in service mode.

5. If the engine speed does not change as described in Step 4A or Step 4B, perform the following:

    a. Stop the engine and disconnect the diagnostic code tool or scan tool.

    b. Remove the IAC as described in Chapter Nine. Clean and inspect the connecting wiring, IAC motor plunger and plunger opening in the throttle body.

    c. Install the IAC as described in Chapter Nine.

    d. Repeat the test to check for proper IAC operation. Replace the IAC if it fails to perform as specified.

6. Disconnect the code tool or scan tool and install the cap onto the DLC (**Figure 80**).

POWER STEERING SYSTEM

This section describes troubleshooting the cable-actuated power steering system used with Indmar inboard marine engines.

The power steering system is very reliable, and malfunction is usually due to low fluid level or improper installation of the steering cable. At the first sign of trouble, check and correct the fluid level as described in Chapter Three. Check the cable installation as described in the steering cable installation instructions. Refer to *Steering Cable and Helm*. Also, check the items listed in **Table 5**. Refer to the cause listed next to the symptom that best describes the malfunction. Check the items or perform the suggested repair listed under the corrective action.

Stiff or Binding Cable or Helm

A binding steering cable or helm can lead the operator to believe the power steering system is not operating. The cable must move the control valve for steering assist to occur. Always check for a faulty steering cable or helm before repair or replacement of other steering system components.

1. Temporarily disconnect the steering cable from the actuator and steering lever. Refer to *Steering Cable and Helm* in Chapter Eleven.

2. Rotate the steering wheel to the full port and starboard directions. The wheel must turn in both directions without excessive effort, binding or roughness. Otherwise, replace the steering cable and helm as described in Chapter Eleven.

3. Reconnect the steering cable to the actuator and steering lever as described in Chapter Eleven.

Power Steering Fluid Cooler

A faulty power steering fluid cooler can allow water into the power steering fluid, leak power steering fluid into the cooling water, restrict cooling water flow or re-

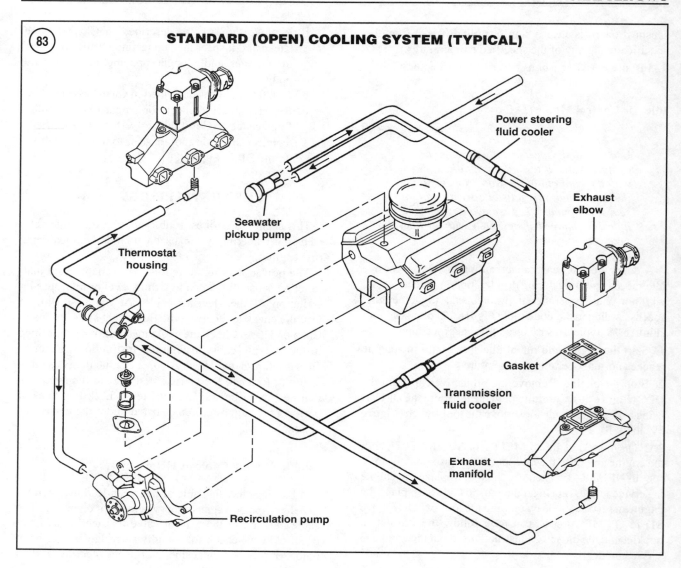

83 **STANDARD (OPEN) COOLING SYSTEM (TYPICAL)**

Power steering
fluid cooler

Seawater
pickup pump

Exhaust
elbow

Thermostat
housing

Gasket

Transmission
fluid cooler

Exhaust
manifold

Recirculation pump

strict power steering fluid flow. If these symptoms occur, remove the fluid cooler as described in Chapter Eight.

Direct air through the passages to check for and remove restrictions. If it is suspected of leaking, have the cooler tested and repaired at a radiator repair shop.

COOLING SYSTEM

Malfunction of the cooling system results in overheating or overcooling.

Overheating is almost always caused by insufficient water flowing through the engine or heat exchanger (models with a closed cooling system), or the water fails to absorb heat from the engine. Poor idle quality or stalling at idle can also occur when overheating.

If overheating is occurring, first refer to the cooling system operation description in the following section. Many times the system is operating as designed, and the operator is unaware of the special features designed into the system. The system description will usually indicate by symptom which components are suspect.

Most overheating problems are directly related to excessive wear or failure of water pump components. Inspect and repair the water pump prior to inspecting any other cooling system components. Verify the engine temperature as described in this section before beginning the troubleshooting procedure. The dash gauge, engine temperature sender or wiring might be faulty and falsely indicate overheating. If overheating is verified, refer to Chapter Eight for water pump inspection and repair instructions.

Refer to **Table 6** for a list of items to check. Refer to the causes listed next to the symptom that best describes the malfunction. Other useful information and tips are described with the specific test instructions.

Overcooling is almost always caused by failure of the thermostat. First verify the engine temperature as described in this section. If necessary, test the thermostat as described in this section.

Cooling System Operation

On models equipped with a standard (open) cooling system, water in which the boat is operated is picked up at the drive unit by the seawater pump and circulated through the engine to absorb heat. The heated water is transferred to the exhaust manifold(s) where it is expelled overboard with the exhaust gasses.

Some engines are equipped with a closed cooling system that is divided into two separate subsystems. One subsystem is a closed system of coolant (antifreeze and water mixture) circulating in the engine and absorbing the engine heat. Heat absorbed by the coolant is then transferred (exchanged) to the seawater in the heat exchanger. Water in which the boat is operated is picked up at the drive unit by the seawater pump and transferred through the heat exchanger where the seawater absorbs heat from the coolant. The heated seawater from the exchanger is transferred to the exhaust manifold(s) where it is expelled overboard with the exhaust gasses. **Figure 83** shows a typical standard (open) cooling system. **Figure 84** shows a typical closed cooling system. The location of the pumps and path of flow might differ slightly from those shown in the illustrations.

Verifying engine temperature

Always verify the actual temperature of the engine using thermomelt sticks or a digital pyrometer before testing other cooling system components. Thermomelt sticks (**Figure 85**) resemble crayons and are designed to melt at specific temperatures. The melting temperatures are listed on the sides of the sticks or the labels. Purchase the Thermomelt sticks or digital pyrometer from a tool supplier.

Troubleshooting an overheating or overcooling problem using a flush attachment is difficult if not impossible. Water supplied by the flushing adapter tends to mask problems with the cooling system. Perform this test with the boat in the water under actual operating conditions.

If using Thermomelt sticks, hold the sticks against the brass body of the temperature sender (**Figure 86**), overheat switch or engine temperature sensor (EFI models). Refer to Chapter Nine to locate these components. Try to check the temperature immediately after or during the suspected overheat condition. Hold different temperature sticks to the engine to determine the temperature the engine is reaching.

If using a pyrometer, attach the sender to or aim the pyrometer at the brass body of the temperature sender, overheat switch or engine temperature sensor (EFI models). Refer to Chapter Nine to locate these components. Monitor the engine temperature as the engine warms.

Stop the engine if the temperature exceeds 195° F (90° C). Normal operating temperature is 140-180° F (60-88° C). Overheating is evident if higher temperature is noted. Test the temperature sender or switch if an alarm or gauge indicates overheating but the Thermomelt sticks or pyrometer indicate normal operating temperature.

Compare the actual engine temperature with the temperature on the dash instruments. A faulty sender, gauge or faulty wiring is evident if the readings are substantially different.

Overcooling is evident if the engine fails to reach normal operating temperature. Due to the variations in temperature of the water in which the engine is operating, it might take as few as 5 minutes or as many as 20 minutes of operating at idle speed to reach normal operating temperature. If operating at low speed only in very cold water, the engine might never reach normal temperature. This occurs because the very cool water flowing through the thermostat bypass is able to absorb more heat than the engine produces at a lower throttle setting.

Thermostat test

Test the thermostat if the engine overheats or runs too cool. A thermometer, piece of string and a container of water that can be heated are required.

1. Remove the thermostat as described in Chapter Eight. Note the temperature value stamped on the thermostat (**Figure 87**). Suspend the thermostat into the container of water with the string tied to the thermostat as shown in **Figure 88**.

2. Place the liquid thermometer in the container and begin heating the water. Observe the temperature of the water and the thermostat while heating the water.

3. The thermostat must start opening within a few degrees of the number stamped on the thermostat (**Figure 87**). If not, discontinue testing and replace the thermostat.

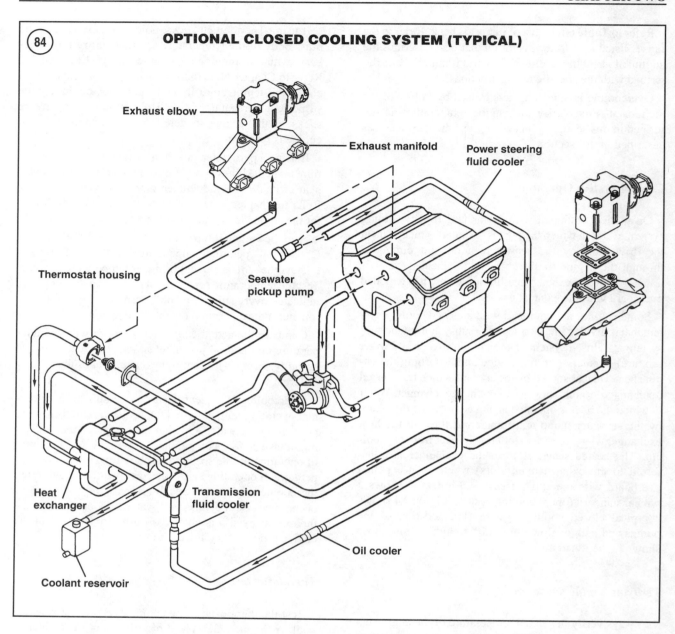

OPTIONAL CLOSED COOLING SYSTEM (TYPICAL)

Exhaust elbow

Exhaust manifold

Power steering fluid cooler

Thermostat housing

Seawater pickup pump

Heat exchanger

Transmission fluid cooler

Oil cooler

Coolant reservoir

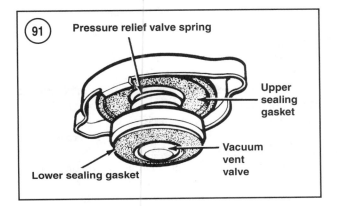

Pressure relief valve spring

Upper sealing gasket

Vacuum vent valve

Lower sealing gasket

Pressure test (closed cooling system)

If the coolant reservoir in a closed cooling system requires frequent filling, it probably has a leak. Small leaks might not be easy to locate because the hot coolant evaporates as quickly as it leaks out and prevents the formation of telltale rusty or grayish-white staining. A pressure test of the coolant side of the closed cooling system will usually locate the leak. This procedure tests the pressure cap for leakage and proper unseating pressure and tests the closed cooling system for leaking. A cooling system pressure tester (**Figure 89**) is required for this procedure. Purchase the tester from a tool supplier.

1. Allow the engine to cool completely. Never remove the pressure cap from a warm or hot engine.

2. Remove the pressure cap from the heat exchanger or integrated reservoir (**Figure 90**). Wash the cap in clean water to remove debris and deposits. Inspect the cap for cut, cracked or a deteriorated seal and gasket (**Figure 91**, typical). Make sure the locking tabs on the cap are not bent or damaged. Replace the cap if these or other defects are evident.

3. Attach the cap to the pressure tester (**Figure 92**). Dip the pressure cap into clean water.

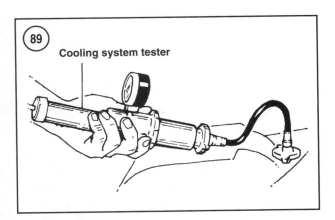

Cooling system tester

4. Heat the water to 25° F above the number stamped on the thermostat. The thermostat must be fully open at this temperature. If not, replace the thermostat.

5. Discontinue the testing and install the thermostat as described in Chapter Eight.

4. Observe the cap and gauge while pumping the tester to apply pressure against the cap. Note the pressure in which bubbles indicate the pressure cap is unseating. Small bubbling does not indicate unseating. Large bubbles coupled with a rapid pressure drop indicate unseating. The cap should unseat at 13-15 psi (90-103 kPa). Replace the cap if unseating occurs at a higher or lower pressure.

5. Remove the cap from the water. Pump the gauge to apply 14 psi (96 kPa) pressure against the cap. Wait approximately 30 seconds and check the gauge. Replace the cap if the pressure has dropped to less than 11 psi (76 kPa).

6. Remove the cap from the pressure tester.

7. Inspect the filler neck and sealing surfaces (**Figure 93**) for nicks, distortion and dirty or contaminated surfaces. Wipe the surfaces clean. Make sure the locking cams are not bent or damaged.

8. Check and correct the coolant level as described in Chapter Three.

9. Connect the pressure tester to the filler neck (**Figure 89**). Pump the tester to apply 17 psi (116 kPa) to the system. Wait 2 minutes and then check the gauge. Any noticeable pressure drop indicates leaking. If there is a leak, check all hoses, drain plugs, core plugs, the thermostat housing, intake manifold and recirculation pump for leaking coolant. Listen for hissing while the system is under pressure. If hissing is noted, apply soapy water around the pressure tester connection to check for leaking.

10. If not, external coolant leaks are evident, the leakage is related to a leaking heat exchanger or internal leak in the engine. Remove the heat exchanger and have it pressure tested at a reputable radiator shop. If the heat exchanger is not leaking but the coolant requires frequent filling, the leak is evidently in the engine cooling system. Typically, such a leak is due to a blown head gasket, cracked or porous cylinder head, leaking intake manifold gasket, cracked or porous intake manifold, or cracked or porous cylinder block. Check the oil for a milky appearance and inspect the spark plugs for crystalline deposits to verify internal leakage. Internal leakage will almost always allow coolant into the oil pan or combustion chamber(s).

11. Remove the tester.

12. If removed, reinstall the heat exchanger.

13. Correct any external leaks or internal leaks.

14. Check and correct the coolant level as described in Chapter Three.

WARNING SYSTEM

The warning system alerts the operator if a cooling or lubrication system failure occurs. Continued operation with the warning system activated can lead to serious and expensive engine damage.

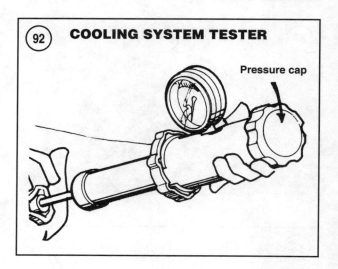

92 COOLING SYSTEM TESTER

Pressure cap

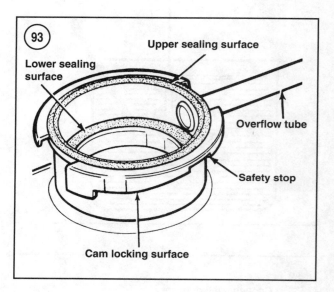

93

Upper sealing surface

Lower sealing surface

Overflow tube

Safety stop

Cam locking surface

If the warning horn is sounding, first check the oil pressure and engine temperature displayed on the dash instruments. Then stop the engine. If the oil pressure and engine temperature are within the normal ranges, the alarm is probably due to overheating of the transmission fluid. Refer to *Warning System Operation* in this section and the owner's manual for specific warning system operations. Many times the system is operating correctly, and the operator is unaware of the system features. The system description and gauges will usually indicate by symptom which system has failed. If the gauge indicates overheating, troubleshoot the cooling system as described in this chapter. If the gauge indicates low oil pressure, test the oil pressure as described in this chapter. Refer to *Engine*.

If the warning horn is sounding and the cooling and lubrication systems are operating properly, or if the gauges

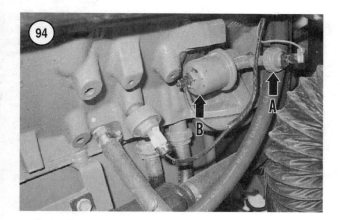

2

Warning System Operation

Carburetor-equipped models

The warning system components used on carburetor-equipped models include the oil pressure switch, engine overheat switch, transmission overheat switch and the warning horn.

Battery voltage is applied to the positive terminal of the warning horn by the purple wire connected to the ignition circuit. The tan/blue warning horn wire connects to the negative terminal of the warning horn and to each of the switches (oil pressure, engine overheat and transmission overheat). The sensors control operation of the warning horn by completing or removing the ground circuit for the warning horn.

The oil pressure switch (A, **Figure 94**) threads into the cylinder block and is exposed to oil pressure developed by the lubrication system. Do not confuse the oil pressure switch with the larger oil pressure sender (B, **Figure 94**). With the engine at rest, no oil pressure is developed, and the switch is closed. The closed switch grounds the tan/blue wire and completes the ground circuit for the warning horn. When the key switch is turned to ON or RUN, battery voltage is applied to the positive terminal on the warning horn, and it sounds to indicate that the warning horn, tan/blue wire and oil pressure switch are operational. This is commonly referred to as the self-test feature. When the engine is started and the oil pressure exceeds 5 psi (34.4 kPa), the oil pressure switch opens and removes the ground circuit for the horn, and the horn stops sounding. If the oil pressure should drop below the specification, the switch will close, complete the ground circuit and sound the horn. The horn will continue sounding until the minimum oil pressure is restored or the key switch is turned to OFF or STOP.

The engine overheat switch (**Figure 95**, typical) threads into the intake manifold, thermostat housing or cylinder head, and the tip of the switch is exposed to the water or coolant in the engine. The engine overheat switch is normally open. If the switch is exposed to water or coolant with a temperature exceeding 190-200° F (88-93° C), the switch closes and grounds the tan/blue wire to complete the circuit and cause the warning horn to sound. The horn will continue sounding until the engine temperature drops below 150-170° F (66-77° C) or the key switch is turned to OFF or STOP.

The transmission overheat switch (**Figure 96**, typical) threads into the transmission body and extends into the internal fluid return passage. The switch is normally open. If the transmission fluid temperature reaches or exceeds 220-240° F (105-115° C), the transmission overheat

indicate overheating or low oil pressure and the warning horn is not sounding, refer to **Table 7** for a list of items to check. Refer to the causes listed next to the symptom that best describes the malfunction. Perform the test or adjustment suggested under corrective action. Other useful information and tips are described with the specific test instructions.

switch closes and grounds the tan/blue wire to complete the circuit and cause the warning horn to sound. The horn will continue sounding until the transmission fluid temperature drops below 180-200° F (82-92° C) or the key switch is turned to OFF or STOP.

Electronic fuel injection (EFI) models

The warning system components used on electronic fuel injection (EFI) models include the oil pressure switch, transmission overheat switch, warning horn and engine control unit (ECU).

Battery voltage is applied to the positive terminal of the warning horn by the purple wire connected to the ignition ON circuit of the key switch. The tan/blue wire connects to the negative terminal of the warning horn and the ECU (**Figure 97**). A tan/blue wire connects to the oil pressure switch and the transmission overheat switch. The transmission overheat switch has a separate black ground wire to ground the switch body. The switches activate the warning system in the event of low oil pressure or high transmission fluid temperature.

The ECU controls the warning horn by completing or removing the warning horn ground using internal circuitry. The ECU uses input from the oil pressure switch, transmission overheat switch and engine temperature sensor to determine whether overheating or low oil pressure is evident.

When the key switch is turned to ON or RUN, the ECU sounds the warning horn for approximately 2 seconds to indicate the warning horn and ECU are operational. This is commonly referred to as the self-test feature.

The oil pressure switch (A, **Figure 94**) threads into the cylinder block and is exposed to oil pressure developed by the lubrication system. Do not confuse the oil pressure switch with the larger oil pressure sender (B, **Figure 94**). With the engine at rest, no oil pressure is developed, and the switch is closed. The closed switch grounds the tan/blue wire leading to the ECU. The ECU will not sound the warning horn because of the closed oil pressure switch unless input from the ignition system indicates the engine is running. When the engine is started and the oil pressure exceeds 5 psi (34.4 kPa), the oil pressure switch opens the grounded tan/blue wire. If the oil pressure should drop below the specification with the engine running, the switch will close and ground the tan/blue wire leading to the ECU. The ECU will then sound the warning horn. The horn will continue sounding until the minimum oil pressure is restored or the key switch is turned to OFF or STOP.

The transmission overheat switch (**Figure 96**, typical) threads into the transmission body and extends into the in-

ternal fluid return passage. The switch is normally open. If the transmission fluid temperature reaches or exceeds 220-240° F (105-115° C), the transmission overheat switch closes and grounds the tan/blue wire leading to the ECU. The ECU will then sound the warning horn. The horn will continue sounding until the transmission fluid temperature drops below 180-200° F (82-92° C) or the key switch is turned to OFF or STOP.

The ECU uses input from the engine temperature sensor (**Figure 98**) to continuously monitor the temperature of the water or coolant in the engine. If the water or coolant temperature exceeds 200° F (93° C), it completes the ground circuit to sound the horn. The horn will continue sounding until the engine shuts off, the engine temperature drops below 180° F (82° C) or the key switch is turned to OFF or STOP.

Warning Horn Test

1. Remove the warning horn as described in Chapter Nine.
2. Using jumper leads, connect the leads of the horn to the battery terminals (**Figure 99**). Polarity is not important for the this test. Replace the warning horn if it fails to emit a loud tone.

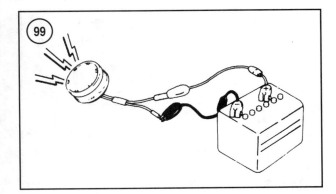

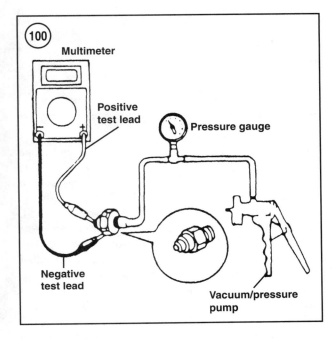

Multimeter

Positive
test lead

Pressure gauge

Negative
test lead

Vacuum/pressure
pump

3. Install the warning horn as described in Chapter Nine.

4. If the engine uses two warning horns, test the other horn using the same procedure.

Oil Pressure Switch Test

This test requires a multimeter and a vacuum/pressure pump. Purchase the vacuum/pressure pump from a local automotive parts or tool supply store. Test the switch as follows:

1. Remove the oil pressure switch as described in Chapter Nine.

2. Carefully slide an appropriately sized hose over the threaded fitting of the oil pressure switch (**Figure 100**). Apply a clamp over the hose to ensure an airtight connection. Do not apply pressure at this time.

3. Connect the ohmmeter leads to the switch terminals and the body of the switch as shown in **Figure 100**. If necessary, use a clamp to secure the test lead to the switch body. The meter must indicate continuity. If not, the switch has failed open and must be replaced.

4. Observe the meter and the pressure gauge while *slowly* applying pressure to the switch. Note the pressure gauge reading when the meter reading changes to no continuity.

5. Observe the meter and pressure gauge while *slowly* relieving the pressure. Note the pressure gauge reading when the reading changes to continuity.

6. Repeat Step 4 and Step 5 several times to check for an intermittent switch failure. The meter must change to no continuity each time the pressure reaches approximately 5 psi (34.4 kPa) and to continuity each time the pressure drops below the specification. Replace the oil pressure switch if it fails to perform as specified.

7. Remove the test leads and pressure/vacuum pump from the oil pressure switch. Clean all hose material from the threaded section of the switch.

8. Install the oil pressure switch as described in Chapter Nine.

Engine Overheat Switch Test

A defective engine overheat switch can cause the warning horn to sound when the engine is not overheating or prevent the warning horn from sounding if the engine overheats.

This test requires a multimeter, liquid thermometer and a container of water that can be heated.

1. Remove the engine overheat switch as described in Chapter Nine.

2. Fill the container with cool water and suspend the tip of the overheat switch in the water (**Figure 101**). Make sure the switch does not contact the bottom or sides of the container. Place a liquid thermometer in the container with the overheat switch as shown in **Figure 101**.

3. Connect one of the ohmmeter leads to the brass body of the switch. Use a clamp to secure the test lead as needed. Connect the other test lead to the switch terminal. The meter must indicate no continuity if placed in cool water. If the meter indicates continuity, the switch is shorted and must be replaced. No further testing is required for a shorted switch.

4. Begin heating and gently stirring the water while observing the meter. Note the temperature at which the meter switches from no continuity to continuity. This should occur at approximately 190-200° F (88-93° C). Replace the switch if the water boils before the meter reading changes.

5. Allow the water to cool gradually and note the temperature at which the meter changes from continuity to no continuity. This should occur at 150-170° F (66-77° C).

6. Replace the engine overheat switch if it does not perform as specified.

7. Install the engine overheat switch as described in Chapter Nine.

Transmission Overheat Switch Test

A faulty transmission overheat switch can cause the warning horn to sound when the transmission is not overheating or prevent the warning horn from sounding if the transmission overheats.

This test requires a multimeter, liquid thermometer and a container of engine oil that can be heated. Water cannot be used as the test medium because the switching temperature can occur at temperatures exceeding the boiling point of plain water.

1. Remove the transmission overheat switch as described in Chapter Nine.

2. Fill the container with cool engine oil and suspend the tip of the overheat switch in the oil (**Figure 101**). Make sure the switch does not contact the bottom or sides of the container. Place a liquid thermometer in the container with the overheat switch shown in **Figure 101**.

3. Connect the ohmmeter leads to the two switch terminals. The meter must indicate no continuity if placed in cool oil. If the meter indicates continuity, the switch is shorted and must be replaced.

4. Begin heating and gently stirring the oil while observing the meter. Note the temperature at which the meter switches from no continuity to continuity. This should occur at 220-240° F (105-115° C). Discontinue the test and replace the switch if the oil temperature exceeds the maximum specification.

5. Allow the oil to cool gradually and note the temperature at which the meter changes from continuity to no continuity. This should occur at 180-200° F (82-92° C).

6. Replace the overheat switch if it does not perform as specified.

7. Install the transmission overheat switches as described in Chapter Nine.

Walters V-Drive Unit

The Walters V-drive unit uses a separate low fluid-pressure warning system. The V-drive low oil-pressure switch (**Figure 102**) threads into a fitting on the side of the V-drive unit housing, and the tip is exposed to the pressure developed by the internal oil pump system. A connection

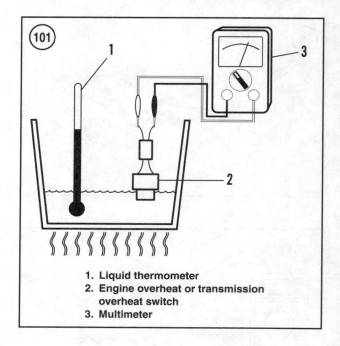

1. Liquid thermometer
2. Engine overheat or transmission overheat switch
3. Multimeter

to the ON circuit of the key switch supplies voltage to one terminal of the dash-mounted warning lamp. A tan/blue wire connects the other terminal of the warning lamp to the V-drive low oil-pressure switch. With the engine at rest, no oil pressure is developed, and the switch is closed. The closed switch grounds the tan/blue wire to complete the ground circuit for the warning lamp. When the key switch is turned to ON or RUN, battery voltage is applied to the positive terminal on the lamp, and it illuminates to indicate the lamp, tan/blue wire and V-drive low oil-pressure switch are operational. This is commonly referred to as the self-test feature. When the engine is started and the V-drive oil pressure exceeds the predetermined value, the switch opens the circuit and removes the ground circuit for the lamp, which causes it to extinguish. If the oil pressure should drop below the limit, the switch will close to complete the ground circuit, and the lamp will illuminate. The lamp will remain illuminated until the minimum oil pressure is reached or the key switch is turned to OFF or STOP.

Under normal idle speed operating conditions, the oil pressure developed by the Walters V-drive is not sufficient to open the switch. This will cause the lamp to illuminate, particularly when the fluid in the V-drive unit reaches full operating temperature. The pressure reaches the switching pressure when the engine speed reaches approximately 1500 rpm, and the lamp will extinguish.

If the lamp illuminates at engine speeds exceeding 1500 rpm, stop the engine and check the V-drive fluid level as described in Chapter Three. Replace the switch if the fluid

level is correct. Run the engine to check for proper warning system operation. Have the V-drive unit repaired at a marine transmission repair facility if the fault persists with the replacement switch.

If the lamp does not illuminate with the key switch in ON or RUN or at idle speed, disconnect the lead from the switch and connect it to an engine ground. Place the key switch in ON or RUN and observe the lamp.

If the lamp does not illuminate with the switch lead grounded, check for faulty wiring or connections at the lamp. Replace the lamp if no fault is found with the wiring.

If the lamp illuminates only with the lead grounded, replace the low oil-pressure switch.

Engine Temperature Sensor Test

The engine temperature sensor provides input to the ECU to operate the fuel injection and warning systems. If it is suspected of causing a malfunction of the warning system, test the engine temperature sensor as described under *Electronic Fuel Injection System* in this chapter.

ENGINE

This section provides instructions to determine whether an engine malfunction is caused by mechanical failure. Cylinder compression and oil pressure testing are included in this section.

Engine Noises

Some engine noise is generated during normal operation. A ticking noise or a heavy knocking noise intensifying when accelerating are reasons for concern.

If a worn or damaged component is suspected of causing an engine noise, consider having a professional technician listen to the engine. In many cases, only the trained ear of the technician can determine what component has failed.

Engine repairs can be costly and time consuming. Investigate all noises thoroughly before disassembling the engine.

A broken or loose bracket or fastener can cause a noise that is easily mistaken for an internal engine failure.

Ticking noise

The ticking noise is common when valve adjustment is required, a rocker arm fastener is loose or a valve train component has failed. Adjust the valves or tighten the rocker arm fasteners as described in Chapter Six. Then listen to the engine.

A ticking noise can also result from a damaged piston. Inspect the spark plugs for damage or aluminum deposits (**Figure 103**). Complete engine disassembly and repair are required if metal deposits are found on the spark plug. Perform a compression test as described in this chapter. Remove the cylinder head and inspect the valves, gaskets, pistons and cylinders if low compression is noted. Cylinder head removal and installation are provided in Chapter Six.

Refer to *Valve Train Failure* in this section for additional information if the spark plugs and compression are good, but the ticking noise persists.

> *CAUTION*
> *Running the engine with an abnormal noise can result in increased damage dramatically increasing the cost of repairs.*

Whirring or squealing noise

A whirring or squealing noise is usually related to a problem with main or connecting rod bearings. Often, the noise becomes louder if the throttle is abruptly reduced to idle from a higher speed.

Sometimes the cylinder creating the noise can be identified using a mechanic's stethoscope. Touch the tip of the probe to the engine while listening. Compare the noise from one area of the engine, cylinder head or crankcase with the noise from the same area but different cylinder. A noise common to one cylinder only indicates a problem with the connecting rod bearing. A noise common to all cylinders indicates a problem with crankshaft main bearings. Test the oil pressure as described in this section to determine whether the noise is caused by insufficient lubrication. Be aware that the accessory drive belts, timing chain or gear, and pulleys can generate considerable noise. Before proceeding with an engine repair, use the stethoscope to make sure the noise is from the engine.

> *WARNING*
> *Use extreme caution when working on or around a running engine. Never wear loose clothing. Take all necessary precautions to make sure no one contacts the pulleys or drive belts. Never allow anyone near the propeller or propeller shaft while the engine is running.*

Knocking noise

Use a mechanic's stethoscope to determine whether the noise is emanating from the engine or elsewhere. The noise will be more pronounced in the crankcase area if a problem exists in the crankshaft and connecting rods. Special insulated pliers allowing spark plug wire removal while running the engine are available. The noise might lessen when the spark plug wire is removed from the suspected cylinder. This procedure is difficult to do and can result in damage to the electrical system. Ground the spark plug promptly to reduce the chance of damage to the ignition system. Another method of isolating the cylinder is to remove one spark plug wire and attach it to an engine ground. Start the engine and listen to the noise. Install the spark lead and repeat the process for another cylinder. If the noise is less when one lead is grounded when compared with another, that cylinder is suspect. The stethoscope method of isolating cylinders is more effective for an amateur technician.

Always perform an oil pressure test as described in this section if a knocking noise is detected. Knocking noise combined with low or unstable oil pressure generally indicate a problem with the crankshaft main and/or connecting rod bearings.

Bearing failure causes metal particles to accumulate in the oil pan. These particles are picked up by the oil pump where they are deposited in the oil filter. Inspect the oil filter if bearing failure is suspected. Remove the filter as described in Chapter Three. Cut open the filter and inspect the filter element. Bearing failure is likely if a significant amount of metal debris is found.

Lubrication System Failure

A lubrication system failure can result in catastrophic engine failure. Lubrication system failure leads to scuffed pistons (**Figure 104**), excessive wear of valve train components (**Figure 105**) and eventual engine failure.

Failure of the lubrication system results from the following common causes:
1. Incorrect oil level.
2. Oil leakage or high oil consumption.
3. Using contaminated, diluted or the wrong type of oil.
4. Failure of the oil pump or pump drive system.

> *CAUTION*
> *Damage can occur in a matter of seconds if the lubrication system fails. To help prevent serious engine damage, slow down and stop the engine at once if low oil pressure is indicated by the warning system.*

Incorrect oil level

Incorrect oil level can result from improperly filling the engine or improperly checking the engine oil level.

If the oil level is too high, the crankshaft and other components can agitate the oil and cause the formation of bubbles or foam. This foamy oil can cause a drop in oil pressure and lead to activation of the low oil pressure

warning system. In some cases, the oil pressure can remain above the low oil pressure activation point, yet the engine will still suffer from inadequate lubrication.

Oil level check and oil filling instructions are provided in Chapter Three.

Oil leakage or high oil consumption

A rapid drop in oil level can result from oil leakage or from high oil consumption. In most cases, oil leakage is easily detected and corrected. Common leakage points are at the rocker arm/valve cover area, oil filter mounting surface, fuel pump mounting surface or oil pan-to-cylinder block mating surfaces. Finding the point of leakage can be difficult. Air flowing around the engine often distributes a thin film of oil on all external surfaces. To locate the point of leakage, carefully clean the engine using a shop towel and degreasing agent. Run the engine until it reaches operating temperature. Turn the engine off and then wipe a white towel across all surfaces of the engine. Oil leakage is readily detected on the towel when the leakage point is contacted. Pinholes or casting flows can cause leakage to occur at other points on the engine. Many times, simply tightening fasteners corrects oil leakage. Replace gaskets, seals or other affected components if the leakage continues.

All engines consume some oil while running. Some of the oil lubricating the cylinders and valves is drawn into the combustion chamber and subsequently burned. Oil consumption rates vary by model, condition of the engine and how the engine is used. Engines with high operating hours or engines with worn internal components generally burn much more oil than new or low-hour engines. Damage to the pistons and cylinders from detonation or preignition can cause increased oil consumption. New or recently rebuilt engines generally consume oil during the break-in period. After the break-in period, the oil consumption should drop to a normal level.

A typical symptom of excessive oil consumption is blue smoke coming from the exhaust during hard acceleration or high-speed operation. Inspection of the spark plugs usually reveals fouling or an oily film on the spark plug electrodes.

Perform a compression test if excessive smoke or an oil-fouled plug is noted. Worn or damaged components will generally cause a low compression reading. Compression test instructions are provided in this section.

Contaminated, diluted or wrong type of oil

Contaminants enter the engine oil during normal operation. Dirt or dust enters the engine along with the air used during normal operation. Other particles form during the combustion process. Dirt, dust and other particles are captured by the lubricating oil and circulated throughout the engine. Most of the larger particles are captured in the oil filter. Smaller particles circulate through the engine with the lubricating oil. Frequent oil changes flush these particles from the oil before they reach high concentrations. High concentrations of these particles cause increased wear of internal engine components.

During normal operation, unburned fuel and water vapor accumulate in the lubricating oil. Oil also absorbs heat from the engine during operation. This heating causes the unburned fuel and water to evaporate from the oil and form crankcase vapor. The crankcase ventilation system returns the vapor to the combustion chamber where it burns or exits through the exhaust.

A faulty fuel system can dramatically increase the amount of unburned fuel in the oil. High levels of unburned fuel might not evaporate quickly enough to prevent oil dilution.

Failure to reach normal engine operating temperature prevents the fuel and water vapor from evaporating. Failure to reach normal operating temperature is generally caused by a faulty or improperly installed thermostat.

Wipe a sample of the oil from the dipstick between your finger and thumb. Compare the thickness of the oil with a sample of new oil. Smell the oil. Then check for a white or light color residue.

A very thin feel, fuel smell in the oil or white residue indicates oil dilution. If oil dilution is indicated, test the cooling and fuel systems as described in this chapter.

Using the wrong grade, type or weight of oil can lead to increased engine wear and/or complete engine failure. Poor-quality oil might not provide the level of protection required by the engine. Using the wrong type of oil usually leads to serious engine damage. Never use two-stroke outboard oil in a four-stroke engine. Using the improper weight of oil can also prevent correct oil circulation during cold-engine operation or allow excessive thinning of the oil at higher temperatures. Oil recommendations are provided in Chapter Three.

Failure of the oil pump system

Failure of the lubrication system results in rapid wear of internal components and eventual engine seizure. Causes of oil pump system failure include:
1. Worn, damaged or broken oil pump components.
2. Worn or damaged crankshaft or connecting rod bearings.
3. A blocked, damaged or loose oil pickup tube or screen.
4. A faulty or stuck oil pressure relief valve.

Failure of the lubrication system causes a loss of oil pressure and activation of the low oil pressure warning system. Continued operation results in rapid wear of internal components followed by eventual engine seizure. Check the oil pressure as described in this section if the warning system activates and low oil level is ruled out as the cause.

Detonation

Detonation damage is the result of the heat and pressure in the combustion chamber becoming too great for the fuel that is used. Fuel normally burns a controlled rate during normal combustion. The fuel explodes violently if the heat and pressure become too high. These violent explosions in the combustion chamber cause serious damage to internal engine components. The piston typically suffers the brunt of the damage. Detonation usually occurs only at higher engine speeds or during heavy acceleration. When detonation is occurring, a pinging noise emanates from the engine accompanied by a loss of power. Inspect the spark plug if detonation damage is suspected. Aluminum deposits (**Figure 103**) or a melted electrode (**Figure 106**) indicate probable detonation damage. Perform a compression test to determine the extent of damage to the engine. Repair the engine if low compression is indicated. Correct the causes of detonation to prevent additional engine damage or repeat failures.

Conditions that promote detonation include:
1. Using a fuel with too low of an octane rating.
2. Excessive carbon deposits in the combustion chamber.
3. Overheating of the engine.
4. Using the incorrect propeller or overloading the engine.
5. Excessively lean fuel/air mixture.

6. Overadvanced ignition timing.

Preignition

Preignition is caused by a glowing object inside the combustion chamber causing early ignition. The flame from the early ignition collides with the flame front initiated by the spark plug. A violet explosion occurs as these flame fronts collide. The piston suffers the brunt of the damage caused by this explosion. Inspect the spark plug and perform a compression test if preignition is suspected. Aluminum deposits on the spark plugs are likely when preignition has occurred. Repair the engine if low compression is revealed. Correct the causes of preignition to prevent additional engine damage or repeat failures.

Conditions that promote preignition include:
1. Excessive carbon deposits in the combustion chamber.
2. Using the wrong heat range of spark plug (too hot).
3. Engine overheating.

Engine Seizure

Engine seizure results from failure of internal engine components. This can occur at any engine speed. Should the failure occur at higher engine speeds, the engine might abruptly stop or gradually slow down and stall. Typically, the seizure is caused by a crankshaft, connecting rod or piston failure. Although not as common, engine seizure also occurs from a failure of the valve train components. Engine seizure prevents the electric starter from cranking the engine. Major repair is almost always required when engine seizure occurs.

Failure of the transmission or seizure of the V-drive unit or propeller shaft can also prevent flywheel rotation. Before suspecting the engine, inspect the transmission fluid as described in this chapter. Refer to *Drive System*. Water in the cylinders can also cause engine seizure. The water will cause a hydraulic lock on the piston as it comes up on the compression stroke. Remove the spark plugs to the check for this condition.

Water Entering the Cylinder

Water can enter the cylinder in a number of ways including:

1. Water entering the carburetor or throttle body openings.
2. Shutting the engine off at higher engine speeds.
3. Inadequate exhaust elbow height.
4. Engine dieseling.
5. Leaking cylinder head gaskets.
6. Cracked cylinder head.
7. Leaking water jacket in cylinder head.
8. Leaking exhaust manifold(s).
9. Leaking water jacket in the cylinder block.
10. Leaking water jacket in the intake manifold.

CAUTION
Never operate the engine without first providing cooling water. Use a flush device or operate the engine under actual conditions (boat in the water). Operating the engine without providing adequate cooling water will quickly damage the seawater pump and can result in serious engine damage.

The typical symptom is rough running, especially at idle. The engine might run correctly at higher speed because a small amount of water might not prevent normal combustion at higher speeds. If water enters the cylinders, remove the spark plugs and ground the spark plug leads. Crank over the engine to remove residual water from the cylinders. Change the engine oil. Then start the engine and operate a minimum of 20 minutes to evaporate residual water from the oil passages.

Water entering the carburetor or throttle body opening

The presence of water in the throttle body opening indicates water is entering the cylinders through these means. This occurs from submersion, a leaking engine cover or subjecting the engine to a considerable amount of water spray. Water in the fuel allows water to enter along with the fuel and incoming air. The heavier, less volatile water usually settles in the intake manifold or other passages. Inspect the fuel for water as described in this chapter. Refer to *Inspecting the Fuel*.

Shutting off the engine at higher engine speeds

Unless necessary to prevent an accident, never shut off the engine at speeds higher than idle. High vacuum forms in the intake manifold under this circumstance. This vacuum is applied to the exhaust passages due to camshaft overlap. High vacuum in the exhaust passages causes water in the exhaust system to flow into the cylinders. Serious engine damage can occur in this event.

Inadequate exhaust elbow height

The top of the exhaust elbow must extend a minimum of 15 in. (381 mm) above the water line. Otherwise, water can siphon into the engine through the exhaust system. Measure the distance with the boat in the water under normal loading and with a full fuel tank(s). Install exhaust riser kits if the water line-to-exhaust elbow is less than the minimum specification.

Engine dieseling

Dieseling is a condition in which the engine runs after the ignition is turned OFF. Dieseling occurs if the fuel in the combustion chamber ignites from a source other than the spark plugs. It can be caused by excessive engine temperature, excessive combustion chamber deposits, poor-quality fuel and improper carburetor adjustment. Excessive idle speed is a primary cause for dieseling. The engine might run for several seconds after the ignition is turned OFF and might actually run backwards briefly at the end of the event. The backward engine rotation will draw water into the engine from the exhaust system. If sufficient water enters the engine, it will experience hydraulic lock. If dieseling occurs, check the cooling system, spark plug and carburetor adjustments.

Leaking cylinder head gasket or cracked/ leaking cylinder head water jacket

A leaking cylinder head gasket results from failure of the gasket that seals the cylinder head to the cylinder block. Damage to the gasket is likely if the engine has overheated. A cracked cylinder head is usually caused by expansion as water freezes in the cylinder head. A crack can also occur from rapid expansion and contraction that occurs from overheating. A leaking cylinder head water jacket is usually the result of overheating or corrosion damage. Symptoms of these faults include:

1. Water in the oil.
2. Water entering the cylinder(s).

3. Overheating (particularly at higher engine speeds).

4. Rough running (particularly at lower engine speeds).

5. External water or exhaust leakage at the cylinder head-to-cylinder block mating surfaces.

Perform a compression test if any of these symptoms are noted. Bear in mind that cylinder head gasket leakage is not always verified by a compression test. Slightly lower compression typically is noted on two adjoining cylinders. Only removal and inspection of the gasket and mating surfaces verify a gasket failure.

Remove the cylinder head and inspect the cylinders and piston domes if water is entering the cylinders. Compare the appearance of the affected cylinder with other cylinders in the engine. Cylinders with water intrusion usually have significantly fewer carbon deposits on the piston and cylinders. Rusting or corrosion of the valves, valve seats, cylinders and piston dome is common when this condition occurs. A complete engine repair is required if rusting or pitting is noted on the cylinders or piston domes. Refer to Chapter Seven for cylinder head removal and installation instructions.

Leaking exhaust manifold water jacket

A leaking exhaust manifold allows water to enter the cylinders from the exhaust passages. High-performance four-stroke engines, such as marine engines, have an aggressive camshaft lift, duration and valve overlap. Valve overlap allows reverse exhaust flow (reversion) under certain conditions. Reverse exhaust flow can increase the chance of water entering the cylinders through the exhaust valves if water is present in the exhaust passages. Leaking exhaust elbow gaskets allow water into the exhaust passages. Repair leaking gaskets if external leakage is evident at the mating surfaces. Removal and installation of the exhaust system components are described in Chapter Eight.

Leaking cylinder block water jacket

Leakage from the cylinder block water jacket can allow water to enter the cylinders or oil. Water leaking from the cylinder block water jackets is almost always due to cracks caused by freezing the water in the jacket. Porosity or excessive corrosion damage are other common causes. Leaking water jackets in the cylinder block can be difficult to find. Casting flaws, pinholes and cracks might or might not be visible. Replace the cylinder block if water is entering the cylinder, all other causes are ruled out and no visible defects in the gaskets or mating surface can be

found. Continued operation with water intrusion results in eventual engine failure.

Leaking intake manifold water jacket

Failure of the intake manifold water jacket can allow water to enter the cylinder(s) or oil. This failure is almost always due to gasket failure at the cylinder head-to-intake manifold mating surfaces. Failure of the gasket is common after the engine has overheated. Remove the intake manifold as described in Chapter Seven. Inspect the gasket if water is entering the cylinder(s) or oil and other causes are ruled out.

Water Entering the Oil

Normal condensation causes water to form in the oil. This is especially common if the engine is operated in cool and humid environments. Regular oil changes remove normal amounts of water before the engine suffers serious harm. Excessive amounts of water will dilute the oil and cause serious engine damage. Symptoms of excessive water in the oil include:

1. Water on the dipstick.

2. Water in oil drained from the crankcase.

3. A light color or milky oil appearance.

Excessive amounts of water in the crankcase are generally caused by water entering the cylinders; leaking water jackets in the cylinder block, cylinder heads or intake manifold; or internal leakage in the oil cooler.

If the described symptoms occur, check for water entering the cylinders as described in this section. If water is not entering the cylinders, remove the oil cooler (on models so equipped) as described in Chapter Eight. Have the oil cooler pressure tested at a radiator repair shop. If the cooler is not leaking, check for a leaking intake manifold. Replace the cylinder block if the intake manifold is not leaking and all other causes are ruled out.

Valve Train Failure

Failure of the valve train can cause low compression, excessive engine noise or an inability to start the engine. Valve train components include the camshaft, lifters, timing gear, timing chain, valves, valve springs and the cylinder head. This section describes common causes of valve train failure.

Timing chain, sprocket or gear failure

> *CAUTION*
> *Attempts to start the engine with improper valve timing or a failed timing gear, sprocket or chain can lead to damage of valves, pistons and other engine components.*

Failure of the timing components will result in an inability to start the engine, rough running or poor performance.

An excessively worn timing chain or sprockets might allow the chain to jump over one or more of the teeth on the sprockets. This results in improper valve timing causing rough operation and poor performance. Complete failure of the timing chain or sprocket prevents camshaft rotation. If failure of the sprocket or chain is suspected of causing a no-start condition, check for distributor rotation as described in this chapter. Refer to *Basic Ignition System Troubleshooting*.

Sticking, worn or damaged valves

Sticking, worn or damaged valves cause low compression, rough operation, poor performance and/or backfiring.

Corrosion or heavy carbon deposits can cause valves to stick in the open position. Valves can become bent or damaged from contacting the top of the piston or foreign objects in the combustion chamber.

Any of these conditions result in an inability to fully close the affected valve. Rough operation at lower engine speed is common with a sticking, worn or damaged valve. Backfiring occurs when a leaking valve allows the burning fuel to enter the intake manifold or exhaust passages. Backfiring or a popping noise coming from the intake manifold usually is the result of a stuck, worn or damaged intake valve. Backfiring or a popping noise coming from the exhaust is usually the result of a stuck, worn or damaged exhaust valve.

Perform a compression test if any the listed symptoms are noted.

Improper valve adjustment can cause the same symptoms as sticking, worn or damaged valves. Check the valve adjustment before disassembling the engine. Valve adjustment is described in Chapter Six.

If backfiring is noted, run the engine with one spark plug wire at a time grounded. The backfire will stop when the spark plug wire is grounded on the affected cylinder. Remove the cylinder head and inspect the valves if backfiring and low compression are evident on the same cylinder and improper valve adjustment is ruled out.

Sticking valves are often the result of improper long-term storage, water entering the cylinders or submersion of the engine. Using the wrong type of oil, improper fuel system operation or lugging the engine all contribute to increased deposits or wear of the valve and seat area.

Oil recommendations are provided in Chapter Three. Prevent lugging by selecting the correct propeller for the given engine-and-boat combination. Refer to Chapter One for propeller selection.

Worn valve guides

Worn valve guides prevent consistent closing of the valves. A compression test usually does not generally verify an excessively worn valve guide because the valve tends to seat normally at cranking speed. Continued operation with worn valve guides will cause the valve seats to wear unevenly and eventually cause low compression and poor performance.

High oil consumption, fouled spark plugs and blue exhaust smoke during deceleration are typical symptoms of excessively worn valve guides and valve stem seals. Only disassembly of the cylinder head and subsequent measurement can confirm excessively worn valve guides. Refer to Chapter Seven.

Camshaft failure

Failure of the camshaft lobes (**Figure 105**) can cause the same symptoms as a sticking or damaged valve. Excessively worn camshaft lobes are generally the result of improper valve adjustment, using the incorrect type, grade or weight of oil, a high number of operating hours and/or oil dilution. Refer to *Lubrication System Failure*, in this section, for additional information on oil dilution. Check for excessively worn camshaft lobes by measuring the camshaft lobe lift as described in Chapter Six.

Oil Pressure Test

An oil pressure gauge, T-fitting adapter and a shop tachometer are required to perform an oil pressure test. This test must be performed under actual operating conditions.

Test the oil pressure at the threaded opening for the oil pressure sender (**Figure 107**). Refer to *Oil Pressure Sender Replacement* in Chapter Nine to locate the sender.

Use a T-fitting adapter with the same threads as the oil pressure sender on the male and female ends. One of the female ends must have the same thread size and pitch as the oil pressure gauge. Oil pressure gauges and threaded adapters are available from most automotive parts stores. Securely tighten the adapters before running the engine.

> *WARNING*
> *Safely performing on-water testing or adjustments requires two people: one person to operate the boat and the other to monitor the gauges or test equipment and make necessary adjustments. All personnel must remain seated inside the boat at all times. Do not lean over the transom while the boat is underway. Use extensions to allow all gauges and test equipment to be located in normal seating areas.*

Test the oil pressure as follows:

1. Run the engine until it reaches normal operating temperature.

2. Remove the oil pressure sender as described in Chapter Nine.

3. Install the male end of the adapter into the oil pressure sender opening (**Figure 108**). Securely tighten the adapter.

4. Install the oil pressure sender into one of the female openings of the adapter (**Figure 108**). Securely tighten the oil pressure sender.

5. Connect the wire connector to the oil pressure sender to allow verification of the dash-mounted oil pressure gauge during testing.

6. Install the threaded adapter of the oil pressure gauge (**Figure 108**) into the remaining female opening of the adapter. Securely tighten all fittings. Secure the oil pressure gauge hose to prevent it from contacting any moving components.

7. Following the manufacturer's instructions, attach the shop tachometer to the engine.

8. Start the engine and immediately check for and correct any oil leakage at the gauge and adapter fittings.

9. Shift the engine into FORWARD. Observe the oil pressure gauge while an assistant operates the engine in FORWARD at idle speed. Stop the engine *immediately* if the gauge indicates no oil pressure. The gauge must indicate a minimum of 4 psi (28 kPa) at idle speed. Note the pressure while the assistant advances the throttle 2000 rpm. The gauge must indicate 30-60 psi (207-414 kPa) oil pressure with the engine at normal operating temperature. A slightly higher reading might be indicated if the engine is cool. Compare the actual engine oil pressure with the pressure displayed on the dash-mounted oil pressure gauge. A faulty sender, gauge or wiring is evident if the readings are substantially different. Refer to the following:

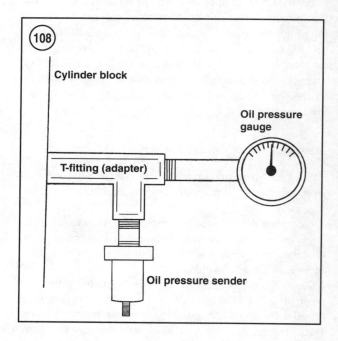

a. If the oil pressure exceeds 60 psi (414 kPa) at idle speed, the engine is not reaching normal operating temperature, or the oil pressure relief valve is stuck. Verify the engine temperature as described in this chapter. Refer to *Cooling System Troubleshooting*. Replace the oil pump as described in Chapter Six if the oil pressure at idle exceeds the specification at normal operating temperature.

b. If the oil pressure is less than 4 psi (28 kPa) at idle speed, the engine is running too hot, the oil is too thin or diluted, the oil pump is faulty, or the crankshaft, camshaft or bearings have worn or failed. Verify the engine temperature as described in this chapter. Refer to *Cooling System Troubleshooting*. Inspect the oil for dilution as described in this section. Refer to *Lubrication System Failure*. Replace the oil pump as described in Chapter Six if the en-

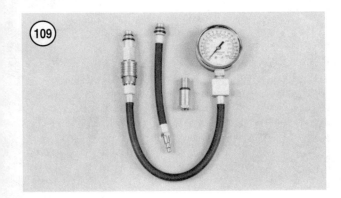

gine is operating at the correct temperature and the oil is not diluted. Faulty bearings, crankshaft or camshaft is evident if the oil pressure is not corrected with the replacement oil pump. Replacement of these components is described in Chapter Six.

c. If the oil pressure exceeds 60 psi (414 kPa) at 2000 rpm, the engine is not reaching normal operating temperature, or the oil pressure relief valve is stuck. Verify the engine temperature as described in this chapter. Refer to *Cooling System Troubleshooting*. Replace the oil pump as described in Chapter Six if the oil pressure at 2000 rpm exceeds the specification at normal operating temperature.

d. If the oil pressure is less than 30 psi (207 kPa) at 2000 rpm, the engine is running too hot, the oil is too thin or diluted, the oil pump is excessively worn, or the engine has worn or failed bearing(s), crankshaft, or camshaft. Verify the engine temperature as described in this chapter. Refer to *Cooling System Troubleshooting*. Inspect the oil for dilution as described in this section. Refer to *Lubrication System Failure*. Replace the oil pump as described in Chapter Six if the engine is operating at the correct temperature and the oil is not diluted. Faulty bearings, crankshaft or camshaft is evident if the oil pressure is not corrected with the replacement oil pump. Replacement of these components is described in Chapter Six.

10. Remove the shop tachometer, oil pressure gauge and adapter. Install the oil pressure sender as described in Chapter Nine.

Compression Test

A good quality compression gauge and adapters (**Figure 109**) are required for accurate compression testing. They are available at automotive part stores and from tool suppliers. A small can of engine oil might also be required.

1. Remove all of the spark plugs as described in Chapter Three. Refer to *Spark plug removal*. Connect the spark plug leads to a suitable engine ground. Activate the lanyard safety switch to further disable the ignition system.

2. Install the compression gauge into the No. 1 spark plug hole. To locate the No. 1 cylinder, refer to the following:

a. On models using an in-line transmission, the drive belt side of the engine faces the bow (front) of the boat, and the front cylinder on the port bank is the No. 1 cylinder. The front cylinder on the starboard bank is the No. 2 cylinder. Odd-numbered cylinders are on the port cylinder bank, and even-numbered cylinders are on the starboard bank.

b. On models using a V-drive transmission, the drive belt side of the engine faces the stern (rear) of the boat, and the rear cylinder on the starboard bank is the No. 1 cylinder. The rear cylinder on the port bank is the No. 2 cylinder. Odd-numbered cylinders are on the starboard cylinder bank, and even-numbered cylinders are on the port bank.

3. Securely tighten the hose adapter. Position the throttle in the wide-open position during testing.

4. Stay clear of the remaining spark plug openings during testing. Observe the compression gauge and operate the electric starter. Crank the engine a minimum of five revolutions at normal cranking speed. Record the compression reading.

5. Repeat Step 3 and Step 4 for the remaining cylinders. Record all compression readings.

6. Low compression is evident if the compression pressure varies more than 10 percent between cylinders or if any cylinder pressure is less than 100 psi (690 kPa).

7. If low compression is noted, squirt approximately 1 teaspoon of clean engine oil into the suspect cylinder through the spark plug hole. Rotate the engine several revolutions to distribute the oil in the cylinder. Then repeat Step 3 and Step 4.

a. If the compression increases significantly, the piston rings and cylinder are excessively worn.

b. If the compression does not increase, the compression leakage is the result of a worn valve face or seat.

8. Remove the compression gauge. Place the remote control in the idle position.

9. Install the spark plugs as describe in Chapter Three. Refer to *Spark plug installation*. Place the lanyard safety switch in RUN.

DRIVE SYSTEM

Failure of the drive system will cause shifting difficulty, dark, burned or water-contaminated fluid, unusual noise or vibration. This section describes the causes of drive system failure and describes the troubleshooting procedures to pinpoint the cause.

Shifting Difficulty

Shifting difficulty can cause an inability to shift the engine into one or both gears, delayed shifting, shifting into or out of gear without moving the remote control lever or excessive shifting effort.

Inability to shift into gear or delayed shifting

Inability to shift into gear or delayed shifting is generally caused by improper shift cable adjustment, a faulty shift cable or failure of internal transmission components. To isolate the cause, first inspect the transmission fluid level as described in Chapter Three. Excessively high or too low fluid levels will allow air to enter the hydraulic passages and cause low fluid pressure. The resulting low fluid pressure will cause no shifting or delayed shifting. Inspect a sample of the transmission fluid as described in this section.

If the fluid level is correct, run the engine using a flush device or with the boat in the water until it reaches normal operating temperature. If the boat is in the water, make sure it is in an area clear of other boats, obstacles or other hazards. Stop the engine and disconnect the shift cable from the shift lever (**Figure 110**). Move the shift lever on the transmission to NEUTRAL. Have an assistant start the engine and run at idle speed. Manually shift the transmission into FORWARD and REVERSE. Adjust or replace the cable if the transmission shifts properly only when manually moving the lever. Remove the transmission as described in Chapter Ten and have it rebuilt by a marine transmission repair facility if it cannot be shifted into gear or the shift is delayed while manually moving the lever. Reconnect the shift cable as described in Chapter Five. Refer to *Shift Cable Adjustment.*

Shifting into or out of gear without moving the remote control lever

Shifting into or out of gear without moving the control lever is generally caused by improper shift cable adjustment, a faulty shift cable or failure of internal transmission components. If these symptoms are evident, first

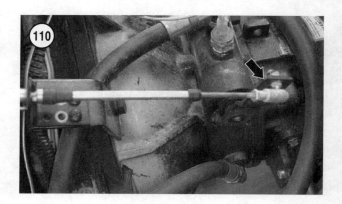

inspect the transmission fluid level as described in Chapter Three.

To isolate the cause, first adjust the shift cable as described in Chapter Five. Run the engine and check for normal transmission operation. If the boat is stored in the water, make sure it is in an area clear of other boats, obstacles or other hazards before starting the engine. If adjusting the shift cable does not correct the shifting problem, the control valve in the transmission is probably defective. Remove the transmission, as described in Chapter Ten and have it rebuilt by a marine transmission repair facility. Reconnect the shift cable as described in Chapter Five. Refer to *Shift Cable Adjustment.*

Excessive shifting effort

Excessive shifting effort is generally caused by a damaged or worn shift cable, faulty remote control or transmission shift lever. To determine which, first disconnect the battery cables to prevent accidental starting. Then disconnect the shift cable from the shift lever (**Figure 110**).

Move the transmission shift lever to check for binding. The transmission shift lever should move without binding, and the ball and spring behind the lever must provide a positive detent for each gear position. If the lever binds or the detent is not positive, remove the lever and clean dirt, corrosion or other contaminants from the ball and spring. Apply a light coat of marine grease to the ball, spring and detent stops in the lever. Install the lever and securely tighten the retaining bolt. If the binding and positive gear detent are not corrected, the fault is probably within the transmission control valve. Have the transmission repaired by a marine transmission repair facility.

If the transmission lever is moving correctly, move the remote control lever to FORWARD, NEUTRAL and then REVERSE. If binding or stiffness is evident, replace the shift cable as described in Chapter Twelve. Disassemble, repair and lubricate the remote control if the binding condition is not corrected with the replacement cable. Reconnect the shift cable as described in Chapter Five. Refer to *Shift Cable Adjustment*.

Inspecting the Transmission Fluid

Remove the dipstick as described in Chapter Three. Refer to *Checking the Transmission Fluid Level*. Inspect the fluid on the dipstick for dark color, a burning odor, water contamination or a milky appearance.

Dark coloration and burned odor

Failure of the transmission will almost always cause the transmission fluid to have a distinct burned odor and a dark coloration. If uncertain, compare a sample of the transmission fluid with a sample of new fluid. A burned odor with dark coloration indicates the transmission fluid has overheated due to failure of the clutch disc, operating the transmission at higher throttle settings in REVERSE, improper shift cable adjustment or failure of other internal transmission components. If the fluid smells burned along with the dark coloration, the transmission probably has suffered internal damage and must be rebuilt. Remove the transmission as described in Chapter Ten and have it repaired by a marine transmission repair facility.

Water-contaminated fluid or a milky appearance

Water contamination or a milky appearance indicates water has mixed with the transmission fluid. Water contaminates the fluid from two basic sources: an internal leak in the transmission fluid cooler or water entering the transmission housing through the vent opening.

To isolate the fault, first remove the transmission fluid cooler as described in Chapter Eight. Have the cooler pressure tested at a radiator repair facility. If the cooler is good, the water entered the transmission from the vent opening due to a high water level in the engine compartment or from water dripping onto the transmission near the vent opening. Correct the leak that allowed high water in the engine compartment or the source of dripping. Then change the transmission fluid as described in Chapter Three. Start the engine and operate for approximately 30 minutes at idle speed. Repeatedly cycle the transmission through all three gear positions to distribute the fresh fluid through all internal passages. Stop the engine. Change the transmission fluid to remove residual moisture.

Unusual Drive System Noise

Normal drive system noise is barely noticeable over normal engine noise. A rough growling, grinding, knocking or loud high-pitched whine is a reason for concern. These noises usually indicate failure of bearings, gears or other drive system components. If any unusual noise is present, inspect the transmission fluid as described in this section.

Knocking noise

A knocking noise is generally caused by low idle speed, a damaged propeller, bent propeller shaft, improper engine alignment, corroded or damaged drive plate spring, or failure of the transmission.

First check and adjust the idle speed as described in Chapter Five. If correcting the idle speed does not correct the knocking noise, inspect the propeller for bent or damaged blades. Then inspect the propeller shaft for bending as described in Chapter Ten.

Inspect the transmission fluid as described in this section. Check the engine alignment as described in Chapter Six. If the knocking noise is not corrected by aligning the engine, remove the transmission as described in Chapter Ten and inspect the drive plate for corroded or broken springs. A defective drive plate will usually cause a knocking noise only at lower engine speeds.

Growling or grinding noise

A grinding noise indicates failure of gears, bearings or shafts in the transmission or failure of the propeller shaft support strut bearing. Remove the bolts that secure the transmission output flange to the propeller shaft flange. Rotate the propeller shaft to check for binding or excessive looseness. Inspect the transmission fluid as described in this section. Failure of internal components will likely distribute metal particles throughout the transmission. If in question, insert a magnet firmly attached to an extension into the transmission dipstick opening until it reaches the bottom of the fluid reservoir. Withdraw the magnet and check for metal contamination. If large metal particles are found on the magnet, the transmission probably has suffered internal damage and must be rebuilt. Remove the transmission as described in Chapter Ten and have it repaired by a marine transmission repair facility.

High-pitched whine

During normal operation, the transmission generates a high-pitched whine. The whine is most prevalent when a unirotational transmission is shifted into REVERSE. The REVERSE whine, though audible, is a normal occurrence and does not indicate a problem with the transmission. A loud high-pitched whine normally indicates a faulty bearing, improper bearing preload or misaligned gears. To check for internal damage, first inspect the transmission fluid as described in this section. Failure of internal components will usually distribute metal particles throughout the transmission. If uncertain, insert a magnet firmly attached to an extension into the transmission dipstick opening until it reaches the bottom of the fluid reservoir. Withdraw the magnet and check for metal contamination. If large metal particles are found on the magnet, the transmission probably has suffered internal damage and must be rebuilt. Remove the transmission as described in Chapter Ten and have it repaired by a marine transmission repair facility.

Vibration

Never operate the engine if excessive vibration is present. The vibration places excessive stress on gears, bearings, shafts and other engine components. Operating the engine with excessive vibration can seriously compromise the durability of the entire drive system.

Excessive vibration is usually due to improper engine alignment, a damaged propeller or bent propeller shaft. First check and correct the engine alignment as described in Chapter Six. If the vibration is not corrected with engine alignment, inspect the propeller for bent or damaged blades. Then inspect the propeller shaft for bending as described in Chapter Ten. Have the propeller(s) checked at a propeller repair shop. The propeller can appear to be in perfect condition but still be unbalanced. Another option is simply to try a different propeller.

Table 1 STARTING SYSTEM TROUBLESHOOTING

Symptom	Possible causes	Corrective action
Starter does not operate	Engine not in neutral	Shift into neutral
	Weak or discharged battery	Charge and test the battery (Chapter Nine)
	Loose battery cable at starter	Tighten battery cable terminal
	Dirty or corroded battery terminals	Thoroughly clean battery terminals
	Faulty neutral start switch	Test neutral start switch
	Faulty key switch	Test key switch
	Faulty starter solenoid	Test the starter solenoid
	Faulty starter relay	Test starter relay
	Faulty slave solenoid	Test slave solenoid
	Loose or dirty wire connection	Clean and tighten starter wire connections
	Faulty electric starter	Test starter motor cranking voltage
	Faulty instrument harness wiring	Check for open or shorted wiring
	Faulty engine wiring harness	Check for open or shorted wiring
	Faulty instrument harness plug	Check for faulty terminals in plug
Starter turns slowly	Weak or discharged battery	Charge and test the battery (Chapter Nine)
	Dirty or corroded battery terminals	Thoroughly clean battery terminals
	Loose or dirty wire connections	Clean and tighten starter wire connections
	Engine is in gear	Adjust shift cable (Chapter Five)
	Faulty electric starter	Test starter motor cranking voltage
	Internal engine damage	Check engine compression
	Failed drive system component	Inspect transmission and V-drive fluid
Starter engages flywheel but does not turn	Weak or discharged battery	Charge and test the battery (Chapter Nine)
	Dirty or corroded battery terminals	Thoroughly clean battery terminals
	Loose or dirty wire connections	Clean and tighten starter wire connections
	Water in the cylinder	Inspect spark plug for water contamination
	Oil in the cylinder	Inspect spark plugs for oil contamination
	Damaged starter pinion gear	Inspect starter pinion gear
	Damaged flywheel gear teeth	Inspect flywheel gear teeth
	Faulty electric starter	Test starter motor cranking voltage
	Seized engine	Check engine for damage
	Failed drive system component	Inspect transmission and V-drive fluid
	Improper valve timing or adjustment	Check valve timing and adjustment

(continued)

Table 1 STARTING SYSTEM TROUBLESHOOTING (continued)

Symptom	Possible causes	Corrective action
Noisy starter operation	Dirty or dry starter pinion gear	Repair starter motor (Chapter Nine)
	Damaged starter pinion gear teeth	Repair starter motor (Chapter Nine)
	Damaged or corroded flywheel gear	Inspect flywheel drive gear teeth
	Loose starter mounting bolt	Tighten starter mounting bolt
	Worn or dry starter bearings	Repair starter motor (Chapter Nine)
Starter operates in forward or reverse gear	Faulty neutral start switch	Test neutral start switch
	Improper wiring	Check wiring to neutral start switch
Starter operates without turning key switch	Faulty key switch	Test key switch
	Faulty starter relay	Test starter relay
	Faulty slave solenoid	Test slave solenoid
	Faulty starter solenoid	Test starter solenoid
	Loose wiring at starter terminals	Check and correct the wiring
	Faulty instrument harness wiring	Check for open or shorted wiring
	Faulty engine wiring harness	Check for open or shorted wiring
	Faulty instrument harness plug	Check for faulty terminals in plug

Table 2 IGNITION SYSTEM TROUBLESHOOTING

Symptom	Possible causes	Corrective action
Engine will not start	Lanyard switch activated	Check lanyard switch position
	No spark at plugs	Check for spark at spark plug leads
	Dirty contact points	Clean and adjust contact points (Chapter Three)
	Improperly adjusted contact points	Adjust contact points (Chapter Three)
	Faulty condenser	Replace condenser (Chapter Three)
	Faulty distributor rotor	Inspect or replace rotor (Chapter Nine)
	Faulty lanyard switch	Test lanyard switch
	Shorted tachometer	Check for shorted tachometer
	Distributor not rotating	Check for distributor rotation
	Faulty tachometer amplifier	Test the tachometer amplifier
	Faulty EFI system relay	Test EFI system relay
	Low voltage supply to system	Check battery voltage to system
	Low voltage supply to system	Perform ignition system voltage test
	Low voltage supply to system	Troubleshoot ignition system
	Faulty crankshaft position sensor	Replace the sensor (Chapter Nine)
	Faulty ignition module	Troubleshoot ignition system
	Faulty pickup coil	Test pickup coil
	Fouled spark plugs	Check or replace spark plug(s)
	Faulty ignition coil	Troubleshoot ignition system
	Faulty engine control unit (ECU)	Check for diagnostic trouble codes
Stalls or runs rough at idle	No spark at plugs	Check for spark at spark plug leads
	Dirty contact points	Clean and adjust contact points (Chapter Three)
	Improperly adjusted contact points	Adjust contact points (Chapter Three)
	Faulty condenser	Replace condenser (Chapter Three)
	Fouled spark plug(s)	Check or replace spark plug(s)
	Faulty distributor rotor	Inspect or replace rotor (Chapter Nine)
	Faulty distributor cap	Inspect or replace rotor (Chapter Nine)
	Faulty spark plug wires	Inspect spark plug wires
	Low voltage supply to system	Troubleshoot ignition system

(continued)

Table 2 IGNITION SYSTEM TROUBLESHOOTING (continued)

Symptom	Possible causes	Corrective action
Stalls or runs rough at idle (continued)	Faulty lanyard switch	Test lanyard switch
	Shorted tachometer	Check for shorted tachometer
	Faulty tachometer amplifier	Test the tachometer amplifier
	Faulty ignition coil	Troubleshoot ignition system
Idle speed too high	Incorrect ignition timing	Check and adjust ignition timing (Chapter Five)
	Incorrect sensor-to-sender air gap	Refer to *Ignition module replacement* (Chapter Nine)
	Faulty engine temperature sender	Check for diagnostic trouble codes
	Faulty throttle position sensor	Check for diagnostic trouble codes
Idle speed too low	Incorrect ignition timing	Check and adjust ignition timing (Chapter Five)
	Incorrect sensor-to-sender air gap	Refer to *Ignition module replacement* (Chapter Nine)
Misfire or poor high-speed performance	No spark at plugs	Check for spark at spark plug leads
	Dirty contact points	Clean and adjust contact points (Chapter Three)
	Improperly adjusted contact points	Adjust contact points (Chapter Three)
	Faulty condenser	Replace condenser (Chapter Three)
	Incorrect ignition timing	Check and adjust ignition timing (Chapter Five)
	Incorrect sensor-to-sender air gap	Refer to *Ignition module replacement* (Chapter Nine)
	Engine reaching rev limit	Check full speed engine rpm
	Fouled spark plug(s)	Inspect or replace spark plug(s)
	Faulty distributor rotor	Inspect or replace rotor (Chapter Nine)
	Faulty distributor cap	Inspect or replace rotor (Chapter Nine)
	Faulty spark plug wires	Inspect spark plug wires
	Low voltage supply to system	Troubleshoot ignition system
	Faulty lanyard switch	Test lanyard switch
	Shorted tachometer	Check for shorted tachometer
	Faulty tachometer amplifier	Test the tachometer amplifier
	Faulty ignition coil	Troubleshoot ignition system

Table 3 FUEL SYSTEM TROUBLESHOOTING

Symptom	Possible causes	Corrective action
Engine will not start	Plugged fuel tank vent	Check the fuel tank vent
	Old or contaminated fuel	Inspect the fuel
	Air or fuel leaks in hose fittings	Inspect the hoses and fitting
	Restricted fuel supply	Check for restricted fuel supply
	Blocked fuel filter	Inspect the fuel filters (Chapter Seven)
	Faulty mechanical fuel pump	Test the mechanical fuel pump
	Faulty low-pressure electric pump	Test the low-pressure electric pump
	Faulty high-pressure electric pump*	Test the fuel pressure
	Faulty EFI system relay*	Test the EFI system relay
	Flooding carburetor	Check for flooding carburetor
	Choke valve malfunction	Check the choke valve operation
	Fuel injectors not operating*	Check for fuel injector operation
	Faulty engine temperature sensor*	Test the engine temperature sensor
	Stuck carburetor inlet needle	Repair the carburetor (Chapter Seven)
	Improper float level adjustment	Repair the carburetor (Chapter Seven)
	Blocked carburetor passages	Repair the carburetor (Chapter Seven)
	Faulty accelerator pump	Repair the carburetor (Chapter Seven)

(continued)

Table 3 FUEL SYSTEM TROUBLESHOOTING (continued)

Symptom	Possible causes	Corrective action
Engine will not start (continued)	Faulty EFI sensor*	Check for diagnostic trouble codes
	Faulty idle air control motor (IAC)*	Test the idle air control motor (IAC)
Stalls or runs rough at idle	Improper idle speed adjustment	Adjust idle speed (Chapter Five)
	Old or contaminated fuel	Inspect the fuel
	Plugged fuel tank vent	Check the fuel tank vent
	Blocked carburetor passages	Repair the carburetor (Chapter Seven)
	Faulty idle air control motor (IAC)*	Test the IAC
	Air or fuel leaks in hose fittings	Inspect the hoses and fittings
	Restricted fuel supply	Check for restricted fuel supply
	Blocked fuel filter	Inspect the fuel filters (Chapter Seven)
	Faulty mechanical fuel pump	Test the mechanical fuel pump
	Faulty low-pressure electric pump	Test the low-pressure electric pump
	Faulty high-pressure electric pump*	Test the fuel pressure
	Faulty EFI system relay	Test the EFI system relay
	Flooding carburetor	Check for flooding carburetor
	Choke valve malfunction	Check the choke valve operation
	Faulty engine temperature sensor*	Test the engine temperature sensor
	Sticking carburetor inlet needle	Repair the carburetor (Chapter Seven)
	Improper float level adjustment	Repair the carburetor (Chapter Seven)
	Faulty EFI sensor*	Check for diagnostic trouble codes
	Leaking or blocked fuel injectors*	Check the fuel injectors
Idle speed too high	Improper throttle cable adjustment	Adjust the throttle cable
	Improper idle speed adjustment	Adjust idle speed (Chapter Five)
	Faulty idle air control motor (IAC)*	Test the IAC
	Faulty engine temperature sensor*	Test the engine temperature sensor
	Faulty EFI system sensor*	Check for diagnostic trouble codes
	Faulty throttle position sensor (TPS)	Check the TPS
Hesitation during acceleration	Improper carburetor adjustment	Adjust the carburetor (Chapter Five)
	Faulty accelerator pump	Repair the carburetor (Chapter Seven)
	Faulty throttle position sensor*	Check for diagnostic trouble codes
	Blocked carburetor passages	Repair carburetor (Chapter Seven)
	Improper idle speed adjustment	Adjust idle speed (Chapter Five)
	Old or contaminated fuel	Inspect the fuel
	Plugged fuel tank vent	Check the fuel tank vent
	Air or fuel leaks in hose fittings	Inspect the hoses and fittings
	Restricted fuel supply	Check for restricted fuel supply
	Blocked fuel filter	Inspect the fuel filters (Chapter Seven)
	Faulty mechanical fuel pump	Test the mechanical fuel pump
	Faulty low-pressure electric pump	Test the low-pressure electric pump
	Faulty high-pressure electric pump*	Test the fuel pressure
	Flooding carburetor	Check for flooding carburetor
	Choke valve malfunction	Check the choke valve operation
	Sticking carburetor inlet needle	Repair the carburetor (Chapter Seven)
	Improper float level adjustment	Repair the carburetor (Chapter Seven)
	Faulty EFI system sensor*	Check for diagnostic trouble codes
	Leaking or blocked fuel injectors*	Check the fuel injectors
Misfire or poor high-speed performance	Plugged fuel tank vent	Check the fuel tank vent
	Old or contaminated fuel	Inspect the fuel
	Air or fuel leaks in hose fittings	Inspect the hoses and fittings
	Restricted fuel supply	Check for restricted fuel supply
	Blocked fuel filter	Inspect the fuel filters (Chapter Seven)
	Choke valve malfunction	Check the choke valve operation
	Faulty mechanical fuel pump	Test the mechanical fuel pump

(continued)

Table 3 FUEL SYSTEM TROUBLESHOOTING (continued)

Symptom	Possible causes	Corrective action
Misfire or poor high-speed performance (continued)	Faulty low-pressure electric pump	Test the low-pressure electric pump
	Faulty high-pressure electric pump*	Test the fuel pressure
	Blocked fuel injectors*	Check the fuel injectors
	Flooding carburetor	Check for flooding carburetor
	Sticking carburetor inlet needle	Repair the carburetor (Chapter Seven)
	Improper float level adjustment	Repair the carburetor (Chapter Seven)
	Blocked carburetor passages	Repair the carburetor (Chapter Seven)
	Faulty EFI sensor*	Check for diagnostic trouble codes
Excessive exhaust smoke	Improper carburetor adjustment	Adjust the carburetor (Chapter Five)
	Flooding carburetor	Check for flooding carburetor
	Choke valve malfunction	Check the choke valve operation
	Sticking carburetor inlet needle	Repair the carburetor (Chapter Seven)
	Improper float level adjustment	Repair the carburetor (Chapter Seven)
	Faulty engine temperature sensor*	Test the engine temperature sensor
	Faulty manifold air pressure sensor (MAP)*	Check for diagnostic trouble codes
	Leaking fuel injectors*	Check the fuel injectors
	Fault intake air temperature sensor (IAT)	Test the IAT
	Faulty mechanical fuel pump	Test the mechanical fuel pump
	Faulty low-pressure electric pump	Test the low-pressure electric pump
	Faulty high-pressure electric pump*	Test the fuel pressure
	Faulty EFI sensor*	Check for diagnostic trouble codes

*Applies only to electronic fuel injection (EFI) models.

Table 4 CHARGING SYSTEM TROUBLESHOOTING

Symptom	Possible causes	Corrective action
Low charging output	Loose drive belt	Adjust drive belt tension (Chapter Nine)
	Faulty battery	Charge and test the battery (Chapter Nine)
	Dirty or loose battery cables	Clean and check terminals (Chapter Nine)
	Blown fuse	Check fuses
	Tripped circuit breaker	Check circuit breaker
	Excitation circuit fault	Test the excitation circuit
	Faulty sensing circuit	Test the sensing circuit
	Faulty voltage regulator	Perform alternator output test
	Faulty diode trio	Perform diode trio test
	Faulty alternator	Perform alternator output test
Battery is overcharging	Dirty or loose battery cables	Clean and check terminals (Chapter Nine)
	Faulty sensing circuit	Test the sensing circuit
	Faulty voltage regulator	Perform alternator output test
	Faulty alternator	Perform alternator output test
Battery discharges at rest	Faulty battery	Charge and test the battery (Chapter Nine)
	Shorted boat accessory wiring	Check accessory wiring
	Shorted boat accessory	Check accessories
	Faulty voltage regulator	Perform alternator output test
	Faulty diode trio	Perform diode trio test
	Faulty alternator	Perform alternator output test
	Shorted instrument harness wiring	Check wiring
	Shorted engine harness wiring	Check wiring

(continued)

Table 4 CHARGING SYSTEM TROUBLESHOOTING (continued)

Symptom	Possible causes	Corrective action
Battery is overcharging (continued)	Excitation circuit fault	Test the excitation circuit
	Faulty sensing circuit	Test the sensing circuit

Table 5 POWER STEERING SYSTEM TROUBLESHOOTING

Symptom	Possible causes	Corrective action
Steers hard in both directions	Low fluid level	Check fluid level (Chapter Three)
	Loose drive belt	Adjust belt tension (Chapter Eleven)
	Improper cable installation	Check cable installation (Chapter Eleven)
	Binding cable or helm	Check cable and helm
	Air in system	Bleed the system (Chapter Eleven)
	Faulty pump	Repair pump (Chapter Eleven)
	Faulty actuator	Replace actuator
Steers hard in one direction only	Improper cable installation	Check cable installation (Chapter Eleven)
	Binding cable or helm	Check cable and helm
	Faulty actuator	Replace actuator
Noisy pump	Low fluid level	Check fluid level (Chapter Three)
	Loose drive belt	Adjust belt tension (Chapter Eleven)
	Air in system	Bleed the system (Chapter Eleven)
	Contaminated fluid	Inspect the fluid
	Loose pump	Check the pump mounting (Chapter Eleven)
	Sticking flow control valve	Repair pump (Chapter Eleven)
	Faulty pump	Repair pump (Chapter Eleven)
Noisy pump (only in full turn)	Low fluid level	Check fluid level (Chapter Three)
	Improper cable installation	Check cable installation (Chapter Eleven)
	Steering lever interference	Check lever clearance
Steering wheel jerks while turning	Low fluid level	Check fluid level (Chapter Three)
	Loose drive belt	Adjust belt tension (Chapter Eleven)
	Improper cable installation	Check cable installation (Chapter Eleven)
	Binding cable or helm	Check cable and helm
	Air in system	Bleed the system (Chapter Eleven)
	Faulty pump	Repair pump (Chapter Eleven)
	Faulty actuator	Replace actuator
Steers hard only when turning quickly	Low fluid level	Check fluid level (Chapter Three)
	Loose drive belt	Adjust belt tension (Chapter Eleven)
	Binding cable or helm	Check cable and helm
	Sticking flow control valve	Repair pump (Chapter Eleven)
	Faulty pump	Repair pump (Chapter Eleven)
	Faulty actuator	Replace actuator
Fluid appears milky	Water in system	Inspect fluid and check fluid cooler
	Air in system	Bleed the system (Chapter Eleven)
Losing fluid	External leak	Inspect hoses and fittings
	Leaking fluid cooler	Inspect fluid cooler
Rising fluid level	Leaking fluid cooler	Inspect fluid cooler
Steering wheel creeps or rotates without assistance	Improper cable installation	Check cable installation (Chapter Eleven)
	Faulty actuator	Replace actuator

Table 6 COOLING SYSTEM TROUBLESHOOTING

Symptom	Possible causes	Corrective action
Engine is overheating (all engine speeds)	Faulty seawater pump	Repair the water pump (Chapter Eight)
	Loose seawater pump drive belt	Check the belt tension (Chapter Eight)
	Blocked water inlets	Inspect the water inlets
	Faulty thermostat	Test the thermostat
	Blocked thermostat housing	Inspect thermostat housing (Chapter Eight)
	Blocked power steering fluid cooler	Remove and inspect cooler (Chapter Eight)
	Blocked or collapsed hoses	Inspect hoses (Chapter Eight)
	Blocked oil cooler	Remove and inspect cooler (Chapter Eight)
	Blocked heat exchanger	Inspect heat exchanger (Chapter Three)
	Blocked exhaust elbow	Remove and inspect elbow (Chapter Eight)
	Blocked exhaust manifold	Remove and inspect manifold (Chapter Eight)
	Blown cylinder head gasket	Perform compression test
	Cracked or porous cylinder head	Inspect the oil for milky appearance
		Inspect the spark plugs for water
	Cracked or porous cylinder block	Inspect the oil for milky appearance
		Inspect the spark plugs for water
	Cracked or porous intake manifold	Inspect the oil for milky appearance
		Inspect the spark plugs for water
Engine is overheating (lower speeds only)	Faulty thermostat	Test the thermostat
	Loose seawater pump drive belt	Check the belt tension (Chapter Eight)
	Blocked thermostat housing	Inspect thermostat housing (Chapter Eight)
	Faulty seawater pump	Repair the water pump (Chapter Eight)
	Damaged recirculation pump	Remove and inspect pump (Chapter Eight)
Engine is overheating (higher speeds only)	Faulty seawater pump	Repair the water pump (Chapter Eight)
	Loose seawater pump drive belt	Check the belt tension (Chapter Eight)
	Blocked water inlets in hull fitting	Inspect the water inlets
	Faulty thermostat	Test the thermostat
	Blocked thermostat housing	Inspect thermostat housing (Chapter Eight)
	Blocked power steering fluid cooler	Remove and inspect cooler (Chapter Eight)
	Blocked or collapsed hoses	Inspect hoses (Chapter Eight)
	Blocked oil cooler	Remove and inspect cooler (Chapter Eight)
	Blocked heat exchanger	Inspect heat exchanger (Chapter Three)
	Blocked exhaust elbow	Remove and inspect elbow (Chapter Eight)
	Blocked exhaust manifold	Remove and inspect manifold (Chapter Eight)
	Blown cylinder head gasket	Perform compression test
	Cracked or porous cylinder head	Inspect the oil for milky appearance
		Inspect the spark plugs for water
	Cracked or porous cylinder block	Inspect the oil for milky appearance
		Inspect the spark plugs for water
	Cracked or porous intake manifold	Inspect the oil for milky appearance
		Inspect the spark plugs for water
Engine is running too cool (lower speeds only)	Normal cold water operation	Check operation in warmer water
	Faulty thermostat	Test the thermostat
	Faulty thermostat housing	Replace thermostat housing
Engine is running too cool (higher speeds only)	Faulty thermostat	Test the thermostat
	Faulty thermostat housing	Replace thermostat housing
Engine is running too cool (all engine speeds)	Faulty thermostat	Test the thermostat

(continued)

Table 6 COOLING SYSTEM TROUBLESHOOTING (continued)

Symptom	Possible causes	Corrective action
Engine is running too cool (all engine speeds) (continued)	Faulty thermostat housing	Replace thermostat housing
Temperature gauge does not match actual temperature	Faulty engine temperature sender	Replace engine temperature sender (Chapter Eight)
	Faulty sender or gauge wiring	Check the wiring
	Faulty temperature gauge	Replace the gauge
Oil pressure gauge does not match actual oil pressure	Faulty oil pressure sender	Replace oil pressure sender (Chapter Eight)
	Faulty sender or gauge wiring	Check the wiring
	Faulty oil pressure gauge	Replace the gauge

Table 7 WARNING SYSTEM TROUBLESHOOTING

Symptom	Possible causes	Corrective action
Warning horn sounding	Engine is overheating	Check temperature gauge
	Low oil pressure	Check oil pressure gauge
	Transmission is overheating	Check transmission temperature
	Faulty engine overheat switch	Test engine overheat switch
	Faulty engine temperature sensor (EFI)	Test engine temperature sensor
	Faulty oil pressure switch	Test oil pressure switch
	Shorted tan/blue switch wire	Check wiring
	Shorted tan/blue ECU wire (EFI)	Check wiring
	Shorted tan/blue warning horn wire	Check wiring
Warning horn does not self test	Faulty key switch	Test key switch
	Faulty oil pressure switch	Test oil pressure switch
	Open tan/blue switch wire	Check wiring
	Open tan/blue ECU wire (EFI)	Check wiring
	Open tan/blue warning horn wire	Check wiring
	Open purple warning horn wire	Check wiring
	Faulty ECU	Check for diagnostic trouble codes
Engine overheating and warning horn not sounding	Faulty engine overheat switch	Test engine overheat switch
	Faulty engine temperature sensor (EFI)	Test engine temperature sensor
	Open tan/blue ECU wire (EFI)	Check wiring
	Open tan/blue warning horn wire	Check wiring
	Open purple warning horn wire	Check wiring
	Faulty ECU	Check for diagnostic trouble codes
Transmission overheating and warning horn not sounding	Faulty transmission overheat switch	Test overheat switch
	Open tan/blue warning horn wire	Check wiring
	Open purple warning horn wire	Check wiring
Low oil pressure and warning horn not sounding	Faulty oil pressure switch	Test oil pressure switch
	Open tan/blue ECU wire (EFI)	Check wiring
	Open tan/blue warning horn wire	Check wiring
	Open purple warning horn wire	Check wiring
	Faulty ECU	Check for diagnostic trouble codes

Table 8 IGNITION AND PICKUP COIL RESISTANCE SPECIFICATIONS

Model	Specification
Standard point ignition system	
Ignition coil	
Primary resistance	0.9-1.5 ohms
Secondary resistance	7500-15,000 ohms
Prestolite BID ignition system	
Ignition coil	
Primary resistance	1.25-1.40 ohms
Secondary resistance	9400-11,700 ohms
Delco EST ignition system	
Ignition coil	
Distributor pickup coil	500-1500 ohms

Table 9 FUEL PRESSURE SPECIFICATIONS

Model	Specification
Electric boost pump (EFI models)	4.9-8.5 psi (33.8-58.6 kPa)
Electric low-pressure fuel pump	4.9-8.5 psi (33.8-58.6 kPa)
(carburetor-equipped models)	
High-pressure electric fuel pump (EFI models)	
Throttle body injection (TBI) models	27-31 psi (186-214 kPa)
Multiport injection (MPI) models	35-47 psi (241-324 kPa)
Mechanical low-pressure fuel pump	3-7 psi (20.7-48.3 kPa)

Table 10 DIAGNOSTIC TROUBLE CODES (ALL EFI MODELS)

Code	Fault
12	Normal condition (diagnostic system is operational)
14	
MEFI 1 or MEFI 2 ECU	Engine coolant temperature sensor (ECT) out of range
MEFI 3 or MEFI 4 ECU	ECT reading too low
15	ECT reading too high
21	
MEFI 1 or MEFI 2 ECU	Throttle position sensor (TPS) out of range
MEFI 3 or MEFI 4 ECU	TPS reading too high
22	TPS reading too low
23	Intake air temperature sensor (IAT) reading too low
25	IAT reading too high
33	
MEFI 1 or MEFI 2 ECU	Manifold air pressure (MAP) sensor out of range
MEFI 3 or MEFI 4 ECU	MAP reading too high
34	MAP reading too low
41	Open ignition control circuit
42	Shorted ignition control or bypass circuit
43	Incorrect knock sensor module voltage
44	Knock sensor not operating
51	Engine control unit (ECU) calibration failure
81	Fuel pump driver circuit failure
	Injector driver circuit failure
	Sensor reference voltage out of range

Table 11 ENGINE TEMPERATURE SENSOR RESISTANCE SPECIFICATIONS

Model	Temperature	Resistance (ohms)
All models	212° F (100° C)	177
	158° F (70° C)	467
	104° F (40° C)	1800
	68° F (20° C)	3520
	41° F (5° C)	7500

Table 12 AIR TEMPERATURE SENSOR RESISTANCE SPECIFICATIONS

Model	Temperature	Resistance (ohms)
All models	104° F (40° C)	1459
	95° F (35° C)	1802
	86° F (30° C)	2238
	77° F (25° C)	2296
	68° F (20° C)	3520
	59° F (15° C)	4450
	50° F (10° C)	5670
	41° F (5° C)	7280
	32° F (0° C)	9420

Table 13 WARNING SYSTEM TEST SPECIFICATIONS

Test	Specification
Engine overheat switch	
Switches to closed circuit	190-200° F (88-93° C)
Switches back to open circuit	150-170° F (66-77° C)
Oil pressure switch	
Switches to open circuit	5 psi (34.4 kPa) and higher
Switches to closed circuit	Below 5 psi (34.4 kPa)
Oil pressure specifications	
Idle speed	4-60 psi (28-414 kPa)*
2000 rpm	30-60 psi (207-414 kPa)*
Transmission overheat switch	
Switches to closed circuit	220-240° F (105-115°C)
Switches back to open circuit	180-200° F (82-92° C)

*Under load at normal operating temperature.

Table 14 TROUBLESHOOTING TORQUE SPECIFICATIONS

Fastener	in.-lb.	ft.-lb.	N•m
Distributor hold-down clamp bolt	–	30	41
Fuel line fittings			
Low-pressure or boost pump outlet fitting	177-212	–	20-24
Fuel delivery line to throttle body fitting	204	–	23
Spark plug			
5.0L and 5.7L models			
With used cylinder head	–	15	20
With new cylinder head	–	22	30
7.4L and 8.2L models	–	15-20	20-28
8.1L models	–	15	20

Chapter Three

Lubrication, Maintenance and Tune-up

When operating properly, the Indmar inboard marine engine provides smooth operation, reliable starting and excellent performance. This chapter describes the procedures necessary to keep the engine and drive system in peak condition.

Table 1 lists torque specifications for fasteners and plugs. Tighten fasteners or plugs not listed in **Table 1** to the general tightening torque specifications in Chapter One. **Table 2** lists service intervals for all engine systems and components. Service intervals are also listed in the Quick Reference Data section at the front of the manual. If the boat is used for continuous heavy-duty, high speed operation or under other severe operating conditions, all maintenance operations, including lubrication procedures, should be performed more frequently. **Tables 3-5** list fluid capacities and spark plug recommendations. **Tables 1-5** are located at the end of this chapter.

If the engine becomes partially or completely submerged, refer to *Submersion* in this chapter for service instructions. Service the engine as soon as possible to minimize the damage.

If the boat is not used regularly, moisture and dirt will collect in and on the engine. Irregular use will eventually lead to corrosion and other damage. It is a good practice to keep the engine free of dirt and grease buildup. Frequent cleaning allows detection and correction of leaks before serious damage occurs.

BEFORE EACH USE

Certain items must be checked before use to avoid engine damage or equipment failure. This section describes inspection of the following fluids and components.

1. Fuel system leakage.
2. Engine oil level.
3. Transmission and V-drive fluid level.
4. Power steering fluid level.
5. Propeller and propeller shaft.
6. Steering system.
7. Coolant level.
8. Lanyard (emergency stop) switch operation.

NOTE
If the boat is stored in a wet slip, it might be impractical to perform inspection of drive system components such as the propeller

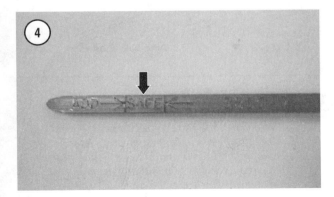

3

and shaft. In such instances, perform the inspections when the boat is removed from the water for routine maintenance.

Fuel Leakage Check

Before starting the engine for the first time each day, remove the engine cover or hatch and check for the presence of gasoline fumes or visual evidence of fuel leakage. Operate the bilge blower for a few minutes. If strong fumes can be smelled, determine the source and correct the leakage before operating or servicing the engine.

Engine Oil Level Check

> *CAUTION*
> *Never operate the engine with the oil level above or below the fill line on the dipstick. Overfilling can result in foaming of the oil. Operation with a low or high oil level can result and inadequate lubrication and certain engine damage.*

To avoid overfilling the oil, wait until the engine has been switched off for 30 minutes or more. This allows the oil to drain back into the oil pan.

The dipstick (A, **Figure 1**) is located on the port or starboard side of the engine near the rocker arm cover. On later models, the dipstick grip is red or yellow for easier identification.

On 5.0L, 5.7L, 7.4L and 8.2L models, the oil fill cap attaches to the rocker arm cover (B, **Figure 1**). On 8.1L models, the oil fill cap attaches to a tube that leads into the intake manifold (**Figure 2**).

Check the oil level as follows:

1. Pull the dipstick out of the tube (**Figure 3**).
2. Wipe the dipstick with a clean shop towel.
3. Insert the dipstick fully into the tube.
4. Wait a few minutes. Then *slowly* pull the dipstick from the tube and note the oil level. It should fall within the safe area (**Figure 4**).
5. Inspect the oil for the presence of water, a milky appearance or significant fuel odor. Refer to *Engine* in Chapter Two if any of these conditions is noted. Refer to *Water Entering the Oil* and *Lubrication System Failure.*
6. If necessary, add oil until the level is even with the upper safe mark. Do not overfill the engine. It is better for the oil level to be slightly low than overfilled. If the engine is overfilled, drain the excess oil as described under *Changing the Oil* in this chapter.
7. Insert the dipstick fully into the tube.

Transmission Fluid and V-Drive
Unit Fluid Level Check

Indmar inboard marine engines may be equipped with a number of different transmissions. Identify the transmission and drive system before checking the fluid level.

Most models use a Borg-Warner, Regal Beloit (Velvet-Drive) or ZF Hurth inline transmission that positions the front of the engine (pulley side) toward the front of the boat. See **Figure 5**. This drive system uses a single dipstick (**Figure 6**, typical) to check fluid level. Some models are equipped with a Walters V-drive unit attached to the end of a Borg-Warner or Regal Beloit (Velvet-Drive) transmission. See **Figure 7**. The Walters V-drive can be identified by the large rectangular cover (A, **Figure 8**) on the top of the unit. This arrangement positions the front of the engine (pulley side) toward the rear of the boat. These models use a dipstick to check the transmission fluid level (**Figure 6**, typical) and a dipstick (B, **Figure 8**) to check the V-drive unit fluid level. Other models use a ZF Hurth integral V-drive transmission. See **Figure 9**. This arrangement also positions the front of the engine facing the rear of the boat. These models use a single dipstick (**Figure 6**, typical) to check the fluid level.

Transmission

> *WARNING*
> *Stay clear of the propeller and propeller shaft while running an engine on a flush adapter.*

> *CAUTION*
> *Use a flush device or other means to supply the engine with cooling water if running the engine with the boat out of the water. The seawater pump is quickly damaged if operated without adequate cooling water.*

1. Clean all debris from the area surrounding the dipstick. If the dipstick cannot be located, refer to the owner's manual for the particular engine model. An owner's manual may be purchased from an Indmar dealership.

2. On models with a Borg-Warner or Regal Beloit (Velvet-Drive) transmission, twist the dipstick handle counterclockwise to loosen the seal. This allows quick removal of the dipstick.

3. Run the engine for approximately 10 minutes or until the engine reaches normal operating temperature. Shift the engine from NEUTRAL to FORWARD and REVERSE to purge any air from the fluid passages.

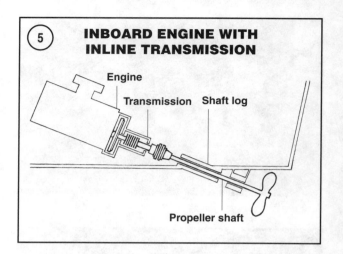

⑤ INBOARD ENGINE WITH INLINE TRANSMISSION

Engine
Transmission   Shaft log
Propeller shaft

⑥

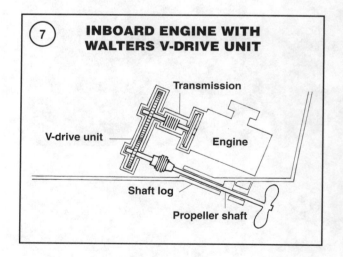

⑦ INBOARD ENGINE WITH WALTERS V-DRIVE UNIT

Transmission
V-drive unit
Engine
Shaft log
Propeller shaft

> *CAUTION*
> *For accurate fluid level readings, the dipstick must be removed as soon as the engine is stopped. Have a qualified assistant stop the engine for you to avoid any delay in removing the dipstick.*

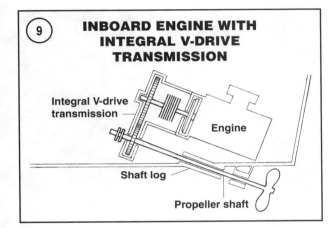

INBOARD ENGINE WITH INTEGRAL V-DRIVE TRANSMISSION

Integral V-drive transmission

Engine

Shaft log

Propeller shaft

4. Shift the engine into NEUTRAL. Have an assistant stop the engine. Then quickly pull the dipstick out of the transmission (**Figure 10**).

5. The fluid on the dipstick must be even with the full mark on the dipstick. Note the fluid level and condition. Then refer to the following:

   a. If the fluid has a milky appearance, water probably has contaminated the fluid. Refer to *Drive System* in Chapter Two. Before operating the engine, correct

the cause and change the transmission fluid as described in this chapter.

   b. If the fluid level reaches the full mark, wipe a sample of the fluid on the sealing surfaces or O-ring on the neck of the dipstick opening. Then insert the dipstick and fully seat it into the opening. On models with a Borg-Warner or Regal Beloit (Velvet-Drive) transmission, twist the dipstick handle clockwise to tighten the seal. Tug on the dipstick to make sure there is a secure fit.

   c. If the fluid level is above the full mark, use a common engine oil pump-out device and suitable tube to draw excess fluid from the dipstick tube. Recheck the fluid level.

   d. If the fluid level is below the full mark, add a small amount of the recommended fluid through the dipstick opening. Refer to *Transmission Fluid Change* in this chapter to determine the proper transmission fluid. Install the dipstick and repeat the fluid level check.

Walters V-drive unit

1. Clean all debris from the area surrounding the dipstick (B, **Figure 8**).

2. Run the engine for approximately 10 minutes or until the engine reaches normal operating temperature. Shift the engine from NEUTRAL to FORWARD and REVERSE to purge any air from the fluid passages.

3. Shift the engine into NEUTRAL. Stop the engine. Then pull the dipstick out of the V-drive unit.

4. The fluid on the dipstick must be even with the top mark on the dipstick. Note the fluid level and condition. Then refer to the following:

   a. If the fluid has a milky appearance, water probably has contaminated the fluid. Refer to *Drive System* in Chapter Two. Before operating the engine, correct the cause and change the fluid as described in this chapter.

   b. If the fluid level reaches the full mark, wipe a sample of the fluid on the sealing surfaces or O-ring on the neck of the dipstick opening. Then insert the dipstick and fully seat into the opening.

   c. If the fluid level is above the full mark, use a common engine oil pump-out device and suitable tube to draw excess fluid from the dipstick tube. Recheck the fluid level.

   d. If the fluid level is below the mark, remove the cap (C, **Figure 8**) from the elbow. Then add a small amount of the recommended fluid through the elbow opening. Refer to *Transmission Fluid Change* in this chapter to determine the proper fluid. Reinstall the cap and dipstick and then repeat the fluid level check. Continue adding fluid and checking the level until the fluid level just reaches the full mark.

Power Steering Fluid

Use only Dexron III automatic transmission fluid in the power steering system. Under normal operation, the power steering system does not require additional fluid or periodic fluid change. Inspect the system for a leak if frequent filling is required.

1. Locate the power steering pump on the front starboard or front port side of the engine (**Figure 11**).

2. Position the steering wheel and rudder in the straight forward position.

3. Remove the fill cap (**Figure 12**). Wipe the dipstick with a clean shop towel and reinstall it into the pump reservoir.

4. Remove the cap and note the fluid level on the dipstick (**Figure 13**). Correct the fluid level as follows:

   a. If no fluid is detected on the dipstick, add a small amount of fluid. Then cycle the steering wheel several turns lock to lock to purge air from the system. Place the steering wheel and rudder in the straight forward position and recheck the fluid level. Continue this step until the fluid level is correct.

   b. If the fluid has a milky appearance, water probably has contaminated the fluid. Refer to *Steering System* in Chapter Two.

   c. If the engine is warm, add fluid until the level just reaches the upper end of the range (**Figure 13**).

   d. If the engine is cold, add fluid until the level just reaches the groove below the add mark (**Figure 13**).

   e. If the fluid level is too high (warm or cold engine), use a syringe or other means to remove excess fluid.

5. With the engine off, cycle the steering several times to the full port and starboard limits. Place the steering wheel and rudder in the straight-ahead position and recheck the fluid level. Correct the level as necessary.

6. Install the fill cap.

Propeller and Propeller Shaft Inspection

Inspect the propeller (**Figure 14**, typical) for cracked, damaged or missing blades. Operating the engine with a damaged propeller results in decreased performance, excessive vibration and increased wear of the drive components. Straighten small bent areas with locking pliers. Repair small nicks with a metal file. To prevent an unbalanced condition, do not remove excessive amounts of ma-

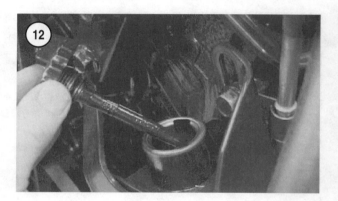

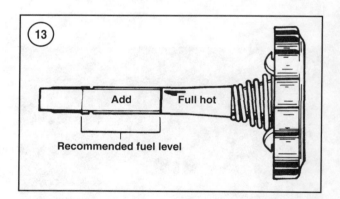

Recommended fuel level

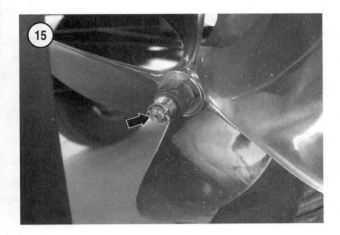

terial from the propeller. If significant damage is evident, have the propeller repaired at a propeller repair shop.

To check for a bent propeller shaft, disconnect the battery cables. Shift the transmission into NEUTRAL. Slowly spin the propeller while observing the end of the propeller shaft (**Figure 15**). If the shaft wobbles noticeably, the propeller shaft is bent and must be replaced. Refer to *Propeller Shaft* in Chapter Ten.

Steering System Inspection

Before starting the engine, rotate the steering wheel to the clockwise and counterclockwise limits. Note any binding or excessive slack as the wheel changes direction. Inspect and repair worn or faulty components. Never operate the engine if the steering is binding or loose.

Coolant Level Check

Coolant level inspection applies only to engines equipped with a closed cooling system. The engine coolant section of the closed cooling system must be filled with a 50:50 solution of pure water and ethylene glycol-based antifreeze. The antifreeze mixture does not require draining during winter months unless the engine will be subjected to temperatures below the rating of the water and antifreeze mixture. However, the raw water section *must* be drained *completely* before exposing the engine to freezing temperatures.

Allow the engine to cool completely before checking the coolant level. The coolant level drops as the engine cools.

Some closed cooling systems are equipped with a separate overflow reservoir (**Figure 16**). The translucent reservoir allows visual inspection of the coolant level. On other systems, the reservoir is integrated into the heat exchanger (**Figure 17**). With this design, the fill cap must be removed to check the coolant level.

> *WARNING*
> *Stay clear of the propeller and propeller shaft while running an engine on a flush adapter.*

> *WARNING*
> *Do not remove the pressure cap from a closed cooling system if the engine is warm. Hot coolant can spray out and cause serious injury.*

> *CAUTION*
> *Use a flush test device or other means to supply the engine with cooling water if running the engine with the boat out of the water. The seawater pump is quickly damaged if operated without adequate cooling water.*

> *NOTE*
> *Closed cooling system kits are available from numerous sources. Cooling system design, hose routing and fluid capacity will vary by manufacturer. Refer to information supplied by the cooling system manufacturer for specific information. This section*

describes maintenance on a typical closed cooling system.

Separate overflow reservoir

1. Allow the engine to cool completely before checking the coolant level. The coolant level drops as the engine cools.

2. Check the coolant level in the translucent reservoir. The level must be between the add and full lines. Correct the coolant level as follows:

   a. If the reservoir is empty, check for loose hose clamps, faulty hoses or a leaking recirculation pump. If the source of the leak is not visually apparent, pressure test the cooling system as described in Chapter Two. Refill the cooling system as described in this chapter (refer to *Changing the Engine Coolant*).

   b. If the reservoir is not empty but the coolant level is low, carefully remove the cap and add the required amount of coolant to the reservoir. Replace the cap.

   c. If the reservoir is overfilled, use a syringe or other means to remove excess coolant.

3. Start the engine. After the engine reaches normal operating temperature, check the level in the overflow reservoir. Cool the engine and correct the coolant level as needed.

Integrated reservoir

1. Allow the engine to cool completely before removing the pressure cap.

2. Cover the cap (**Figure 18**, typical) with a heavy shop towel. Using gloves, push down on the pressure cap. Rotate the cap counterclockwise until the tabs are clear of the cam locking surfaces. Lift the cap from the reservoir.

3. Wipe debris and crystallized coolant from the cap and filler neck opening. Inspect the upper and lower gaskets (**Figure 19**) for cracked, missing or otherwise damaged surfaces. Make sure the cam locking surfaces on the filler neck and cap are not damaged. Replace the cap or repair the filler neck if necessary. Damaged seals on the cap or filler neck surfaces will allow coolant leakage.

4. The coolant level should be within 1 in. (25 mm) of the filler neck opening. If necessary, *slowly* pour the coolant into the opening until full. If more than a few ounces are required, check for loose hose clamps, faulty hoses or a leaking recirculation pump. If the source of the leak is not visually apparent, pressure test the cooling system as described in Chapter Two.

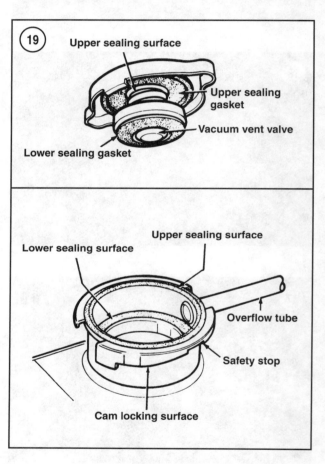

NOTE
To prevent the false indication of leakage, always wipe spilled coolant from the filler neck before installing the cap.

5. Align the locking tabs on the cap with the notches on the filler neck. Push down on the cap to clear the cam locking surfaces. Then rotate the cap clockwise until it touches the stop (**Figure 19**). Release the cap.

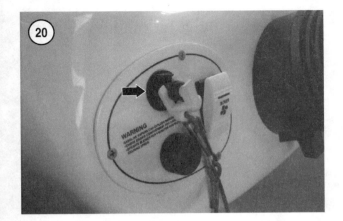

6. If coolant was added, start the engine and allow it to reach operating temperature. Allow the engine to completely cool. Then check and correct the coolant level.

7. After starting the engine, check for coolant leaking around the cap and filler neck and correct leakage as needed.

Emergency Stop (Lanyard) Switch Operation

CAUTION
Use a flush test device or other means to supply the engine with cooling water if running the engine with the boat out of the water. The seawater pump is quickly damaged if operated without adequate cooling water.

This switch is either incorporated in the remote control or mounted on the dashboard (**Figure 20**). Check the operation of the switch before getting underway.

1. Make sure the lanyard cord is connected to the switch. Start the engine. Do not shift into gear.

2. Pull the lanyard cord from the switch.

3. If the engine fails to stop, turn the key switch OFF. Repair or replace the switch before operating the engine.

AFTER EACH USE

Certain maintenance must be performed after each outing. Observing these requirements can dramatically reduce corrosion and extend the life of the engine.

1. Flush the cooling system.

2. Clean debris or contaminants from the engine surfaces.

Cooling System Flush

Flush the cooling system after each use to prevent deposit buildup and corrosion in the cooling passages. This is even more important if the engine was operated in saltwater, brackish water or polluted water.

Engines equipped with a closed cooling system also benefit from regular flushing because it reduces deposit buildup and corrosion in the heat exchanger, exhaust manifold(s) and fluid coolers.

Many models are equipped with a freshwater flushing system (**Figure 21**, typical). This system allows connection of a garden hose to the cooling system and flushing of the cylinder block (standard cooling system only) and exhaust manifold(s) with the boat in the water. Never start the engine while using the freshwater flushing system because the seawater pump will introduce contaminated water into the freshwater.

For boats stored on a trailer, flush the engine using a flush adapter connected to a garden hose (**Figure 22**, typical). Available from marine dealerships or marine supply stores, the adapter cup fits over the seawater inlet grate on the bottom of the hull (**Figure 23**). The adjustable-length pole of the adapter contacts the surface below the inlet to keep the cup in firm contact with the hull and fitting. This adapter allows flushing of the seawater side of the cooling system, including the water passages in the transmission, V-drive and power steering fluid coolers. The engine may also be flushed by connecting a garden hose to the seawater inlet hose that connects to the inlet fitting inside the boat (**Figure 24**).

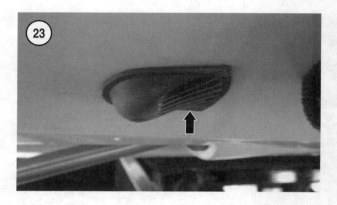

WARNING
Stay clear of the propeller and propeller shaft while running an engine on a flush adapter.

CAUTION
Use a flush device or other means to supply the engine with cooling water if running the engine with the boat out of the water. The seawater pump is quickly damaged if operated without adequate cooling water.

Using a flush adapter

WARNING
Stay clear of the propeller and propeller shaft while running an engine on a flush adapter.

1. Connect the garden hose to the adapter.

2. Position the rubber adapter cup over the inlet grate (**Figure 23**) on the bottom of the hull. If the boat has multiple inlet fittings, trace the seawater pump inlet hose (**Figure 25** or **Figure 26**) to the corresponding inlet fitting inside the boat (**Figure 24**). Select the inlet grate that aligns with the inlet fitting.

3. Adjust the length of the adapter pole to allow full compression of the cup with the end of the pole positioned on the hard surface directly below the inlet grate. If necessary, secure the adapter to the hull with duct tape.

4. Turn on the water. Make sure the flush adapter cup remains positioned over the water inlet. Start the engine and run at fast idle (approximately 1500 rpm) in NEUTRAL until the engine reaches full operating temperature.

5. Continue to run the engine until the water exiting the exhaust opening is clear and the engine has run for a minimum of 5 minutes. Monitor the engine temperature. Stop the engine if it begins to overheat or water is not exiting the exhaust.

6. Throttle back to idle and stop the engine. Remove the flush adapter.

Using the inlet fitting

WARNING
Stay clear of the propeller and propeller shaft while running an engine on a flush adapter.

1. Disconnect the battery cables to prevent accidental starting.

2. Trace the seawater pump inlet hose (**Figure 25** or **Figure 26**) to the corresponding inlet hose inside the boat (**Figure 24**).

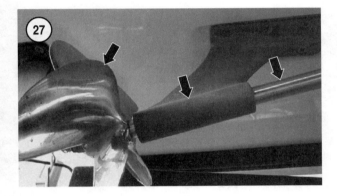

3. Loosen the hose clamps and then pull the hose off the inlet fitting.

4. Insert the water hose fitting into the inlet hose. Position one of the clamps on the hose to cover the hose fitting inside the hose. Securely tighten the clamp. Tug on the water hose to make sure there is a tight fit to the inlet hose.

5. Turn on the water and check for leakage at the hose connections. Reposition the hoses or tighten the clamp to eliminate leakage. Route the water hose and seawater pump inlet hose to prevent contact with the belts, pulleys and other moving components on the engine. Secure the hoses with plastic locking clamps as needed.

6. Connect the battery cables. Start the engine and run at fast idle (approximately 1500 rpm) in NEUTRAL until the engine reaches full operating temperature.

7. Continue to run the engine until the water exiting the exhaust opening is clear and the engine has run for a minimum of 5 minutes. Monitor the engine temperature. Stop the engine if it begins to overheat or water is not exiting the exhaust.

8. Throttle back to idle and stop the engine. Disconnect the battery cables to prevent accidental starting.

9. Loosen the clamp and pull the water hose out of the seawater pump inlet hose. Push the inlet hose fully over the inlet fitting in the boat hull. Position the clamp over

the hose to clamp against the inlet fitting. Then fully tighten the clamp.

10. Connect the battery cables.

Using the freshwater flushing system

1. Remove the cap (A, **Figure 21**) from the flushing system hose.

2. Locate the brass adapter (B, **Figure 21**) that is attached to the hose. Detach the adapter from the clamp and carefully thread it onto the hose fitting. Thread the garden hose onto the adapter.

3. Turn on the water. Immediately check for leakage from the adapter. Tighten the adapter fittings if leaking.

4. Leave the water on for a minimum of 5 minutes. Turn off the water and disconnect the water hose.

5. Remove the brass adapter from the flush hose. Connect the adapter to the clamp. Thread the cap onto the hose and securely tighten.

Cleaning the Engine

Clean any dirt or vegetation from all external drive system components such as the propeller, propeller shaft and strut (**Figure 27**). This step slows corrosion, reduces wear on bearings in the propeller shaft strut and makes worn or damaged components easier to see.

Never use strong cleaning solutions or solvents to clean the engine. Mild dish soap and pressurized water adequately clean most debris from external components. To prevent water intrusion, never direct water into the exhaust openings.

Rinse all external surfaces with clean water to remove soap residue.

Use a dry cloth to wipe oil or debris from components inside the engine compartment. Never direct water onto any electrical or fuel system components on the engine. These components are not waterproof.

LUBRICATION

Proper lubrication is absolutely critical to engine operation. Lubricant helps prevent wear to the engine, transmission and other areas; guards against corrosion; and provides smooth operation of moving parts.

Inboard marine engines operate in a corrosive environment and often require special lubricants. Using the wrong type of lubricant can cause serious engine damage or substantially shorten the life of the engine.

Special lubricant pumps are required for some of the procedures described in this section. The lubricants and pumps described in these procedures are available from most marine suppliers or marine dealerships.

Engine Oil and Filter Change

Change the engine oil and filter after the initial 20 hours of operation and then after every 100 hours of operation or once a season, whichever comes first. Always replace the filter when changing the oil to prevent contaminants in the filter from mixing with the fresh oil.

The manufacturer recommends using a Pennzoil PZ3 oil filter on all models covered in this manual. If this filter is not available, use a filter designed for use on General Motors-produced V-8 inboard marine engines. These filters are available from marine suppliers or marine dealerships. Oil filters designed for an automotive application might not meet the filtration requirements for the engine. Using the wrong filter can cause increased engine wear or seriously damage the engine.

Indmar recommends using a *marine-grade* SAE 15W-40 motor oil in all 5.0L and 5.7L models. SAE 40 marine-grade oil is recommended for 7.4L, 8.1L and 8.2L models. Make sure the oil used is of good quality and meets or exceeds the SG/CD service classification and meets or exceeds General Motors standard GM-6094-M. The classification is usually printed on the container label or cap (**Figure 28**, typical). If applicable, the GM standard is usually printed on the container label.

> *NOTE*
> *In some instances, the oil fill cap is imprinted with engine oil and service classification specifications. The information on the cap might or might not reflect the actual engine oil requirements. Disregard the specification on the oil fill cap.*

Oil filter

> *WARNING*
> *Stay clear of the propeller and propeller shaft while running an engine on a flush adapter.*

> *CAUTION*
> *Use a flush device or other means to supply the engine with cooling water if running the engine with the boat out of the water. The seawater pump is quickly damaged if operated without adequate cooling water.*

Use an oil filter wrench to loosen and tighten the oil filter. Other tools can damage the filter. Never overtighten

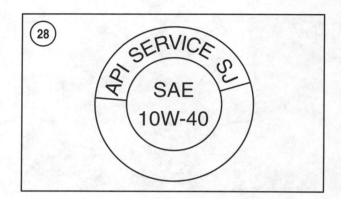

the replacement filter because overtightening will make future removal difficult and can damage the filter. A damaged filter can rupture while underway and cause oil leakage and possible engine damage. Oil filter mounting locations vary by model.

On most models, the oil filter mounts on the rear port side of the cylinder block (**Figure 29**). On V-drive models, the oil filter is on the front starboard side. An optional remote oil filter mounting kit (**Figure 30**, typical) is available and is factory-installed on some EFI models. The kit repositions the oil filter to an accessible location on the

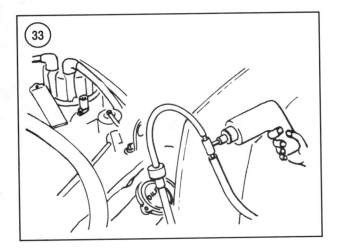

drain from the filter. Turn the filter until free from the threaded adapter.

3. Remove the gasket (**Figure 31**) from the cylinder block or adapter if it does not come off with the filter.

4. Empty the filter into a suitable container. Dispose of the filter in an environmentally responsible manner. Contact a marine dealership, auto repair shop or automotive parts store for information on the proper disposal of the oil filter.

5. Thoroughly clean the filter mating surface on the cylinder block or remote filter adapter. Apply a light coat of oil to the gasket (**Figure 31**) on the new filter.

6. For reference, write the engine operating hours and/or date on the filter body using a permanent marker.

7. Thread the filter onto the threaded adapter until the gasket just touches the mating surface. Use a filter wrench and tighten the filter exactly one turn. Do not overtighten the filter.

8. Change the engine oil as described in this chapter.

9. Start the engine and immediately check for oil leakage. Monitor the oil pressure gauge. The oil pressure must rise within a few seconds of starting the engine. Correct oil leakage or low oil pressure before operating the engine.

Engine oil

If easily accessible, remove the drain plug from the oil pan and drain the oil into a suitable container. This method allows complete draining of the oil and most of the contaminants that rest on the bottom the pan. In most boats, it is difficult if not impossible to place a container under the pan. Some models are equipped with an oil drain hose (**Figure 32**) that attaches to the oil pan drain opening. To use the drain hose, simply route the hose end into a suitable container positioned below the level of the oil pan. If the boat is stored on a trailer, the hose can be routed through the bilge drain and into a container positioned below the boat. The most common method of removing the oil is to pump the oil from the pan through the dipstick tube. This requires an oil-pumping device (**Figure 33**) that can be attached to the dipstick tube. This device is available from marine dealerships, marine supply stores and most automotive parts stores. Because the dipstick tube reaches the bottom of the oil pan, most of the oil and contaminants can be removed by this method. If all the oil cannot be drawn from the dipstick tube, insert a section of small diameter stiff tubing into the dipstick tube until it contacts the bottom of the oil pan. Connect the tube to the pump hose to draw the remaining oil out of the pan. The required tubing is usually included with the oil pumping device.

1. Change the oil filter as described in this chapter.

top of the engine or onto a stable boat structure near the engine. Consider adding this kit if boat structure prevents reasonable access to the filter.

1. Place a suitable container or shop towel under the filter to capture spilled oil.

2. Loosen the filter until the filter just breaks contact with the mating surface. Allow a few minutes for the oil to

2. Remove the oil fill cap (B, **Figure 1** or **Figure 2**) to allow air into the pan as the oil is removed.

3A. To drain oil directly from the pan:

   a. Place a suitable container under the oil drain plug.

   b. Slowly loosen and remove the plug and drain the oil. Remove the sealing washer from the drain plug or oil pan surface.

   c. Clean the plug, sealing washer and oil pan fitting.

   d. Fit the sealing washer onto the plug. Install the plug and tighten it to 221 in.-lb. (25 N•m) for 5.0L/5.7L models, 20 ft.-lb. (27 N•m) for 7.4L/8.2L models and 21 ft.-lb. (28 N•m) for 8.1L models.

3B. To pump oil using the dipstick tube:

   a. Remove the dipstick.

   b. Attach the oil pump hose to the dipstick tube or stiff tubing inserted into tube. Make sure the stiff tubing contacts the bottom of the oil pan.

   c. Pump the oil out of the pan until the pump starts to ventilate. This indicates the oil has been sufficiently removed and air is being drawn into the dipstick tube.

   d. Wipe clean and then install the dipstick.

3C. To drain oil using the oil drain hose:

   a. Place a suitable drain pan in a location lower than the oil pan. If the boat is stored on a trailer, place the drain pan under the bilge drain plug. Remove the bilge drain plug.

   b. Route the oil drain hose (**Figure 32**) into the drain pan. If the boat is stored on a trailer, route the hose through the bilge drain plug opening.

   c. Remove the cap from the end of the drain hose and *quickly* direct the hose into the drain pan. Allow the oil to drain completely.

   d. Apply a light coating of Permatex gasket sealing compound to the threads of the drain hose cap. Thread the cap onto the end of the hose. Securely tighten the cap.

   e. Route the drain hose to position the end in a location higher than the top of the oil pan. Secure the end of the hose in position with a plastic locking clamp. Make sure the hose is routed to prevent contact with belts, pulleys or other moving engine components.

   f. If removed, reinstall the bilge drain plug and securely tighten.

4. Refer to **Table 3** to determine the engine oil capacity. Slowly pour 90 percent of this amount into the oil fill opening. Install the oil fill cap.

WARNING
Stay clear of the propeller and propeller shaft while running an engine on a flush adapter.

CAUTION
Use a flush device or other means to supply the engine with cooling water if running the engine with the boat out of the water. The seawater pump is quickly damaged if operated without adequate cooling water.

5. Start the engine and monitor the oil pressure gauge. The pressure must rise within a few seconds of starting the engine. Otherwise, check for an improperly installed oil filter.

6. Inspect the oil filter mounting area and drain plug for leakage. If there is leakage, stop the engine and correct any leaking before operating the engine.

7. Stop the engine and allow at least 30 minutes for the oil to drain back into the oil pan. Check and correct the oil level as described in this chapter.

Transmission Fluid Change

Change the transmission fluid after the initial 20 hours of operation and then after every 100 hours of operation or once a season, whichever comes first.

Use Dexron III automatic transmission fluid in all of the Borg-Warner or Regal Beloit (Velvet-Drive) and ZF Hurth transmissions used on the models covered in this manual. On models so equipped, use Exxon Spartan EP-68 gear oil or a heavy-duty SAE 30 SE, SF or SG classification engine oil in the Walters V-drive unit. **Table 4** lists approximate fluid capacities for the transmission and V-drive unit.

Most transmissions are equipped with a drain plug on the bottom of the transmission case. However, the drain plug is used primarily to drain the unit after removing it from the boat because the plug is not generally accessible with the transmission mounted in the boat. The most common method of removing the transmission fluid is to pump it from the sump through the dipstick tube. This requires an oil-pumping device (**Figure 33**) that can be attached to a tube inserted into the dipstick. This device is available from marine dealerships, marine supply stores and most automotive parts stores. Because the dipstick reaches the bottom of the sump, most of the oil can be removed by this method. The required section of tubing is usually included with the oil pump.

Borg-Warner, Regal Beloit (Velvet-Drive)
and ZF Hurth transmissions

1. Disconnect the battery cables.

2. Remove the dipstick as described in this chapter. Refer to *Transmission Fluid and V-Drive Unit Fluid Level Check*.

3. Insert a section of tubing into the dipstick until it reaches the bottom of the housing sump. Compare the length of the tubing to the height of the transmission to determine whether the tubing is reaching the bottom.

4. Connect the pump to the tubing. Operate the pump until it starts to ventilate. This indicates the fluid has been sufficiently removed and air is being drawn into the pump-out tubing.

5. Wait approximately 30 minutes. Then operate the pump to remove any residual fluid remaining in the transmission. Remove the tubing from the dipstick.

6. Refer to **Table 4** to determine the approximate transmission fluid capacity. *Slowly* add 90 percent of this amount of Dexron III automatic transmission fluid (ATF) through the dipstick.

7. Wait a few minutes for any trapped air in passages to purge and then check the fluid level as described in this chapter. Add fluid until the level is correct.

8. Wipe clean and then install the dipstick.

> *WARNING*
> *Stay clear of the propeller and propeller shaft while running an engine on a flush adapter.*

> *CAUTION*
> *Use a flush device or other means to supply the engine with cooling water if running the engine with the boat out of the water. The seawater pump is quickly damaged if operated without adequate cooling water.*

9. Connect the battery cables.

10. Start the engine and allow it to reach full operating temperature. Shift the transmission into all three positions to purge any air from the internal passages.

11. Stop the engine and check the fluid level as described in this chapter. Correct the fluid level as needed.

Walters V-drive unit

1. Disconnect the battery cables.

2. Remove the dipstick as described in this chapter. Refer to *Transmission Fluid and V-Drive Unit Fluid Level Check*.

3. Insert a stiff section of tubing into the dipstick until it reaches the bottom of the housing sump. Compare the length of the tubing to the height of the V-drive unit to determine whether the tubing is reaching the bottom.

4. Connect the pump to the tubing. Operate the pump until it starts to ventilate. This indicates the fluid has been sufficiently removed and air is being drawn into the pump-out tubing.

5. Wait approximately 30 minutes and then operate the pump to remove any residual fluid remaining in the V-drive unit.

6. Remove the cap (C, **Figure 8**) from the elbow. *Do not install the dipstick tube at this time.*

7. Refer to **Table 4** to determine the approximate oil capacity. *Slowly* add 90 percent of this amount of the recommended oil into the unit through the elbow.

8. Wait approximately 10 minutes and then install the cap and dipstick. Check the fluid level as described in this chapter.

    a. If the fluid level is low, remove the dipstick and cap. Then add a small quantity of fluid and check the level. Continue adding fluid and checking the level until the fluid level just reaches the full mark.

    b. If the fluid level is high, use the pump to remove excess fluid.

9. Wipe clean and then install the dipstick.

> *WARNING*
> *Stay clear of the propeller and propeller shaft while running an engine on a flush adapter.*

> *CAUTION*
> *Never run the engine without first providing cooling water. Use a flush adapter or other means to supply water to the seawater pump before starting the engine.*

10. Connect the battery cables.

11. Start the engine and allow it to reach full operating temperature. Shift the transmission into all three positions to purge any air from the internal passages.

12. Stop the engine and check the fluid level as described in this chapter. Correct the fluid level as needed.

Steering Cable Lubrication

Apply a good-quality water-resistant grease to the steering cable ram (**Figure 34**, typical) after the first 20 hours of operation and then after every 50 hours of operation or 60 days, whichever comes first.

1. Disconnect the battery cables.

2. Rotate the steering wheel clockwise to the full starboard limit.

3. Apply a light coat of grease to the exposed ram of the steering cable (**Figure 34**).

4. Rotate the steering wheel to the full port and starboard limits several times to distribute the grease.

5. Rotate the steering wheel to the straight-ahead position.

6. Connect the battery cable.

Checking Engine Alignment

Check the engine alignment once a year or every 100 hours of use, whichever comes first. Engine alignment is described in Chapter Six.

FUEL SYSTEM MAINTENANCE

Fuel Requirements

> *CAUTION*
> *Never run the engine on stale fuel. Varnish-like deposits form in the fuel system as the fuel deteriorates. These deposits block fuel passages and cause a lean condition in the combustion chamber. Damage to the pistons, valves and other engine components results from operating the engine with an excessively lean fuel mixture.*

Petroleum-based fuels have a short shelf life. Some fuels begin to lose potency in as few as 14 days.

Purchase fuel from busy fuel stations, which usually have a high turnover of fuel, to make sure that the fuel will be fresh. Always use the fuel well before it becomes stale. Refer to *Lay-Up* in Chapter Four for information on fuel additives.

All models covered in this manual are designed to use regular unleaded fuel. Use fuel with an average octane rating of 91 or higher for 5.7L LT-1 and 8.1L models, Use a fuel with a rating of 89 or higher for all other models. Using fuel with a lower octane rating can result in power loss and/or serious engine damage.

Fuel Filter Maintenance

Debris can enter the fuel tank when adding fuel, from the fuel tank vent, during manufacture of the tank or when the tank was installed in the boat. Although the engine can have multiple fuel filters, the primary filter captures this material before it contaminates the carburetor, fuel pump or other fuel system components. Other filters on the engine are designed to capture debris or material that forms within the engine-mounted fuel system components.

Most of the models covered in this manual are equipped with a spin-on water-separating fuel filter (**Figure 35**) as

the primary fuel filter in the system. This filter is readily accessible and easy to service. On some carburetor-equipped models, the primary filter is located in the carburetor inlet fitting. Refer to Chapter Seven to service the fuel filter on these models.

Water-separating fuel filter

Although the fuel filter is reusable, it is a good practice to replace the filter after the first 20 hours of operation and then once a year or every 100 hours, whichever comes first.

1. Disconnect the battery cables.

2. Place a suitable container or shop towels under the water-separating fuel filter to capture spilled fuel.

3. Using an oil filter wrench or other suitable tool, carefully loosen the filter.

4. Remove the filter. Then promptly clean up any spilled fuel. Remove the seal from the filter housing if not found on the filter.

5. Empty the filter into a transparent container. Inspect the fuel sample for the presence of water, rust or other contaminants. If a significant amount of rust is present, inspect the fuel tank. Drain and refill the tank if a significant

amount of water is present. Replace the filter if significant contamination is evident.

6. Inspect the filter for rusted or damaged surfaces. Replace the filter if any damage or evidence of leakage is present.

7. Apply a light coat of engine oil to the filter seal (**Figure 36**).

NOTE
Always fill the spin-on fuel filter with clean, fresh fuel prior to installation. Otherwise,

the air introduced into the system might prevent proper priming of the fuel system and create starting difficulty.

8. Carefully pour clean, fresh fuel into the filter until the fuel level just reaches the threaded opening. Install the filter onto the adapter until the seal just contacts the housing. Tighten the filter exactly one additional turn.

9. Clean up any spilled fuel. Wipe the filter dry to allow easy detection of leaking fuel.

10. Connect the battery cables.

WARNING
Stay clear of the propeller and propeller shaft while running an engine on a flush adapter.

CAUTION
Use a flush device or other means to supply the engine with cooling water if running the engine with the boat out of the water. The seawater pump is quickly damaged if operated without adequate cooling water.

11. Start the engine and immediately check for leakage at the filter. Stop the engine and correct the leakage if present. Allow the engine to reach normal operating temperature and then stop the engine. Wait a few minutes. Then check for fuel leakage at the filter. Correct any leakage before putting the engine into service.

Flame Arrestor

During normal engine operation, belt material, engine compartment insulation, oily deposits from the crankcase ventilation system and other material contaminate the flame arrestor screen (**Figure 37**, typical). Not only does this contamination restrict air flow and decrease engine power, it also presents a fire hazard if subjected to an engine backfire. To help maintain maximum performance and minimize the fire hazard, clean the flame arrestor after every 50 hours of operation and if significant debris is noted on the screen.

1. Disconnect the battery cables.

2A. On carburetor-equipped models, remove the flame arrestor as follows:

    a. If so equipped, disconnect the breather tube (C, **Figure 38**) from the flame arrestor (B).

    b. Unthread the screw (A, **Figure 38**). Then lift the flame arrestor off the carburetor (**Figure 39**).

2B. On throttle body injection (TBI) models, unthread the screw (A, **Figure 40**) and then lift the plastic cover (B) off the flame arrestor. Remove the flame arrestor (**Figure 37**, typical) from the throttle body. Work carefully to

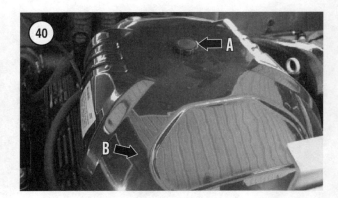

avoid snagging the fuel injector wire harness while re-moving the flame arrestor.

2C. On 5.0L and 5.7L multiport injection (MPI) models with a center-mounted throttle body (**Figure 41**), remove the plastic cover and then unthread the screw that secures the flame arrestor to the throttle body. Remove the flame arrestor from the throttle body.

2D. On multiport injection (MPI) models with a front-mounted flame arrestor (**Figure 42**, typical), loosen the clamp screw (**Figure 43**) and then carefully pull the flame arrestor off the throttle body flange.

3. On carburetor-equipped models using a mechanical fuel pump, inspect the clear or translucent sight tube (**Figure 44**) connected to the carburetor for the presence of fuel. If fuel is in the sight tube, replace the mechanical fuel pump. Disconnect the sight tube from the carburetor fitting. Inspect the sight tube for brittle, deteriorated or cracked surfaces. Replace the sight tube with the recommended tube if these or other defects are evident. *Do not replace the tube with any other type of hose or tubing.*

4. Use compressed air to clear any loose material from the flame arrestor screen.

> *WARNING*
> *Replace the flame arrestor if any physical damage is evident. Operating the engine with a damaged flame arrestor might allow an engine backfire to ignite fuel vapor or other flammable material in the engine compartment.*

5. Use solvent to thoroughly clean the flame arrestor. Use a plastic brush to remove fiber material from the fins or screen. Never use a wire brush to clean the arrestor. After cleaning, dry the flame arrestor with compressed air.

6. Inspect the flame arrestor for damage to the screen or mating surfaces. Replace the flame arrestor if any damage is evident.

7A. On carburetor-equipped models, install the flame arrestor as follows:

a. Fit the flame arrestor onto the carburetor (**Figure 39**).

b. Insert the screw (A, **Figure 38**) into the flare arrestor opening and guide it into the threaded opening at the top of the carburetor. If necessary, lift the flame arrestor slightly to guide the screw. Securely tighten the screw.

c. If so equipped, connect the breather tube (C, **Figure 38**) to the flame arrestor (B).

7B. On throttle body injection (TBI) models, install the flame arrestor as follows:

a. Without snagging the fuel injector wiring (A, **Figure 45**) or connectors (B), carefully fit the flame arrestor onto the throttle body unit. Rotate the arrestor to align the stud with the opening and then seat the arrestor onto the throttle body.

b. Install the plastic cover (B, **Figure 40**) onto the flame arrestor. Guide the screw (A, **Figure 40**) into the cover, flame arrestor and throttle body openings. Lift the cover and flame arrestor slightly to assist with aligning the screw with the threaded opening.

c. Align the plastic cover and then securely tighten the screw.

7C. On 5.0L and 5.7L multiport injection (MPI) models with a center-mounted throttle body (**Figure 41**), install the flame arrestor as follows:

a. Fit the flame arrestor onto the throttle body.

b. Insert the screw into the flame arrestor opening and guide it into the threaded opening in the throttle body. Lift the flame arrestor slightly to assist with aligning the screw with the threaded opening.

c. Thread the screw into the throttle body and then securely tighten it.

d. If so equipped, fit the plastic cover onto the throttle body.

7D. On multiport injection (MPI) models with a front-mounted flame arrestor (**Figure 42**, typical), install the flame arrestor as follows:

a. Carefully fit the flame arrestor over the throttle body flange.

b. Rotate the flame arrestor on the flange to a position that prevents contact with the motor cover, belts, pulleys or other moving components.

c. Securely tighten the clamp screw (**Figure 43**).

d. If so equipped, install any plastic covers onto the engine.

8. Route any loose wiring to prevent interference with the throttle linkage and other moving components. Secure the wiring with plastic locking clamps as needed.

9. Connect the battery cables.

PCV Valve

Clean the positive crankcase ventilation (PCV) valve once a year or every 100 hours, whichever comes first. A PCV valve is not used on 8.1L and many earlier models; a crankcase ventilation valve is located on the breather hose at the opening to the rocker arm cover (**Figure 46**, typical).

1. Disconnect the battery cables.

2. Carefully pull the valve and hose from the rocker arm grommet (**Figure 47**).

3. Carefully pull the PCV valve from the hose fitting. Inspect the connecting hose for splitting, deterioration or other defects. Inspect the plastic hose fitting of cracks or a loose fit on the valve. Replace the hose and/or fitting as needed.

4. Inspect the rubber grommet in the rocker arm cover for split or deteriorated surfaces. A damaged grommet allows oil leakage and prevents proper operation of the crankcase ventilation system. Make sure the opening in the rocker arm cover fits into the slot in the grommet. For easier installation, apply a soap-and-water solution to the grommet prior to installation.

5. Direct aerosol carburetor cleaner into the PCV valve and opening on the opposite end. Wait a few minutes. Then blow compressed air into the valve to remove the cleaner and contaminants. Repeat this step several times until all deposits are removed.

6. Shake the valve to check for a stuck check valve. The check valve must rattle while shaking the PCV valve. Replace the PCV valve if the check valve cannot be freed by cleaning.

7. Carefully insert the PCV valve into the grommet. The hose-fitting must face upward. Carefully seat the valve until the lip contacts the grommet.

8. Connect the plastic fitting and hose to the valve.

9. Connect the battery cables.

10. After starting the engine, immediately check for oil leakage at the rocker arm cover grommet. Replace the grommet if any oil leakage is evident.

ENGINE COOLANT

Change the engine coolant every 2 years or 200 hours, whichever comes first. Replace the coolant anytime it is drained for other service.

Over time, certain chemicals in the coolant react with minerals in the water mixed with the coolant or metals in the cylinder block to form crystalline deposits that coat the passages in the heat exchanger and cylinder block. These deposits insulate the coolant from the components and prevent efficient heat transfer. As they build, these deposits restrict coolant flow, which further compromises the cooling system, and cause the engine to overheat.

Change the coolant on a regular basis to minimize these deposits. Heavy deposits can be removed using a cooling system cleaner. Always follow the manufacturer's instructions when using these products.

The manufacturer recommends using an ethylene glycol-based, extended-life coolant in the closed cooling system. Read the container label carefully and make sure the

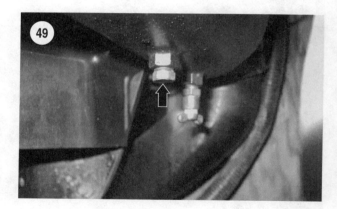

coolant meets these requirements. If this type of coolant is not available, use a good-quality ethylene glycol-based coolant. Do not use propylene glycol-based coolant in the closed cooling system.

Dilute the coolant with an equal amount of clear purified water. The cooling system must operate with a 50:50 mixture for efficient cooling and protection against freezing. Read the container carefully. Some brands of coolant are premixed and do not require dilution with water.

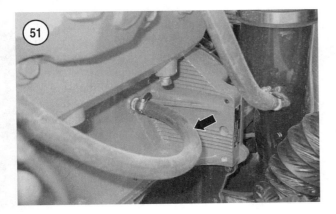

3

Draining the Coolant

WARNING
Do not remove the pressure cap, drain plugs
or hoses from the closed cooling system if
the engine is warm. Hot coolant might spray
out and cause serious injury.

The old coolant must be drained from the heat exchanger, cylinder block and hoses. Some closed cooling systems also flow coolant through the exhaust manifold(s). If applicable, the exhaust manifold must also be drained. If in doubt, remove the manifold drain plug or cap to check for coolant. Exhaust manifold draining is described in Chapter Four. Refer to *Winterizing*.

1. Disconnect the battery cables.

2. Cover the cap (**Figure 48**, typical) with a heavy shop towel. Using gloves, push down on the pressure cap. Rotate the cap counterclockwise until the tabs are clear of the cam locking surfaces. Lift the cap from the reservoir.

3. Wipe debris and crystallized coolant from the cap and filler neck opening. Inspect the upper and lower gaskets (**Figure 19**) for cracks or other damage. Make sure the cam locking surfaces on the filler neck and cap are not damaged. Replace the cap or repair the filler neck if necessary.

4. Locate the drain plug (**Figure 49**, typical) on the bottom of the heat exchanger. The heat exchanger is located on the front of the engine directly above the drive belts or on the back of the engine directly above the flywheel. If two plugs are present, the plug nearest the end usually drains seawater, and the other plug drains coolant.

5. Place a suitable container under the fitting. Then remove the plug and allow the exchanger to drain fully.

6. Locate the block drain plugs (**Figure 50**) or petcock on each side of the cylinder block. If the engine is equipped with block drain/flush hoses (**Figure 51**), locate the cap on the end of the drain hose. Place a suitable container under the hoses or fittings. Then remove the plug(s) from the block, open the petcocks, or remove the cap from the drain hose.

7. Allow the coolant to drain fully. Make sure the boat is level to ensure complete draining.

8. If the system has a separate overflow reservoir (**Figure 52**), place a suitable container under the reservoir. Remove the clamp and disconnect the hose from the fitting on the bottom of the reservoir. Drain the reservoir and hose. Reconnect the hose and secure with the clamp.

9. If the closed cooling system passes coolant through the exhaust manifolds, place a suitable container under the manifold drain plug (**Figure 53**, typical). Then remove the plug. Allow the manifold to drain completely. Then

NOTE
Closed cooling system kits are available from numerous sources. Cooling system design, hose routing and fluid capacity will vary by manufacturer. Refer to the information supplied by the cooling system manufacturer for specific information. This section describes maintenance on the typical closed cooling system.

drain the other exhaust manifold using the same procedure.

Filling with Coolant

1. Recap or reconnect hoses, close petcocks and install all plugs into the cylinder block, manifold and heat exchanger.

2. *Slowly* pour the coolant-and-water mixture into the fill neck until the level is within 1 in. (25 mm) of the top of the filler neck opening. Wait a few minutes for trapped air to purge and the level to drop. Then add additional coolant. Continue until the coolant level stabilizes.

3. If the system has a separate overflow reservoir, *slowly* pour the coolant-and-water mixture into the reservoir until the level reaches the full mark.

4. Wipe spilled coolant from the filler neck. Align the locking tabs on the cap with the notches on the filler neck. Push down on the cap to clear the cam locking surfaces, then rotate the cap clockwise until it touches the stop. Release the cap.

> *WARNING*
> *Stay clear of the propeller and propeller shaft while running an engine on a flush adapter.*

> *CAUTION*
> *Use a flush device or other means to supply the engine with cooling water if running the engine with the boat out of the water. The seawater pump is quickly damaged if operated without adequate cooling water.*

5. Connect the battery cables.

6. Start the engine and immediately check for coolant leaking around the cap and filler neck. Correct any leakage before operating the engine.

7. Stop the engine and allow the engine to cool completely.

8. Check and correct the coolant level as described in this chapter.

9. If the thermostat housing has an air-bleed fitting (**Figure 54**, typical), bleed air from the closed cooling system as follows:

   a. Start the engine and operate at 1500 rpm until the engine reaches normal operating temperature.

   b. Return the engine to idle speed. Then *slowly* loosen the fitting. Wear a glove for hand protection.

   c. Securely tighten the fitting when coolant just starts flowing from the fitting opening.

   d. Stop the engine.

TUNE-UP

A tune-up is a series of adjustments, tests and parts replacements performed to restore performance lost from wear, corrosion or deterioration of one or more engine components. Perform all of the operations listed in this section to perform a complete tune-up. Simply replacing the spark plugs and adjusting the carburetor might not provide the desired results. Only a complete tune-up will provide the expected performance and smooth running characteristics.

Compression Test

No tune-up is complete without a compression test. An engine with low compression on one or more cylinders cannot be properly tuned or expected to deliver satisfactory performance. Perform a compression test before replacing any components or performing any adjustments. Correct the cause of low compression before proceeding with the tune-up. Compression testing is described in Chapter Two.

Spark Plugs

Many of the Indmar inboard marine engines covered in this manual use a transistorized ignition system. These systems produce higher energy than conventional breaker-point systems used on earlier products. The transistorized systems provide longer spark plug life and less chance of spark plug fouling. Nevertheless, spark plugs operate in a harsh environment and eventually require replacement.

Generally, the spark plugs should be cleaned and regapped or replaced once a season or every 100 hours when performing a complete tune-up if the engine is misfiring or a decrease in performance is evident.

An engine that is used primarily at mid-range cruising speed under normal operating conditions might not require spark plug replacement until after 200 or more hours of operation. However, an engine operated primarily at idle speed in very cold operating conditions might require spark plug replacement every 50 hours or less of operation. Later-model engines with multiport fuel injection are factory-equipped with platinum-tipped spark plugs that usually do not require replacement until the engine has logged 300 or more hours of normal use. Generally, an engine operated under heavy load or in extreme climates will require more frequent spark plug replacement.

Spark plug condition can reveal much about the condition of the engine. Regular inspection allows problems to be identified and corrected before expensive engine damage occurs. After removing the spark plugs, compare them to the ones shown in **Figure 55**.

Be sure to correct any engine-related problems before installing new spark plugs. Operating the engine with an incorrectly adjusted carburetor, dirty flame arrestor, sticking choke valve, ignition system or fuel injection system malfunction will usually result in rapid fouling of the new spark plugs.

Spark plug removal

1. Disconnect the battery cables.

2. Mark the cylinder number on the spark plug wire leads before disconnecting them from the spark plug. Refer to the following:

   a. On models using an inline transmission, the pulley end of the engine faces the bow (front) of the boat. The No. 1 cylinder is the front cylinder on the port side, and the No. 2 cylinder is the front cylinder on the starboard side. Odd-numbered cylinders are on the port side, and even-numbered cylinders are on the starboard side.

   b. On models using a V-drive transmission, the pulley end of the engine faces the stern (rear) of the boat. The No. 1 cylinder is the rear cylinder on the starboard side and the No. 2 cylinder is the rear cylinder on the port side. Odd numbered cylinder are on the starboard side and even numbered cylinder are on the port side.

> *CAUTION*
> *Never use pliers or other tools with serrated grips to disconnect spark plug boots. The serrated surfaces pierce the spark plug boots. The piercing causes a misfire by allowing arcing to the exhaust manifolds and other engine components. The arcing and misfiring occur primarily at higher throttle settings.*

3. Disconnect the spark plug wires by carefully twisting and pulling on the wire boot (**Figure 56**). If working on a hot engine and/or in cramped quarters, grip the boot with spark plug boot pliers. (**Figure 57**).

4. Use compressed air to blow debris from around the spark plugs before removing them. If the spark plug threads are corroded, apply a penetrating oil and allow it to soak in.

5. Sometimes the threads in the cylinder head are damaged during spark plug removal. This condition can be repaired without removing the cylinder head by installing a special threaded insert. Have the repair performed by a professional if you are unfamiliar with the procedure or do not have access to the equipment.

6. Clean the spark plug openings with a thread chaser (**Figure 58**). Thread the chaser by hand into each spark plug opening. Several passes might be required to remove all carbon or corrosion deposits from the threads. Flush all debris from the openings with compressed air.

Spark plug inspection

Compare the spark plugs with those shown in **Figure 55**. Sometimes, spark plugs can give a clear indication of problems in the engine before symptoms occur. Additional inspection and testing might be required if an abnormal condition is evident. Refer to Chapter Two for troubleshooting instructions.

Spark plug installation

Use a gap-adjusting tool (**Figure 59**) to adjust the spark plug gap (**Table 5**). Never tap the plug against a hard object to close the gap. The ceramic insulator can crack and

SPARK PLUG CONDITION

NORMAL

- Identified by light tan or gray deposits on the firing tip.
- Can be cleaned.

GAP BRIDGED

- Identified by deposit buildup closing gap between electrodes.

OIL FOULED

- Identified by wet black deposits on the insulator shell bore and electrodes.
- Caused by too much oil entering combustion chamber through worn rings and pistons, excessive clearance between valve guides and stems, or worn or loose bearings. Can be cleaned. If engine is not repaired, use a hotter plug.

CARBON FOULED

- Identified by dry, fluffy black carbon deposits on insulator tips, exposed shell surfaces and electrodes.
- Caused by a too-cold plug, weak ignition, dirty air cleaner, too-rich fuel mixture or excessive idling. Can be cleaned.

LEAD FOULED

- Identified by dark gray, yellow, tan or black deposits or a fused glazed coating on the insulator tip.
- Caused by highly leaded gasoline.

WORN

- Identified by severely eroded or worn electrodes.
- Caused by normal wear. Should be replaced.

FUSED SPOT DEPOSIT

- Identified by melted or spotty deposits resembling bubbles or blisters.
- Caused by sudden acceleration. Can be cleaned.

OVERHEATING

- Identified by a white or light gray insulator with small black or gray-brown spots with bluish-burnt appearance of electrodes.
- Caused by engine overheating, wrong type of fuel, loose spark plugs, a too-hot plug or incorrect ignition timing. Replace the plug.

PREIGNITION

- Identified by melted electrodes and possibly blistered insulator. Metallic deposits on insulator indicate engine damage.
- Caused by wrong type of fuel, incorrect ignition timing or advance, a too-hot plug, burned valves or engine overheating. Replace the plug.

3

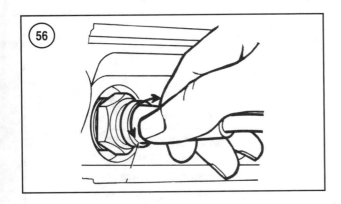

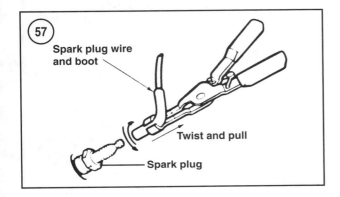

Spark plug wire
and boot

Twist and pull

Spark plug

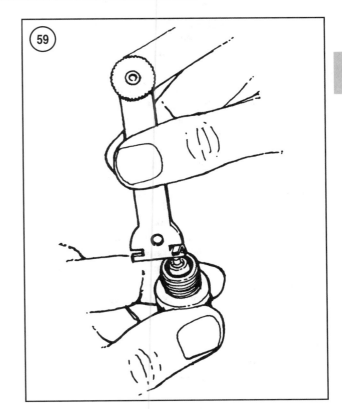

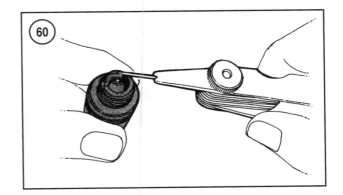

break away. Gap-adjusting tools are available at most automotive parts stores.

1. Refer to **Table 5** to determine the spark plug gap.

2. Check the gap using a wire feeler gauge (**Figure 60**) of the same thickness as the recommended gap. The gauge should pass between the electrodes (**Figure 61**) with a slight drag.

3. Open or close the gap as necessary.

4. Inspect the spark plugs for parallel surfaces (**Figure 61**). Carefully bend the electrode until the surfaces are parallel and the gap is correct.

NOTE
On some brands of spark plugs, the terminal end must be installed before installing the spark plug. Thread the terminal onto the spark plug as shown in **Figure 62**.

5. Apply a very light coat of oil to the spark plug threads and thread them in by hand. Use a torque to tighten the spark plug as follows:

    a. .On 5.0L and 5.7L models, tighten the spark plugs to 22 ft.-lb. (30 N•m) if the cylinder head is new and 15 ft.-lb. (20 N•m) if the cylinder head is used.

b. On 7.4L and 8.2L models, tighten the spark plugs to 15-20 ft.-lb. (20-28 N•m).

c. On 8.1L models, tighten the spark plugs to 15 ft.-lb. (20 N•m).

6. Apply a light coat of silicone lubricant to the inner surface of the spark plug boots. Carefully slide the boot over the correct spark plug. Snap the connector in the boot fully onto the spark plug terminal.

7. Connect the battery cables.

Distributor Cap, Spark Plug Wires and Rotor

Inspect the distributor cap, spark plug wires and rotor during the tune-up. Numerous types of distributors are used on the models covered in this manual. Look for an identification tag, stamp or decal on the distributor body (**Figure 63**, typical). Any mark or stamp on the distributor might be required when purchasing replacement parts.

1. Mark the cylinder number on the spark plug wires and distributor cap prior to removing the wires from the cap. Transfer the cylinder number to the replacement cap or wires prior to installation.

2. Wipe all ignition wires with a cloth slightly moistened with silicone lubricant. Carefully bend each wire and inspect the insulation, cable nipple and spark plug boot for abrasions, cracks, burned areas or deterioration. Replace any wire that is not in excellent condition.

3. Unsnap, unscrew or turn the distributor cap attachment as required to remove the distributor cap. See **Figure 64**. Pull the cap straight up and off the distributor to prevent damage to the rotor.

4. Check the center carbon contact and electrodes inside the cap for burning, corrosion, arcing or pitted surfaces. Inspect the cap for cracks, carbon tracks or other defects. See **Figure 65**. Replace the cap and rotor if these or other defects are evident.

5. Lift the rotor straight up and off the distributor shaft (**Figure 66**). Wipe the rotor clean with a damp cloth and dry with compressed air. Inspect the rotor for cracks, carbon tracks, and corroded or burned contacts. Replace the cap and rotor if these or other defects are evident.

6. On models using a breaker-point ignition system, service the breaker points as described in this section before installing the rotor and distributor cap.

7. To install the rotor, align the tang in the rotor bore with the groove in the distributor shaft. Then carefully press the rotor onto the shaft until fully seated.

8. On models with a breaker-point ignition system, grasp the rotor and twist it clockwise. Release the rotor. The centrifugal advance mechanism is sticking if the rotor does not quickly return to the original location. If neces-

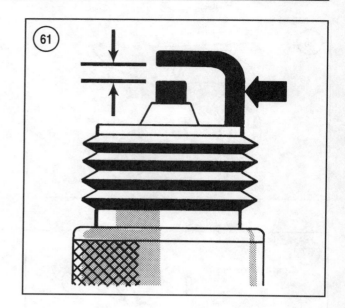

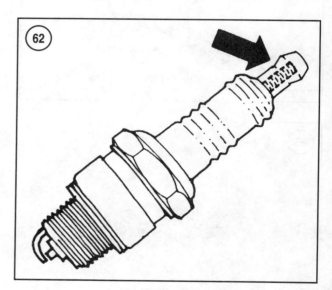

3

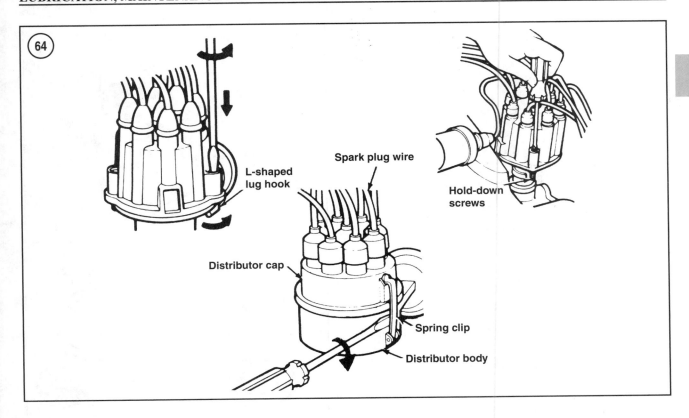

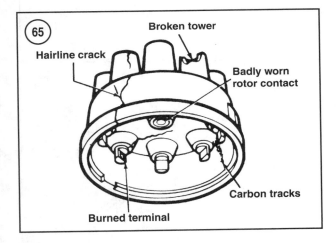

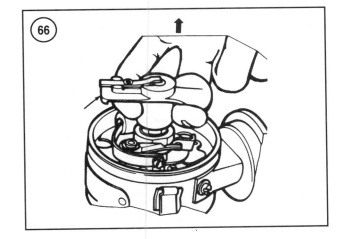

sary, have the distributor advance mechanism repaired at a reputable marine dealership.

9. To install the distributor cap, align the locating boss in the mating surface of the cap with the corresponding notch in the distributor body. Then seat the cap onto the distributor. Snap the clips in place, turn the latches or tighten the screws to secure the cap. See **Figure 64**.

10. If removed, connect the spark plug wires to the corresponding distributor cap terminals.

Breaker Points and Condenser Replacement

Replace the breaker points and condenser during a tune-up or if suspected of causing an ignition misfire. Consider reusing the points only if they are in excellent condition and a replacement set is not available. Although condenser failure is relatively rare, it is a good practice to replace it along with the ignition points.

A feeler gauge and an accurate dwell meter are required to adjust the breaker-point gap properly.

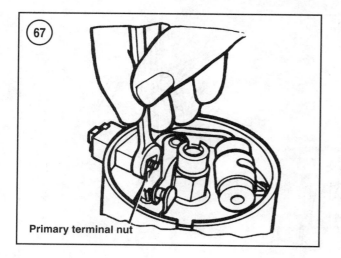

Primary terminal nut

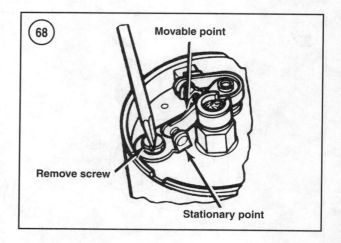

Movable point

Remove screw

Stationary point

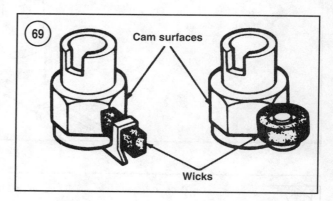

Cam surfaces

Wicks

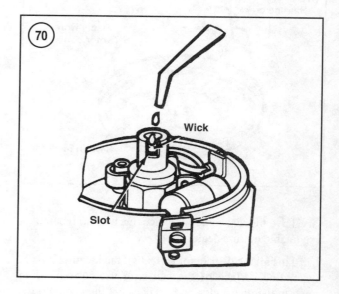

Wick

Slot

1. Disconnect the battery cables.

2. Remove the distributor cap and rotor as described in this section.

3. Loosen the primary wire nut (**Figure 67**, typical). Disconnect the primary lead and condenser lead or strap from the terminal block in the distributor or on the breaker assembly. Note all wire routing and connections prior to disconnecting the wiring.

4. Remove the screws (**Figure 68**, typical). Then lift the breaker assembly out of the distributor.

5. Remove the screw and then lift the condenser and clamp out of the distributor.

6. Clean debris and the oily film from the breaker plate and cam on the distributor shaft.

7A. On distributors using the type of lubricating wicks shown in **Figure 69**, remove the used wick from the slot or post. Install the new wick included with the replacement breaker assembly. Make sure the wick lightly contacts the cam.

7B. On distributors with a felt wick inside the distributor shaft (**Figure 70**), apply two drops of SAE 30 engine oil to the wick.

7C. On distributors *not* using a lubricating wick (**Figure 69** or **Figure 70**), lightly coat the distributor cam lobes with special distributor grease. A quantity of this grease is usually included with the replacement breaker assembly and can be purchased from most automotive parts stores. Never use oil or common grease; they will not provide the needed lubricating quality and are likely to migrate to the breaker-point contacts.

8. Install the *new* breaker assembly onto the breaker plate. Lightly tighten the screws (**Figure 68**).

9. If the replacement condenser does not have a hold-down clamp, remove the clamp from the used condenser and snap it onto the body of the replacement con-

denser. Install the condenser onto the breaker plate and install the clamp screw. Position the condenser to make sure it does not contact the sides of the distributor or the distributor cam lobes. Then tighten the screw.

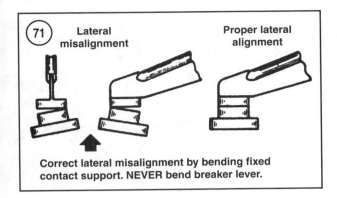

(71) Lateral misalignment   Proper lateral alignment

Correct lateral misalignment by bending fixed contact support. NEVER bend breaker lever.

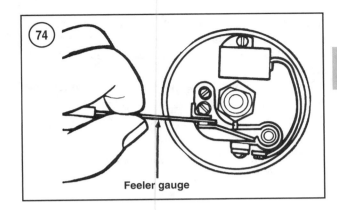

(74)

Feeler gauge

(72)

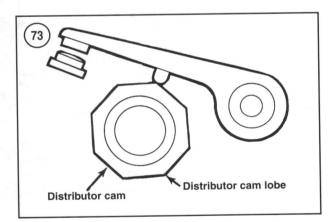

(73)

Distributor cam lobe

Distributor cam

3

10. Route the primary lead and condenser lead or strap to the primary nut terminal (**Figure 67**, typical). If the condenser uses an insulated strap instead of a wire, make sure the lower side of the strap is not contacting the breaker plate. Reposition the strap as needed. Make sure all wiring is routed correctly to prevent contact with moving components and then securely tighten the terminal nut.

11. Move the breaker assembly on the pivot until the points are closed (contacting). Check the alignment of the contact points (**Figure 71**). If necessary, carefully bend the stationary contact support on the breaker assembly to achieve proper alignment. Never bend the breaker lever. Replace the breaker assembly if the contacts cannot be properly aligned.

12. Adjust the breaker-point gap as described in this section.

13. Install the rotor and distributor cap as described in this section.

14. Connect the battery cables.

15. Adjust the ignition timing as described in Chapter Five.

Breaker-Point Gap and Dwell Adjustment

A remote starter switch, feeler gauge and an accurate dwell meter are required to adjust the breaker-point gap properly. The dwell meter indicates the number of degrees of distributor shaft rotation at which the points are *closed* and provides more accuracy than feeler gauge adjustment.

1. Disconnect the ignition coil secondary wire (**Figure 72**) from the distributor cap. Connect the wire to an engine ground to prevent arcing.

2. Following the manufacturer's instructions, connect a remote starter switch to the starter solenoid or slave solenoid. Bump the switch button until the starter rotates the engine just enough to align the breaker-point rubbing block *precisely* with the point on the distributor cam lobe as shown in **Figure 73**. At this point, the contact points are fully open.

3. Insert a 0.015-in. feeler gauge between the contact points as shown in **Figure 74**. Proper gap adjustment will allow the feeler gauge to slide between the contacts with a slight drag without moving the breaker-point lever. If adjustment is required, turn the eccentric adjusting screw or move the stationary bracket with a screwdriver inserted into the adjustment slot. See **Figure 75**. When the gap is correct, securely tighten the screw (**Figure 68**, typical) to

secure the stationary bracket. Recheck the gap and correct as needed.

4. Install the rotor and distributor cap as described in this section.

5. Connect the dwell meter to the negative coil terminal and engine ground following the manufacturer's instructions.

> **WARNING**
> *Stay clear of the propeller and propeller shaft while running an engine on a flush adapter.*

> **CAUTION**
> *Use a flush device or other means to supply the engine with cooling water if running the engine with the boat out of the water. The seawater pump is quickly damaged if operated without adequate cooling water.*

> **CAUTION**
> *Never adjust the point gap or dwell after adjusting the ignition timing. Changing the point gap or dwell will affect the ignition timing. Ignition timing does not affect the point gap or dwell.*

6. Start the engine and note the dwell meter. The meter should indicate 24-30° dwell. Refer to the following:
   a. If the dwell is lower than the specification, stop the engine and decrease the point gap. Repeat the dwell measurement.
   b. If the dwell is greater than the specification, stop the engine and adjust the points, as described in this section, to a greater gap and repeat the dwell measurement.
   c. If the dwell meter reading is within the specification, proceed to Step 7.

7. Adjust the ignition timing as described in Chapter Five.

8. Stop the engine. Remove the timing light and dwell meter.

Valve Adjustment

The models covered in this manual use hydraulic lifters, and periodic valve adjustment is not required during a periodic tune-up. The valves can be adjusted on all 5.0L/5.7L models and 7.4/8.2L models (with a two-piece rear main seal). All 7.4L/8.2L models with a one-piece rear main seal and all 8.1L models use nonadjustable valve train hardware.

Excessive valve clearance causes valve system noise and may increase wear on some valve train components.

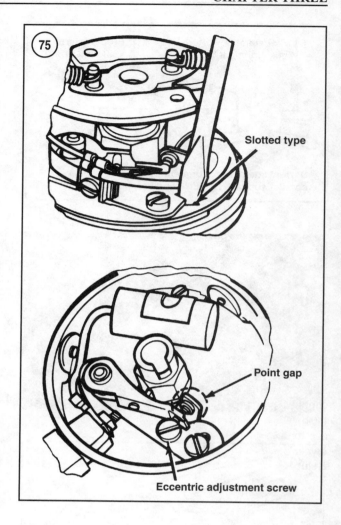

Insufficient clearance can result in rapid wear of valve train components, reduced power and rough engine operation. Valve noise or insufficient clearance is generally the result of improper assembly or damaged components. If valve noise is evident or improper valve adjustment is suspected, adjust the valves as described in Chapter Six.

Carburetor Adjustment

Proper carburetor adjustment is essential for smooth and efficient operation. Carburetor adjustments performed during a tune-up include idle mixture and idle speed. Carburetor adjustment is described in Chapter Five.

Ignition Timing Adjustment

The ignition timing is automatically set by the engine control unit (ECU) on 5.7L LT-1 and 8.1L models. The initial timing must be adjusted on all other models. On electronic fuel injection (EFI) models, special procedures must be followed. Failure to follow these procedures can result in poor performance or serious engine damage. Ignition timing adjustment is described in Chapter Five.

Water Testing the Engine

NOTE
Perform this test with an average load in the boat.

1. Connect a shop tachometer to the engine following the manufacturer's instructions.
2. Start the engine and run at fast idle (approximately 1500 rpm) in NEUTRAL until it reaches normal operating temperature.
3. Return the engine to idle speed. Note the idle speed while an assistant operates the boat. Adjust the idle speed as described in Chapter Five.
4. Accelerate to wide-open throttle and note the engine speed. Compare the speed on the shop tachometer with the speed indicated on the dash-mounted speedometer. Check for improper adjustment of the dash-mounted tachometer if the speeds vary more than 200 rpm. Refer to the owner's manual for the specific boat and engine package to determine the correct engine operating range. An owner's manual may be purchased from an Indmar dealership. Check the propeller for damage or incorrect pitch if the engine speed is not within the recommended range. Refer to *Preliminary Inspection* in Chapter Two if the correct propeller is installed but the engine fails to reach the recommended speed range.
5. Try rapid acceleration and run the engine at various speed ranges. Refer to *Preliminary Inspection* in Chapter Two if rough operation is noted at any speed range or hesitation occurs during rapid acceleration.

SUBMERSION

If the engine has been submerged, three factors need to be considered. Was the engine running when the submersion occurred? Was the engine submerged in saltwater, brackish water or polluted water? How long has the engine been retrieved from the water?

Complete disassembly and inspection of the engine is required if the engine was submerged when running. Internal damage to the engine (bent connecting rod) is likely. Refer to Chapter Six for engine repair instructions.

Many components of the engine suffer the corrosive effects of submersion in saltwater, brackish water or polluted water. The symptoms might not occur for some time

after the event. Salt crystals form in many areas of the engine and promote intense corrosion in that area. The wire harness and the connections are usually damaged very quickly. It is difficult to remove all of the salt from the harness connectors. Replace the wire harness and clean all electrical connections to ensure a reliable repair. The starter motor, relays and any switch on the engine usually fail if they are not thoroughly cleaned of all salt residue.

Retrieve and service the engine as soon as possible. Vigorously wash all debris from the engine with freshwater after retrieval. Complete engine disassembly and inspection is required if sand, silt or other gritty material is noted inside the throttle opening. Refer to Chapter Six for engine repair instructions.

Service the engine quickly to make sure it is running within a few hours after retrieval. This is especially important if the engine was submerged in saltwater, brackish water or polluted water.

Completely disassemble and inspect the internal components if the engine was not serviced in a timely manner.

Perform the following steps as soon as the engine is retrieved from the water:

1. Remove the engine cover and flame arrestor and vigorously wash all material from the engine using freshwater. Completely disassemble and inspect the engine if sand, silt or gritty material is present inside the throttle opening.

2. Dry the exterior of the engine with compressed air. Remove the spark plugs and ground all spark plug leads.

3. Change the transmission fluid as described in this chapter.

4. Drain all water and fuel from the fuel system. Replace all fuel filters on the engine. Refer to Chapter Seven.

5. Drain the oil from the crankcase and remove the oil filter. Disconnect the battery cables.

6. Manually rotate the harmonic balancer (clockwise on a standard-rotation engine and counterclockwise on a counter-rotation engine) to force water from the cylinders. Rotate the flywheel several times and note whether the engine is turning freely. Completely disassemble and inspect the engine if interference is noted.

7. Pour approximately one teaspoon of engine oil into each spark plug opening. Repeat Step 6 to distribute the oil in the cylinders.

8. Disconnect all electrical connections and inspect the terminals. Dry all exterior surfaces and wire connectors with compressed air. Remove, disassemble and inspect the starter motor as outlined in Chapter Nine. Service and test the battery (refer to Chapter Nine). Have the alternator cleaned and inspected at a reputable starter and alternator repair shop.

9. Replace the oil filter and fill the engine with fresh oil. Clean and install the spark plugs. Reconnect all wire harnesses and battery terminals.

10. Provide the engine with a fresh supply of fuel. Start the engine and run it at a low speed for a few minutes. Refer to Chapter Two for troubleshooting instructions if the engine cannot be started. Stop the engine immediately and investigate if unusual noises are noted.

11. Allow the engine to run at low speed for a minimum of 30 minutes to dry any residual water from the engine. Promptly investigate any unusual noises or unusual running conditions.

12. Change the engine oil again and replace the oil filter.

13. Change the transmission fluid.

14. Perform all maintenance items listed in **Table 2**.

Table 1 MAINTENANCE TORQUE SPECIFICATIONS

Fastener	in.-lb.	ft.-lb.	N•m
Oil drain plug			
5.0L and 5.7L models	221	–	25
7.4L and 8.2L models	–	20	27
8.1L models	–	21	28
Spark plug			
5.0L and 5.7L models			
With used cylinder head	–	15	20
With new cylinder head	–	22	30
7.4L and 8.2L models	–	15-20	20-28
8.1L models	–	15	20

Table 2 MAINTENANCE INTERVALS

Before each use	Check engine oil level
	Check transmission fluid level
	Check power steering fluid level*
	Check propeller for damage
	Check propeller shaft for bending
	Inspect steering system
	Check coolant level (closed cooling system)*
	Check emergency stop (lanyard) switch operation
After each use	Flush the cooling system
	Clean the engine
	Inspect the propeller for damage
First 20 hours of operation	Change the engine oil and oil filter
	Change the transmission fluid
	Check power steering fluid level*
	Clean or replace primary fuel filter
	Adjust shift cable (refer to Chapter Five)
	Lubricate steering cable ram*
	Check drive belt tension (refer to Chapter Nine)
	Tighten hose clamps and engine mounts
Every 50 hours of operation	Check drive belt tension (refer to Chapter Nine)
	Clean flame arrestor
	Check rubber hoses for deterioration
Every 60 days or 50 hours of operation	Lubricate the steering cable ram*
	(continued)

Table 2 MAINTENANCE INTERVALS (continued)

Once a year or every 100 hours of operation	Change the engine oil and oil filter
	Change the transmission fluid
	Clean or replace primary fuel filter
	Check shift cable adjustment (refer to Chapter Five)
	Check engine alignment (refer to Chapter Six)
	Clean PCV valve*
	Clean and inspect spark plugs
	Replace breaker points and condenser*
Every two years or 200 hours of operation	Replace water pump impeller (refer to Chapter Eight)
	Change closed cooling system coolant*

*This maintenance item does not apply to all models.

Table 3 ENGINE OIL CAPACITIES

Model	Approximate capacity	
5.0L and 5.7L models	5 qt. (4.7 L)	
7.4L and 8.2L models	7 qt. (6.6 L)	
8.1L models	9 qt. (8.5 L)	

Table 4 TRANSMISSION FLUID CAPACITIES

Model	Approximate capacity	
Borg-Warner or Regal Beloit		
71C (inline transmission)	64 oz. (1.4 L)	
72C (V-drive transmsission)	3.0 qt. (2.8 L)	
5000A series	2.5 qt. (2.4 L)	
5000V series	3.0 qt. (2.8 L)	
Hurth/ZF		
360	47 oz. (1.4 L)	
450	2.0 qt. (1.8 L)	
630V	4.5 qt. (4.3 L)	
630A	3.25 qt. (3.1 L)	
800A	5.75 qt. (5.4 L)	
Walters V-drive		
RV-36	32 oz. (0.95 L)	

Table 5 SPARK PLUG RECOMMENDATIONS

Model	Spark plug No.	Spark plug gap
5.0L and 5.7L models		
With 12-bolt intake manifold		
AC plug	MR43T	0.035 in. (0.9 mm)
Champion plug	RV12YC	0.035 in. (0.9 mm)

(continued)

Table 5 SPARK PLUG RECOMMENDATIONS (continued)

Model	Spark plug No.	Spark plug gap
5.0L and 5.7L models		
With 12-bolt intake manifold (continued)		
NGK plug		
1983-1987	UR5	0.035 in. (0.9 mm)
1988-1997	BR6FS	0.035 in. (0.9 mm)
With 8-bolt intake manifold		
1998-2001		
AC plug	MR43LTS	0.045 in. (1.1 mm)
Champion plug	RS12YC	0.045 in. (1.1 mm)
NGK plug	BPR6EFS	0.045 in. (1.1 mm)
2002-2003		
AC plug	41-932	0.060 in. (1.5 mm)
7.4L and 8.2L models		
1983-1997		
AC plug	MR43T	0.035 in. (0.9 mm)
Champion plug	RV8C	0.035 in. (0.9 mm)
NGK plug	BR6FS	0.035 in. (0.9 mm)
1998-2000		
AC plug	MR43LTS	0.045 in. (1.1 mm)
NGK plug	BPR6EFS	0.045 in. (1.1 mm)
Champion plug	RS12YC	0.045 in. (1.1 mm)
8.1L models		
Nippon Denso plug	TJ14R-P15	0.060 in. (1.5 mm)

Chapter Four

Lay-Up, Winterizing and Fitting Out

All major engine systems require some preparation before storage. Perform the procedures described in *Lay-Up* if the engine will not be operated for several weeks or longer and especially if the engine is used or stored in saltwater or heavily polluted water.

The engine must be winterized before being exposed to freezing temperatures. Water remaining in the cooling system can freeze and expand and cause serious damage to the cylinder block, manifolds, heat exchanger(s) and other components. Always winterize the engine before transporting or storing the boat in high-elevation areas that might experience freezing temperatures even during the summer months.

Fitting out prepares the engine for operation. Perform these procedures before returning the engine to service.

LAY-UP

When preparing the engine for long-term storage, the objective is to prevent corrosion or deterioration during the storage period.

Refer to Chapter Three and perform any maintenance due during the storage period.

External Surfaces

Use pressurized water to clean the propeller, propeller shaft and support strut (**Figure 1**). Wipe the components clean and apply a good corrosion-prevention spray available from most marine dealerships and marine supply stores.

Fuel

Serious problems can be avoided if the fuel system is properly prepared for storage. Start by draining as much fuel as possible from the fuel tank. Then inspect or replace all fuel filters as described in Chapter Three and Chapter Seven. Treat the fuel system with a fuel stabilizer as described in this section.

Fuel stabilizer

NOTE
*Inspect the fuel fill hose for dips or low places (**Figure 2**) that may prevent all of the*

fuel stabilizer from flowing into the fuel tank.

Use a fuel stabilizer to help prevent the formation of gum or varnish during the storage period. Be aware that some stabilizers may adversely affect some fuel system components if mixed or used incorrectly. Deterioration of hoses, check valves and other nonmetallic components may occur. Never mix the stabilizer at a rate greater than specified on the label.

Always inspect the fuel fill hose for dips or low spots (**Figure 2**) before pouring a fuel stabilizer into the tank. Dips or low spots may prevent all of the stabilizer from flowing into the tank. If necessary, lift the hose after pouring the stabilizer into the hose or add fresh fuel into the fill cap to wash the stabilizer into the tank.

Before storage, run the engine for a minimum of 15 minutes to distribute the stabilizer throughout the fuel system. If the engine is equipped with a four-barrel carburetor (**Figure 3**), the engine must be operated for several minutes under actual operating conditions and at a high throttle setting to transfer the treated fuel into the secondary fuel metering passages.

Fogging the Engine

Treat the cylinders with a fogging oil if the engine will not be used for several weeks or longer. The fogging oil is available from marine dealerships and marine supply stores. This procedure can prevent corrosion inside the engine during the storage period. This is especially important if the engine is used or stored in saltwater or polluted water. The oil used and method for application depends on the type of fuel system used on the engine. Refer to Chapter Seven to identify the fuel system components.

> *WARNING*
> *Stay clear of the propeller and propeller shaft while running the engine on a flush adapter.*

> *CAUTION*
> *Use a flush device or other means to supply the engine with cooling water if running the engine with the boat out of the water. The seawater pump is quickly damaged if operated without adequate cooling water.*

Carburetor-equipped engines

1. Add the required amount of fuel stabilizer to the fuel tank.

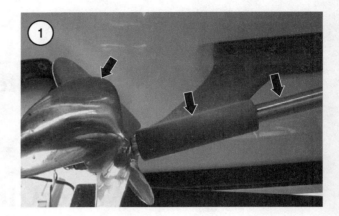

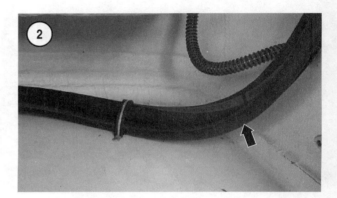

2. Remove the flame arrestor (**Figure 4**) as described in Chapter Three. Refer to *Cleaning the Flame Arrestor.*

3. Raise the engine speed to approximately 1500 rpm. Spray the fogging oil into the carburetor throat in 5-10 second intervals (**Figure 5**). Continue to spray the oil into the engine until heavy smoke comes from the exhaust. This indicates the oil has passed through the engine. Stop the engine at this point.

4. Spray more of the fogging oil into the carburetor. Activate the lanyard switch to prevent accidental starting. Operate the starter for a few seconds to distribute the oil into the cylinders. Reset the lanyard switch.

5. Install the flame arrestor as described in Chapter Three. Refer to *Cleaning the Flame Arrestor*.

Throttle body injection (TBI) models

On throttle body injection (TBI) models, the fogging oil is introduced into the engine through the throttle bores in the throttle body.

1. Add the required amount of fuel stabilizer to the fuel tank. Refer to *Fuel stabilizer*.

2. Remove the cover and flame arrestor (**Figure 6**) as described in Chapter Three. Refer to *Cleaning the Flame Arrestor*.

3. Spray the fogging oil into the throttle body openings (**Figure 7**) in 5-10 second intervals. Continue to spray the oil into the engine until heavy smoke comes from the exhaust. This indicates the oil has passed through the engine. Stop the engine at this point.

4. Spray one more shot of the fogging oil into the throttle bores. Activate the lanyard switch to prevent accidental starting. Operate the starter for a few seconds to distribute the oil over the cylinder walls. Reset the lanyard switch.

5. Install the flame arrestor (**Figure 6**) as described in Chapter Three. Refer to *Cleaning the Flame Arrestor*.

Multiport injection (MPI) models (center-mounted throttle body)

On multiport injection (MPI) models with a center-mounted throttle body, the fogging oil is introduced into the engine through the throttle body.

1. Add the required amount of fuel stabilizer to the fuel tank. Refer to *Fuel stabilizer*.

2. Remove the cover and flame arrestor as described in Chapter Three. Refer to *Cleaning the Flame Arrestor*.

3. Spray the fogging oil into the throttle body opening (**Figure 8**, typical) in 5-10 second intervals. Continue to spray the oil into the engine until heavy smoke comes from the exhaust. This indicates the oil has passed through the engine. Stop the engine at this point.

4. Spray one more shot of the fogging oil into the throttle bore. Activate the lanyard switch to prevent accidental starting. Operate the starter for a few seconds to distribute the oil over the cylinder walls. Reset the lanyard switch.

5. Install the flame arrestor as described in Chapter Three. Refer to *Cleaning the Flame Arrestor*.

4

Multiport injection (MPI) models (front-mounted throttle body [engine-mounted electric fuel pump])

On MPI models with a front-mounted throttle body (**Figure 9**), the fogging oil is introduced into the engine through the fuel injectors. This procedure requires a portable outboard fuel tank, 26 oz. of fogging oil and enough fuel stabilizer to treat the fuel in the tank plus an additional 2 gal. (7.6 L). Liquid fogging oil may be difficult to locate in some areas. If necessary, purchase the fogging oil from a marine dealership.

1. Add the required amount of fuel stabilizer to the fuel tank. Refer to *Fuel stabilizer*.

2. Turn the engine off and disconnect the battery cables.

3. Pour a mixture of 2 gal. (7.6 L) of fresh fuel, enough fuel stabilizer for 2 gal. (7.6 L) of fuel and 26 oz. (766 mL) of fogging oil into a portable outboard fuel tank. Rock the tank for several minutes to thoroughly mix the contents.

4. Refer to the information in Chapter Seven to identify the fuel supply line on the engine. Trace the fuel supply line from the fuel tank to the inlet fitting on the water-separating fuel filter or boost pump (if so equipped). Loosen the clamp screw (**Figure 10**, typical) and carefully pull the supply line off the fitting. Drain the line into the portable fuel tank.

5. Connect the portable fuel tank hose to the inlet and secure with the hose clamp. Route the hose to prevent interference with belts or other moving components on the engine. Squeeze the primer bulb to transfer treated fuel into the system in preparation for starting.

6. Connect the battery cable.

7. Start the engine and operate at 1500 rpm for 10 minutes to distribute the fogging mixture throughout the fuel system and into the cylinders. A hint of smoke should be detected in the exhaust indicating the mixture is distributed throughout the engine. If necessary, run the engine for a few more minutes or until smoking is evident.

8. Stop the engine and disconnect the portable fuel tank hose. Drain the hose into the portable tank.

9. Connect the boat fuel supply line to the inlet fitting and secure with the hose clamp. Route the supply hose to prevent interference with belts or other moving components. Secure the hose with clamps as necessary.

Multiport injection (MPI) models (front-mounted throttle body [tank-mounted electric fuel pump])

On MPI models with a front-mounted throttle body, the fogging oil is introduced into the engine through the fuel injectors. This procedure requires enough liquid fogging oil and fuel stabilizer to treat the fuel in the tank. If neces-

sary, drain the fuel from the tank but leave a minimum of 2 gal. (7.6 L). Liquid fogging oil might be difficult to locate in some areas. If necessary, purchase the fogging oil from a marine dealership.

1. Add enough fuel stabilizer for the fuel in the tank plus enough for one additional gallon into the boat fuel tank. Refer to *Fuel stabilizer*.

2. Pour enough fogging oil for the fuel into the boat fuel tank plus enough for one additional gallon of fuel into a portable fuel tank. Add one gallon of fuel to the portable

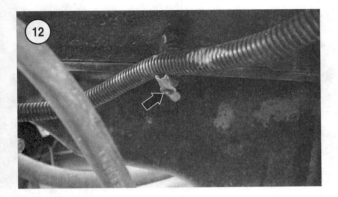

tank. Rock the portable tank to thoroughly mix the fogging oil and fuel.

3. Pour the oil-and-fuel mixture into the boat fuel tank.

4. Start the engine and operate at 1500 rpm for 10 minutes to distribute the fogging mixture throughout the fuel system and into the cylinders. A hint of smoke should be detected in the exhaust to indicate the mixture is distributed throughout the engine. If necessary, run the engine for a few more minutes or until smoking is evident.

5. Stop the engine.

Transmission Storage

> *CAUTION*
> *Never direct pressurized water onto the transmission housing. Pressurized water might bypass seals or enter vent openings and contaminate the transmission fluid.*

The transmission requires only that all water is removed from the transmission fluid cooler, the fluid is changed, and debris, salt crystals or other contamination is removed from the external surfaces. Drain the fluid cooler as described in *Winterizing* in this chapter. Check and/or change the transmission fluid as described in Chapter

Three. Use a soap-and-water solution to remove grease and other contaminants from the transmission housing. Do not allow water near the vent cap (**Figure 11**, typical) as it can enter the opening and contaminate the transmission fluid. After cleaning the transmission housing, apply a corrosion-prevention spray onto the housing.

Battery Storage

After treating the fuel system and fogging the engine, remove the battery and recharge at 30-day intervals as described in Chapter Nine. A discharged battery can freeze and rupture.

WINTERIZING

Winterizing is a series of steps to drain all water from the cooling system. The exhaust manifolds and seawater pump must be drained on all models. The cylinder block must also be drained on all models equipped with an open cooling system. The heat exchanger must be drained on all models equipped with a closed cooling system. On models with a closed cooling system, the cylinder block is filled with a coolant-and-water solution and does not require draining for storage, provided that the coolant mixture can withstand the lowest anticipated temperature without freezing. Some closed cooling systems flow coolant through the cylinder block and exhaust manifolds. If uncertain, loosen the drain fittings for the exhaust manifolds to check for water or coolant.

> *NOTE*
> *Manufacturers often make changes in production that affect hose routing or water drain locations. Always refer to the owner's manual for specific drain locations. An owner's manual may be purchased from an Indmar dealership.*

> *NOTE*
> *Closed cooling system kits are available from numerous sources. Cooling system design, hose routing and fluid capacity will vary by manufacturer. Refer to the information supplied by the cooling system manufacturer for specific information. This section describes draining water from the typical closed cooling system.*

Drain Locations

Carburetor-equipped models have cylinder block drain petcocks (**Figure 12**) or removable plugs (**Figure 13**) on

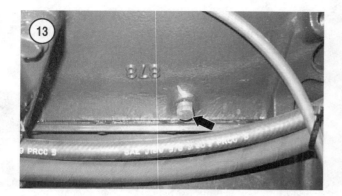

the port and starboard sides of the cylinder block. Electronic fuel injection (EFI) models have a drain plug (**Figure 13**) on one side of the cylinder block. The water must be drained from the other side of the cylinder block by removing the knock sensor (A, **Figure 14**).

Some late models might be equipped with a freshwater flushing system that also is used to drain the cylinder block. The system consists of block drain hoses (B, **Figure 14**) connected to a common drain hose fitting (**Figure 15**, typical).

On early models, the exhaust manifold drain petcock or plug is located on the bottom (**Figure 16**) or end (**Figure 17**) of each manifold. Some late models might be equipped with a water drain hose connected to each exhaust manifold (**Figure 18**). Drain the manifolds by disconnecting the hose coupling (**Figure 19**).

Early models use a belt-driven seawater pump (**Figure 20**). Late models use a crankshaft-driven seawater pump (**Figure 21**). The inlet and outlet hoses must be removed to drain either type of seawater pump.

The large recirculation pump hose (**Figure 22**, typical) must be removed to drain the recirculation pump.

On models with a closed cooling system, the seawater drain plug for the heat exchanger (**Figure 23**) is located on the bottom near the end of the heat exchanger. The

coolant drain plug is located farther from the end of the exchanger. The heat exchanger end cap (**Figure 24**, typical) can also be removed to drain seawater from the heat exchanger. Use this method if the drain plug is inaccessible. Removing the end cap will also allow a visual inspection for debris or excessive deposit buildup.

The transmission fluid cooler (**Figure 25**, typical) is located along the hose connecting the seawater pump outlet fitting to the thermostat housing. The water hose must be removed from the cooler fitting to drain the water. The transmission fluid cooler is similar in appearance to the power steering fluid cooler used on models with power steering. The transmission fluid cooler is larger than the power steering fluid cooler and uses flare nut connections to secure the fluid hoses to the cooler. The power steering fluid cooler uses screw type hose clamps to secure the fluid hoses onto the cooler.

On models with power steering, the fluid cooler (**Figure 26**, typical) is located along the hose connecting the seawater pump outlet fitting to the thermostat housing. The water hose must be disconnected from the cooler to drain the water.

CAUTION
After removing any plug, always insert a stiff piece of wire into the opening to clear sand or other debris from the opening.

Models with a Standard (Open) Cooling System

1. Treat the fuel system and fog the engine as described in this chapter. Disconnect the battery cables. Make sure the engine is level. Tilting can prevent proper draining.

CAUTION
The inlet and outlet hoses connected to the seawater pump are the same diameter. Always mark the hoses and pump prior to disconnecting them to make sure they are not switched when reconnected. Running the engine with the hoses switched will damage the impeller or other pump components.

2. Loosen the hose clamps and then disconnect the inlet and outlet hoses from the seawater pump (**Figure 20** or **Figure 21**). Push the hoses off the seawater pump using a blunt tool. Work carefully to avoid damaging the hoses or pump. Drain all water from the hoses. Use compressed air to clear residual water from the hoses and pump.

3. If the boat is stored in the water and is equipped with a shutoff valve on the seawater pickup, turn the valve off and loosen the clamp that secures the inlet hose to the pickup. Disconnect the hose from the pickup and drain the water from the hose.

4A. On models using a Walters V-drive unit, trace the seawater inlet hose from the seawater pickup (**Figure 27**, typical) to the fitting on the side of the V-drive unit (**Figure 28**). The inlet hose may be attached to either side. Loosen the clamp and carefully push the inlet hose off the pickup. If the boat is stored in the water, secure the disconnected end of the hose to a location higher than the water level *and* insert a plug into the end of the hose to

prevent water from siphoning into the bilge. Secure the plug in the hose with a clamp.

4B. On models without a Walters V-drive unit that are stored in the water, route the water pump end of the inlet hose to a location higher than the water level *and* insert a plug into the end of the inlet hose to prevent water from siphoning into the bilge. Identify the seawater inlet hose by tracing it to the seawater pickup (**Figure 27**, typical). Secure the plug in the hose with a clamp.

5A. On models with drain petcocks or drain plugs in the bottom of the exhaust manifolds, open the petcock or remove the plug from each manifold (**Figure 16**, typical). Insert a stiff wire into the plug opening to clear sand and other debris. Continue clearing debris until each manifold is fully drained.

5B. On models with drain plugs on the ends of the exhaust manifolds (**Figure 17**, typical), use a 1/2-in. drive ratchet or breaker bar to remove the plug from the end of each manifold. Insert a stiff wire into the plug opening to clear sand and other debris. Continue clearing debris until each manifold is fully drained.

5C. On models with drain hoses on the exhaust manifolds (**Figure 18**), unthread the hose coupler (**Figure 19**) and then direct the coupler to a location in the bilge that is lower than the oil pan. Make sure water drains from both

4

couplers. If not, disconnect the coupler hose from the exhaust manifold fitting and insert a stiff piece of wire into the manifold fitting to clear debris.

6. Remove the water hose (**Figure 29**) from the opposite end of both exhaust manifolds. Direct compressed air into the manifolds to clear residual water and debris from the manifold cooling passages.

7A. On carburetor-equipped models with block drain petcocks (**Figure 12**) or removable drain plugs (**Figure 13**), open the drain petcock or remove the brass drain plugs from the port and starboard sides of the cylinder block. Remove the petcock from the block if it does not drain water when opened. Insert a stiff wire into the plug or petcock openings to clear sand and other debris. Continue clearing debris until both sides of the cylinder block are fully drained.

7B. On EFI models with removal drain plugs (**Figure 13**), remove the drain plug from the side of the cylinder block. Then remove the knock sensor (A, **Figure 14**) as described in Chapter Nine. Insert a stiff wire into the plug or knock sensor openings to clear sand and other debris. Continue clearing debris until both sides of the cylinder block are fully drained.

7C. On late models with block drain hoses (B, **Figure 14**), remove the brass cap (**Figure 15**, typical) from the

freshwater flush hose. Route the hose to a location lower than the oil pan and allow the water to drain fully from the block. While draining the block, trace the water drain hoses to the fittings on each side of the cylinder block. Both hoses must be warm, which indicates water is flowing from the cylinder block. If one of the hoses is cool or water does not drain from the fitting, remove the suspect hose(s) from the fitting(s) and insert a stiff wire into the fitting(s) to clear debris. Use compressed air to clear debris from the hoses. After they have fully drained, reconnect the drain hoses to the fitting(s).

8. Loosen the clamp and then disconnect the C-shaped hose (**Figure 22**) from the recirculation pump. Bend the bottom of the hose to drain residual water from the low spot in the hose.

9. Loosen the clamp and disconnect the lower hose from the transmission cooler (**Figure 25**). Drain all water from the cooler. Route the disconnected hose to a location in the bilge that is lower than the oil pan to drain residual water from the hose. If the boat is stored in the water, secure the disconnected end of the hose to a location higher than the water level *and* insert a plug into the end of the inlet hose to prevent water from siphoning into the bilge. Secure the plug in the hose with a clamp.

10. On models with power steering, loosen the clamp and disconnect the lower hose from the fluid cooler (**Figure 26**). Drain all water from the cooler. Route the disconnected hose to a location in the bilge that is lower than the oil pan to drain residual water from the hose. If the boat is stored in the water, secure the disconnected end of the hose to a location higher than the water level *and* insert a plug into the end of the inlet hose to prevent water from siphoning into the bilge. Secure the plug in the hose with a clamp.

11. Direct compressed air into all open fittings and hoses to clear debris or residual water from the passages.

12. If the boat is stored in the water and is equipped with a shutoff valve on the seawater pickup, drain any water from the hose. Then connect the inlet hose to the pickup. Securely tighten the hose clamp. *Do not* open the shutoff valve.

13. If the boat is equipped with a water heater, disconnect the water heater hoses from the engine (**Figure 30**, typical). Drain all water from the hoses. Drain the water heater following the manufacturer's instructions.

14. If the boat is stored in the water, observe all disconnected hoses and fittings for evidence of water siphoning into the engine compartment. Plug hoses or tighten clamps as needed to prevent siphoning. Wait at least 30 minutes and again check for siphoning. Do not store the boat in the water until all siphoning is eliminated.

15A. If the boat is stored on a trailer, remove the battery and store in a cool and dry location. Charge the battery every 30-45 days, as described in Chapter Nine. A discharged battery can freeze and rupture.

15B. If the boat is stored in the water, remove the battery and charge every 30-45 days as described in Chapter Nine. A preferable alternative is to install an onboard charger that connects to shore power to maintain the battery charge level.

16. If the boat is stored on a trailer or the exhaust outlets are above the water level, cover the exhaust outlets to prevent small animals or insects from entering the exhaust system. If necessary, insert a sponge into each outlet.

Models with a Closed Cooling System

1. Treat the fuel system and fog the engine as described in this chapter. Disconnect the battery cables. Make sure the engine is level. Tilting may prevent proper draining.

> *CAUTION*
> *The inlet and outlet hoses connected to the seawater pump are the same diameter. Always mark the hoses and pump prior to disconnecting them to make sure they are not switched when reconnected. Running the engine with the hoses switched will damage the impeller or other pump components.*

2. Loosen the hose clamps and then disconnect the inlet and outlet hoses from the seawater pump (**Figure 20** or **Figure 21**). Push the hoses off the seawater pump fittings using a blunt tool. Work carefully to avoid damaging the hoses or pump. Drain all water from the hoses. Use compressed air to clear water from the hoses and fittings.

3. If the boat is stored in the water and is equipped with a shutoff valve on the seawater pickup, turn the valve off and loosen the clamp that secures the inlet hose to the pickup. Disconnect the hose from the pickup and drain the water from the hose.

4A. On models using a Walters V-drive unit, trace the seawater inlet hose from the pickup (**Figure 27**, typical) to the V-drive unit (**Figure 28**). The inlet hose may be attached to either side. Loosen the clamp and push the inlet hose off the V-drive unit. If the boat is stored in the water, secure the disconnected end of the hose to a location higher than the water level *and* insert a plug into the end of the inlet hose to prevent water from siphoning into the bilge. Secure the plug in the hose with a clamp.

4B. On models without a Walters V-drive unit that are stored in the water, route the water pump end of the inlet hose to a location higher than the water level *and* insert a plug into the end of the inlet hose to prevent water from si-

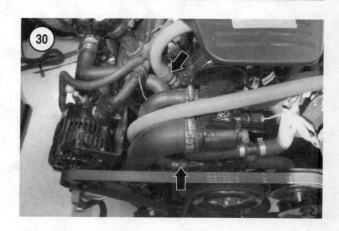

phoning into the bilge. Identify the seawater inlet hose by tracing it to the seawater pickup fitting (**Figure 27**, typical). Secure the plug to the hose with a clamp.

> *NOTE*
> *Some models are equipped with a closed cooling system that directs coolant through the exhaust manifolds. If uncertain, carefully loosen one of the exhaust manifold drain petcocks or plugs to check for coolant. If water is present, the exhaust manifolds are cooled with seawater and must be drained in preparation for exposure to freezing temperature. If coolant is present, the exhaust manifolds are included in the closed system and do not require draining. However, the exhaust elbow/riser must be drained because exiting seawater passes through the elbow/riser.*

5A. If the exhaust manifolds are cooled with seawater and are equipped with drain petcocks or drain plugs, open the petcock or remove the plug from each manifold (**Figure 16**, typical). Insert a stiff wire into the plug opening to clear sand and other debris. Continue clearing debris until each manifold is fully drained.

5B. If the manifolds are cooled with seawater and are equipped with drain plugs on the ends of the exhaust manifolds (**Figure 17**, typical), use a 1/2-in. drive ratchet or breaker bar to remove the plugs from the end of each manifold. Insert a stiff wire into the plug opening to clear sand and other debris. Continue clearing debris until each manifold is fully drained.

5C. On models with drain hoses on the exhaust manifolds (**Figure 18**), unthread the hose coupler (**Figure 19**) and then direct the coupler to a location in the bilge that is lower than the oil pan. Make sure water drains from both couplers. If not, disconnect the coupler hose from the exhaust manifold and insert a stiff piece of wire into the manifold to clear debris.

6. Remove the water hose (**Figure 29**) from the end of both exhaust manifolds. Direct compressed air into the manifolds to clear water and debris from the manifold cooling passages.

7. If the exhaust manifolds are cooled with seawater, disconnect the hoses from each exhaust elbow/riser. Drain all water from the hoses. Direct compressed air into the elbow/riser hose fitting to clear debris and water.

8. Loosen the clamp. Then disconnect the lower hose from the transmission cooler (**Figure 25**). Drain all water from the cooler. Route the disconnected hose to a location in the bilge that is lower than the oil pan to drain water from the hose. If the boat is stored in the water, secure the disconnected end of the hose to a location higher than the water level *and* insert a plug into the end of the inlet hose to prevent water from siphoning into the bilge. Secure the plug in the hose with a clamp.

9. On models with power steering, loosen the clamp and then disconnect the lower hose from the fluid cooler (**Figure 26**). Drain all water from the cooler. Route the disconnected hose to a location in the bilge that is lower than the oil pan to drain water from the hose. If the boat is stored in the water, secure the disconnected end of the hose to a location higher than the water level *and* insert a plug into the end of the inlet hose to prevent water from siphoning into the bilge. Secure the plug in the hose with a clamp.

10. Remove the drain plug from the heat exchanger (**Figure 23**, typical). The water drain fitting is generally located near the end of the heat exchanger. Insert a stiff wire into the plug opening to clear sand and other debris. Continue clearing debris until the exchanger is fully drained. If the drain plug is inaccessible, damaged or seized, remove the bolt (**Figure 24**, typical) and carefully pry the cap from the heat exchanger. Replace the gasket in the cap upon installation.

11. Direct compressed air into all open fittings and hoses to clear debris or water from the passages.

12. If the boat is stored in the water and is equipped with a shutoff valve on the seawater pickup, drain any water from the hose and then connect the inlet hose to the pickup. Securely tighten the hose clamp. *Do not* open the shutoff valve. Observe all disconnected hoses and fittings for evidence of water siphoning into the engine compartment. Plug hoses or tighten clamps as needed to prevent siphoning. Wait at least 30 minutes and again check for siphoning. Do not store the boat in the water until all siphoning is eliminated.

13. If the boat is equipped with a water heater, drain any water from the heater following the heater manufacturer's instructions.

14A. If the boat is stored on a trailer, remove the battery and store in a cool and dry location. Charge the battery every 30-45 days, as described in Chapter Nine. A discharged battery can freeze and rupture.

14B. If the boat is stored in the water, remove the battery and charge every 30-45 days or install an onboard charger that connects to shore power to maintain the battery charge level.

15. If the boat is stored on a trailer, or the exhaust outlets are above the water level, cover the exhaust outlets to prevent small animals or insects from entering the exhaust system. If necessary, insert a sponge into each outlet.

FITTING OUT

Fitting out is a series of steps that prepares the engine for operation after storage or winterization.

1. Perform all required maintenance as described in Chapter Three.

2. Service the water pump as described in Chapter Eight.

3. Check all fluid levels as described in Chapter Three.

4. Fill the fuel tank with fresh fuel.

5. Remove any covers from the exhaust outlets.

6. Service and install the battery as described in Chapter Nine.

7. If removed for draining, install the drain plug into the heat exchanger or fit the end cap (with new gasket) onto the heat exchanger. Secure the end cap with the bolt. Do not overtighten the bolt.

8. If the boat was winterized and then stored in the water, remove the plugs from the inlet water hoses to the seawater pump, V-drive unit, transmission fluid cooler and power steering fluid cooler.

9. If removed for winterization, connect the water hoses to the seawater pump, V-drive unit, transmission fluid cooler, power steering fluid cooler, exhaust manifolds and exhaust elbows.

10. Install any drain plug or close any petcock in the cylinder block and exhaust manifold(s).

11. If the exhaust manifolds are equipped with water drain hoses, Thread the hose couplings together until securely tightened. Route the hoses and coupling to a location directly above the transmission.

12. Install the cap onto the freshwater flush/drain system and securely tighten. Secure the freshwater flush hose to prevent interference with belts or other moving components.

13. If the boat is equipped with a water heater, reconnect the hoses to the engine and securely tighten the clamps. Route the heater hoses to prevent interference with belts, pulleys and other moving components.

4

14. If so equipped, open the valve on the seawater pickup.

> *WARNING*
> *Stay clear of the propeller and propeller shaft while running the engine on a flush adapter.*

> *CAUTION*
> *Use a flush device or other means to supply the engine with cooling water if running the engine with the boat out of the water. The seawater pump is quickly damaged if operated without adequate cooling water.*

15. Supply cooling water and then start the engine. Immediately check for leaking fuel, water, coolant, oil or other fluids. Stop the engine and correct any leakage before operating the engine.

16. Run the engine at low speed until the engine reaches normal operating temperature. Check for proper operation of the cooling, electrical and warning systems. Refer to Chapter Two for troubleshooting procedures if a malfunction is indicated.

> *CAUTION*
> *If the engine must be shifted into gear with the boat stored on a trailer, have an assis-*

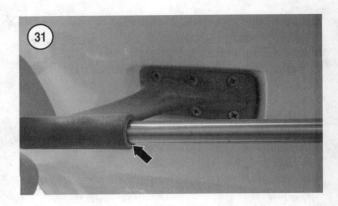

*tant spray water onto the propeller shaft surface, where it passes into the support strut (**Figure 31**), anytime the transmission is shifted into gear. The water spray is required to lubricate the cutlass bearing in the support strut.*

17. With the engine running at idle speed, shift the transmission into FORWARD and REVERSE and cycle the steering to the port and starboard limits. Advance the throttle slightly and then return to the idle setting. Do not operate the engine if a malfunction is evident in the shifting, steering or throttle control systems.

Chapter Five

Adjustments

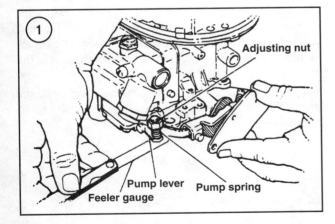

Pump lever   Pump spring
Feeler gauge

This chapter describes adjustments for the carburetor, ignition timing, throttle cable and shift cable. **Table 1** lists tightening specifications for most fasteners. Use the general tightening specifications listed in Chapter One for fasteners not listed in **Table 1**. **Table 2** lists service specifications for the procedures performed in this chapter. **Table 1** and **Table 2** are located at the end of this chapter.

CARBURETOR

This section describes accelerator pump clearance, idle speed, idle mixture and final float level adjustment.

Accelerator Pump Clearance Adjustment

Adjust the accelerator pump lever clearance if hesitation or backfiring occurs during rapid acceleration.
1. Disconnect the battery cables.
2. Place the throttle in FORWARD gear wide-open position.
3. Manually depress the accelerator pump lever on the throttle cable side of the carburetor.
4. Use a feeler gauge to measure the clearance between the pump lever and the head of the screw on the pump arm (**Figure 1**). The clearance must be 0.010-0.015 in. (0.25-0.38 mm). If adjustment is needed, hold the screw to prevent rotation and turn the adjusting nut to achieve the required clearance.
5. Return the throttle to NEUTRAL idle.
6. Connect the battery cables.

Idle Mixture Screw Adjustment

WARNING
Safely performing on-the-water adjustments requires two people: one who is qualified to operate the boat and another to perform the adjustment(s). Always route hoses and harnesses from test equipment to prevent entanglement with drive belts, linkages and other moving components. Both persons must remain seated at all times. Add extension harnesses or hoses on test equipment to allow adjustment while remaining seated.

Improper idle mixture screw adjustment will generally cause rough idle, excess exhaust smoke, hard starting or hesitation during rapid acceleration.

On early models the idle mixture screws (**Figure 2**) are located on each side of the primary float bowl. On late models, the idle mixture screws are factory-adjusted and a plug (**Figure 3**) is installed over the opening to prevent tampering.

1. Disconnect the battery cables.

2. On later models with a tamper-resistant plug, carefully pry the plugs out of the idle mixture screw openings on the sides of the metering block (**Figure 3**).

3. Turn the mixture screws *clockwise* until lightly seated. Do not force the screws into the seats.

4. Turn the mixture screws out three-quarters of a turn.

5. Connect the battery cables.

6. Connect a shop tachometer to the engine following the manufacturer's instructions. Do not rely on the boat tachometer for carburetor adjustments.

7. Prepare the boat and engine for operation under normal conditions. The idle mixture screws cannot be adjusted accurately using a flush device for cooling water with the propeller out of the water. Start the engine and operate at fast idle (1200-1500 rpm) in NEUTRAL until it reaches normal operating temperature.

8. Return the engine to idle. Have an assistant shift the engine into FORWARD. Allow a few minutes for the idle to stabilize. Then note the tachometer reading. The tachometer must indicate an idle speed of 600-650 rpm. If not, adjust the idle speed as described in this chapter.

9. Turn one mixture screw clockwise until the idle speed just begins to drop (too lean). Repeat for the remaining mixture screw.

10. While noting the number of turns required, slowly turn one mixture screw counterclockwise until the idle speed increases and then just begins to drop again (too rich). Repeat for the other mixture screw.

11. Slowly turn one mixture screw clockwise to the midpoint between the too lean drop and the too rich drop. This setting should provide the best idle quality and idle speed. If acceptable idle quality cannot be obtained, check for incorrect ignition timing, malfunctioning ignition, fuel and fuel delivery problems and low compression. If all other systems are operating properly, disassemble and clean the carburetor as described in Chapter Seven.

12. On late models with tamper-resistant plugs, press the plugs (**Figure 3**) into the idle mixture screw openings to prevent tampering.

13. Adjust the idle speed as described in this section.

14. Stop the engine and remove the shop tachometer.

Idle speed adjustment

WARNING
Safely performing on-the-water adjustments requires two people: one who is qualified to operate the boat and another to perform the adjustment(s). Always route hoses and harnesses from test equipment to prevent entanglement with drive belts, linkages and other moving components. Both persons must remain seated at all times.

Add extension harnesses or hoses on test equipment to allow adjustment while remaining seated.

CAUTION
Do not attempt to adjust the idle speed on electronic fuel injection (EFI) models. On EFI models, the idle speed is controlled by the engine control unit (ECU) and the idle air control motor (IAC). Do not tamper with the factory-adjusted idle stop screw on the throttle body. Tampering with the screw might prevent the EFI system from properly controlling the idle speed and cause hard starting, high idle speed or stalling. The throttle body must be replaced if tampering is causing these or other symptoms. The manufacturer does not provide an adjustment procedure for the idle stop screw on EFI models.

1. Following the manufacturer's instructions, connect a shop tachometer to the engine. Do not rely on the boat tachometer for carburetor adjustments.

2. Prepare the boat and engine for operation under normal conditions. The idle speed cannot be adjusted accurately using a flush device for cooling water with the propeller out of the water. Start the engine and operate at fast idle (1200-1500 rpm) in NEUTRAL until it reaches normal operating temperature.

3. Return the engine to idle. Have an assistant shift the engine into FORWARD.

NOTE
It might be necessary to disconnect the throttle cable from the linkage so the throttle lever on the carburetor remains in contact with the stop screw with the drive in FORWARD.

4. Allow a few minutes for the idle to stabilize and then note the tachometer reading. The tachometer must indicate 600-650 rpm. If not, adjust as follows:
   a. Make sure the throttle stop is firmly against the idle speed-adjusting screw. If not, temporarily disconnect the throttle cable from the carburetor linkage and hold the linkage *firmly* against the screw. The stop and speed-adjusting screw are located on the same side of the carburetor as the throttle cable attaching points.
   b. Observe the tachometer and turn the idle speed screw (**Figure 4**) to achieve the middle of the specified range (600-650 rpm). Make sure the stop is in *firm* contact with the adjusting screw during the adjustment.

5. Stop the engine. If disconnected, reconnect the throttle cable to the carburetor linkage. Make sure the throttle stop is against the idle speed-adjusting screw. If not, adjust the throttle cable as described in this chapter.

6. Start the engine and note the idle speed. Readjust the idle speed as necessary. Have an assistant shift the engine into FORWARD. Motor to a safe area and then have the assistant advance the throttle and return to idle speed. Wait a few minutes and note the idle speed. Repeat this operation several times. The idle speed must return to 600-650 rpm within a few minutes each time the throttle returns to idle. If not, adjust the throttle cable as described in this chapter.

7. Remove the shop tachometer.

Float level adjustment (models with a center-hinged float)

Perform the float adjustment after a carburetor repair or if improper float level is causing the engine to run poorly. Refer to the *Carburetor* in Chapter Seven to identify the center-hinge float.

WARNING
Stay clear of the propeller and propeller shaft while running an engine on a flush adapter.

CAUTION
Use a flush device or other means to supply the engine with cooling water if running the engine with the boat out of the water. The seawater pump is quickly damaged if operated without adequate cooling water.

1. Following the manufacturer's instructions, connect a shop tachometer to the engine. Do not rely on the boat tachometer for carburetor adjustments.

5

2. Start the engine and operate at fast idle (1200-1500 rpm) in NEUTRAL until it reaches normal operating temperature.

3. Return the engine to idle.

4. Place a shop towel under the float bowl to capture spilled fuel.

5. Carefully remove the sight plug (A, **Figure 5**) from the side of the float bowl.

6. The fuel must be even with the bottom of the threaded opening. If adjustment is required, loosen the screw (B, **Figure 5**) and *slowly* rotate the adjusting nut (C) until the fuel level is correct. Hold the nut to prevent rotation and then tighten the screw. Check the fuel level and correct as needed.

7. Install the sight plug and securely tighten.

8. On models with accessible idle mixture screws (**Figure 2**), adjust the idle mixture as described in this section.

9. Adjust the idle speed as described in this section.

10. Stop the engine and remove the shop tachometer.

IGNITION TIMING ADJUSTMENT

This section describes the ignition timing adjustment procedures for carburetor and electronic fuel injection models. The ignition timing is not adjustable on 5.7L LT-1 and 8.1L models because these models are not equipped with a distributor.

Operating the engine with incorrect ignition timing will result in loss of power, poor fuel economy or serious engine damage. Ignition timing adjustment varies by the type of fuel and ignition systems used. Refer to Chapter Seven and Chapter Nine to identify the fuel and ignition systems used on the engine.

WARNING
Stay clear of the propeller and propeller shaft while running an engine on a flush adapter.

CAUTION
Use a flush device or other means to supply the engine with cooling water if running the engine with the boat out of the water. The seawater pump is quickly damaged if operated without adequate cooling water.

Carburetor-Equipped Models

Early carburetor-equipped models use either a breaker-point ignition system or a Prestolite BID ignition system. Late carburetor-equipped models use a Delco EST ignition system. Refer to *Ignition System* in Chapter Two to identify the ignition system.

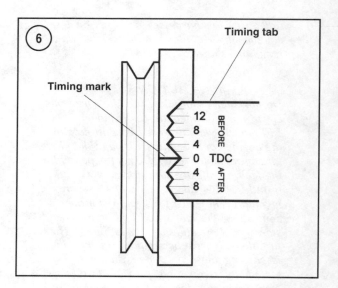

On models using the Delco EST ignition system, a timing adapter is required to set the electronic timing control circuits to base mode. The adapter can be purchased from a Volvo Penta (part No. 885163-6) or OMC (part No. 986662) dealership. The ignition timing cannot be accurately adjusted without the adapter.

1. Disconnect the battery cables.

2. Following the manufacturer's instructions, connect a suitable timing light to the No. 1 cylinder spark plug wire. On models using an inline transmission, the pulleys face the front of the boat and the No. 1 spark plug and wire are on the port side closest to the pulley end of the engine. On models using a V-drive transmission, the pulleys face the rear of the boat, and the No. 1 spark plug and wire are on the starboard side closest to pulley end of the engine.

3. Locate the timing marks and pointer on the engine. On early models, the numbers are stamped into a tab that is attached to the timing cover. The timing mark is machined into the harmonic balancer (**Figure 6**). On later models,

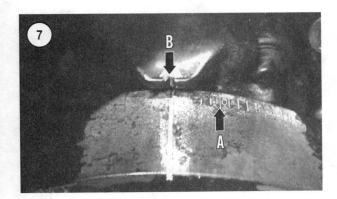

the numbers are stamped into the harmonic balancer (A, **Figure 7**) or printed onto a decal affixed to the balancer. The timing mark is located in a notch in the timing cover (B, **Figure 7**). If necessary, clean the timing marks. Apply white paint or chalk on the timing cover mark to make it more visible.

> *NOTE*
> *On counter-rotation models, the crankshaft turns in the opposite direction of the much more common standard-rotation models. The before top dead center (BTDC) and after top dead center (ATDC) marks on the timing tab are reversed right to left for counter-rotation models. Refer to **Engine Rotational Direction** in Chapter Six if the engine rotational direction is in question.*

4. Connect the battery cables.

5. Start the engine and operate at fast idle (1200-1500 rpm) in NEUTRAL until it reaches normal operating temperature. Return the engine to idle.

6. On models using a Delco EST ignition system, set the ignition timing control circuits to base mode as follows:

   a. Stop the engine.

   b. Attach the adapter (Volvo Penta part No. 885163-6 or OMC part No. 986662) to the distributor module connector (**Figure 8**). The locking tab on the adapter must engage the tab on the module connector.

   c. Connect the wire end of the adapter to a battery positive power source. The large red wire terminal on the starter motor is a suitable connection point.

   d. Start the engine and run at idle speed.

7. Direct the timing light at the timing marks. The flash of the timing light will make the moving marks appear to stand still. The actual timing is indicated by the scale on the tab (**Figure 6**) or harmonic balancer (A, **Figure 7**) that aligns with the machined mark on the harmonic balancer (**Figure 6**) or notch on the timing cover (B, **Figure 7**). The machined mark on the harmonic balancer or notch on the cover must align with the 10° before top dead center (BTDC) mark on all models covered in this manual.

> *NOTE*
> *Use a special distributor wrench to loosen the distributor clamp bolt. Purchase the special wrench from a tool supplier or automotive parts store. Attempting to tighten the bolt using makeshift tools will usually cause the distributor to rotate and disturb the timing adjustment.*

8A. On models using a breaker-point ignition system:

   a. Stop the engine.

   b. Remove the distributor cap and adjust the breaker-point gap and dwell as described in Chapter Three.

   c. Install the distributor cap and start the engine.

   d. Support the distributor to prevent free rotation. Then use a special distributor wrench to loosen the distributor clamp bolt (**Figure 9**). Observe the timing marks while *slowly* rotating the distributor (**Figure 10**) until the 10° BTDC mark aligns with the timing mark. Hold the distributor in position and tighten the clamp bolt to 30 ft.-lb. (41 N•m).

   e. Check the ignition timing. Readjust the timing if it changed while tightening the bolt. Continue adjusting until the ignition timing is correct and the clamp bolt is tight.

8B. On models using a Prestolite BID ignition system:

   a. Stop the engine.

   b. Remove the distributor cap and adjust the air gap between the sensor and impulse sender as described in Chapter Nine. Refer to *Ignition Module Replacement*. Improper air gap can change the ignition timing. Always correct the air gap before attempting to adjust the ignition timing.

   c. Install the distributor cap and start the engine.

5

d. Support the distributor to prevent free rotation. Then use a special distributor wrench to loosen the distributor clamp bolt (**Figure 9**). Observe the timing marks while *slowly* rotating the distributor (**Figure 10**) until the 10° BTDC mark aligns with the timing mark. Hold the distributor in position and tighten the clamp bolt to 30 ft.-lb. (41 N•m).

e. Check the ignition timing. Readjust the timing if it changed while tightening the bolt. Continue adjusting until the ignition timing is correct and the clamp bolt is tight.

8C. On models using a Delco EST ignition system:

a. Support the distributor to prevent free rotation. Then use a special distributor wrench to loosen the distributor hold-down clamp bolt (**Figure 9**).

b. Observe the timing marks while *slowly* rotating the distributor (**Figure 10**) until the 10° BTDC mark aligns with the timing mark. Hold the distributor in position and tighten the hold-down clamp bolt to 30 ft.-lb. (41 N•m).

c. Check the ignition timing. Readjust the timing if it changed while tightening the bolt. Continue adjusting until the ignition timing is correct and the clamp bolt is tight.

9. Stop the engine. Disconnect the timing light.

10. On models using a Delco EST ignition system, remove the adapter from the distributor module connector (**Figure 8**). Then disconnect the wire end of the adapter from the battery positive power source.

Electronic Fuel Injection (EFI) Models

Ignition timing adjustment for EFI models requires a marine diagnostic trouble code tool. If the tool is not available, a suitable tool can be fashioned with a short section of fine wire or a paper clip.

CAUTION
Purchase the marine diagnostic trouble code tool from a tool supplier. If the supplier does not offer the tool, purchase the tool from a Mercruiser, OMC or Volvo Penta dealership. Make sure the tool is suitable for use on the engine. The diagnostic tools available for automobile applications might not be suitable for marine engines and might damage the EFI system.

1. Disconnect the battery cables.

2. Connect a suitable timing light to the No. 1 cylinder spark plug wire following the manufacturer's instruction. On models using an inline transmission, the pulleys face the front of the boat and the No. 1 spark plug and wire are

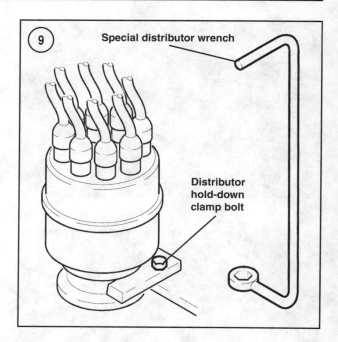

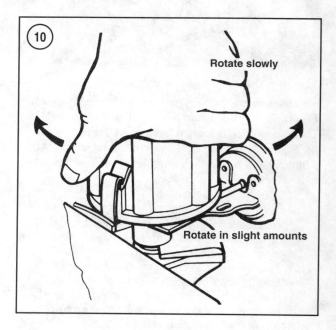

on the port side closest to the pulley end of the engine. On models using a V-drive transmission, the pulleys face the rear of the boat, and the No. 1 spark plug and wire are on the starboard side and closest to the pulley end of the engine.

3. Locate the timing marks and pointer on the engine. On early models, the numbers are stamped into a tab that is attached to the timing cover. The timing mark is machined into the harmonic balancer (**Figure 6**). On later models,

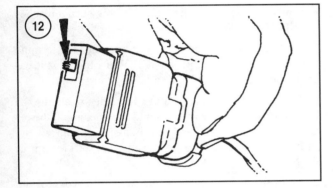

the numbers are stamped into the harmonic balancer (A, **Figure 7**) or printed onto a decal affixed to the balancer. The timing mark is located in a notch in the timing chain cover (B, **Figure 7**). If necessary, clean the timing marks. Apply white paint or chalk to the timing cover marking to make it more visible.

4. Connect the battery cables.

5. Start the engine and operate at fast idle (1200-1500 rpm) in NEUTRAL until it reaches normal operating temperature. Return the engine to idle.

6A. If using a marine diagnostic trouble code tool, place the engine in service mode as follows:

    a. Remove the protective cap from the diagnostic link connector (DLC) (**Figure 11**).

    b. Plug the tool onto the DLC.

    c. Move the tool switch (**Figure 12**) to ON.

6B. If *not* using a diagnostic code tool, place the engine in service mode as follows:

    a. Remove the protective cap from the DLC (**Figure 11**).

    b. Insert a small-diameter jumper wire or paper clip into the plug openings for the white/black and black wires. The wire terminals are labeled *A* and *B*. The terminal lettering is molded into the side of the plug.

7. The idle speed should increase automatically within a few seconds after putting the engine into service mode. If it does not or the engine dies, check for proper tool or jumper wire connections. If the tool or jumper is properly connected, the engine is equipped with an ECU that does not feature automatic idle speed increase for timing adjustment. On such models, advance the engine speed to approximately 1200 rpm before connecting the code tool or installing the jumper wire.

8. Direct the timing light at the timing marks. The flash of the timing light will make the moving marks appear to stand still. The actual timing is indicated by the scale on the tab (**Figure 6**) or harmonic balancer (A, **Figure 7**) that aligns with the machined mark on the harmonic balancer (**Figure 6**) or notch on the timing cover (B, **Figure 7**). The machined mark on the harmonic balancer or notch on the cover must align with the 10° before top dead center (BTDC) mark on all models covered in this manual.

9. If ignition timing requires adjustment, proceed as follows:

    a. Support the distributor to prevent free rotation. Then use a special distributor wrench to loosen the distributor clamp bolt (**Figure 9**).

    b. Observe the timing marks while *slowly* rotating the distributor (**Figure 10**) until the 10° BTDC mark aligns with the timing mark. Hold the distributor in position and tighten the clamp bolt to 30 ft.-lb. (41 N•m).

    c. Check the ignition timing. Readjust the timing if it changed while tightening the bolt. Continue adjusting until the ignition timing is correct and the clamp bolt is tight.

10. Switch the diagnostic trouble code tool to OFF and disconnect the tool from the DLC. If using a jumper wire or clip, remove it from the DLC.

11. The engine speed should slowly drop to the idle position. If the idle speed was raised in Step 7, return the throttle to idle.

12. Attach the protective cap onto the DLC (**Figure 11**). The locking tab must engage the tab on the connector.

13. Stop the engine. Do not remove the timing light at this time.

WARNING
Safely performing on-the-water adjustments requires two people: one who is qualified to operate the boat and another to perform the adjustment(s). Always route hoses and harnesses from test equipment to prevent entanglement with drive belts, linkages and other moving components. Both persons must remain seated at all times. Add extension harness or hoses on test

5

equipment to allow adjustment while remaining seated.

14. Prepare the boat and engine for operation under actual operating conditions.

15. Start the engine and operate in NEUTRAL at fast idle (1200-1500 rpm) until the engine reaches normal operating temperature. Have the assistant return the engine to idle and then shift the engine into FORWARD. Motor to a safe operating area. Observe the ignition timing and tachometer while an assistant slowly advances the throttle to wide-open. The timing must advance as the engine speed increases.

16. Observe the ignition timing as the assistant returns to idle and shifts into NEUTRAL gear. The timing advance must drop as the engine speed is reduced. The idle timing must vary several degrees with the engine in NEUTRAL at idle speed and from warmed to normal operating temperature.

17. The timing advance is controlled by the ECU and varies widely according to temperature, barometric pressure and engine load. The actual timing is not relevant for this test. It is only important that the timing does advance as the speed increases and varies under normal NEUTRAL idle speeds. If the timing does not advance as speed increases and the engine performs poorly, replace the ignition module as described in Chapter Nine. If the ignition timing is not variable at NEUTRAL idle speed, recheck the ignition timing as described in this procedure.

18. Remove the timing light.

SHIFT CABLE ADJUSTMENT

Adjust the shift cable after replacing the shift cable, remote control cable and transmission or if improper adjustment is causing a shifting system malfunction.

1. Disconnect the battery cables.

2. Place the remote control NEUTRAL.

3. Push the cable end retainer (A, **Figure 13**) toward the cable anchor (B). Then pull the cable end off the shift lever pin.

4. Move the shift lever (D, **Figure 13**) toward the engine until it reaches the in-gear detent. Make match marks on the lever and transmission to indicate the lever position when it reaches the in-gear detent.

5. Move the shift lever (D, **Figure 13**) away from the engine until it reaches the other in-gear detent. Make match marks on the lever and transmission to indicate the lever position when it reaches the in-gear detent.

6. Move the shift lever (D, **Figure 13**) to the location between the two in-gear detent positions until it reaches the NEUTRAL detent. Make match marks on the lever and

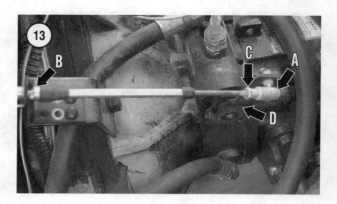

transmission to indicate the lever position when it reaches the NEUTRAL detent.

7. Push and pull on the cable end retainer to determine the midpoint of the free play in the cable. Maintain the cable at the midpoint of play during the adjustment.

8. Loosen the jam nut (C, **Figure 13**). Then rotate the cable end retainer on the threads until the opening in the retainer aligns perfectly with the ball-shaped end on the shift lever pin. Make sure the transmission shift lever is in the NEUTRAL detent and the match markings align.

9. Mark the threaded end of the cable at the edge of the retainer. Then thread the retainer off the cable. Measure the distance from the threaded end to the mark to determine the amount of thread engagement in the retainer. The retainer must thread onto a cable a minimum of 3/8 in. (9.5 mm). If the thread engagement is less than specified, move the remote control end of the cable to a different attaching point on the shift arm in the remote control to achieve the minimum engagement.

10. Push the cable end retainer (A, **Figure 13**) toward the cable anchor (B). Then fit the cable end fully over the ball-shaped shift lever pin. Rotate the retainer to align the slot in the back of the retainer with the pin. Then slide the slot in the retainer over the pin. The internal spring holds the retainer in position. Tug lightly on the cable end to verify a secure connection.

11. Hold the cable end retainer in position and securely tighten the jam nut (C, **Figure 13**).

12. Shift the remote control into FORWARD. Check the alignment of the match marks to make sure the transmission shift lever is reaching the in-gear detent. Shift the remote control into REVERSE. Check the alignment of the match marks to make sure the transmission shift lever is reaching the in-gear detent. Shift the remote control into NEUTRAL. Check the alignment of the match marks to make sure the transmission is reaching the NEUTRAL detent. Refer to the following:

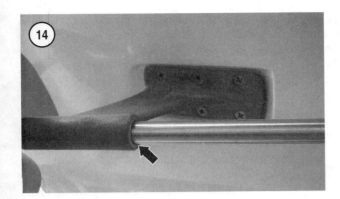

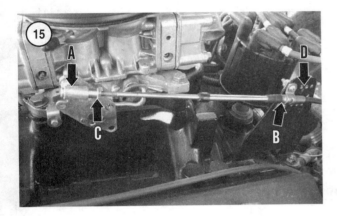

WARNING
Stay clear of the propeller and propeller shaft while running an engine on a flush adapter.

CAUTION
Use a flush device or other means to supply the engine with cooling water if running the engine with the boat out of the water. The seawater pump is quickly damaged if operated without adequate cooling water.

CAUTION
If the engine must be shifted into gear with the boat stored on a trailer, have an assistant spray water onto the propeller shaft surface, where it passes into the support strut (Figure 14), anytime the transmission is shifted into gear. The water spray is required to lubricate the cutlass bearing in the support strut.

14. Start the engine and operate at fast idle (1200-1500 rpm) in NEUTRAL until it reaches normal operating temperature. Return the engine to idle.

15. With the engine running at idle, shift the engine repeatedly into FORWARD and REVERSE. Repeat the adjustment procedures if improper or delayed shifting is noted while shifting.

16. Make sure the propeller rotates in the proper direction to move the boat forward in FORWARD and reverse in REVERSE. If otherwise, the cable is attached to the wrong shift arm, or the transmission is malfunctioning. If the cable orientation in the remote control and propeller rotational direction are correct, refer to *Drive System* in Chapter Two. *Do not* operate the engine if any shifting malfunction is evident.

17. Stop the engine.

THROTTLE CABLE ADJUSTMENT

1. Disconnect the battery cables.
2. Remove the plastic carburetor or engine cover to access the throttle cable attaching points.
3. Place the remote control into NEUTRAL idle.
4. Push the cable end retainer (A, **Figure 15**) toward the cable anchor (B). Then pull the cable end off the shift lever pin.
5. Loosen the jam nut (C, **Figure 15**) on the throttle cable to allow free rotation of the cable retainer.
6. Hold the carburetor or throttle body linkage against the idle speed adjusting screw or throttle stop.
7. *Lightly* push the threaded end of the cable into the cable jacket to remove any slack.

a. If the shift lever reaches the detent in all three positions, the shift adjustment is correct. Proceed to Step 13.

b. If the shift lever does not reach the detent in both in-gear positions, move the remote control end of the cable to an attaching point farther from the remote control shift arm pivot to achieve more shift cable movement.

c. If the shift lever moves past the detent in both in-gear positions, move the remote control end of the cable to an attaching point closer to the remote control shift arm pivot to achieve less shift cable movement.

d. If the shift lever reaches the detent in one in-gear position and does not reach or exceeds the detent in the other position, readjust the shift cable. Make sure the cable maintains the midpoint of free play during the adjustment.

e. If the shift lever reaches the detent in both in-gear positions but does not reach the NEUTRAL, readjust the shift cable. Make sure the cable maintains the midpoint of free play during the adjustment.

13. Connect the battery cables.

8. Maintain light pressure on the cable to remove slack. Then rotate the cable end retainer on the threads until the opening in the retainer aligns perfectly with the ball-shaped end on the shift lever pin.

9. Mark the threaded end of the cable at the edge of the retainer. Then thread the retainer off the cable. Measure the distance from the threaded end to the mark to determine the amount of thread engagement in the retainer. The retainer must thread onto the cable a minimum of 3/8 in. (9.5 mm). If the thread engagement is less than the specification, reattach the cable anchor (B, **Figure 15**) onto the mount using a different screw opening (D).

10. Push the cable end retainer (A, **Figure 15**) toward the cable anchor (B). Then fit the cable end fully over the ball-shaped shift lever pin. Rotate the retainer to align the slot in the back of the retainer with the pin. Then slide the slot in the retainer over the pin. The internal spring holds the retainer in position. Tug lightly on the cable end to verify a secure connection.

11. Hold the cable end retainer in position and securely tighten the jam nut (C, **Figure 15**).

12. Verify that the carburetor or throttle body lever is lightly contacting the idle speed adjusting screw or stop screw. Using light pressure, attempt to push the throttle linkage away from the adjusting screw or throttle stop. The linkage must not move with light pressure. If the linkage moves, adjust the retainer to provide more distance between the pivot points. Do not increase the distance enough to excessively preload the cable or allow less than 3/8 in. (9.5 mm) thread engagement. Preloading the cable will cause remote control binding and excessive cable and linkage wear.

13. Move the throttle to the wide-open position and back to idle several times while observing the throttle linkage. The throttle linkage arm on the carburetor or throttle body must be very close or lightly contacting the wide-open throttle stop at full throttle and must fully contact the idle speed adjusting screw or idle stop at idle. If more or less throttle travel is needed from the remote control, connect the remote control end of the throttle cable to a different attaching point on the remote control throttle arm.

14. Install the plastic carburetor or engine cover.

15. Connect the battery cables.

Table 1 ADJUSTMENT TORQUE SPECIFICATIONS

Fastener	in.-lb.	ft.-lb.	N•m
Distributor hold-down clamp bolt	–	30	41
Spark plug			
5.0L and 5.7L models			
With used cylinder head	–	15	20
With new cylinder head	–	22	30
7.4L and 8.2L models	–	15-20	20-28
8.1L models	–	15	20

Table 2 ADJUSTMENT SPECIFICATIONS

Adjustment	Specification
Accelerator pump arm clearance	0.010-0.015 in. (0.25-0.38 mm)
Idle mixture screw adjustment	One-half turn to one turn out from a light seat
Idle speed	600-650 rpm (in gear)
Ignition timing (idle only)	10° BTDC
Breaker point gap	0.015 in. (0.38 mm)
Breaker point dwell	24-30°

Chapter Six

Engine

Tightening specifications for most fasteners are listed in **Table 1**. Use the general torque specifications in Chapter One for fasteners not listed in **Table 1**. **Tables 2-8** list engine service specifications. **Tables 1-8** are at the end of this chapter.

ENGINE OPERATION

This chapter covers repair to the GM base engines used to produce Indmar marine inboard engines.

On 5.0L, 5.7L, 7.4L and 8.2L V-8 models, the cylinders are numbered from front to rear (1-3-5-7 on the port side and 2-4-6-8 on the starboard side). The firing order is 1-8-4-3-6-5-7-2 for standard-rotation engines and 1-2-7-5-6-3-4-8 for counter-rotation engines.

On 8.1L V-8 models, the cylinders are numbered from front to rear (1-3-5-7 on the port side and 2-4-6-8 on the starboard side). The firing order is 1-8-7-2-6-5-4-3. All 8.1L models are standard-rotation engines.

The intake and exhaust valves (one each per cylinder) are operated via pushrods and rocker arms by a camshaft located in the cylinder block. Camshaft motion is transferred through hydraulic lifters to the rocker arms by pushrods. The rocker arms move on ball pivots located on individual shoulder studs or shoulder bolts.

On 5.0L, 5.7L, 7.4L and 8.2L models, the camshaft is chain-driven on standard-rotation engines and gear-driven on counter-rotation engines. The camshaft is located between the two cylinder banks. The camshaft is supported by five bearings. The oil pump, mounted at the bottom rear of the cylinder block, is driven by the distributor shaft or oil pump drive assembly (5.7L LT-1 models) by a gear on the camshaft.

On 8.1L models, the camshaft is chain-driven and is located between the two cylinder banks. The camshaft is supported by five bearings. All 8.1L models are equipped with a distributorless ignition system. The oil pump, mounted at the bottom rear of the cylinder block, is driven by the oil pump drive assembly by a gear on the camshaft.

All models covered in this manual use pressed-in exhaust valve seats. This allows replacement of the seat in the event that it cannot be reconditioned to the specification.

The crankshaft is supported by five main bearings. The rear main bearing provides crankshaft thrust control. The crankshaft drives the camshaft using a chain and sprocket. The camshaft turns at one-half crankshaft speed.

On standard-rotation engines, crankshaft rotation is counterclockwise when viewed from the flywheel end of the engine. On counter-rotation engines, crankshaft rotation is clockwise as viewed from the flywheel end of the engine.

On vessels with twin engines, a standard or right-hand propeller is generally used for the starboard engine, and a counter-rotation or left-hand propeller is used on the port engine. This setup describes *outboard* turning propellers. See **Figure 1**. Some vessels perform better when using a left-hand propeller on the starboard side and a right-hand propeller on the port side. This arrangement describes *inboard* turning propellers. See **Figure 2**. The oppositely rotating propellers balance inherent propeller torque that otherwise would adversely affect vessel handling and efficiency.

Because the transmission used on early models is not suitable for full-power operation in REVERSE, a counter-rotation engine and transmission must be used on one side, and a standard-rotation engine and transmission must be used on the other side. The remote control cables are arranged to shift both transmissions into FORWARD for forward thrust and REVERSE for reverse thrust. To provide the correct direction of thrust, a propeller with the correct direction must be installed onto the corresponding propeller shaft.

Later models use a birotational transmission that can be operated at full power in either direction. This allows counter-rotating propellers without the need for a special engine or transmission. The remote control cables are arranged to shift one transmission into FORWARD and the other into REVERSE for forward thrust. For reverse thrust, the transmissions are shifted into the opposite gears.

SPECIAL TOOLS

If special tools are required or recommended, the tool part numbers are provided in the procedure. Some of the tools are offered by Indmar. The remaining tools are offered by Kent-Moore. Purchase or rent Indmar tools from a local Indmar dealership. Purchase Kent-Moore tools from Kent-Moore Special Tools, 29784 Little Mack, Roseville, MI 48066.

REPLACEMENT PARTS

There are several differences between automotive engines and engines adapted for marine applications. For example, the cylinder head gasket must be corrosion-resistant. Marine engines use stainless steel or composite gaskets instead of the standard steel gasket used in automotive blocks. Brass core plugs must be used instead of the steel plugs used in automotive blocks. Because marine engines run at or near maximum speed most of the time,

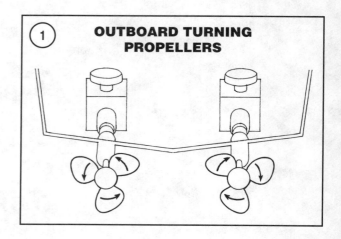

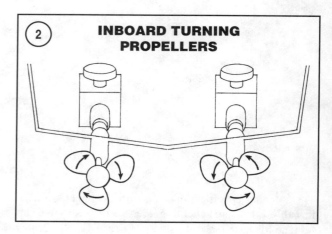

they use special lifters, valve springs, pistons, bearings, camshaft and other heavy-duty components.

SPECIAL SERVICE PRECAUTIONS

When working on the engine, taking basic precautions will make your work easier, faster and more accurate.
1. Always make notes, drawings or photographs of all external engine components *before* beginning disassembly. An incorrectly routed hose or wire can interfere with linkage movement and result in a dangerous lack of throttle control. Wiring or hoses can short or abrade and leak if allowed to contact sharp, hot or moving parts. Check for components that can be installed in two or more positions and mark them accordingly.
2. Mark the up and forward directions of all components before removing them. If a cluster of components share common wires or hoses, try to remove the entire assembly intact. This reduces the time required to disassemble and assemble the engine and reduces the chance of improper connections during assembly.

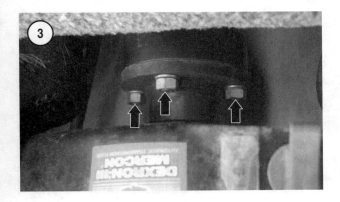

3. Mount the engine to an engine stand if the repair involves the pistons, rods or crankshaft. Support the engine with an overhead lift or blocks as needed for other repairs.

4. Use muffin tins or egg cartons to organize fasteners as they are removed. Mark all fasteners to make sure they are reinstalled in the correct locations.

5. Use special tools where noted. In some cases, it might be possible to perform the procedure with makeshift tools, but this is not recommended. Makeshift tools can damage components or cause serious injury.

6. Use a vise with protective jaws to hold housings or components. If protective jaws are not available, insert wooden blocks on each side of the part before clamping them in the vise. Never clamp on thin castings, such as the piston skirt, which can be damaged by the clamping force.

7. Remove and install pressed-on parts with the appropriate mandrel, support and hydraulic press. Do not try to pry or hammer them from the component.

8. Tighten all fasteners to the specification in **Table 1**. Use the general tightening specifications listed in the *Quick Reference Data* section at the front of the manual for fasteners not listed in **Table 1**.

9. Apply the recommended sealant or threadlocking compound to the outer surface of seals. Lubricate seal lips during assembly.

10. Prior to installation, apply engine oil or other recommended lubricant to all internal components.

11. Work in a clean area and where there is good lighting and sufficient space for storing components. Keep small containers on hand for storing small parts. Cover parts with clean shop towels when not working with them.

12. Replace all seals, gaskets and O-rings during assembly. These parts are inexpensive compared to the damage they will cause if they fail.

WARNING
The engine is heavy, is awkward to handle and has numerous sharp edges. It can shift or drop suddenly during removal. To pre-

vent serious injury, never place the body where any sudden or unexpected engine movement can contact the body.

13. Never place any part of the body where a moving or falling engine can trap, cut or crush it.

14. If it is necessary to push the engine during removal or installation, use a board or similar tool to keep hands and arms out of danger.

15. Make sure any lifting device, such as a hoist, is designed to lift engines and has enough capacity to lift the engine.

16. Make sure the lifting device is securely attached to safe lifting points on the engine.

17. If difficulty is encountered while removing the engine, stop lifting, lower the engine back onto the mounts and make sure the engine has completely separated from the vessel.

ENGINE REMOVAL AND INSTALLATION

Removal

Some service procedures can be performed with the engine in the boat; others require removal. Boat design and the service procedure determines whether the engine must be removed.

1. Remove the engine hatch, seating and any panels or structures that might interfere with engine removal or access to any of the engine mounts.

2. Disconnect the battery cables. As a precaution, remove the batteries from the boat.

3. Remove the bolts and nuts securing the transmission output shaft flange (**Figure 3**) to the propeller shaft flange. The flange is located on the rear or bottom of the transmission. Tap on the side of the propeller shaft flange to separate the flanges. Use a rubber mallet with light force to prevent damage to the flanges.

4. On models with a water-cooled propeller shaft seal, loosen the clamp and disconnect the water hose from the fitting on the shaft log. Drain water from the hose and secure it to the engine to prevent entanglement during engine removal.

5. On models with a ZF Hurth integral V-drive transmission, remove the propeller shaft as described in Chapter Ten.

NOTE
In many instances, boat design or added structure can prevent removal of the engine as an assembly. In such cases, remove the exhaust manifold or other readily accessi-

ble external components to achieve the needed clearance.

6. Disconnect the throttle cable from the carburetor or throttle body and the cable anchor point (**Figure 4**, typical).

7. Disconnect the shift cable from the transmission shift lever and the cable anchor point (**Figure 5**, typical).

8. Loosen the clamp (**Figure 6**, typical) and detach the instrument harness from the engine harness.

9. On models equipped with a closed cooling system, drain coolant from the system as described in Chapter Three.

10. If so equipped, disconnect the hot water heater hoses (**Figure 7**, typical) from the thermostat housing and recirculation pump. Heater hoses are red.

11. On models equipped with power steering, disconnect the power steering hoses from the control valve. The control valve is located near the steering cable and rudder lever connection. Drain all fluid from the hoses. Cap the hose and plug the corresponding opening in the control valve to prevent contamination.

12A. On early carburetor-equipped models using a mechanical fuel pump, disconnect the fuel supply hose from the fuel pump (**Figure 8**, typical) or fuel filter inlet (**Fig-**

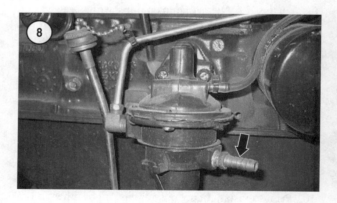

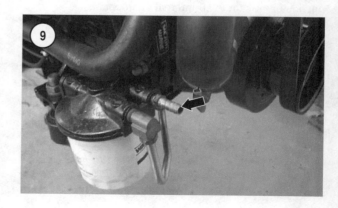

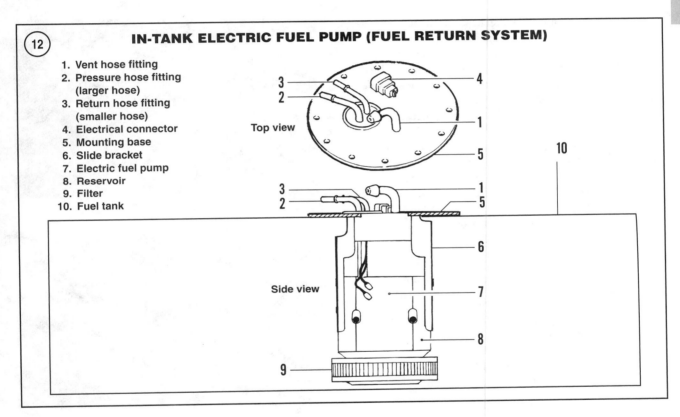

IN-TANK ELECTRIC FUEL PUMP (FUEL RETURN SYSTEM)

1. Vent hose fitting
2. Pressure hose fitting (larger hose)
3. Return hose fitting (smaller hose)
4. Electrical connector
5. Mounting base
6. Slide bracket
7. Electric fuel pump
8. Reservoir
9. Filter
10. Fuel tank

Top view

Side view

ure **9**, typical). Plug the hose and fitting to prevent leakage and contamination.

12B. On later carburetor-equipped models using an electric fuel pump, disconnect the fuel supply hose from the fuel pump (**Figure 10**). The fuel pump is located on the front starboard side of the engine. On V-drive models, the fuel pump is on the port side. Plug the hose and pump to prevent leakage and contamination.

13. On electronic fuel injection (EFI) models, relieve the fuel pressure as described in Chapter Seven.

14A. On electronic fuel injection models equipped with an engine-mounted electric fuel pump, disconnect the fuel

supply hose from the filter assembly (**Figure 11**). The filter assembly is located on the front starboard side of the engine. On V-drive models the assembly is on the port side. Plug the hose and pump to prevent leakage and contamination.

14B. On EFI models equipped with a fuel tank-mounted pump, disconnect the fuel supply hose from the fitting (2, **Figure 12**), fuel return hose from the fitting (3) and fuel pump harness from the fuel pump connector (4). Some models do not use a fuel return hose. Plug all disconnected hoses and fittings to prevent contamination. Use a quick-connect tool commonly available from automotive

parts stores to disconnect the fuel hoses from the pump fitting(s).

15. Loosen the hose clamp and detach the seawater inlet hose (**Figure 13**, typical) from the seawater pump. Identify the seawater inlet hose by tracing it to the seawater pickup (**Figure 14**, typical). Drain all water from the hose.

16. Loosen the clamps (two on each bank) that secure the exhaust hose to the exhaust elbow (**Figure 15**, typical). Carefully insert a pry bar between the hose and exhaust elbow. Work the bar around the hose to break the bond between the hose and elbow. Use a blunt pry bar and work carefully to avoid damaging the exhaust hose. If the exhaust hose is weathered, charred or melted, remove the remaining hose clamps. Then carefully cut the hose and peel it off the elbow and exhaust tube.

> *WARNING*
> *Failure of the exhaust hose(s) creates a dangerous fire, explosion, asphyxiation and sinking hazard. If damaged or deteriorated, replace exhaust hose(s) with high-quality wet marine exhaust hose. Other types of rubber hose might fail prematurely and allow water, flame and exhaust gasses into the engine compartment.*

17. Detach any wires, hoses or accessories that can interfere with engine removal. Accessory ground wires are often connected to the flywheel housing ground studs and are not usually apparent at a quick glance. Check thoroughly for overlooked wiring before lifting the engine.

> *NOTE*
> *At this point, there should be no hoses, wires or linkages connecting the engine to the boat. Make sure nothing remains to interfere with engine removal.*

18A. On carburetor-equipped models, unthread the screw (A, **Figure 16**, typical). Then lift the flame arrestor (B, **Figure 16**) off the carburetor. If attached to the flame

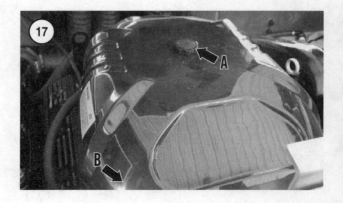

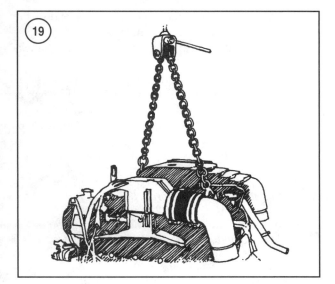

6

18B. On throttle body injection (TBI) electronic fuel injection models, unthread the screw (A, **Figure 17**) and then lift the plastic flame arrestor cover (B) off the engine. Then lift the flame arrestor (**Figure 18**) off the throttle body. If attached to the flame arrestor, pull the breather tube and PCV valve or fitting out of the rocker arm cover. To prevent contamination, cover the rocker arm cover opening(s) with masking tape. Cover the entire top of the throttle body assembly with plastic film or other suitable material and tape it securely in place.

19. Attach a suitable overhead hoist to the front and rear engine lifting brackets (**Figure 19**). The hoist must have a minimum lift capacity of 1500 lb. (680 kg). Raise the hoist just enough to just remove slack from the chain. *Do not* lift the engine at this time.

20. Remove the bolts (**Figure 20**, typical) securing the port and starboard engine side mounts to the boat structure.

21. Remove the bolts (**Figure 21**, typical) securing the transmission mounts to the boat structure.

NOTE
Do not loosen or move the alignment adjusting nuts, or complete realignment will be required when the engine is reinstalled. Engine alignment should not be disturbed if the engine mounts are detached as described in Step 19 and Step 20.

22. Lift the engine just enough to relieve pressure on the engine and transmission mounts.

23. Again check for any wiring, cables or hoses that can interfere with engine removal and detach if necessary.

24. Carefully move the engine forward or rearward enough the pull the exhaust elbow outlets out of the exhaust tubes. If boat structure prevents adequate forward or rearward movement, loosen the remaining exhaust hose clamps and slide the exhaust hose down and over the exhaust tube until the elbow opening is visible. If the exhaust hose cannot slide over the exhaust tube, lift slightly

arrestor, pull the breather tube (C, **Figure 16**) and PCV valve or fitting out of the rocker arm cover opening. To prevent contamination, cover the rocker arm cover opening with masking tape. Cover the entire top of the carburetor with plastic film or other suitable material and tape it securely in place.

and pull on the opposite end of the assembly while lifting the engine and transmission out of the boat. Lifting and pulling at a slight angle allow the elbow to slide out of the exhaust hose.

25. Carefully lift the engine from the boat.

26. Use a suitable detergent to remove oily deposits from the bilge area.

27. Use a wire brush to remove resin material, sealant or other contaminants from the engine and transmission mount lag bolts. Inspect the bolts for corrosion, damaged threads or other defects. Replace damaged or corroded bolts with suitable stainless steel units. Do not use steel or zinc-plated bolts. Only good quality stainless steel lag bolts will withstand the potential for corrosion in this area.

28. Inspect the mount bolt openings in the boat structure for stripped or oversized openings and a deteriorated or questionable condition of the surrounding structure. Have questionable boat structure repaired by a qualified fiberglass repair technician before reinstalling the engine.

Installation

1. If the exhaust hose must be replaced, install the new hose before installing the engine. To ease installation and prevent damage to the rubber, apply a soap-and-water solution to the inner exhaust hose surface before installing the engine.

2. Position any wires, hoses, cables or accessories to prevent interference or damage during engine installation.

3. Carefully lower the engine and transmission into the vessel until the transmission output flange is aligned with the propeller shaft flange. Make sure the engine is positioned forward enough to prevent the transmission output flange from resting on the propeller shaft flange. If boat structure prevents adequate forward or rearward movement, lift the opposite end of the assembly while guiding the exhaust hose over the exhaust elbow while lowering the engine into position. Do not relieve the support from the hoist at this time.

4. Move the engine to align the bolt openings in the engine and transmission mounts with the corresponding openings in the mount pad or stringers. Then slowly lower the engine until a slight amount of slack is present in the lifting chain.

5A. If lag bolts are used to secure the engine and transmission, apply a light coat of marine-grade silicone sealant to the threads. Then install the lag bolts into the mounts and boat structure openings. Securely tighten the lag bolts.

5B. If bolts and locknuts are used, insert the bolts and washers into the mount and boat structure openings.

Thread the washers and nuts onto the lower end of the bolts. Securely tighten the bolts and washers.

6. Detach the lifting chain from the engine-lifting brackets.

7. On models with a ZF Hurth integral V-drive transmission, install the propeller shaft as described in Chapter Ten.

8. Check the engine alignment as described in this chapter.

> *NOTE*
> *The fasteners that secure the transmission output flange to the propeller shaft flange must be SAE Grade 8 (Metric Grade 10.9) or better. The shoulder of the bolts must be long enough to pass through both flanges. Always use an equivalent grade of lockwashers and nuts with the bolts and tighten to the recommended specification.*

9. Install the bolts and nuts securing the transmission output shaft flange (**Figure 3**) to the propeller shaft flange. Hold the nut and tighten each bolt to 50 ft.-lb. (68 N•m).

10. On models equipped with a water-cooled propeller shaft seal, connect the water hose to the shaft log fitting and secure with a hose clamp. Route the water hose to prevent contact with the propeller shaft, steering system components, rotating flanges and moving components on the engine. Secure the hose with plastic locking clamps as needed.

11. Position the exhaust hoses fully over the exhaust elbows. Position the clamps (**Figure 15**) to apply force over the elbow tube. Then securely tighten. Wait a few minutes for the hose material to relax and then retighten the clamps. Using the same procedure, tighten the clamps that secure the exhaust hose to the exhaust tube.

12. Inspect the pins and corresponding openings in the instrument harness and engine harness connectors (**Figure 22**) to identify the pin orientation. If the pin halves are completely closed from clamping force, use a small blade

and spread the pin halves just enough to create clearance. If spread too much, the pin will not pass into the engine harness opening. Align the two or three larger pins with the corresponding openings and then carefully plug the instrument harness fully onto the engine harness. Position the clamp over the plug as shown in **Figure 6**. Then lightly tighten the clamp. Overtightening the clamp damages the connectors.

13. Apply a soap-and-water solution to the surfaces and push the seawater inlet hose (**Figure 13**, typical) fully onto the seawater pump inlet fitting. Install the clamp and then securely tighten the clamp. Wait a few minutes for the hose material to relax and then retighten the clamp.

14. On models equipped with power steering, remove the plugs and caps. Then attach the power steering hose to the corresponding control valve openings. Position the hoses to prevent interference with the steering components. Hold the hoses in position and then tighten the fittings to 25 ft.-lb. (34 N•m). Fill the power steering system with fluid as described in Chapter Three.

15. If so equipped, connect the hot water heater hoses (**Figure 7**, typical) to the thermostat housing and recirculation pump fittings. Securely tighten the heater hose clamps.

16. Connect the throttle cable to the carburetor or throttle body and the cable anchor point (**Figure 4**, typical).

17. Connect the shift cable to the transmission shift lever and the cable anchor point (**Figure 5**, typical).

18. Adjust the throttle and shift cables as described in Chapter Five.

19. On models equipped with a closed cooling system, refill the system as described in Chapter Three.

20A. On early carburetor-equipped models using a mechanical fuel pump, remove the plugs and caps and then connect the fuel supply hose to the fuel pump (**Figure 8**, typical) or fuel filter inlet (**Figure 9**, typical). Securely tighten the hose clamp.

20B. On later carburetor-equipped models using an electric fuel pump, remove any plugs and clamps. Then connect the fuel supply hose to the fuel pump (**Figure 10**). Securely tighten the hose clamp.

20C. On EFI models equipped with an engine-mounted electric fuel pump, remove any plugs and caps then connect the fuel supply hose onto the filter assembly fitting (**Figure 11**). Securely tighten the hose clamp.

20D. On EFI models equipped with a fuel tank-mounted pump, connect the fuel supply hose to the tank (2, **Figure 12**), fuel return hose to the fitting (3) and fuel pump harness to the fuel pump (4). Some models do not use a fuel return hose. The hose connectors are push-on connectors. After pushing the hose fitting(s) fully onto the fitting(s), tug on the hose(s) to verify a secure connection.

21A. On carburetor-equipped models, remove the cover material from the carburetor. Then install the flame arrestor (B, **Figure 16**). Thread the screw (A, **Figure 16**, typical) into the flame arrestor and carburetor opening and hand-tighten. If the breather tube or PCV hose is attached to the flame arrestor, lubricate the surfaces with engine oil. Then press the fitting or PCV valve into the rocker arm cover.

21B. On throttle body injection (TBI) electronic fuel injection models, remove the cover material and then install the flame arrestor (**Figure 18**) onto the throttle body assembly. Fit the plastic flame arrestor cover (B, **Figure 17**) onto the flame arrestor and then thread the screw (A, **Figure 17**), into the plastic cover, flame arrestor and throttle body. Hand-tighten the screw. If the breather tube or PCV hose is attached to the flame arrestor, lubricate the surfaces with engine oil. Then press the fitting or PCV valve into the rocker arm cover.

22. Install the battery. Then reconnect the positive and then negative battery cables.

23. Supply the engine with cooling water as described in Chapter Three. Refer to *Flushing the Cooling System*.

24. Start the engine and immediately check for fuel, oil or water leakage. Stop the engine and correct any leakage before running the engine. Check for proper steering, shifting, throttle and cooling system operation. Correct any malfunction before putting the engine into service.

25. Install any engine hatch, seating and panels or structure that were removed to access the engine mounts.

ENGINE ALIGNMENT

The engine alignment must be checked and, if necessary, corrected anytime the engine, transmission, propeller shaft or propeller shaft flange is removed. Incorrect alignment will result in excessive vibration and rapid wear of the propeller shaft and transmission output shaft components. If the vessel is moored, the alignment must be rechecked after the vessel is left in the water for a minimum of 48 hours with a normal load of fuel and water. This allows the vessel structure to settle to the normal in-the-water position. The in-the-water engine alignment might be significantly different from the alignment while on a trailer.

NOTE
The manufacturer produces engines equipped with an inline transmission, integral V-drive transmission or Walters V-drive attached to an inline transmission. Although the location and orientation of propeller shaft and flanges are different for each type,

6

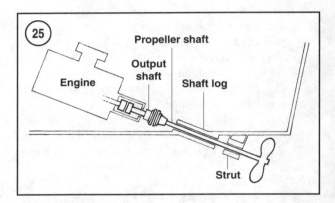

the engine alignment procedures are very similar for all three types of transmissions.

1. Disconnect the battery cables to prevent accidental starting.

2. Remove any seating or other boat structure necessary to access the transmission output and propeller shaft flange. Remove the four bolts, washers and nuts (**Figure 23**) securing the output flange to the propeller shaft flange. Tap the side of the propeller shaft flange to separate the flanges. Use a rubber mallet with light force to prevent damage to the flanges or shaft.

3A. If the propeller shaft flange is equipped with square setscrews (**Figure 24**), cut the safety wire and then remove the setscrews.

3B. If the propeller shaft flange is equipped with recessed Allen setscrews, remove the setscrews. If necessary, heat the flange near the setscrews to soften the threadlocking compound.

4. Slide the propeller shaft flange down the propeller shaft enough to access the mating surfaces. Clean any corrosion or debris from the surfaces with solvent and dry with compressed air.

5. Push up and down on the propeller shaft and note the midpoint of the movement. Next, move the shaft from side to side and again note the midpoint of the movement. Position the shaft in the middle of the up-and-down and side-to-side movement. The shaft log and cutlass bearing in the strut (**Figure 25**) allow some lateral and vertical movement to compensate for mount and shaft deflection while under power.

6. Slide the propeller shaft flange toward the transmission output shaft flange. If the propeller shaft flange has a raised shoulder, it should align with the corresponding recess in the output shaft flange with no resistance. If not, check for proper engagement after performing the following alignment procedure. Some propeller shaft flanges are not equipped with the raised shoulder. Although desirable, the raised shoulder is not required to align the engine

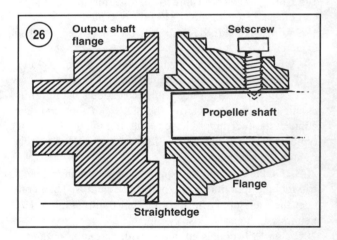

and secure the shafts flanges. Correct engine alignment allows the flange to enter the recess easily.

7. Slide the propeller shaft flange up the shaft until it contacts the output shaft flange. Rotate the flange to position one of the setscrews facing upward. Use a straightedge to check the alignment of the side of the flanges at the bottom of the flange (**Figure 26**). Rotate the propeller shaft 90°. Then check the alignment at locations 90° from the setscrew (**Figure 27**). The flange side surfaces must align

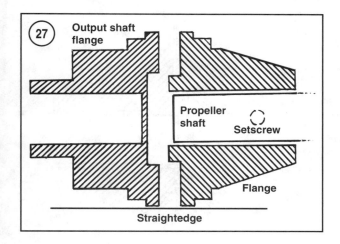

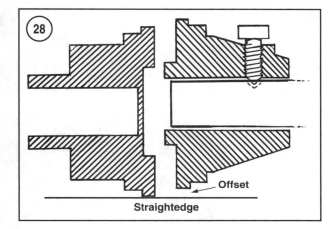

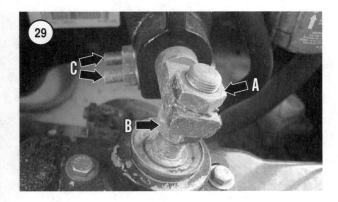

turn the lower nut the same amount on each side of the engine. *Do not* tighten the upper nut at this time.

b. To raise or lower the rear of the engine, locate the mounts on each side of the transmission. Loosen the nut on the bottom of the round trunnion bars. Turn the upper nut (A, **Figure 30**) clockwise to raise the rear of the engine and counterclockwise to lower the engine. To keep the rear of the engine level from side to side, turn the upper nut the same amount on each side of the transmission. *Do not* tighten the lower nut at this time.

c. To move the engine and transmission laterally in the boat, loosen the trunnion bar clamp bolts and nuts (C, **Figure 29**) on each side of the engine. Then loosen the transmission trunnion bar clamp bolts or nuts (B, **Figure 30**) on each side of the transmission. Move the engine and transmission in the direction necessary to align the flange surfaces as shown in **Figure 26** and **Figure 27**. Make sure each trunnion is fully supported within the engine and transmission mount. Inadequate support prevents adequate clamping and might allow the mount to loosen or fail while underway. If necessary, reposition the engine mounts on the boat structure to make sure ample trunnion engagement. Do not tighten the trunnion clamp bolts and nuts at this time.

8. Slide the propeller shaft flange up the shaft until it contacts the output shaft flange. Rotate the flange to position one of the setscrews facing upward. Use feeler gauges to check for a gap at the mating surfaces at a point aligned with the setscrew and a location at the bottom of the flange (**Figure 31**). Then check for a gap at locations 90° from the setscrew (**Figure 32**). Align the engine if the gap difference on the opposite side of the flange (**Figure 33**) exceeds 0.003 in. (0.08 mm).

a. Correct excessive gap at the top or bottom of the flange by raising or lowering the engine. Loosen the upper nut (A, **Figure 29**) on each side of the engine.

at both locations. If the straightedge indicates the surfaces are offset (**Figure 28**), correct as follows:

a. To raise or lower the front of the engine, loosen the upper nut (A, **Figure 29**) on each side of the engine. Turn the lower nut (B, **Figure 29**) clockwise to lower the engine and counterclockwise to raise the engine. To keep the engine level from side to side,

Turn the lower nut (B, **Figure 29**) clockwise to lower the engine and counterclockwise to raise the engine. To keep the engine level from side to side, turn the lower nut the same amount on each side of the engine.

b. Correct excessive gap at either side of the flange by moving the engine and transmission laterally in the boat, loosen the trunnion bar clamp bolts and nuts (C, **Figure 29**) on each side of the engine. Then loosen the transmission trunnion bar clamp bolts or nuts (B, **Figure 30**) on each side of the transmission. Move the engine and transmission in the direction necessary to correct excessive gap. Make sure each trunnion is fully supported within the engine and transmission mount. Inadequate support prevents adequate clamping and might allow the mount to loosen or fail while underway. If necessary, reposition the engine mounts on the boat structure to ensure sufficient trunnion engagement.

c. After correcting the gap, check the output shaft and propeller shaft flange alignment as described in Step 7. If adjustment is required, check the mating surface gap and correct as needed.

9. Engine alignment is correct when both the flange alignment and mating surface gap are within the specification at the same time. Readjust as necessary before continuing.

10. Remove the setscrews from the propeller shaft flange. Then hold the flange in firm contact with the output shaft flange. Use a center punch to mark the propeller shaft in the center of each setscrew opening. Slide the propeller shaft flange down the shaft to expose the marks. Then use a suitable drill to create shallow depressions at the marks. Clean any cuttings or contaminants from the shaft. Then slide the propeller shaft flange up the shaft until it contacts the output shaft flange. Rotate the flange to align the threaded openings with the depressions.

11A. If the propeller shaft flange is equipped with square setscrews (**Figure 24**), secure the flange to the propeller shaft as follows:

a. Thread the screws by hand. Make sure the tip of the screws engage the depressions in the propeller shaft. Proper engagement prevents the flange from rotating on the propeller shaft.

b. Securely tighten the screws.

c. Pass a single strand of stainless steel safety wire through the openings in the setscrews. Make a loop and then twist the wire to prevent the screws from loosening. See **Figure 34**.

11B. If the propeller shaft is equipped with recessed Allen setscrews, secure the flange to the propeller shaft as follows:

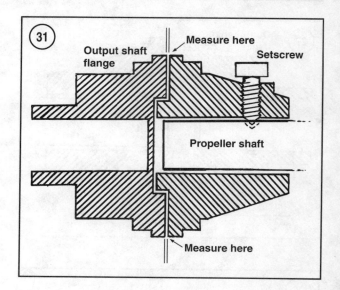

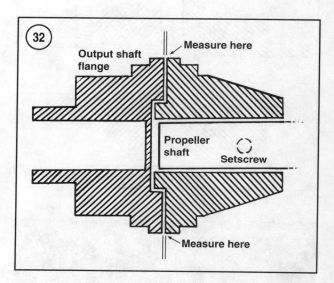

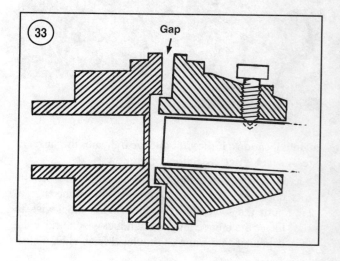

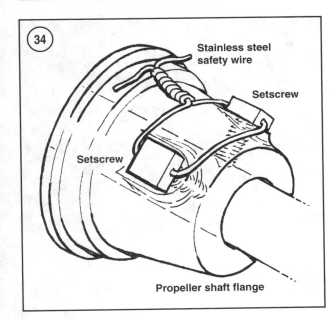

Stainless steel safety wire

Setscrew

Setscrew

Propeller shaft flange

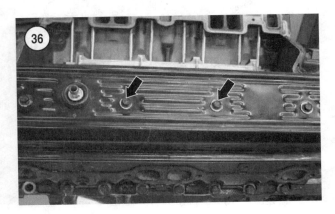

a. Apply a coat of Loctite 271 or equivalent to the threads and then thread the screws into the flange by hand. Make sure the tips of the screws enter the depressions in the propeller shaft. Proper engagement

prevents the flange from rotating on the propeller shaft.

b. Securely tighten the setscrews.

12. Tighten all four of the trunnion clamping bolts and nuts (C, **Figure 29** and B, **Figure 30**) to 50 ft.-lb. (68 N•m).

13. Securely tighten the upper nut (A, **Figure 29**) on each side of the engine. *Do not* inadvertently turn the lower nut (B, **Figure 29**) while tightening the upper nut.

14. Locate the mounts on each side of the transmission. Securely tighten the nuts on the bottom of the round trunnion bars. *Do not* inadvertently turn upper nuts (A, **Figure 30**) while tightening the lower nuts.

NOTE
The fasteners that secure the transmission output flange to the propeller shaft flange must be SAE Grade 8 (Metric Grade 10.9) or better. The shoulder of the bolts must be long enough to pass through both flanges. Always use an equivalent grade of lockwashers and nuts with the bolts and tighten to the recommended specification.

15. Rotate the propeller shaft to align the openings and then install the bolts and nuts securing the transmission output shaft flange (**Figure 23**) to the propeller shaft flange. Hold the nut and tighten each bolt to 50 ft.-lb. (68 N•m).

16. Install any engine hatch, seating and panels or structure that were removed to access the engine mounts.

17. Reconnect the battery cables.

ROCKER ARM COVER

The rocker arm cover must be removed to adjust the valves, measure camshaft lobe lift or service the cylinder head. On earlier 5.0L and 5.7L models, the rocker arm cover retaining screws are located around the perimeter of the cover (**Figure 35**). On later 5.0L and 5.7L models, the screws are located in the center of the cover. (**Figure 36**). On all 7.4L, 8.1L and 8.2L models, the screws are located around the perimeter of the cover. On many early models, a bead of RTV sealant is used to seal the cover to the cylinder head. A cork gasket, rubber gasket or O-ring seals the cover on later models.

Removal and Installation

NOTE
Mark the rocker arm covers to identify the port and starboard sides. The oil fill cap ori-

entation will be incorrect if the covers are installed in the wrong locations.

1. Disconnect the battery cables to prevent accidental starting.

2. Disconnect or remove any hoses, wiring or other components that can interfere with removal of the rocker arm cover. On 8.1L models, mark the cylinder number on the wiring and then disconnect the engine wire harness from the ignition coils. The coils are positioned directly above their corresponding cylinders.

3. Remove the fasteners and lift the rocker arm cover (**Figure 37**) from the cylinder head.

4. Remove the oil fill cap and breather tube/PCV grommet from the cover. Clean the rocker arm cover(s) with solvent and dry with compressed air.

5A. If the cover is sealed with RTV sealant, carefully scrape all sealant from the cover and cylinder head surfaces. Clean the surfaces with aerosol carburetor cleaner to remove any oil residue.

5B. If the cover is sealed with a cork gasket, remove and discard the gasket. Use aerosol carburetor cleaner to remove any gasket adhesive from the rocker cover and cylinder head surfaces.

5C. If the cover is sealed with a rubber gasket or O-ring, inspect the gasket or O-ring for torn, deteriorated or irregular surfaces. Replace the rubber gasket unless it is in excellent condition.

6A. If the cover is sealed with RTV sealant, apply a 3/16-in. (4.8 mm) bead of RTV along the valve cover mating surface on the cylinder head rail. Make sure to apply the bead on the inner side of the screw openings.

6B. If the cover is sealed with a cork or rubber gasket, apply a very light coat of 3M Weatherstrip Adhesive to the gasket surface on the rocker arm cover. Fit the gasket onto the cover and hold in place until it adheres to the cover.

6C. If the cover is sealed with an O-ring, apply a light coat of engine oil to the O-ring and press it into the rocker cover groove.

7. Position the rocker cover onto the cylinder head. Do not press down on or slide the rocker cover on the cylinder head surfaces.

8. On early models with perimeter cover screws, fit the load spreaders over the rocker cover screws. Thread the screws into the cover and cylinder head. The rounded side of the load spreaders must fit into the rounded recess in the side of the cover.

9. Tighten the cover fasteners as follows:

    a. On early 5.0L and 5.7L models with perimeter cover screws (**Figure 35**), tighten the cover screws

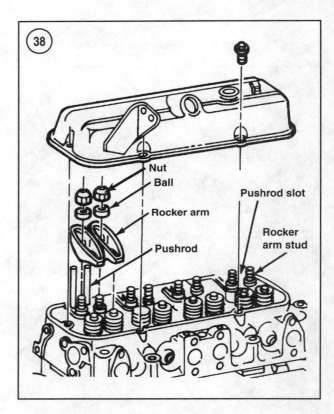

in a crossing pattern starting from the center and working outward, to 60 in.-lb. (6.8 N•m).

b. On later 5.0 and 5.7L models with center screws (**Figure 36**), tighten the rocker arm cover screws, starting in the center and working outward, to 106 in.-lb. (12 N•m).

c. On 7.4L and 8.2L models, tighten the cover screws in a crossing pattern, starting from the center and working outward, to 71 in.-lb. (8.0 N•m).

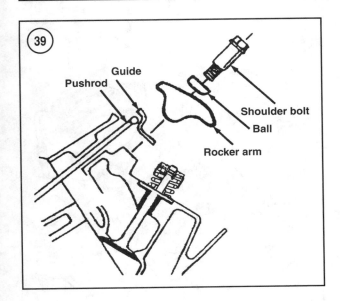

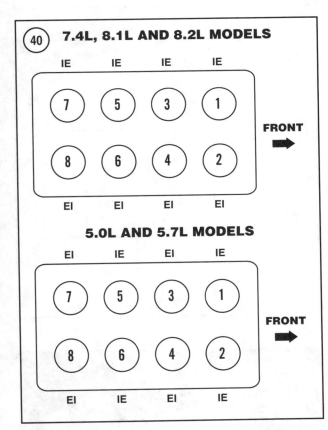

10. Apply a soap-and-water solution to the surfaces. Then insert the breather tube/PCV valve grommet into the rocker cover. Install the oil fill cap.

11. Install or reposition the components removed to access the rocker arm cover(s). On 8.1L models, connect the wiring harness connectors to the corresponding ignition coils.

12. Connect the battery cables.

VALVE ADJUSTMENT

Adjust the valves if lifter noise is present and if replacing the cylinder head, camshaft, lifters, pushrods or other valve train components.

Valve adjustment is required on all 5.0L, 5.7L, early 7.4L and early 8.2L models. These models use a nut (**Figure 38**) to hold the rocker arm and pivot ball onto the rocker arm stud. Later 7.4L, later 8.2L and all 8.1L models use a shoulder bolt (**Figure 39**) to hold the rocker arm and pivot ball on the cylinder head, and the valves are not adjustable. However, on such models, the shoulder bolt must be tightened in the proper sequence (refer to *Cylinder Head Replacement*). If necessary, remove the rocker arm cover and visually inspect the components to determine the need for adjustment.

Early 5.0L, 5.7L and 7.4L models were produced in both standard- and counter-rotation models.

Adjust the valves as follows:

1. Disconnect the negative battery cable and remove the spark plugs.

2. Determine the engine rotation and place the No. 1 piston at TDC as described in this chapter.

3. Remove both rocker arm covers as described in this chapter.

4A. On standard-rotation models, adjust these valves as described in Step 5 (**Figure 40**).

    a. No. 1 cylinder intake.
    b. No. 1 cylinder exhaust.
    c. No. 2 cylinder intake.
    d. No. 3 cylinder exhaust.
    e. No. 4 cylinder exhaust.
    f. No. 5 cylinder intake.
    g. No. 7 cylinder intake.
    h. No. 8 cylinder exhaust.

4B. On counter-rotation models, adjust these valves as described in Step 5 (**Figure 40**).

    a. No. 1 cylinder intake.
    b. No. 1 cylinder exhaust.
    c. No. 2 cylinder exhaust.
    d. No. 3 cylinder intake.
    e. No. 4 cylinder intake.
    f. No. 5 cylinder exhaust.

6

    d. On 8.1L models, tighten the rocker arm cover screws in a crossing pattern, starting in the center and working outward, to 53 in.-lb. (6 N•m). Then tighten the fasteners a final time in sequence to 106 in.-lb. (12 N•m).

g. No. 7 cylinder exhaust.

h. No. 8 cylinder intake.

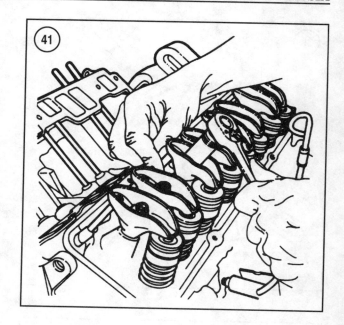

NOTE
Turn the pushrod to determine whether there is any lash between the rocker arm and pushrod. The pushrod will turn freely if lash is present.

5. To adjust the valve lash, loosen the adjusting nut until some lash is felt at the pushrod (**Figure 41**). While turning the pushrod, slowly tighten the adjusting nut until all lash is just removed. Then tighten the nut exactly one turn.

6. Rotate the crankshaft in the normal direction of rotation exactly one turn to place the No. 6 piston at TDC. On early models, align the timing mark on the harmonic balancer with the 0 mark on the timing tab (**Figure 42**). On later models, align the 0 mark on the harmonic balancer with the notch molded into the timing cover (**Figure 43**).

CAUTION
Do not rotate the crankshaft opposite the normal direction of rotation, or the seawater pump will be damaged.

7A. On standard-rotation models, adjust these valves as described in Step 5 (**Figure 40**).

   a. No. 2 cylinder exhaust.

   b. No. 3 cylinder intake.

   c. No. 4 cylinder intake.

   d. No. 5 cylinder exhaust.

   e. No. 6 cylinder intake.

   f. No. 6 cylinder exhaust.

   g. No. 7 cylinder exhaust.

   h. No. 8 cylinder intake

7B. On counter-rotation models, adjust these valves as described in Step 5 (**Figure 40**).

   a. No. 2 cylinder intake.

   b. No. 3 cylinder exhaust.

   c. No. 4 cylinder exhaust.

   d. No. 5 cylinder intake.

   e. No. 6 cylinder intake.

   f. No. 6 cylinder exhaust.

   g. No. 7 cylinder intake.

   h. No. 8 cylinder exhaust.

8. Install the rocker arm covers as described in this chapter.

9. Install the spark plugs and tighten to 22 ft.-lb. (30 N•m) if the cylinder head is new or 15 ft.-lb. (20 N•m) if the cylinder head is used. Connect the plug wires and install or reposition any components removed to access the rocker arm cover.

10. Connect the battery cables.

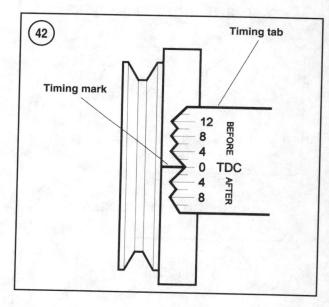

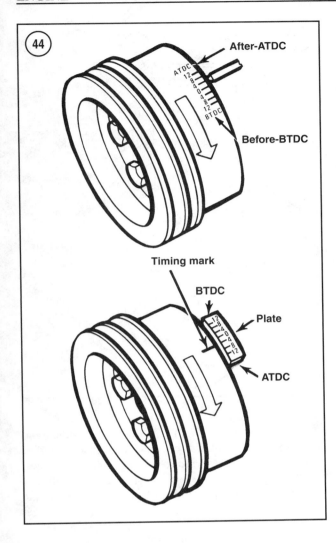

**TOP DEAD CENTER (TDC)
FIRING POSITION**

This section describes the procedure for placing the No. 1 cylinder piston and valves in the top dead center (TDC) firing position. This procedure must be performed before adjusting the valves, routing spark plug wires or installing the distributor. Before beginning this procedure, determine the engine rotation as described in this section.

Intake Manifold Installed

1. Determine the engine rotational direction as described in this section.

2. Disconnect the negative battery cable and remove the spark plugs.

3. Place a thumb over the No. 1 cylinder spark plug opening. The No. 1 cylinder is on the port side closest to the front of the engine (**Figure 40**, typical).

NOTE
*On early 5.0L and 5.7L models, the timing mark is located on the harmonic balancer, and the timing scale is stamped into a tab on the timing cover (**Figure 42**). On later models, the timing scale is printed on the decal on the harmonic balancer, and the timing mark is molded into the timing cover (**Figure 43**).*

4A. On 5.0L, 5.7L, 7.4L and 8.2L models, observe the timing marks (**Figure 44**) and turn the harmonic balancer in the normal direction of engine rotation until compression forms in the No. 1 cylinder. This indicates the cylinder is on the compression stroke. Continue rotating the balancer until the timing mark just aligns with the 0 mark (TDC).

NOTE
8.1L models are not equipped with a timing pointer because the ignition timing is controlled by the ECU and is not adjustable. However, this procedure is accurate enough to allow pushrod and rocker arm installation without valve interference.

4B. On 8.1L models, turn the harmonic balancer clockwise until compression forms on the No. 1 cylinder. This indicates the cylinder is on the compression stroke.

5A. On 5.0L and 5.7L models, install the spark plugs and tighten to 22 ft.-lb. (30 N•m) if the cylinder head is new and 15 ft.-lb. (20 N•m) if the cylinder head is used.

5B. On 7.4L and 8.2L models, install the spark plugs and tighten to 15-20 ft.-lb. (20-28 N•m).

5C. On 8.1L models, install the spark plugs and tighten to 15 ft.-lb. (20 N•m).

6. Connect the spark plug wires.

7. Connect the battery cables.

Intake Manifold Removed

1. Determine the engine rotational direction as described in this section.

2. Disconnect the negative battery cable and remove the spark plugs.

3. Refer to **Figure 40** and locate the No. 1 cylinder.

4. Attach a large breaker bar and socket onto the harmonic balancer bolt. If a bolt is not used in this location, rotate the engine in the normal direction of rotation by

engaging a large pry bar between the pulley mounting bolts.

NOTE
*On early 5.0L and 5.7L models, the timing mark is located on the harmonic balancer, and the timing scale is stamped into a tab on the timing cover (**Figure 42**). On later models, the timing scale is printed on a decal on the harmonic balancer, and the timing mark is molded into the timing cover (**Figure 43**).*

5A. On 5.0L, 5.7L, 7.4L and 8.2L models, observe the rocker arm for the No. 1 intake valve while rotating the harmonic balancer clockwise for standard-rotation engines and counterclockwise for counter-rotation engines. Stop when the No. 1 intake valve rocker arm starts moving downward. Observe the timing marks (**Figure 44**) and turn the harmonic balancer clockwise until the timing mark aligns with the 0 mark.

NOTE
8.1L models are not equipped with a timing pointer because the ignition timing is controlled by the ECU and is not adjustable. However, this procedure is accurate enough to allow pushrod and rocker arm installation without valve interference.

5B. On 8.1L models, observe the No. 1 intake rocker arm while rotating the harmonic balancer clockwise. Stop when the No. 1 intake valve rocker arm starts moving downward. Continue rotating the harmonic balancer clockwise until the lifter roller is positioned at the base (lowest point) of the cam lobe (**Figure 45**). The lifter and cam lobe are visible through the oil drain openings in the lifter valley.

6A. On 5.0L and 5.7L models, install the spark plugs and tighten to 22 ft.-lb. (30 N•m) if the cylinder head is new and 15 ft.-lb. (20 N•m) if the cylinder head is used.

6B. On 7.4L and 8.2L models, install the spark plugs and tighten to 15-20 ft.-lb. (20-28 N•m).

6C. On 8.1L models, install the spark plugs and tighten to 15 ft.-lb. (20 N•m).

7. Connect the spark plug wires.

Engine Rotational Direction

Early 5.0L, 5.7L and 7.4L models were produced in both standard- and counter-rotation versions. The rotation must be determined before adjusting the valves, routing spark plug wires and performing other repair procedures. The easiest way to determine the engine rotation is to simply inspect the timing scale on the timing cover. **Figure 42**

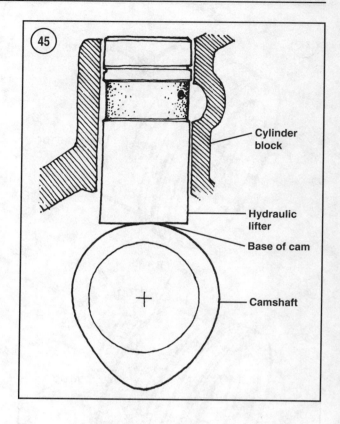

shows the before and after TDC orientation for the more common standard-rotation engines. The before and after TDC orientation is reversed for counter-rotation engines. Another method to determine rotation is to simply observe the crankshaft pulley while an assistant operates the electric starter. On standard-rotation engines, the flywheel rotates counterclockwise as viewed from the rear and the crankshaft pulley rotates clockwise. On counter-rotation engines, the flywheel rotates clockwise as viewed from the rear, and the crankshaft pulley rotates counterclockwise.

CAMSHAFT LOBE LIFT

This measurement checks for excessive camshaft wear. This procedure requires a dial indicator and a clamp for attaching the indicator to the cylinder head or block. A magnetic mount or mount that can be attached to the rocker arm stud will perform well for this measurement. Before removing them, mark the original location of all valve train components. *All* parts must be reinstalled in their original locations.

Early 5.0L, 5.7L and 7.4L models were produced in both standard- and counter-rotation models. Before beginning this procedure, refer to *Top Dead Center (TDC)*

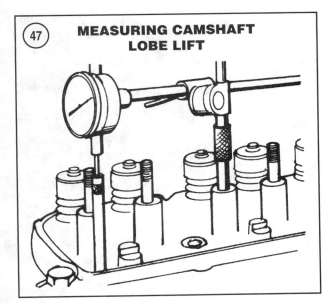

MEASURING CAMSHAFT LOBE LIFT

Firing Position in this chapter for instructions and identify the engine rotation before beginning this procedure.

NOTE
On 7.4L, 8.1L and 8.2L models, the exhaust pushrods are longer than the intake pushrods.

NOTE
7.4L models are produced in both standard- and high-output models that must be identified before beginning this procedure. If the identification decal is missing from the engine or the output specification is in question, remove the intake manifold as described in Chapter Seven. Then inspect the intake manifold and cylinder head intake ports. The standard-output models use round or oval ports. The high-output models use rectangular ports.

1. Disconnect the negative battery cable and remove the spark plugs.
2. Remove the rocker arm as described in this chapter.
3. Remove the intake manifold as described in Chapter Seven.

NOTE
*Late models are equipped with roller lifters. Roller lifters require a lifter retainer as shown in **Figure 46**. Early models are equipped with flat lifters and do not require the retainer.*

6

4A. On 5.0L/5.7L and earlier 7.4L/8.2L models, remove the adjusting nut and pivot ball (**Figure 38**) from each rocker arm. Mark the original locations and remove the rocker arms and pushrods from the cylinder heads.

4B. On later 7.4L, later 8.2L and all 8.1L models, remove the shoulder bolt and pivot ball (**Figure 39**) from each rocker arm. Mark the original locations and remove the rocker arm, guide and pushrods from the cylinder heads.

5. Roll the pushrods across a flat surface to check for bending. Replace bent pushrods.

6. Attach a breaker bar and socket to the harmonic balancer attaching bolt.

7. Observe the No. 1 exhaust valve lifter (see **Figure 40**) while turning the harmonic balancer in the normal direction of rotation (refer to *Engine Rotational Direction*). Stop when the lifter drops in the bore and the base of the cam lobe aligns with the bottom of the lifter (**Figure 45**). On later models using roller lifters, the lobe must align with the center of the roller on the bottom of the lifter.

8. Insert the pushrod into the corresponding slot in the cylinder head and seat it into the recess in the lifter.

9. Attach the dial indicator to the cylinder head using a suitable mount (**Figure 47**). Align the plunger of the dial indicator with the tip of the pushrod. Rotate the face of the dial indicator to align the needle with the 0 mark.

10. Observe the dial indicator while rotating the harmonic balancer exactly one revolution in the normal direction of engine rotation. The amount of needle movement equals camshaft lobe lift. Record the lobe lift.

11. Repeat Steps 7-10 for the remaining camshaft lobes. Record each measurement.

12A. On 5.0L and 5.7L models with flat lifters, the camshaft lobe lift must be 0.263-269 in. (6.680-6.833 mm) for the intake valve lobes and 0.269-0.276 in. (6.833-7.010 mm) for the exhaust valve lobes.

12B. On 5.0L and 5.7L models with roller lifters (except 5.7L LT-1), the camshaft lobe lift must be 0.274-0.278 in. (6.970-7.070 mm) for the intake valve lobes and 0.278-0.283 in. (7.061-7.188 mm) for the exhaust valve lobes.

12C. On 7.4L standard-output models with flat lifters, the camshaft lobe lift must be 0.280-0.284 in. (7.112-7.214 mm) for the intake valve and 0.269-0.273 in. (6.833-6.934 mm) for the exhaust valve lobes.

12D. On 7.4L standard-output models with roller lifters, the camshaft lobe lift must be 0.280-0.284 in. (7.112-7.214 mm) for the intake valve lobes and 0.282-0.286 in. (7.163-7.264 mm) for the exhaust valve lobes.

12E. On 7.4L high-output models with flat lifters and all 8.2L models with flat lifters, the camshaft lobe lift must be 0.298-0.302 in.(7.569-7.671 mm) for the intake and exhaust valve lobes.

12F. On 7.4L high-output models with roller lifters and all 8.2L models with roller lifters, the camshaft lobe lift must be 0.340-0.344 in. (8.636-8.738 mm) for the intake and exhaust valve lobes.

12G. On 8.1L standard-output models, the camshaft lobe lift must be 0.273-0.277 in. (6.934-7.036 mm) for the intake valve lobes and 0.275-0.279 in. (6.985-7.087 mm) for the exhaust valve lobes.

12H. On 8.1L high-output models, the camshaft lobe lift must be 0.298-0.302 in. (7.569-7.671 mm) for the intake and exhaust valve lobes.

13. Replace the camshaft as described in this chapter if any of the measurements are less than the minimum specification.

14. Install the pushrods, roller rocker arms and nuts as described in this chapter.

15. On 5.0L, 5.7L and earlier 7.4/8.2L models, adjust the valves as described in this chapter.

16. Install the intake manifold as described in Chapter Seven.

17. Install the rocker arm covers as described in this chapter.

18A. On 5.0L and 5.7L models, install the spark plugs and tighten to 22 ft.-lb. (30 N•m) if the cylinder head is new and 15 ft.-lb. (20 N•m) if the cylinder head is used.

18B. On 7.4L and 8.2L models, install the spark plugs and tighten to 15-20 ft.-lb. (20-28 N•m).

18C. On 8.1L models, install the spark plug and tighten to 15 ft.-lb. (20 N•m).

19. Connect the plug wires and install or reposition any components removed to access the rocker arm covers.

20. Connect the negative battery cable.

ROCKER ARM AND PUSHROD

All 5.0L/5.7L models and early 7.4L/8.2L models use a nut to hold the rocker arm and pivot ball to the rocker arm stud. Later 7.4L, later 8.2L and all 8.1L models use a shoulder bolt to hold the rocker arm and pivot ball on the cylinder head, and the valves are not adjustable. However,

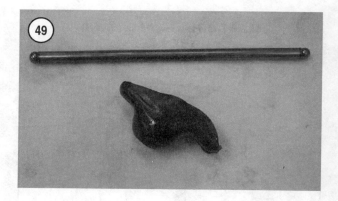

on such models, the shoulder bolt must be tightened in the proper sequence (refer to *Cylinder Head Replacement*). If necessary, remove the rocker arm cover and visually inspect the components to determine the need for adjustment.

Removal (5.0L/5.7L and Earlier 7.4L/8.2L Models)

1. Remove the rocker arm cover(s) as described in this chapter.

2. Place the No. 1 piston in the TDC firing position as described in this chapter.

3. Remove the nut and pivot ball (**Figure 48**) from each rocker arm. Mark the original locations and remove the rocker arms and pushrods (**Figure 49**) from the cylinder head studs.

4. Clean the components with solvent and dry with compressed air.

5. Inspect all parts for excessive, wear or damage and replace if necessary. Inspect the rocker arm studs for excessive wear on the sides. Replace the cylinder head if any of the studs are heavily worn on one side. This condition usually affects only a single stud.

50

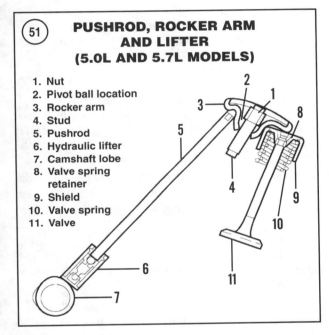

51

PUSHROD, ROCKER ARM
AND LIFTER
(5.0L AND 5.7L MODELS)

1. Nut
2. Pivot ball location
3. Rocker arm
4. Stud
5. Pushrod
6. Hydraulic lifter
7. Camshaft lobe
8. Valve spring
    retainer
9. Shield
10. Valve spring
11. Valve

6. Roll the pushrods across a flat surface (**Figure 50**) to check for bending. Replace bent pushrods.

Installation

1. If disturbed, place the No. 1 cylinder in the TDC firing position as described in this chapter.
2. Insert the pushrods (5, **Figure 51**) through their respective slots in the cylinder head. Used pushrods must be installed into the original locations in the cylinder head.
3. Fit the lower end of the pushrods into the recesses in the lifters (6, **Figure 51**). Make sure the rollers are seated against the camshaft lobes (7, **Figure 51**). Push down on each lifter to verify proper seating.
4. Install each rocker arm (3, **Figure 51**) over the rocker arm studs. Fit the upper end of the pushrods into the slot in

the tip of the rocker arms. The other end of the rocker arms must align with the top of the valve stems.
5. Fit the pivot ball over the stud with the rounded side facing the rocker arm. Set the pivot ball into the recess in the rocker arm.
6. Thread the adjusting nut (1, **Figure 51**) onto the stud. Do not tighten the nut at this time.
7A. On standard-rotation models, identify the adjusting nuts for the following valves (**Figure 40**):
    a. No. 1 cylinder intake.
    b. No. 1 cylinder exhaust.
    c. No. 2 cylinder intake.
    d. No. 3 cylinder exhaust.
    e. No. 4 cylinder exhaust.
    f. No. 5 cylinder intake.
    g. No. 7 cylinder intake.
    h. No. 8 cylinder exhaust.
7B. On counter-rotation models, identify the adjusting nuts for the following valves (**Figure 40**):
    a. No. 1 cylinder intake.
    b. No. 1 cylinder exhaust.
    c. No. 2 cylinder exhaust.
    d. No. 3 cylinder intake.
    e. No. 4 cylinder intake.
    f. No. 5 cylinder exhaust.
    g. No. 7 cylinder exhaust.
    h. No. 8 cylinder intake.
8. Tighten the adjusting nuts until a slight amount of lash exists between the rocker arm and pushrod. Do not remove all of the lash.
9. Rotate the crankshaft exactly one turn in the normal direction of engine rotation and align the timing pointer with the 0° TDC marking on the harmonic balancer (**Figure 44**). The No. 6 piston is now at TDC.
10A. On standard-rotation models, identify the adjusting nuts for the following valve (**Figure 40**):
    a. No. 2 cylinder exhaust.
    b. No. 3 cylinder intake.
    c. No. 4 cylinder intake.
    d. No. 5 cylinder exhaust.
    e. No. 6 cylinder intake.
    f. No. 6 cylinder exhaust.
    g. No. 7 cylinder exhaust.
    h. No. 8 cylinder intake.
10B. On counter-rotation models, identify the adjusting nuts for the following valve (**Figure 40**):
    a. No. 2 cylinder intake.
    b. No. 3 cylinder exhaust.
    c. No. 4 cylinder exhaust.
    d. No. 5 cylinder intake.
    e. No. 6 cylinder intake.
    f. No. 6 cylinder exhaust.

6

g. No. 7 cylinder intake.

h. No. 8 cylinder exhaust.

11. Tighten the adjusting nuts until a slight amount of lash exists between the rocker arm and pushrod. Do not remove all of the lash.

12. Rotate the crankshaft exactly one turn in the normal direction of engine rotation and align the notch in the harmonic balancer with the 0 mark on the timing tab (**Figure 42**). The No. 1 piston is now at TDC.

13. Adjust the valves as described in this chapter.

14. To provide initial lubrication, coat the rocker arms, pushrods, pivot balls and lifters with engine oil.

15. Install the intake manifold as described in Chapter Seven.

16. Install the rocker arm cover(s) as described in this chapter.

17A. On 5.0L and 5.7L models, install the spark plugs and tighten to 22 ft.-lb. (30 N•m) if the cylinder head is new and 15 ft.-lb. (20 N•m) if the cylinder head is used.

17B. On 7.4L and 8.2L models, install the spark plugs and tighten to 15-20 ft.-lb. (20-28 N•m).

18. Connect the plug wires and install or reposition any components removed to access the rocker arm covers.

19. Connect the negative battery cable.

Removal (Later 7.4L/8.2L and All 8.1L Models)

These models use a shoulder bolt to retain the rocker arm and pivot ball onto the cylinder head and the valves are not adjustable. However, the shoulder bolt must be tightened in the proper sequence as described in this section.

1. Disconnect the negative battery cable and remove the spark plugs.

2. Remove the rocker arm cover(s) as described in this chapter.

3. Remove the intake manifold as described in Chapter Seven.

4. Place the engine in the TDC position for the No. 1 cylinder as described in this chapter.

5. Remove the shoulder bolt and pivot ball (**Figure 39**) from each rocker arm. Mark the original locations and remove the rocker arms, guides and pushrods from the cylinder head studs.

6. Clean the components with solvent and dry with compressed air.

7. Roll the pushrods across a flat surface to check for bending. Replace bent pushrods. Inspect all parts for excessive wear or damage and replace if necessary.

Installation

NOTE
On 7.4L, 8.1L and 8.2L models, the exhaust valve pushrods are longer than the intake valve pushrods.

NOTE
7.4L models are produced in both standard- and high-output models that must be identified before beginning the installation procedure. If the identification decal is missing from the engine or the output specification is in question, remove the intake manifold as described in Chapter Seven. Then inspect the intake manifold and cylinder head intake ports. The standard-output models use round or oval ports. The high-output models use rectangular ports.

1. Inspect the lifters and camshaft lobes of the No. 1 cylinder for proper alignment. The roller on the lifters must align with the base of the camshaft lobes (**Figure 45**). If otherwise, the crankshaft must be rotated to position the No. 1 piston in the TDC firing position.

2. Insert the pushrods (**Figure 39**) for the No. 1 cylinder through their respective slots in the cylinder head. Used pushrods must be installed into the original locations in the cylinder head.

3. Fit the lower end of the pushrods into the recesses in the roller lifters. Make sure the lifter rollers are seated against the camshaft lobes. Push down on each lifter to verify proper seating.

4. Fit the slot in the guides over the pushrods with the offset facing upward. Align the shoulder bolt opening in the guide with the corresponding threaded openings in the cylinder head.

5. Slide the pivot balls over the shoulder bolts with the rounded side facing away from the bolt head. Guide the shoulder bolts and pivot balls into the openings in the rocker arms. Seat the balls and bolts into the recesses in the rocker arms.

6. Install the No. 1 cylinder rocker arm assemblies onto the cylinder head. The upper end of the pushrods must align the depression in the tip of the rocker arms. The other end of the rocker arms must align with the top of the valve stems.

7. Thread the shoulder bolts into the corresponding openings in the cylinder head. Tighten both shoulder bolts evenly to 40 ft.-lb. (52 N•m) for standard output 7.4L models, 45 ft.-lb. (61 N•m) for high output 7.4L models, 19 ft.-lb. (26 N•m) for 8.1L models and 45 ft.-lb. (61 N•m) for 8.2L models.

8. Rotate the harmonic balancer *exactly* 90° clockwise. Do not rotate the balancer counterclockwise, or the water pump will be damaged. Inspect the lifters and camshaft lobes for proper alignment. The roller on the lifters must align with the base of the camshaft lobes (**Figure 45**). If otherwise, the crankshaft must be rotated to position the piston for the selected cylinder in the TDC firing position.

9. Refer to **Figure 40** to locate the valve train components for the next cylinder in the firing order. On 7.4L and 8.2L models, the firing order is 1-8-4-3-6-5-7-2. On 8.1L models, the firing order is 1-8-7-2-6-5-4-3.

10. Insert the pushrods (**Figure 39**) for the selected cylinder through their respective slots in the cylinder head. Used pushrods must be installed into the original locations in the cylinder head.

11. Fit the lower end of the pushrods into the recesses in the roller lifters. Make sure the lifter rollers are seated against the camshaft lobes. Push down on each lifter to verify proper seating.

12. Fit the slot in the guides over the pushrods (**Figure 39**) with the offset facing upward. Align the shoulder bolt opening in the guide with the corresponding threaded openings in the cylinder head.

13. Slide the pivot balls over the shoulder bolts with the rounded side facing away from the bolt head. Guide the shoulder bolts and pivot balls into the openings in the rocker arms. Seat the balls and bolts into the recesses in the rocker arms.

14. Install the rocker arm assemblies onto the cylinder head. The upper end of the pushrods must align the depression in the tip of the rocker arms. The other end of the rocker arms must align with the top of the valve stems.

15. Thread the shoulder bolts into the corresponding openings in the cylinder head. Tighten both shoulder bolts evenly to the following specification:
   a. On 7.4L standard-output models, tighten the bolts to 40 ft.-lb. (52 N•m).
   b. On 7.4L high-output models and all 8.2L models, tighten the bolts 45 ft.-lb. (61 N•m).
   c. On all 8.1L models, tighten the bolts to 19 ft.-lb. (26 N•m).

16. Repeat Steps 8-15 for the remaining cylinders.

17. Install the intake manifold as described in Chapter Seven.

18. Install the rocker arm covers as described in this chapter.

19. Connect the spark plug wires and engine wire harness to the ignition coils.

20A. On 7.4L and 8.2L models, install the spark plugs and tighten to 15-20 ft.-lb. (20-28 N•m).

20B. On 8.1L models, install the spark plugs and tighten to 15 ft.-lb. (20 N•m).

21. Connect the plug wires and install any other components removed to access the rocker arm covers.

22. Connect the negative battery cable.

CYLINDER HEAD

The cylinder head(s) can be removed and installed without removing the engine from the boat.

Take photographs or make sketches of bracket orientation, hose and wire routing before removing the cylinder head(s). This step saves a great deal of time and helps prevent incorrect assembly.

Mark the mounting locations and orientations of the pushrods, rocker arm and mounting hardware prior to removing them.

Valve and valve seat repair requires special knowledge, training and expensive equipment. Although the procedures and specifications are provided in this chapter, it is far more practical to have valve and valve seat repairs performed at a reputable machine shop.

The cylinder head uses bolts of different lengths. Label the bolts or make a diagram to show the location of each bolt as it is removed from the cylinder head.

Use a wire brush to remove all sealant from the cylinder head bolts. Use a thread chaser to clean any sealant or corrosion from the bolt openings in the cylinder block. Apply a light coat of GM Sealant (GM part No. 12346004) or equivalent to the cylinder head bolt threads prior to installing them. Purchase the sealant from a GM automobile dealership.

Replace the head gasket each time the cylinder head bolts are loosened. Apply a light coat of Permatex Gasket Sealing Compound or equivalent to both sides of the stainless steel ribbed gaskets. Do not apply sealant to composition gaskets. Purchase the gasket sealing compound from an automotive parts store.

Follow the specified head bolt tightening sequence and procedure. Many later models use a torque-and-turn tightening sequence. The bolts are tightened in sequence to a specified torque and then turned an additional amount. Use a torque angle gauge and tighten the bolts the specified degrees of rotation. Purchase the torque angle gauge from a tool supplier or automotive parts store.

NOTE
7.4L models are produced in both standard- and high-output models that must be identified before beginning the repair procedure. If the identification decal is missing from the engine or the output specification is in question, remove the intake manifold as described in Chapter Seven. Then inspect the

6

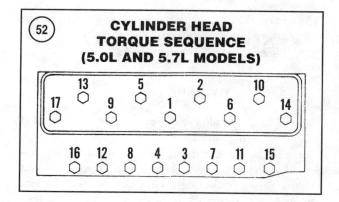

CYLINDER HEAD TORQUE SEQUENCE (5.0L AND 5.7L MODELS)

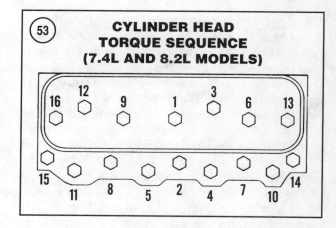

CYLINDER HEAD TORQUE SEQUENCE (7.4L AND 8.2L MODELS)

intake manifold and cylinder head intake ports. The standard-output models use round or oval ports. The high-output models use rectangular ports.

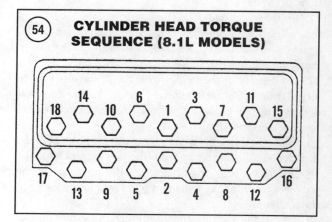

CYLINDER HEAD TORQUE SEQUENCE (8.1L MODELS)

Removal

1. Disconnect the battery cables.

2A. On open cooling system models, drain water from the cylinder block and manifold as described in Chapter Three.

2B. On closed cooling system models, drain water from the exhaust manifolds and heat exchanger as described in Chapter Three. Drain coolant from the system as described in Chapter Three.

3. Remove the exhaust manifold as described in Chapter Eight.

4. Remove the intake manifold as described in Chapter Seven.

5. Remove the rocker arm cover(s), rocker arms and pushrods as described in this chapter.

6. Relocate or remove any bracket, hoses, lines or other components that will interfere with cylinder head removal.

7. Remove the spark plugs.

8. Refer to the appropriate diagrams (**Figures 52-54**) and loosen the cylinder head bolts in the reverse order of the tightening sequence.

9. Remove the cylinder head bolts. Note each bolt length upon removal. On 8.1L models, note which length of bolt is used in each location. Then discard the cylinder head bolts. The cylinder head bolts used on these models are not designed for reuse.

10. Have an assistant support the cylinder head and then tap on the end of the cylinder head with a rubber mallet to break the gasket seal. If this does not loosen the head, carefully pry the cylinder head away from the cylinder

block. Use a blunt pry bar and work carefully to avoid damaging the mating surfaces.

11. Remove the gasket from the cylinder block or head. Carefully scrape all gasket material from the mating surfaces. Do not scratch or gouge the mating surfaces. Clean the surfaces with aerosol carburetor cleaner.

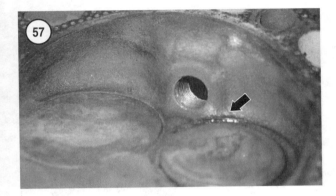

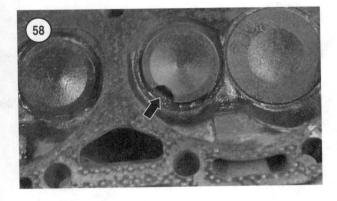

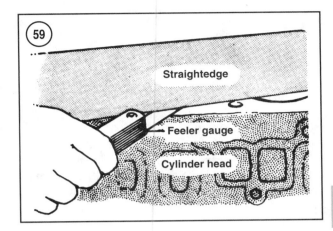

6

3. Inspect the cylinder head for surface cracks (**Figure 55**), especially near the valve seats (**Figure 56**) and spark plug openings (**Figure 57**). Replace the cylinder head if cracked.

4. Inspect the valves for damage and chipped or burned edges (**Figure 58**). Have the cylinder head repaired if these or other defects are present.

5. Check for valve recession. Compare the valve depth in the valve seat with other valves in the cylinder head. The valve is recessed if it appears to be lower in the seat than the others. Have the cylinder head repaired if valve recession is evident.

6. Check for cylinder head warpage by placing a straightedge at various positions across the cylinder head mating surface (**Figure 59**). Hold the straightedge firmly against the surface and using a feeler gauge, check the gap at various points along the straightedge. The thickness of the feeler gauge that can pass under the straightedge indicates the amount of warpage. Have the cylinder head resurfaced if surface damage is evident or if the warpage exceeds the limit. Do not remove more than 0.010 in. (0.254 mm) of material from the cylinder head surface. Replace the cylinder head if a greater amount of material must be removed to true the surface. Warpage specifications follow:

    a. On 5.0L and 5.7L models, the warpage must not exceed 0.004 in. (0.102 mm) at any point along the length of the cylinder head.

    b. On 7.4L standard-output models, the warpage must not exceed 0.003 in. (0.076 mm) at any 6 in. (152 mm) span or 0.004 in. (0.102 mm) along the length of the cylinder head.

    c. On 7.4L high-output models, 8.1L models and 8.2L models, the warpage must not exceed 0.003 in. (0.076 mm) at any 6 in. (152 mm) span or 0.007 in. (0.178 mm) along the length of the cylinder head.

12. Inspect the piston crowns for damage or excessive carbon deposits. Remove carbon deposits with a blunt scraper. Disassemble the cylinder block and replace damaged pistons as described in this chapter.

Inspection

1. Using a blunt scraper, scrape all carbon deposits from the combustion chamber. Do not nick or gouge the cylinder head.

2. Use solvent and thoroughly clean the cylinder head.

7. Check the cylinder block for warpage by placing a straightedge at various points on the cylinder head mating surface (**Figure 60**). Hold the straightedge firmly against the head and using a feeler gauge, check the gap at various points along the straightedge. The thickness of the feeler gauge that can pass under the straightedge indicates the amount of warpage. Have the cylinder block resurfaced if the warpage exceeds 0.004 in. (0.100 mm) along the length of the straightedge or 0.002 in. (0.050 mm) within a 6 in. (152 mm) span or if other surface damage is evident. Do not remove more than 0.010 in. (0.254 mm) of material from the cylinder block surface. Replace the cylinder block if a greater amount of material must be removed to true the surface.

8. Position the cylinder head so the ports are higher than the valves. Pour light solvent into the ports (**Figure 61**). Check for solvent leaking between the valves and seats. Have the cylinder head repaired if solvent leaks from the valves.

9. Inspect the dowel pins in the cylinder block. They must fit tightly in the openings. Replace damaged or loose-fitting pins.

10. Check the rocker arm studs, if so equipped, for worn or damaged surfaces and replace if necessary. Studs with a hex head are threaded into the head. Studs without a hex head are pressed into the head, and a suitable puller and installation tool must be used to replace them. Oversized studs are available to replace loose-fitting pressed-in studs. Have pressed-in studs installed at a reputable machine shop.

Installation

The cylinder head bolt tightening procedure for early 5.0L and 5.7L models are different from the procedure used for later models. Early models use 12 bolts to secure the intake manifold to the cylinder head. Later models use eight bolts to secure the manifold and are commonly referred to as Gen+ models. The later 5.0L/5.7L Gen+ and all 8.1L models use a torque-and-turn bolt tightening procedure that requires a torque angle gauge (**Figure 62**). Purchase the torque angle gauge from a tool supplier. Follow the tool manufacturer's instructions when using the tool.

1. Use an aerosol carburetor cleaner or other suitable solvent and thoroughly clean the cylinder head and cylinder block mating surfaces. Any residual gasket material or other contaminants may allow water, coolant or exhaust to leak.

2A. If a stainless steel gasket is used, apply a light coating of Permatex Gasket Sealing Compound or equivalent

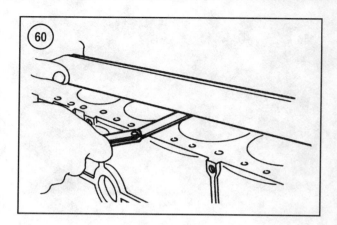

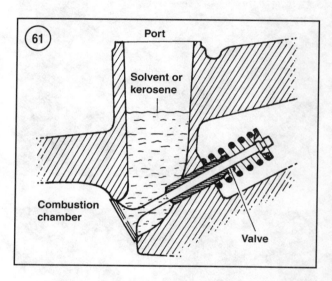

to both sides of the new gasket(s). Purchase the gasket sealing compound from an automotive parts store.

2B. If a composition gasket is used, do not apply sealant to the gasket or mating surfaces.

3. Thoroughly inspect the gasket for marks indicating which side of the gasket faces upward. The *up* or *this side up* inscription is sometimes difficult to locate. Align the cylinder bore and dowel pin openings and place the gasket(s) onto the cylinder block.

4. Align the openings with the dowel pins and carefully fit the cylinder head(s) onto the cylinder block.

CAUTION
The cylinder head bolts used on 8.1L models are not designed for reuse. Install new cylinder head bolts each time they are loosened. The bolts stretch during the tightening process and can break if reused.

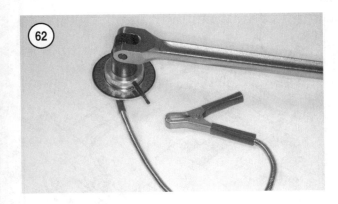

5. Apply a light coat of GM Sealant (GM part No. 12346004) or equivalent to the cylinder head bolt threads prior to installing them. Purchase the sealant from a GM automobile dealership. Install the bolts and hand-thread them into the cylinder head and cylinder block. Bolts of different lengths are used. Make sure they are installed in the original locations.

CAUTION
The cylinder heads used on 5.7L LT-1 models are made of aluminum alloy and require a special procedure, equipment and practical experience to properly tighten the cylinder head bolts. Improper tightening can crack or damage the cylinder head. After installing the cylinder head and tightening the bolts by hand, have the cylinder head bolts tightened at an Indmar dealership.

6A. On early 5.0L and 5.7L models with a 12-bolt intake manifold, tighten the head bolts as follows:
   a. Tighten the head bolts in sequence (**Figure 52**) to 20 ft.-lb. (27 N•m).
   b. Tighten the head bolts in sequence (**Figure 52**) a second time to 40 ft.-lb. (54 N•m).
   c. Tighten the head bolts in sequence (**Figure 52**) a final time to 65 ft.-lb. (88 N•m).

6B. On later 5.0L and 5.7L models (except 5.7L LT-1) with an eight-bolt intake manifold (Gen+ models), tighten the head bolts as follows:
   a. Tighten the head bolts in sequence (**Figure 52**) to 22 ft.-lb. (30 N•m).
   b. Use a torque angle gauge and tighten the bolts in sequence (**Figure 52**) a final time. Tighten the short bolts an additional 55°. Tighten the medium-length bolts an additional 65°. Tighten the long bolts an additional 75°.

6C. On 7.4L standard-output models, tighten the head bolts as follows:

   a. Tighten the head bolts in sequence (**Figure 53**) to 20 ft.-lb. (27 N•m).
   b. Tighten the head bolts in sequence (**Figure 53**) a second time to 50 ft.-lb. (68 N•m).
   c. Tighten the head bolts in sequence (**Figure 53**) a final time to 85 ft.-lb. (115 N•m).

6D. On 7.4L high-output models, tighten the head bolts as follows:
   a. Tighten the head bolts in sequence (**Figure 53**) to 20 ft.-lb. (27 N•m).
   b. Tighten the head bolts in sequence (**Figure 53**) a second time to 50 ft.-lb. (68 N•m).
   c. Tighten the head bolts in sequence (**Figure 53**) a final time to 89 ft.-lb. (120 N•m) for the short bolts and 92 ft.-lb. (125 N•m) for the long bolts.

6E. On 8.1L models, tighten the head bolts as follows:
   a. Tighten the head bolts in sequence (**Figure 54**) to 22 ft.-lb. (30 N•m).
   b. Use a torque angle gauge and tighten the bolts in sequence (**Figure 54**) an additional 120°.
   c. Use a torque angle gauge and tighten the bolts in sequence (**Figure 54**) a final time. Tighten the long bolts an additional 60°. Tighten the medium-length bolts an additional 45°. Tighten the short bolts an additional 30°.

6F. On 8.2L models, tighten the head bolts as follows:
   a. Tighten the head bolts in sequence (**Figure 53**) to 20 ft.-lb. (27 N•m).
   b. Tighten the head bolts in sequence (**Figure 53**) a second time to 50 ft.-lb. (68 N•m).
   c. Tighten the head bolts in sequence (**Figure 53**) a final time to 89 ft.-lb. (120 N•m) for the short bolts and 92 ft.-lb. (125 N•m) for the long bolts.

7. Install the pushrods and rocker arms as described in this chapter. Do not install the rocker arm covers at this time.

8. On all 5.0L/5.7L and earlier 7.4/8.2L models, adjust the valves as described in this chapter.

9. Install the intake manifold as described in Chapter Seven.

10. Install the rocker arm covers as described in this chapter.

11. Install the exhaust manifold as described in Chapter Eight.

12. On models with a closed cooling system, fill the cooling system with the proper coolant-and-water mixture as described in Chapter Three.

13A. On 5.0L and 5.7L models, install the spark plug and tighten to 22 ft.-lb. (30 N•m) if the cylinder head is new and 15 ft.-lb. (20 N•m) if the cylinder head is used.

13B. On 7.4L and 8.2L models, install the spark plugs and tighten to 15-20 ft.-lb. (20-28 N•m).

6

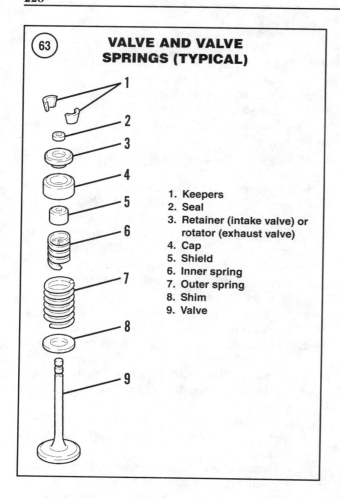

VALVE AND VALVE SPRINGS (TYPICAL)

1. Keepers
2. Seal
3. Retainer (intake valve) or rotator (exhaust valve)
4. Cap
5. Shield
6. Inner spring
7. Outer spring
8. Shim
9. Valve

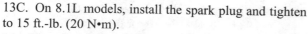

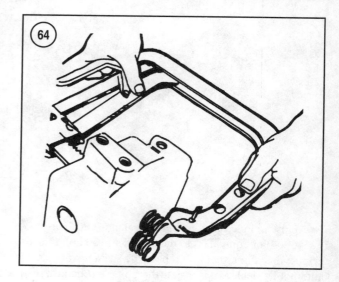

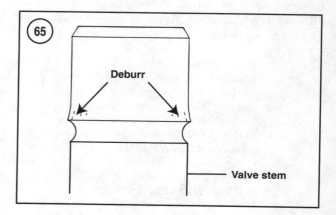

Deburr

Valve stem

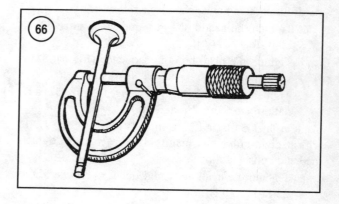

13C. On 8.1L models, install the spark plug and tighten to 15 ft.-lb. (20 N•m).
14. Connect the plug wires and install or reposition any components removed to access the rocker arm covers.
15. Connect the battery cables.

VALVES AND VALVE SEATS

Valve and valve seat repair requires special knowledge, training and expensive equipment. Although the procedures are described in this section, it is far more practical to have valve and valve seat repairs performed at a reputable machine shop.

Valve Removal

Refer to **Figure 63** for this procedure.
1. Remove the cylinder head as described in this chapter.
2. Remove the rocker arms, pivot balls and guides as described in this chapter.

3. Use a valve spring compressor tool (**Figure 64**) to fully compress the valve spring. Remove the valve keepers (1, **Figure 63**) from the valve stem. Then release the spring tension. Remove the valve spring retainer or rotator (3, **Figure 63**) and cap (4). Then lift the valve springs (6 and 7, **Figure 63**) and shield (5) from the head.

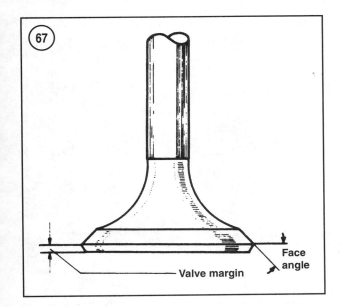

67

Valve margin

Face angle

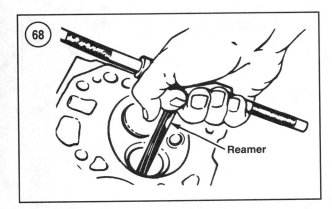

68

Reamer

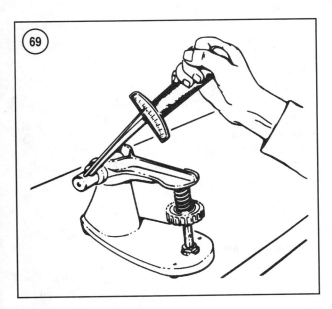

69

4. Pull the small valve stem seal (2, **Figure 63**) and the umbrella seal off the cylinder head. Discard the seals. On some models, the exhaust valve might not use valve stem seals.

5. If so equipped, remove the shim (8, **Figure 63**) from the head.

CAUTION
Remove any burrs from the valve stem keeper groove before pulling the valve out of the cylinder head. Any burrs will damage the valve guide bore as the valve is removed.

6. Inspect the valve stems for burrs near the keeper grooves (**Figure 65**). Carefully file or polish away any burrs before removing the valve.

7. Pull the valve out of the cylinder head.

8. Remove the remaining valves as described in Steps 3-7.

9. Arrange all parts in order so they can be returned to the original location during assembly.

Valve Inspection

1. Clean the valves with a fine wire brush or buffing wheel. Discard any valves with cracked, warped or burned surfaces.

2. Measure the valve stems (**Figure 66**) at the top, center and bottom. Replace any valve if the stem diameter is less than the specification in **Table 4**.

3. Measure the thickness of each valve edge or margin (**Figure 67**). Replace any valve with a margin less than the specification in **Table 4**.

4. Use a stiff spiral wire brush to remove any carbon and varnish from the valve guides.

5. Insert each valve into the original guide in the cylinder head. Be sure to use the replacement valve for this procedure if the original valve has excessive valve stem wear. Hold the valve slightly off the seat and rock it back and forth in a direction parallel to the rocker arms. This is the direction in which the greatest wear occurs. A slight amount of rocking movement is acceptable. Significant rocking motion indicates worn guides that must be reamed (**Figure 68**) to the next oversized diameter. Valves with oversized stems are available in either two or three sizes. Valve guide reaming requires special tooling and training and should be performed at a reputable machine shop.

6. Check valve spring pressure using a valve spring testing tool (**Figure 69**). Replace any spring with a pressure that is less than the specification in **Table 5**.

7. Check each spring on a flat surface with a steel square (**Figure 70**). Slowly rotate the spring while noting the

6

space between the top of the coil and the square. Replace the spring if the space exceeds 5/16 in. at any point.

8. Measure the lengths of the valve springs. Compare the length to the specification in **Table 5**. Replace any valve spring that measures less than the specification.

9. Inspect the valve seats for excessive wear, pitting or other surface imperfections. Have the seats reconditioned at a reputable machine shop if these or other surface defects are evident.

10. After any machining operation on the valve and valve seat, coat the face of the valve with Prussian Blue marking compound. Insert the valve into the valve guide. Apply light pressure to the valve to ensure contact with the valve seat. Then while maintaining light pressure, rotate the valve approximately one-quarter turn. Lift out the valve and inspect the valve and seat mating surfaces.

   a. If the dye transfers evenly to the valve seat surfaces (**Figure 71**), the valve is seating properly. No further machining is required.

   b. If the dye transfers toward the top of the valve seat, machine the seat using the dressing stone specified to lower the seat.

   c. If the dye transfers toward the bottom of the valve seat, machine the seat using the dressing stone specified to raise the seat.

Valve Installation

Refer to **Figure 63** for this procedure.

1. Coat the valve stem with engine oil and carefully insert the valve into the cylinder head.

2. Install the shim (8, **Figure 63**) around the valve guide boss and seat onto the cylinder head.

3. If so equipped, apply engine oil to the surfaces and then fit a *new* seal (3, **Figure 63**) into the recess in the valve guide opening. Make sure the seal is not twisted and remains flat in the groove.

4. If so equipped, install the *new* umbrella type seal over the valve stem and seat it lightly against the valve guide.

5. Install the valve springs (7 and 8, **Figure 63**) over the valve stem and then seat against the spacer. Guide the shield (5, **Figure 63**) over the valve stem and fit it between the springs and valve guide boss.

6. Install the cap (4, **Figure 63**) and then the valve spring retainer or rotator (3) over the stem and seat it against the spring.

7. Use a valve spring compressor (**Figure 64**) to compress the valve springs. Compress the springs enough to fully expose the grooves in the valve stem.

8. Fit the two keepers into the upper groove in the valve stem (**Figure 72**) with the tapered ends facing down.

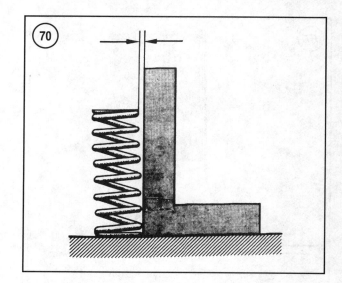

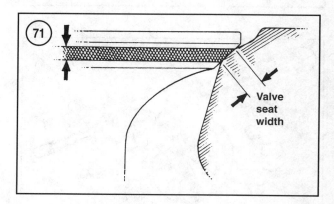

Make sure the ridges in both keepers are fully seated in the groove in the valve stem.

9. *Slowly* release pressure on the valve spring compressor. Make sure both keepers are fully seated in the valve stem groove and spring retainer opening. If questionable, compress the spring and check the installation.

10. Measure the installed valve spring height between the top of the valve spring base and the underside of the valve spring retainer or rotator as shown in **Figure 73**. Compare the measurement with the specification in **Table 5**. If the measurement exceeds the specification, remove the valve and install a 1/16-in. (1.59 mm) shim. Reinstall the valve and repeat the measurement.

OIL PAN

Removal and Installation

In some cases, the boat design and engine installation allow sufficient clearance for oil pan removal without re-

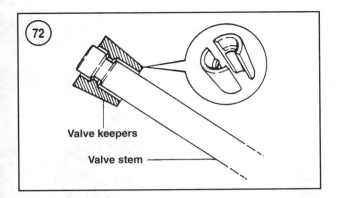

72

Valve keepers

Valve stem

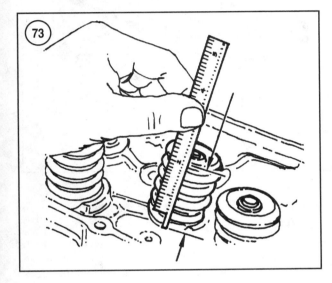

73

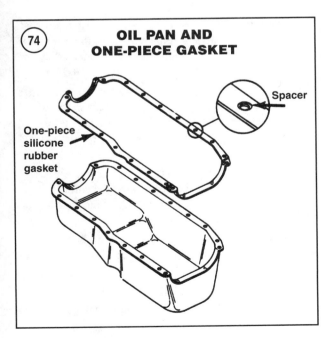

74

**OIL PAN AND
ONE-PIECE GASKET**

Spacer

**One-piece
silicone
rubber
gasket**

moving the engine. In others, the engine must be removed. Remove the engine if the clearance is in question. Inadequate clearance might allow pan removal but prevent proper alignment of the gasket during assembly and result in oil leakage.

All 1983-1985 models use a two-piece cork gasket with rubber front and rear seals. All 1986-2003 models use a one piece oil pan gasket (**Figure 74**, typical). At the fastener openings, this type of gasket has molded-in metal spacers, which prevent excessive gasket crushing and resulting oil leakage. The one-piece oil pan gasket is used as the replacement gasket on 1983-1985 models in place of the earlier four-piece gasket. Although the one-piece gasket is designed for reuse, it is a good practice to replace the gasket anytime the oil pan is removed. Small tears might not be easy to see but will still allow oil to leak into the bilge.

All 1983-1985 5.0L/5.7L models and 1983-1990 7.4L/8.2L models use a two-piece rear main seal. All 1986-2003 5.0L/5.7L models and 1991-2003 7.4L/8.2L models use a one-piece rear main seal. Although the oil pan replacement procedure is the same for either type of seal, the tightening specifications for the oil pan fasteners might differ by the type of seal used. Refer to *Rear Main Seal* in this chapter and identify the type of seal used before tightening the fasteners. All 8.1L models use a one-piece rear main seal.

1. Disconnect the battery cables.

2. Drain the engine oil as described in Chapter Three.

3. If necessary, remove the engine as described in this chapter.

4. Remove the starter motor as described in Chapter Nine.

5. Support the oil pan and remove the fasteners. Remove the reinforcement (4, **Figure 75**) if one is present. Carefully pull the oil pan from the cylinder block. If necessary, use a dull scraper and pry the pan from the cylinder block. Do not damage the gasket or mating surface.

6. Carefully remove the gasket from the oil pan or cylinder block. Work carefully to avoid damaging the gasket surface.

   a. If using a four-piece oil pan gasket, discard the gasket and replace it with the later one-piece gasket. Make sure to remove all of the old gasket material from the mating surfaces.

   b. If using a one-piece oil pan gasket, inspect the gasket for torn or damaged surfaces and replace if necessary.

7. Thoroughly clean the oil pan with solvent and dry with compressed air. Inspect the oil pan for cracks, dents or corrosion damage and replace if necessary.

6

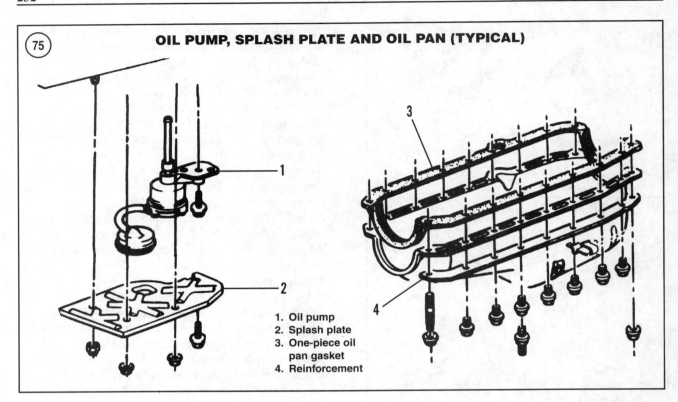

OIL PUMP, SPLASH PLATE AND OIL PAN (TYPICAL)

1. Oil pump
2. Splash plate
3. One-piece oil
   pan gasket
4. Reinforcement

8. Inspect the oil pump pickup screen for debris or sludge deposits. Clean the screen with solvent if necessary.

9. Clean the gasket sealant from the mating surfaces.

10. Apply a bead of RTV sealer to the corners where the oil pan gasket surface joins the timing cover and rear main seal retainer (**Figure 76**). Apply just enough sealant to fill the gap. Place the gasket on the cylinder block. Align the openings in the metal spacers with the fastener openings. Align the front of the gasket with the groove in the timing cover. Align the rear of the gasket with the groove in the rear main seal retainer.

11. Carefully guide the oil pump screen into position while fitting the oil pan onto the cylinder block. The grooves at the front and rear of the pan must fit over the gasket.

12. Install the fasteners. If so equipped, install the reinforcement (4, **Figure 75**). Tighten the oil pan fasteners starting from the center and working outward as follows:

   a. On 5.0L and 5.7L models with a two-piece rear main seal, tighten the fasteners at the corners to 168 in.-lb. (19 N•m). Tighten the fasteners on the sides of the pan to 84 in.-lb. (9.5 N•m).

   b. On 5.0L and 5.7L models with a one-piece rear main seal, tighten the fasteners at the corners of the pan to 177 in.-lb. (20 N•m). Tighten the fasteners on the sides to 106 in.-lb. (21 N•m).

   c. On 7.4L models with a two-piece rear main seal, tighten the fasteners at the corners of the pan to 168 in.-lb. (19 N•m). Tighten the fasteners on the sides of the pan to 84 in.-lb. (9.5 N•m).

   d. On 7.4L models with a one-piece rear main seal, tighten the fasteners at the corners of the pan to 204 in.-lb. (23 N•m). Tighten the fasteners that run down the sides of the pan to 84 in.-lb. (9.5 N•m).

   e. On 8.1L models, tighten the oil pan screws in a crossing pattern starting from the center and working outward to 89 in.-lb. (10 N•m). Tighten the oil pan screws in the same sequence a final time to 221 in.-lb. (25 N•m).

   f. On 8.2L models with a two-piece or one-piece rear main seal, tighten the fasteners at the corners of the pan to 204 in.-lb. (23 N•m). Tighten the fasteners on the sides of the pan to 84 in.-lb. (9.5 N•m).

13. Install the starter motor as described in Chapter Nine.

14. Install the sealing washer onto the oil pan drain plug or drain hose. Then thread the plug or fitting into the oil pan. Tighten the oil drain plug or fitting as follows:

   a. On 5.0L and 5.7L models, tighten the plug/fitting to 221 in.-lb. (25 N•m).

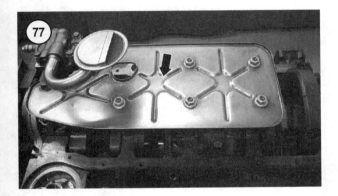

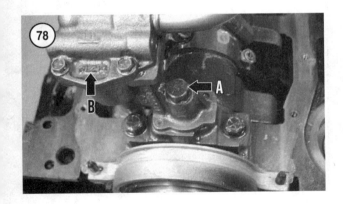

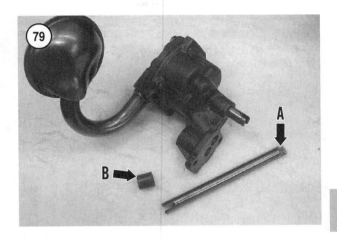

OIL PUMP

The oil pump (1, **Figure** 75) is attached to the rear main bearing cap. On 8.1L models, the oil pump is driven by the pump drive assembly via a gear on the camshaft. On all other models, the oil pump is driven by the distributor shaft gear. Some models are equipped with a splash plate (**Figure 77**) that is secured to the engine by the oil pump retaining bolt and the retaining studs for the main bearing caps.

NOTE
On 5.0L and 5.7L models, the oil pump pickup tube and screen are a press fit in the pump housing. Do not remove the tube and screen unless either must be replaced. On 7.4L, 8.1L and 8.2L models, the tube and screen assembly cannot be removed from the pump.

Removal/Installation

1. Remove the oil pan as described in this chapter.
2. On models with a splash plate, remove the nuts that hold the plate (2, **Figure 75**) onto the main bearing cap and oil pump stud. Then lift the plate off the engine.
3. Remove the bolt that secures the oil pump (A, **Figure 78**) and remove the pump (B, **Figure 78**).
4. Remove the oil pump drive shaft (A, **Figure 79**) and plastic shaft coupling (B) from the oil pump.
5. Inspect the oil pump for damage or excessive wear as described in this chapter (refer to *Oil pump disassembly, inspection and assembly*).
6. Carefully insert the oil pump drive shaft into the opening in the cylinder block. If the distributor or oil pump drive is installed, rotate the shaft to align the slot in the shaft with the pin in the distributor or drive assembly.

b. On 7.4L and 8.2L models, tighten the plug/fitting to 20 ft.-lb. (27 N•m).

c. On 8.1L models, tighten the plug/fitting to 21 ft.-lb. (28 N•m).

15. Fill the crankcase with fresh oil as described in Chapter Three. Inspect the drain plug or fitting for leakage and correct before proceeding.

16. If removed, install the engine as described in this chapter.

17. Start the engine and immediately check for oil leakage. Correct any leakage before operating the engine.

6

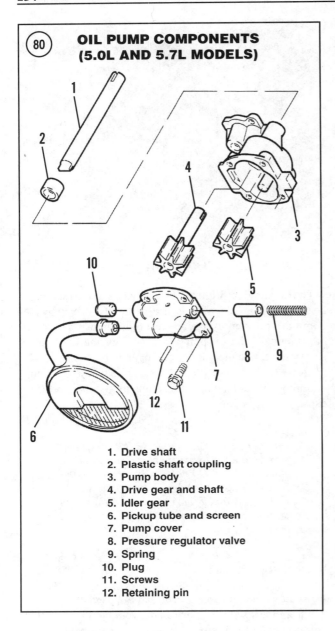

⑧⓪ **OIL PUMP COMPONENTS**
(5.0L AND 5.7L MODELS)

1. Drive shaft
2. Plastic shaft coupling
3. Pump body
4. Drive gear and shaft
5. Idler gear
6. Pickup tube and screen
7. Pump cover
8. Pressure regulator valve
9. Spring
10. Plug
11. Screws
12. Retaining pin

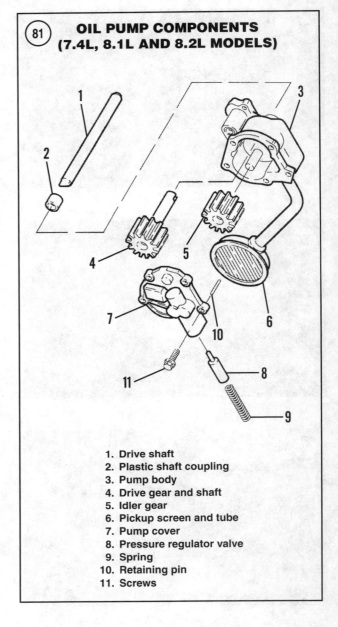

⑧① **OIL PUMP COMPONENTS**
(7.4L, 8.1L AND 8.2L MODELS)

1. Drive shaft
2. Plastic shaft coupling
3. Pump body
4. Drive gear and shaft
5. Idler gear
6. Pickup screen and tube
7. Pump cover
8. Pressure regulator valve
9. Spring
10. Retaining pin
11. Screws

7. If removed, install the distributor or oil pump drive into the cylinder block opening. Rotate the oil pump body and align the pump with the shaft, distributor or oil pump drive (8.1L and 5.7L LT-1 models). The oil pump will seat against the bearing cap as the shafts align.

NOTE
All 1983-1985 5.0L/5.7L models and 1983-1990 7.4L/8.2L models use a two-piece rear main seal. All 1986-2003 5.0L/5.7L models and 1991-2003 7.4L/8.2L models use a one-piece rear main seal. All 8.1L models use a one-piece rear main seal. Although the oil

pump replacement procedures are the same for either type of seal, the tightening specifications for the oil pump mounting bolt might differ by the type of seal used. Refer to **Rear Main Seal** *in this chapter and identify the type of seal used before tightening the fasteners.*

8. Rotate the oil pump and align the mounting bolt openings. Thread the mount bolt(s) into the pump and cylinder block. Refer to the following:

   a. On 5.0L and 5.7L models, tighten the oil pump mounting bolt to 66 ft.-lb. (89 N•m).

b. On 7.4L and 8.2L models with a two-piece rear main seal, tighten the oil pump mounting bolt to 65 ft.-lb. (88 N•m).

c. On 7.4L and 8.2L models with a one-piece rear main seal, tighten the oil pump mounting bolt to 70 ft.-lb. (95 N•m).

d. On 8.1L models, tighten the mounting bolt to 56 ft.-lb. (76 N•m).

9. Install the splash plate (**Figure 77**) and secure with the fasteners as follows:

a. On 5.0L and 5.7L models with a two-piece rear main seal, tighten the nuts and single bolt to 25 ft.-lb. (34 N•m).

b. On 5.0L and 5.7L models with a one-piece rear main seal, tighten the nuts and single bolt to 30 ft.-lb. (41 N•m).

c. On 7.4L and 8.2L models, tighten the splash plate retaining nuts in a crossing pattern to 25 ft.-lb. (34 N•m).

d. On 8.1L models, tighten the eight splash plate retaining nuts in a crossing pattern to 37 ft.-lb. (50 N•m).

10. Install the oil pan as described in this chapter.

Oil Pump Disassembly, Inspection and Assembly

Internal oil pump components are not available separately. Refer to **Figure 80** or **Figure 81** during this procedure. Use a pickup tube installation tool (Kent-Moore part No. J21882) to install the pickup tube and screen assembly, if removed, into the pump cover. Otherwise, the tube might fit improperly and cause low oil pressure and engine damage.

CAUTION
On 7.4L, 8.1L and 8.2L models, the pickup tube and screen are welded to the oil pump body. The oil pump assembly must be replaced if the pickup tube or screen requires replacement.

1. Remove the screws and carefully pull the cover from the pump body (**Figure 82**).

2. Make match marks on the drive gear and idler gear teeth (**Figure 83**) prior to removing them from the pump housing. If reused, the teeth on one gear must align with the corresponding teeth on the other gear, or the gears will wear and fail prematurely.

3. Pull the drive gear (**Figure 84**) and then the idler (**Figure 85**) gear from the pump body.

6

4. Use a pin punch to drive the retaining pin carefully from the pump cover (**Figure 86**). Remove the spring and pressure regulator valve (**Figure 87**) from the cover.

5. Clean all components in solvent and dry with compressed air. Inspect the components as follows:

  a. Inspect the gears for wear, rough surfaces, excessive polishing or discoloration.

  b. Inspect the cover (**Figure 88**) and pump body (**Figure 89**) for wear, grooves, discoloration or rough surfaces.

  c. Inspect the pressure regulator valve for worn or rough surfaces.

  d. Inspect the spring for corrosion or weak spring tension.

  e. Inspect the drive shaft bore in the pump body for excessive wear, elongation of the bore or other damage.

  f. Replace the oil pump assembly if these or other defects are evident.

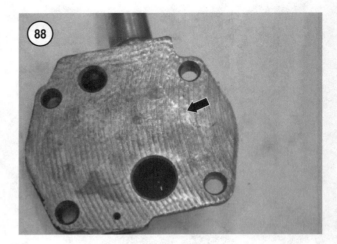

6A. On 5.0L and 5.7L models, inspect the pickup tube and screen for corrosion or other damage. If either the pickup tube or screen is defective, replace the assembly as follows:

  a. Make match marks on the pickup tube and oil pump cover.

  b. Clamp the cover in a vise with protective jaws.

  c. Carefully twist the tube and screen assembly out of the cover.

  d. Transfer the match marks onto the replacement tube and screen assembly.

  e. Fit the pickup tube into the cover.

  f. Align the match marks and then drive the pickup tube into the cover until the bead on the tube contacts the cover. Use a pickup tube installation tool (Kent-Moore tool part No. J21882) to install the tube. See **Figure 90**.

6B. On 7.4L, 8.1L and 8.2L models, inspect the pickup tube and screen for corrosion or other damage. Replace the oil pump assembly if damage is evident.

7. Align the match marks (**Figure 83**) and install the drive gear and idler gear into the pump body. The gears must spin freely in the pump body. If not, replace the oil pump assembly.

8. Insert the pressure regulator valve and then the spring into the pump body. Depress the spring until it is below

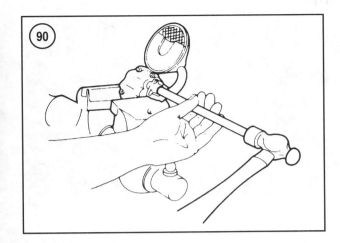

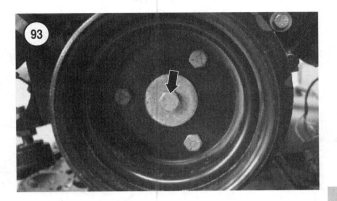

6

b. On 5.0L and 5.7L models with a one-piece rear main seal, tighten the screws to 106 in.-lb. (12 N•m).

c. On 7.4L and 8.2L models with a two-piece rear main seal, tighten the screws in a crossing pattern to 84 in.-lb. (9.5 N•m).

d. On 7.4L and 8.2L models with a one-piece rear main seal, tighten the screws in a crossing pattern to 106 in.-lb. (12 N•m).

e. On 8.1L models, tighten the screws to 106 in.-lb. (12 N•m).

HARMONIC BALANCER

Removal/Inspection/Installation

Use a balancer removal and installation tool such as Kent-Moore part No. J-23523-E for this operation Do not use makeshift tools, which can damage the balancer or other engine components.

If boat structure prevents access to the balancer, remove the engine as described in this chapter.

NOTE
5.7L LT-1 models use a reluctor ring in place of the balancer. The removal and installation instructions are similar.

1. Disconnect the battery cables.
2. Loosen the tension and remove the alternator drive belt as described under *Alternator* in Chapter Nine.

3A. On models with a belt-driven seawater pump (**Figure 91**), loosen the tension and remove the water pump drive belt as described in Chapter Eight.

3B. On models with a crankshaft pulley-driven water pump (**Figure 92**), remove the water pump as described in Chapter Eight.

4. Remove the center bolt and large washer (**Figure 93**) from the crankshaft pulley. On some models, the crank-

the retaining pin bore. Then carefully drive the retaining pin into the opening in the pump body.

9. Apply engine oil to the gears. Rotate the drive shaft to distribute the oil.

10. Fit the pump cover onto the pump body. Install and tighten the screws as follows:

a. On 5.0 and 5.7L models with a two-piece rear main seal, tighten the screws in a crossing pattern to 84 in.-lb. (9.5 N•m).

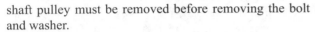

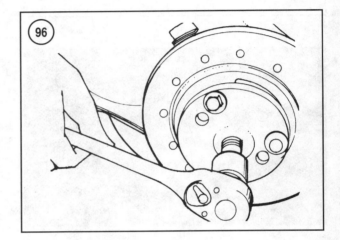

shaft pulley must be removed before removing the bolt and washer.

5. Remove the three bolts (**Figure 94**) and then pull the crankshaft pulley off the harmonic balancer (**Figure 95**). If necessary, tap on the side of the pulley with a rubber hammer to free the pulley.

6. On 5.7L LT-1 models, remove the crankshaft position sensors as described in Chapter Nine.

7. Attach the removal tool to the balancer or reluctor ring (5.7L LT-1 models). Thread the appropriate bolts from the removal tool into the tool and balancer. Be careful not to crossthread the bolts. The openings use fine threads. Securely tighten the bolts.

8. Thread the puller bolt into the removal tool until it contacts the crankshaft. Use the bolt with a tip that matches the crankshaft. Most of the models covered in this manual are tapered at the bolt opening.

9. Turn the puller bolt (**Figure 96**) and remove the balancer or reluctor ring (5.7L LT-1 models) from the crankshaft. Use solvent to clean the balancer and exposed end of the crankshaft.

10. Inspect the drive key in the crankshaft (**Figure 97**) for corrosion or damage and replace as needed.

11. Inspect the balancer at the seal contact surface (**Figure 98**). Replace the balancer if deeply grooved or pitted at this surface.

12. Inspect the balancer for protruding rubber material, cracks or other defects. Replace the balancer if these or other defects are evident. Cracking of the paint covering the rubber material is normal and does not indicate a defective balancer.

NOTE
If the harmonic balancer is replaced, the seal in the timing cover must also be replaced.

13. Inspect the seal in the timing cover (**Figure 99**) for wear or damage. Replace the seal if defective or if replacing the balancer. Refer to *Timing Cover*.

14. Apply a bead of RTV sealant to the key slot. Apply engine oil to the seal lip and the exposed end of the crankshaft.

15. Align the key slot with the crankshaft drive key. Fit the balancer or reluctor ring (5.7L LT-1 models) onto the crankshaft (**Figure 100**).

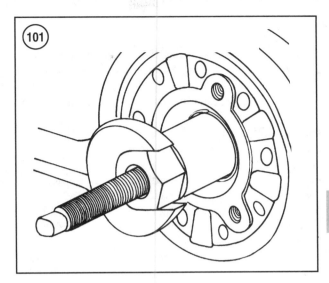

16. Fully thread the bolt from the installation tool into the crankshaft threads. Thread the puller hub onto the bolt until it contacts the balancer. Turn the puller hub (**Figure 101**) until the balancer fully seats against the crankshaft. Do not allow the balancer or center bolt to rotate during balancer installation. Remove the installation tool.

17. On 5.7L LT-1 models, install the crankshaft position sensor described in Chapter Nine.

18. On 5.0L and 5.7L models, install the crankshaft pulley onto the balancer. Install the three bolts and washers and tighten evenly to 35 ft.-lb. (47 N•m).

19. Thread the balancer retaining bolt and washer into the crankshaft. Tighten the bolt as follows:

   a. On 5.0L and 5.7L models with a steel pulley, tighten the bolt to 60 ft.-lb. (81 N•m).

   b. On 5.0L and 5.7L models with an aluminum pulley, tighten the bolt to 40 ft.-lb. (54 N•m).

   c. On 7.4L and 8.2L models, tighten the bolt to 110 ft.-lb. (149 N•m).

   d. On 8.1L models, tighten the bolt to 188 ft.-lb. (255 N•m).

20. On 7.4L, 8.1L, and 8.2L models, install the crankshaft pulley. Tighten the pulley bolts to 35 ft.-lb. (47 N•m).

21. On models with a belt-driven seawater pump (**Figure 91**), install the water pump drive belt and adjust the tension as described in Chapter Eight.

22. On models with a crankshaft-driven water pump (**Figure 92**), install the water pump as described in Chapter Eight.

23. Install the alternator drive belt and adjust the tension as described in Chapter Nine.

24. Connect the battery cables.

TIMING COVER

Remove the cover for seal replacement or as necessary to access the timing sprockets and chain. On 5.0L/5.7L with an eight-bolt intake manifold and all 8.1L models, the timing cover is manufactured from a composite material. If removed, it must be replaced, or the cover might leak oil. On all other models, the cover is made of metal and can be reinstalled.

6

Removal

1. Remove the oil pan as described in this chapter.
2. Remove the harmonic balancer as described in this chapter.
3. Remove the recirculation pump as described in Chapter Eight.
4A. On 5.7L LT-1 models, remove the crankshaft position sensor mounting bracket as described in Chapter Nine.
4B. On 8.1L models, remove the camshaft position sensor as described in Chapter Nine.
5. Remove the bolts from the timing cover. Use a blunt scraper and carefully pry the cover from the cylinder block (**Figure 102**).
6. Carefully scrape gasket material from the cover mating surfaces.
7. On 5.0L, 5.7L or 8.1L models with a composite (plastic) cover, discard the timing chain cover. The cover is not reusable.

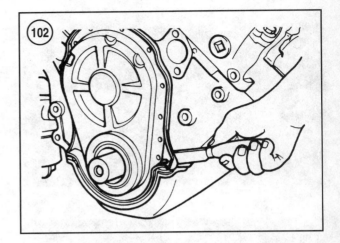

Installation

1. On models with a steel cover, replace the seal as follows:
    a. Thoroughly clean the cover with solvent and dry with compressed air.
    b. Carefully pry the seal from the cover. Discard the seal. Clean the seal bore with aerosol carburetor cleaner. Remove all remnants of sealing compound or adhesive from the bore.
    c. Apply a light coat of Loctite 271 to the seal bore and outer diameter of the new seal.
    d. Place the cover on a suitable work surface with the inner side facing downward. Place a wooden block under the seal bore for support.
    e. Set the new seal into the bore with the lip side facing downward. Using a suitable mandrel, fully drive the seal into the bore (**Figure 103**).
    f. Wipe excess Loctite from the seal bore.

2A. On 5.0L, 5.7L, 7.4L and 8.2L models with a steel cover, apply a light coat of gasket sealing compound to both surfaces of the new gasket. Fit the gasket onto the cover. Also apply a light coat to the cylinder block surface that contacts the gasket.

2B. On 8.1L models, apply a light coat of gasket sealing compound to both surfaces of the new gasket. Fit the gasket onto the cover. Then apply a bead of RTV sealant to the two cylinder block surfaces where the cover, oil pan and cylinder block mate. This is necessary to prevent oil leakage in the corner where the oil pan gasket and cover gasket do not contact.

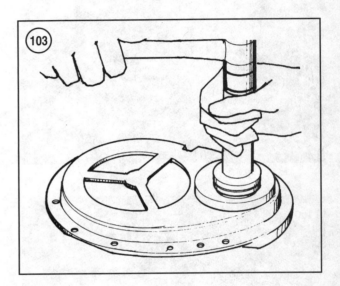

3A. On 5.0L and 5.7L models with a steel cover, apply a coat of engine oil to the seal surface. Then while carefully guiding the seal over the crankshaft, fit the cover onto the cylinder block. Move the gasket as necessary to align the screw openings in the cover, gasket and cylinder block. Apply a light coat of gasket sealing compound to the threads. Then install the cover screws. Tighten the cover screws in a crossing pattern to 84 in.-lb. (9.5 N•m).

3B. On 5.0L and 5.7L models with a composite (plastic) cover, apply a coat of engine oil to the seal lip. Then while carefully guiding the seal over the crankshaft, seat the cover against the cylinder block. Install the cover screws and tighten in a crossing pattern, starting from the center and working outward, to 106 in.-lb. (21 N•m).

3C. On 7.4L and 8.2L models, apply a coat of engine oil to the seal surface. Then apply a bead of RTV sealant to the two cylinder block surfaces where the cover, oil pan

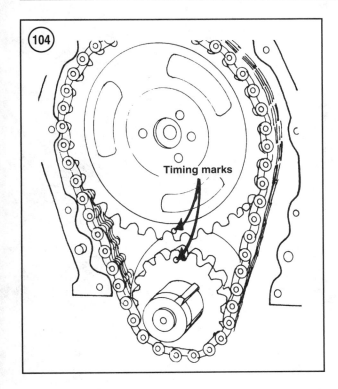

Timing marks

and cylinder block mate. This is necessary to prevent oil leakage in the corner where the oil pan gasket and cover gasket do not contact. Carefully guide the seal over the crankshaft and then position the cover toward the down side to prevent wiping the sealant from the oil pan. Move the cover toward the block until it contacts and then push the cover upward to align the locating pins. Seat the cover against the cylinder block. Install the cover screws and tighten in a crossing pattern to 120 in.-lb. (13.6 N•m).

3D. On 8.1L models, apply a coat of engine oil to the seal lip. Then carefully guide the seal over the crankshaft. To avoid wiping the RTV sealant from the cylinder block surfaces, position the cover toward the down side while guiding the cover into position. When the cover contacts the locating pins, carefully move the cover upward to align the pin openings. Then seat the cover against the cylinder block. Tighten the bolts to 53 in.-lb. (6 N•m). Tighten the bolts a final time to 106 in.-lb. (12 N•m).

4. Install the recirculation pump as described in Chapter Eight.

5A. On 5.7L LT-1 models, install the crankshaft position sensor mounting bracket as described in Chapter Nine.

5B. On 8.1L models, install the camshaft position sensor as described in Chapter Nine.

6. Install the harmonic balancer as described in this chapter.

7. Install the oil pan as described in this chapter.

TIMING GEAR, CHAIN AND SPROCKETS

A timing chain and sprockets are used on all standard-rotation engines. Timing gears are used on counter-rotation engines (refer to *Engine Operation* in this chapter). Use a crankshaft timing gear removal tool, such as Kent-Moore part No. J-8105, or another suitable two-bolt puller to remove the gear. Use Kent-Moore part No. J21058-20 to install the crankshaft timing gear. Do not use makeshift tools, which can damage the gear, crankshaft or other engine components.

Removal/Inspection/Installation (Standard-Rotation Engines)

1. Disconnect the battery cables. Position the No. 1 piston at the TDC firing position as described in this chapter.

2. To prevent possible interference between the pistons and valves, remove the rocker arms and pushrods as described in this chapter.

3. Remove the timing cover as described in this chapter.

4. Measure the timing chain deflection as follows:
   a. Rotate the crankshaft counterclockwise to tighten the chain on the starboard side.
   b. Scribe a reference marking on the cylinder block that aligns with the tight side of the chain at a point midway between the sprockets.
   c. Rotate the crankshaft clockwise to tighten the chain on the port side.
   d. Pull the loose side of the chain (on the starboard side) toward the starboard side. Scribe a reference marking on the cylinder block that aligns with the chain. The distance between the two marks indicates the timing chain deflection. Replace the timing chain and both sprockets if the deflection exceeds 0.625 in. (16 mm).

5. Rotate the crankshaft to align the marks on the camshaft and crankshaft sprockets (**Figure 104**). This places the engine in the No. 1 cylinder TDC firing position.

6. Remove the bolts and then carefully pull the camshaft sprocket and timing chain from the engine.

7. Use a two-jaw puller to remove the crankshaft sprocket.

8. Clean the chain and sprockets with solvent and dry with compressed air.

9. Inspect the timing chain and both sprockets for wear, cracks or damage. Replace all three components if any defects are evident.

10. Inspect the drive key in the crankshaft for corrosion, bending or other damage and replace as needed.

11. Install the crankshaft sprocket as follows:

6

a. Guide the crankshaft sprocket over the end of the crankshaft with the timing mark side facing outward.

b. Align the key slot in the crankshaft sprocket with the crankshaft key.

c. Using a suitable driver, tap the crankshaft sprocket onto the crankshaft until it seats against the shoulder on the crankshaft.

12. Align the locating pin and fit the camshaft sprocket without the chain onto the camshaft. Do not install the bolts at this time. Rotate the camshaft and crankshaft sprockets as needed to align the timing marks (**Figure 104**). Remove the camshaft sprocket. Do not inadvertently rotate the camshaft or crankshaft.

13. Fit the timing chain onto the camshaft sprocket and crankshaft sprocket while installing the camshaft sprocket onto the camshaft. The timing marks must align as shown in **Figure 104**. Do not drive the camshaft sprocket onto the camshaft, which can dislodge the plug at the rear of the engine. If necessary, use the three bolts to draw the sprocket onto the camshaft.

NOTE
*All 1983-1985 5.0L/5.7L models and 1983-1990 7.4L/8.2L models use a two-piece rear main seal. All 1986-2003 5.0L/5.7L models and 1991-2003 7.4L/8.2L models use a one-piece rear main seal. All 8.1L models use a one-piece rear main seal. Although the sprocket and chain replacement procedures are the same, the tightening torque specifications might differ by the type of seal used. Refer to **Rear Main Seal** in this chapter and identify the type of seal used before tightening the fasteners.*

14. Install the camshaft sprocket fasteners and tighten as follows:

a. On 5.0L and 5.7L models with a two-piece rear main seal, tighten the bolts to 20 ft.-lb. (27 N•m).

b. On 5.0L and 5.7L models with a one-piece rear main seal, tighten the bolts to 25 ft.-lb. (34 N•m).

c. On 7.4L and 8.2L models, tighten the bolts to 25 ft.-lb. (35 N•m).

d. On 8.1L models, tighten the bolts to an initial torque of 132 in.-lb. (11 N•m). Tighten the bolts a second time to 22 ft.-lb. (30 N•m). Tighten the bolts a final time to 22 ft.-lb. (30 N•m).

15. Lubricate the timing chain and sprockets with engine oil.

16. Install the timing chain cover as described in this chapter.

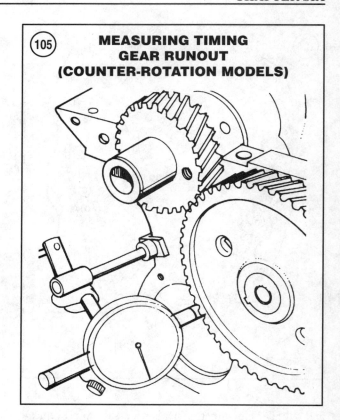

(105) MEASURING TIMING GEAR RUNOUT (COUNTER-ROTATION MODELS)

17. Install the rocker arms and pushrods as described in this chapter.

18. Tighten the rocker arm nuts or adjust the valves as described in this chapter.

Removal/Inspection/Installation (Counter-Rotation Engines)

Use a crankshaft timing gear removal tool, such as Kent-Moore part No. J-8105, or another suitable two-bolt puller to remove the gear. Use Kent-Moore part No. J21058-20 to install the crankshaft timing gear. Do not use makeshift tools, which can damage the gear, crankshaft or other engine components.

1. Disconnect the battery cables. Position the No. 1 piston at the TDC firing position as described in this chapter.

2. To prevent possible interference between the pistons and valves, remove the rocker arms and pushrods as described in this chapter.

3. Remove the timing gear cover as described in this chapter.

4. Measure the camshaft timing gear runout before removing the gears.

a. Clamp a dial indicator mount onto the cylinder block.

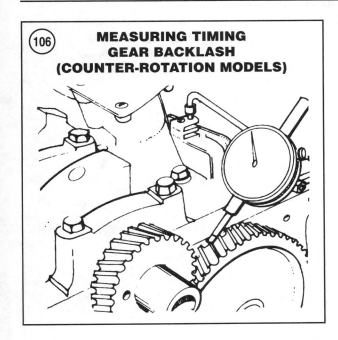

MEASURING TIMING GEAR BACKLASH (COUNTER-ROTATION MODELS)

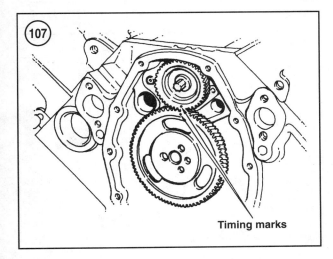

Timing marks

b. Position the dial indicator plunger perpendicular to the front surface of the camshaft timing gear (**Figure 105**). The plunger must contact the flat surface of the gear as closely as possible to the gear teeth.

c. Zero the dial indicator.

d. Observe the dial indicator while rotating the crankshaft through two complete revolutions. The needle movement indicates the camshaft gear runout.

e. Remove the camshaft as described in this chapter and inspect the camshaft bearings if the runout exceeds 0.004 in. (0.102 mm). Replace both the camshaft and crankshaft timing gears if the camshaft bearings are in acceptable condition.

5. Measure the crankshaft timing gear runout before removing the gears.

a. Clamp a dial indicator mount to the cylinder block.

b. Position the dial indicator plunger perpendicular to the front surface of the crankshaft timing gear. The plunger must contact the flat surface of the gear as closely as possible to the gear teeth.

c. Zero the dial indicator.

d. Observe the dial indicator while rotating the crankshaft through one complete revolution. The needle movement indicates the crankshaft timing gear runout.

e. Remove the crankshaft, as described in this chapter and inspect the crankshaft main bearings if the runout exceeds 0.003 in. (0.076 mm). Replace both the camshaft and crankshaft timing gears if the main bearings are in good condition.

6. Measure the timing gear backlash before removing the gears. Instructions follow:

a. Clamp a dial indicator mount onto the cylinder block.

b. Position the plunger in contact with one of the timing gear teeth (**Figure 106**).

c. Zero the dial indicator.

d. Observe the dial indicator while gently rotating the camshaft timing gear clockwise and counterclockwise. Do not drive the crankshaft timing gear. The needle movement indicates the gear backlash.

e. The gear backlash must be 0.004-0.008 in. (0.102-0.203 mm). Remove the camshaft and crankshaft and inspect the bearings if the backlash is not within the specification. Replace both the camshaft and crankshaft timing gears if the backlash exceeds the specification but the bearings are in good condition.

7. Rotate the camshaft to align the timing marks on the camshaft and crankshaft gears (**Figure 107**). This places the No. 1 piston in the TDC firing position.

8A. On 5.0L and 5.7L models, remove the three bolts that hold the camshaft timing gear to the camshaft. Carefully pull the timing gear off the camshaft. If necessary, tap on the lower edge of the gear with a plastic hammer to dislodge the gear.

8B. On 7.4L models, remove the camshaft and timing gear as an assembly as described in this chapter. Do not press the gear off the camshaft at this time.

9. Guide the two bolts of the gear removal tool (Kent-Moore part No. J-8105) through the two slots in the puller bar. Fully thread the two bolts into the crankshaft timing gear. Thread the puller bolt with the tapered tip through the puller bar and into the tapered opening in the crankshaft. Turn the puller bolt to pull the timing gear off the crankshaft.

6

10. Clean the gears with solvent and dry with compressed air. Inspect the gears for damaged or missing teeth, cracks, excessive wear or corrosion damage. Replace both the camshaft and crankshaft timing gears if these or other defects are evident.

11. On 7.4L models, inspect the camshaft thrust plate (**Figure 108**) and mating surface on the camshaft for uneven wear, rough surfaces or discoloration. If these or other defects are evident, replace the thrust plate and/or camshaft and lifters as described in this chapter.

12. On 7.4L models, use feeler gauges and measure the gap between the thrust plate and camshaft surfaces (**Figure 108**). The gap indicates the amount of camshaft end play necessary for maintaining a film of lubricant on the thrust surfaces. Replace the timing gear and thrust plate if the end play measurement exceeds 0.005 in. (0.127 mm) or is less than 0.001 in. (0.025 mm).

13. Inspect the drive key in the crankshaft for corrosion, bending or other damage and replace as needed.

14. Install the crankshaft gear as follows:
   a. Guide the crankshaft gear over the end of the crankshaft with the timing mark side facing outward.
   b. Align the key slot in the gear with the crankshaft key.
   c. Guide the sleeve of the installation tool (Kent-Moore part No. J21058-20) over the crankshaft and seat the open end against the gear.
   d. Guide the puller bolt and pusher nut assembly into the sleeve opening. Then thread the puller bolt into the crankshaft threads.
   e. Hold the puller bolt to prevent rotation. Then rotate the pusher nut clockwise until the gear fully seats against the step on the crankshaft.
   f. Remove the installation tool.

15A. On 5.0L and 5.7L models, install the camshaft timing gear as follows:
   a. Align the locating pin and fit the camshaft gear onto the camshaft.
   b. Rotate the camshaft and crankshaft sprockets as needed to align the timing marks (**Figure 107**). Then use hand pressure to seat the camshaft gear onto the camshaft. Do not drive the camshaft sprocket onto the camshaft, which can dislodge the plug at the rear of the engine. If necessary, use the three bolts to draw the sprocket onto the camshaft.
   c. Check for correct timing mark alignment. If necessary, pull the gear off the shaft and rotate the crankshaft to achieve correct alignment.
   d. Install the camshaft gear bolts and tighten evenly to 20 ft.-lb. (27 N•m).

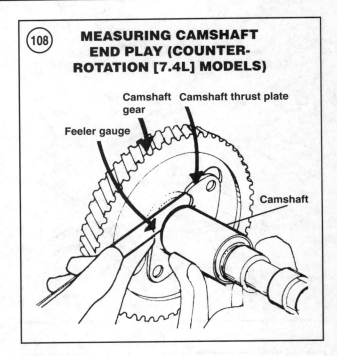

108 MEASURING CAMSHAFT END PLAY (COUNTER-ROTATION [7.4L] MODELS)

Camshaft thrust plate gear

Camshaft thrust plate

Feeler gauge

Camshaft

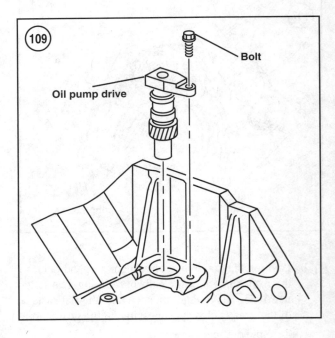

109

Bolt

Oil pump drive

15B. On 7.4L models, install the camshaft and timing gears as an assembly as described in this chapter.

16. Lubricate the timing gears with engine oil.

17. Install the timing cover as described in this chapter.

18. Install the rocker arms and pushrods as described in this chapter.

19 Tighten the rocker arm nuts or adjust the valves as described in this chapter.

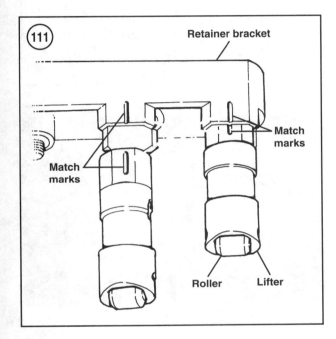

CAMSHAFT AND LIFTERS

Always replace the lifters if replacing the camshaft. Operating the engine with used lifters will damage a new camshaft. If reusing lifters, always install them in the original locations. Otherwise, the camshaft and lifters will wear excessively and fail.

Apply General Motors Cam and Lifter Prelube to the camshaft lobes and lifters prior to installation.

Only a mechanic with the proper equipment and experience shoudl attempt to repair defective camshaft bearings. The bearings and cylinder block are easily damaged without the proper equipment, and the installation equipment is more expensive than having the bearings professionally replaced. Improper bearing installation can also result in camshaft failure.

Removal

1. Remove the oil pan and timing chain/gear cover as described in this chapter.

2. Remove the intake manifold as described in Chapter Seven.

3. On 8.1L models, remove the bolt and carefully lift the oil pump drive (**Figure 109**) from the cylinder block. The gear on the oil pump drive must turn freely. If not, replace the oil pump drive.

4. Remove the rocker arm covers as described in this chapter.

5. On models with a mechanical fuel pump, remove the pump and pushrod as described in Chapter Seven.

6A. On models with flat lifters (**Figure 110**), remove the lifters from the cylinder block and note the original locations.

6B. On models with roller lifters, scribe match marks on the roller lifters, guides and retainers (**Figure 111**) to make sure the roller turns in the original direction after installation. Remove the bolts and carefully lift the lifter guides and retainers (**Figure 112**) from the cylinder block. Keep all components arranged in a manner consistent with the original mounting locations. Remove the lifters from the cylinder block.

7A. On standard-rotation models, remove the timing chain and camshaft sprocket as described in this chapter. It is not necessary to remove the crankshaft sprocket unless it is defective.

7B. On 5.0L and 5.7L counter-rotation models, remove the camshaft timing gear as described in this chapter.

8. On 5.0L/5.7L models with roller lifters and all 8.1L models, remove the two bolts and then remove the thrust plate from the cylinder block.

9A. On standard-rotation models and 5.0L/5.7L counter-rotation models, thread two 5/16—18 bolts into the camshaft bolt openings. Carefully pull the camshaft from the cylinder block. Support the camshaft during removal to prevent damage to the camshaft bearings.

9B. On 7.4L counter-rotation models, remove the camshaft and camshaft timing gear assembly as follows:

    a. Rotate the crankshaft gear until the timing marks align as shown in **Figure 113**. Remove the thrust plate bolts through the access holes in the timing gear (**Figure 113**).

    b. Carefully remove the camshaft and gear assembly from the cylinder block. Support the camshaft during removal. Otherwise, the camshaft bearings might be damaged as the lobes pass through them.

Inspection

1. Inspect the camshaft bearings in the cylinder block for roughness, uneven wear or discoloration. Have the bearings replaced if these or other defects are evident.

2A. On models with flat lifters, inspect the lifters for wear on the lobe-contact surfaces and scuffing on the sides or other defects. Replace all lifters if any of them are defective.

2B. On models with roller lifters, inspect the lifters for discoloration, loose-fitting rollers, scuffing on the sides or other defects. Replace all of the lifters if any are defective.

3. Inspect the camshaft lobes for wear or rounded surfaces (**Figure 114**). Replace the camshaft, lifters and bearings if any of the lobes are worn excessively or damaged.

4. On models with roller lifters, inspect the lifter guides and retainers for wear or damage. Replace any defective components.

5. Inspect the lifter bores in the cylinder block for excessive wear, scuffing or discoloration. Replace the cylinder block if any imperfections in the bore cannot be dressed by polishing with crocus cloth.

6. On 7.4L counter-rotation models, inspect the timing gear and thrust surfaces. Then measure the camshaft end play as described in this chapter (refer to *Timing Gear, Chain and Sprockets*). If any of the components are defective, press the timing gear off the camshaft as follows:

    a. Place the camshaft on a press with the gear resting on the press table and the camshaft in the table opening.

    b. Support the camshaft. Press the camshaft from the gear using a suitable mandrel. The mandrel must contact only the end of the camshaft.

    c. Remove the thrust plate from the camshaft or timing gear.

    d. Remove the Woodruff key from the camshaft. Discard the Woodruff key.

7. Measure a camshaft bearing journal at several locations around the diameter (**Figure 115**). Record all measurements. The difference between the largest and smallest measurement is the amount the journal is out of

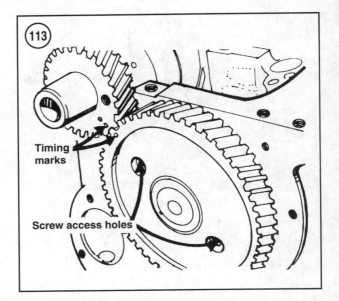

round. Measure each journal and determine the out-of-round measurement for each journal. Replace the camshaft, lifters and bearings if any of the journals have a diameter less than the specification in **Table 2** or if any journal is out of round more than 0.001 in. (0.025 mm).

8. Support the camshaft on V-blocks as shown in **Figure 116**. Set the plunger of a dial indicator so it touches one of the middle camshaft journals. Observe the dial indicator while slowly rotating the camshaft. The needle movement indicates the amount of camshaft runout. Replace the camshaft, lifters and bearings if the runout exceeds 0.002 in. (0.051 mm).

9. Inspect the distributor/oil pump drive gear on the camshaft for uneven wear, discoloration and excessive wear. Replace the camshaft if these or other defects are evident on the gear.

10. On 5.0L/5.7L models with roller lifters and all 8.1L models, inspect the thrust plate for uneven wear, rough-

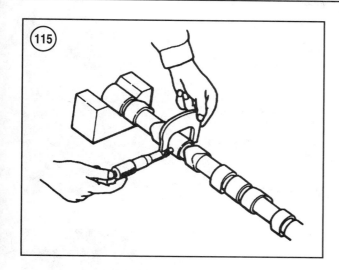

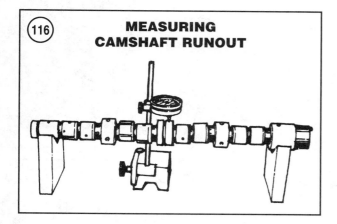

MEASURING
CAMSHAFT RUNOUT

ness or discoloration. Replace the thrust plate if these or other defects are evident.

Installation

1. On 7.4L counter-rotation models, install the camshaft timing gear and thrust plate onto the camshaft as follows:

   a. Fit a new Woodruff key into the slot in the camshaft with the flat side facing outward.

   b. Place the new gear on the table of the press with the timing mark facing downward.

   c. Align the new thrust plate with the camshaft bore of the gear. Align the key slot in the gear with the key in the camshaft. Apply engine oil to the gear bore. Insert the camshaft into the gear bore.

   d. Press the camshaft into the gear until fully seated. Make sure the thrust plate remains centered over the gear bore during the procedure.

2. Apply engine oil to the camshaft bearings. Apply General Motors Cam and Lifter Prelube to the camshaft lobes and bottom of the lifters or lifter rollers.

3A. On 5.0L, 5.7L, 7.4L (standard-rotation), 8.1L and 8.2L models, carefully guide the camshaft into the bearings Support the camshaft during installation to prevent damaged bearings.

3B. On counter-rotation 7.4L models, carefully guide the camshaft and timing gear assembly into the cylinder block and bearings. Support the camshaft to prevent damaged bearings. Align the timing marks (**Figure 113**) and gear teeth. Then seat the camshaft into the cylinder block. Align the thrust plate with the access holes in the gear (**Figure 113**). Install the thrust plate bolts and tighten evenly to 96 in.-lb. (11 N•m).

4. On 5.0L/5.7L with roller lifters and all 8.1L models, install the camshaft thrust plate and bolts. Tighten the thrust plate bolts evenly to 106 in.-lb. (12 N•m).

5A. On standard-rotation models, install the timing chain and gears as described in this chapter.

5B. On 5.0L and 5.7L counter-rotation models, install the camshaft timing gear as described in this chapter.

6A. On models with flat lifters, install the lifters into the cylinder block. If reused, the lifters must be installed in the original locations. Seat the lifters against the camshaft lobes.

6B. On models with roller lifters, install the lifters into the respective locations in the cylinder block. Seat the lifter rollers against the camshaft lobes. Align the match marks and install the guides and retainers. Tighten the retainer bolts to 18 ft.-lb. (24.4 N•m) on 5.0L and 5.7L models. Tighten the retainer bolts to 19 ft.-lb. (25.8 N•m) on 7.4L, 8.1L and 8.2L models.

7. Install the pushrods and rocker arm as described in this chapter.

8. On 8.1L models, lubricate the oil pump drive (**Figure 109**) with engine oil and install it into the cylinder block. Rotate the camshaft as necessary to align the gear teeth and oil pump drive shaft. When aligned, the drive will drop into position and seat against the cylinder block. Install the drive mounting bolt and tighten to 221 in.-lb. (25 N•m).

9. Install the timing cover, oil pan and harmonic balancer as described in this chapter.

10. Install the mechanical fuel pump on models so equipped. Refer to Chapter Seven.

11. Tighten the rocker arm nuts/bolts or adjust the valves as described in this chapter.

12. Install the rocker arm covers as described in this chapter.

13. Install the intake manifold as described in Chapter Seven.

6

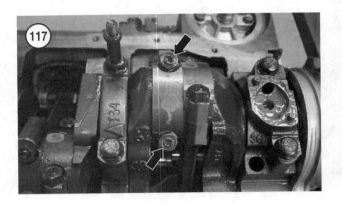

14. Connect the battery cables.

15. Adjust the ignition timing as described in Chapter Five.

PISTONS AND CONNECTING RODS

Removal

1. Remove the cylinder head(s), oil pan, oil pump and timing cover as described in this chapter.

2. Rotate the crankshaft until one of the pistons is at the bottom of the stroke.

3. Evenly loosen and remove the connecting rod nuts (**Figure 117**). Tap on the bottom of the connecting rod cap until it is free of the connecting rod (**Figure 118**). Reinstall the insert bearing (**Figure 119**) if it dislodges from the rod cap.

4. Using a wooden dowel, carefully push the piston and connecting rod from the cylinder block (**Figure 120**). Install the rod cap onto the rod and secure with the nuts. The bearing tangs must align as shown in **Figure 121**. Mark the cylinder number on the sides of the connecting rod and cap (**Figure 122**).

5. Mark the cylinder number on the inner surface of the piston. Do not scratch the top or side of the piston. Re-

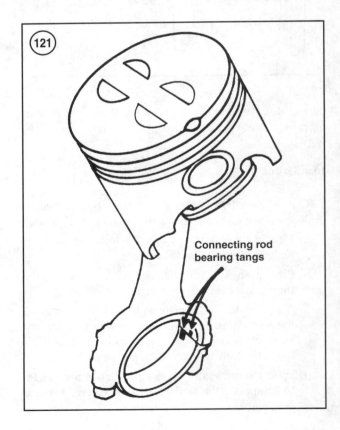

Connecting rod
bearing tangs

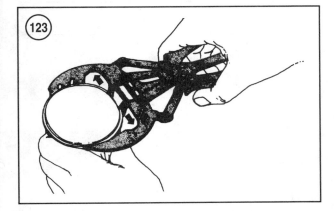

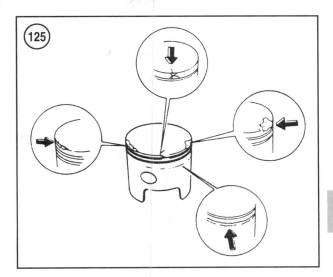

6

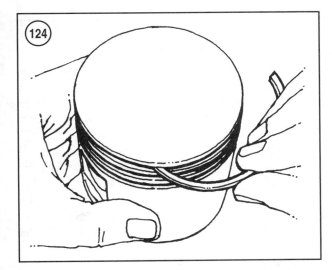

move and mark all pistons and connecting rods as described.

6. Remove the drive plate, flywheel and crankshaft as described in this chapter.

7. Use a piston ring expander (**Figure 123**) and remove the rings from the pistons. Use a broken ring to scrape car-

bon carefully from the ring grooves (**Figure 124**). Do not remove aluminum material from the ring groove.

Piston, Connecting Rod and Cylinder Bore Inspection

1. Clean the pistons and rods with solvent. Use a plastic-bristle brush to remove carbon from the piston surfaces. Never use a wire brush because small pieces of wire can become embedded in the piston dome and cause preignition or detonation damage.

2. Inspect the edge of the piston crowns for cracks, erosion or missing sections (**Figure 125**). Inspect the sides of the pistons for scuffing (**Figure 126**), deep scratches or other damage. Rock each piston on the connecting rod while checking for binding or a loose fit of the piston pin and piston. Replace the piston and pin if the pin fits loosely or if other defects are evident.

3. Inspect the cylinder bore for cracking, deep scratches, transferred piston material or corrosion pitting. Replace the cylinder block if cracks are visible. Have the cylinder bored to accept oversized pistons if it is deeply scratched or pitted. Remove transferred piston material with a blunt scraper.

NOTE
The piston used on 8.1L models has a friction-reducing coating on the sides that prevents accurate measurement of the piston. It is not necessary to determine the piston-to-cylinder bore clearance on 8.1L models. The clearance is acceptable if the piston is not excessively worn and the cylinder bore is within the specification.

NOTE
7.4L models are produced in both standard- and high-output models that must be identified before beginning the repair procedure. If the identification decal is missing from the engine or the output specification is in question, remove the intake manifold as described in Chapter Seven. Then inspect the intake manifold and cylinder head intake ports. The standard-output models use round or oval ports. The high-output models use rectangular ports.

NOTE
On 8.1L models, the piston, piston pin and connecting rod are not available separately. The piston and connecting rod assembly must be replaced if any of the components are defective.

4. On 5.0L, 5.7L, 7.4L and 8.2L models, use an outside micrometer to measure the piston diameter at two points: aligned with the piston pin and at 90° to the pin (**Figure 127**). Record the measurement for each piston.

5. Check the piston and piston rings for proper fit as follows:
   a. Temporarily install new rings onto the pistons.
   b. Use a feeler gauge and measure the clearance between the sides of the ring and the ring groove (**Figure 128**). The clearance equals the thickness of the feeler gauge that passes between the ring and groove with a slight drag.
   c. Compare the clearance with the ring groove clearance specification in **Table 6**. Replace the piston if the clearance exceeds the specification.
   d. Remove the piston rings.

6. Measure the cylinder-bore diameter, taper and out-of-round as follows:

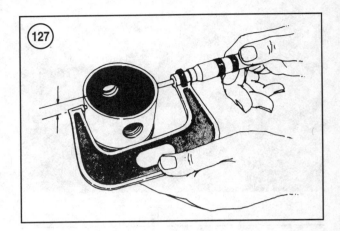

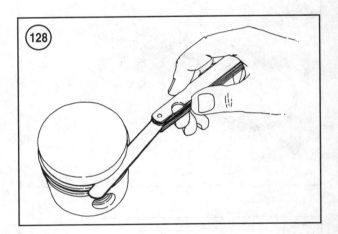

   a. Use a cylinder-bore gauge (**Figure 129**) to measure the cylinder-bore diameter. Take the measurements at three or more evenly spaced depths in the bore and then again at 90° to the first measurement (**Figure 130**). Take the top measurement at a point even with the upper travel of the rings.
   b. Subtract the smallest diameter at the bottom of the bore from the largest diameter at the top of the bore. This calculation indicates the amount of cylinder-bore taper. Record the cylinder-bore taper.
   c. Subtract the smallest diameter from the largest-diameter measurement at each depth in the cylinder bore. This calculation indicates the amount the cylinder is out of round. Record the cylinder out-of-round calculation.
   d. Repeat this step for the remaining cylinders. Record all measurements.

7. Compare the cylinder diameter measurements, cylinder taper and out-of-round calculations to the specification in **Table 7**. If any of the measurements exceed the specifications, have a reputable machine shop bore the

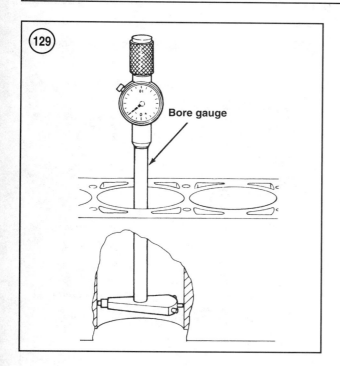

Bore gauge

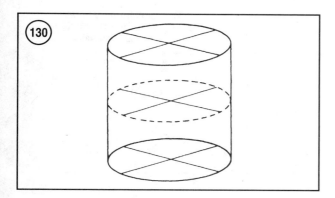

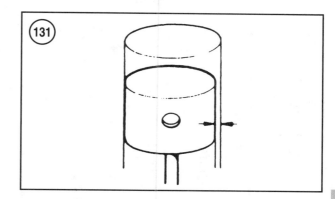

6

c. Compare the minimum and maximum clearances with the piston skirt clearance specification in **Table 6**.

d. If the piston skirt clearance is less than specified, the piston diameter is at or above the maximum diameter specification, and/or the cylinder bore is at or below the minimum diameter. Repeat the measurement and replace the piston or bore the cylinder to accept an oversized piston as necessary to achieve the required clearance.

e. If the piston skirt clearance exceeds the specification, the piston diameter is at or below the minimum diameter specification, and/or the cylinder bore is at or above the maximum diameter. Repeat the measurement and replace the piston or bore the cylinder to accept an oversized piston as necessary to achieve the required clearance.

f. Repeat this step for the remaining cylinders.

9. Hone the cylinders to achieve a 45-60° crosshatch pattern before installing the pistons. Have a reputable machine shop hone the cylinders if you are unfamiliar with the honing operation or lack the proper equipment. Thoroughly clean the cylinders with warm soapy water after the honing operation. Wipe a clean white shop towel through the bore to check for residual material. Any residual abrasive material from the honing process will result in rapid wear and improper seating of the piston rings. To prevent corrosion, coat the cylinder walls and other unpainted surfaces with engine oil.

10. Remove the insert bearings from the connecting rods. Inspect the rod surfaces for discoloration, corrosion pitting, roughness or other damage. Have a reputable machine shop remove the piston and replace the connecting rod if defective. Inspect the crankshaft for defects if discoloration, scratches, corrosion pitting or transferred material is found on the bearings.

11. Inspect the rod bolts and nuts for stretched or damaged threads. Replace the rod bolts and nuts unless they are in excellent condition.

cylinder to accept an oversized piston. It is not necessary to bore all of the cylinders because the oversized pistons weigh the same as standard pistons. Oversized piston availability varies by model. Always buy the oversized piston and supply it to the machine shop before boring the cylinder. This allows the machinist to precisely fit the piston to the cylinder bore.

8. On 5.0L, 5.7L, 7.4L and 8.2L models, determine the piston-to-piston skirt clearance as follows:

a. Subtract the piston skirt diameter (Step 4) from the smallest cylinder diameter to determine the minimum skirt clearance for the cylinder (**Figure 131**).

b. Subtract the piston diameter from the largest cylinder diameter to determine the maximum skirt clearance for the cylinder.

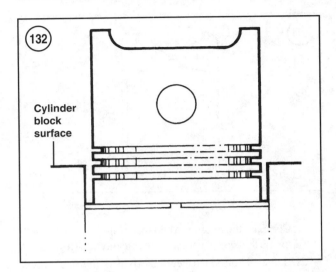

Cylinder block surface

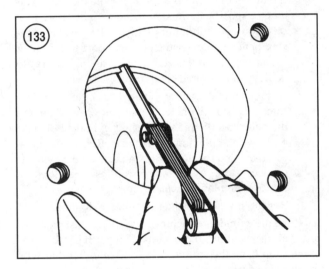

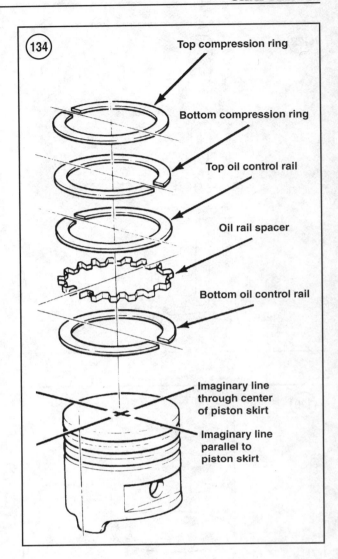

Top compression ring

Bottom compression ring

Top oil control rail

Oil rail spacer

Bottom oil control rail

Imaginary line through center of piston skirt

Imaginary line parallel to piston skirt

12. Inspect the connecting rod for bending or twisting at the I-beam section. Have a reputable machine shop remove the piston and replace the rod if bent or twisted.

Installation

1. Install the crankshaft, flywheel and drive plate as described in this chapter.

2. Measure the piston ring end gap as follows:

   a. Insert one of the new compression (upper) rings into one of the cylinder bores. Use a piston without rings to push the ring into the bore to a depth near the lowest point of ring travel (**Figure 132**).

   b. Measure the ring end gap (**Figure 133**) using a feeler gauge. Compare the end gap measurement with the specification in **Table 6**.

   c. If the ring end gap is incorrect, remove the ring and try a different ring. Continue until a ring with the correct gap is located for the cylinder. If unable to find rings with the correct gap, check the cylinder-bore diameter.

   d. Measure and select the second compression ring and both oil ring rails as described. Attach a tag with the cylinder number to the selected rings.

   e. Select rings for each cylinder.

3. Coat the cylinder bore with engine oil.

4. Use a ring expander (**Figure 123**) to install the rings onto the piston as shown in **Figure 134**. The marks on the compression rings must face the top of the piston.

5. Locate the piston ring gaps as shown in **Figure 135**. The ring gaps must be positioned correctly for proper engine operation and minimum oil consumption.

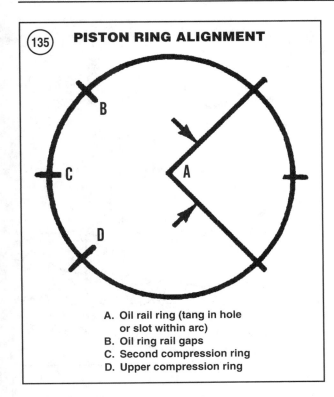

PISTON RING ALIGNMENT

A. Oil rail ring (tang in hole
   or slot within arc)
B. Oil ring rail gaps
C. Second compression ring
D. Upper compression ring

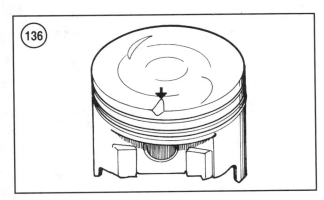

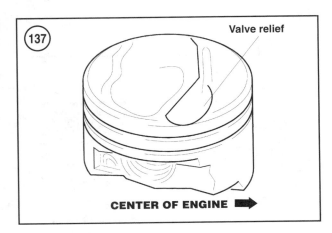

Valve relief

CENTER OF ENGINE ➡

6. Make sure the piston is correctly attached to the connecting rod. If not, have a machine shop remove the piston pin and reinstall the connecting rod. On all models, the connecting rod bearing tangs (**Figure 121**) must face the port side in odd-numbered cylinders and the starboard side in even-numbered cylinders.

   a. On 5.0L and 5.7L standard-rotation models, the notch in the piston dome (**Figure 136**) must face toward the front of the engine or away from the flywheel when installed.

   b. On 5.0L and 5.7L counter-rotation models, the notch in the piston dome (**Figure 136**) must face toward the rear of the engine or toward the flywheel when installed.

   c. On 7.4L standard-output/standard-rotation models, Inspect the piston dome for a notch, single valve relief depression or small reference hole. If the piston has a notch in the piston dome (**Figure 136**), it must face toward the front of the engine or away from the flywheel. If the piston does not have a notch, the single valve relief depression in the piston dome (**Figure 137**) must face toward the center of the engine. If the piston does not have the notch or single valve relief depression, the small reference hole in the piston dome must face toward the outside of the engine on cylinder No. 2, 4, 6 and 8. The hole must face toward the center of the engine on cylinder No. 1, 3, 5 and 7.

   d. On 7.4L standard-output/counter-rotation models, inspect the piston dome for a notch, single valve relief depression or small reference hole. If the piston has a notch in the piston dome (**Figure 136**), it must face toward the rear of the engine and toward the flywheel. If the piston does not have a notch, the single valve relief depression in the piston dome (**Figure 137**) must face toward the center of the engine. If the piston does not have the notch or single valve relief depression, the small reference hole in the piston dome must face toward the center of the engine on cylinder No. 2, 4, 6 and 8. The hole must face toward the outside of the engine on cylinder No. 1, 3, 5 and 7.

   e. On 7.4L high-output and all 8.2L models, the valve relief depression in the piston dome must face toward the center of the engine.

7. Remove the rod cap and bearings. Wipe all oil or debris from the connecting rod. To prevent the rod bolts from damaging the crankshaft, fit short pieces of rubber tubing over the rod bolts.

8. Rotate the crankshaft to position the crankpin of the selected cylinder at the bottom of the stroke.

6

9. Fit a ring compressor over the piston. Tighten the compressor until the rings fully compress into the grooves. Do not overtighten the compressor. The piston must slide from the compressor during installation.

10. Carefully guide the connecting rod and piston skirt into the cylinder block (**Figure 120**). Rotate the piston and position the notch, valve relief or reference hole as described in Step 6. On 8.1L models, the flange on the connecting rod cap and bolt must face the front of the block on the port cylinders and the rear of the block on the starboard cylinders.

11. Hold the ring compressor tightly against the cylinder head mating surface (**Figure 138**). Use a wooden dowel and soft mallet to carefully tap the piston into the bore. Do not use excessive force. Check for insufficient ring compression if the piston will not enter the bore with light tapping.

12. Carefully guide the connecting rod toward the crankshaft while pushing the piston down in the bore. Fit the new bearing into the connecting rod. The bearing tang must fit into the notch in the connecting rod (**Figure 121**). Seat the rod and bearing against the crankpin.

13. Place a section of Plastigage (**Figure 139**) onto the crankpin journal. The Plastigage must be as long as the width of the bearing and aligned with the bottom of the journal (**Figure 140**).

14. Fit the new bearing into the connecting rod cap (**Figure 119**). The bearing tang must fit into the notch in the cap. Install the rod cap onto the connecting rod (**Figure 118**). The bearing tangs must align on the same side of the rod. Carefully seat the cap onto the rod. To check for proper alignment, drag a sharpened pencil tip along the machined side of the cap and rod (**Figure 141**). The pencil tip must not catch on the split line. If the cap and rod do not align, make sure the correct cap is installed. The connecting rod cap might also be distorted. Replace the connecting rod if necessary.

15. Tighten the connecting rod fasteners as follows:

   a. On 5.0L and 5.7L models with a 12-bolt intake manifold, tighten the rod cap nuts to 45 ft.-lb. (61 N•m).

   b. On 5.0L and 5.7L models with an eight-bolt intake manifold, tighten the connecting rod nuts evenly to 20 ft.-lb. (27 N•m). Check for proper rod cap alignment as described in Step 14. Use an angle torque gauge and tighten the rod nuts an additional 55° of rotation.

   c. On 7.4L and 8.2L models with 3/8—24 nuts, tighten the connecting rod nuts evenly to 47 ft.-lb. (64 N•m).

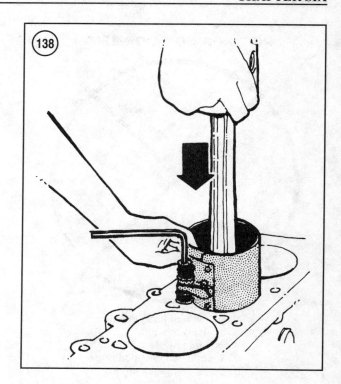

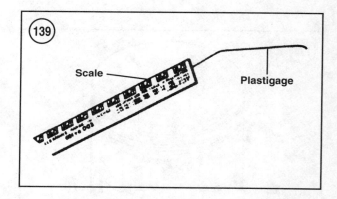

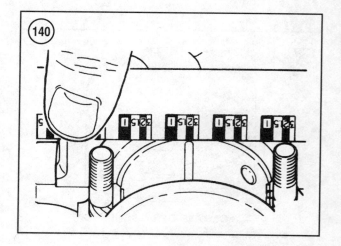

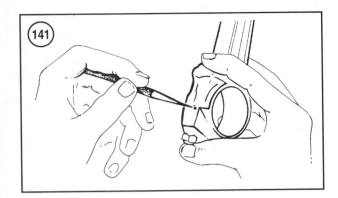

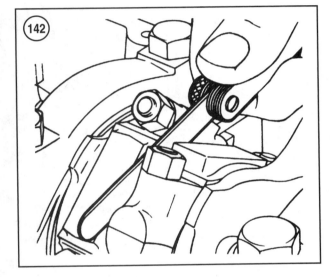

6

ance. Never install bearings with an undersized amount that exceeds the out-of-round measurement of the crankpin. Otherwise, inadequate clearance could occur at the wider crankpin diameter. Repeat the bearing clearance measurement.

b. If the bearing clearance is less than the specification, remove the piston and connecting rod as described in this section. Then measure the crankpin as described in this chapter (refer to *Crankshaft Removal and Inspection*). If the crankpin diameter is within the specification, check for improper rod cap or bearing installation and debris or an oil film between the rod or rod cap and bearings. Install the piston and connecting rod as described in this section. Repeat the bearing clearance measurement.

c. If the bearing clearance is within the specification, use a fingernail to scrape the Plastigage from the journal and bearing. Apply engine oil to the crankshaft and bearing surfaces. Install the rod cap and tighten the nuts as described in Step 15.

17. Rotate the crankshaft several revolutions. If the crankshaft binds or turns roughly, check for improper piston or connecting rod installation.

18. Repeat Steps 4-17 for the remaining pistons and connecting rods.

19. Measure the connecting rod side clearance as follows:

a. Push each connecting rod on the selected journal toward the crankshaft contact surfaces. Insert a feeler gauge between the two connecting rods (**Figure 142**). The clearance equals the thickness of the feeler gauge that passes between the connecting rods with a slight drag.

b. The connecting rod side clearance must be 0.006-0.024 in. (0.152-0.609 mm) on 5.0L and 5.7L models, 0.013-0.023 in. (0.330-0.584 mm) on 7.4L and 8.2L models or 0.015-0.027 in. (0.381-0.685 mm) on 8.1L models. If the clearance exceeds the specification, check for excessive wear on the corresponding connecting rod and crankshaft surfaces. Disassemble the engine and replace the pair of connecting rods and recheck the clearance. If this does not correct the excessive clearance, replace the crankshaft. If the clearance is less than the specification, check for improper installation of the connecting rod, connecting rod cap or piston.

c. Repeat this step for the remaining pairs of connecting rods.

20. Install the oil pump, timing cover, oil pan and cylinder head(s) as described in this chapter.

d. On 7.4L and 8.2L models with 7/16—20 nuts, tighten the connecting rod nuts evenly to 73 ft.-lb. (99 N•m).

e. On 8.1L models, tighten the connecting rod nuts evenly to 22 ft.-lb. (30 N•m). Check for proper rod cap alignment as described in Step 14. Use an angle torque gauge and tighten the rod nuts an additional 90° of rotation.

16. Evenly loosen the nuts and remove the rod cap. Gauge the connecting rod bearing clearance by comparing the width of the flattened Plastigage with the scale on the envelope (**Figure 140**). Compare the clearance with the specifications in **Table 8**. Refer to the following:

a. If the bearing clearance exceeds the specification, remove the piston and connecting rod as described in this section. Then measure the crankpin as described in this chapter (refer to *Crankshaft Removal and Inspection*). If the crankpin diameter is within the specification in **Table 8**, install either a 0.001 or 0.002 in. undersized bearing to correct the clear-

FLYWHEEL HOUSING, FLYWHEEL AND DRIVE PLATE

Removal, Inspection and Installation

Refer to **Figure 143** for this procedure.

1. Remove the engine as described in this chapter.

2. Remove the starter motor as described in Chapter Nine.

3. Remove the transmission from the engine as described in Chapter Ten.

4. Suspend the rear of the engine with a suitable lift to allow flywheel housing removal. It is acceptable to rest the engine on the side engine mounts, but *do not* rest the engine on the oil pan. Doing so will probably damage the oil pan and does not provide enough stability.

5. Remove the screws (15, **Figure 143**) and washers (16) that hold the shield (14) onto the flywheel housing.

6. Carefully pull the shield off the flywheel housing. Remove the seal (13, **Figure 143**) from the shield or cylinder block. Inspect the seal for deterioration or damage and replace as needed.

7. If so equipped, remove the nut and lockwasher. Then disconnect the battery ground cable from the flywheel housing stud.

8. Remove the gasket (12, **Figure 143**) from the shield or flywheel housing. Discard the gasket.

9. Note the original locations and bolt lengths. Then support the flywheel housing while removing the bolts, nuts and washers (1-4, **Figure 143**) that secure the housing to the cylinder block. Carefully pull the flywheel housing from the cylinder block. If difficulty is encountered, check for overlooked fasteners. If necessary, carefully pry the housing loose. Do not damage the mating surfaces.

10. Use soap and water to remove grease and contaminants from the flywheel housing and shield. Dry the housing and shield with compressed air.

11. Engage a flywheel holding tool (**Figure 144**) onto the teeth of the flywheel to prevent flywheel rotation in the counterclockwise direction. Support the drive plate and then remove the six bolts (7, **Figure 143**) and washers (8) that secure the drive plate (9) to the flywheel. Carefully remove the drive plate from the flywheel. If difficulty is encountered, carefully pry the drive plate loose.

NOTE
Minor surface corrosion of the drive plate surfaces is normal and does not indicate a need for replacement. Heavy corrosion or corrosion that impedes spring movement or proper transmission drive shaft engagement indicates a need to replace the drive plate.

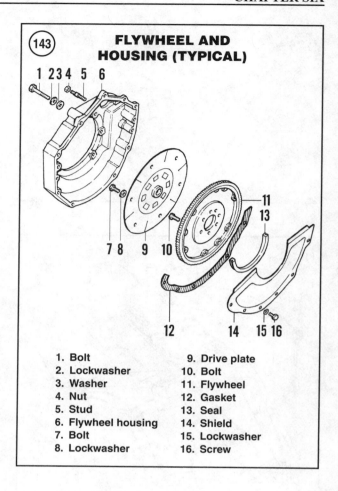

FLYWHEEL AND HOUSING (TYPICAL)

143

1 2 3 4 5   6

7 8   9 10

11
13

12   14 15 16

1. Bolt	9. Drive plate
2. Lockwasher	10. Bolt
3. Washer	11. Flywheel
4. Nut	12. Gasket
5. Stud	13. Seal
6. Flywheel housing	14. Shield
7. Bolt	15. Lockwasher
8. Lockwasher	16. Screw

12. Inspect the drive plate for worn or damaged splines in the center opening, broken springs, cracks or corrosion damage. Replace the drive plate if these or other defects are evident.

13. Engage a flywheel holding tool (**Figure 144**) on the teeth of the flywheel to prevent flywheel rotation in the counterclockwise direction. Support the flywheel and then remove the six bolts (10, **Figure 143**) or six nuts and washers that hold the flywheel to the crankshaft flange. Carefully pull the flywheel off the crankshaft. If removal is difficult, rock the flywheel on the alignment dowel until free. If necessary, pry between the cylinder block and flywheel. Work carefully to avoid damaging the flywheel teeth or cylinder block.

CAUTION
Make sure the mating surfaces of the crankshaft, flywheel and drive plate are completely clean and the surfaces are true. Debris or uneven surfaces will prevent proper seating of the mating surfaces and allow the fasteners to loosen.

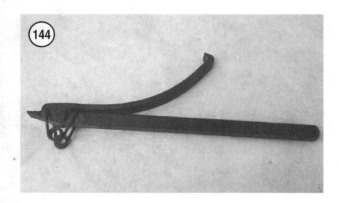

14. Use a suitable solvent to clean grease and other contaminants from the flywheel and crankshaft mating surfaces.

15. Inspect the flywheel-to-crankshaft mating surfaces for transferred material (rough or uneven mating surfaces) or other defects. If transferred material or other defects are found on the flywheel, have the mating surfaces machined. Do not remove more than 0.020 in. (0.5 mm) from the surface. Replace the flywheel if surface defects cannot be removed by machining. If transferred material is found on the crankshaft, remove the crankshaft as described in this chapter and have it machined to remove the imperfection. Do not remove more than 0.020 in. (0.5 mm) from the surface.

16. Inspect the alignment dowel (**Figure 145**) for wear, bending or other defects and replace as necessary. Using locking pliers, carefully twist and pull the dowel from the crankshaft. Carefully tap the replacement dowel into the opening. Drive gently to avoid damaging the replacement dowel.

17A. On models with a two-piece rear main seal, inspect the studs in the crankshaft for wear, cracks or damage and replace as needed.

17B. On models with a one-piece rear main seal, inspect the bolt openings in the crankshaft for damaged threads or cracking toward the outside of the flange. Cracking occurs from improperly tightening the flywheel attaching bolts. Renew damaged threads as needed using a proper tap. If cracking is evident, replace the crankshaft as described in this chapter.

18. Use a thread chaser or tap to remove corrosion or threadlocking compound from the studs, bolts, nuts and bolt openings in the crankshaft.

19. Align the dowel with the corresponding opening. Then fit the flywheel onto the crankshaft. Seat the flywheel against the crankshaft flange.

NOTE
*All 1983-1985 5.0L/5.7L models and 1983-1990 7.4L/8.2L models use a two-piece rear main seal. All 1986-2003 5.0L/5.7L models and 1991-2003 7.4L/8.2L models use a one-piece rear main seal. All 8.1L models use a one-piece rear main seal. Although the flywheel removal and installation procedures are similar for either type of seal, the tightening specifications might differ by the type of seal used. Refer to **Rear Main Seal** in this chapter and identify the type of seal used before tightening the fasteners.*

20. Apply Loctite 271 to the threads. Then thread the six bolts into the flywheel or six nuts and washers onto the crankshaft studs. Engage a flywheel holding tool (**Figure 144**) onto the teeth of the flywheel to prevent flywheel rotation in the clockwise direction. Then tighten the fasteners as follows:

  a. On 5.0L and 5.7L models with a two-piece rear main seal, tighten the nuts and washers in a crossing pattern to 70 ft.-lb. (95 N•m).

  b. On 5.0L and 5.7L models with a one-piece rear main seal, tighten the bolts in a crossing pattern to 75 ft.-lb. (102 N•m).

  c. On 7.4L and 8.2L models, tighten the nuts and washers or bolts in a crossing pattern to 65 ft.-lb. (88 N•m).

  d. On 8.1L models, tighten the bolts in a crossing pattern to 74 ft.-lb. (100 N•m).

21. Fit the drive plate (9, **Figure 143**) onto the flywheel. Then install the six washers (8, **Figure 142**) and bolts (7) into the drive plate and flywheel. Engage a flywheel holding tool (**Figure 144**) on the teeth of the flywheel to prevent flywheel rotation in the clockwise direction. Then tighten the bolts in a crossing pattern to 35 ft.-lb. (47 N•m).

6

22. Carefully fit the flywheel housing (6, **Figure 143**) over the flywheel. Align the large locating pin on each side and then seat the housing against the cylinder block. Make sure that no wiring, hoses or clamps are pinched between the mating surfaces and then thread the fasteners. Tighten the fasteners in a crossing pattern to 30 ft.-lb. (41 N•m).

23. If so equipped, attach the battery ground cable terminal onto the flywheel housing stud. Secure the terminal with a lockwasher and nut.

24. Apply a coat of 3M WeatherStrip Adhesive to the surfaces. Then install the new gasket (12, **Figure 143**) and seal (13) onto the shield (14). Wait for the adhesive to cure and then install the shield onto the flywheel housing. Thread the screws (16, **Figure 143**) and washers (15) into the shield and flywheel housing. Tighten the screws in a crossing pattern to 80 in.-lb. (9 N•m).

25. Install the transmission from the engine as described in Chapter Ten.

26. Install the starter motor as described in Chapter Nine.

27. Install the engine as described in this chapter.

REAR MAIN SEAL

All 1983-1985 5.0L/5.7L models and 1983-1990 7.4L/8.2L models use a two-piece rear main seal. The seal is located under the rear main bearing cap and can be replaced without removing the crankshaft from the cylinder block. However, the rear main bearing cap must be removed to replace the seal.

All 1986-2003 5.0L/5.7L models and 1991-2003 7.4L/8.2L models use a one-piece rear main seal. All 8.1L models use a one-piece rear main seal.

On 5.0L and 5.7L models, the one-piece seal is pressed into a seal retainer that bolts onto the cylinder block. The seal can be replaced without removing the oil pan or rear main bearing cap. The one-piece seal is identified by the seal retainer (**Figure 146**) on the rear of the engine.

On 7.4L, 8.1L and 8.2L models, the one-piece seal is pressed into the cylinder block and rear main bearing cap counterbore. The one-piece seal is pressed into the counterbore after the crankshaft is installed and can be replaced without removing the oil pan or rear main bearing cap.

Rear Main Seal Replacement (Two-Piece Seal)

Refer to **Figure 147** for this procedure.
1. Remove the engine as described in this chapter.
2. Remove the flywheel housing, drive plate and flywheel as described in this chapter.

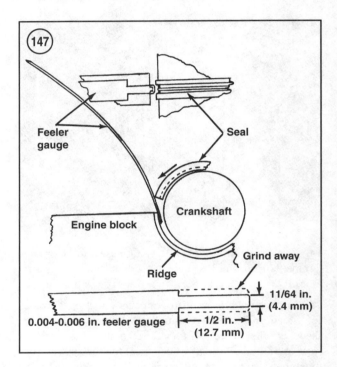

3. Remove the oil pan and oil pump as described in this chapter.

4. Remove the bolts and then carefully pull the rear main bearing cap off the crankshaft and cylinder block.

5. Carefully pull the seal out of the groove in the bearing cap.

6. Tap one end of the upper seal with a brass punch until the other end of the seal protrudes far enough to be pulled out with pliers. Discard the seals.

7. Use solvent to clean all sealant and oil from the rear main bearing cap, crankshaft and cylinder block surfaces.

8. Apply a light coat of engine oil to the lip and bead of the new seals. Do not allow oil to contact the mating ends or parting line surfaces.

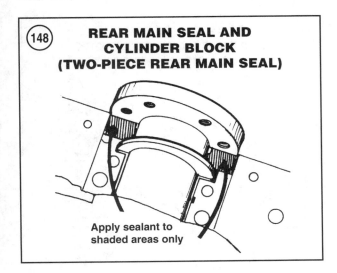

REAR MAIN SEAL AND CYLINDER BLOCK (TWO-PIECE REAR MAIN SEAL)

Apply sealant to shaded areas only

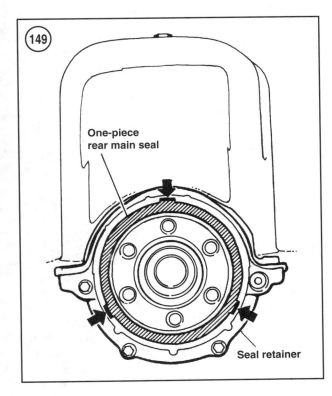

One-piece rear main seal

Seal retainer

9. Carefully fit the new seal into the groove in the bearing cap. Make sure the sharp edges of the bearing cap do not cut the bead in the center of the seal surface. The lip side of the seal must face toward the inside of the engine when installed.

10. Make a seal installation tool by grinding and bending a 0.004-0.006 in. feeler gauge (**Figure 147**) until it will fit in the *U* shape of the seal without scraping the seal sides. File the ground edges to prevent seal damage.

11. Wipe all debris and oil from the crankshaft surface. Apply a light coat of engine oil to the lip and bead of the new seals. Do not allow oil to contact the mating ends or parting line surfaces.

12. Insert the seal installation tool between the block and crankshaft as shown in **Figure 147**. Then insert the new seal between the tool and crankshaft. The lip side of the seal must face toward the inside of the engine when installed. Hold the feeler gauge while feeding the new seal into the opening until the ends are flush with the cylinder block surfaces on each side of the crankshaft. Remove the installation tool.

13. Apply a light coat of Permatex Gasket Sealing Compound to the block surfaces shown in **Figure 148**. Purchase the sealing compound from an automotive parts store.

14. Install the rear main bearing cap with a new seal onto the crankshaft and cylinder block. Tighten the cap bolts to 120-144 in.-lb. (13.6-16.3 N•m). Tap on the front (harmonic balancer end) and then the flywheel end of the crankshaft with a rubber mallet to align the thrust surfaces on the rear main bearing. Tighten the rear main cap bolts evenly to 80 ft.-lb. (108 N•m) for 5.0L/5.7L models and 110 ft.-lb. (149 N•m) for 7.4L and 8.2L models.

15. Install the oil pump and oil pan as described in this chapter.

16. Install the flywheel, drive plate and flywheel housing as described in this chapter.

17. Install the engine as described in this chapter.

Rear Main Seal Replacement (One-Piece Seal)

The rear main seal can be replaced without removing the oil pan or seal retainer.

1. Remove the flywheel housing, drive plate and flywheel as described in this chapter.

2A. On 5.0L, 5.7L, 7.4L and 8.2L models, insert a pry bar into one of the three seal retainer slots (**Figure 149**). Carefully pry the seal from the retainer or block and rear main counterbore. Do not allow the pry bar to contact the crankshaft surface. Discard the seal.

2B. On 8.1L models, use the seal removal tool (Kent-Moore part No. J-43320) to pull the seal from the cylinder block and rear main bearing cap counterbore. Instructions follow:

   a. Insert the guide pins from the tool into the two openings in the crankshaft.

   b. Fit the seal puller plate over the guide pins and seat against the crankshaft.

   c. Thread the eight self-tapping screws (included with the tool) into the puller plate and seal casing.

   d. Thread the puller bolt into the plate.

6

e. Turn the bolt until the seal is free from the engine.

f. Discard the seal.

g. Remove the guide pins from the crankshaft.

3. Use a quick-drying solvent, such as carburetor cleaner, to clean the seal contact surfaces in the seal retainer. Allow the solvent to dry completely before installing the new seal.

4. Lubricate the seal lip with engine oil. Then insert the new seal into the bore with the lip side facing the crankshaft. Make sure the seal is not cocked in the bore.

5A. On 5.0L and 5.7L models, use the seal installation tool (Kent-Moore part No. J-35621-B) and push the seal into the retainer until fully seated.

5B. On 7.4L and 5.7L models, use the seal installation tool (Kent-Moore part No. J-38841) and push the seal into the counterbore until fully seated.

5C. On 8.1L models, use the seal installation tool (Kent-Moore part No. J-42849) to push the new seal into the cylinder block and counterbore until fully seated.

6. Install the flywheel, drive plate and flywheel housing as described in this chapter.

Rear Main Seal Retainer Replacement

NOTE
A rear main seal retainer is used on 5.0L and 5.7L models with a one-piece rear main seal. On 7.4L, 8.1L and 8.2L models with a one-piece rear main seal, the seal fits into a recess in the cylinder block and rear main bearing cap.

1. Remove the flywheel housing, drive plate and flywheel as described in this chapter.

2. Remove the oil pan as described in this chapter.

3. Remove the rear main seal from the retainer as described in this chapter.

4. Remove the fasteners and carefully pry the retainer (6, **Figure 150**) from the rear main bearing. Remove and discard the gasket (7, **Figure 150**).

5. Clean any gasket material or sealant from the retainer and rear main bearing.

6. Fit a new gasket onto the seal retainer. Do not apply sealant to the gasket.

7. Align the locating pin and studs and then fit the retainer onto the rear main bearing.

8. Apply a light coat of Loctite Pipe Sealant with Teflon to the threads of the retainer fasteners. Install the fasteners and tighten evenly to 106 in.-lb. (12 N•m).

9. Install the rear main seal into the retainer as described in this chapter.

10. Install the oil pan as described in this chapter.

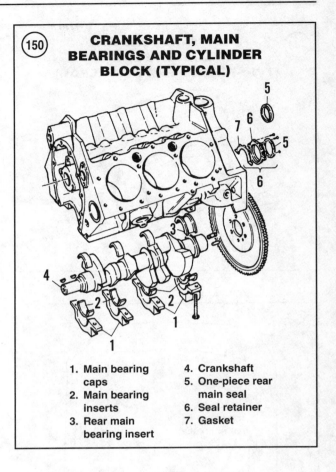

CRANKSHAFT, MAIN BEARINGS AND CYLINDER BLOCK (TYPICAL)

1. Main bearing caps
2. Main bearing inserts
3. Rear main bearing insert
4. Crankshaft
5. One-piece rear main seal
6. Seal retainer
7. Gasket

11. Install the flywheel, drive plate and flywheel housing as described in this chapter.

CRANKSHAFT AND MAIN BEARINGS

Replace the rear main seal (5, **Figure 150**, typical) and crankshaft main bearings (2) if the crankshaft is removed. The main bearing caps (1, **Figure 150**, typical) are machined to match the cylinder block. The caps must be installed in the proper location with the arrows on the casting (**Figure 151**) facing forward or away from the flywheel. Otherwise, the crankshaft will bind in the cylinder block, wear rapidly and fail. The cap from one cylinder block cannot be installed onto a different cylinder block.

To compensate for manufacturing variations, some engines are equipped with 0.009 in. undersized main bearing inserts. On such engines, the cylinder block is stamped with a 009 mark on the middle forward crankshaft flyweight. However, because 0.009 in. undersized bearings are not available separately, replace the bearings with 0.010 in. undersized main bearing inserts and check the main bearing clearance during assembly. On an engine

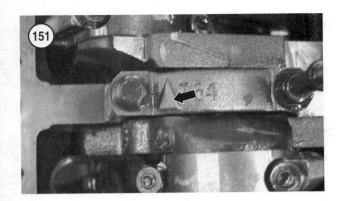

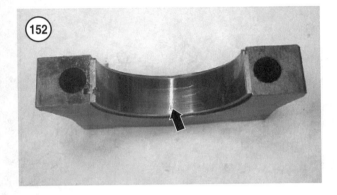

with very low operating hours, the crankshaft might require machining to accept the 0.010 in. undersized bearings.

To fit precise factory tolerances, some engines are equipped with a 0.001 in. undersized and a standard bearing insert on the same journal. On such engines, use standard or 0.001 in. undersized bearings for service replacement.

NOTE
7.4L models are produced in both standard- and high-output models that must be identified before beginning the repair procedure. If the identification decal is missing from the engine or the output specification is in question, remove the intake manifold as described in Chapter Seven. Then inspect the intake manifold and cylinder head intake ports. The standard-output models use round or oval ports. The high-output models use rectangular ports.

Crankshaft Removal

1. Remove the flywheel housing, drive plate and flywheel as described in this chapter.

2. Remove the oil pan, oil pump, timing components and cylinder head(s) as described in this chapter.

3. Remove the pistons and connecting rods as described in this chapter.

4. Remove the lifters and camshaft as described in this chapter.

5. Position the cylinder block with the crankshaft facing upward. Number the main bearing caps to indicate the locations on the cylinder block. Note the cast-in arrows (**Figure 151**) or triangle marks on the bearing caps. The arrows or triangles must face the front of the engine or away from the flywheel.

6A. On 5.0L, 5.7L, 7.4L and 8.2L models with a two-piece rear main seal, remove the rear main bearing cap and lower main seal half as described in this chapter. Do not remove the upper main seal half at this time.

6B. On 5.0L and 5.7L models with a one-piece rear main seal, remove the rear main seal and then the rear main seal retainer as described in this chapter.

6C. On 7.4L and 8.2L models with a one-piece rear main seal and all 8.1L models, remove the rear main seal as described in this chapter.

7. Remove the main bearing caps (1, **Figure 150**) one at a time. Note the original mounting locations of each cap. Remove the lower bearing inserts (**Figure 152**) from the main bearing caps.

8. Carefully lift the crankshaft from the cylinder block. Place the crankshaft on a sturdy work surface with good lighting. Remove the upper main bearing inserts from the cylinder block.

9. On 5.0L, 5.7L, 7.4L and 8.2L models with a two-piece rear main seal, remove the upper main seal half from the upper rear main bearing.

10. Remove any remaining fittings, brackets or other components from the cylinder block. Thoroughly clean the cylinder block with pressurized soap and water. Direct the spray through all passages and into any crevices. Rinse the block with clean water and dry with compressed air. Direct air through all passages to remove residual water or debris. To prevent corrosion, promptly coat all unpainted surfaces with engine oil.

11. If the engine is equipped with an oil cooler, remove the cooler as described in Chapter Eight and thoroughly flush all debris from the cooler and connecting hoses.

Crankshaft Inspection

1. Inspect the main bearing inserts for discolored, scratches, corrosion, pits or roughness. Inspect the crankshaft for damage if these or other defects are found with the bearings.

6

2. Inspect the crankshaft main bearing and crankpin journals for cracks, discoloration, corrosion pitting, scratches or transferred bearing material. If the surfaces are lightly discolored, scratched, corroded, rough or pitted, have a reputable machine shop machine the crankshaft to accept undersized bearings. Contact an Indmar dealership for undersized bearing availability before machining the crankshaft. Replace the crankshaft if cracks or heavy discoloration is evident.

3. Use an accurate outside micrometer to measure the diameter of the main and crankpin journals (**Figure 153**). Take measurements at several points along the length of the journals and at several points around the circumference of the journals. Record all measurements for each journal. Refer to the following:

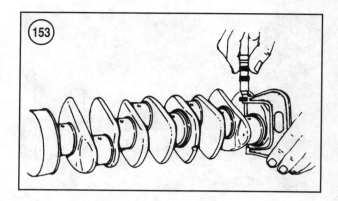

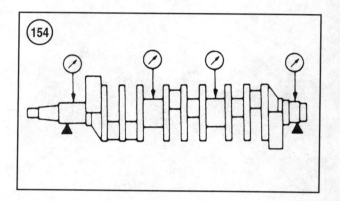

a. To determine the amount of journal taper, subtract the smallest diameter at one end of the journal from the largest diameter at the other end of the journal. If the journal taper exceeds 0.001 in. (0.025 mm), have the crankshaft machined to accept the next undersized bearing inserts. Contact an Indmar dealership for undersized bearing availability before machining the crankshaft.

b. Subtract the smallest diameter at one point along the length of the journal from the largest diameter taken around the circumference of the journal (and at the same point along the length) to determine the amount of journal out-of-round. If the journal out-of-round exceeds 0.001 in. (0.025 mm), have the crankshaft machined to accept the next undersized bearing inserts. Contact an Indmar dealership for undersized bearing availability before machining the crankshaft.

c. Compare the journal measurement with the specification in **Table 8**. Have the crankshaft machined to accept the next undersized bearing inserts if any of the measurements are below the minimum specification. Contact an Indmar dealership for undersized bearing availability before machining the crankshaft.

4. Support the crankshaft with V-blocks under the front and rear main bearing journals (**Figure 154**). Mount a dial indicator so the plunger touches one of the center main bearing journals. Zero the dial indicator. Observe the needle movement while slowly rotating the crankshaft. The needle movement indicates the amount of crankshaft runout. Replace the crankshaft if the runout exceeds 0.002 in. (0.051 mm).

Crankshaft Installation

CAUTION
Failure of the crankshaft, bearings or other internal engine components will deposit bearing material and other debris into the oil cooler and hoses connecting the cooler to the oil filter adapter. To avoid repeat engine failure, thoroughly flush all debris from the cooler and connecting hoses prior to connecting them to the engine.

An angle torque gauge is required to properly tighten the main bearing caps on 5.0L and 5.7L models with an eight-bolt intake manifold and all 8.1L models.

1. Install the new main bearing inserts into the cylinder block. The inserts with the grooves fit into the cylinder block. The inserts without grooves fit into the main bearing caps. Do not lubricate the inserts at this time.

2. Carefully lower the crankshaft into the cylinder block. Seat the crankshaft against the main bearings. Do not rotate the crankshaft.

3. Place a section of Plastigage (**Figure 139**) onto each of the main bearing journals. The Plastigage must span the length of the journals and align with the bottom of the journals (**Figure 140**).

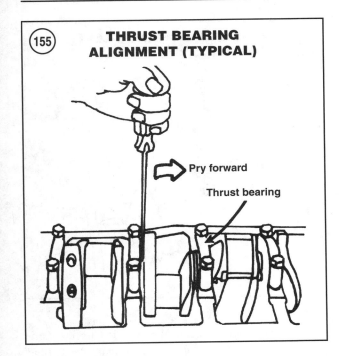

THRUST BEARING ALIGNMENT (TYPICAL)

Pry forward

Thrust bearing

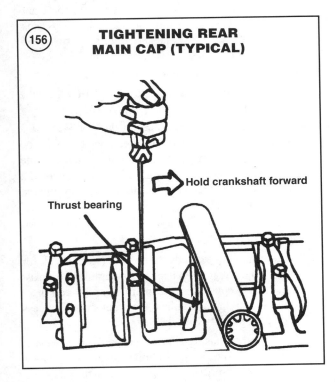

TIGHTENING REAR MAIN CAP (TYPICAL)

Hold crankshaft forward

Thrust bearing

4. Fit the bearing inserts into the main bearing caps. The bearing tang must fit into the notch in the cap. Install the main bearing caps over the crankshaft journal and rest on the cylinder block. The arrow (**Figure 151**) or triangle mark must point toward the front of the engine.

CAUTION
Do not tighten the rear main bearing cap bolts in Step 5. The rear main thrust surfaces must be aligned before tightening the rear main bearing cap, or the thrust surfaces will wear excessively and fail the bearing. Tighten the front and center main bearings as described in Step 5. Then align the bearing and tighten the rear main bearing as described in Step 6.

5. Thread the bolts into the main bearing caps. Do not rotate the crankshaft. Tighten the bolts as follows:

   a. On 5.0L and 5.7L models with a 12-bolt intake manifold, tighten the bolts evenly to 80 ft.-lb. (108 N•m).

   b. On 5.0L and 5.7L models with an eight-bolt intake manifold and two-bolt main bearing caps, tighten each pair of bolts evenly to 15 ft.-lb. (20.3 N•m). Use an angle torque gauge to tighten each pair of bolts an additional 73° of rotation.

   c. On 5.0L and 5.7L models with an eight-bolt intake manifold and four-bolt main bearing caps, tighten the four bolts on each bearing cap evenly to 15 ft.-lb. (20.3 N•m). Tighten each pair of inner bolts (closest to the crankshaft journal) an additional 73° of rotation. Tighten each pair of outer bolts (farthest from the crankshaft) an additional 43° of rotation.

   d. On 7.4L standard-output models with a two-piece rear main seal, tighten the bolts evenly to 110 ft.-lb. (149 N•m).

   e. On 7.4L standard-output models with a one-piece rear main seal, tighten the bolts evenly to 102 ft.-lb. (138 N•m).

   f. On 7.4L high-output models, tighten the bolts evenly to 110 ft.-lb. (149 N•m).

   g. On 8.1L models, tighten the four bolts on each main bearing cap evenly to 22 ft.-lb. (30 N•m). Use an angle torque gage to tighten the inner bolts (closest to the journal) an additional 90° of rotation. Use an angle torque gage to tighten the outer bearing stud bolts an additional 80° of rotation.

   h. On 8.2L models, tighten the bolts evenly to 110 ft.-lb. (149 N•m).

6. Insert a pry bar between one of the center main bearing caps and a crankshaft flyweight (**Figure 155**). Carefully pry the crankshaft toward the rear of the cylinder block. Move the pry bar to the other side of the bearing cap and carefully pry the crankshaft toward the front of the cylinder block (**Figure 156**). Maintain moderate pressure on the pry bar while tightening the rear main bearing cap as follows:

6

a. On 5.0L and 5.7L models with a 12-bolt intake manifold, tighten the rear main bearing cap bolts evenly to 80 ft.-lb. (108 N•m).

b. On 5.0L and 5.7L models with an eight-bolt intake manifold and two-bolt main bearing caps, tighten the rear main bearing cap bolts evenly to 15 ft.-lb. (20.3 N•m). Use an angle torque gauge to tighten each bolt an additional 73° of rotation.

c. On 5.0L and 5.7L models with an eight-bolt intake manifold and four-bolt main bearing caps, tighten the four bolts on the rear main bearing cap to 15 ft.-lb. (20.3 N•m). Tighten the two inner bolts (closest to the crankshaft journal) an additional 73° of rotation. Tighten the two outer bolts (farthest from the crankshaft) an additional 43° of rotation.

d. On 7.4L standard-output models with a two-piece rear main seal, tighten the rear main bearing cap bolts evenly to 110 ft.-lb. (149 N•m).

e. On 7.4L standard output models with a one-piece rear main seal, tighten the rear main bearing cap bolts evenly to 102 ft.-lb. (138 N•m).

f. On 7.4L high-output models, tighten the rear main bearing cap bolts evenly to 110 ft.-lb. (149 N•m).

g. On 8.1L models, tighten the four rear main bearing cap bolts evenly to 22 ft.-lb. (30 N•m). Use an angle torque gauge to tighten the two inner bolts (closest to the journal) an additional 90° of rotation. Use an angle torque gauge to tighten the two outer bearing stud bolts an additional 80° of rotation.

h. On 8.2L models, tighten the rear main bearing cap bolts evenly to 110 ft.-lb. (149 N•m).

7. Evenly loosen the bolts and studs. Remove the main bearing caps. Determine the main bearing clearance by comparing the width of the flattened Plastigage (**Figure 140**) with the marks on the envelope. Compare the clearance to the specification in **Table 8**. Refer to the following:

a. If the clearance exceeds the specification, measure the crankshaft as described in this chapter (refer to *Crankshaft Inspection*). Install either 0.001- or 0.002-in. undersized bearings to correct excessive clearance. Never install bearings with an undersized amount that exceeds the out-of-round measurement of the journal. Otherwise, inadequate clearance could occur at the wider journal diameter.

b. If the clearance is less than the specification, measure the crankshaft as described in this chapter (refer to *Crankshaft Inspection*). Check for improper bearing cap or bearing insert installation, debris or an oil film between the cap or cylinder block and the bearings.

(157) **MEASURING CRANKSHAFT END PLAY (TYPICAL)**

c. If the clearance is within the specification, use a fingernail to scrape the Plastigage from the journal and bearings. Apply engine oil to the crankshaft and bearing surfaces. Install the main bearing caps. Tighten the bearing caps and align the thrust bearing surfaces as described in Steps 5 and 6.

8. Measure the crankshaft end play as follows:

a. Use a pry bar to gently pry the crankshaft toward the front of the cylinder block (**Figure 157**).

b. Maintain moderate pressure on the pry bar. Use a feeler gauge to measure the clearance between the rear main bearing and the thrust surface on the crankshaft. The crankshaft end play equals the thickness of the feeler gauge that passes through the gap with a slight drag.

c. Compare the gap measurement with the crankshaft end play specification in **Table 8**.

d. If the end play exceeds the specification, check for wear on the rear main bearing and crankshaft thrust surfaces. Replace the rear main bearing and repeat the measurement. Replace the crankshaft if excess end play persists with the new bearing.

e. If the end play is less than the specification, loosen the rear main bearing cap bolts and align the thrust bearing as described in Step 6. Tighten the rear main bolts as described and repeat the measurement. Replace the rear main bearing if inadequate clearance persists.

9. Rotate the crankshaft several revolutions. Check for improper main bearing installation or inadequate clearance if binding or roughness is evident.

10A. On 5.0L, 5.7L, 7.4L and 8.2L models with a two-piece rear main seal, remove the rear main bearing cap and install the rear main seal as described in this chapter. Align the thrust bearing and tighten the rear main bearing cap as described in Step 6.

10B. On 5.0L and 5.7L models with a one-piece rear main seal, install the rear main seal retainer and then the rear main seal as described in this chapter.

10C. On 7.4L and 8.2L models with a one-piece rear main seal and all 8.1L models, install the rear main seal as described in this chapter.

11. Install the pistons and connecting rods as described in this chapter.

12. Install the camshaft and lifters as described in this chapter.

13. Install the timing components as described in this chapter.

14. Install the timing cover as described in this chapter.

15. Install the oil pump and oil pan as described in this chapter.

16. Install the cylinder head(s) as described in this chapter.

17. Install the flywheel, drive plate and flywheel housing as described in this chapter.

18. Install any remaining fittings, brackets or other components that were removed from the cylinder block.

BREAK-IN PROCEDURE

Perform the break-in procedure any time internal components are replaced. During the first few hours of running, many of the engine components cannot handle full load until fully seated. Failure to properly break in the engine can result in engine failure, decreased performance, shortened engine life and increased oil consumption.

An engine needs approximately 20 hours of running time to be fully broken in. Increased oil consumption can be expected during this period. During break-in, check the oil level frequently as described in Chapter Three. Also, check the tightness of all external fasteners during the break-in period.

1. During the first 10 minutes of operation, start the engine and immediately advance the throttle to 1500 rpm in NEUTRAL. After the engine reaches operating temperature, reduce the throttle to idle for 1-2 minutes and then return to 1500 rpm for 1-2 minutes.

2. After the first 10 minutes, return the engine to idle and shift into FORWARD. Advance the throttle quickly to plane the boat. Then immediately reduce the throttle to just maintain the boat on plane. Do not exceed 3500 rpm after planing the boat. During the next 2 hours of operation, repeatedly advance the throttle to three-quarters open for 3 minutes followed by a return to planing speed for 3 minutes. Continue this procedure during the 2-hour period.

3. During the next 8 hours of the break-in period, operate the engine at wide-open throttle for no more than 2 minutes at a time followed by a few minutes of operation at idle to allow a cooling down period. Otherwise, operate the engine at varying speeds of less than three-quarters open.

4. During the next 10 hours of operation, operate the engine at wide-open throttle for no more than 10 minutes at a time followed by operation at a lower speed. Otherwise, operate the engine at three-quarters open throttle or less. Periodically reduce the engine to idle for a few minutes to allow a cooling down period.

Table 1 ENGINE TORQUE SPECIFICATIONS

Fastener	in.-lb.	ft.-lb.	N•m
Camshaft thrust plate			
5.0L, 5.7L and 8.1L models	106	–	12
7.4L counter-rotation models	96	–	11
Camshaft timing sprocket			
5.0L and 5.7L models			
With two-piece rear main seal	–	20	27
With one-piece rear main seal	–	25	34
7.4L and 8.2L models	–	25	34
8.1L models			
First step	132	11	15
Second step	–	22	30
Final step	–	22	30
(continued)			

Table 1 ENGINE TORQUE SPECIFICATIONS (continued)

Fastener	in.-lb.	ft.-lb.	N•m
Camshaft timing gear			
5.0L and 5.7L models	–	20	27
Connecting rod nuts			
5.0L and 5.7L models			
With 12-bolt intake manifold	–	45	61
With 8-bolt intake manifold	240*	20*	27*
7.4L and 8.2L models			
With 3/8-24 nuts	–	47	64
With 7/16-20 nuts	–	73	99
8.1L models	264*	22*	30*
Crankshaft pulley	–	35	47
Cylinder head bolts			
5.0L and 5.7L models (except 5.7L LT-1)			
12-bolt intake			
First step	–	20	27
Second step	–	40	54
Final step	–	65	88
8-bolt intake (Gen +)			
First step*	–	22*	30*
7.4L standard-output models			
First step	–	20	27
Second step	–	50	68
Final step	–	85	115
7.4L high-output models			
First step	–	20	27
Second step	–	50	68
Final step			
Short bolts	–	89	120
Long bolts	–	92	125
8.1L models			
First step*	–	22*	30*
8.2L models			
First step	–	20	27
Second step	–	50	68
Final step			
Short bolts	–	89	120
Long bolts	–	92	125
Drive plate to flywheel	–	35	47
Flywheel			
5.0L and 5.7L models			
With two-piece rear main seal	–	70	95
With one-piece rear main seal	–	75	102
7.4L and 8.2L models	–	65	88
8.1L models	–	74	100
Flywheel housing	–	30	41
Flywheel shield	80	–	9
Harmonic balancer			
5.0L and 5.7L models			
With aluminum pulley	–	40	54
With steel pulley	–	60	81
7.4L and 8.2L models	–	110	149
8.1L models	–	188	255
Main bearing caps			
5.0L and 5.7L models			
With 12-bolt intake manifold	–	80	108
With 8-bolt intake manifold	180*	15*	20.3*
7.4L models			
Standard-output models			
With two-piece rear main seal	–	110	149

(continued)

Table 1 ENGINE TORQUE SPECIFICATIONS (continued)

Fastener	in.-lb.	ft.-lb.	N•m
Main bearing caps			
7.4L models			
Standard-output models (continued)			
With one-piece rear main seal	–	102	138
High-output models	–	110	149
8.1L models	–	22*	30*
8.2L models	–	110	149
Mount trunnion bolts	–	50	68
Oil drain plug/fitting			
5.0L and 5.7L models	221	–	25
7.4L and 8.2L models	–	20	27
8.1L models	–	21	28
Oil pan			
5.0L and 5.7L models			
With two-piece rear main seal			
Corner nuts or screws	168	–	19
Side screws	84	–	9.5
With one-piece rear main seal			
Corner nuts or screws	177	–	20
Side screws	106	–	21
7.4L models			
With two-piece rear main seal			
Corner nuts or screws	168	–	19
Side screws	84	–	9.5
With one-piece rear main seal			
8.1L models			
First step	89	–	10
Final step	221	–	25
8.2L models			
Corner nuts or screws	204	–	23
Side screws	84	–	9.5
Oil pump cover screws			
5.0L and 5.7L models			
With two-piece rear main seal	84	–	9.5
With one-piece rear main seal	106	–	12
7.4L and 8.2L models			
With two-piece rear main seal	84	–	9.5
With one-piece rear main seal	106	–	12
8.1L models	106	–	12
Oil pump mounting bolt			
5.0L and 5.7L models	–	66	89
7.4L and 8.2L models			
With two-piece rear main seal	–	65	88
With one-piece rear main seal	–	70	95
8.1L models	–	56	76
Oil pump drive gear assembly			
8.1L models	221	–	25
Oil splash plate			
5.0L and 5.7L models			
With two-piece rear main seal	–	25	34
With one-piece rear main seal	–	30	41
7.4L and 8.2L models	–	25	34
8.1L models	–	37	50
Power steering hose fittings	–	25	34
Rear main seal retainer			
5.0L and 5.7L models	106	–	12
Rocker arm cover			
5.0L and 5.7L models			
With perimeter screws	60	–	6.8

(continued)

6

Table 1 ENGINE TORQUE SPECIFICATIONS (continued)

Fastener	in.-lb.	ft.-lb.	N•m
Rocker arm cover			
5.0L and 5.7L models (continued)			
With center screws	106	–	12
7.4L and 8.2L models	71	–	8.0
8.1L models			
First step	53	–	6
Final step	106	–	12
Rocker arm shoulder bolt			
7.4L standard-output models	–	40	52
7.4L high-output models	–	45	61
8.1L models	–	19	26
8.2L models	–	45	61
Roller lifter guide/retainer bolts			
5.0L and 5.7L models	216	18	24.4
7.4L, 8.1L and 8.2L models	228	19	25.8
Spark plugs			
5.0L and 5.7L models			
New cylinder head	–	22	30
Used cylinder head	–	15	20
7.4L and 8.2L models	–	15-20	20-28
8.1L models	–	15	20
Timing chain/gear cover			
5.0L and 5.7L models			
With composite (plastic) cover	106	–	12
With steel cover	84	–	9.5
7.4L and 8.2L models	120	–	13.6
8.1L models			
First step	53	–	6
Final step	106	–	12
Transmission output flange	–	50	68

*This value represents the first tightening sequence only. Perform the final torque using a torque angle gauge as described in Chapter Six.

Table 2 CAMSHAFT SERVICE SPECIFICATIONS

Measurement	Specification
Camshaft end play	
Counter-rotation 7.4L models	0.001-0.005 in. (0.025-0.127 mm)
Camshaft journal diameter	
5.0L and 5.7L models	1.8682-1.8692 in. (47.452-47.478 mm)
7.4L and 8.2L models	1.9482-1.9492 in. (49.484-49.510 mm)
8.1L models	1.9477-1.9479 in. (49.472-49.477 mm)
Camshaft journal out-of-round (maximum)	0.001 in. (0.025 mm)
Camshaft lobe lift	
5.0L and 5.7L models	
With flat lifters	
Intake valve lobes	0.263-269 in. (6.680-6.833 mm)
Exhaust valve lobes	0.269-0.276 in. (6.833-7.010 mm)
With roller lifters	
Intake valve lobes	0.274-0.278 in. (6.970-7.070 mm)

(continued)

Table 2 CAMSHAFT SERVICE SPECIFICATIONS (continued)

Measurement	Specification
Camshaft lobe lift	
5.0L and 5.7L models	
With roller lifters (continued)	
Exhaust valve lobes	0.278-0.283 in. (7.070-7.200 mm)
7.4L standard-output models	
With flat lifters	
Intake valve lobes	0.280-0.284 in. (7.112-7.214 mm)
Exhaust valve lobes	0.269-0.273 in. (6.833-6.934 mm)
With roller lifters	
Intake valve lobes	0.280-0.284 in. (7.112-7.214 mm)
Exhaust valve lobes	0.282-0.286 in. (7.163-7.264 mm)
7.4L high-output models	
With flat lifters	
Intake valve lobes	0.298-0.302 in. (7.569-7.671 mm)
Exhaust valve lobes	0.298-0.302 in. (7.569-7.671 mm)
With roller lifters	
Intake valve lobes	0.340-0.344 in. (8.636-8.738 mm)
Exhaust valve lobes	0.340-0.344 in. (8.636-8.738 mm)
8.1L standard-output models	
Intake valve lobes	0.273-0.277 in. (6.934-7.036 mm)
Exhaust valve lobes	0.275-0.279 in. (6.985-7.087 mm)
8.1L high-output models	
Intake valve lobes	0.298-0.302 in. (7.569-7.671 mm)
Exhaust valve lobes	0.298-0.302 in. (7.569-7.671 mm)
8.2L models	
With flat lifters	
Intake valve lobes	0.298-0.302 in. (7.569-7.671 mm)
Exhaust valve lobes	0.298-0.302 in. (7.569-7.671 mm)
With roller lifters	
Intake valve lobes	0.340-0.344 in. (8.636-8.738 mm)
Exhaust valve lobes	0.340-0.344 in. (8.636-8.738 mm)
Camshaft runout (maximum)	0.002 in. (0.051 mm)
Timing gear backlash (maximum)	0.004-0.008 in. (0.102-0.203 mm)
Timing gear runout (maximum)	
Camshaft gear	0.004 in. (0.102 mm)
Crankshaft gear	0.003 in. (0.076 mm)

Table 3 CYLINDER HEAD WARP LIMITS

Cylinder head	Maximum gap
5.0L and 5.7L models	
Overall length	0.004 in. (0.102 mm)
7.4L standard-output models	
6-in. (152 mm) span	0.003 in. (0.076 mm)
Overall length	0.004 in. (0.102 mm)
7.4L high-output models	
6-in. (152 mm) span	0.003 in. (0.076 mm)
Overall length	0.007 in. (0.178 mm)
8.1L and 8.2L models	
6-in. (152 mm) span	0.003 in. (0.076 mm)
Overall length	0.007 in. (0.178 mm)

Table 4 VALVE AND VALVE SEAT SERVICE SPECIFICATIONS

Measurement	Specification
Face angle	45°
Seat angle	46°
Seat runout (maximum)	0.002 in. (0.051 mm)
Seat width	
5.0L models	
Models with 12-bolt intake manifold	
Intake valve	0.0311-0.0625 in. (0.788-1.588 mm)
Exhaust valve	0.0625-0.0937 in. (2.381-1.588 mm)
Models with 8-bolt intake manifold	
Intake valve	0.0449-0.0701 in. (1.140-1.780 mm)
Exhaust valve	0.0650-0.0980 in. (1.651-2.489 mm)
5.7L models	
Models with 12-bolt intake manifold	
Intake valve	0.0311-0.0625 in. (0.788-1.588 mm)
Exhaust valve	0.0625-0.0937 in. (2.381-1.588 mm)
Models with 8-bolt intake manifold	
Intake valve	0.0402-0.0650 in. (1.140-1.780 mm)
Exhaust valve	0.0591-0.1008 in. (1.501-2.560 mm)
7.4L models	
With two-piece rear main seal	
Intake valve	0.0311-0.0625 in. (0.788-1.588 mm)
Exhaust valve	0.0625-0.0937 in. (2.381-1.588 mm)
With one-piece rear main seal	
Standard-output models	
Intake valve	0.0300-0.0600 in. (0.772-1.524 mm)
Exhaust valve	0.0600-0.0950 in. (1.524-2.413 mm)
High-output models	
Intake valve	0.0311-0.0625 in. (0.788-1.588 mm)
Exhaust valve	0.0625-0.0937 in. (2.381-1.588 mm)
8.1L models	
Intake valve	0.0300-0.0600 in. (0.772-1.524 mm)
Exhaust valve	0.0600-0.0950 in. (1.524-2.413 mm)
8.2L models	
With two-piece rear main seal	
Intake valve	0.0311-0.0625 in. (0.788-1.588 mm)
Exhaust valve	0.0625-0.0937 in. (2.381-1.588 mm)
With one-piece rear main seal	
Intake valve	0.0300-0.0600 in. (0.772-1.524 mm)
Exhaust valve	0.0600-0.0950 in. (1.524-2.413 mm)
Stem-to-guide clearance	
5.0L and 5.7L models	
Models with 12-bolt intake manifold	
Intake valve	0.0010-0.0037 in. (0.025-0.094 mm)
Exhaust valve	0.0010-0.0047 in. (0.025-0.119 mm)
Models with 8-bolt intake manifold	
Intake valve	0.0010-0.0037 in. (0.025-0.094 mm)
Exhaust valve	0.0010-0.0037 in. (0.025-0.094 mm)
7.4L models	
Intake valve	0.0010-0.0037 in. (0.025-0.094 mm)
Exhaust valve	0.0010-0.0049 in. (0.025-0.124 mm)
8.1L models	
Intake valve	0.0010-0.0029 in. (0.025-0.074 mm)
Exhaust valve	0.0012-0.0031 in. (0.030-0.079 mm)
8.2L models	
Intake valve	0.0010-0.0037 in. (0.025-0.094 mm)
Exhaust valve	0.0010-0.0049 in. (0.025-0.124 mm)
Valve stem diameter	
5.0L and 5.7L models	
Intake valve	
Standard diameter	0.3410-0.3417 in. (8.661-8.679 mm)

(continued)

Table 4 VALVE AND VALVE SEAT SERVICE SPECIFICATIONS (continued)

Measurement	Specification
Valve stem diameter	
5.0L and 5.7L models	
Intake valve (continued)	
Oversize diameter	0.3715 in. (9.436 mm)
Exhaust valve	
Standard diameter	0.3410-0.3417 in. (8.661-8.679 mm)
Oversize diameter	0.3715 in. (9.436 mm)
7.4L and 8.2L models	
Intake valve	
Standard diameter (minimum)	0.372 in. (9.489 mm)
Oversize diameter (minimum)	0.387 in. (9.830 mm)
Exhaust valve	
Standard diameter (minimum)	0.372 in. (9.489 mm)
Oversize diameter (minimum)	0.387 in. (9.830 mm)
8.1L models	
Intake valve	0.3715-0.3722 in. (9.436-9.454 mm)
Exhaust valve	0.3713-0.3720 in. (9.431-9.449 mm)
Valve margin	
5.0L and 5.7L models	
Models with 12-bolt intake manifold	
Intake and exhaust valve (minimum)	0.031 in. (0.787 mm)
Models with 8-bolt intake manifold	
Intake valve (minimum)	0.031 in. (0.787 mm)
Exhaust valve	0.060-0.080 in. (1.524-2.032 mm)
7.4L, 8.1L and 8.2L models	
Intake and exhaust valve (minimum)	0.031 in. (0.787 mm)

Table 5 VALVE SPRING SERVICE SPECIFICATIONS

Measurement	Specification
Valve spring free length	
5.0L and 5.7L models	
With two-piece rear main seal	
Inner spring (damper)	1.86 in. (47.244 mm)*
Lavender stripe spring	2.03 in. (51.562 mm)*
Two green stripe spring	1.91 in. (48.514 mm)*
With one-piece rear main seal	2.02 in. (51.308 mm)*
7.4L models	
With two-piece rear main seal	
Models with single spring	2.12 in. (53.848 mm)*
Models with two springs	
Outer spring	2.250 in. (57.150 mm)*
Inner spring (damper)	2.125 in. (53.975 mm)*
With one-piece rear main seal	
Standard-output models	
Outer spring	2.12 in. (53.848 mm)*
Inner spring (damper)	1.86 in. (47.244 mm)*
High-output models	
Outer spring	2.15 in. (54.610 mm)*

(continued)

Table 5 VALVE SPRING SERVICE SPECIFICATIONS (continued)

Measurement	Specification
Valve spring free length	
7.4L models	
With one-piece rear main seal	
High-output models (continued)	
Inner spring (damper)	1.86 in. (47.244 mm)*
8.1L models	2.219 in. (56.337 mm)*
8.2L models	
Outer spring	2.15 in. (54.610 mm)*
Inner spring (damper)	1.86 in. (47.244 mm)*
Valve spring out of square (maximum)	5/16 in. (8.0 mm)
Valve spring installed height	
5.0L and 5.7L models	
With two-piece rear main seal	
Lavender stripe spring	1.593 in. (40.462 mm)*
Two green stripe spring	1.718 in. (43.637 mm)*
With one-piece rear main seal	
With 12-bolt intake manifold	1.690-1.710 in. (42.926-43.434 mm)
With 8-bolt intake manifold	1.680-1.700 in. (42.672-43.180 mm)
7.4L models	
Standard-output models	
With two-piece rear main seal	1.875 in. (47.625 mm)*
With one-piece rear main seal	1.760-1.910 in. (44.704-48.514 mm)
High-output models	
With two-piece rear main seal	1.875 in. (47.625 mm)*
With one-piece rear main seal	1.880 in. (47.752 mm)*
8.1L models	1.838-1.869 in. (46.685-47.472 mm)
8.2L models	1.880 in. (47.752 mm*)
Valve spring pressure	
5.0L and 5.7L models	
With two-piece rear main seal	
Lavender stripe spring	
At 1.61 in. (40.89 mm)	76-84 lb. (338-374 N)
At 1.15 in. (29.46 mm)	194-206 lb. (863-916 N)
Two green stripe spring	
At 1.70 in. (43.18 mm)	76-84 lb. (338-374 N)
At 1.25 in. (31.75 mm)	194-206 lb. (863-916 N)
With one-piece rear main seal	
At 1.70 in. (43.18 mm)	76-84 lb. (338-374 N)
At 1.27 in. (32.26 mm)	187-203 lb. (832-903 N)
7.4L models	
With two-piece rear main seal	
Models with single spring	
At 1.88 in. (47.75 mm)	74-86 lb. (329-382 N)
At 1.38 in. (35.05 mm)	288-312 lb. (1281-1387 N)
Models with two springs	
At 1.88 in. (47.75 mm)	115-125 lb. (511-556 N)
At 1.38 in. (35.05 mm)	305-325 lb. (1356-1445 N)
With one-piece rear main seal	
Standard-output models	
At 1.84 in. (46.73 mm)	71-79 lb. (316-351 N)
At 1.38 in. (35.05 mm)	238-262 lb. (1058-1165 N)
High-output models	
At 1.88 in. (47.75 mm)	110 lb. (489 N)*
At 1.34 in. (34.03 mm)	316 lb. (1406 N)*
8.1L models	
At 1.808 in. (45.92 mm)	86-94 lb. (381-419 N)
At 1.338 in. (33.99 mm)	216-236 lb. (962-1058 N)
8.2L models	
At 1.88 in. (47.75 mm)	110 lb. (489 N)*
At 1.34 in. (34.03 mm)	316 lb. (1406 N)*

*This value represents the minimum specification.

Table 6 PISTON SERVICE SPECIFICATIONS

Measurement	Specification
Piston pin diameter	
5.0L and 5.7L models	
With 12-bolt intake manifold	0.9270-0.9273 in. (23.546-23.553 mm)
With 8-bolt intake manifold	0.9269-0.9270 in. (23.543-23.546 mm)
7.4L and 8.2L models	0.9895-0.9898 in. (25.133-24.140 mm)
8.1L models	1.0400-1.0401 in. (26.416-26.419 mm)
Piston pin to pin bore clearance	
5.0L and 5.7L models	0.0005-0.0010 in. (0.127-0.0254 mm)
7.4L and 8.2L models	
With two-piece rear main seal	0.0003-0.0010 in. (0.0076-0.0254 mm)
With one-piece rear main seal	0.0002-0.0010 in. (0.0051-0.0254 mm)
8.1L models	0.0004-0.0006 in. (0.0102-0.0152 mm)
8.2L models	0.0002-0.0010 in. (0.0051-0.0254 mm)
Piston pin to rod (interference)	
5.0L and 5.7L models	0.0008-0.0016 in. (0.020-0.040 mm)
7.4L models	0.0008-0.0016 in. (0.020-0.041 mm)
8.1L models	0.0002-0.0007 in. (0.005-0.018 mm)
8.2L models	0.0008-0.0016 in. (0.020-0.041 mm)
Piston skirt clearance	
5.0L and 5.7L models	0.0007-0.0026 in. (0.0178-0.0660 mm)
7.4L models	
Standard-output models	
With two-piece rear main seal	0.0014-0.0035 in. (0.036-0.089 mm)
With one-piece rear main seal	0.0018-0.0030 in. (0.046-0.076 mm)
High-output models	
With two-piece rear main seal	0.0045-0.0075 in. (0.114-0.1905 mm)
With one-piece rear main seal	0.0025-0.0075 in. (0.064-0.190 mm)
8.2L models	
With two-piece rear main seal	0.0040-0.0065 in. (0.102-0.165 mm)
With one-piece rear main seal	0.0040-0.0060 in. (0.102-0.152 mm)
Ring groove side clearance	
5.0L and 5.7L models	
With two-piece rear main seal	
Top and second ring	0.0012-0.0033 in. (0.030-0.084 mm)
Oil ring	0.0020-0.0080 in. (0.051-0.203 mm)
With one-piece rear main seal	
With 12-bolt intake manifold	
Top and second ring	0.0012-0.0032 in. (0.030-0.081 mm)
Oil ring	0.0020-0.0070 in. (0.051-0.178 mm)
With 8-bolt intake manifold	
Top ring	0.0012-0.0035 in. (0.030-0.089 mm)
Second ring	0.0015-0.0040 in. (0.038-0.102 mm)
Oil ring	0.0020-0.0076 in. (0.051-0.193 mm)
7.4L models	
Standard-output models	
With two-piece rear main seal	
Top and second ring	0.0017-0.0042 in. (0.043-0.107 mm)
Oil ring	0.0050-0.0075 in. (0.127-0.190 mm)
With one-piece rear main seal	
Top and second ring	0.0012-0.0039 in. (0.030-0.099 mm)
Oil ring	0.0050-0.0075 in. (0.127-0.190 mm)
High-output models	
Top and second ring	0.0017-0.0042 in. (0.043-0.107 mm)
Oil ring	0.0050-0.0075 in. (0.127-0.190 mm)
8.1L models	
Top and second ring	0.0012-0.0039 in. (0.030-0.099 mm)
Oil ring	0.0020-0.0080 in. (0.051-0.203 mm)
8.2L models	
Top and second ring	0.0017-0.0042 in. (0.043-0.107 mm)

(continued)

6

Table 6 PISTON SERVICE SPECIFICATIONS (continued)

Measurement	Specification
Ring groove side clearance	
8.2L models (continued)	
Oil ring	0.0050-0.0075 in. (0.127-0.190 mm)
Ring end gap	
5.0L and 5.7L models	
With two-piece rear main seal	
Top compression ring	0.010-0.030 in. (0.254-0.762 mm)
Second compression ring	0.010-0.035 in. (0.254-0.889 mm)
Oil ring	0.015-0.055 in. (0.381-1.397 mm)
With one-piece rear main seal	
With 12-bolt intake manifold	
Top compression ring	0.010-0.020 in. (0.254-0.508 mm)
Second compression ring	0.010-0.025 in. (0.254-0.635 mm)
Oil ring	0.015-0.055 in. (0.381-1.397 mm)
With 8-bolt intake manifold	
Top compression ring	0.009-0.025 in. (0.229-0.635 mm)
Second compression ring	0.010-0.035 in. (0.254-0.889 mm)
Oil ring	0.010-0.030 in. (0.254-0.762 mm)
7.4L models	
Standard-output models	
With two-piece rear main seal	
Top compression ring	0.010-0.030 in. (0.254-0.762 mm)
Second compression ring	0.010-0.030 in. (0.254-0.762 mm)
Oil ring	0.015-0.055 in. (0.381-1.397 mm)
With one-piece rear main seal	
Top compression ring	0.010-0.028 in. (0.254-0.711 mm)
Second compression ring	0.016-0.034 in. (0.406-0.864 mm)
Oil ring	0.010-0.031 in. (0.243-0.787 mm)
High-output models	
With two-piece rear main seal	
Top and second ring	0.010-0.030 in. (0.254-0.762 mm)
Oil ring	0.020-0.045 in. (0.508-1.143 mm)
With one-piece rear main seal	
Top compression ring	0.010-0.028 in. (0.254-0.711 mm)
Second compression ring	0.016-0.034 in. (0.406-0.864 mm)
Oil ring	0.020-0.045 in. (0.508-1.143 mm)
8.1L models	
Top compression ring	0.018-0.027 in. (0.457-0.686 mm)
Second compression ring	0.026-0.039 in. (0.660-0.991 mm)
Oil ring	0.0098-0.0299 in. (0.249-0.759 mm)
8.2L models	
With two-piece rear main seal	
Top and second ring	0.010-0.030 in. (0.254-0.762 mm)
Oil ring	0.020-0.045 in. (0.508-1.143 mm)
With one-piece rear main seal	
Top compression ring	0.011-0.031 in. (0.279-0.787 mm)
Second compression ring	0.016-0.036 in. (0.406-0.914 mm)
Oil ring	0.010-0.035 in. (0.254-0.889 mm)

Table 7 CYLINDER BLOCK SERVICE SPECIFICATIONS

Measurement	Specification
Cylinder bore diameter	
5.0L models	3.7350-3.7384 in. (94.869-94.955 mm)

(continued)

Table 7 CYLINDER BLOCK SERVICE SPECIFICATIONS (continued)

Measurement	Specification
Cylinder bore diameter (continued)	
5.7L models	4.0007-4.0017 in. (101.618-101.643 mm)
7.4L models	
Standard-output models	
With two-piece rear main seal	4.2495-4.2525 in. (107.937-108.013 mm)
With one-piece rear main seal	4.2500-4.2507 in. (107.950-107.968 mm)
High-output models	4.2451-4.2525 in. (107.826-108.013 mm)
8.1L models	4.2496-4.2516 in. (107.940-107.990 mm)
8.2L models	
With two-piece rearmain seal	4.4650-4.4725 in. (113.411-113.601 mm)
With one-piece rear main seal	4.4655-4.4662 in. (113.423-113.441 mm)
Maximum cylinder bore out-of-round	0.002 in. (0.050 mm)
Maximum cylinder bore taper	
5.0L, 5.7L, 7.4L and 8.2L models	0.001 in. (0.025 mm)
8.1L models	0.002 in. (0.050 mm)

6

Table 8 CRANKSHAFT AND CONNECTING ROD SERVICE SPECIFICATIONS

Measurement	Specification
Connecting rod bearing oil clearance	
5.0 and 5.7L models	
With two-piece rear main seal	0.0013-0.0030 in. (0.043-0.076 mm)
With one-piece rear main seal	0.0013-0.0027 in. (0.043-0.068 mm)
7.4L models	
Standard-output models	0.0011-0.0029 in. (0.028-0.073 mm)
High-output models	0.0011-0.0030 in. (0.028-0.076 mm)
8.1L models	0.0008-0.0032 in. (0.020-0.081 mm)
8.2L models	0.0011-0.0030 in. (0.028-0.076 mm)
Connecting rod side clearance	
5.0L and 5.7L models	
With two-piece rear main seal	0.008-0.014 in. (0.203-0.355 mm)
With one-piece rear main seal	0.006-0.024 in. (0.152-0.609 mm)
7.4L models	
With two-piece rear main seal	0.013-0.023 in. (0.330-0.584 mm)
With one-piece rear main seal	0.002-0.023 in. (0.051-0.584 mm)
8.1L models	0.015-0.027 in. (0.381-0.685 mm)
8.2L models	0.013-0.023 in. (0.330-0.584 mm)
Connecting rod journal diameter	
5.0L and 5.7L models	
With two-piece rear main seal	2.0988-2.0998 in. (53.310-53.334 mm)
With one-piece rear main seal	2.0978-2.0998 in. (53.284-53.334 mm)
7.4L and 8.2L models	
With two-piece rear main seal	2.1985-2.1995 in. (55.842-55.867 mm)
With one-piece rear main seal	2.1990-2.1996 in. (55.855-55.869 mm)
8.1L models	2.1990-2.1996 in. (55.855-55.869 mm)
Connecting rod journal out-of-round (maximum)	0.001 in. (0.025 mm)
Connecting rod journal taper (maximum)	0.001 in. (0.025 mm)
Crankshaft end play	
5.0L and 5.7L models	
With two-piece rear main seal	0.002-0.006 in. (0.051-0.152 mm)
With one-piece rear main seal	0.002-0.008 in. (0.051-0.203 mm)
7.4L models	
Standard-output models	0.005-0.011 in. (0.127-0.279 mm)
High-output models	0.001-0.006 in. (0.025-0.152 mm)
	(continued)

Table 8 CRANKSHAFT AND CONNECTING ROD SERVICE SPECIFICATIONS (continued)

Measurement	Specification
Crankshaft end play (continued)	
8.1L models	0.005-0.011 in. (0.127-0.279 mm)
8.2L models	0.001-0.006 in. (0.025-0.152 mm)
Crankshaft runout (maximum)	0.002 in. (0.051 mm)
Main bearing oil clearance	
5.0L and 5.7L models	
With two-piece rear main seals	
Front main bearing	0.0010-0.0015 in. (0.025-0.038 mm)
Center main bearings	0.0010-0.0025 in. (0.025-0.063 mm)
Rear main bearing	0.0025-0.0035 in. (0.063-0.089 mm)
With one-piece rear main seal	
Front main bearing	0.0010-0.0020 in. (0.025-0.051 mm)
Center main bearings	0.0010-0.0025 in. (0.025-0.063 mm)
Rear main bearing	0.0010-0.0030 in. (0.025-0.076 mm)
7.4L models	
With two-piece rear main seal	
Front main bearing	0.0010-0.0015 in. (0.025-0.038 mm)
Center main bearings	0.0010-0.0025 in. (0.025-0.063 mm)
Rear main bearing	0.0025-0.0035 in. (0.063-0.89 mm)
With one-piece rear main seal	
Front main bearing	0.0010-0.0030 in. (0.025-0.076 mm)
Center main bearings	0.0010-0.0030 in. (0.025-0.076 mm)
Rear main bearing	0.0025-0.0040 in. (0.063-0.102 mm)
8.1L models	
Front and center main bearings	0.0008-0.0035 in. (0.020-0.089 mm)
Rear main bearing	0.0014-0.0040 in. (0.036-0.101 mm)
8.2L models	
With two-piece rear main seal	
Front main bearing	0.0010-0.0015 in. (0.025-0.038 mm)
Center main bearings	0.0010-0.0025 in. (0.025-0.063 mm)
Rear main bearing	0.0025-0.0035 in. (0.063-0.89 mm)
With one piece rear main seal	
Front main bearing	0.0010-0.0015 in. (0.025-0.038 mm)
Center main bearings	0.0010-0.0025 in. (0.025-0.063 mm)
Rear main bearing	0.0025-0.0040 in. (0.063-0.102 mm)
Main bearing journal diameter	
5.0L and 5.7L models	
With two-piece rear main seal	
Front main journal	2.4484-2.4493 in. (62.189-62.212 mm)
Center main journals	2.4481-2.4490 in. (62.181-62.205 mm)
Rear main journal	2.4479-2.4488 in. (62.177-62.199 mm)
With one-piece rear main seal	
Front main journal	2.4483-2.4492 in. (62.187-62.210 mm)
Center main journals	2.4480-2.4490 in. (62.179-62.205 mm)
Rear main journal	2.4479-2.4490 in. (62.177-62.205 mm)
7.4L and 8.2L models	
With two-piece rear main seal	
Front main journal	2.7485-2.7494 in. (69.812-69.835 mm)
Center journals	2.7481-2.7490 in. (69.802-69.825 mm)
Rear main journal	2.7478-2.7488 in. (69.794-69.819 mm)
With one-piece rear main seal	
All journals	2.7482-2.7489 in. (69.804-69.822 mm)
8.1L models	
All journals	2.7482-2.7489 in. (69.804-69.822 mm)
Main bearing journal out-of-round (maximum)	0.001 in. (0.025 mm)
Main bearing taper (maximum)	0.001 in. (0.025 mm)

Chapter Seven

Fuel Systems

Review *Safety* in Chapter One before performing any service procedures on the fuel system.

Refer to *Servicing the Fuel System* in this chapter prior to removal and disassembly of any fuel system component. This section provides information needed to perform a safe, reliable and effective repair.

Table 1 lists tightening specifications for most fuel system fasteners. Use the general tightening torque specification in Chapter One for fasteners not listed in **Table 1**. **Table 1** is located at the end of this chapter.

> *WARNING*
> *Use caution when working with the fuel system. Never smoke around fuel or fuel vapor. Make sure no flame or source of ignition is present in the work area. Flame or sparks can ignite fuel or vapor and cause a fire or explosion.*

SERVICING THE FUEL SYSTEM

Always use gloves and eye protection when working with the fuel system. Take all necessary precautions against fire or explosion. To prevent arcing or accidental starting, always disconnect the battery cables *before* servicing any marine engine.

When removing and installing components (especially carburetor components), pay close attention to avoid installing them in the wrong locations during assembly.

Capture fuel from disconnected hoses or fittings using a small container or clean shop towel. Try to use a clear container because it allows visual inspection of the fuel. If water or other contamination is noted in the fuel, clean the fuel tank and all other fuel delivery components.

Before disconnecting any fuel system hose or fitting, always relieve the fuel pressure as described in the removal or disassembly procedures.

Inspect all hoses for leakage or deterioration when servicing the fuel system. Damaged fuel hoses pose a safety hazard. In addition, pieces of deteriorated or damaged hoses can break free and block fuel passages in the system.

Gaskets, Seals and O-rings

To ensure a safe and reliable repair, use only factory-recommended replacement parts. Some commonly available seals or O-rings are not suitable for contact with fuel.

To avoid potential fuel or air leakage, replace all disturbed seals and O-rings anytime a fuel system component is removed from the engine. Consider reusing a seal or O-ring only if a replacement is not available and the original is in excellent condition.

To help avoid the potential for contamination during lengthy downtime, have the required gaskets or repair kit on hand prior to removal and disassembly of the component(s).

Cleaning Fuel System Components

The most important step in carburetor, throttle body and fuel rail repair is the cleaning process. Use only solvents suitable for use on carburetors. Some cleaning agents can damage fuel system components. Aerosol carburetor cleaners are available at most automotive parts stores. They effectively remove most stubborn deposits. Avoid using any solvents not suitable for aluminum.

Remove all plastic or rubber components from the assembly before cleaning them with solvent. Gently scrape away gasket material with a scraper. Never scrape away any metal from the component. Use a stiff parts-cleaning brush and solvent to remove deposits from the carburetor bowl. Never use a wire brush because the sealing surfaces can quickly become damaged. Blow out all passages and orifices with compressed air (**Figure 1**). A piece of straw from a broom works well to clean small passages. Never use stiff wire for this purpose because the wire can enlarge the size of the passage and possibly alter the fuel system calibration. If the deposits are particularly difficult to remove, allow components to soak in the solvent for several hours.

Use great care and patience when removing fuel jets and other threaded or pressed-in components. Clean the passage without removing the jet if it cannot be removed without causing damage. Carburetor fuel jets are easily damaged.

One small particle in the carburetor or fuel injection system can compromise the cleaning process. Continue to clean until *all* deposits and debris are removed.

Fuel System Inspection

Place all components on a clean surface as they are removed. Arrange these components in a manner consistent with the provided illustrations. This arrangement saves time and helps make sure the parts are installed in the correct locations.

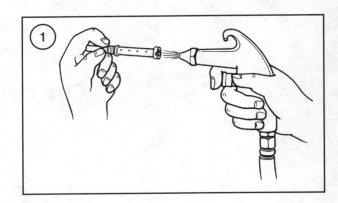

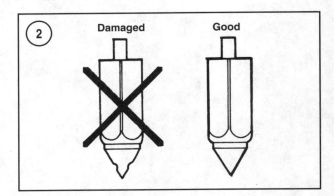

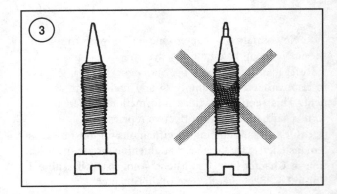

Inspect the inlet needle (carburetor-equipped models) for wear or deterioration (**Figure 2**). Replace the inlet needle unless the tip is perfectly cone-shaped (**Figure 2**). Inspect the inlet needle seat for grooves or damage. Carburetor flooding is likely if a worn or faulty inlet needle or seat is used.

Inspect the tip of the pilot screw (carburetor-equipped models) for wear or damage (**Figure 3**). Damage to the tip usually occurs from improper seating of the screw during adjustment. In many instances, the seat for the tip is also damaged. Damage to the screw or seat will cause rough idle or improper off-idle engine operation. Replace the

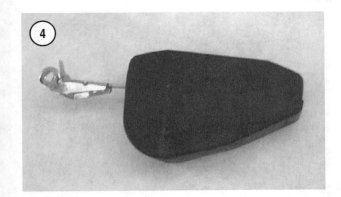

Check the float level settings (**Figure 5**) prior to assembling the carburetor. Use an accurate ruler or a caliper with depth-reading capability. Set the float *exactly* as specified to help ensure proper carburetor operation. Specific instructions are provided in the assembly instructions.

When servicing the carburetor or throttle body, move the throttle lever from closed to wide-open throttle. Remove the throttle plate and repeat this step if binding or rough operation is noted. Continued binding indicates a bent throttle shaft. If free movement is noted with the plate removed, an improperly aligned or damaged throttle plate is evident. Replace the throttle shaft, carburetor or throttle body as necessary to eliminate binding. Apply a suitable threadlocking compound and stake all throttle plate retaining screws to prevent loosening.

Inspecting Fuel Jets

Fuel jets (**Figure 6**) meter the fuel flow through various passages in the carburetor. They along with other components allow the carburetor to deliver the precise amount of fuel needed for the engine. Fuel jet sizes vary by model and carburetor location on the engine. Fuel jets normally have a number stamped on the side or end. Note the fuel jet number and location in the carburetor prior to removal. Always reinstall the fuel jets and other carburetor components in the correct locations.

Purchase replacement jets at an Indmar marine engine dealership or a carburetor specialty shop. For proper engine operation, replacement jets must have the same size and shape of opening as the original fuel jets. Improper engine operation, increased exhaust emissions or potentially serious engine damage can result from using incorrect fuel jets.

Using the engine at higher elevation (5000 ft. [1524 m]) might require alternate fuel jets to achieve optimal engine operation. If necessary, contact an Indmar marine engine dealership in an area with a similar elevation for recommended jet changes.

Never install a damaged jet in the carburetor. The fuel or air flow characteristics might be altered. Altering the fuel and air flow can cause an engine malfunction or potentially serious engine damage.

FUEL PUMP AND FILTER
REPLACEMENT

This section describes replacement of the low-pressure mechanical or electric fuel pump and the filter used on carburetor-equipped models. Replacement of the high-

screw or carburetor if worn or damaged components are noted.

Inspect the float (**Figure 4**, typical) for wear or damage. Some floats are made of a translucent material allowing visual detection of fuel inside the float.

Push a thumbnail gently against the material on nontranslucent floats. A leaking or saturated float is indicated if fuel appears at the thumbnail contact area. Replace the float if visibly damaged, leaking or saturated. Check the float for free movement on the float pin. Replace the float if it does not move freely.

pressure electric fuel pump used on electronic fuel injection models is described in the *Electronic Fuel Injection (EFI)* section in this chapter.

Mechanical Fuel Pump

A mechanical fuel pump (**Figure 7**, typical) is used on 1983-1997 5.0L/5.7L and 1983-1990 7.4L/8.2L carburetor-equipped models. An electric fuel pump is used on all models equipped with electronic fuel injection and 1998-2003 5.0L/5.7L and 1991-2003 7.4L/8.2L carburetor-equipped models. Two bolts secure the mechanical pump to the starboard side of the cylinder block. Replace the pump if faulty. The manufacturer does not offer a repair kit.

WARNING
Avoid the risk of serious bodily injury or death. Use only the manufacturer-recommended part when replacing fuel hoses or tubing. Other types of hoses or tubing might not meet the requirements and might fail prematurely and leak fuel, which causes an extreme fire and explosion hazard.

WARNING
Rust deposits in the fuel filter might indicate rust in the boat fuel tank and the need for immediate inspection or replacement. Rust will eventually allow fuel to leak from the tank and result in a dangerous fire and explosion hazard.

CAUTION
Rust or other deterioration in the fuel tank will migrate to and block filters and other fuel system components. The blockage will restrict fuel flow and lead to a lean operating condition and possible engine damage.

Removal and installation

The fuel pump mounts on the starboard side of the cylinder block directly below the No. 2 spark plug. On V-drive models, the No. 2 spark plug is on the port side.
1. Disconnect the battery cables.
2. Place a suitable container or shop towel under the fuel pump to capture spilled fuel.
3. Loosen the clamp or fitting and then disconnect the supply hose or line from the fuel pump (A, **Figure 7**). Drain residual fuel from the supply hose.
   a. If a hose connects to the fuel pump, inspect the hose for brittleness, cracks, deterioration or damage. Re-

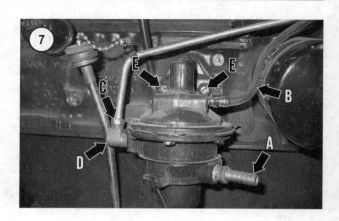

place the fuel supply hose with marine-grade and U.S. Coast Guard-approved hose.
   b. If a metal line connects to the fuel pump, inspect the line for twisted, cracked, corroded, bent or kinked areas. Inspect the fitting for damaged threads, damaged seating surfaces or rounding of the hex section. Replace the line and fitting as an assembly if these or other defects are evident.
4. Disconnect the sight tube (B, **Figure 7**) from the fuel pump fitting. Inspect the sight tube for brittle, deteriorated or cracked surfaces. Replace the sight tube with the manufacturer-recommended tube if these or other defects are evident. *Do not* replace the tube with any other type of hose or tubing.
5. Engage a wrench onto the elbow (D, **Figure 7**) or outlet line fitting that threads into the pump body to prevent rotation. Then use a flare nut wrench to *slightly* loosen the outlet fuel line fitting (C, **Figure 7**). Wrap a shop towel around the fitting and then loosen the fitting by hand. Allow residual fuel to drain from the fuel line. When completely drained, unthread the fitting and disconnect the fuel line from the pump. Cap or plug the hoses or lines to prevent leakage or contamination.
6. Loosen the two pump attaching bolts (E, **Figure 7**) and lockwashers. Do not remove the bolts at this time.
7. Hold the pump in position while an assistant rotates the crankshaft pulley in the normal direction of rotation. Refer to *Determining Engine Rotational Direction* in Chapter Six. Have the assistant stop rotating the engine when you feel a reduction in tension against the pump. This indicates the low point of the camshaft eccentric is aligned with the pump rod.
8. Remove the bolts and pull the pump off the mounting plate (**Figure 8**). Drain any residual fuel from the inlet and outlet fittings. Remove the gasket from the fuel pump or mounting pump mating surface. Discard the gasket.
9. Remove the two screws at the bottom of the mounting plate and then carefully pull the plate off the cylinder

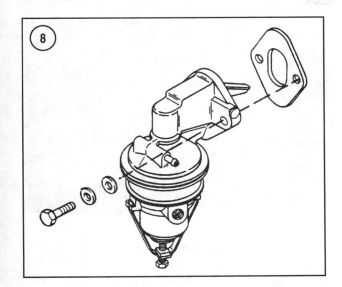

block. Be prepared to capture the pump pushrod as the plate is removed. Note which end of the pump rod was driving against the fuel pump and label or mark accordingly. If reused, the pump rod must be installed with the same end driving against the camshaft eccentric. Remove the gasket from the mounting plate or cylinder block mating surface. Discard the gasket. Promptly clean up any spilled fuel.

10. Inspect the pump rod for excessive wear, discoloration or bending and replace as needed. Discoloration or excessive wear is caused by insufficient lubrication. Insufficient lubrication is usually caused by fuel leaking from the fuel pump and diluting the lubricating oil. Replace the fuel pump if it is suspected of leaking.

11. Thoroughly clean the fuel pump, mounting plate and mounting surface on the cylinder block. Scrape all gasket material and sealant from the mating surfaces. *Do not* damage the mating surfaces.

12. If replacing the pump, remove the inlet and outlet fittings from the pump. Clean all old sealant from the fitting.

13. Apply a heavy coat of clean grease to the end of the pushrod and then insert the pushrod into the bore. If reusing the pump rod, make sure the end that was driving against the pump arm is facing outward. Push on the rod until fully seated against the camshaft eccentric.

14. Apply a coat of Permatex Gasket Sealing Compound to both sides of the *new* mounting plate-to-cylinder block gasket and the threads of the mounting plate bolts. Fit the gasket onto the mounting plate. Then fit the plate and gasket onto the cylinder block. Make sure the gasket is located between the mounting plate and block. Thread the two screws into the lower openings and tighten by hand only.

15. Apply a coat or Permatex Gasket Sealing Compound to both sides of the *new* fuel pump-to-mounting plate gasket and the mounting bolts. Fit the gasket onto the fuel pump mating surface.

16. Position the pump with the pump arm angled downward and toward the mounting plate (**Figure 8**). Carefully guide the pump onto the mounting plate. To avoid dislodging the pump rod, guide the pump arm into the lower end of the elongated opening in the mounting plate. Seat the pump against the mounting plate. Align the mounting bolt openings and then thread the bolts into the pump, mounting plate and cylinder block. Tighten the bolts evenly to 20 ft.-lb. (27 N•m). Then tighten the two lower mounting plate bolts to 15 ft.-lb. (20 N•m).

17. If removed, apply a light coat of Loctite Pipe Sealant with Teflon to the threads of the fuel inlet and outlet fittings. Purchase the sealant from an automotive parts store or GM automobile dealership (GM part No. 12346004). *Do not* allow sealant into the fuel passage of the fittings. Thread the elbow or outlet fitting (D, **Figure 7**) into the fuel pump and tighten to 48-59 in.-lb. (5.4-6.7 N•m). Tighten the elbow *slightly* if necessary to properly align with the fuel outlet line. Thread the fuel inlet barb fitting (A, **Figure 7**) or flare fitting into the fuel pump by hand. Then tighten to 48-59 in.-lb. (5.4-6.7 N•m). If the inlet line is a metal line, tighten the inlet fitting *slightly* to align the fitting with the inlet line.

18. Attach the fuel outlet line to the elbow or outlet fitting on the fuel pump. Engage a wrench onto the fuel pump elbow or fitting to prevent rotation. Then use a flare nut wrench to tighten the fuel line fitting to 177-212 in.-lb. (20-24 N•m).

19A. If a rubber fuel inlet hose is used, install the hose clamp over the end and then push the fuel supply hose fully over the fuel inlet fitting (A, **Figure 7**). Align the hose clamp over the fitting and then securely tighten the clamp.

19B. If a metal fuel inlet line is used, attach the fuel inlet line to the inlet fitting on the fuel pump. Engage a wrench onto the fuel pump inlet fitting to prevent rotation. Then use a flare nut wrench to tighten the fuel line fitting to 177-212 in.-lb. (20-24 N•m).

20. Push the sight tube (B, **Figure 7**) fully over the fuel pump fitting. Secure the tube to the fitting with a plastic locking clamp. Secure the tube to the fuel line with a plastic locking clamp. Do not tighten the clamp to the point that the tube begins to collapse.

21. Connect the battery cables.

CAUTION
Use a flush test device or other method to supply the engine with cooling water if running the engine with the boat out of the wa-

7

ter. The seawater pump is quickly damaged if operated without adequate cooling water.

22. Start the engine and immediately check for fuel leaking from the fitting and oil leaking from the pump-to-cylinder block mating surface. Stop the engine and repair any leaks before operating the engine.

Electric Fuel Pump (Carburetor-Equipped Models)

Two types of electric fuel pumps are used on carburetor-equipped models. The larger and more common Carter pump (**Figure 9**) mounts on the starboard side of the engine next to the side engine mount. The smaller and less common Delco pump (**Figure 10**) mounts on the front starboard side of the engine. To prevent premature failure of the pump, replace the water-separating fuel filter (**Figure 11**) when replacing the pump and at the specified maintenance intervals. Water-separating fuel filter replacement and maintenance intervals are described in Chapter Three.

Removal and installation (Carter pump)

1. Disconnect the battery cables. Use compressed air to blow debris and loose material off the electric fuel pump, electrical connectors, fuel line fittings and mounting bracket.
2. Pull the rubber boots (A and B, **Figure 12**) away from the terminals. Note the wire routing and connection points and then disconnect the wires from the pump.
3. Place a suitable container under the fuel pump to capture spilled fuel.
4. Loosen the clamp or fitting and then disconnect the supply hose or line from the fuel pump (A, **Figure 9**). Allow the fuel to drain fully from the pump supply hose. Inspect the fuel supply hose for cracks, deterioration or damage. Replace the fuel supply hose with marine-grade and U.S. Coast Guard-approved hose if these or other defects are evident.
5. To prevent rotation, engage a wrench onto the brass fitting or elbow on the opposite side of the pump (C, **Figure 12**). Use a flare nut wrench to *slightly* loosen the outlet fuel line fitting. Wrap a shop towel around the fitting and then loosen the fitting by hand. Allow all fuel to drain from the fuel line. When completely drained, unthread the fitting and disconnect the fuel line from the pump. Promptly clean up any spilled fuel.
6. Support the pump. Then remove the three screws (B, **Figure 9**) that secure the pump to the mounting bracket. Remove the pump from the bracket. Remove the sleeves

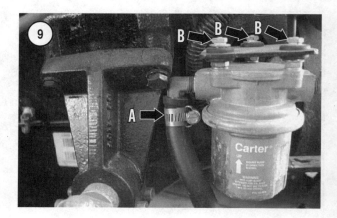

from the grommets. Inspect the grommets in the mounting brackets for damage or deterioration and replace as needed.

7. Drain the fuel from the fuel pump. Plug or cap the disconnected hoses, lines and fittings to prevent leakage and contamination.

8. If the fuel pump will be replaced, remove the pump inlet and outlet fittings. Clean all old sealant from the fitting.

9. If removed, apply a light coat of Loctite Pipe Sealant with Teflon to the threads of the fuel inlet and outlet fit-

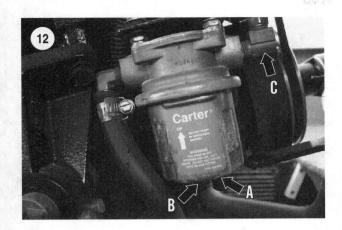

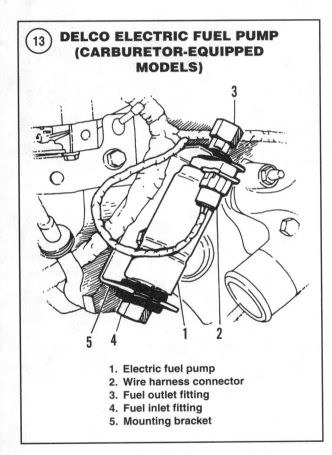

DELCO ELECTRIC FUEL PUMP (CARBURETOR-EQUIPPED MODELS)

1. Electric fuel pump
2. Wire harness connector
3. Fuel outlet fitting
4. Fuel inlet fitting
5. Mounting bracket

grommet and fuel pump. Securely tighten the three screws.

11. Tighten the fuel outlet elbow or fitting *slightly* if necessary to properly align it with the fuel outlet line. Thread the fuel outlet line into the fuel pump by hand. Engage a wrench onto the fuel pump elbow or fitting to prevent rotation. Then use a flare nut wrench to tighten the fuel line fitting to 177-212 in.-lb. (20-24 N•m).

12A. If a rubber fuel inlet hose is used, install the hose clamp over the end and then push the fuel hose fully over the fuel inlet fitting (A, **Figure 9**). Align the hose clamp over the fitting and then securely tighten the clamp.

12B. If a metal fuel inlet line is used, thread the fuel inlet line into the inlet fitting on the fuel pump. Engage a wrench onto the fuel pump inlet fitting to prevent rotation. Then use a flare nut wrench to tighten the fuel line fitting to 177-212 in.-lb. (20-24 N•m).

13. Connect the engine wire harness to the corresponding terminals on the bottom of the pump (A and B, **Figure 12**). Securely tighten the terminal nuts. Then carefully push the insulator boots over the wire terminals. Work carefully to avoid damaging the terminal or tearing the boots.

14. Connect the battery cables.

CAUTION
Use a flush test device or other means to supply the engine with cooling water if running the engine with the boat out of the water. The seawater pump is quickly damaged if operated without adequate cooling water.

15. Start the engine and immediately check for fuel leaking from the fittings, pump body or other fuel system components. Stop the engine and repair any leaks before operating the engine.

Removal and installation (Delco pump)

1. Disconnect the battery cables. Use compressed air to blow debris and loose material off the electric fuel pump, fuel filter and mounting bracket.

2. Depress the locking clip. Then carefully unplug the harness (2, **Figure 13**) from the pump.

3. Place a suitable container under the fuel pump and filter to capture spilled fuel.

4. To prevent rotation, engage a wrench onto the outlet fitting on the top of the pump (3, **Figure 13**). Use a flare nut wrench to *slightly* loosen the outlet line. Wrap a shop towel around the fitting and then loosen the fitting by hand. Allow all fuel to drain from the fuel line. When completely drained, unthread the fitting and disconnect the outlet line from the pump.

tings or elbows. Purchase the sealant from an automotive parts store or GM automobile dealership (GM part No. 12346004). *Do not* allow sealant into the fuel passage of the fittings. Thread the fittings into the fuel pump and tighten to 48-59 in.-lb. (5.4-6.7 N•m).

10. Insert the sleeves into the grommets in the mounting bracket. Fit the replacement pump onto the mounting bracket. Thread the three screws (B, **Figure 9**) into the

7

5. To prevent rotation, engage a wrench onto the inlet fitting on the top of the pump (4, **Figure 13**). Use a flare nut wrench to *slightly* loosen the inlet line. Wrap a shop towel around the fitting and then loosen the fitting by hand. Allow all fuel to drain from the fuel line. When completely drained, unthread the fitting and disconnect the inlet line from the pump. Promptly clean up any spilled fuel.

6. Support the fuel pump. Then remove the two bolts that secure the fuel pump mounting bracket (5, **Figure 13**) to the cylinder head. Carefully pull the fuel pump out of the mounting bracket slots. Remove the grommet from the upper and lower end of the fuel pump. Inspect the grommets for damage or deterioration and replace as needed.

7. Drain the fuel from the fuel pump inlet and outlet. Plug or cap the disconnected hoses, lines and fittings to prevent leakage and contamination.

8. Engage a wrench onto the hex-shaped end at the bottom of the fuel pump. Hold the wrench and use a flare nut wrench to remove the brass outlet fitting (3, **Figure 13**) from the top of the fuel pump. Remove the O-ring from the fitting or pump outlet. Discard the O-ring.

9. Lubricate new O-rings with dishwashing soap and then install O-rings onto the fuel pump outlet fitting. Work carefully to avoid tearing the O-rings.

10. Hand-thread the outlet fitting into the fuel pump. Engage a wrench onto the hex-shaped end at the bottom of the fuel pump. Hold the wrench to prevent the fuel pump from rotating. Then tighten the pump outlet fitting to 60-84 in.-lb. (6.8-9.5 N•m).

11. Fit the grommets onto the upper and lower ends of the fuel pump. Guide the slots in the grommets over the slots in the mounting bracket. Then push the fuel pump fully into the bracket.

12. Align the two bolt openings and then fit the fuel pump mounting bracket onto the cylinder head. Thread the two bolts into the bracket and cylinder head. Tighten the two bolts evenly to 20-25 ft.-lb. (27-34 N•m).

13. Hand-thread the fuel outlet line into the fuel pump (3, **Figure 13**). Engage a wrench onto the outlet fitting and then tighten the fuel line fitting to 177-212 in.-lb. (20-24 N•m).

14. Hand-thread the fuel inlet line fitting into the fuel pump (4, **Figure 13**). Engage a wrench onto the outlet line fitting and then tighten the fuel line fitting to 177-212 in.-lb. (20-24 N•m).

15. Carefully plug the engine harness connector (2, **Figure 13**) onto the fuel pump.

16. Connect the battery cables.

CAUTION
Use a flush test device or other means to supply the engine with cooling water if running the engine with the boat out of the wa-

ter. The seawater pump is quickly damaged if operated without adequate cooling water.

17. Start the engine and immediately check for leaking fuel. Stop the engine and repair any leaks before operating the engine.

CARBURETOR

This section covers removal, repair and installation of the two-barrel and four-barrel carburetors as well as replacement of the carburetor fuel inlet filter.

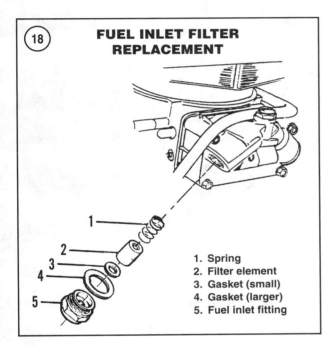

FUEL INLET FILTER REPLACEMENT

1. Spring
2. Filter element
3. Gasket (small)
4. Gasket (larger)
5. Fuel inlet fitting

Fuel Inlet Filter Replacement

Replace the fuel inlet filter if blockage is suspected or if contamination is noted in other fuel system components.

1. Disconnect the battery cables.

2. If so equipped, disconnect the breather tube (C, **Figure 14**) from the flame arrestor (B). Unthread the screw (A, **Figure 14**) and then lift the flame arrestor off the carburetor (**Figure 15**).

3. Use compressed air to blow debris and loose material off the fuel line and carburetor fitting.

NOTE
*Some models use a four-barrel Holley carburetor equipped with twin fuel inlet (**Figure 16**). All other carburetors use a single fuel inlet (**Figure 17**).*

4A. On models using a carburetor with a single fuel inlet fitting (**Figure 17**), disconnect the fuel inlet line as follows:

   a. Hold the inlet fitting (A, **Figure 17**, typical) with a wrench to prevent rotation. Then use a flare nut wrench to *slightly* loosen the fuel line fitting (B, **Figure 17**).

   b. Wrap a shop towel around the fitting and then loosen the fitting by hand. Allow all fuel to drain from the fuel line.

   c. When completely drained, unthread the fitting and disconnect the fuel line from the carburetor.

4B. On models using a carburetor with twin fuel inlets, disconnect the fuel inlet lines as follows:

   a. Hold the fuel line junction (A, **Figure 16**) with a wrench to provide support. Then use a flare nut wrench to *slightly* loosen the fuel line fitting that threads into the junction.

   b. Wrap a shop towel around the fitting and then loosen the fitting by hand. Allow all fuel to drain from the fuel line.

   c. When completely drained, unthread the fitting and disconnect the fuel line from the junction.

   d. Hold the front inlet fitting (A, **Figure 17**, typical) with a wrench to prevent rotation. Then use a flare nut wrench to *slightly* loosen the fuel line fitting (B, **Figure 17**).

   e. Hold the rear inlet fitting (A, **Figure 17**, typical) with a wrench to prevent rotation. Then use a flare nut wrench to *slightly* loosen the fuel line fitting (B, **Figure 17**).

   f. Wrap a shop towel around both fittings and then simultaneously unthread both fittings by hand. Carefully pull the junction line and fittings out of the carburetor inlet.

5. Use a socket to *slightly* loosen the inlet fitting(s) (5, **Figure 18**). Wrap a shop towel around the fitting(s) and then loosen by hand. Allow all fuel to drain from the inlet fitting(s).

6. Unthread and remove the inlet fitting(s). Pull the spring (1, **Figure 18**) out of the carburetor. Inspect the spring(s) for corrosion damage or weak spring tension. Replace the spring if necessary. If corroded, disassemble the carburetor and clean the passages as described in this section.

7. Pull the filter element (2, **Figure 18**) out of the fitting(s). Remove the gaskets (3 and 4, **Figure 18**) from the inlet fitting(s). Discard the gaskets. Clean the inlet fitting(s) with solvent and dry with compressed air.

WARNING
Rust deposits in the fuel filter might indicate rust in the boat fuel tank and the need for

7

immediate inspection or replacement. Rust will eventually allow fuel to leak from the tank and result in a dangerous fire and explosion hazard.

8. Inspect the filter(s) for sediment or rust deposits. If rust is found in the filter, inspect the fuel tank for rust damage. Replace the fuel tank if rust or deterioration is evident. White sediment usually indicates water has contaminated the fuel system. Corrosion of the fuel lines, fuel pump and fuel tank creates the white sediment. Inspect a fuel sample for water. If water is found, drain the tank and refill with fresh fuel before operating the engine. Discard the filter. If the filter must be reused, thoroughly clean the filter with solvent and dry with compressed air. *Do not* reuse the filter if damaged or if it cannot be completely cleaned.

9. Install a *new* gasket (4, **Figure 18**) over the inlet fitting and seat it against the step on the fitting. Install a *new* gasket (3, **Figure 18**) into the inlet fitting and center over the fuel passage. If the carburetor has twin fuel inlet fittings, repeat this step for the remaining fitting.

10. Install the filter element (2, **Figure 18**) into the inlet fitting with the open end facing the smaller gasket. Install the spring (1, **Figure 18**) into the carburetor. If the carburetor has twin fuel inlet fittings, repeat this step for the remaining fitting.

11. Guide the filter element into the carburetor. The closed end of the filter must contact the spring. Thread the inlet fitting into the carburetor by hand. Securely tighten the fitting. If the carburetor has twin fuel inlet fittings, repeat this step for the remaining fitting.

12A. On models using a carburetor with a single fuel inlet, connect the fuel inlet line as follows:

   a. Hand-thread the fuel line into the inlet fitting.

   b. To prevent rotation, engage a wrench onto the inlet fitting (A, **Figure 17**). Then use a flare nut wrench to tighten the fuel line fitting (B, **Figure 17**) to 132-156 in.-lb. (14.9-17.6 N•m).

12B. On models using a carburetor with twin fuel inlets, connect the fuel inlet lines as follows:

   a. Align the fuel lines with the openings in the carburetor.

   b. Simultaneously guide the fuel line fittings into the carburetor. Simultaneously hand-thread both fuel lines into the carburetor.

   c. Hand-thread the fuel line fitting into the fuel line junction (A, **Figure 16**). Do not tighten the fitting at this time.

   d. Engage a wrench onto the rear inlet fitting (A, **Figure 17**) to prevent rotation. Then use a flare nut wrench to tighten the fuel line fitting (B, **Figure 17**) to 132-156 in.-lb. (14.9-17.6 N•m).

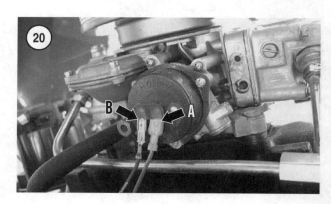

   e. Engage a wrench onto the front inlet fitting (A, **Figure 17**) to prevent rotation, then use a flare nut wrench to tighten the fuel line fitting (B, **Figure 17**) to 132-156 in.-lb. (14.9-17.6 N•m).

   f. Engage a wrench onto the fuel line junction (A, **Figure 16**) to provide support. Then use a flare nut wrench to tighten the fitting (B, **Figure 16**) to 132-156 in.-lb. (14.9-17.6 N•m).

13. Install the flame arrestor onto the carburetor (**Figure 15**). Insert the screw (A, **Figure 14**) into the flame arrestor opening and guide into the threaded opening at the top of the carburetor. If necessary, lift the flame arrestor slightly to guide the screw. Securely tighten the screw. If so equipped, connect the breather tube (C, **Figure 14**) to the flame arrestor (B).

14. Connect the battery cables.

CAUTION
Use a flush test device or other means to supply the engine with cooling water if running the engine with the boat out of the water. The seawater pump is quickly damaged if operated without adequate cooling water.

15. Start the engine and immediately check for leaking fuel. Stop the engine and repair any leaks before operating the engine.

Two-Barrel Carburetor

The two-barrel Holley carburetor (**Figure 19**) can be identified by the single side-mounted float bowl. This section describes removal, repair and installation of the carburetor.

Removal

1. Disconnect the battery cables. Use compressed air to blow debris and loose material off the carburetor and intake manifold.
2. Disconnect the fuel line and remove the fuel inlet filter as described in this section.
3. Carefully unplug the purple or purple/white wire (A, **Figure 20**) and black wire (B) from the electric choke.
4. On models using a mechanical fuel pump, inspect the clear or translucent sight tube connected to the carburetor for the presence of fuel. Replace the mechanical fuel pump as described in this chapter if any trace of fuel is in

the sight tube. Disconnect the sight tube from the carburetor. Replace the sight tube with the recommended tube if any defects are evident. *Do not* replace the tube with any other hose or tubing.
5. If so equipped, unplug the PCV hose (A, **Figure 21**, typical) from the rear of the carburetor.
6. Push the cable end retainer (A, **Figure 22**) toward the cable anchor (B) and then pull the cable end off the carburetor lever pin.
7. Remove the four carburetor mounting nuts (B, **Figure 21**, typical) and then lift the carburetor off the intake manifold.
8. Remove the carburetor mounting gasket from the intake manifold or carburetor base. Discard the gasket. *Carefully* scrape all gasket material from the surfaces. *Do not* damage the mating surfaces.
9. Use an aerosol carburetor cleaner to remove oily deposits from the mating surfaces.

Installation

1. Install a *new* carburetor mounting gasket over the studs and seat it against the intake manifold. Make sure the gasket openings match the intake manifold.
2. Install the carburetor onto the intake manifold. Then thread the four nuts onto the studs. Tighten the nuts in a crossing pattern to 13-19 N•m (115-168 in.-lb.).
3. On models using a mechanical fuel pump, push the sight tube fully over the carburetor fitting. Secure the tube to the fitting with a plastic locking clamp. Do not tighten the clamp to the point where the tube begins to collapse.
4. If so equipped, plug the PCV hose (A, **Figure 21**, typical) fully onto the fitting on the rear of the carburetor.
5. Plug the purple or purple/white (A, **Figure 20**) and black wire (B) onto the electric choke. The wires must fit snugly on the choke terminals. If necessary, remove the wire and squeeze the terminals *slightly* to achieve a snug fit.
6. Push the cable end retainer (A, **Figure 22**) toward the cable anchor (B). Then fit the cable end fully over the ball-shaped carburetor lever pin. Rotate the retainer to align the slot in the back of the retainer with the pin. Then slide the slot in the retainer over the pin. The internal spring holds the retainer in position. Tug lightly on the cable end to verify a secure connection.
7. Install the inlet fuel filter and connect the fuel line as described in this chapter. Refer to *Fuel Inlet Filter Replacement*.
8. Connect the battery cables.

CAUTION
Use a flush test device or other means to
supply the engine with cooling water if run-

7

TWO-BARREL CARBURETOR (HOLLEY)

㉓

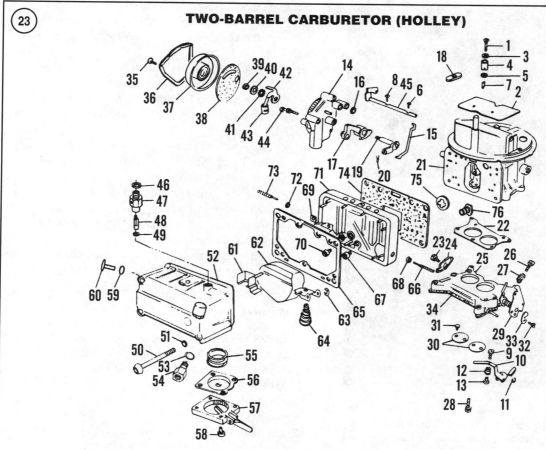

1. Screw	28. Screw	54. Fuel inlet filter nut
2. Choke plate	29. Throttle shaft	55. Spring
3. Gasket	30. Throttle plate	56. Diaphragm
4. Accelerator pump discharge nozzle	31. Screw	57. Accelerator pump cover
5. Gasket	32. Screw	58. Screw and lockwasher
6. Screw	33. Accelerator pump cam	59. Gasket
7. Discharge needle	34. Gasket	60. Fuel level sight plug
8. Screw	35. Screw	61. Baffle plate*
9. Screw	36. Retainer	62. Float*
10. Accelerator pump lever	37. Choke cover	63. E-clip*
11. Retainer	38. Gasket	64. Float spring*
12. Spring	39. Nut	65. Float bowl gasket
13. Sleeve nut	40. Lockwasher	66. Idle mixture screw
14. Choke housing	41. Spacer	67. Main fuel jet
15. Choke rod	42. Choke lever	68. Seal
16. Gasket	43. Choke piston	69. Baffle plate
17. Fast idle cam	44. Screw and washer	70. Main fuel jet
18. Choke rod seal	45. Choke valve shaft	71. Metering block
19. Choke lever	46. Gasket*	72. Seal
20. Retainer	47. Inlet needle seat*	73. Idle mixture screw
21. Carburetor body	48. Inlet needle*	74. Metering block gasket
22. Throttle body gasket	49. Pull clip*	75. Power valve gasket
23. Screw	50. Screw	76. Power valve
24. Diaphragm lever	51. Gasket	
25. Throttle body	52. Float bowl	*Used on carburetor with
26. Idle speed adjusting screw	53. Gasket	side-hinged float assembly.
27. Spring		

ning the engine with the boat out of the water. The seawater pump is quickly damaged if operated without adequate cooling water.

9. Adjust the throttle cable and idle speed as described in Chapter Five.

10. Start the engine and immediately check for leaking fuel. Stop the engine and repair any leaks before operating the engine.

Disassembly

Refer to **Figure 23** for this procedure.

1. Remove the carburetor as described in this section.

2. Remove the four screws (**Figure 24**) securing the float bowl and metering block to the carburetor body. Remove the gaskets from the screws or float bowl. Discard the gaskets. Carefully pull the float bowl (**Figure 25**) and then the metering block (**Figure 26**) off the carburetor body. Pull the plastic baffle (69, **Figure 23**) off the metering block pins.

3. If so equipped, carefully pry the plugs out of the idle mixture screw openings on the sides of the metering block (**Figure 27**). Turn the idle mixture screws (**Figure 28**) inward until *lightly* seated. Record the number of turns required to lightly seat the screws for reference during reassembly. Remove the screws and then remove and discard the seals from the screws.

4. Use a wide screwdriver to remove the main fuel jets (**Figure 29**) from the metering block. Mark each jet to indicate the mounting location in the carburetor. One side might have a differently sized orifice.

5. Loosen and then remove the power valve (76, **Figure 23**) from the metering block. Remove the gasket (75, **Figure 23**) from the valve. Do not discard the gasket at this time. The rebuild kit may have several styles of gaskets. Use the style that matches the original.

6A. On models with a center-hinged float (**Figure 30**), remove the float, inlet needle and seat as follows:

7

a. Loosen the lockscrew (7, **Figure 30**) and then re-move the inlet valve and seat assembly (3) by turn-ing the adjusting nut (5) counterclockwise.

b. Remove the gaskets from under the lockscrew and adjusting nut. Discard the gaskets.

c. Remove the two screws (8, **Figure 30**) and then pull the retaining bracket (9) and float (10) out of the float bowl.

d. Remove the pin (11, **Figure 30**) and then pull the float off the bracket.

6B. On models with a side-hinged float, remove the float, inlet needle and seat as follows:

a. Pull the baffle plate (61, **Figure 23**) out of the float bowl.

b. Use needlenose pliers to pull the E-clip (63, **Figure 23**) off the float shaft.

c. Pull the float (62, **Figure 23**) and spring assembly off the shaft. Pull the spring (64, **Figure 23**) off the float arm.

d. Pull the inlet needle (48, **Figure 23**) and clip (49) out of the seat (47). Remove the clip from the nee-dle.

e. Loosen and then remove the needle seat (47, **Figure 23**). Remove the gasket (46, **Figure 23**) from the seat. Discard the gasket.

7. Remove the four screws and lockwashers (**Figure 31**). Then lift the accelerator pump cover (**Figure 32**), dia-phragm (**Figure 33**) and spring (**Figure 34**) from the float bowl.

8. Inspect the check ball in the float bowl (**Figure 35**) for free movement. For proper accelerator pump operation, the check ball must move freely. Replace the float bowl if the check ball does move freely after cleaning. The check ball is not available separately.

9. Remove the gaskets from the float bowl, metering block and carburetor body. Do not discard the gaskets at this time. The rebuild kit may contain several styles of gaskets. Use the style that matches the original. *Carefully*

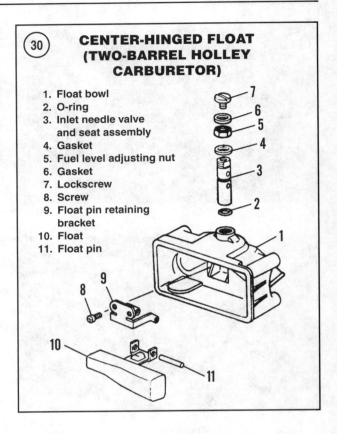

CENTER-HINGED FLOAT (TWO-BARREL HOLLEY CARBURETOR)

1. Float bowl
2. O-ring
3. Inlet needle valve and seat assembly
4. Gasket
5. Fuel level adjusting nut
6. Gasket
7. Lockscrew
8. Screw
9. Float pin retaining bracket
10. Float
11. Float pin

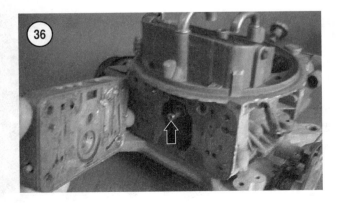

scrape all gasket material off the mating surfaces. *Do not damage the mating surfaces.*

10. Pull the brass accelerator pump tube (**Figure 36**) out of the metering block or carburetor body. Remove the O-rings from the tube. Discard the O-rings.

11. Remove the retainer pin (20, **Figure 23**) from the choke rod (15) and separate the rod from the lever (19).

12. Remove the screws (44, **Figure 23**) and then pull the electric choke off the carburetor. Remove the small gasket (16, **Figure 23**) from the port.

13. Remove the screw (1, **Figure 23**) and then lift the accelerator pump discharge nozzle and gasket. Remove the gaskets from the screw, nozzle or carburetor. Discard the gaskets.

14. Invert the carburetor and capture the discharge needle (7, **Figure 23**) from the nozzle bore.

15. Remove the retainer (11, **Figure 23**) and then remove the accelerator pump operating lever (10).

16. Disassemble the electric choke as follows:

   a. Make match marks on the choke cover and housing (**Figure 37**) for reference during assembly.

   b. Remove the screws (35, **Figure 23**) and retainer (36) and then pull the choke cover (37) off the choke housing (14).

   c. Remove the nut, lockwasher and spacer (39-41, **Figure 23**) and then pull the choke lever (42) and piston (43) out of the choke housing.

   d. Remove the choke rod (15, **Figure 23**) and seal (18). Remove the fast idle cam (17, **Figure 23**) and choke shaft (19).

17. Remove the screws (28, **Figure 23**) and then separate the throttle (25) from the carburetor body (21). Remove the gasket (22, **Figure 23**). If necessary, carefully scrape all gasket material from the mating surfaces. Do not damage the mating surfaces. Do not discard the gasket at this time. The repair kit might contain several styles of gaskets. Use the same gasket as the original.

18. Clean and inspect the carburetor components.

Assembly

Refer to **Figure 23** for this procedure.

1. Install a new gasket (22, **Figure 23**) onto the throttle plate (25). Then fit the throttle plate onto the carburetor body. Install the screws (28, **Figure 23**) and tighten in a crossing pattern to 50 in.-lb. (5.6 N•m).

2. Attach the accelerator pump lever (10, **Figure 23**) to the carburetor body. Secure the lever with the retainer (11, **Figure 23**).

3. Install the accelerator pump discharge nozzle and related components as follows:

   a. Drop the discharge needle (4, **Figure 38**) into the nozzle bore with the pointed tip facing downward.

   b. Install a *new* gasket (2, **Figure 38**) onto the bottom of the pump nozzle (3). Then fit the nozzle onto the carburetor with the discharge openings pointing into the carburetor bore.

   c. Install a *new* gasket (2, **Figure 38**) onto the top of the nozzle. Thread the screw (1, **Figure 38**) into the nozzle and carburetor. Securely tighten the screw.

   d. Stake the screw lightly in place using a punch.

4. Assemble and install the electric choke as follows:

   a. Insert the choke shaft (19, **Figure 23**) into the fast idle cam (17). Guide the threaded end of the choke shaft into the choke housing.

   b. Insert the piston (43, **Figure 23**) into the bore in the choke housing (14) and then fit the lever (42) over the choke shaft. Install the spacer, lockwasher and nut onto the shaft. Securely tighten the nut.

   c. Fit the *new* gasket (16, **Figure 23**) into the carburetor body port that aligns with the choke housing port.

   d. Insert the choke rod (15, **Figure 23**) into the choke shaft lever and then fit the choke housing onto the carburetor. The projection on the rod must be located under the fast idle cam to lift the cam when the choke is closed. Install a *new* retainer (20, **Figure 23**) onto the choke rod. Verify proper alignment and then install the screws and washers (44, **Figure 23**). Securely tighten the screws.

   e. Install a *new* gasket (38, **Figure 23**) onto the choke housing. Make sure the tab on the lever fits into the slot in the gasket. Engage the spring loop over the tab lever (42, **Figure 23**) and then seat the choke cover (37) onto the housing. Fit the retainer (36, **Figure 23**) onto the choke cover. Rotate the retainer to align the screw openings and then install the screws (35, **Figure 23**). Rotate the choke cover to align the match mark made prior to disassembly (**Figure 37**). Then securely tighten the screws.

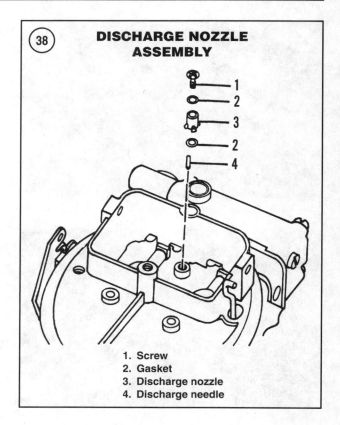

DISCHARGE NOZZLE ASSEMBLY

1. Screw
2. Gasket
3. Discharge nozzle
4. Discharge needle

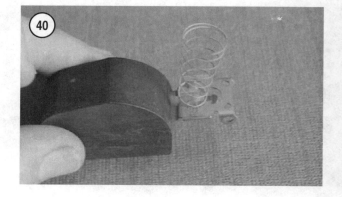

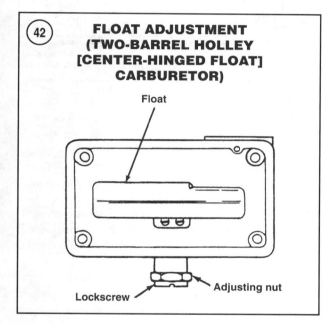

FLOAT ADJUSTMENT (TWO-BARREL HOLLEY [CENTER-HINGED FLOAT] CARBURETOR)

Float

Lockscrew

Adjusting nut

5. Install the accelerator pump components onto the float bowl as follows:

   a. Install the accelerator pump diaphragm onto the cover with the large-lever disc facing the pump lever. Install the spring onto the diaphragm and center over the lever disc.

   b. Without dislodging the spring or diaphragm, fit the cover onto the float bowl. The pump lever must face toward the end of the float bowl.

   c. Make sure the screw openings in the diaphragm align with the cover and float bowl openings.

   d. Install the four screws and lockwashers (**Figure 31**) into the cover and bowl. Do not tighten the screws at this time.

   e. Make sure the diaphragm is centered and then push the lever (**Figure 39**) to fully depress the dia-

phragm. Hold the lever in the compressed position. Then securely tighten the cover screws.

6A. On models with a center-hinged float (**Figure 30**), install the float, inlet needle and seat assembly and bracket into the float bowl as follows:

   a. Align the pin openings in the float arm and retaining bracket and then insert the float pin (11, **Figure 30**).

   b. Guide the retaining bracket and float assembly into the float bowl. Make sure the float pin enters the recess in the float bowl.

   c. Thread the two screws (8, **Figure 30**) into the retainer and float bowl openings. Securely tighten the screws.

   d. Apply a light coat of engine oil to the O-ring (2, **Figure 30**) on the inlet needle and seat assembly (3). Then thread the assembly into the float bowl.

   e. Install a *new* gasket (4, **Figure 30**) onto the needle and seat assembly and then thread the adjusting nut (5) onto the needle and seat assembly.

   f. Install a *new* gasket (6, **Figure 30**) onto the needle and seat assembly and then thread the lockscrews (7) into the needle and seat.

6B. On models with a side-hinged float (62, **Figure 23**), install the float, inlet needle and seat into the float bowl as follows:

   a. Install a new gasket (46, **Figure 23**) and then thread the needle seat (47) into the float bowl. Tighten the seat to 10 in.-lb. (1.1 N•m).

   b. Install a new pull clip (49, **Figure 23**) onto the inlet needle (48). Insert the inlet needle and clip into the seat. Make sure the pull clip wire extends outward.

   c. Install the spring onto the float arm with the small-diameter end fitting over the tabs as shown in **Figure 40**.

   d. Slide the float onto the float shaft. Make sure the spring is seated between the ridges on the boss in the float bowl floor as shown in **Figure 41**. Make sure the pull clip wire enters the slot in the float arm.

   e. Use needlenose pliers to install the E-clip (63, **Figure 23**) onto the float shaft.

   f. Insert the baffle plate (61, **Figure 23**) into the float bowl with the slot over the inlet needle seat.

7A. On models with a center-hinged float (**Figure 30**), adjust the float level as follows:

   a. Invert the float bowl.

   b. Loosen the lockscrew (**Figure 42**) and then turn the adjusting nut until the flat float surface is level with the flat float bowl (inner) surface.

   c. Securely tighten the lockscrew.

7B. On models with a side-hinged float, place the float bowl on a level work surface with the inlet needle side facing downward. The top of the float should be parallel

7

to the flat float bowl surface as shown in **Figure 43**. If adjustment is needed, carefully bend the curved part of the float arm that contacts the inlet needle as necessary.

NOTE
Several different power valves and power valve gaskets might be included in the repair kit. The valves are identified by numbers stamped onto the faces of the valves. Install a valve with the same number as the original. Also, the valve must be installed with the correct gasket. If the power valve has round fuel openings, use the gasket with three internal projections. If the power valve has rectangular fuel openings, use the gasket without internal projections.

8. Install the *new* gasket (75, **Figure 23**) onto the power valve (76). Make sure the power valve and gasket have the same number and style as the originals. Hand-thread the power valve into the metering block opening and then tighten the power valve to 100 in.-lb. (11.3 N•m).

9. Hand-thread the main fuel jets into the metering block (**Figure 29**). Then use a wide screwdriver to tighten the jets to 10 in.-lb. (1.1 N•m).

10. Thread the idle mixture screws (**Figure 28**) into the metering block using *new* seals (66, **Figure 23**). Turn in the needles until lightly seated. Then back the screws out the number of turns recorded during disassembly. The setting is normally one-half to one turn out from lightly seated. If so equipped, install the plugs (**Figure 27**) into the screw openings to prevent tampering.

11. Install the metering block and float bowl as follows:
    a. Install the plastic baffle (69, **Figure 23**) onto the metering block and position over the dowels.
    b. Install a *new* inner gasket (74, **Figure 23**) onto the metering block (71). Use the dowels on the block to align and retain the gasket. Install a *new* O-ring onto the brass accelerator pump tube and then insert the tube into the carburetor body (**Figure 36**).
    c. Fit the metering block and gasket onto the carburetor body (**Figure 26**). Install a *new* outer gasket (65, **Figure 23**) onto the metering block. Use the dowels on the block to align and retain the gasket.
    d. Install the float bowl onto the metering block (**Figure 25**). Use the gasket and dowel to align and retain the float bowl.
    e. Install a *new* gasket (51, **Figure 23**) onto each of the four screws (50). Thread the four screws (**Figure 24**) into the bowl, metering block and carburetor body. Verify proper fuel bowl, metering block and carburetor body alignment and then securely tighten the screws in a crossing pattern.

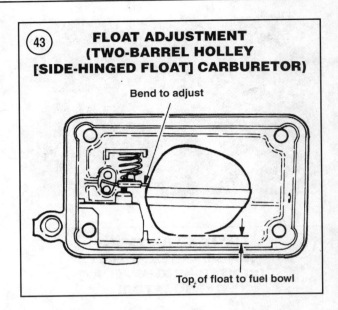

43 **FLOAT ADJUSTMENT (TWO-BARREL HOLLEY [SIDE-HINGED FLOAT] CARBURETOR)**

Bend to adjust

Top of float to fuel bowl

12. Adjust the accelerator pump clearance as follows:
    a. Hold the throttle linkage in the wide-open throttle position.
    b. Manually depress the pump lever.
    c. Use feeler gauges to measure the clearance between the pump lever and the head of the screw on the pump arm (**Figure 44**). The clearance must be 0.010-0.015 in. (0.25-0.38 mm). If adjustment is needed, turn the screw to achieve the required clearance.

13. Install the carburetor as described in this section.

14. On models with a center-hinged float bowl, perform the final float level adjustment as described in Chapter Five.

Four-Barrel Carburetor

The four-barrel Holley carburetor (**Figure 45**) can be identified by the two side-mounted float bowls and the two secondary openings. This section describes removal, repair and installation of the carburetor.

Removal

1. Disconnect the battery cables. Use compressed air to blow debris and loose material from the carburetor and intake manifold.

2. Disconnect the fuel line and remove the fuel inlet filter as described in this section.

3. Carefully unplug the purple/white wire (A, **Figure 20**) and black wire (B) from the electric choke.

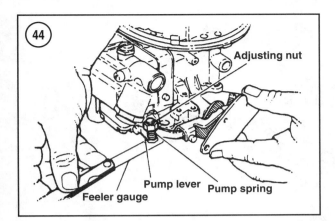

(44)

Adjusting nut

Pump lever   Pump spring

Feeler gauge

(45)

9. Use an aerosol carburetor cleaner to remove oily deposits from the mating surfaces.

Installation

1. Install a *new* carburetor mounting gasket over the studs and seat it on the intake manifold. Make sure the gasket openings match the intake manifold.

2. Install the carburetor onto the intake manifold. Then thread the four nuts onto the studs. Tighten the nuts in a crossing pattern to 115-168 in.-lb. (13-19 N•m).

3. On models using a mechanical fuel pump, push the sight tube fully over the carburetor fitting. Secure the tube using a plastic locking clamp. Do not tighten the clamp to the point when the tube begins to collapse.

4. If so equipped, plug the PCV hose (A, **Figure 21**, typical) fully onto the rear of the carburetor.

5. Plug the purple or purple/white (A, **Figure 20**) and black wire terminal (B) onto the electric choke. The wires must fit snugly on the choke terminals. If necessary, remove the wire and squeeze the terminals *slightly* to achieve a snug fit.

6. Push the cable end retainer (A, **Figure 22**) toward the cable anchor (B) and then fit the cable end fully over the ball-shaped carburetor lever pin. Rotate the retainer to align the slot in the back of the retainer with the pin and then slide the slot in the retainer over the pin. The internal spring holds the retainer in position. Tug lightly on the cable end to verify a secure connection.

7. Install the inlet fuel filter and connect the fuel line as described in this chapter.

8. Connect the battery cables.

CAUTION
Use a flush test device or other means to supply the engine with cooling water if running the engine with the boat out of the water. The seawater pump is quickly damaged if operated without adequate cooling water.

9. Start the engine and immediately check for leaking fuel. Stop the engine and repair any leaks before operating the engine.

Disassembly

Refer to **Figure 46** for this procedure.

1. Remove the carburetor as described in this section.

2. Remove the four screws (**Figure 24**) securing the primary float bowl (12, **Figure 46**) and metering block (18) to the carburetor body. The primary float bowl is on the front of the carburetor and on the same side as the choke

4. On models using a mechanical fuel pump, inspect the clear or translucent sight tube connected to the carburetor for the presence of fuel. Replace the mechanical fuel pump as described in this chapter if any fuel is visible in the sight tube. Disconnect the sight tube from the carburetor. Replace the sight tube with the recommended tube if any defects are evident. *Do not* replace the tube with any other type of hose or tubing.

5. If so equipped, unplug the PCV hose (A, **Figure 21**, typical) from the rear of the carburetor.

6. Push the cable end retainer (A, **Figure 22**) toward the cable anchor (B) and then pull the cable end off the carburetor lever pin.

7. Remove the four carburetor mounting nuts (B, **Figure 21**, typical) and then lift the carburetor off the intake manifold.

8. Remove the carburetor mounting gasket from the intake manifold or carburetor base. Discard the gasket. *Carefully* scrape all gasket material from the surfaces. *Do not* damage the mating surfaces.

7

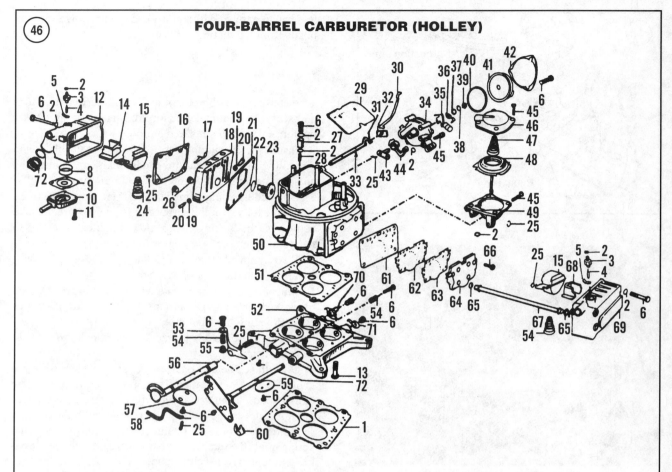

FOUR-BARREL CARBURETOR (HOLLEY)

1. Mounting gasket	26. Main fuel jet	51. Throttle body gasket
2. Gasket*	27. Discharge nozzle	52. Throttle body
3. Inlet needle seat*	28. Discharge needle	53. Accelerator pump operating lever
4. Inlet needle*	29. Choke plate	54. Spring
5. Pull off clip*	30. Choke rod	55. Sleeve nut
6. Screw	31. Choke shaft	56. Secondary throttle shaft
7. Fuel filter nut	32. Choke rod seal	57. Secondary throttle plate
8. Diaphragm spring	33. Screw	58. Throttle connecting rod
9. Diaphragm assembly	34. Choke housing	59. Primary throttle plate
10. Accelerator pump cover	35. Choke link and piston	60. Accelerator pump cam
11. Screw and lockwasher	36. Choke lever	61. Gasket
12. Primary float bowl	37. Spacer	62. Secondary plate
13. Screw	38. Lockwasher	63. Metering body gasket
14. Baffle plate*	39. Nut	64. Secondary metering block
15. Float*	40. Gasket	65. O-ring
16. Float bowl gasket	41. Choke cover	66. Clutch screw
17. Baffle plate	42. Retainer	67. Fuel balance tube
18. Primary metering block	43. Lever	68. Baffle plate
19. Seal	44. Fast idle cam	69. Secondary float bowl
20. Idle mixture screw	45. Screw and washer	70. Fast idle cam lever
21. Metering block gasket	46. Cover	71. Diaphragm lever assembly
22. Power valve gasket	47. Diaphragm spring	72. Primary throttle shaft
23. Power valve	48. Diaphragm assembly	
24. Float spring*	49. Diaphragm housing	*Used on carburetor with
25. E-clip*	50. Carburetor body	side-hinged float assembly.

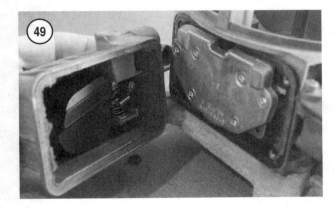

(**Figure 27**). Turn the idle mixture screws (**Figure 28**) inward until *lightly* seated. Record the number of turns required to lightly seat the screws for reference during reassembly. Remove the screws and then remove and discard the seals from the screws.

5. Use a wide screwdriver to remove the main fuel jets (**Figure 29**) from the metering block. Mark each jet to indicate the mounting location in the carburetor. One side might have a differently sized orifice.

6. Loosen and then remove the power valve (23, **Figure 46**) from the metering block. Remove the gasket (22, **Figure 46**) from the valve. Do not discard the gasket at this time. The rebuild kit might have several styles of gaskets. Use the style that matches the original.

7A. On models with a center-hinged float (**Figure 30**), remove the float, inlet needle and seat from the primary float bowl as follows:

   a. Loosen the lockscrew (7, **Figure 30**) and then remove the inlet valve and seat assembly (3) by turning the adjusting nut (5) counterclockwise.

   b. Remove the gaskets from under the lockscrew and adjusting nut. Discard the gaskets.

   c. Remove the two screws (8, **Figure 30**) and then pull the retaining bracket (9) and float (10) out of the float bowl.

   d. Remove the pin (11, **Figure 30**) and then pull the float off the bracket.

7B. On models with a side-hinged float, remove the float, inlet needle and seat from the primary float bowl as follows:

   a. Pull the baffle plate (14, **Figure 46**) out of the float bowl.

   b. Use needlenose pliers to pull the E-clip (25, **Figure 46**) off the float shaft.

   c. Pull the float (15, **Figure 46**) and spring assembly off the shaft. Pull the spring (24, **Figure 46**) off the float arm.

   d. Pull the inlet needle (4, **Figure 46**) and clip (5) out of the seat (3). Remove the clip from the needle.

   e. Loosen and then remove the needle seat (3, **Figure 46**). Remove the gasket (2, **Figure 46**) from the seat. Discard the gasket.

8. Remove the four screws (**Figure 48**) securing the secondary float bowl and metering block to the carburetor body. Remove the gasket from the screws or float bowl. Discard the gaskets. Carefully pull the float bowl off the carburetor body (**Figure 49**).

9. Use a No. 2 clutch (double-D) screwdriver to remove the screws (**Figure 50**). Then separate the secondary metering block (**Figure 51**) and plate (**Figure 52**) from the carburetor body. Work carefully to avoid bending the plate.

valve. Remove the gaskets from the screws or float bowl. Discard the gaskets. Carefully pull the float bowl (**Figure 25**) and then the metering block (**Figure 26**) off the carburetor body. Pull the plastic baffle (17, **Figure 46**) off the metering block pins.

3. On models with a single fuel inlet fitting, carefully pull the balance tube from the primary or secondary float bowl (**Figure 47**). Remove the O-rings (65, **Figure 46**) from the balance tube or bowl openings. Discard the O-rings.

4. If so equipped, carefully pry the plugs out of the idle mixture screw openings on the sides of the metering block

7

10A. On models with a center-hinged float (**Figure 30**), remove the float, inlet needle and seat from the secondary float bowl as follows:

    a. Loosen the lockscrew (7, **Figure 30**) and then remove the inlet valve and seat assembly (3) by turning the adjusting nut (5) counterclockwise.

    b. Remove the gaskets from under the lockscrew and adjusting nut. Discard the gaskets.

    c. Remove the two screws (8, **Figure 30**) and then pull the retaining bracket (9) with float (10) out of the float bowl.

    d. Remove the pin (11, **Figure 30**) and then pull the float off the bracket.

10B. On models with a side-hinged float, remove the float, inlet needle and seat from the secondary float bowl as follows:

    a. Pull the baffle plate (14, **Figure 46**) out of the float bowl.

    b. Use needlenose pliers to pull the E-clip (25, **Figure 46**) off the float shaft.

    c. Pull the float (15, **Figure 46**) and spring assembly off the shaft. Pull the spring (24, **Figure 46**) off the float arm.

    d. Pull the inlet needle (4, **Figure 46**) and clip (5) out of the seat (3). Remove the clip from the needle.

    e. Use a suitable wrench to loosen and then remove the needle seat (3, **Figure 46**). Remove the gasket (2, **Figure 36**) from the seat. Discard the gasket.

11. Remove the screw (6, **Figure 46**) and then remove the accelerator pump discharge nozzle (27) and gasket (2). Remove the gaskets from the screw, nozzle or carburetor. Discard the gaskets.

12. Invert the carburetor and capture the discharge needle (28, **Figure 46**) from the nozzle bore.

13. Remove the retainer (25, **Figure 46**) that attaches the secondary diaphragm link onto the secondary throttle shaft.

14. Remove the screws (13, **Figure 46**) that secure the throttle plate to the carburetor body. Separate the throttle body (52, **Figure 46**) from the carburetor body (50). Remove the gasket (51, **Figure 46**) from the throttle plate or carburetor body. If necessary, carefully scrape all gasket material from the mating surfaces. Do not damage the mating surfaces. Do not discard the gasket at this time. The repair kit might contain several styles of gaskets. Use the same gasket as the original.

15. Remove the four screws and lockwashers (**Figure 31**) and then lift the accelerator pump cover (**Figure 32**), diaphragm (**Figure 33**) and spring (**Figure 34**) from the float bowl.

16. Inspect the check ball in the float bowl (**Figure 35**) for free movement. For proper accelerator pump operation, the check ball must move freely. Replace the float

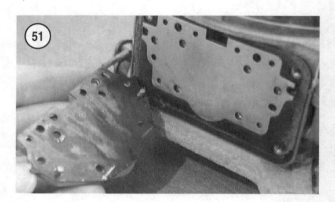

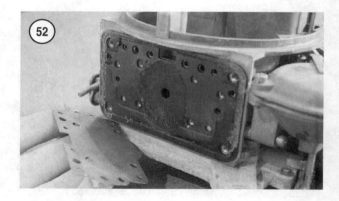

bowl if the check ball does move freely after cleaning. The check ball is not available separately.

17. Pull the brass accelerator pump tube (**Figure 36**) out of the metering block or carburetor body. Remove the O-rings from the tube. Discard the O-rings.

18. Disassemble the electric choke as follows:

    a. Make match marks on the choke cover and housing (**Figure 37**) to assist with proper assembly.

    b. Remove the three screws (6, **Figure 46**) and retainer (42). Then pull the choke cover (41, **Figure 46**) off the choke housing (34).

c. Remove the spacer, lockwasher and nut (37-39, **Figure 46**) and then pull the choke link and piston (35) out of the choke housing.

d. Remove the choke housing (34, **Figure 46**). Remove the small gasket (2, **Figure 46**) from the choke housing or port in the carburetor body.

e. Pull the choke shaft (31, **Figure 46**) and fast idle cam (44) out of the choke housing.

f. Remove the choke rod (30, **Figure 46**) and seal (32).

19. Remove the retainer (25, **Figure 46**) and then remove the accelerator pump operating lever (53).

20. Remove and disassemble the diaphragm housing as follows:

a. Remove the screws (45, **Figure 46**) and then separate the diaphragm housing from the carburetor body (**Figure 53**).

b. Remove the small gasket (2, **Figure 46**) from the diaphragm housing or carburetor body. Discard the gasket.

c. Remove the four screws (**Figure 54**) and then lift the cover off the diaphragm housing.

d. Remove the spring (47, **Figure 46**) and then pull the diaphragm and shaft out of the housing (**Figure 55**).

e. Inspect the diaphragm for tears, stretching or deterioration. Replace the diaphragm and shaft assembly unless in excellent condition.

21. Clean and inspect the carburetor components.

Assembly

Refer to **Figure 46** for this procedure.

1. Install a new gasket (51, **Figure 46**) onto the throttle body (52) and then fit the throttle body onto the carburetor body. Install the screws (13, **Figure 46**) and tighten in a crossing pattern to 50 in.-lb. (5.6 N•m).

2. Attach the accelerator pump lever (53, **Figure 46**) to the carburetor body. Secure the lever with the retainer (25, **Figure 46**).

3. Install the accelerator pump discharge nozzle and related components as follows:

a. Drop the discharge needle (4, **Figure 38**) into the nozzle bore with the pointed tip facing downward.

b. Install a *new* gasket (2, **Figure 38**) onto the pump nozzle (3). Then fit the nozzle onto the carburetor with the discharge openings pointing toward the carburetor bore.

c. Install a *new* gasket (2, **Figure 46**) onto the top of the nozzle. Fit a new gasket (2, **Figure 46**) over the discharge passage in the carburetor air horn.

d. Use needlenose pliers to install the nozzle and screw into the opening (**Figure 46**). Align the discharge openings toward the throttle bores and then securely tighten the screw.

e. Stake the screw lightly in place with a punch.

4. Assemble and install the secondary diaphragm as follows:

a. Install the secondary diaphragm and shaft into the housing (**Figure 55**). Make sure the corner with two openings is properly positioned over the vacuum passage (**Figure 56**).

7

b. Install the spring (47, **Figure 46**) onto the housing (46) with the larger-diameter side against the diaphragm.

c. Fit the cover onto the housing. Do not dislodge the spring or diaphragm.

d. Install the four screws (**Figure 54**) into the cover and housing. *Do not* tighten the screws at this time.

e. Support the housing and pull downward as far as possible on the diaphragm shaft. Hold the shaft in position and then securely tighten the screws. Release the diaphragm.

f. Install a *new* gasket (2, **Figure 46**) over the diaphragm vacuum passage on the carburetor body.

g. Install the secondary diaphragm assembly onto the carburetor body. Do not dislodge the gasket.

h. Install the three screws (45, **Figure 46**) into the diaphragm assembly and carburetor body. Securely tighten the screws.

i. Fit the opening in the diaphragm shaft over the secondary throttle lever. Install a *new* retainer onto the lever to secure the shaft.

5. Fit a new seal (32, **Figure 46**) onto the choke rod (30). Fit the seal with rod into the grooves under the flame arrestor flange.

6. Assemble and install the electric choke as follows:

a. Insert the choke shaft (31, **Figure 46**) into the fast idle cam (44) opening. Guide the threaded end of the choke shaft into the choke housing.

b. Insert the piston (35, **Figure 46**) into the bore in the choke housing (34) and then fit the lever (36) over the choke shaft. Install the spacer, lockwasher and nut onto the shaft. Securely tighten the nut.

c. Fit the *new* gasket (2, **Figure 46**) into the carburetor body port that aligns with the choke housing port.

d. Insert the choke rod (30, **Figure 46**) into the choke shaft lever and then fit the choke housing onto the carburetor. The projection on the rod must be located under the fast idle cam to lift the cam when the choke is closed. Install a *new* retainer onto the choke rod. Verify proper alignment and then install the screws and washers (45, **Figure 46**). Securely tighten the screws.

e. Install a *new* gasket (40, **Figure 46**) onto the choke housing. Make sure the tab on the lever fits into the slot in the gasket. Engage the spring loop over the tab lever and then seat the choke cover (41, **Figure 46**) onto the housing. Fit the retainer (42, **Figure 46**) onto the choke cover. Align the screw openings and then install the screws (6, **Figure 46**). Rotate the choke cover to align the match marks made prior to disassembly (**Figure 37**). Then securely tighten the screws.

7. Install the accelerator pump components onto the primary float bowl as follows:

a. Install the accelerator pump diaphragm onto the cover with the large disc facing the pump lever. Install the spring onto the diaphragm and center it over the lever disc.

b. Without dislodging the spring or diaphragm, fit the cover onto the float bowl. The pump lever must face toward the end of the float bowl.

c. Make sure the screw openings in the diaphragm align with the cover and float bowl opening.

d. Install the four screws and lockwashers (**Figure 31**) into the cover and bowl. Do not tighten the screws at this time.

e. Make sure the diaphragm is centered and then push the lever (**Figure 39**) to fully depress the diaphragm. Hold the lever in the compressed position. Then securely tighten the cover screws.

8. Identify the secondary float bowl as follows:

a. On models with a single fuel inlet, the secondary float bowl does not have a threaded opening. The float bowl has an opening only for the balance tube.

b. On models with twin fuel inlets, the secondary float bowl has a threaded opening on the side opposite the throttle linkage.

9A. On models with a center-hinged float (**Figure 30**), install the float, inlet needle and seat assembly and bracket into the secondary float bowl as follows:

a. Align the pin openings in the float arm and retaining bracket and then insert the float pin (11, **Figure 30**).

b. Guide the retaining bracket and float assembly into the float bowl. Make sure the float pin enters the recess in the float bowl.

c. Thread the two screws (8, **Figure 30**) into the retainer and float bowl openings. Securely tighten the screws.

d. Apply a light coat of engine oil to the O-ring (2, **Figure 30**) on the inlet needle and seat assembly (3). Then thread the assembly into the float bowl.

e. Install a *new* gasket (4, **Figure 30**) onto the needle and seat assembly and then thread the adjusting nut (5) onto the needle and seat.

f. Install a *new* gasket (6, **Figure 30**) onto the needle and seat assembly and then thread the lockscrews (7) into the needle and seat.

9B. On models with a side-hinged float (15, **Figure 46**), install the inlet needle, seat and float into the secondary float bowl as follows:

a. Install a new gasket (2, **Figure 46**) and then thread the needle seat (3) into the float bowl. Tighten the seat to 10 in.-lb. (1.1 N•m).

b. Install a new pull clip (5, **Figure 46**) onto the inlet needle (4). Insert the inlet needle and clip into the seat. Make sure the pull clip wire extends outward.

c. Install the spring onto the float arm with the small-diameter end fitting over the tabs as shown in **Figure 40**.

d. Slide the float onto the float shaft. Make sure the spring is seated between the ridges on the boss in the float bowl floor as shown in **Figure 41**. Make sure the pull clip wire enters the slot in the float arm.

e. Use needlenose pliers to install the E-clip (25, **Figure 46**) onto the float shaft.

f. Insert the baffle plate (68, **Figure 46**) into the float bowl with the slot over the inlet needle seat.

10A. On models with a center-hinged float (**Figure 30**), adjust the float level as follows:

a. Invert the float bowl.

b. Loosen the lockscrew (**Figure 42**) and then turn the adjusting nut until the flat float surface is level with the flat float bowl (inner) surface.

c. Securely tighten the lockscrew.

10B. On models with a side-hinged float, place the float bowl on a level work surface with the inlet needle side facing downward. The top of the float should be parallel to the flat float bowl surface as shown in **Figure 43**. If adjustment is needed, carefully bend the curved part of the float arm that contacts the inlet needle.

11. Install the secondary metering block and float bowl as follows:

a. Install a *new* plate gasket (61, **Figure 46**) onto the secondary side of the carburetor body. The secondary side is opposite the choke valve. Install the plate onto the gasket and carburetor body (**Figure 52**).

b. Install a *new* metering block gasket (63, **Figure 46**) onto the metering block. Install the metering block and gasket onto the plate (**Figure 51**).

c. Align all screw openings, then thread the screws (**Figure 50**) into the block, plate and carburetor body. Use a No. 2 clutch (double-D) screwdriver to securely tighten the screws in a crossing pattern.

d. Install the secondary float bowl onto the carburetor body (**Figure 49**). Install *new* gaskets (2, **Figure 46**) onto the screws. Then thread them into the secondary float bowl and carburetor body (**Figure 48**). Tighten the screws securely in a crossing pattern.

12A. On models with a center-hinged float (**Figure 30**), install the float, inlet needle and seat assembly and bracket into the primary float bowl as follows:

a. Align the pin openings in the float arm and retaining bracket and then insert the float pin (11, **Figure 30**).

b. Guide the retaining bracket and float assembly into the float bowl. Make sure the float pin enters the recess in the float bowl.

c. Thread the two screws (8, **Figure 30**) into the retainer and float bowl. Securely tighten the screws.

d. Apply a light coat of engine oil to the O-ring (2, **Figure 30**) of the inlet needle and seat assembly (3). Then thread the assembly into the float bowl.

e. Install a *new* gasket (4, **Figure 30**) onto the needle and seat assembly and then thread the adjusting nut (5) onto the needle and seat.

f. Install a *new* gasket (6, **Figure 30**) onto the needle and seat assembly and then thread the lockscrews (7) into the needle and seat.

12B. On models with a side-hinged float (15, **Figure 46**), install the inlet needle, seat and float into the primary float bowl as follows:

a. Install a new gasket (2, **Figure 46**) and then thread the needle seat (3) into the float bowl. Tighten the seat to 10 in.-lb. (1.1 N•m).

b. Install a new pull clip (5, **Figure 46**) onto the inlet needle (4). Insert the inlet needle and clip into the seat. Make sure the pull clip wire extends outward.

c. Install the spring onto the float arm with the small-diameter end fitting over the tabs as shown in **Figure 40**.

d. Slide the float onto the float shaft. Make sure the spring is seated between the ridges on the boss in the float bowl floor as shown in **Figure 41**. Make sure the pull clip wire enters the slot in the float arm.

e. Use needlenose pliers to install the E-clip (25, **Figure 46**) onto the float shaft.

f. Insert the baffle plate (68, **Figure 46**) into the float bowl with the slot over the inlet needle seat.

13A. On models with a center-hinged float (**Figure 30**), adjust the float level as follows:

a. Invert the float bowl.

7

b. Loosen the lockscrew (**Figure 42**) and then turn the adjusting nut until the flat float surface is level with the flat float bowl (inner) surface.

c. Securely tighten the lockscrew.

13B. On models with a side-hinged float, place the float bowl on a level work surface with the inlet needle side facing downward. The top of the float should be parallel to the flat float bowl surface as shown in **Figure 43**. If adjustment is needed, carefully bend the curved part of the float arm that contacts the inlet needle.

14. On models with a single fuel inlet, make sure the *used* balance tube O-rings (65, **Figure 46**) are removed from the float bowls. Install *new* O-rings onto each end of the tube. Insert the tube into the opening in the secondary float bowl.

> *NOTE*
> *Several different power valves and power valve gaskets might be included in the repair kit. The valves are identified by numbers stamped onto the faces of the valves. Install a valve with the same number as the original. Also, the valve must be installed with the correct gasket. If the power valve has round fuel openings, use the gasket with three internal projections. If the power valve has rectangular fuel openings, use the gasket without internal projections.*

15. Install the *new* gasket (22, **Figure 46**) onto the power valve (23). Make sure the power valve and gasket have the same number and style as the originals. Hand-thread the power valve into the metering block opening. Tighten the power valve to 100 in.-lb. (11.3 N•m).

16. Hand-thread the main fuel jets into the metering block (**Figure 29**). Then use a wide screwdriver to tighten the jets to 10 in.-lb. (1.1 N•m).

17. Thread the idle mixture screws (**Figure 28**) into the metering block using *new* seals (66, **Figure 23**). Turn in the needles until lightly seated and then back the screws out the number of turns recorded during disassembly. The setting is normally one-half to one turn out from lightly seated. If so equipped, install the plugs (**Figure 27**) into the screw openings to prevent tampering.

18. Install the primary metering block and float bowl as follows:

a. Install the baffle (17, **Figure 46**) onto the metering block and position it over the dowels.

b. Install a *new* inner gasket (21, **Figure 46**) onto the metering block (18). Use the dowels on the block to align and retain the gasket. Install a *new* O-ring onto the brass accelerator pump tube and then insert the tube into the carburetor body (**Figure 36**).

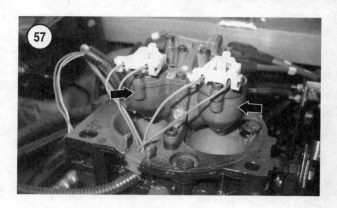

c. Fit the metering block and gasket onto the carburetor body (**Figure 26**). Install a *new* outer gasket (16, **Figure 46**) onto the metering block. Use the dowels on the block to align and retain the gasket.

d. Guide the balance tube, if so equipped, into the opening in the primary float bowl and then install the bowl onto the metering block (**Figure 25**). Use the dowels to align and retain the float bowl.

e. Install a *new* gasket (2, **Figure 46**) onto each of the four screws (6). Thread the four screws (**Figure 24**) into the bowl, metering block and carburetor body. Verify proper fuel bowl, metering block and carburetor body alignment and then tighten the screws securely in a crossing pattern.

19. Adjust the accelerator pump clearance as follows:

a. Hold the throttle linkage in the wide-open throttle position.

b. Manually depress the pump lever.

c. Use feeler gauges to measure the clearance between the pump lever and the head of the screw on the pump arm (**Figure 44**). The clearance must be 0.010-0.015 in. (0.25-0.38 mm). If adjustment is needed, turn the screw to achieve the required clearance.

20. Install the carburetor as described in this section.

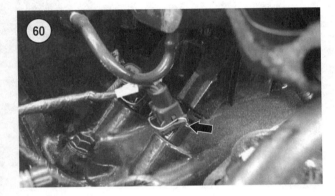

21. On models with a center-hinged float bowl, perform the final float level adjustment as described in Chapter Five.

ELECTRONIC FUEL INJECTION (EFI)

This section describes service procedures for the electronic fuel injection (EFI) components. Two different types of fuel injection systems are used on the engines covered in this manual. The throttle body injection (TBI) system is used on most 5.0L, 5.7L and 7.4L EFI models with a standard output rating. The multiport injection (MPI) system is used on high-output 5.7L and 7.4L and all 8.1L and 8.2L EFI models. Identify the type of system by location of the throttle body. On TBI systems, the throttle body is located on the intake manifold in the same location as the carburetor on models so equipped. The throttle body houses the fuel injectors (**Figure 57**). On MPI systems, the throttle body is located on the intake manifold (**Figure 58**) in the same location as the carburetor on models so equipped or on the front of the intake plenum (**Figure 59**). On MPI systems, the fuel injectors (**Figure**

60) fit into the intake manifold and align with the intake passages for the individual cylinders.

Replacement of the water-separating fuel filter and replacement intervals are described in Chapter Three. Refer to *Fuel Filter Maintenance*. Replacement of the fuel pressure regulator filter used on some MPI models is described in the pressure regulator replacement procedure. Replacement of the injector filters used on TBI and MPI models is described in the injector replacement procedure.

Both the TBI and MPI systems are produced with a return-to-tank, return-to-filter housing or no-return fuel delivery system. Refer to *Electronic Fuel Injection* in Chapter Two. On all models *except* TBI systems with return fuel delivery systems, always relieve the fuel system pressure as described in this section *before* disconnecting any fuel line or removing any EFI component. The TBI models with a return fuel delivery system are equipped with an internal bleed system that automatically relieves the system pressure within a few seconds after stopping the engine.

Take all precautions to prevent contamination and work only in a clean environment when servicing the EFI system. Use only clean solvent and lint-free shop towels when cleaning components. Dry components with compressed air and promptly cover them. Replace all gaskets, seals and O-rings if disturbed. Unless specified otherwise, apply liquid dishwashing soap to all O-rings before installing them.

WARNING
Use caution when working with the fuel system. Never smoke around fuel or fuel vapor. Make sure no flame or source of ignition is present in the work area. Flame or sparks can ignite fuel or fuel vapor and cause in fire and explosion.

CAUTION
Do not use solvents containing methyl ethyl ketone to clean the fuel rail, throttle body and related components. Use only mild solvents designed to clean fuel system components. Harsh solvents can dissolve protective coatings and damage some fuel system components.

Relieving Fuel System Pressure

This procedure is required on all models using an MPI system or TBI system with a no-return fuel delivery system. The TBI models with a return fuel delivery system are equipped with an internal bleed system that automati-

7

cally relieves the system pressure within a few seconds after stopping the engine.

On MPI models, a suitable pressure gauge with a bleed hose (**Figure 61**) (Kent-Moore part No. J-34730-1A) is required for this procedure.

Throttle body injection (TBI) models (with a no-return fuel system)

1. Disconnect the battery cables.

2. Unthread the screw (A, **Figure 62**) and then lift the plastic cover (B) off the flame arrestor.

3. Locate the fuel delivery line connection (**Figure 63**) on the fitting at the rear of the throttle body assembly. Use compressed air to remove debris from the fittings and throttle body.

4. Wrap a suitable shop towel around the fitting to capture spilled fuel.

5. Hold the throttle body using a suitable wrench to prevent rotation. Then use a flare nut wrench to loosen the fuel line fitting.

6. *Slowly* loosen the fuel line fitting by hand until fuel just starts dripping from the connection. Wait until the fuel stops dripping and then unthread the fitting.

7. Drain all fuel in the line into a suitable container. Clean up any spilled fuel at once.

8. Remove the O-ring from the groove at the end of the fuel line fitting. Discard the O-ring.

9. Install a *new* O-ring into the fitting groove. Then hand-thread the line fitting into the throttle body.

10. Hold the throttle body fitting using a wrench to prevent rotation. Then tighten the fuel line fitting to 204 in.-lb. (23 N•m). Do not allow the fuel line to twist during the tightening procedure. Twisting damages the line.

CAUTION
Never start the engine without providing cooling water. Start the engine with the vessel in the water or use an adapter that connects a water hose to the seawater pump inlet hose or fitting.

11. After performing the fuel system service procedure, start the engine and immediately check for fuel leakage at the fuel line-to-throttle body connection. Correct any fuel leakage before operating the engine.

12. Install the plastic cover (B, **Figure 62**) onto the flame arrestor. Guide the screw (A, **Figure 62**) into the cover, flame arrestor and throttle body openings.

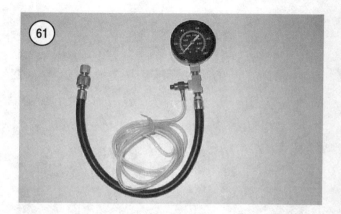

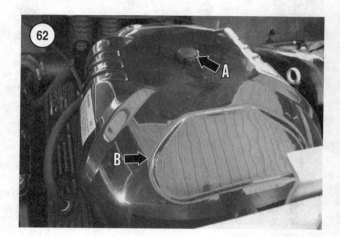

Multiport injection (MPI) models

A suitable pressure gauge with a bleed hose (**Figure 61**) available from Kent-Moore (part No. J-34730-1A) is required for this procedure.

Refer to **Figures 64-67** for this procedure.

1. Disconnect the battery cables.

2. Remove any plastic cover (B, **Figure 62**, typical) from the top of the engine.

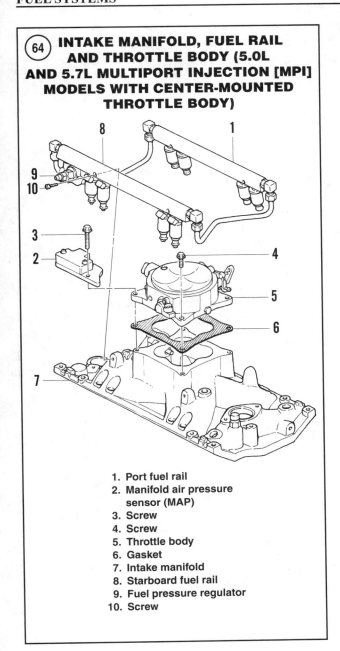

(64) INTAKE MANIFOLD, FUEL RAIL AND THROTTLE BODY (5.0L AND 5.7L MULTIPORT INJECTION [MPI] MODELS WITH CENTER-MOUNTED THROTTLE BODY)

1. Port fuel rail
2. Manifold air pressure sensor (MAP)
3. Screw
4. Screw
5. Throttle body
6. Gasket
7. Intake manifold
8. Starboard fuel rail
9. Fuel pressure regulator
10. Screw

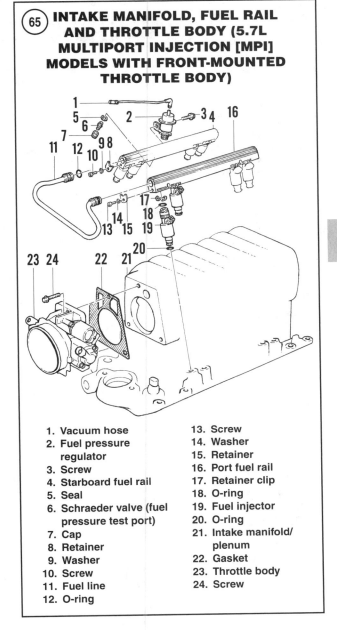

(65) INTAKE MANIFOLD, FUEL RAIL AND THROTTLE BODY (5.7L MULTIPORT INJECTION [MPI] MODELS WITH FRONT-MOUNTED THROTTLE BODY)

1. Vacuum hose
2. Fuel pressure regulator
3. Screw
4. Starboard fuel rail
5. Seal
6. Schraeder valve (fuel pressure test port)
7. Cap
8. Retainer
9. Washer
10. Screw
11. Fuel line
12. O-ring
13. Screw
14. Washer
15. Retainer
16. Port fuel rail
17. Retainer clip
18. O-ring
19. Fuel injector
20. O-ring
21. Intake manifold/plenum
22. Gasket
23. Throttle body
24. Screw

7

3. Locate the high-pressure test port and remove the cap.

   a. On 5.0L and 5.7L models with a center mounted throttle body, the fuel pressure test port is located next to the fuel pressure regulator (9, **Figure 64**) at the rear of the starboard fuel rail (port side fuel rail on V-drive models).

   b. On 5.7L models with a front-mounted throttle body, the fuel pressure test port (6, **Figure 65**) is located under the cap (5) on the bottom of the starboard side fuel rail (port side fuel rail on V-drive models).

   c. On 7.4L and 8.2L models, the fuel pressure test port is located on the aft end (forward end on V-drive models) of the fuel rail (33, **Figure 66**).

   d. On 8.1L models, the fuel pressure test port (8, **Figure 67**) is located on the top of the starboard side fuel rail (port side fuel rail in V-drive models).

4. Remove the cap from the test port. Wrap a suitable shop towel around the test port to capture spilled fuel.

   a. If the test gauge uses a lever to lock the hose fitting onto the test port, pull up on the locking lever and

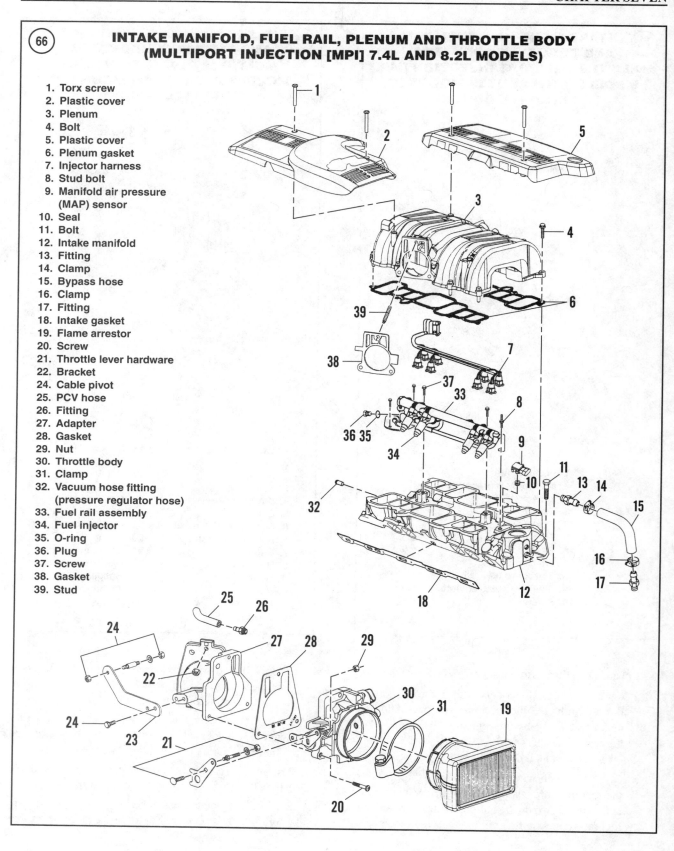

**66 INTAKE MANIFOLD, FUEL RAIL, PLENUM AND THROTTLE BODY
(MULTIPORT INJECTION [MPI] 7.4L AND 8.2L MODELS)**

1. Torx screw
2. Plastic cover
3. Plenum
4. Bolt
5. Plastic cover
6. Plenum gasket
7. Injector harness
8. Stud bolt
9. Manifold air pressure (MAP) sensor
10. Seal
11. Bolt
12. Intake manifold
13. Fitting
14. Clamp
15. Bypass hose
16. Clamp
17. Fitting
18. Intake gasket
19. Flame arrestor
20. Screw
21. Throttle lever hardware
22. Bracket
24. Cable pivot
25. PCV hose
26. Fitting
27. Adapter
28. Gasket
29. Nut
30. Throttle body
31. Clamp
32. Vacuum hose fitting (pressure regulator hose)
33. Fuel rail assembly
34. Fuel injector
35. O-ring
36. Plug
37. Screw
38. Gasket
39. Stud

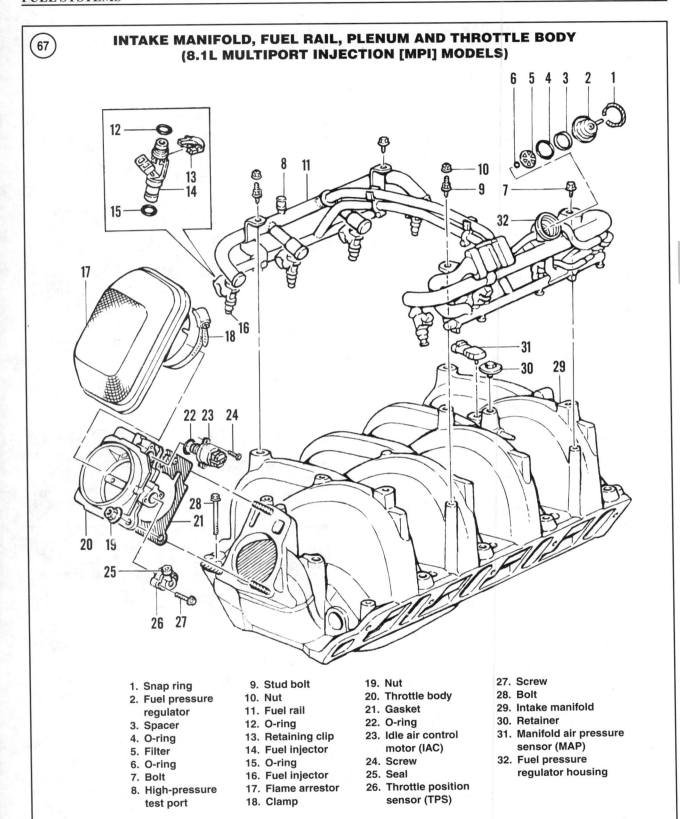

67 INTAKE MANIFOLD, FUEL RAIL, PLENUM AND THROTTLE BODY
(8.1L MULTIPORT INJECTION [MPI] MODELS)

7

1. Snap ring
2. Fuel pressure regulator
3. Spacer
4. O-ring
5. Filter
6. O-ring
7. Bolt
8. High-pressure test port
9. Stud bolt
10. Nut
11. Fuel rail
12. O-ring
13. Retaining clip
14. Fuel injector
15. O-ring
16. Fuel injector
17. Flame arrestor
18. Clamp
19. Nut
20. Throttle body
21. Gasket
22. O-ring
23. Idle air control motor (IAC)
24. Screw
25. Seal
26. Throttle position sensor (TPS)
27. Screw
28. Bolt
29. Intake manifold
30. Retainer
31. Manifold air pressure sensor (MAP)
32. Fuel pressure regulator housing

then *quickly* push the connector onto the test port and release the locking lever.

    b. If the test gauge threads onto the test port, hold the hose fitting in firm contact with the test port. Then *quickly* thread the hose fitting onto the test port.

5. Direct the bleed hose into a container suitable for holding fuel. Open the valve on the gauge until the pressure is completely relieved. Allow all fuel to drain from the hose.

    a. If the test gauge uses a lever to lock the hose fitting onto the test port, lift the locking lever and pull the connector off the test port.

    b. If the test gauge threads onto the test port, wrap a shop towel around the test point. Then *slowly* unthread the fitting.

6. Clean up any spilled fuel and replace the cap. Open the valve and allow all fuel to drain from the bleed hose.

7. Inspect the fuel for contamination. If not contaminated, empty the fuel into the boat fuel tank. Dispose of contaminated fuel in an environmentally responsible manner. Contact a marine dealership or local government official for information on the proper disposal of fuel.

8. Connect the battery cables only after completing the fuel system service procedure.

Throttle Body Removal and Installation

This section describes throttle body removal and installation. Replace the mounting gasket anytime the throttle body mounting fasteners are removed.

Throttle body injection (TBI) models

Refer to **Figure 68** for this procedure.

1. Disconnect the battery cables.

2. Remove the screw (A, **Figure 62**) and plastic cover (B) from the flame arrestor.

3. Remove the flame arrestor (A, **Figure 69**) from the throttle body.

4. Relieve the fuel system pressure as described in this section.

5. Disconnect the injector wire harness from the throttle position sensor (A, **Figure 70**), idle air control motor (B) and both fuel injectors. Pinch the two white plastic arms (A, **Figure 71**) to unplug the fuel injector connectors. Pull the injector harness grommet (B, **Figure 71**) out of the notch in the throttle body.

6. Disconnect the pressure line from the throttle body as follows:

    a. Engage a wrench onto the throttle body pressure line fitting (B, **Figure 69**) to prevent rotation. The pressure line fitting is on the port side.

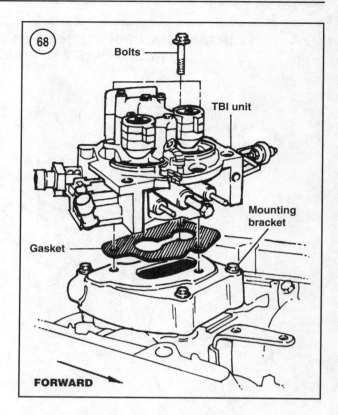

    b. Wrap a shop towel around the fitting to capture spilled fuel.

    c. Use a flare nut wrench to loosen the pressure line. Allow the line to drain completely and then unthread the pressure line. Remove the O-ring from the line or throttle body. Discard the O-ring.

7. On models with a return fuel delivery system, disconnect the return line from the throttle body as follows:

    a. Engage a wrench onto the throttle body return line (C, **Figure 69**) to prevent rotation. The return line fitting is on the starboard side (port side on V-drive models).

9. Push the cable end retainer (A, **Figure 72**) toward the cable anchor (B) and then pull the cable end off the throttle arm.

10. Disconnect the PCV hose from the rear of the throttle body. Disconnect the manifold air pressure (MAP) sensor hose from the throttle body.

11. Remove the three bolts (**Figure 68**) and then lift the TBI unit off the mounting bracket.

12. Remove the gasket (**Figure 68**) from the mounting bracket or throttle body. Carefully scrape all gasket material from the mating surfaces. Do not damage the surfaces. Residual gasket material or damaged surfaces will allow air leakage and cause poor idle characteristics and a lean operating condition. Use aerosol carburetor cleaner to remove oily deposits or other material from the mating surfaces.

13. If the throttle body requires repair or replacement, refer to *Fuel Rail and Injectors* in this section.

14. Fit a new gasket (**Figure 68**) onto the mounting plate. Align the mounting bolt and throttle bore openings.

15. Install the TBI unit (**Figure 68**) onto the mounting bracket.

16. Hand-thread the three mounting bolts (**Figure 68**) into the throttle body and mounting bracket. Tighten the bolts evenly to 142 in.-lb. (16 N•m).

17. Connect the pressure line onto the throttle body as follows:

    a. Lubricate a new O-ring with dishwashing soap and then install it onto the pressure line. Do not cut the O-ring on the threads during installation.

    b. Remove the caps and plugs from the fittings and then hand-thread the pressure line into the port side of the throttle body.

    c. Rotate the fitting to prevent line stress or kinking. Engage a wrench onto the throttle body fitting to prevent rotation.

    d. Hold the elbow section of the line in position. Then tighten the pressure line to 204 in.-lb. (23 N•m). Do not allow the throttle body fitting to rotate while tightening the pressure line.

18. On models with a return fuel delivery system, connect the return line to the throttle body as follows:

    a. Lubricate a new O-ring with dishwashing soap and then install the O-ring onto the return line. Do not cut the O-ring on the threads during installation.

    b. Remove the caps and plugs from the fittings. Then hand-thread the return line into the starboard side throttle body.

    c. Rotate the fitting to prevent line stress or kinking. Engage a wrench onto the throttle body fitting to prevent rotation.

    b. Wrap a shop towel around the fitting to capture spilled fuel.

    c. Use a flare nut wrench to loosen the return line fitting. Allow the line to drain completely and then unthread the return line. Remove the O-ring from the line or throttle body. Discard the O-ring.

8. Drain all fuel in the pressure and return lines into a suitable container. Plug the lines and throttle body to prevent contamination.

d. Hold the elbow section of the line in position and then tighten the return line to 204 in.-lb. (23 N•m). Do not allow the throttle body fitting to rotate while tightening the return line.

19. Connect the PCV hose to the rear of the throttle body. Connect the MAP sensor hose to the remaining fitting at the rear of the throttle body.

20. Fit the injector wire harness grommet into the notch in the throttle body (B, **Figure 71**). Pinch the white plastic arms and then plug the injector harness connectors (A, **Figure 71**) onto the fuel injectors. The connectors can attach to either injector.

21. Connect the engine wire harness to the throttle position sensor (A, **Figure 70**) and idle air control motor (B).

22. Push the cable end retainer (A, **Figure 72**) toward the cable anchor (B). Then fit the cable end fully over the ball-shaped end of the throttle lever. Rotate the retainer to align the slot in the back of the retainer with the pin. Then slide the slot in the retainer over the pin. The internal spring holds the retainer in position. Tug lightly on the cable end to verify a secure connection.

23. Route the wiring to prevent interference with the throttle linkage and other moving components. Secure the wiring with plastic locking clamps as needed.

24. Adjust the throttle cable as described in Chapter Five.

25. Connect the battery cables.

CAUTION
Use a flush test device or other means to supply the engine with cooling water if running the engine with the boat out of the water. The seawater pump is quickly damaged if operated without adequate cooling water.

26. Start the engine and immediately check for fuel leakage at all fuel line and hose connections, throttle body injector housing mating surfaces and the fuel pressure regulator cover. Stop the engine and repair any leaks before operating the engine.

27. Carefully install the flame arrestor (A, **Figure 69**) onto the throttle body. Do not pinch the fuel injector wires between the throttle body and flame arrestor.

28. Install the plastic cover (B, **Figure 62**) onto the flame arrestor. Guide the screw (A, **Figure 62**) into the cover, flame arrestor and throttle body openings. Lift the cover and flame arrestor slightly to align the screw with the threaded opening.

5.0L and 5.7L multiport injection (MPI) models (with a center-mounted throttle body)

Refer to **Figure 64** for this procedure.

1. Disconnect the battery cables.

2. Remove the plastic cover and flame arrestor from the throttle body.

3. Disconnect the engine wire harness from the throttle position sensor and idle air control (IAC) motor. The IAC is located on the rear of the throttle body. The throttle position sensor is located on the side of the throttle body.

4. Push the cable end retainer (A, **Figure 72**) toward the cable anchor (B) and then pull the cable end off the throttle arm.

5. Disconnect the PCV hose from the fitting on the rear of the throttle body.

6. Remove the screw (3, **Figure 64**) and then move the MAP sensor bracket away from the throttle body.

7. Remove the three screws (4, **Figure 64**) and then lift the throttle body (5) off the intake manifold.

8. Remove the gasket (6, **Figure 64**) from the intake manifold or throttle body. Carefully scrape all gasket material from the mating surfaces. Do not damage the surfaces. Residual gasket material or damaged surfaces will allow air leakage and cause poor idle characteristics and a lean operating condition. Use aerosol carburetor cleaner to remove oily deposits or other material from the mating surfaces.

9. Remove the throttle position sensor (TPS) and IAC as described in Chapter Nine.

10. Soak the throttle body in a mild solvent and blow dry with compressed air. Inspect the throttle body for cracks, loose throttle shaft or plate, or other defects. Replace the throttle body if these or other defects are evident.

11. After cleaning and inspection, install the TPS and IAC as described in Chapter Nine.

12. Fit a new gasket (6, **Figure 64**) onto the intake manifold.

13. Install the throttle body (5, **Figure 64**) onto the gasket and intake manifold.

14. Hand-thread the three mounting screws (4, **Figure 64**) into the throttle body, gasket and intake manifold.

15. Fit the MAP sensor bracket (2, **Figure 64**) onto the boss for the fourth mounting screw. Install the screw (3, **Figure 64**) into the bracket, throttle body, gasket and intake manifold.

16. Tighten the four throttle body mounting screws in a crossing pattern to 132 in.-lb. (15 N•m).

17. Connect the PCV hose to the rear of the throttle body.

18. Connect the engine wire harness to the TPS and IAC connectors. The IAC is located on the rear of the throttle body. The TPS is located on the side of the throttle body.

19. Push the cable end retainer (A, **Figure 72**) toward the cable anchor (B) and then fit the cable end fully over the ball-shaped end of the throttle lever. Rotate the retainer to align the slot in the back of the retainer with the pin. Then slide the slot in the retainer over the pin. The internal

spring holds the retainer in position. Tug lightly on the cable end to verify a secure connection.

20. Adjust the throttle cable as described in Chapter Five.

21. Install the flame arrestor and plastic cover. Route the wiring to prevent interference with the throttle linkage and other moving components. Secure the wiring with plastic locking clamps as needed.

22. Connect the battery cables.

5.0L and 5.7L multiport injection (MPI) models (with a front-mounted throttle body)

Refer to **Figure 65** for this procedure.

1. Disconnect the battery cables.

2. Loosen the hose clamp and then carefully pull the flame arrestor off the throttle body flange.

3. Disconnect the engine wire harness from the TPS and IAC. Both components are located on the side of the throttle body opposite the throttle cable.

4. Push the cable end retainer (A, **Figure 72**) toward the cable anchor (B) and then pull the cable end off the throttle arm.

5. Support the throttle body and then remove the three screws (24, **Figure 65**). Pull the throttle body (23, **Figure 65**) off the plenum (21).

6. Remove the gasket (22, **Figure 65**) from the plenum or throttle body. Carefully scrape all gasket material from the mating surfaces. Do not damage the surfaces. Residual gasket material or damaged surfaces will allow air leakage and cause poor idle characteristics and a lean operating condition. Use aerosol carburetor cleaner to remove oily deposits or other material from the mating surfaces.

7. Remove the TPS and IAC as described in Chapter Nine.

8. Soak the throttle body in a mild solvent and blow dry with compressed air. Inspect the throttle body for cracks, loose throttle shaft or plate, or other defects. Replace the throttle body if these or other defects are evident.

9. After cleaning and inspection, install the TPS and IAC as described in Chapter Nine.

10. Insert the three screws (24, **Figure 65**) into the throttle body and then fit the *new* gasket (22) onto the throttle body. Make sure the openings in the gasket match the openings in the throttle body and plenum.

11. Install the throttle body (23, **Figure 65**) onto the plenum.

12. Install the three mounting screws and tighten evenly to 132 in.-lb. (15 N•m).

13. Connect the engine wire harness to the TPS and IAC. Both components are located on the side of the throttle body opposite the throttle cable.

14. Push the cable end retainer (A, **Figure 72**) toward the cable anchor (B) and then fit the cable end fully over the ball-shaped end of the throttle lever. Rotate the retainer to align the slot in the back of the retainer with the pin and then slide the slot in the retainer over the pin. The internal spring holds the retainer in position. Tug lightly on the cable end to verify a secure connection.

15. Adjust the throttle cable as described in Chapter Five.

16. Install the flame arrestor over the throttle body flange. Securely tighten the hose clamp to retain the flame arrestor.

17. Route the wiring to prevent interference with the throttle linkage and other moving components. Secure the wiring with plastic locking clamps as needed.

18. Connect the battery cables.

7.4L and 8.2L multiport injection (MPI) models

Refer to **Figure 66** for this procedure.

1. Disconnect the battery cables.

2. Remove the plastic covers (2 and 5, **Figure 66**, typical) from the engine.

3. Loosen the hose clamp (31, **Figure 66**) and then carefully pull the flame arrestor (19) off the throttle body flange.

4. Disconnect the engine wire harness from the TPS and IAC. Both components are located on the side of the throttle body opposite the throttle cable.

5. Push the cable end retainer (A, **Figure 72**) toward the cable anchor (B) and then pull the cable end off the throttle arm.

6. Support the throttle body and then remove the three screws (20, **Figure 66**). Pull the throttle body (30, **Figure 66**) off the plenum (3).

7. Remove the gasket (28, **Figure 66**) from the plenum or throttle body. Carefully scrape all gasket material from the mating surfaces. Do not damage the surfaces. Residual gasket material or damaged surfaces will allow air leakage and cause poor idle characteristics and a lean operating condition. Use aerosol carburetor cleaner to remove oily deposits or other material from the mating surfaces.

8. Remove the TPS and IAC as described in Chapter Nine.

9. Soak the throttle body in a mild solvent and blow dry with compressed air. Inspect the throttle body for cracks, loose throttle shaft or plate or other defects. Replace the throttle body if these or other defects are evident.

10. After cleaning and inspection, install the TPS and IAC as described in Chapter Nine.

11. Insert the three screws (20, **Figure 66**) into the throttle body and then fit the *new* gasket (28) onto the throttle body.

7

12. Install the throttle body (30, **Figure 66**) onto the plenum.

13. Install the three mounting screws and tighten evenly to 132 in.-lb. (15 N•m).

14. Connect the engine wire harness connectors onto the TPS and IAC connectors. Both components are located on the side of the throttle body opposite the throttle cable.

15. Push the cable end retainer (A, **Figure 72**) toward the cable anchor (B) and then fit the cable end fully over the ball-shaped end of the throttle lever. Rotate the retainer to align the slot in the back of the retainer with the pin and then slide the slot in the retainer over the pin. The internal spring holds the retainer in position. Tug lightly on the cable end to verify a secure connection.

16. Adjust the throttle cable as described in Chapter Five.

17. Install the flame arrestor (19, **Figure 66**) over the throttle body flange. Securely tighten the hose clamp (31, **Figure 66**) to retain the flame arrestor.

18. Route the wiring to prevent interference with the throttle linkage and other moving components. Secure the wiring with plastic locking clamps as needed.

19. Install the plastic covers (2 and 5, **Figure 66**, typical) onto the engine. Securely tighten the cover retaining screws.

20. Connect the battery cables.

8.1L multiport injection (MPI) models

Refer to **Figure 67** for this procedure.

1. Disconnect the battery cables.

2. Loosen the hose clamp (18, **Figure 67**) and then carefully pull the flame arrestor (17) off the throttle body flange.

3. Disconnect the engine wire harness from the TPS (26, **Figure 67**) and IAC (23).

4. Push the cable end retainer (A, **Figure 72**) toward the cable anchor (B) and then pull the cable end off the throttle arm.

5. Support the throttle body (20, **Figure 67**) and then remove the three nuts (19). Pull the throttle body off the intake manifold (29, **Figure 67**).

6. Remove the gasket (21, **Figure 67**) from the intake manifold or throttle body. Carefully scrape all gasket material from the mating surfaces. Do not damage the surfaces. Residual gasket material or damaged surfaces will allow air leakage and cause poor idle characteristics and a lean operating condition. Use aerosol carburetor cleaner to remove oily deposits or other material from the mating surfaces.

7. Remove the TPS and IAC motor as described in Chapter Nine.

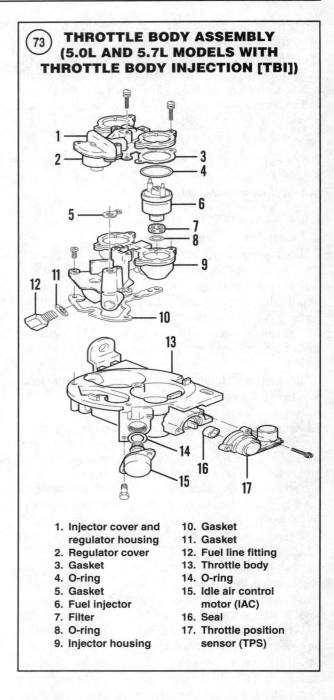

73 **THROTTLE BODY ASSEMBLY (5.0L AND 5.7L MODELS WITH THROTTLE BODY INJECTION [TBI])**

1. Injector cover and regulator housing
2. Regulator cover
3. Gasket
4. O-ring
5. Gasket
6. Fuel injector
7. Filter
8. O-ring
9. Injector housing
10. Gasket
11. Gasket
12. Fuel line fitting
13. Throttle body
14. O-ring
15. Idle air control motor (IAC)
16. Seal
17. Throttle position sensor (TPS)

8. Soak the throttle body in a mild solvent and blow dry with compressed air. Inspect the throttle body for cracks, loose throttle shaft or plate, or other defects. Replace the throttle body if these or other defects are evident.

9. After cleaning and inspection, install the TPS and IAC as described in Chapter Nine.

10. Fit a new gasket (21, **Figure 67**) over the studs and seat it onto the intake manifold (29).

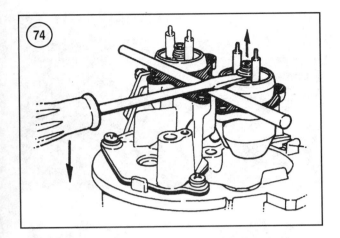

11. Install the throttle body (20, **Figure 67**) onto the intake manifold.

12. Hand-thread the three nuts (19, **Figure 67**) onto the studs. Then tighten the nuts evenly to 89 in.-lb. (10 N•m).

13. Connect the engine wire harness to the TPS (26, **Figure 67**) and IAC (23).

14. Push the cable end retainer (A, **Figure 72**) toward the cable anchor (B) and then fit the cable end fully over the ball-shaped end of the throttle lever. Rotate the retainer to align the slot in the back of the retainer with the pin, then slide the slot in the retainer over the pin. The internal spring holds the retainer in position. Tug lightly on the cable end to verify a secure connection.

15. Adjust the throttle cable as described in Chapter Five.

16. Install the flame arrestor (17, **Figure 67**) over the throttle body flange. Securely tighten the hose clamp (18, **Figure 67**) to retain the flame arrestor.

17. Route the wiring to prevent interference with the throttle linkage and other moving components. Secure the wiring with plastic locking clamps as needed.

18. Connect the battery cables.

Fuel Rail and Injectors
Removal and Installation

This section describes removal and installation of the fuel injectors and fuel rail. Repair of the throttle body assembly used on TBI models is also described in this section. Replace all O-rings and gaskets anytime they are removed. Consider reusing a gasket only if it is in excellent condition and a *new* replacement is not available. Never reuse O-rings.

5.0L and 5.7L throttle body injection (TBI) models

Failure of the fuel pressure regulator is almost always the result of debris under the diaphragm and housing seats. Cleaning the seats usually corrects the fault. Replace the throttle body assembly if the regulator diaphragm or seating surfaces are damaged. The housing, cover, spring and diaphragm are not available separately.

Refer to **Figure 73** for this procedure.

1. Disconnect the battery cables.

2. Relieve the fuel system pressure as described in this section.

3. Remove the throttle body as described in this section.

4. Remove the screws. Then *carefully* lift the injector cover and regulator housing (1, **Figure 73**) off the injector housing (9). Do not remove the regulator unless it must be replaced. Refer to *Fuel Pressure Regulator Replacement* in this section.

5. Leave the gasket (3, **Figure 73**) in place during injector removal to protect the injector housing.

6. Use a screwdriver as a fulcrum as shown in **Figure 74** and pry the injectors from the housing.

7. Remove the gaskets (3 and 5, **Figure 73**) from the injector housing or injector cover and regulator housing. Discard the gaskets.

8. Remove the O-rings (4 and 8, **Figure 73**) from the fuel injectors (6) or injector bores in the housing (9). Discard the O-rings.

9. Carefully slide the filter (7, **Figure 73**) off the injectors.

10. Remove the pressure and return fittings (12, **Figure 73**) and gaskets (11) from the housing. Discard the gaskets. If the throttle body does not use a return line, remove the plug and gasket from the opening used for the return line fitting. Remove and discard the gasket for the plug also.

11. Remove the screws and then lift the injector housing out of the throttle body (13).

12. Remove the TPS (17, **Figure 73**) and IAC (15) from the throttle body as described in Chapter Nine.

13. Remove the gasket (10, **Figure 73**) from the throttle body or injector housing. Carefully scrape all gasket material from the surfaces. Do not damage the surfaces. Surface damage will allow air or fuel leakage.

14. Soak the injector housing and throttle body in mild solvent and dry using compressed air. *Do not* soak the injector cover and regulator housing or injectors in solvent. Solvent will damage these components.

15. Inspect the passages in the injector cover and regulator housing for gummy deposits or other contaminants. If contaminated, remove the fuel pressure regulator as described in this section.

7

16. Inspect the filters for blockage or damage. Replace filters that are damaged or cannot be completely cleaned with solvent.

17. Inspect the throttle body for cracks, loose throttle shaft or plate, or other defects. Replace the throttle body assembly if these or other defects are evident.

18. Inspect the injector housing and injector cover and regulator housing for cracks or damaged mating surfaces. Replace the throttle body assembly if these or other defects are evident.

19. If removed, install the fuel pressure regulator as described in this section.

20. Install a *new* gasket (10, **Figure 73**) onto the throttle body (13). Install the injector housing (9, **Figure 73**) into the throttle body and seat it against the gasket.

21. Apply a light coat of Loctite 262 to the injector housing screw threads. Install the screws into the housing, gasket and throttle body. Tighten the screws in a crossing pattern to 35 in.-lb. (4.0 N•m).

22. Carefully slide the filters over the injector bodies and position over the openings. Lubricate the new O-rings with dishwashing soap and fit the O-ring (4 and 8, **Figure 73**) into the injector housing. Rest the smaller O-rings in the recess at the bottom of the injector bore. Rest the larger O-ring on the step at the top of the bore.

23. Without dislodging the O-rings, insert the injectors into the housing. Push down on the injectors until fully seated.

24. Install *new* gaskets (3 and 5, **Figure 73**) onto the injector housing (9) and then install the injector cover and regulator housing.

25. Align the screw openings. Apply a light coat of Loctite 262 to the threads of the injector housing screws and then install the screws. Tighten the screws in a crossing pattern to 27 in.-lb. (3.0 N•m).

26. Install the TPS (17, **Figure 73**) and IAC (15) onto the throttle body as described in Chapter Nine.

27. Fit a *new* gasket (11, **Figure 73**) onto the pressure and return fittings (12). Thread the fittings into the injector housing. Tighten the pressure line to 30 ft.-lb. (40 N•m). Tighten the return line to 21 ft.-lb. (29 N•m). If the throttle body does not use a return line fitting, install a new gasket onto the plug and thread into the opening used by the return fitting. Tighten the plug to 21 ft.-lb. (29 N•m).

28. Install the throttle body as described in this section.

5.0L and 5.7L multiport injection (MPI) models (with a center-mounted throttle body)

Early models use threaded flare nut fuel line connections (**Figure 75**) for the pressure and return lines. Later models use quick-connect fittings (**Figure 76**). A special

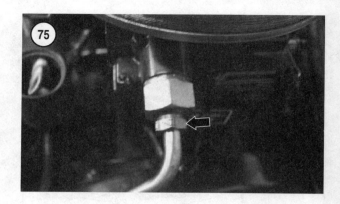

quick-connect separator tool is required to disconnect the lines on models so equipped. Purchase the separator tool from an automotive parts store or marine dealership (Volvo Penta part No. 885384).

Refer to **Figure 64** for this procedure.

1. Disconnect the battery cables.

2. Relieve the fuel system pressure as described in this section.

3. Remove the plastic cover and flame arrestor from the throttle body.

4. Disconnect the engine wire harness from the TPS and IAC. The IAC is located on the rear of the throttle body. The TPS is located on the side of the throttle body.

5. Push the cable end retainer (A, **Figure 72**) toward the cable anchor (B) and then pull the cable end off the throttle arm.

6. Place a shop towel under the fuel line fittings to capture spilled fuel. The pressure line connects to the fitting in the crossover tube at the rear of the assembly. The return line connects to the fuel pressure regulator. Models with the fuel pump mounted inside the fuel tank and a no-return fuel system do not use a return line fitting. Do not loosen the fittings at this time.

7. Unplug the vacuum hose from the regulator (9, **Figure 64**). If fuel is found in the vacuum hose, replace the regu-

lator as described in this section. This indicates the diaphragm in the regulator is leaking.

8. Mark the cylinder number on each fuel injector harness connector (**Figure 77**, typical). The fuel injectors are located above the respective cylinders. On models using an inline transmission with the pulleys and belts facing the front of the boat, odd-numbered cylinders are located on the port bank with the No. 1 cylinder at the front followed by No. 3, 5 and 7. Even-numbered cylinders are located on the starboard bank with the No. 2 cylinders at the front followed by No. 4, 6 and 8. On models using a V-drive transmission with the pulleys and belts facing the rear of the boat, odd-numbered cylinders are located on the starboard bank with the No. 1 cylinder at the rear working forward with No. 3, 5 and 7. Even-numbered cylinders are located on the port bank with the No. 2 cylinder at the rear working forward with No. 4, 6 and 8. Depress the locking clip and then unplug the connector from each injector. Route the injector harness to a location that prevents interference during fuel rail removal and installation.

9. Use compressed air to blow all debris from the intake manifold, fuel rail and hose fittings. Mark the fuel line fittings to identify the connection points prior to removal.

10A. On early models (flare nut fuel line connectors) (**Figure 75**), disconnect the pressure line as follows:
   a. Engage a wrench onto the fuel rail fitting to prevent rotation.
   b. Wrap a shop towel around the fitting to capture spilled fuel.
   c. Use a flare nut wrench to loosen the pressure line fitting. Allow the line to drain completely and then unthread the pressure line. Remove the O-ring from the line fitting. Discard the O-ring.

10B. On late models (quick-connect fuel line connectors) (**Figure 76**), disconnect the pressure line from the fuel rail as follows:
   a. Fit the separator tool over the male fitting (**Figure 78**).
   b. Insert the projection on the separator tool into the opening in the female end of the fitting.
   c. Push the tool to expand the retaining spring and then separate the fuel line from the fuel rail. Allow the line to drain completely.
   d. Inspect the O-ring(s) in the male end of the quick-connect fitting for damage or excessive wear. Replace the O-rings unless in excellent condition.

11A. On models with a return fuel delivery system using flare nut fuel line connectors, disconnect the return line from the fuel pressure regulator as follows:
   a. Engage a wrench onto the fuel pressure regulator fitting to prevent rotation.
   b. Wrap a shop towel around the fitting to capture spilled fuel.
   c. Use a flare nut wrench to loosen the return line fitting. Allow the line to drain completely and then unthread the return line. Remove the O-ring from the line fitting or pressure regulator fitting. Discard the O-ring.

11B. On models with a return fuel delivery system using quick-connect fuel line connectors, disconnect the return line from the fuel pressure regulator as follows:
   a. Fit the separator tool over the male fitting (**Figure 78**).
   b. Insert the projection on the separator tool into the opening in the female fitting.
   c. Push the tool to expand the retaining spring and then separate the fuel line from the regulator. Allow the line to drain completely.
   d. Inspect the O-ring(s) in the male end of the quick-connect fitting for damage or excessive wear. Replace the O-rings unless in excellent condition.

11C. On models with a no-return fuel delivery system using quick-connect fuel line connectors, disconnect the cap from the fuel pressure regulator as follows:

7

a. Fit the separator tool over the cap fitting (**Figure 78**).

b. Insert the projection on the separator tool into the opening in the female fitting.

c. Push the tool to expand the retaining spring and then separate the cap from the fuel pressure regulator. Allow the line to drain completely.

d. Inspect the O-ring(s) in the male end of the quick-connect fitting for damage or excessive wear. Replace the O-rings unless in excellent condition.

12. Drain all fuel from the fuel lines into a suitable container. Plug all openings to prevent contamination.

13. Remove the four screws (10, **Figure 64**) and then lift the fuel rail assembly and injectors off the intake manifold.

14. Remove the seal (**Figure 79**) from the injectors or corresponding openings in the intake manifold. Discard the seals.

15. Use aerosol solvent to thoroughly clean the intake manifold openings and dry with compressed air. Cover the openings to prevent contamination.

CAUTION
*Remove the fuel injector filter (**Figure 79**) only if it has a flange of sufficient diameter to rest against the top of the injector. Do not remove the filter if it does not have the flange or is located completely inside the opening. The filter without the flange is not designed for removal.*

16. Remove the injectors from the fuel rails as follows:

a. Slide the small metal clip along the grooves in the rail until the slot in the clip is free from the groove in the injector body.

b. Pull the injector out of the fuel rail.

c. Remove the grommet (**Figure 79**) from the injector. Some models do not use the grommet.

d. Remove the O-ring (**Figure 79**) from the groove at the top of the injector. Discard the O-ring.

e. If the flange at the top of the filter (**Figure 79**) extends from the opening, carefully pull the filter out of the injector. Discard the filter.

f. Repeat this step for the remaining injectors. Place the injectors in a sealed container to prevent contamination.

17. Remove the fuel pressure regulator as described in this section.

18. Use mild solvent to flush the fuel rail passages. Do not apply solvent to the injectors or fuel pressure regulator. Solvent may damage these components. Direct pressurized air into the passages to remove solvent and contaminants.

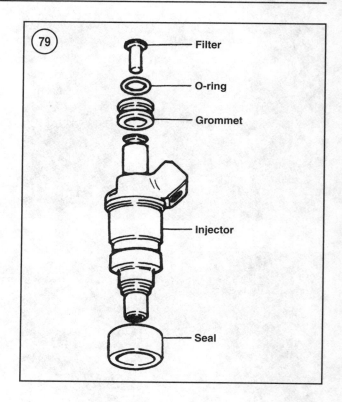

19. Install the fuel pressure regulator as described in this section.

20. Install the fuel injectors into the fuel rail as follows:

a. If removed, insert the new filters (**Figure 79**) into the injectors. Seat the filter flange against the top of the injector.

b. Lubricate the new O-rings with engine oil and then install the *new* O-ring (**Figure 79**) into the groove near the top of the fuel injector.

c. If used, install the grommet (**Figure 79**) over the inlet end of the fuel injector and seat against the step in the injector bodies.

d. Position the small metal clip into the grooves in the fuel rail with the slot facing the corresponding fuel injector groove.

e. Without dislodging or pinching the O-ring, insert the injector into the fuel rail opening.

f. Hold the injector in position and then slide the retainer along the grooves in the rail until the slot in the retainer seats into the corresponding groove in the injector body. Tug on the injector to verify a secure connection.

g. Lubricate with engine oil and then fit the *new* seal (**Figure 79**) over the lower end of the injector. Seat the seal against the step on the injector body.

h. Repeat this step for the remaining injectors.

21. *Slowly* rotate the injector to position the harness connector side of the injector facing away from the fuel rail.

22. Remove the covering and then apply a light coat of oil into the injector openings in the intake manifold.

23. Carefully guide all of the injectors into the respective intake manifold openings while installing the fuel rail onto the intake manifold. Verify that all injectors have entered their openings then seat the fuel rail onto the intake manifold.

24. Apply a coat of Loctite 243 onto the threads. Then install the four screws (10, **Figure 64**) into the fuel rail and intake manifold. Tighten the screws to 180 in.-lb. (20 N•m).

25A. On models using flare nut fuel line connectors (**Figure 75**), connect the pressure line to the fuel rail as follows:

a. Lubricate with liquid dish soap and then install a *new* O-ring onto the pressure line fitting. Do not cut the O-ring on the threads during installation.

b. Remove the caps and plugs from the fittings and then hand-thread the pressure line into the fuel rail.

c. Rotate the fitting to prevent line stress or kinking. Engage a wrench onto the fuel rail fitting to prevent rotation.

d. Have an assistant hold the fuel line in position to prevent twisting. Then tighten the pressure line to 115 in.-lb. (13 N•m). Do not allow the fuel rail fitting to rotate while tightening the pressure line.

25B. On models using quick-connect fuel line connectors (**Figure 76**), connect the pressure line to the fuel rail as follows:

a. Remove any caps or plugs from the connectors.

b. Apply a light coat of engine oil to the O-ring in the male end of the quick connect fitting.

c. Guide the male end of the fitting into the female fitting. Push the fittings together until they lock. Tug on the pressure line to verify a secure connection.

26A. On models with a return fuel delivery system using flare nut fuel line connectors, connect the return line to the fuel pressure regulator as follows:

a. Lubricate with liquid dish soap and then install a *new* O-ring onto the return line fitting. Do not cut the O-ring on the threads during installation.

b. Remove the caps and plugs from the fittings and then hand-thread the return line into the fuel pressure regulator.

c. Rotate the fitting to prevent line stress or kinking. Engage a wrench onto the fuel pressure regulator fitting to prevent rotation.

d. Have an assistant hold the fuel line in position to prevent twisting and then tighten the return line to 156 in.-lb. (17.6 N•m). Do not allow the fuel pres-

sure regulator fitting to rotate while tightening the return line fitting.

26B. On models with a return fuel delivery system using quick-connect fuel line connectors, connect the return line to the fuel pressure regulator as follows:

a. Remove any cap or plugs from the connectors.

b. Apply a light coat of engine oil to the O-ring in the male end of the quick-connect fitting.

c. Guide the male end of the pressure regulator fitting into the female fitting. Push the fittings together until they lock. Tug on the return line to verify a secure connection.

26C. On models with a no-return type fuel delivery system, using quick connect type fuel line connectors, connect the cap onto the fuel pressure regulator as follows:

a. Remove any cap or plugs from the connectors.

b. Apply a light coating of engine oil onto the O-ring in the male end of the quick connect fitting.

c. Guide the male end of the fitting into the cap. Push the cap onto the fuel rail fitting until they lock. Tug on the cap to verify a secure connection.

27. Depress the locking clip and then plug the injector harness connectors onto the respective injectors.

28. Plug the vacuum hose onto the fuel pressure regulator.

29. Connect the PCV hose to the fitting at the rear of the throttle body.

30. Connect the engine wire harness to the TPS and IAC connectors. The IAC is located on the rear of the throttle body. The TPS is located on the side of the throttle body.

31. Push the cable end retainer (A, **Figure 72**) toward the cable anchor (B) and then fit the cable end fully over the ball-shaped end of the throttle lever. Rotate the retainer to align the slot in the back of the retainer with the pin and then slide the slot in the retainer over the pin. The internal spring holds the retainer in position. Tug lightly on the cable end to verify a secure connection.

32. Adjust the throttle cable as described in Chapter Five.

33. Connect the battery cables.

CAUTION
Use a flush test device or other means to supply the engine with cooling water if running the engine with the boat out of the water. The seawater pump is quickly damaged if operated without adequate cooling water.

34. Start the engine and immediately check for fuel leakage at the regulator housing, fuel rail, injectors, and all fuel line and hose connections. Stop the engine and repair any leaks before operating the engine.

7

35. Stop the engine. Route the wiring to prevent interference with throttle linkages and other moving components. Secure the wiring with plastic locking clamps as needed.

36. Install the flame arrestor and plastic cover. Securely tighten the flame arrestor nut(s).

5.0L and 5.7L multiport injection (MPI) models (with front-mounted throttle body)

Early models use threaded flare nut fuel line connections (**Figure 75**) for the pressure and return lines. Later models use quick-connect fittings (**Figure 76**) for the pressure line and return line. On these models, a special separator tool is required to disconnect the lines. Purchase the separator tool from an automotive parts store or Volvo Penta stern drive dealership (Volvo Penta part No. 885384).

Refer to **Figure 65** for this procedure.

1. Disconnect the battery cables.

2. Relieve the fuel system pressure as described in this section.

3. Place a shop towel under the fuel line fittings to capture spilled fuel. The pressure line connects to the fitting in the middle of the starboard side fuel rail (port side on V-drive models). The return line connects to the fuel pressure regulator. Models with the fuel pump mounted inside the fuel tank and with a no-return fuel system do not use a return line fitting. Do not loosen the fittings at this time.

4. Unplug the vacuum hose (1, **Figure 65**) from the fuel pressure regulator (2). Replace the regulator as described in this section if fuel is found in the vacuum hose. This indicates the diaphragm in the regulator is leaking.

5. Mark the cylinder number on each fuel injector harness connector (**Figure 77**, typical). The fuel injectors are located above the respective cylinders. On models using an in-line transmission with the pulleys and belts facing the front of the boat, odd-numbered cylinders are located on the port bank with the No. 1 cylinder at the front followed by No. 3, 5 and 7. Even-numbered cylinders are located on the starboard bank with the No. 2 cylinders at the front followed by No. 4, 6 and 8. On models using a V-drive transmission with the pulleys and belts facing the rear of the boat, odd-numbered cylinders are located on the starboard bank with the No. 1 cylinder at the rear working forward with No. 3, 5 and 7. Even-numbered cylinders are located on the port bank with the No. 2 cylinder at the rear working forward with No. 4, 6 and 8. Depress the locking clip and unplug the connector from each injector. Route the injector harness to a location that prevents interference during fuel rail removal and installation.

6. Use compressed air to blow all debris from the intake manifold, fuel rail and hose fittings. Mark the fuel line fittings to identify the connection points prior to removal.

7A. On models using flare nut fuel line connectors (**Figure 75**), disconnect the pressure line as follows:

   a. Engage a wrench onto the fuel rail fitting to prevent rotation.

   b. Wrap a shop towel around the fitting to capture spilled fuel.

   c. Use a flare nut wrench to loosen the pressure line fitting. Allow the line to drain completely and then unthread the pressure line. Remove the O-ring from the line or fuel rail fitting. Discard the O-ring.

7B. On models using quick-connect fuel line connectors (**Figure 76**), disconnect the pressure line from the fuel rail as follows:

   a. Fit the separator tool over the male fitting (**Figure 78**).

   b. Insert the projection on the separator tool into the opening in the female fitting.

   c. Push the tool to expand the retaining spring and then separate the fuel line from the fuel rail. Allow the line to drain completely.

   d. Inspect the O-ring(s) in the male end of the quick-connect fitting for torn, flattened or deteriorated surfaces. Replace the O-rings unless found to be in excellent condition.

8A. On models with a return fuel delivery system using flare nut fuel line connectors, disconnect the return line from the fuel pressure regulator as follows:

   a. To prevent rotation, engage a wrench onto the fuel pressure regulator fitting.

   b. Wrap a shop towel around the fitting to capture spilled fuel.

   c. Use a flare nut wrench to loosen the return line fitting. Allow the line to drain completely and then unthread the return line. Remove the O-ring from the line or regulator fitting. Discard the O-ring.

8B. On models with a return fuel delivery system using quick-connect fuel line connectors, disconnect the return line from the fuel pressure regulator as follows:

   a. Fit the separator tool over the male fitting (**Figure 78**).

   b. Insert the projection on the separator tool into the opening in the female fitting.

   c. Push the tool to expand the retaining spring and then separate the fuel line from the pressure regulator. Allow the line to drain completely.

   d. Inspect the O-ring(s) in the male end of the quick-connect fitting for torn, flattened or deteriorated surfaces. Replace the O-rings unless in excellent condition.

8C. On models with a no-return fuel delivery system using quick-connect fuel line connectors, disconnect the cap from the fuel pressure regulator as follows:

    a. Fit the separator tool over the cap fitting (**Figure 78**).

    b. Insert the projection on the separator tool into the opening in the female fitting.

    c. Push the tool to expand the retaining spring and then separate the cap from the fuel pressure regulator. Allow the line to drain completely.

    d. Inspect the O-ring(s) in the male end of the quick-connect fitting for torn, flattened or deteriorated surfaces. Replace the O-rings unless in excellent condition.

9. Drain residual fuel from the fuel lines into a suitable container. Plug all openings to prevent contamination.

10. Remove the four screws (two on each side) that secure the fuel rails. Then lift the fuel rail assembly and injectors off the intake manifold/plenum (21, **Figure 65**). Carefully guide the fuel rail assembly under the throttle body during removal.

11. Remove the seals (**Figure 79**) from the injectors or intake manifold. Discard the seals.

12. Use aerosol solvent to thoroughly clean the intake manifold openings and dry with compressed air. Cover the openings to prevent contamination.

CAUTION
*Remove the fuel injector filter (**Figure 79**) only if it has a flange of a sufficient diameter to rest against the top of the injector. Do not remove the filter if it does not have the flange or is located completely inside the opening. The filter without the flange is not designed for removal.*

13. Remove the injectors from the fuel rails as follows:

    a. Slide the small metal clip along the grooves in the rail until the slot in the clip is free from the groove in the injector body.

    b. Pull the injector out of the fuel rail opening.

    c. Remove the grommet (**Figure 79**) from the injector. Some models do not use the grommet.

    d. Remove the O-ring (**Figure 79**) from the groove at the top of the injector. Discard the O-ring.

    e. If the flange at the top of the filter (**Figure 79**) extends from the opening, carefully pull the filter out of the injector. Discard the filter.

    f. Repeat this step for the remaining injectors. Place the injectors in a sealed container to prevent contamination.

14. Remove the fuel pressure regulator as described in this section.

15. Remove the screw (10, **Figure 65**), washer (14) and retainer (15) from each fuel rail. Carefully pull the fuel line (11, **Figure 65**) fittings out of the fuel rail. Remove the O-ring (12, **Figure 65**) from the line fittings or fuel rail. Discard the O-rings.

16. Use mild solvent to flush the fuel rail and fuel line passages. Do not apply solvent to the injectors or fuel pressure regulator. Solvent can damage these components. Direct pressurized air into the passages to remove solvent and contaminants.

17. Install the fuel pressure regulator as described in this section.

18. Remove any covers or caps from the fuel rail openings.

19. Attach the crossover fuel line (11, **Figure 65**) to the fuel rails as follows:

    a. Lubricate with liquid dish soap and then install *new* O-rings (12, **Figure 65**) onto the fuel line fittings. Do not cut the O-rings while sliding them over the fitting.

    b. Align the fuel line with the fuel rail as shown in **Figure 65**. Then guide the lines into the fuel rail. Seat the fittings into the fuel rail openings.

    c. Hold the fuel line in position and then fit the retainers (15, **Figure 65**) over the fuel line fittings. Seat the retainer against the fittings and rotate to align the screw openings.

    d. Hand-thread the screws (13, **Figure 65**) with washers (14) into the retainers and fuel rails. Make sure the retainers fully engage the fuel line fittings and then tighten the screws to 62 in.-lb. (7 N•m).

20. Install the fuel injectors into the fuel rail as follows:

    a. If removed, insert the new filter (**Figure 79**) into the injector opening. Seat the filter flange against the top of the injector.

    b. Lubricate with engine oil and then install the *new* O-ring (**Figure 79**) into the groove near the top of the fuel injector.

    c. If used, install the grommet (**Figure 79**) over the inlet end of the fuel injector and seat against the step in the injector body.

    d. Position the small metal clip into the grooves in the fuel rail with the slot facing the corresponding fuel injector groove.

    e. Without dislodging or pinching the O-ring, insert the injector into the fuel rail opening.

    f. Hold the injector in position and then slide the retainer along the grooves in the rail until the slot in the retainer seats into the corresponding groove in the injector body. Tug on the injector to verify a secure connection.

7

g. Lubricate with engine oil and then fit the *new* seal (**Figure 79**) over the lower end of the injector. Seat the seal against the step on the injector body.

h. Repeat this step for the remaining injectors.

21. *Slowly* rotate the injector to position the harness connector side of the injector facing away from the fuel rail.

22. Remove the covering and then apply a light coat of oil into the injector openings in the intake manifold.

23. Carefully guide the fuel rail under the throttle body and then align all of the injectors with the respective intake manifold openings. Verify that all injectors have entered the openings and then seat the fuel rail.

24. Thread the four screws (two on each side) into the fuel rail and intake manifold/plenum. Tighten the screws to 88 in.-lb. (10 N•m).

25A. On models using flare nut fuel line connectors (**Figure 75**), connect the pressure line onto the fuel rail as follows:

a. Lubricate with liquid dish soap and then install a *new* O-ring onto the pressure line fitting. Do not cut the O-ring on the threads during installation.

b. Remove the caps and plugs from the fittings and then hand-thread the pressure line into the fuel rail fitting.

c. Rotate the fitting to prevent line stress or kinking. Engage a wrench onto the fuel rail fitting to prevent rotation.

d. Have an assistant hold the fuel line in position to prevent twisting and then tighten the pressure line to 115 in.-lb. (13 N•m). Do not allow the fuel rail fitting to rotate while tightening the pressure line.

25B. On models using quick-connect fuel line connectors (**Figure 76**), connect the pressure line onto the fuel rail as follows:

a. Remove any caps or plugs from the connectors.

b. Apply a light coat of engine oil to the O-ring in the male end of the quick-connect fitting.

c. Guide the male end of the fitting into the female fitting. Push the fittings together until they lock. Tug on the pressure line to verify a secure connection.

26A. On models with a return fuel delivery system using flare nut fuel line connectors, connect the return line to the fuel pressure regulator as follows:

a. Lubricate with liquid dish soap and then install a *new* O-ring onto the return line fitting. Do not cut the O-ring on the threads during installation.

b. Remove the caps and plugs from the fittings and then hand-thread the return line fitting into the fuel pressure regulator fitting.

c. Rotate the fitting to prevent line stress or kinking. Engage a wrench onto the fuel pressure regulator fitting to prevent rotation.

d. Have an assistant hold the fuel line in position to prevent twisting and then tighten the return line fitting to 115 in.-lb. (13 N•m). Do not allow the fuel pressure regulator fitting to rotate while tightening the return line fitting.

26B. On models with a return fuel delivery system using quick-connect fuel line connectors, connect the return line onto the fuel pressure regulator as follows:

a. Remove any cap or plugs from the connectors.

b. Apply a light coat of engine oil to the O-ring in the male end of the quick connect fitting.

c. Guide the male end of the pressure regulator fitting into the female fitting. Push the fittings together until they lock. Tug on the return line to verify a secure connection.

26C. On models with a no-return fuel delivery system using quick-connect fuel line connectors, connect the cap onto the fuel pressure regulator as follows:

a. Remove any caps or plugs from the connectors.

b. Apply a light coat of engine oil to the O-ring in the male end of the quick-connect fitting.

c. Guide the male end of the fitting into the cap. Push the cap onto the fuel pressure regulator fitting until it locks. Tug on the cap to verify a secure connection.

27. Depress the locking clip and then plug the injector harness connectors onto the respective injectors.

28. Plug the vacuum hose (1, **Figure 65**) onto the fuel pressure regulator fitting.

29. Connect the battery cables.

CAUTION
Use a flush test device or other means to supply the engine with cooling water if running the engine with the boat out of the water. The seawater pump is quickly damaged if operated without adequate cooling water.

30. Start the engine and immediately check for fuel leakage at the regulator housing, fuel rail, injectors, and all fuel line and hose connections. Stop the engine and repair any leaks before operating the engine.

31. Stop the engine. Route the wiring to prevent interference with throttle linkage and other moving components. Secure the wiring with plastic locking clamps as needed.

7.4L and 8.2L multiport injection (MPI) models

Early models use threaded flare nut fuel line connections (**Figure 75**) for the pressure line and return line. Later models use quick-connect fittings (**Figure 76**) for the pressure line and return line. On these models, a special separator tool is required to disconnect the lines. Purchase the separator tool from an automotive parts store or Volvo Penta stern drive dealership (Volvo Penta part No. 885384).

Refer to **Figure 66** for this procedure.

1. Disconnect the battery cables.

2. Relieve the fuel system pressure as described in this section.

3. Remove the throttle body as described in this section.

4. Disconnect the engine wire harness from the intake air temperature sensor (IAT). The air temperature sensor threads into an opening in the port side of the plenum (3, **Figure 66**). On V-drive models, the sensor is located on the starboard side.

5. Disconnect the crankcase breather tube from the fitting next to the air temperature sensor.

6. Remove the bolts (4, **Figure 66**) and lift the plenum (3) off the intake manifold (12). Remove and discard the gaskets (6, **Figure 66**).

7. Place a shop towel under the fuel line fittings to capture spilled fuel. The pressure line connects to the lower fitting on the aft end of the fuel rail (forward end on V-drive models). The return line connects to the upper fitting at the end of the fuel rail. Models with the fuel pump mounted inside the fuel tank and a no-return fuel system do not use a return line fitting. Do not loosen the fittings at this time.

8. Unplug the vacuum hose from the fuel pressure regulator. Replace the regulator as described in this section if fuel is found in the vacuum hose. This indicates the diaphragm in the regulator is leaking.

9. Mark the cylinder number on each fuel injector harness connector (**Figure 77**, typical). The fuel injectors are located above the respective cylinders. On models using an in-line transmission with the pulleys and belts facing the front of the boat, odd-numbered cylinders are located on the port bank with the No. 1 cylinder at the front followed by No. 3, 5 and 7. Even-numbered cylinders are located on the starboard bank with the No. 2 cylinders at the front followed by No. 4, 6 and 8. On models using a V-drive transmission with the pulleys and belts facing the rear of the boat, odd-numbered cylinders are located on the starboard bank with the No. 1 cylinder at the rear working forward with No. 3, 5 and 7. Even-numbered cylinders are located on the port bank with the No. 2 cylinder at the rear working forward with No. 4, 6 and 8. Depress the locking clip and then unplug the connector from each injector. Route the injector harness (7, **Figure 66**) to a location that prevents interference during fuel rail removal and installation.

10. Use compressed air to blow all debris from the intake manifold, fuel rail and hose fittings. Mark the fuel line to identify the connection points prior to removal.

11A. On models using flare nut fuel line connectors (**Figure 75**), disconnect the pressure line as follows:

   a. Engage a wrench onto the fuel rail fitting to prevent rotation.

   b. Wrap a shop towel around the fitting to capture spilled fuel.

   c. Use a flare nut wrench to loosen the pressure line fitting. Allow the line to drain completely and then unthread the pressure line. Remove the O-ring from the line or fuel rail fitting. Discard the O-ring.

11B. On models using quick-connect fuel line connectors (**Figure 76**), disconnect the pressure line from the fuel rail as follows:

   a. Fit the separator tool over the fuel rail fitting (**Figure 78**).

   b. Insert the projection on the separator tool into the opening in the female fitting.

   c. Push the tool to expand the retaining spring and then separate the fuel line from the fuel rail. Allow the line to drain completely.

   d. Inspect the O-ring(s) in the male end of the quick-connect fitting for torn, flattened or deteriorated surfaces. Replace the O-rings unless in excellent condition.

12A. On models with a return fuel delivery system using flare nut fuel line connectors, disconnect the return line from the fuel rail as follows:

   a. Engage a wrench onto the fuel rail fitting to prevent rotation.

   b. Wrap a shop towel around the fitting to capture spilled fuel.

   c. Use a flare nut wrench to loosen the return line fitting. Allow the line to drain completely and then unthread the return line. Remove the O-ring from the line or fuel rail fitting. Discard the O-ring.

12B. On models with a return fuel delivery system, using quick-connect fuel line connectors, disconnect the return line from the fuel rail as follows:

   a. Fit the separator tool over the fuel rail fitting (**Figure 78**).

   b. Insert the projection on the separator tool into the opening in the female fitting.

   c. Push the tool to expand the retaining spring and then separate the fuel line from the fuel rail. Allow the line to drain completely.

   d. Inspect the O-ring(s) in the male end of the quick-connect fitting for torn, flattened or deteriorated surfaces. Replace the O-rings unless in excellent condition.

12C. On models with a no-return fuel delivery system using quick-connect fuel line connectors, disconnect the cap from the fuel rail fitting as follows:

7

a. Fit the separator tool over the cap fitting (**Figure 78**).

b. Insert the projection on the separator tool into the opening in the female fitting.

c. Push the tool to expand the retaining spring and then separate the cap from the fuel rail. Allow the line to drain completely.

d. Inspect the O-ring(s) in the male end of the quick-connect fitting for torn, flattened or deteriorated surfaces. Replace the O-rings unless in excellent condition.

13. Drain all fuel from the fuel lines into a suitable container. Plug all openings to prevent contamination.

14. Remove the stud bolts (8, **Figure 66**) and screws (37) and then carefully lift the fuel rail and injectors from the intake manifold.

15. Remove the seal (**Figure 79**) from the injectors or openings in the intake manifold. Discard the seals.

16. Use aerosol solvent to thoroughly clean the intake manifold openings and dry with compressed air. Cover the openings to prevent contamination.

CAUTION
*Remove the fuel injector filter (**Figure 79**) only if it has a flange of sufficient diameter to rest against the top of the injector. Do not remove the filter if it does not have the described flange or is located completely inside the opening. The filter without the flange is not designed for removal.*

17. Remove the injectors from the fuel rail as follows:

a. Expand the arms of the metal retaining clip to disengage it from the tabs on the fuel rail. Then pull the injector out of the fuel rail opening.

b. Remove the grommet (**Figure 79**) from the injector. Some models do not use the grommet.

c. Remove the O-ring (**Figure 79**) from the groove at the top of the injector. Discard the O-ring.

d. If the flange at the top of the filter (**Figure 79**) extends from the opening, carefully pull the filter out of the injector. Discard the filter.

e. Repeat these steps for the remaining injectors. Place the injectors in a sealed container to prevent contamination.

18. Remove the fuel pressure regulator as described in this section.

19. Use mild solvent to flush the fuel rail and fuel line passages. Do not apply solvent to the injectors or fuel pressure regulator. Solvent can damage these components. Direct pressurized air into the passages to remove solvent and contaminants.

20. Remove the IAT from the plenum as described in Chapter Nine.

21. Use soap and water to remove oily deposits or other contamination from the plenum (3, **Figure 66**). Dry the plenum with compressed air. Direct air into all passages to remove residual moisture.

22. Remove all gasket material from the intake to plenum and throttle body to plenum mating surfaces.

23. Install the IAT into the plenum as described in Chapter Nine.

24. Install the fuel pressure regulator as described in this section.

25. Remove any covers or caps from fuel rail openings.

26. Install the fuel injectors into the fuel rail as follows:

a. If removed, insert the new filter (**Figure 79**) into the injector opening. Seat the filter flange against the top of the injector.

b. Lubricate with engine oil and install the *new* O-ring (**Figure 79**) into the groove near the top of the fuel injector.

c. If used, install the grommet (**Figure 79**) over the inlet end of the fuel injector and seat against the step in the injector body.

d. Without dislodging or pinching the O-ring, insert the injector into the fuel rail.

e. Hold the injector in position. Then push the injector toward the rail until the metal arms on the retaining clip snap over the tabs on the fuel rail. Tug on the injector to verify a secure connection.

f. Lubricate with engine oil and then fit the *new* seal (**Figure 79**) over the lower end of the injector. Seat the seal against the step on the injector body.

g. Repeat this step for the remaining injectors.

27. *Slowly* rotate the injector to position the harness connector side of the injector facing upward.

28. Remove the covering and then apply a light coat of oil to the injector openings in the intake manifold.

29. Carefully guide the fuel rail under the throttle body. Then align all of the injectors with the respective intake manifold openings. Verify that all injectors enter the openings and then seat the fuel rail.

30. Hand-thread the stud bolts (8, **Figure 66**) and screws (37) into the fuel rail and intake manifold. Tighten the stud bolts and screws to 28 in.-lb. (3.2 N•m).

31A. On models using flare nut fuel line connectors (**Figure 75**), connect the pressure line to the fuel rail as follows:

a. Lubricate with liquid dish soap and then install a *new* O-ring onto the pressure line fitting. Do not cut the O-ring on the fitting threads during installation.

b. Remove the caps and plugs from the fittings. Then hand-thread the pressure line fitting into the fuel rail.

c. Rotate the fitting to prevent line stress or kinking. Engage a wrench onto the fuel rail fitting to prevent rotation.

d. Have an assistant hold the fuel line in position to prevent twisting and then tighten the pressure line fitting to 216 in.-lb. (24 N•m). Do not allow the fuel rail fitting to rotate while tightening the pressure line.

31B. On models using quick-connect fuel line connectors (**Figure 76**), connect the pressure line to the fuel rail as follows:

a. Remove any caps or plugs from the connectors.

b. Apply a light coating of engine oil to the O-ring in the male end of the quick-connect fitting.

c. Guide the male end of the fitting into the female fitting. Push the fittings together until they lock. Tug on the pressure line to verify a secure connection.

32A. On models using flare nut fuel line connectors (**Figure 75**), connect the return line to the fuel rail as follows:

a. Lubricate the surfaces with liquid dish soap and then install a *new* O-ring onto the return line fitting. Do not cut the O-ring on the fitting threads during installation.

b. Remove the caps and plugs from the fittings and then hand-thread the return line fitting into the fuel rail fitting.

c. Rotate the fitting to prevent line stress or kinking. Engage a wrench onto the fuel rail fitting to prevent rotation.

d. Have an assistant hold the fuel line in position to prevent twisting and then tighten the return line fitting to 216 in.-lb. (24 N•m). Do not allow the fuel rail fitting to rotate while tightening the return line fitting.

32B. On models using quick-connect fuel line connectors (**Figure 76**), connect the return line to the fuel rail as follows:

a. Remove any caps or plugs from the connectors.

b. Apply a light coat of engine oil to the O-ring in the male end of the quick connect fitting.

c. Guide the male end of the fitting into the female fitting. Push the fittings together until they lock. Tug on the return line to verify a secure connection.

32C. On models with a no-return fuel delivery system, using quick-connect fuel line connectors, connect the cap onto the fuel rail fitting as follows:

a. Remove any caps or plugs from the connectors.

b. Apply a light coat of engine oil to the O-ring in the male end of the quick connect fitting.

c. Guide the male end of the fitting into the cap. Push the cap onto the fuel rail fitting until they lock. Tug on the cap to verify a secure connection.

33. Depress the locking clip and then plug the injector harness connectors onto the respective injectors. Route the injector harness wiring to prevent pinching or interference with other components.

34. Plug the vacuum hose onto the fuel pressure regulator.

35. Install new gaskets (6, **Figure 66**) onto the intake manifold (12). Install the plenum (3, **Figure 66**) onto the intake manifold. Install the bolts (4, **Figure 66**) into the plenum, gaskets and intake manifold. Tighten the bolts in a crossing pattern to 30 ft.-lb. (41 N•m).

36. Lift the locking tab and then plug the engine wire harness onto the IAT.

37. Connect the crankcase breather tube to the fitting next to the air temperature sensor. Secure the tube with a plastic locking clamp.

38. Install the throttle body as described in this section.

39. Connect the battery cables.

CAUTION
Use a flush device or other means to supply the engine with cooling water if running the engine with the boat out of the water. The seawater pump is quickly damaged if operated without adequate cooling water.

40. Start the engine and immediately check for fuel leakage at the regulator housing, fuel rail, injectors and all fuel line and hose connections. Stop the engine and repair any leaks before operating the engine.

41. Stop the engine. Route the wiring to prevent interference with throttle linkage and other moving components. Secure the wiring with plastic locking clamps as needed.

42. Install the plastic covers (2 and 5, **Figure 66**, typical) onto the engine. Securely tighten the cover retaining screws.

8.1L models

All 8.1L models use quick-connect fittings (**Figure 76**) for the pressure and return lines. A special separator tool is required to disconnect the lines. Purchase the separator tool from an automotive parts store or Volvo Penta stern drive dealership (Volvo Penta part No. 885384).

Refer to **Figure 67** for this procedure.

1. Disconnect the battery cables.

2. Relieve the fuel system pressure as described in this section.

7

3. Push the cable end retainer (A, **Figure 72**) toward the cable anchor (B) and then pull the cable end off the throttle arm.

4. Place a shop towel under the fuel line fittings to capture spilled fuel. The pressure line connects to the lower fitting on the aft end of the port rail (forward end of starboard rail on V-drive models). The return line connects to the upper fitting at the end of the fuel rail. Models with the fuel pump mounted inside the fuel tank and a no-return fuel system do not use a return line fitting. Do not loosen the fittings at this time.

5. Unplug the vacuum hose from the fuel pressure regulator. Replace the regulator as described in this section if fuel is found in the vacuum hose. This indicates the diaphragm in the regulator is leaking.

6. Mark the cylinder number on each fuel injector harness connector (**Figure 77**, typical). The fuel injectors are located above the respective cylinders. On models using an inline transmission with the pulleys and belts facing the front of the boat, odd-numbered cylinders are located on the port bank with the No. 1 cylinder at the front followed by No. 3, 5 and 7. Even-numbered cylinders are located on the starboard bank with the No. 2 cylinders at the front followed by No. 4, 6 and 8. On models using a V-drive transmission with the pulleys and belts facing the rear of the boat, odd-numbered cylinders are located on the starboard bank with the No. 1 cylinder at the rear working forward with No. 3, 5 and 7. Even-numbered cylinders are located on the port bank with the No. 2 cylinders at the rear working forward with No. 4, 6 and 8. Depress the locking clip and then unplug the connector from each injector. Route the injector harness (7, **Figure 66**) to a location that prevents interference during fuel rail removal and installation.

7. Use compressed air to blow all debris from the intake manifold, fuel rail and hose fittings. Mark the fuel line to identify the connections prior to removal.

8. Disconnect the pressure line from the fuel rail as follows:
   a. Fit the separator tool over the fuel rail fitting (**Figure 78**).
   b. Insert the projection on the separator tool into the opening in the female fitting.
   c. Push the tool to expand the retaining spring and then separate the fuel line from the fuel rail. Allow the line to drain completely.

9A. On models with a return fuel delivery system, disconnect the return line from the fuel rail as follows:
   a. Fit the separator tool over the fuel rail fitting (**Figure 78**).
   b. Insert the projection on the separator tool into the opening in the female fitting.

   c. Push the tool to expand the retaining spring and then separate the fuel line from the fuel rail. Allow the line to drain completely.

9B. On models with a no-return fuel delivery system, disconnect the cap from the fuel rail fitting as follows:
   a. Fit the separator tool over the cap fitting (**Figure 78**).
   b. Insert the projection on the separator tool into the opening in the female fitting.
   c. Push the tool to expand the retaining spring and then separate the cap from the fuel rail. Allow the line to drain completely.

10. Inspect the O-ring(s) in the male end of the quick-connect fitting. Replace the O-rings unless in excellent condition.

11. Drain all fuel from the fuel lines into a suitable container. Plug all openings to prevent contamination.

12. Remove the two bolts (7, **Figure 67**) and two stud bolts (9) and then lift the fuel rail assembly off the intake manifold (29). Remove the seal (**Figure 79**) from the injectors or intake manifold. Discard the seals.

13. Use aerosol solvent to thoroughly clean the intake manifold openings and dry with compressed air. Cover the openings to prevent contamination.

CAUTION
*Remove the fuel injector filter (**Figure 79**) only if it has a flange of sufficient diameter to rest against the top of the injector. Do not remove the filter if it does not have the described flange or is located completely within the opening. The filter without the flange is not designed for removal.*

14. Remove the injectors from the fuel rail as follows:
   a. Use needlenose pliers to pull the retaining clip (13, **Figure 67**) off the injector and fuel rail pods.
   b. Carefully pull the injector out of the fuel rail.
   c. Remove the grommet (**Figure 79**) from the injector. Some models do not use the grommet.
   d. Remove the O-ring (**Figure 79**) from the groove at the top of the injector. Discard the O-ring.
   e. If the flange at the top of the filter (**Figure 79**) extends from the opening, carefully pull the filter out of the injector. Discard the filter.
   f. Repeat this step for the remaining injectors.

15. Remove the fuel pressure regulator as described in this section.

16. Use mild solvent to flush the fuel rail and pressure regulator housing. Do not apply solvent to the injectors or fuel pressure regulator. Solvent can damage these components. Direct pressurized air into the passages to remove solvent and contaminants.

17. Install the fuel pressure regulator as described in this section.

18. Remove any covers or caps from the fuel rail openings.

19. Install the fuel injectors into the fuel rail as follows:

    a. Lubricate with engine oil and then install the *new* O-ring (12, **Figure 67**) into the groove near the fuel inlet end of the injector.

    b. If removed, insert the new filter (**Figure 79**) into the injector opening. Seat the filter flange against the top of the injector.

    c. If used, install the grommet (**Figure 79**) over the inlet end of the fuel injector and seat against the step in the injector body.

    d. Without dislodging or pinching the O-ring, insert the injector into the fuel rail. *Slowly* rotate the injector to position the harness connector side of the injector facing away from the fuel rail. Then seat the injector in the fuel rail.

    e. Snap the retaining clip (13, **Figure 67**) onto the injector. The lips on the clip must fit over the groove in the injector and fuel rail pods. Tug on the injector to verify a secure connection.

    f. Install the remaining fuel injectors as described in this step.

20. Remove the covering and then apply a light coat of oil to the injector openings in the intake manifold.

21. While installing the fuel rail onto the intake manifold, carefully guide all of the injectors into the respective intake manifold openings. Verify that all injectors enter the openings and then seat the fuel rail onto the intake manifold.

22. Apply a coat of GM threadlock (GM part No. 1234582) to the threads. Then install the two stud bolts (9, **Figure 67**) and two bolts (7) into the fuel rail bracket and intake manifold. Purchase the threadlock from a GM automobile dealership. Tighten the two bolts and two stud bolts to 106 in.-lb. (12 N•m).

23. Connect the pressure line to the lower fuel rail fitting as follows:

    a. Remove any caps or plugs from the connectors.

    b. Apply a light coat of engine oil to the O-ring in the male end of the quick-connect fitting.

    c. Guide the male end of the fitting into the female fitting. Push the fittings together until they lock. Tug on the pressure line to verify a secure connection.

24A. On models with a return fuel delivery system, connect the return line to the upper fuel rail fitting as follows:

    a. Remove any caps or plugs from the connectors.

    b. Apply a light coat of engine oil to the O-ring in the male end of the quick-connect fitting.

    c. Guide the male end of the fitting into the female fitting. Push the fittings together until they lock. Tug on the return line to verify a secure connection.

24B. On models with a no-return fuel delivery system, connect the cap to the upper fuel rail fitting as follows:

    a. Remove any caps or plugs from the connectors.

    b. Apply a light coat of engine oil to the O-ring in the male end of the quick-connect fitting.

    c. Guide the male end of the fitting into the cap. Push the cap onto the fuel rail fitting until they lock. Tug on the cap to verify a secure connection.

25. Depress the locking clip and then plug the injector harness connectors onto the respective injectors. Route the injector harness wiring to prevent pinching or interference with other components.

26. Plug the vacuum hose onto the fuel pressure regulator fitting.

27. Push the cable end retainer (A, **Figure 72**) toward the cable anchor (B) and then fit the cable end fully over the ball-shaped end of the throttle lever. Rotate the retainer to align the slot in the back of the retainer with the pin and then slide the slot in the retainer over the pin. The internal spring holds the retainer in position. Tug lightly on the cable end to verify a secure connection.

28. Adjust the throttle cable as described in Chapter Five.

29. Connect the battery cables.

> *CAUTION*
> *Use a flush device or other means to supply the engine with cooling water if running the engine with the boat out of the water. The seawater pump is quickly damaged if operated without adequate cooling water.*

30. Start the engine and immediately check for fuel leakage at the regulator housing, fuel rail, injectors and all fuel line and hose connections. Stop the engine and repair any leaks before operating the engine.

31. Stop the engine. Route the wiring to prevent interference with throttle linkages and other moving components. Secure the wiring with plastic locking clamps as needed.

Fuel Pressure Regulator
Removal and Installation

The fuel pressure regulator can be replaced without removing the throttle body or fuel rail. Replace all O-rings and gaskets anytime they are removed. Consider reusing a gasket only if it is in excellent condition and a *new* replacement is not available. Never reuse O-rings.

On TBI models, the fuel pressure regulator is incorporated into the throttle body assembly. On 5.7L models with MPI, the fuel pressure regulator (**Figure 80**, typical) mounts on the starboard side fuel rail. On V-drive models, the regulator is located on the port side fuel rail. On 7.4L, 8.1L and 8.2L models with MPI, the fuel pressure regulator is integrated into the fuel rail.

5.0L and 5.7L models (TBI)

Failure of the fuel pressure regulator is almost always the result of debris under the diaphragm and housing seats. Cleaning the seats usually corrects the problem. Replace the throttle body assembly if the regulator diaphragm or seating surfaces are damaged. The housing, cover, spring and diaphragm are not available separately.

Refer to **Figure 73** for this procedure.

1. Disconnect the battery cables.
2. Unthread the screw (A, **Figure 62**) and then lift the plastic cover (B) off the flame arrestor.
3. Remove the flame arrestor (A, **Figure 69**) from the throttle body.
4. Relieve the fuel system pressure as described in this section.
5. Disconnect the injector wire harness from the throttle position sensor (A, **Figure 70**), idle air control motor (B) and both fuel injectors. Pinch the two white plastic arms (A, **Figure 71**) to unplug the fuel injector connectors. Pull the injector harness grommet (B, **Figure 71**) out of the notch in the throttle body.
6. Place shop towels into the throttle bores to capture spilled fuel.
7. Remove the screws and then *carefully* lift the injector cover and regulator housing (1, **Figure 73**) off the injector housing (9).
8. Remove the gaskets (3 and 5, **Figure 73**) from the injector housing or injector cover and regulator housing. Discard the gaskets.
9. Fit a C-clamp against the regulator cover (2, **Figure 73**) and the top side of the injector cover and regulator housing. Tighten the C-clamp just enough to lightly clamp the components.
10. Place the injector cover and regulator housing on a clean work surface with the regulator cover facing upward. Remove the screws that secure the regulator cover onto the injector cover. Then *slowly* loosen the clamp to relieve the internal spring tension.
11. Remove the clamp. Then lift the cover, spring and diaphragm from the injector housing.
12. Soak the cover, housing and spring in a mild solvent. Use mild dishwashing soap to clean the diaphragm. Dry the components with compressed air.
13. Inspect the diaphragm for tears, missing sections or other defects. Inspect the seating surfaces on the dia-

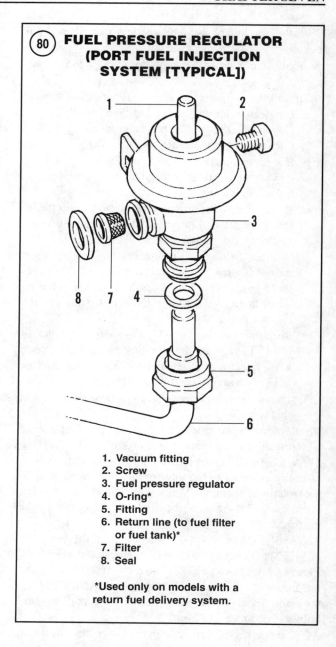

FUEL PRESSURE REGULATOR (PORT FUEL INJECTION SYSTEM [TYPICAL])

1. Vacuum fitting
2. Screw
3. Fuel pressure regulator
4. O-ring*
5. Fitting
6. Return line (to fuel filter or fuel tank)*
7. Filter
8. Seal

*Used only on models with a return fuel delivery system.

phragm and housing for pitting or other defects. Make sure the pivoting seat on the diaphragm moves freely. Inspect the spring for corrosion damage or broken loops. Replace the throttle body assembly if the diaphragm, spring or the seating surfaces are defective. The parts are not available separately.

14. Fit the diaphragm onto the injector cover and regulator housing. The pivoting seat on the diaphragm must fit against the seat in the cover.

15. Install the spring onto the diaphragm and center over the metal support. Fit the cover (2, **Figure 73**) over the

spring. Rotate the spring and diaphragm to align the screw openings.

16. Fit a C-clamp against the regulator cover (2, **Figure 73**) and the top side of the injector cover and regulator housing. *Slowly* tighten the C-clamp to compress the spring and bring the regulator cover in contact with the housing. Make sure the screw openings in the regulator cover, diaphragm and housing remain aligned while tightening the clamp.

17. Verify proper alignment of the openings. Apply a light coat of Loctite 271 to the threads and then install the screws into the regulator cover and housing. Tighten the screws securely in a crossing pattern. Lightly stake the screws to prevent loosening.

18. Install *new* gaskets (3 and 5, **Figure 73**) onto the injector housing (9). Then install the injector cover and regulator housing.

19. Align the screw openings in the cover and throttle body. Apply a light coat of Loctite 262 to the threads and then install the screws. Tighten the screws in a crossing pattern to 27 in.-lb. (3.0 N•m).

20. Fit the injector wire harness grommet into the notch in the throttle body (B, **Figure 71**). Pinch the white plastic arms and then plug the injector harness connectors (A, **Figure 71**) onto the fuel injectors. The connectors can attach to either injector.

21. Remove the shop towels from the throttle bores.

22. Connect the battery cables.

CAUTION
Use a flush device or other means to supply the engine with cooling water if running the engine with the boat out of the water. The seawater pump is quickly damaged if operated without adequate cooling water.

23. Start the engine and immediately check for fuel leakage at all fuel line and hose connections, throttle body injector housing mating surfaces and the fuel pressure regulator cover. Stop the engine and repair any leaks before operating the engine.

24. Carefully install the flame arrestor (A, **Figure 69**) onto the throttle body. Do not pinch the fuel injector wires between the throttle body and flame arrestor.

25. Install the plastic cover (B, **Figure 62**) onto the flame arrestor. Guide the screw (A, **Figure 62**) into the cover, flame arrestor and throttle body openings. Lift the cover and flame arrestor slightly to align the screw with the opening.

5.0L and 5.7L models (MPI)

Early models use threaded flare nut fuel line connections (**Figure 75**) for the fuel return line. Later models use quick-connect fittings (**Figure 76**) for the return line. A special separator tool is required to disconnect the lines. Purchase the separator tool from an automotive parts store or Volvo Penta stern drive dealership (Volvo Penta part No. 885384).

Refer to **Figure 80** for this procedure.

1. Disconnect the battery cables.

2. On models with a center-mounted throttle body, remove the plastic cover and flame arrestor from the throttle body.

3. Relieve the fuel system pressure as described in this section.

4. Use compressed air to blow debris or loose material from the intake manifold and fuel rail. Place a shop towel under the regulator (9, **Figure 64** or 2, **Figure 65**) to capture spilled fuel.

5. Unplug the vacuum hose from the fuel pressure regulator (1, **Figure 80**). Replace the regulator if fuel is found in the vacuum hose. This indicates the diaphragm in the regulator has failed.

6A. On models with a return fuel delivery system, using flare nut fuel line connectors, disconnect the return line from the fuel pressure regulator as follows:

    a. To prevent rotation, engage a wrench onto the fuel pressure regulator (3, **Figure 80**) hex fitting.

    b. Wrap a shop towel around the fitting to capture spilled fuel.

    c. Use a flare nut wrench to loosen the return line fitting (5, **Figure 80**). Allow the line to drain completely and then unthread the return line. Remove the O-ring (4, **Figure 80**) from the line or regulator. Discard the O-ring.

6B. On models with a return fuel delivery system using quick-connect fuel line connectors, disconnect the return line from the fuel pressure regulator as follows:

    a. Fit the separator tool over the male fitting (**Figure 78**).

    b. Insert the projection on the separator tool into the opening in the female fitting.

    c. Push the tool to expand the retaining spring and then separate the fuel line from the pressure regulator. Allow the line to drain completely.

    d. Inspect the O-ring(s) in the male end of the quick-connect fitting for damage. Replace the O-rings unless in excellent condition.

6C. On models with a no-return fuel delivery system using flare nut fuel line connectors, remove the cap fitting from the fuel pressure regulator as follows:

7

a. To prevent rotation, engage a wrench onto the fuel pressure regulator (3, **Figure 80**) hex fitting.

b. Use a flare nut wrench to loosen the cap fitting. Allow the line to drain completely and then unthread the fitting. Remove the O-ring (4, **Figure 80**) from the line or cap fitting. Discard the O-ring.

6D. On models with a no-return fuel delivery system using quick-connect fuel line connectors, disconnect the cap from the fuel pressure regulator as follows:

a. Fit the separator tool over the cap fitting (**Figure 78**).

b. Insert the projection on the separator tool into the opening in the female fitting.

c. Push the tool to expand the retaining spring and then separate the cap from the fuel pressure regulator. Allow the line to drain completely.

d. Inspect the O-ring(s) in the male end of the quick-connect fitting for damage. Replace the O-rings unless in excellent condition.

7. Drain all fuel from the fuel lines into a suitable container. Plug all openings to prevent contamination.

8. Support the fuel pressure regulator and then remove the screw (2, **Figure 80**). Carefully pull the regulator off the fuel rail. Drain all fuel from the regulator into a suitable container. Promptly clean up any fuel that spills from the fuel rail opening.

9. Remove the seal (8, **Figure 80**) from the fuel pressure regulator or area around the fuel rail opening. Discard the seal.

10. Carefully pull the filter (7, **Figure 80**) out of the fuel pressure regulator.

11. Soak the filter in mild solvent and dry with compressed air. *Do not* soak the regulator. Solvent can damage the regulator.

12. Inspect the filter for blockage or damaged. Replace the filter if damaged or if it cannot be completely cleaned with solvent.

13. Inspect the openings in the fuel pressure regulator for gummy deposits or other contaminants. If contaminated, replace the fuel pressure regulator. Then remove the fuel rail and injectors and clean the passages as described in this section. Refer to *Fuel Rail and Injectors*.

14. Carefully insert the filter (7, **Figure 80**) into the fuel pressure regulator. The open side must face out.

15. Lubricate with engine oil and then install the *new* seal (8, **Figure 80**) onto the fuel pressure regulator.

16. Align the regulator and fuel rail openings and then fit the fuel pressure regulator onto the fuel rail. Hold the regulator in position and then thread the screw (2, **Figure 80**) into the regulator and fuel rail. Hand-tighten only at this time.

17A. On models with a return fuel delivery system using flare nut fuel line connectors, connect the return line to the fuel pressure regulator as follows:

a. Lubricate with liquid dish soap and install a *new* O-ring onto the return line. Do not cut the O-ring on the fitting threads during installation.

b. Hand-thread the return line (6, **Figure 80**) into the fuel pressure regulator. Do not tighten the fitting at this time.

17B. On models with a return fuel delivery system using quick-connect fuel line connectors, connect the return line to the fuel pressure regulator as follows:

a. Apply a light coat of engine oil onto the O-ring in the male end of the quick-connect fitting.

b. Guide the male end of the pressure regulator fitting into the female fitting. Push the fittings together until they lock. Tug on the return line to verify a secure connection.

17C. On models with a no-return fuel delivery system using flare nut fuel line connectors, install the cap fitting onto the fuel pressure regulator as follows:

a. Apply a light coat of engine oil to the *new* O-ring and then install it into the fuel pressure regulator. Make sure the O-ring fits fully into the groove. Do not cut the O-ring on the fitting threads during installation.

b. Thread the cap onto the fuel pressure regulator. Do not tighten the fitting at this time.

17D. On models with a no-return fuel delivery system using quick-connect fuel line connectors, connect the cap onto the fuel pressure regulator as follows:

a. Apply a light coat of engine oil to the O-ring in the male end of the quick-connect fitting.

b. Guide the male end of the fitting into the cap. Push the cap onto the regulator fitting until they lock. Tug on the cap to verify a secure connection.

18A. On models with a return fuel delivery system using flare nut fuel line connectors, tighten the fuel return line as follows:

a. Rotate the fitting (5, **Figure 80**) to prevent line stress or kinking.

b. To prevent rotation, engage a wrench onto the fuel pressure regulator (3, **Figure 80**) hex fitting.

c. Have an assistant hold the fuel line in position to prevent twisting and then tighten the return line to 156 in.-lb. (17.6 N•m) on models with a center-mounted throttle body and 115 in.-lb. (13 N•m) on models with a front-mounted throttle body. Do not allow the fuel pressure regulator fitting to rotate while tightening the return line.

18B. On models with a no-return fuel delivery system using flare nut fuel line connectors, tighten the cap fitting as follows:

    a. To prevent rotation, engage a wrench onto the fuel pressure regulator (3, **Figure 80**) hex fitting.

    b. Tighten the cap fitting to 156 in.-lb. (17.6 N•m) on models with a center-mounted throttle body and 115 in.-lb. (13 N•m) on models with a front-mounted throttle body.

19. Tighten the fuel pressure regulator retaining screw (2, **Figure 80**) to 84 in.-lb. (9.5 N•m).

20. Plug the vacuum hose onto the fuel pressure regulator (1, **Figure 80**).

21. Connect the battery cables.

CAUTION
Use a flush device or other means to supply the engine with cooling water if running the engine with the boat out of the water. The seawater pump is quickly damaged if operated without adequate cooling water.

22. Start the engine and immediately check for fuel leakage at the regulator housing, fuel rail, injectors and all fuel line and hose connections. Stop the engine and repair any leaks before operating the engine.

23. Stop the engine. Route the wiring to prevent interference with throttle linkages and other moving components. Secure the wiring with plastic locking clamps as needed.

24. Install the flame arrestor and plastic cover.

7.4L, 8.1L and 8.2L models

Refer to **Figure 66** or **Figure 67** for this procedure.

1. Disconnect the battery cables.

2. Relieve the fuel system pressure as described in this section.

3. On 7.4L and 8.2L models, remove the plastic covers (2 and 5, **Figure 66**) from the top of the engine.

4. Use compressed air to blow debris or loose material from the intake manifold and fuel rail. Place a shop towel under the regulator housing (32, **Figure 67**, typical) to capture spilled fuel.

5. Unplug the vacuum hose from the fuel pressure regulator. Replace the regulator if fuel is found in the vacuum hose. This indicates the diaphragm in the regulator has failed.

6. Push the regulator (2, **Figure 67**, typical) toward the regulator housing (32) and then remove the snap ring (1) from the groove in the housing.

7. Pull the regulator, spacer, large O-ring, filter and small O-ring (3-6, **Figure 67**, typical) out of the regulator housing. Separate the components. Discard the O-rings.

8. Soak the spacer and filter in mild solvent and dry in compressed air. *Do not* soak the regulator. Solvent can damage the regulator.

9. Inspect the filter for blockage or damage. Replace the filter if damaged or if it cannot be completely cleaned with solvent.

10. Inspect the regulator housing for gummy deposits or other contaminants. If contaminated, remove the fuel rail and injectors and then clean the passages as described in this section. Refer to *Fuel Rail and Injectors*.

11. Fit the spacer (3, **Figure 67**, typical) over the regulator (2) and seat against the flange. Install a *new* large O-ring (4, **Figure 67**, typical) over the regulator and rest on the spacer.

12. Fit the filter (5, **Figure 67**, typical) over the tube on the regulator and rest against the O-ring and spacer. Fit the *new* small O-ring (6, **Figure 67**, typical) over the tube on the regulator and seat against the filter.

13. Apply a light coat of engine oil to the O-rings, regulator, filter and spacer.

14. Insert the regulator and filter assembly into the housing. Guide the regulator tube into the opening at the bottom of the housing and then seat the assembly into the housing.

15. Push the regulator toward the regulator housing and then install the snap ring (1, **Figure 67**, typical) into the groove in the housing. Make sure the snap ring is seated fully in the groove. Release the regulator. Tug on the regulator to verify a secure connection.

16. Plug the vacuum hose onto the regulator.

17. Connect the battery cables.

18. Start the engine and immediately check for fuel leakage at the regulator housing and all fuel line and hose connections. Stop the engine and repair any leaks before operating the engine.

19. Stop the engine. Route the wiring to prevent interference with the throttle linkage and other moving components. Secure the wiring with plastic locking clamps as needed.

20. On 7.4L and 8.2L models, install the plastic covers (2 and 5, **Figure 66**, typical) onto the engine. Securely tighten the cover retaining screws.

Electric Fuel Pump Replacement (Electronic Fuel Injection [EFI] Models)

The high-pressure fuel pump systems used on EFI models are divided into the fuel return system and no-return fuel system. The type of fuel delivery system used determines the mounting location for the pump(s).

On models with the fuel return system, the fuel pressure regulator is mounted on the throttle body on TBI models

7

or the fuel rail on MPI models. It directs fuel not used by the fuel injectors through a dedicated line back to the fuel tank or water-separating fuel filter housing on the engine. The high-pressure electric fuel pump (A, **Figure 81**) used with the fuel return system is mounted on the engine or located in the boat fuel tank.

Some fuel return system models are equipped with a low-pressure electric boost pump in addition to the high-pressure electric pump. The boost pump assists with drawing fuel out of the fuel tank to provide the additional fuel necessary on higher output models. Two different types of low-pressure pumps are used. The larger and more common Carter pump (A, **Figure 82**) mounts on the starboard side of the engine and next to the side engine mount. The smaller and less common Delco pump (1, **Figure 83**, typical) mounts on the front starboard side of the engine. To prevent premature failure of the pump, replace the water-separating fuel filter when replacing the pump and at the specified maintenance intervals. Water-separating fuel filter replacement and maintenance intervals are described in Chapter Three.

On models with a no-return fuel system, the fuel pressure regulator is integrated into the fuel tank-mounted electric fuel pump. Excess fuel delivered by the fuel pump is directed back into the fuel tank through internal passages. A fuel pressure regulator is also incorporated into the throttle body assembly on TBI models or the fuel rail on MPI models. The return line fitting on the throttle body unit, fuel rail or fuel pressure regulator is blocked because the fuel pressure is regulated by the in-tank fuel pump. However, the diaphragm in the fuel pressure regulator is able to move within the housing and dampen pressure fluctuation that can occur during normal fuel injector operation. This feature offers smoother operation, improved fuel economy and reduced exhaust emissions.

Refer to *Electronic Fuel Injection* in Chapter Two for a description of the fuel systems and fuel injection system operation.

Carter boost pump (removal/installation)

1. Disconnect the battery cables. Use compressed air to blow debris and loose material off the electric fuel pump, electrical connectors, fuel line fittings and mounting bracket.
2. Pull the rubber boots (A and B, **Figure 84**) away from the terminals. Note the wire routing and connections. Then disconnect the wires from the pump.
3. Place a suitable container under the fuel pump to capture spilled fuel.
4. Loosen the clamp or fitting and then disconnect the supply hose from the fuel pump inlet fitting (B, **Figure**

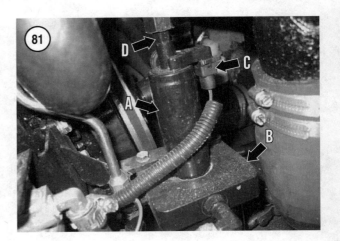

82). The hose connecting to the inlet fitting leads to the fuel tank. Allow the fuel to fully drain from the fuel pump and supply hose. Inspect the fuel supply hose for cracks, deterioration or damage. Replace the fuel supply hose with marine-grade and U.S. Coast Guard-approved hose if these or other defects are evident.

5. To prevent rotation, engage a wrench onto the brass fitting or elbow on the opposite side of the pump (C, **Figure 84**). Use a flare nut wrench to *slightly* loosen the outlet fuel line fitting. The outlet line leads to the water-separating fuel filter housing. Wrap a shop towel around the fitting and then loosen the fitting by hand. Allow all fuel to drain from the fuel line. When completely drained, unthread the fitting and disconnect the fuel line from the pump. Promptly clean up any spilled fuel.

6. Support the pump and then remove the three screws (C, **Figure 82**) that secure the pump to the mounting bracket. Remove the pump from the bracket. Remove the sleeves from the grommets. Inspect the grommets in the mounting brackets for damage and replace as needed.

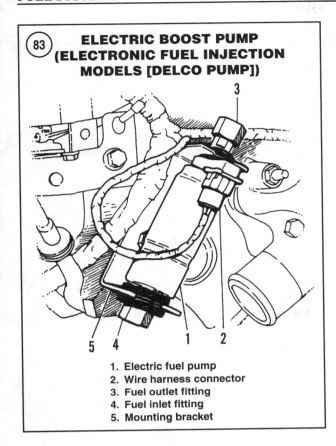

83 **ELECTRIC BOOST PUMP (ELECTRONIC FUEL INJECTION MODELS [DELCO PUMP])**

1. Electric fuel pump
2. Wire harness connector
3. Fuel outlet fitting
4. Fuel inlet fitting
5. Mounting bracket

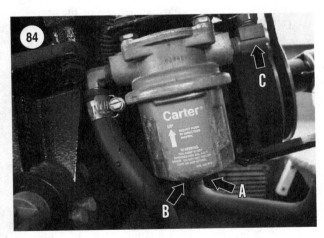

84

outlet fittings or elbows. Purchase the sealant from an automotive parts store or GM automobile dealership (GM part No. 12346004). *Do not* allow sealant into the fuel passage of the fittings. Thread the fittings into the fuel pump and tighten to 48-59 in.-lb. (5.4-6.7 N•m).

10. Insert the sleeves into the grommet openings in the mounting bracket. Fit the replacement pump onto the mounting bracket. Align the openings and install the three screws (C, **Figure 82**) into the grommet and fuel pump. Securely tighten the three screws.

11. Tighten the fuel outlet elbow or fitting *slightly* if necessary to properly align with the fuel outlet line. Thread the fuel outlet line into the fuel pump by hand. Engage a wrench onto the fuel pump elbow or fitting to prevent rotation. Then use a flare nut wrench to tighten the fuel line fitting to 177-212 in.-lb. (20-24 N•m).

12. Install the hose clamp over the end and then push the fuel supply hose fully over the fuel inlet (B, **Figure 82**). Align the hose clamp over the fitting. Then securely tighten the clamp.

13. Connect the engine wire harness to the corresponding terminals on the bottom of the pump (A and B, **Figure 84**). Securely tighten the terminal nuts. Then carefully push the insulator boots over the wire terminals. Work carefully to avoid damaging the terminal or tearing the boots.

14. Connect the battery cables.

CAUTION
Use a flush device or other means to supply the engine with cooling water if running the engine with the boat out of the water. The seawater pump is quickly damaged if operated without adequate cooling water.

15. Start the engine and immediately check for fuel leaking from the fittings, pump body or other fuel system components. Stop the engine and repair any leaks before operating the engine.

Delco boost pump (removal/installation)

1. Disconnect the battery cables. Use compressed air to blow debris and loose material off the electric fuel pump, fuel filter and mounting bracket.

2. Depress the locking clip and then carefully unplug the harness connector (2, **Figure 83**) from the pump.

3. Place a suitable container under the fuel pump and filter to capture spilled fuel.

4. To prevent rotation, engage a wrench onto the outlet fitting on the top of the pump (3, **Figure 83**). Use a flare nut wrench to *slightly* loosen the outlet line. Wrap a shop towel around the fitting; then loosen the fitting by hand.

7. Drain all fuel from the fuel pump. Plug or cap the disconnected hoses, lines and fittings to prevent leakage and contamination.

8. If the fuel pump will be replaced, remove the pump inlet and outlet fittings. Clean all old sealant from the fittings.

9. If removed, apply a light coat of Loctite Pipe Sealant with Teflon to the threaded section of the fuel inlet and

Allow all fuel to drain from the fuel line. When completely drained, unthread the fitting and disconnect the outlet line from the pump.

5. To prevent rotation, engage a wrench onto the inlet fitting on the top of the pump (4, **Figure 83**). Use a flare nut wrench to *slightly* loosen the inlet line. Wrap a shop towel around the fitting and then loosen the fitting by hand. Allow all fuel to drain from the fuel line. When completely drained, unthread the fitting and disconnect the inlet line from the pump. Promptly clean up any spilled fuel.

6. Support the fuel pump and then remove the two bolts that secure the fuel pump mounting bracket (5, **Figure 83**) to the engine. Carefully pull the fuel pump out of the mounting bracket slots. Remove the grommet from the upper and lower end of the fuel pump. Inspect the grommets for excessive wear or damage and replace as needed.

7. Drain all fuel from the fuel pump. Plug or cap the disconnected hoses, lines and fittings to prevent leakage and contamination.

8. Engage a wrench onto the hex-shaped end at the bottom of the fuel pump. Hold the wrench and use a flare nut wrench to remove the brass outlet fitting (3, **Figure 83**) from the top of the fuel pump. Remove the O-ring from the fitting or pump outlet. Discard the O-ring.

9. Lubricate with dishwashing soap and then install *new* O-rings onto the fuel pump outlet fitting. Work carefully to avoid tearing the O-rings.

10. Hand-thread the outlet fitting into the fuel pump. Engage a wrench onto the hex-shaped end at the bottom of the fuel pump. Hold the wrench to prevent the fuel pump from rotating. Then tighten the pump outlet fitting to 60-84 in.-lb. (6.8-9.5 N•m).

11. Fit the grommets onto the upper and lower ends of the fuel pump. Guide the slots in the grommets over the slots in the mounting bracket and then push the fuel pump fully into the bracket.

12. Fit the fuel pump mounting bracket onto the engine. Install the two bolts and tighten evenly to 20-25 ft.-lb. (27-34 N•m).

13. Hand-thread the fuel outlet line fitting into the fuel pump outlet (3, **Figure 83**). Engage a wrench onto the outlet fitting and then tighten the fuel line to 177-212 in.-lb. (20-24 N•m).

14. Hand-thread the fuel inlet line into the fuel pump inlet (4, **Figure 83**). Engage a wrench onto the outlet line fitting and then tighten the fuel line to 177-212 in.-lb. (20-24 N•m).

15. Depress the locking clip and then carefully plug the engine harness connector (2, **Figure 83**) onto the fuel pump.

16. Connect the battery cables.

CAUTION
Use a flush device or other means to supply the engine with cooling water if running the engine with the boat out of the water. The seawater pump is quickly damaged if operated without adequate cooling water.

17. Start the engine and immediately check for leaking fuel. Stop the engine and repair any leaks before operating the engine.

Engine-mounted high-pressure electric fuel pump (removal/installation)

1. Disconnect the battery cables. Use compressed air to blow debris and loose material off the high-pressure electric fuel pump (A, **Figure 81**), water-separating fuel filter and filter housing (B).

2. Depress the locking clip and then carefully unplug the harness connector (C, **Figure 81**) from the pump.

3. Place a suitable container under the fuel pump and filter to capture spilled fuel. Remove the water-separating fuel filter as described in Chapter Three. The filter mounts on the bottom of the filter housing.

4. To prevent rotation, engage a wrench onto the hex-shaped surface on the top of the pump (D, **Figure 81**). Use a flare nut wrench to *slightly* loosen the outlet line. Wrap a shop towel around the fitting and then loosen the fitting by hand. Allow all fuel to drain from the fuel line. When completely drained, unthread the fitting and disconnect the outlet line from the pump.

5. To prevent rotation, engage a wrench onto the hex-shaped surface on the top of the pump (D, **Figure 81**). Use a wrench to loosen the nut/fitting that holds the pump inlet fitting to the filter housing. The nut is located on the bottom of the housing and is only accessible with the filter removed. Allow all fuel to drain from the pump. Then remove the nut and lift the pump off the filter housing. Promptly clean up any spilled fuel.

6. Remove the O-ring from the pump inlet fitting or filter housing. Discard the O-ring.

7. Drain all fuel from the fuel pump. Plug or cap the disconnected hoses, lines and fittings to prevent leakage and contamination.

8. Engage a wrench onto the hex-shaped end at the bottom of the fuel pump. Hold the wrench and use a flare nut wrench to remove the brass outlet fitting from the top of the fuel pump. Remove the O-ring from the fitting or pump outlet opening. Discard the O-ring.

9. Clean all debris or oily deposits from the pump-to-filter housing mating surfaces.

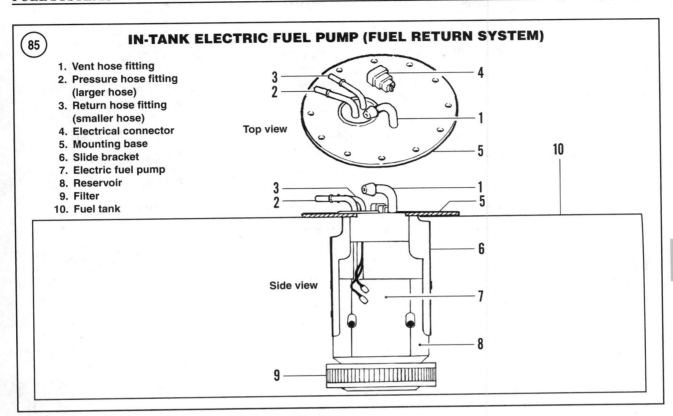

IN-TANK ELECTRIC FUEL PUMP (FUEL RETURN SYSTEM)

85

1. Vent hose fitting
2. Pressure hose fitting (larger hose)
3. Return hose fitting (smaller hose)
4. Electrical connector
5. Mounting base
6. Slide bracket
7. Electric fuel pump
8. Reservoir
9. Filter
10. Fuel tank

Top view

Side view

7

10. Lubricate with dishwashing soap and then install a *new* O-ring onto the fuel pump outlet fitting. Work carefully to avoid tearing the O-ring.

11. Hand-thread the outlet fitting into the fuel pump. Engage a wrench onto the hex-shaped end at the bottom of the fuel pump. Hold the wrench to prevent the fuel pump from rotating. Then tighten the pump outlet to 60-84 in.-lb. (6.8-9.5 N•m).

12. Lubricate with dishwashing soap and install a *new* O-ring over the fuel pump inlet fitting.

13. Insert the pump into the filter housing. Thread the nut/fitting onto the pump inlet. To prevent rotation, engage a wrench onto the hex-shaped end at the bottom of the pump. Use a wrench to securely tighten the nut/fitting that holds the pump inlet fitting onto the filter housing.

14. Hand-thread the fuel outlet line into the fuel pump. Engage a wrench onto the hex-shaped end at the bottom of the pump. Then tighten the fuel line to 177-212 in.-lb. (20-24 N•m). Do not allow the fuel pump outlet fitting to rotate while tightening the fuel line.

15. Depress the locking clip and then carefully plug the engine harness connector (C, **Figure 81**) onto the fuel pump.

16. Install the water-separating fuel filter as described in Chapter Three.

17. Connect the battery cables.

CAUTION
Use a flush device or other means to supply the engine with cooling water if running the engine with the boat out of the water. The seawater pump is quickly damaged if operated without adequate cooling water.

18. Start the engine and immediately check for leaking fuel. Stop the engine and repair any leaks before operating the engine.

Fuel tank-mounted electric fuel pump (removal/installation)

Quick-connect fittings (**Figure 76**) are used to attach the pressure line and the return line to the fuel pump. A special separator tool is required to disconnect the lines. Purchase the separator tool from an automotive parts store or Volvo Penta stern drive dealership (Volvo Penta part No. 885384).

The fuel pump assembly is not serviceable and, if defective, must be replaced as an assembly.

Refer to **Figure 85** or **Figure 86** for this procedure.

1. Disconnect the battery cables.

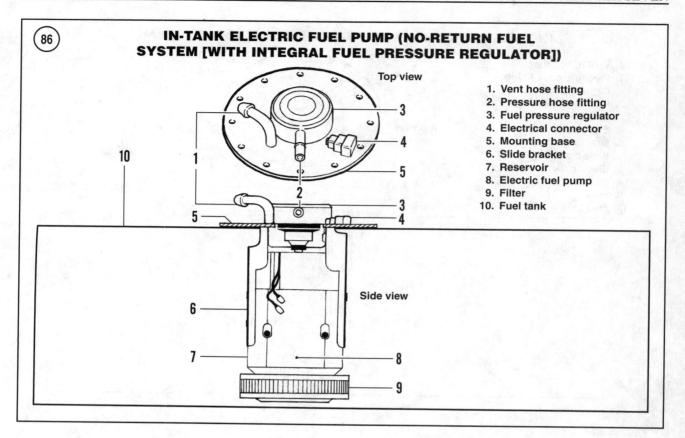

86 IN-TANK ELECTRIC FUEL PUMP (NO-RETURN FUEL SYSTEM [WITH INTEGRAL FUEL PRESSURE REGULATOR])

Top view

Side view

1. Vent hose fitting
2. Pressure hose fitting
3. Fuel pressure regulator
4. Electrical connector
5. Mounting base
6. Slide bracket
7. Reservoir
8. Electric fuel pump
9. Filter
10. Fuel tank

2. Relieve the fuel system pressure as described in this section.

3. Remove seating, floor panels or other boat structure as needed to access the top of the fuel tank.

4. Use compressed air to remove all debris from the external fuel pump and surrounding fuel tank surfaces.

5. Place a shop towel under the fuel pump fittings to capture spilled fuel.

6. Disconnect the vapor vent hose from the fuel pump (1, **Figure 85** or 1, **Figure 86**).

7. Disconnect the fuel pump wire harness from the pump (4, **Figure 85** or 4, **Figure 86**).

8. Disconnect the pressure line from the fuel pump pressure line fitting (2, **Figure 85** or 2, **Figure 86**) as follows:

  a. Fit the separator tool over the fuel pump fitting (**Figure 78**).

  b. Insert the projection on the separator tool into the opening in the female fuel line fitting.

  c. Push the tool to expand the retaining spring and then separate the fuel line from the fuel fitting. Allow the line to drain into a suitable container.

  d. Inspect the O-ring(s) in the fuel pump fitting for torn, flattened or deteriorated surfaces. Replace the O-rings unless in excellent condition.

9. On models with a return fuel delivery system (**Figure 85**), disconnect the return line from the fuel pump return fitting as follows:

  a. Fit the separator tool over the fuel pump fitting (**Figure 78**).

  b. Insert the projection on the separator tool into the opening in the female fuel line fitting.

  c. Push the tool to expand the retaining spring. Then separate the fuel line from the fuel pump fitting (3, **Figure 85**). Allow the line to drain into a suitable container.

  d. Inspect the O-ring(s) in the fuel pump fitting for torn, flattened or deteriorated surfaces. Replace the O-rings unless in excellent condition.

10. Cap or plug the fuel lines to prevent contamination.

11. Remove the 12 screws that hold the fuel pump assembly in the fuel tank. Then carefully lift the fuel pump out of the fuel tank. Place the fuel pump in a suitable, clean container to capture residual fuel.

12. Remove the rubber seal from the fuel pump or fuel tank mating surface. Inspect the seal for torn, creased or deteriorated surfaces and replace as needed.

13. Cover the fuel tank opening to prevent contamination.

14. Use mild solvent to clean loose material and deposits from the fuel pump assembly. Dry the fuel pump with compressed air.

15. Inspect the filter (9, **Figure 85**, or 9, **Figure 86**) at the bottom of the pump for debris or damage. Replace the filter if it is damaged or cannot be completely cleaned.

16. If the fuel pump assembly must be replaced, adjust the slide assembly on the replacement pump to match the fuel tank. Refer to the following:

   a. Insert a ruler into the tank opening and measure the distance from the top of the fuel tank to the bottom of the tank.

   b. Loosen the screws on the side of the slide bracket (6, **Figure 85**, or 6, **Figure 86**).

   c. Slide the filter end of the pump up or down until the distance from the bottom of the filter to the bottom of the mounting flange is approximately 1/2 in. (12.7 mm) less than the depth of the fuel tank. This should position the filter approximately 1/2 in. (12.7 mm) off the bottom of the fuel tank with the pump installed.

   d. Hold the slide assembly in position and then securely tighten the screws on the side of the slide bracket.

   e. Measure the length to verify proper adjustment and correct as needed.

17. Install the rubber gasket over the filter end of the pump and seat against the bottom of the mounting flange.

18. Remove the cover and then carefully guide the fuel pump assembly with rubber seal into the fuel tank. Rotate the pump to align the fittings with the corresponding fuel lines and then seat the fuel pump onto the tank. If the fuel pump flange does not seat against the tank, remove the pump and adjust the slide bracket as described in Step 16.

19. Rotate the pump and rubber seal to align the screw openings with the corresponding openings in the fuel tank. Thread the 12 screws into the pump, seal and tank. Using a crossing pattern, securely tighten the screws.

NOTE
The pressure line fitting connected to the in-tank electric fuel pump fitting is larger in diameter than the return line fitting.

20. Connect the pressure line to the fuel pump as follows:

   a. Remove any caps or plugs from the connectors.

   b. Apply a light coat of engine oil to the O-ring in the pressure fitting (2, **Figure 85**, or 2, **Figure 86**).

   c. Guide the pressure line fitting over the fuel pump fitting. Push the fittings together until they lock. Tug on the pressure line to verify a secure connection.

21. On models with a fuel return system, connect the return line to the fuel pump fitting as follows:

   a. Remove any caps or plugs from the connectors.

   b. Apply a light coat of engine oil to the O-ring on the return line fitting (3, **Figure 85**).

   c. Guide the return line fitting over the fuel pump fitting. Push the fittings together until they lock. Tug on the return line to verify a secure connection.

22. Connect the vapor vent hose to the fuel pump (1, **Figure 85**, or 1, **Figure 86**).

23. Connect the fuel pump wire harness to the fuel pump (4, **Figure 85**, or 4, **Figure 86**). Route the wiring to prevent pinching or interference with fasteners or other components that can damage the wiring. Secure the wiring with clamps as needed.

24. Connect the battery cables.

CAUTION
Use a flush device or other means to supply the engine with cooling water if running the engine with the boat out of the water. The seawater pump is quickly damaged if operated without adequate cooling water.

25. Start the engine and immediately check for leaking fuel at the fittings and hoses. Stop the engine and repair any leaks before operating the engine.

INTAKE MANIFOLD

This section describes removal and installation of the intake manifold. Remove the intake manifold if leaking or as necessary to remove the cylinder head(s), camshaft, lifters, pushrods or oil pump drive on 8.1L models. Always replace the manifold gaskets anytime the manifold is removed. Although the used gasket might appear to be in excellent condition, small tears will allow exhaust, oil, air, water or coolant leakage. The resulting damage would exceed the cost of the gaskets. *Never* use automotive gaskets on the intake manifold. Purchase the new gasket set from an Indmar marine engine dealership. RTV sealant is required for this procedure to seal the front and rear intake manifold mating surfaces. Purchase the RTV sealant from an automotive parts store or GM automobile dealership (GM part No. 12346141). Make sure the sealer is fresh. Old sealer might not cure properly and might allow oil leakage.

Intake Manifold Removal

1. Disconnect the battery cables.

7

2. Use compressed air to blow debris and loose material from the intake manifold and attached components.

3A. On carburetor-equipped models, remove the carburetor as described in this chapter.

3B. On throttle body injection (TBI) models, remove the throttle body as described in this section.

3C. On 5.0L and 5.7L multiport injection (MPI) models with a center-mounted throttle body, remove the throttle body and then fuel rail and injectors as described in this chapter.

3D. On 5.7L models with a front-mounted throttle body, remove the fuel rail and injectors as described in this chapter.

3E. On 7.4L, 8.1L and 8.2L models with MPI, remove the fuel rail and injectors as described in this chapter.

4. On 5.7L models with a front-mounted throttle body and all 8.1L models, push the cable end retainer (A, **Figure 72**) toward the cable anchor (B). Then pull the cable end off the throttle arm.

5. On all MPI models, remove the air pressure sensor as described in Chapter Nine.

6A. On open cooling system models, drain water from the cylinder block and manifold as described in Chapter Three.

6B. On closed cooling system models, drain water from the exhaust manifolds and heat exchanger as described in Chapter Three. Drain coolant from the system as described in Chapter Three.

7. On all models except 5.7L LT-1 and 8.1L, remove the distributor as described in Chapter Nine.

8. On 5.7L LT-1 models, remove the oil pump drive assembly as follows:

    a. Locate the oil pump drive assembly at the rear of the intake manifold and in the location used for the distributor on other models.

    b. Loosen the bolt (A, **Figure 87**) and then move the clamp (B) away from the clamping flange.

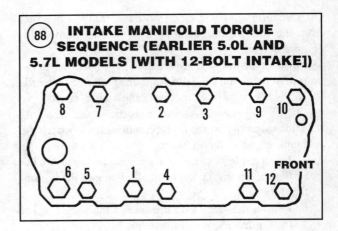

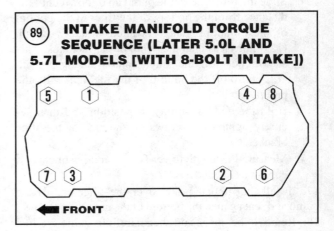

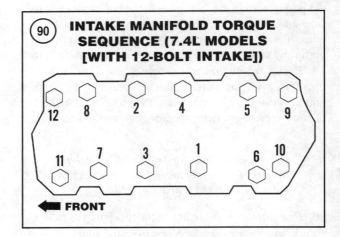

c. Carefully lift the oil pump drive out of the intake manifold. Remove and discard the gasket from the bottom of the clamping flange.

d. Inspect the gear on the bottom of the drive for worn, cracked or missing teeth. Replace the oil pump

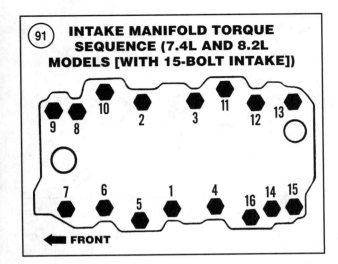

INTAKE MANIFOLD TORQUE SEQUENCE (7.4L AND 8.2L MODELS [WITH 15-BOLT INTAKE])

FRONT

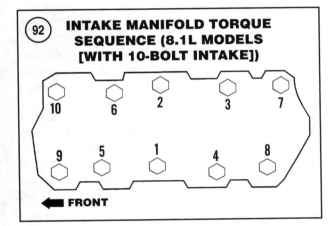

INTAKE MANIFOLD TORQUE SEQUENCE (8.1L MODELS [WITH 10-BOLT INTAKE])

FRONT

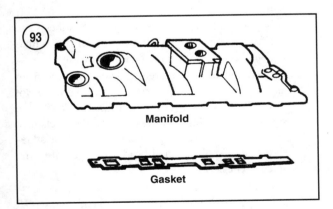

Manifold

Gasket

drive assembly if these or other defects are evident. If teeth are missing, remove the oil pan, as described in Chapter Six. Then remove the gear remnants. To prevent repeat failure of the gear, remove and inspect the oil pump as described in Chapter

Six. Install the oil pump and oil pan as described in Chapter Six.

    e. Rotate the gear on the bottom of the drive to check for smooth operation. Then check for excessive side play in the shaft supporting the gear. Replace the oil pump drive if it does not rotate freely or if excessive side play is evident.

9. On 5.0L, 5.7L, 7.4L and 8.2L models, remove the thermostat and thermostat housing as described in Chapter Eight.

10. On 5.0L, 5.7L, 7.4L and 8.2L models, remove the engine temperature sensor as described in Chapter Nine.

11. Remove any remaining brackets or components that may interfere with manifold removal. Route wiring away from the manifold.

12. Loosen the intake manifold bolts in the opposite of the tightening sequence.

    a. For early 5.0L and 5.7L models with a 12-bolt intake manifold, refer to **Figure 88**.

    b. For later 5.0L and 5.7L models with an eight-bolt intake manifold, refer to **Figure 89**.

    c. For 7.4L models with a 12-bolt intake manifold, refer to **Figure 90**.

    d. On 7.4L and 8.2L models with a 15-bolt intake manifold, refer to **Figure 91**.

    e. On 8.1L models, with a 10-bolt intake manifold, refer to **Figure 92**.

13. Fit a pry bar into the gap at the front of the manifold and carefully pry the manifold from the cylinder heads and block. Remove and discard the gaskets.

14. Remove the intake port and water crossover gaskets (**Figure 93**, typical) from the intake manifold or cylinder head surfaces.

15. On 7.4L, 8.1L and 8.2L models, remove the neoprene manifold gaskets from the front and rear of the cylinder block.

16. On 8.1L models, remove the metal splash shield from the lifter valley.

17. Cover the cylinder head openings and place clean shop towels into the valley between the cylinder heads. Then carefully scrape gasket material and sealant from the cylinder head and cylinder head surfaces.

18A. On TBI models, remove the four bolts and lift the mounting bracket (**Figure 68**) off the intake manifold. Remove the gasket from the mating surfaces. Discard the gasket. Carefully scrape all gasket material from the surfaces.

18B. On 5.7L models with a front-mounted throttle body and all 8.1L models, remove the throttle body as described in this chapter.

19. Use clean solvent and a plastic bristle brush to remove carbon and oil residue from the intake manifold and

7

bracket (TBI models). Dry the manifold and bracket with compressed air. Direct the air into all passages to remove debris and contaminants.

20. Inspect the mating surfaces for deep corrosion pitting, cracks or gouges. Defective mating surfaces will allow water, coolant, air, oil or exhaust leakage.

CAUTION
Never apply muriatic acid onto aluminum intake manifolds or other aluminum components. The acid will rapidly destroy exposed surfaces.

21. Inspect the water or coolant passages in the manifold for corrosion or mineral deposits. Have a machine shop soak the manifold in a special cleaning vat to remove the deposits. The manifolds used on some models are constructed of aluminum, and some acids will damage the material.

Intake Manifold Installation

1. Remove any shop towels or other covers from the cylinder head ports or valley between the cylinder heads. Remove any gasket material from these areas.

2. On 8.1L models, fit the metal splash shield into the lifter valley and rest the bent tabs on the shield against the cylinder heads. The gasket-locating tab openings must face upward.

3A. On early 5.0L and 5.7L models with a 12-bolt intake, install the gaskets and apply sealant as follows:

   a. Apply a small bead of RTV to the front and rear corners where the cylinder head and cylinder block mate.

   b. Coat the gasket mating surfaces on the cylinder heads with Permatex Gasket Sealing Compound.

   c. Install the *new* intake port and water crossover passage gaskets (**Figure 93**) onto the cylinder heads. The *TOP* marks on the gaskets must face up. Position the gaskets to perfectly align the gasket and cylinder head port openings.

   d. Apply a 3/16 in. (4.8 mm) diameter bead of RTV sealant onto the front and rear manifold-to-cylinder block mating surfaces. (**Figure 94**). Extend the bead up to the intake gaskets approximately 1/2 in. (13 mm).

   e. Apply a coat of Permatex Gasket Sealing Compound to the gasket mating surfaces of the intake manifold. *Do not* apply the compound to the manifold surfaces that will contact the bead of RTV sealant.

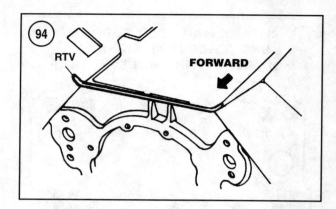

3B. On later 5.0L and 5.7L models with an eight-bolt intake manifold, install the gaskets and apply the sealant as follows:

   a. Apply a small bead of RTV to the front and rear corners where the cylinder head and cylinder block mate.

   b. Fit the locating pins into the cylinder head openings while installing the *new* intake manifold gaskets onto the cylinder heads. The *TOP* marks on the gaskets must face up.

   c. Apply a 3/16 in. (4.8 mm) diameter bead of RTV sealant to the front and rear manifold-to-cylinder block mating surfaces (**Figure 94**). Extend the bead to the intake gaskets approximately 1/2 in. (13 mm).

3C. On 7.4L, 8.1L and 8.2L models, install the intake manifold gaskets and apply sealant as follows:

   a. Apply a small bead of RTV to the front and rear corners where the cylinder head and cylinder block mate.

   b. Apply a small bead of Scotch grip 1300 adhesive to the front and rear manifold-to-cylinder block mating surfaces. Purchase the adhesive locally.

   c. *Quickly* install the neoprene gaskets onto the front and rear cylinder block surfaces. Make sure the slot in the bottom fits over the cylinder block and the square recesses for the intake manifold gaskets face upward. Hold the gaskets in position until the adhesive dries. Apply a small bead RTV sealant to the square recesses.

   d. Install the *new* intake port and water crossover gaskets (**Figure 93**) onto the cylinder heads with *TOP* marks facing upward.

   e. On 8.1L models, guide the locating tabs at the bottom of the gaskets into the corresponding openings in the metal splash shield.

   f. Fit the tabs at the lower front and rear of the gaskets into the square recesses in the neoprene gaskets.

g. On 7.4L and 8.2L models, apply a coat of Permatex Gasket Sealing Compound to the gasket mating surfaces of the intake manifold. *Do not* apply the compound onto the manifold surfaces that will contact the bead or RTV sealant.

h. Apply a 3/16 in. (4.8 mm) diameter bead of RTV sealant that extends approximately 1/2 in. (13 mm) over the ends of the cylinder head-mounted gaskets and down onto the neoprene cylinder block-mounted gaskets.

4. Use aerosol carburetor cleaner to remove all oily deposits from the manifold mating surfaces. Deposits can prevent the RTV sealant from bonding. Wipe the surfaces dry with a clean shop towel.

5. Carefully lower the manifold into position on the cylinder heads. Do not remove the manifold, or the RTV sealant must be reapplied.

6. Apply a coat of GM threadlock (GM part No. 12345382) to the manifold bolts. Purchase the hreadlock from a GM automobile dealership.

7. If necessary to align the openings, move the manifold or gaskets *slightly*. Then hand-thread the bolts into the manifold and cylinder head.

8A. On 5.0L and 5.7L models with a 12-bolt intake manifold, tighten the intake manifold bolts as follows:

a. Tighten the intake manifold bolts in the sequence shown in **Figure 88** to 180 in.-lb. (20 N•m).

b. Tighten the intake manifold bolts in sequence (**Figure 88**) a final time to 30 ft.-lb. (41 N•m).

8B. On 5.0L and 5.7L models with an eight-bolt intake manifold, tighten the intake manifold bolts in three steps as follows:

a. Tighten the bolts in the sequence shown in **Figure 89** to 27 in.-lb. (3 N•m).

b. Wait a few minutes. Then tighten the bolts in sequence a second time to 106 in.-lb. (12 N•m).

c. Wait a few minutes. Then tighten the bolts in sequence a final time to 133 in.-lb. (15 N•m).

8C. On 7.4L models with a 12-bolt intake manifold, tighten the manifold bolts as follows:

a. Tighten the intake manifold bolts in the sequence shown in **Figure 90** to 180 in.-lb. (20 N•m).

b. Tighten the intake manifold bolts in sequence (**Figure 90**) a final time to 30 ft.-lb. (41 N•m).

8D. On 7.4L and 8.2L models with a 14-bolt intake manifold, tighten the manifold bolts as follows:

a. Tighten the intake manifold bolts in the sequence shown in **Figure 91** to 210 in.-lb. (24 N•m).

b. Tighten the intake manifold bolts in sequence (**Figure 91**) a final time to 35 ft.-lb. (47 N•m).

8E. On 8.1L models with a 10-bolt intake manifold, tighten the intake manifold bolts in four steps as follows:

a. Tighten the bolts in the sequence shown in **Figure 92** to 18 in.-lb. (2 N•m).

b. Wait a few minutes. Then again tighten the bolts in sequence (**Figure 92**) to 18 in.-lb. (2 N•m).

c. Wait a few minutes. Then tighten the bolts in sequence (**Figure 92**) a third time to 89 in.-lb. (10 N•m).

d. Wait a few minutes. Then tighten the bolts in sequence (**Figure 92**) a final time to 106 in.-lb. (12 N•m).

9. On 5.0L and 5.7L throttle body injection (TBI) models, install the throttle body mounting bracket as follows:

a. Install a *new* gasket onto the intake manifold. Fit the bracket (**Figure 68**) onto the gasket and manifold.

b. Align the throttle bore openings and bolt holes. Install the four bolts and securely tighten in a crossing pattern.

10A. On carburetor-equipped models, install the carburetor as described in this chapter.

10B. On TBI models, install the throttle body as described in this section.

10C. On 5.0L and 5.7L MPI models with a center-mounted throttle body, install the fuel rail and injectors and then the throttle body as described in this chapter.

10D. On 5.7L models with a front-mounted throttle body, install the fuel rail and injectors as described in this chapter.

10E. On 7.4L, 8.1L and 8.2L models with MPI, install the fuel rail and injectors as described in this chapter.

11. On 5.7L models with a front-mounted throttle body and all 8.1L models, install the throttle body as described in this chapter.

12A. On all models except 5.7L LT-1 and 8.1L, install the distributor as described in Chapter Nine.

12B. On 5.7L LT-1 models, install the oil pump drive assembly as follows:

a. Install a new gasket over the gear end of the assembly and seat against the step on the bottom of the clamping flange.

b. Guide the oil pump drive assembly into the intake manifold and cylinder block.

c. Apply light pressure to the top of the assembly while an assistant manually rotates the crankshaft pulley in the clockwise direction. Continue until the oil pump drive gear teeth engage the camshaft gear teeth and the slot in the bottom of the drive engages the oil pump drive shaft. The assembly will drop down and seat against the intake manifold when all components align.

d. Position the clamp (B, **Figure 87**, typical) over the clamping flange. Then tighten the bolt (A, **Figure 87**) to 216 in.-lb. (24 N•m).

13. On all MPI models, install the air pressure sensor as described in Chapter Nine.

14. On 5.0L, 5.7L, 7.4L and 8.2L models, install the thermostat and thermostat housing as described in Chapter Eight.

15. On 5.0L, 5.7L, 7.4L and 8.2L models, install the engine temperature sensor as described in Chapter Nine.

16. Install any brackets and clamps that were removed for manifold removal.

17. Route all wiring to prevent interference with moving components. Clamp the wiring as needed. Do not install the plastic engine cover at this time.

18. On 5.7L models with a front-mounted throttle body, push the cable end retainer (A, **Figure 72**) toward the cable anchor (B). Then fit the cable end fully over the ball-shaped end of the throttle lever. Rotate the retainer to align the slot in the back of the retainer with the pin and then slide the slot in the retainer over the pin. The internal spring holds the retainer in position. Tug lightly on the cable end to verify a secure connection.

19. Adjust the throttle cable as described in Chapter Five.

20. On models with a closed cooling system, fill the cooling system with the proper coolant-and-water mixture as described in Chapter Three.

21. Connect the battery cables.

22. Start the engine and immediately check for water, coolant, fuel, air or oil leakage. Stop the engine and correct any leaks before proceeding.

23. On all models except 5.7L LT-1 and 8.1L, adjust the ignition timing as described in Chapter Five.

24. Install the plastic cover onto the engine.

Table 1 FUEL SYSTEM TORQUE SPECIFICATIONS

Fastener	in.-lb.	ft.-lb.	N•m
Carburetor			
Inlet needle seat	10	–	1.1
Main fuel jets	10	–	1.1
Mounting nuts or bolts	115-168	–	13-19
Power valve	100	–	11.3
Throttle body to carburetor body	50	–	5.6
Electric fuel pump (carburetor models)			
Mounting bracket	–	20-25	27-34
Fuel line fittings	177-212	–	20-24
Fuel pump fittings			
Carter fuel pump			
Inlet and outlet fitting	48-59	–	5.4-6.7
Delco fuel pump			
Outlet fitting	60-84	–	6.8-9.5
Electric boost pump (EFI models)			
Mounting bracket	–	20-25	27-34
Fuel line fittings	177-212	–	20-24
Fuel pump fittings			
Carter fuel pump			
Inlet and outlet fitting	48-59	–	5.4-6.7
Delco fuel pump			
Outlet fitting	60-84	–	6.8-9.5
Fuel rail			
Crossover fuel line retainers			
5.7L models			
With front-mounted throttle body	62	–	7
Fuel rail to intake manifold			
5.0L and 5.7L models			
With center-mounted throttle body	180	–	20
With front-mounted throttle body	88	–	10
7.4L and 8.2L models	28	–	3.2
8.1L models	106	–	12
Fuel line fittings (EFI models)			
5.0L and 5.7L models			
With center-mounted throttle body			
Pressure line	115	–	13
Return line	156	–	17.6

(continued)

Table 1 FUEL SYSTEM TORQUE SPECIFICATIONS (continued)

Fastener	in.-lb.	ft.-lb.	N•m
Fuel line fittings (EFI models)			
5.0L and 5.7L models (continued)			
With front-mounted throttle body			
Pressure and return lines	115	–	13
7.4L and 8.2L models			
Pressure and return lines	216	18	24
Fuel pressure regulator to fuel rail			
5.0L and 5.7L models	84	–	9.5
High-pressure electric fuel pump (EFI models)			
Engine-mounted pump			
Pump outlet fitting	60-84	–	6.8-9.5
Outlet line fitting	177-212	–	20-24
Intake manifold			
5.0L and 5.7L models			
With 12-bolt intake			
First step	180	–	20
Final step	–	30	41
With 8-bolt intake			
First step	27	–	3
Second step	106	–	12
Final step	133	–	15
7.4L models			
With 12-bolt intake			
First step	180	–	20
Final step	–	30	41
With 15-bolt intake			
First step	–	210	24
Final step	–	35	47
8.1L models			
First step	18	–	2
Second step	18	–	2
Third step	89	–	10
Final step	106	–	12
8.2L models			
First step	–	210	24
Final step	–	35	47
Mechanical fuel pump			
Mounting bolts	240	20	27.1
Fuel pump mounting plate	180	15	20.3
Inlet and outlet fitting	48-49	–	5.4-6.7
Fuel line fittings	177-212	–	20-24
Plenum to intake manifold			
7.4L and 8.2L models	–	30	41
Oil pump drive			
5.7L LT-1	216	18	24
Throttle body			
Fuel line to TBI unit	204	17	23
Injector cover and regulator housing	27	–	3.0
Injector housing to TBI unit	35	–	4.0
Pressure line fitting into TBI unit	–	30	40
Return line fitting into TBI unit	–	21	29
Return passage plug into TBI unit	–	21	29
Throttle body to manifold adapter			
TBI models	142	–	16
Throttle body to intake manifold			
5.0L and 5.7L MPI models	132	11	15
8.1L models	89	–	10
Throttle body to plenum			
5.7L, 7.4L and 8.2L models	132	11	15

7

Chapter Eight

Cooling and Exhaust System

This chapter covers service procedures for the thermostat, engine recirculation pump, hoses, seawater pump, oil and power steering fluid coolers, exhaust elbow and exhaust manifold. Procedures for flushing the cooling system and maintaining closed cooling systems are described in Chapter Three.

On models equipped with a standard (open) cooling system (**Figure 1**, typical), water in which the boat is being operated is picked up at the seawater pickup (**Figure 2**) and circulated throughout the engine to absorb heat. The heated water is transferred to the exhaust manifold(s) where it is expelled overboard with the exhaust gasses.

Some models are equipped with an optional closed cooling system (**Figure 3**), which consists of a closed subsystem and a raw water subsystem. The closed subsystem contains coolant (antifreeze-and-water mixture) that circulates throughout the engine cooling passages and absorbs engine heat. The heat absorbed by the coolant is transferred (exchanged) to the seawater in the heat exchanger (raw water subsystem). Water in which the boat is being operated is picked up at the seawater pickup (**Figure 2**) and transferred through the passages in the heat exchanger, where it absorbs heat from the coolant.

The heated seawater from the exchanger is transferred to the exhaust manifold(s) where it is expelled overboard with the exhaust gasses. Several manufacturers offer closed cooling systems. The hose connection points and routing on the standard open and closed systems may differ slightly from the illustrations.

Table 1 lists tightening specifications for most cooling and exhaust system fasteners. Use the general tightening torque specifications provided in Chapter One for cooling or exhaust system fasteners not listed in **Table 1**. **Table 1** is located at the end of this chapter.

> *WARNING*
> *Stay clear of the propeller and propeller shaft while running an engine on a flush adapter.*

> *CAUTION*
> *Use a flush device or other means to supply the engine with cooling water if running the engine with the boat out of the water. The seawater pump is quickly damaged if operated without adequate cooling water.*

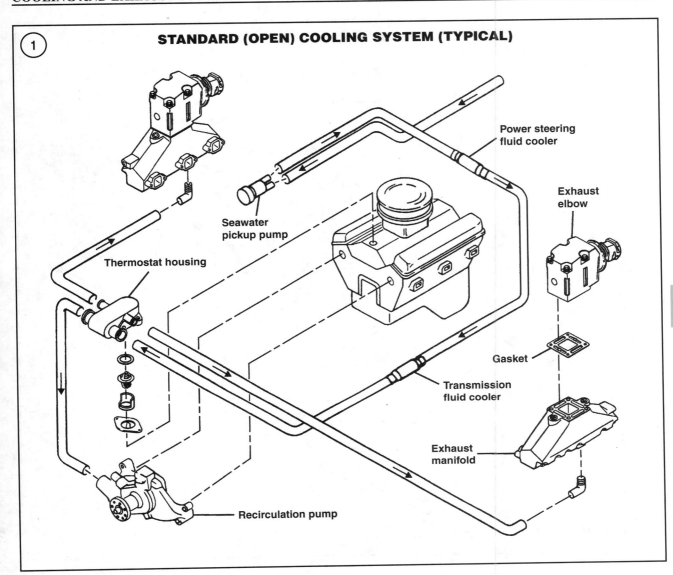

① STANDARD (OPEN) COOLING SYSTEM (TYPICAL)

Power steering fluid cooler

Exhaust elbow

Seawater pickup pump

Thermostat housing

Gasket

Transmission fluid cooler

Exhaust manifold

Recirculation pump

8

②

THERMOSTAT

The thermostat controls water or coolant circulation to provide quick engine warm up and maintain a consistent operating temperature.

On a standard (open) cooling system, the thermostat controls seawater flow through the cylinder block and then the cylinder heads to control engine temperature. When the engine is cold, the thermostat is closed and water cannot exit the cylinder block and cylinder heads. The closed thermostat directs the incoming water to the exhaust manifolds where it is expelled. When the engine warms up, the thermostat opens, and water can flow through the block and heads where it absorbs excess heat before exiting through the exhaust manifolds.

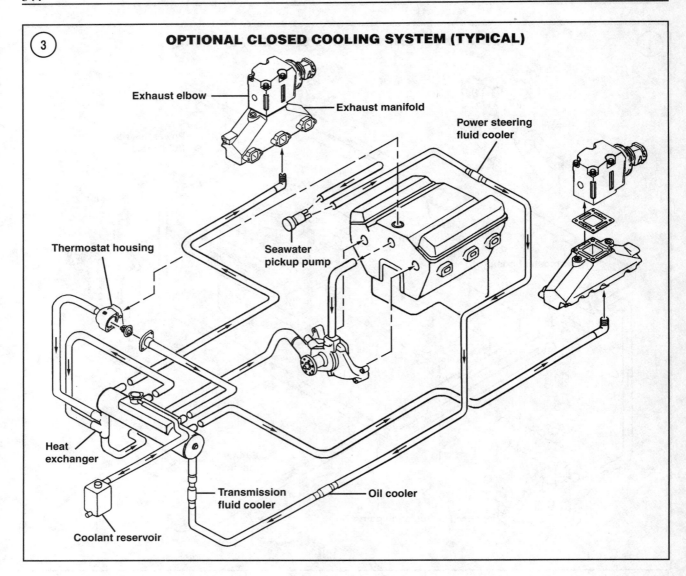

OPTIONAL CLOSED COOLING SYSTEM (TYPICAL)

③

Exhaust elbow

Exhaust manifold

Power steering fluid cooler

Thermostat housing

Seawater pickup pump

Heat exchanger

Transmission fluid cooler

Oil cooler

Coolant reservoir

On a closed cooling system, the thermostat controls coolant flow through the cylinder block and heat exchanger to control engine temperature. When the engine is cold, the thermostat is closed, and the coolant bypasses the heat exchanger. This allows the cylinder block to warm to normal operating temperature. When the engine warms up, the thermostat opens, and coolant flows through the heat exchanger to remove excess heat.

On 5.7L LT-1 models, a special thermostat housing and recirculation pump are used to create a reverse flow cooling system. On this model, water flows through the cylinder heads and then the cylinder block. This arrangement increases overall performance by lowering the cylinder head temperature compared to other models. The special thermostat housing contains two thermostats to offer a two-stage cooling system that provides optimum control of the engine temperature.

CAUTION
Never operate the engine with a faulty or missing thermostat. Either condition can cause the engine to overheat or fail to reach normal operating temperature. Operating too cool for an extended period of time can result in oil dilution and possible engine damage from inadequate lubrication. Operating the engine at excessive temperature can result in serious damage to all engine components.

Thermostats are rated according to the opening temperatures. The opening temperature value is stamped in the

thermostat flange (**Figure 4**) or other area. The thermostat should start to open at the temperature stamped on the thermostat and be fully opened at 25° F above that temperature. The manufacturer does not recommend installing a thermostat with a higher or lower temperature rating than the original equipment. Doing so can adversely affect engine operation, durability and exhaust emissions.

CAUTION
Do not substitute an automotive thermostat in place of the original equipment. The higher rating will cause the engine to overheat and

can cause serious engine damage. Make sure any thermostat installed in the engine is approved for use in an Indmar marine engine.

Thermostat Removal

1A. On models with a standard (open) cooling system, drain all water from the cylinder block as described in Chapter Four. Refer to *Winterizing*.
1B. On models with a closed cooling system, drain coolant from the cylinder block as described in Chapter Three. Refer to *Changing the Engine Coolant*.
2. Loosen the hose clamps and disconnect all hoses (A, **Figure 5**, typical) from the thermostat/distribution housing.
3. Note the wire routing and connections. Then disconnect the engine wire harness from the engine temperature sender, overheat switch or engine temperature sensor that might be mounted in the thermostat/distribution housing.
4. Remove the two bolts (B, **Figure 5**, typical) that secure the thermostat housing to the intake manifold.
5. Lift the thermostat housing off the intake manifold. If necessary, tap lightly on the side of the housing with a rubber mallet to break the gasket bond.
6. Note which end is facing up. Then remove the thermostat from the intake manifold or thermostat housing. If necessary, grip the thermostat with pliers and twist lightly to free the thermostat.
7. Scrape all gasket material from the thermostat housing and intake mating surface. Any material on the mating surfaces will allow water or coolant leakage.
8. Remove all corrosion, salt or mineral deposits from the thermostat flange recess in the thermostat/distribution housing. Any material on the flange surface will allow water or coolant to bypass the thermostat and greatly increase the warm-up time.
9. Use a wire brush to remove all corrosion or mineral deposits from the thermostat housing bolts. Use a tap or thread chaser to remove corrosion or deposits from the bolt openings in the housing. Use compressed air to clear debris from the openings.
10. Test the thermostat as described in Chapter Two. Refer to *Cooling System*.

Thermostat Installation

1. If a new thermostat is being installed, test it as described in Chapter Two. A faulty new thermostat is a common occurrence.
2. Install the thermostat into the intake manifold or thermostat housing. Make sure the thermostat is installed in the correct direction. On most models, the element end (**Figure 6**) must face down or toward the intake manifold.

8

Make sure the flange fully seats into the recess in the housing.

3. Apply a light coat of gasket sealing compound to the mating surfaces. Then fit a *new* gasket onto the thermostat housing.

4. Install the thermostat housing onto the intake manifold. Apply a light coat of gasket sealing compound to the threads and then install the bolts (B, **Figure 5**, typical) into the housing and intake manifold. Tighten the bolts evenly to 20-25 ft.-lb. (27-34 N•m).

5. Connect all hoses (A, **Figure 5**, typical) to the thermostat housing. Securely tighten the hose clamps.

6. Connect any disconnected wires to the engine temperature sender, overheat switch or engine temperature sensor that is mounted in the thermostat/distribution housing. Route the wiring to prevent entanglement in the drive belt(s) or other moving components.

7. On models with a closed cooling system, refill with coolant as described in Chapter Three. Refer to *Changing the Engine Coolant*.

8. Start the engine and immediately check for water or coolant leakage from the thermostat housing. Correct the leakage before continuing operation.

9. Monitor the engine and temperature gauge while the engine warms to operating temperature. Stop the engine if overheating or continued low temperature is evident. Correct the cause of overheating or overcooling before putting the engine into service.

HOSE REPLACEMENT

Replace any hoses that are cracked, brittle, mildewed or very soft and spongy. Always replace hoses in questionable condition. Attention to hose condition can prevent failure while offshore. Some of the hoses are difficult to access under normal working conditions with all of the necessary tools available. It might be impossible to change the hose at sea with a limited supply of tools.

Hose manufacturers generally recommend replacing the hoses every 2 years. How long the hoses last depends a great deal on how much the boat is used and how well it is maintained. However, it is a good practice to replace hoses at the recommended 2-year intervals. Always replace cooling system hoses with the same type as the original. Pleated rubber hoses do not allow the same amount of water or coolant flow and do not have the same strength as reinforced molded hoses. Straight hose is not an acceptable substitute for curved or molded hoses. In such applications, the straight hose can kink and prevent adequate water or coolant flow.

Always check the condition of the hose clamps and install new worm screw clamps if necessary. A damaged

clamp can loosen while underway and result in coolant loss, overheating and serious engine damage.

When replacing hoses that connect only to the upper part of the engine, it is acceptable to partially drain the seawater or coolant. Always fully drain the system when replacing hoses connecting to the recirculation pump, heat exchanger or exhaust manifold(s).

1. Loosen the clamp at each end of the hose. Grasp the hose and twist it off the fitting with a pulling motion. Avoid using a sharp instrument to remove the hose. Doing so can damage the reinforcement material in the hose and might not be visually apparent. The hose might fail while at sea.

2. If the hose is corroded onto the fitting and will not twist free, cut it off with a sharp knife about 1.0 in. (25.4 mm) beyond the fitting. Remove the clamp and slit the remaining piece of hose lengthwise. Then peel it off the fitting.

3. Clean any rust or corrosion from the fitting by wrapping a piece of medium-grit sandpaper around it and rotating until the fitting is clean and smooth. Turn carefully to avoid removing too much material when cleaning composite or plastic fittings.

4. Wipe the inside diameter of the replacement hose with a soap-and-water solution. Never apply grease or oil to

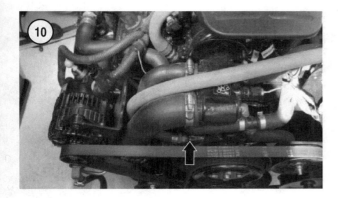

the hose or fitting. Grease or oil can cause the surfaces to deteriorate at a rapid rate or allow the hose to slip off the fitting, even while securely clamped.

5. Fit the hose over the fittings with a twisting motion. Align the hose to prevent kinking or twisting and then push the hose fully onto the fittings.

6. Position the clamps approximately 1/4 in. (6.3 mm) from the end of the hose, Make sure the clamp screw is oriented for easy access and does not contact other engine components. Tighten the clamp securely.

7. On models with a closed cooling system, check the coolant level or refill the system as described in Chapter Four.

WARNING
Stay clear of the propeller and propeller shaft while running an engine on a flush adapter.

CAUTION
Use a flush device or other means to supply the engine with cooling water if running the engine with the boat out of the water. The seawater pump is quickly damaged if operated without adequate cooling water.

8. Start the engine and immediately check for leakage. Tighten the clamps if leaking. Check for residual debris on the fittings if leakage cannot be corrected by tightening the clamps.

RECIRCULATION PUMP REMOVAL AND INSTALLATION

If the recirculation pump is making noise, it might be an indication of impending failure. If the seal is defective, seawater or coolant can leak from behind the pump pulley. The pump is serviced as an assembly and can be replaced with the engine in the boat. Marine recirculation pumps contain stainless steel components and use a special shaft seal. *Do not* replace it with an automotive pump.

1. Disconnect the battery cables.

2. Loosen but do not remove the four bolts (**Figure 7**) that secure the pulley to the pump shaft. The tension of the drive belt(s) will help limit pulley rotation while loosening the bolts.

3A. On models with a standard (open) cooling system, drain seawater from the cylinder block as described in Chapter Four. Refer to *Winterizing*.

3B. On models with a closed cooling system, drain the coolant as described in Chapter Three. Refer to *Changing the Coolant*.

4. Remove the alternator drive belt as described in Chapter Nine. Refer to *Alternator Removal*.

5. Remove the pump pulley bolts (**Figure 7**) and carefully pull the pulley from the pump shaft. Clean rust or corrosion from the pulley surfaces. Rust or corrosion pitting on the belt contact surfaces will allow slippage and quickly wear a new belt. Clean and repaint the pulley as necessary.

6. Loosen the clamps and disconnect the large hose (**Figure 8**) from the pump.

7. On 7.4L and 8.2L models, loosen the clamp. Then disconnect the bypass hose (**Figure 9**) from the fitting on the top of the recirculation pump.

8. If the boat is equipped with a hot water heater, loosen the clamp. Then disconnect the water heater hose (**Figure 10**, typical) from the recirculation pump.

9. Remove any accessory brackets or clamps attached to the recirculation pump or those which might interfere with pump removal.

10. Note the locations of the stud bolts used on most models. The stud bolts must be installed in the original locations for proper accessory bracket and clamp alignment.

11. Support the pump while removing the four pump fasteners (**Figure 11**, typical). Tap on the body with a rubber mallet to free the pump from the cylinder block.

8

12. Carefully scrape all gasket material and old sealant from the cylinder block and recirculation pump mating surfaces. Be thorough. Residual gasket material is easy to overlook and will cause the pump to leak after installation. Use a thread chaser to remove corrosion and old sealant from the pump fastener openings. Use a wire brush to clean the fastener threads.

13. If the boat is equipped with a water heater, remove the plug from the replacement recirculation pump. Then remove the fitting from the opening in the used pump. Apply gasket sealing compound to the fitting and then install it into the replacement pump. Securely tighten the fitting.

14. Apply gasket sealing compound to the mating surfaces and then install a new gasket(s) onto the pump. The sealant should hold the gaskets in position. On 5.0L and 5.7L models, the port side replacement gasket does not perfectly match the openings. Although the gasket will protrude on the bottom, the gasket will seal satisfactorily.

15. Insert the pump bolts through the pump body and gasket(s) to help retain the gasket(s). Make sure the stud bolts are in the proper openings as noted in Step 10. Apply a light coat of gasket sealing compound to the bolt threads.

16. Fit the pump onto the cylinder block. Thread the bolts (**Figure 11**) into the cylinder block. Make sure the gaskets are properly positioned before tightening the bolts. Tighten the bolts in a crossing pattern to 33 ft.-lb. (45 N•m). for 5.0L and 5.7L models, 30 ft.-lb. (41 N•m) for 7.4L and 8.2L models and 37 ft.-lb. (50 N•m) for 8.1L models.

17. Install the pulley onto the water pump shaft. Rotate the pulley to align the four bolt openings. The replacement pump might have eight bolt openings. Rotate the pulley until all four openings align. Install the four bolts into the openings and tighten by hand. The bolts are easier to tighten with the drive belt(s) installed. Make sure the pulley is fully seated on the shaft flange.

18. Connect the large hose to the water pump (**Figure 8**) and secure with the worm screw clamp.

19. On 7.4L and 8.2L models, connect the bypass hose (**Figure 9**) to the recirculation pump fitting. Securely tighten the hose clamp.

20. If the boat is equipped with a water heater, connect the water heater hose to the pump fitting (**Figure 10**). Route the hose to prevent contact with the belts and pulleys. Secure the hose with plastic locking clamps as needed.

21. Install any accessory bracket or clamp removed to access the pump.

22. Install the alternator drive belt as described in Chapter Nine. Refer to *Alternator Installation*.

23. Tighten the four pulley bolts in a crossing pattern to the general tightening specification provided in Chapter One for 3.0L, 4.3L, 5.0L or 5.7L models and 18 ft.-lb. (25 N•m) for 8.1L models. Check and readjust the drive belt tension. Refer to *Alternator Installation* in Chapter Nine.

24. On models with a closed cooling system, refill the engine with coolant as described in Chapter Three.

25. Connect the battery cables.

WARNING
Stay clear of the propeller and propeller shaft while running an engine on a flush adapter.

CAUTION
Use a flush device or other means to supply the engine with cooling water if running the engine with the boat out of the water. The seawater pump is quickly damaged if operated without adequate cooling water.

26. Start the engine and immediately check for leakage at the hoses and water pump. If leaking from a hose connection, remove the hose, clean the hose and fitting and install the hose. If leaking from the mating surfaces, remove the pump and remove residual gasket material from the pump and cylinder block mating surfaces.

SEAWATER PUMP

A seawater pump with a replaceable rubber impeller is used on all models. Two different types of pumps are used. Early models use a belt-driven seawater pump (**Figure 12**) that mounts onto the lower front of the engine. Later models use a crankshaft driven seawater pump (**Figure 13**) located on the lower front side of the engine. The pump attaches to and is driven by the crankshaft pulley. A bracket attaches to the cylinder block and the pump body to provide support and prevent the body from rotating

with the crankshaft. This section describes pump removal, repair and installation for both types of pumps.

CAUTION
The seawater pump is quickly damaged if the inlet and outlet hoses are connected to the wrong seawater pump fittings. Early 5.0L, 5.7L and 7.4L models were produced in both standard- and counter-rotation models, and the seawater pump hose connections on counter-rotation models are the reverse of standard rotation models. Identify the engine rotation before beginning this procedure.

NOTE
The manufacturer uses several different designs for the belt-driven and crankshaft-driven seawater pump. Removal, repair and installation of the various designs are very similar. This section describes removal, repair and installation of the typical seawater pumps. The illustrations might vary slightly for the actual equipment.

Removal (Belt-Driven Seawater Pump)

1A. On standard-rotation models, loosen the clamps. Then carefully pull the inlet (A, **Figure 14**) and outlet (B) hoses from the pump.

1B. On counter-rotation models, loosen the clamps. Then carefully pull the outlet (A, **Figure 14**) and inlet (B) hoses from the pump.

2. Rotate the pulley if necessary to align the bolt access holes in the pulley with the mounting bolts (**Figure 15**, typical). Loosen but do not remove the mounting bolts.

3. Slide the pump toward the crankshaft pulley to relieve belt tension and then slip the belt off the pump pulley. Inspect the belt for wear, damage or deterioration and replace as needed.

4. Remove the mounting bolts and carefully slide the pump assembly out of the mounting bracket.

Impeller replacement

The water pump repair kit includes a new impeller and gaskets. Some kits include a new cam element and lubrication for the water pump impeller. Several styles of gaskets are included in the kit. Use the style that perfectly matches the original gasket.

1. Remove the belt-driven water pump as described in this chapter.

8

2. Place the water pump on a suitable work surface with the pulley side facing down.

3. Remove the screws (**Figure 16**, typical). Then carefully pull the cover off the pump body (**Figure 17**). Do not pry off the cover. The gasket surfaces are easily damaged. If necessary, carefully twist the cover loose.

4. Use two blunt screwdrivers to pry the impeller out of the pump body (**Figure 18**). Work carefully to avoid damaging the pump body or gasket mating surfaces.

5. On models with a removable cam element, remove the single screw (**Figure 19**) on the side of the pump body. Carefully remove the cam element (**Figure 20**) from the pump body. Always replace the cam element with the new element included in the repair kit. The design of the element is sometimes changed to match the impeller in the kit.

6. Use compressed air to clear all water and debris from the pump body.

7. Inspect the impeller contact surfaces in the pump body and cover (**Figure 21**) for deep corrosion pitting, deep scratches, cracking or roughness. Replace the water pump assembly if these defects are evident.

8. Grasp the water pump body and rotate the pump pulley to check for roughness or excessive play in the pump bearings. Replace the pump body if these defects are evident.

9. Inspect the shaft seal (**Figure 22**) for cracking at the seal lip, missing sections or other defects. Replace the seal if these or other defects are evident. Make sure the seal is available before removing it from the housing. The seal is not available separately on some models.

10. Inspect the impeller for worn, charred or missing sections. Replace the impeller unless a new replacement is not available and the impeller is in like-new condition. Charred surfaces indicate the water pump was operated with insufficient water. Check for blocked passages, loose hose clamps, damaged or kinked hoses, or other defects that allow air to enter the pump or restrict water flow. If

sections are missing, remove all hoses and the thermostat. Then check all cooling system passages for remnants. Missing sections are usually lodged in the water pump-to-thermostat hose or in the thermostat housing.

11. Fit the cam element into the pump body. Work carefully to avoid bending the element fingers. Reposition the element if necessary to align the screw opening with the corresponding opening in the pump body.

12. Apply a light coat of gasket sealing compound to the threads. Then install and carefully tighten the screw (**Figure 19**). Do not overtighten the screw. The screw will break if overtightened.

13. Coat the inner surfaces of the pump body and the impeller with the impeller lubricant included in the repair kit. If the lubricant is not included in the kit, coat the surfaces with liquid dishwashing soap.

14A. On standard-rotation models, align the shaft and impeller splines. Then carefully fit the impeller into the pump body. Rotate the pump pulley clockwise as viewed from the pulley side to make sure all of the impeller vanes curl in the clockwise direction as shown in **Figure 23**. Remove and reinstall the impeller if necessary.

14B. On counter-rotation models, align the shaft and impeller splines. Then carefully fit the impeller into the pump body. Rotate the pump pulley counterclockwise as viewed from the pulley side to make sure all of the impeller vanes curl in the counterclockwise direction. Remove and reinstall the impeller if necessary.

15. Carefully match the original gasket with the correct replacement gasket from the repair kit. Some of the gaskets are very similar. Fit the new gasket onto the pump body (**Figure 24**). Do not apply sealant to the gasket. Sealant will cause the gasket to slide out of position while tightening the cover screws.

16. Carefully fit the cover onto the pump body. Do not dislodge the gasket.

17. Apply a light coat of gasket sealing compound to the threads. Then carefully thread the screws (**Figure 16**) into the cover, gasket and pump body. Verify that the gasket is in position and then tighten the cover screws. Do not overtighten the screws. Overtightening will break the screws.

18A. On standard-rotation models, rotate the water pump pulley clockwise, as viewed from the pulley side to check for smooth operation. Do not rotate the pulley counterclockwise. Doing so might cause one or more of the impeller vanes to curl in the wrong direction and result in inefficient water pump operation, a damaged impeller and/or overheating. Disassemble the pump and check for improper assembly or damaged components if binding or roughness is evident.

8

18B. On counter-rotation models, rotate the water pump pulley counterclockwise as viewed from the pulley side to check for smooth operation. Do not rotate the pulley clockwise. Doing so might cause one or more of the impeller vanes to curl in the wrong direction and result in inefficient water pump operation, a damaged impeller and/or overheating. Disassemble the pump and check for improper assembly or damaged components if binding or roughness is evident.

19. Install the belt-driven seawater pump as described in this chapter.

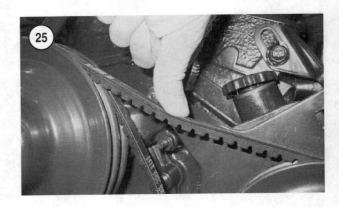

Installation (Belt-Driven Seawater Pump)

1. Carefully slide the pump into the mounting bracket and align the pump pulley with the crankshaft pulley.

2. Thread the mounting bolts (**Figure 15**) into the bracket and pump body openings. Do not tighten the bolts at this time.

3. Move the pump toward the crankshaft pulley and then slip the drive belt onto the pump and crankshaft pulleys. Make sure the belt is not twisted and fits into the groove in each pulley.

4. Rotate the pump pulley to align the openings in the pulley with the mounting bolts.

5. Move the pump away from the crankshaft pulley to apply tension to the drive belt. When properly tensioned, the belt will deflect approximately 1/4-1/2 in. (6-13 mm) with thumb pressure applied at a point midway between the pulleys (**Figure 25**).

6. Hold the pump in position to maintain belt tension while tightening the mounting bolts to 30 ft.-lb. (41 N•m).

7A. On standard-rotation models, fit the clamps over the ends. Then push the inlet (A, **Figure 14**) and outlet hoses (B) onto the pump. The inlet hose leads to the seawater pickup fitting (**Figure 26**). The outlet hose leads to the thermostat housing (**Figure 27**). The transmission cooler (A, **Figure 28**) is installed along the inlet hose on some models and the outlet hose on others.

7B. On counter-rotation models, fit the clamps over the ends. Then push the outlet (A, **Figure 14**) and inlet hoses (B) onto the pump. The inlet hose leads to the seawater pickup fitting (**Figure 26**). The outlet hose leads to the thermostat housing (**Figure 27**). The transmission cooler (A, **Figure 28**) is installed along the inlet hose on some models and the outlet hose on others.

8. Position the hose clamps approximately 1/4 in. (6 mm) from the ends of the hoses. Then securely tighten the clamps.

WARNING
Stay clear of the propeller and propeller shaft while running an engine on a flush adapter.

CAUTION
Use a flush device or other means to supply the engine with cooling water if running the engine with the boat out of the water. The seawater pump is quickly damaged if operated without adequate cooling water.

9. Connect the battery cables.

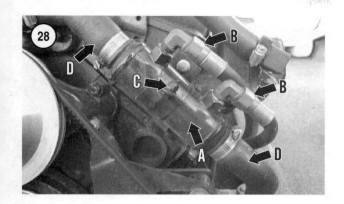

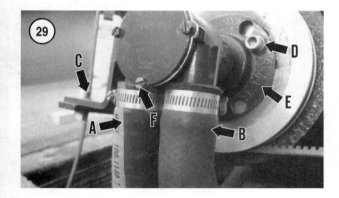

Removal and inspection

1. Disconnect the battery cables.

CAUTION
Do not pry the hoses off the seawater pump. Doing so will damage the pump. If necessary, carefully twist the hoses to break the bond and then push the hoses off with a blunt-tip instrument.

2A. On standard-rotation models, loosen the hose clamps. Then carefully pull the inlet (A, **Figure 29**) and outlet (B) hoses from the pump.

2B. On counter-rotation models, loosen the hose clamps. Then carefully pull the outlet (A, **Figure 29**) and inlet (B) hoses from the pump.

3. Remove the four screws (F, **Figure 29**) that secure the cover to the pump body. Carefully pry the impeller out of the pump body with two blunt screwdrivers. Work carefully to avoid damaging the pump body.

4. Remove the O-ring from the groove in the pump body. Discard the O-ring.

5. Remove the bolt(s) (C, **Figure 29**) to free the pump body from the support bracket.

6. Use compressed air to clear all water and debris from the pump body.

7. Inspect the impeller contact surfaces in the pump body and cover for deep corrosion pitting, deep scratches, cracking or roughness. Replace the pump body or cover if these or other defects are evident.

8. Inspect the impeller for worn, charred or missing sections. Replace the impeller unless a new replacement is not available and the impeller is in like-new condition. Charred surfaces indicate the water pump was operated without sufficient water. Check for blocked passages, loose hose clamps, damaged or kinked hoses or other defects that allow air to enter the pump or restrict water flow. If sections of the impeller are missing, remove all hoses and the thermostat. Then check all cooling system passages for remnants. Missing sections are usually lodged in the water pump-to-thermostat hose, fluid cooler or thermostat housing.

9. If the pump body must be replaced or removed to access other engine components, remove as follows:
   a. Make match marks on the crankshaft pulley and pump body mount to ensure correct orientation during assembly. If the body must be replaced, transfer the marks to the replacement part.
   b. Support the pump body and then remove the Allen-head bolts (D, **Figure 29**).
   c. Carefully pull the body off the crankshaft pulley.

10. Start the engine and immediately check for leakage from the hoses and end plate mating surfaces. If leaking from the hoses, remove the hoses, clean the fittings, and reinstall the hoses. If leaking from the mating surfaces, the gasket likely slipped out of position during assembly. Replace the gasket to correct the leak.

11. Monitor the engine temperature while allowing the engine to reach normal operating temperature. If the engine begins to overheat, refer to Chapter Two for troubleshooting procedures.

12. Stop the engine and disconnect the battery cables.

13. Check the belt tension as described in Step 5 and readjust as necessary.

14. Connect the battery cables.

Crankshaft-Driven Seawater Pump

The pump mounts on the front of the crankshaft pulley. The pump must be partially disassembled for impeller removal. The pump repair kit includes a new impeller, O-ring and sealing ring. On some models, the kit includes a tube of water pump impeller lubricant.

8

d. Clean all threadlocking compound from the Allen-head bolts and the threaded openings in the crankshaft pulley.

Assembly and installation

Refer to **Figure 29** for this procedure.

1. Note the bracket orientation, then remove the bolts and seawater pump support bracket from the cylinder block.

2. If the pump body (E, **Figure 29**) was removed from the crankshaft pulley, install as follows:

    a. Fit the pump body mount onto the crankshaft pulley. Rotate the mount to align the match marks.

    b. Apply a light coat of Loctite 271 or equivalent to the threads of the Allen-head bolts.

    c. Rotate the pump body mount as needed to align the bolt openings and then thread the bolts (D, **Figure 29**) into the mount and pulley. Tighten the bolts evenly to 35-40 ft.-lb. (47-54 N•m).

3. Coat the inner surfaces of the pump body and the replacement impeller with the impeller lubricant included in the repair kit. If the lubricant is not included in the kit, coat the surfaces with liquid dishwashing soap.

4. Carefully align the shaft bore in the impeller with the shaft in the pump body. Do not attempt to install the impeller into the body at this time. The following procedures must be followed to make sure the impeller vanes curl in the proper direction when installed.

5A. On standard-rotation models, push on the end of the impeller while rotating the pump body counterclockwise until the vanes curl enough to allow the shaft in the body to engage the corresponding bore in the impeller. Continue pushing and turning until the impeller enters the body and fully seats in the bore. Do not rotate the pump body clockwise with the impeller installed. Doing so will cause the impeller vanes to reverse direction and cause decreased cooling system efficiency and overheating.

5B. On counter-rotation models, push on the end of the impeller while rotating the pump body clockwise until the vanes curl enough to allow the shaft in the body to engage the corresponding bore in the impeller. Continue pushing and turning until the impeller enters the body and fully seats in the bore. Do not rotate the pump body counterclockwise with the impeller installed. Doing so will cause the impeller vanes to reverse direction and cause decreased cooling system efficiency and overheating.

6. Temporarily hold the pump support bracket onto the cylinder block. Then rotate the pump in the direction noted in Step 5A or Step 5B until the support bolt opening in the pump body aligns with the corresponding opening the pump support bracket.

7. Thread the bolts into the support bracket and cylinder block. Do not tighten the bolts at this time.

8. Thread the bolt (C, **Figure 29**) into the support bracket and pump body mount opening.

9. Tighten the pump body-to-support bolt to 20-25 ft.-lb. (27-34 N•m). Then tighten the bracket-to-cylinder block bolts to 20-25 ft.-lb. (27-34 N•m).

10. Inspect the impeller vanes to make sure that none have reversed direction during pump assembly. Remove the impeller and reinstall as needed.

11. Lubricate with grease. Then fit the new O-ring into the groove on the pump body.

12. Fit the cover onto the pump body. Install the screws (F, **Figure 29**) into the cover and body. Lightly tighten the screws. Do not overtighten the screws. Overtightening will break the screws.

13A. On standard-rotation models, fit the clamps over the ends. Then push the inlet (A, **Figure 29**) and outlet hoses (B) onto the pump. The inlet hose leads to the seawater pickup (**Figure 26**). The outlet hose leads to the thermostat housing (**Figure 27**). The transmission cooler (A, **Figure 28**) is installed along the inlet hose on some models and the outlet hose on others.

13B. On counter-rotation models, fit the clamps over the ends. Then push the outlet (A, **Figure 29**) and inlet hoses (B) onto the pump. The inlet hose leads to the seawater pickup (**Figure 26**). The outlet hose leads to the thermostat housing (**Figure 27**). The transmission cooler (A, **Figure 28**) is installed along the inlet hose on some models and the outlet hose on others.

14. Position the hose clamps approximately 1/4 in. (6 mm) from the ends of the hoses. Then securely tighten the clamps.

15. Connect the battery cables.

> *WARNING*
> *Stay clear of the propeller and propeller shaft while running an engine on a flush adapter.*

> *CAUTION*
> *Use a flush device or other means to supply the engine with cooling water if running the engine with the boat out of the water. The seawater pump is quickly damaged if operated without adequate cooling water.*

16. Start the engine and immediately check for leakage from the hoses and body-to-cover mating surfaces. If the hoses leak, stop the engine, remove the hoses, and clean the fittings. Reinstall the hoses and run again to check for leaking. If the pump leaks from the cover-to-body mating surfaces, the O-ring probably slipped out of the groove

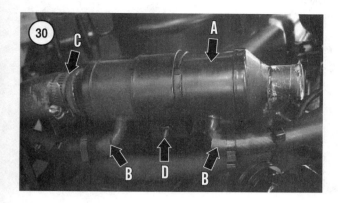

while installing the cover. Stop the engine and reposition or replace the O-ring to correct the leak.

17. Monitor the engine temperature while allowing the engine to reach normal operating temperature. If the engine begins to overheat, refer to Chapter Two for troubleshooting procedures.

18. Stop the engine.

TRANSMISSION FLUID, POWER STEERING FLUID AND OIL COOLERS

A transmission fluid cooler (A, **Figure 28**, typical) is used on all models covered in this manual. The transmission fluid cooler is mounted onto the front or side of the engine. The transmission fluid cooler can be identified by the flare nut hose fittings (B, **Figure 28**) and hoses leading to the transmission.

A power steering fluid cooler (A, **Figure 30**, typical) is used only on models equipped with power steering. The power steering fluid cooler can be identified by the power steering pump return hoses connecting to the barbed fittings and secured with worm screws or plastic hose clamps (B, **Figure 30**).

An oil cooler is only used on some high-output models. The oil cooler is located on the side of the engine and near the oil filter adapter near the flywheel housing on the side of the cylinder block. The oil cooler is very similar in appearance to the transmission fluid cooler and uses similar flare nut hose fittings. The oil cooler can be identified by smaller hoses connected to the oil filter adapter.

The transmission fluid, power steering fluid and oil coolers are one-piece, welded designs, and cooler replacement is usually required due to freeze or corrosion damage. Internal pressure from freezing water usually pushes the end piece off the cooler. In most instances, the end can be reinstalled and soldered in place at a reputable radiator repair shop. Always have the shop pressure test the cooler after the repair to make sure other parts of the

cooler are not damaged. Replace the cooler if it leaks due to corrosion damage.

Transmission Fluid Cooler Removal and Installation

1. Disconnect the battery cables.

2. Mark all hoses and connections on the cooler to ensure proper assembly. Transfer marks to the replacement cooler.

3. Loosen the clamps and then carefully pull the large seawater hoses (D, **Figure 28**) from the cooler. Do not attempt to pry or cut the hoses off the fittings. Doing so will damage the thin fitting material. If necessary, use a blunt instrument to carefully push the hoses off the fittings. If the boat is stored in the water, plug the disconnected hoses to prevent water from siphoning into the bilge.

NOTE
Always mark the hose connections before disconnecting the hoses from the cooler. The fluid hoses can be installed onto either connection on the cooler. However, for maximum cooling efficiency, they must be connected to the fitting that will flow the fluid through the cooler in the opposite direction of the water flow.

4. Place a suitable container under the cooler to capture spilled transmission fluid. Hold the elbow fitting with a wrench and then use another wrench to loosen the fluid hose (B, **Figure 28**). Allow the fluid to fully drain and then unthread the hose fitting. Using the same procedure, disconnect the other hose fitting. Drain the hoses and then plug the ends to prevent contamination.

5. Loosen the clamp bolt and then spread the clamp enough to pull the cooler out of the mounting bracket (C, **Figure 28**).

6. Drain all water and transmission fluid from the cooler. If the cooler will be replaced, remove the elbow fittings and install them into the replacement cooler. Make sure the fittings are securely tightened and oriented properly to align with the hoses.

7. Spread the clamp and slide the replacement cooler into the mounting bracket (C, **Figure 28**). Rotate the cooler in the bracket to align the fittings with the fluid hoses. Then tighten the clamp bolt to secure the cooler. Make sure the cooler is oriented properly and is not in contact with any moving components, electrical terminals and sharp or pointed surfaces.

8. Thread the transmission fluid hose fitting onto the cooler. Hold the elbow fittings with a wrench to prevent rotation. Then securely tighten the hoses (B, **Figure 28**).

8

Make sure the hoses are not kinked or in contact with sharp or pointed objects.

9. Fit the clamps over the ends then push the seawater hoses (D, **Figure 28**) onto the cooler fittings. Position the clamps approximately 1/4 in. (6 mm) from the end of the hose, then securely tighten the clamps. Make sure the clamps are not in contact with moving components, wiring or wire terminals.

10. Check the transmission fluid level as described in Chapter Three.

11. Connect the battery cables.

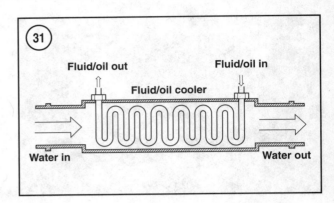

WARNING
Stay clear of the propeller and propeller shaft while running an engine on a flush adapter.

CAUTION
Use a flush device or other means to supply the engine with cooling water if running the engine with the boat out of the water. The seawater pump is quickly damaged if operated without adequate cooling water.

12. Start the engine and immediately check for water or transmission fluid leakage from the cooler or hoses. Correct any leakage before continuing operation.

13. Stop the engine. Check the transmission fluid level.

14. Start the engine and allow it to reach full operating temperature. Grasp each of the transmission fluid hoses and note which feels warmer to the touch. The cooler hose contains transmission fluid that is returning to the transmission from the cooler. The warmer hose contains fluid that is exiting the transmission and flowing to the cooler. Trace the seawater hoses (D, **Figure 28**) to determine the direction water is flowing through the cooler. For maximum cooling efficiency, the cooler hose should be connected to the fitting nearest the water inlet end of the cooler. See **Figure 31**. Switch the hoses as needed.

Power Steering Fluid Cooler
Removal and Installation

1. Disconnect the battery cables.

2. Mark all hoses and connections on the cooler to ensure proper assembly. Transfer marks to the replacement cooler.

3. Loosen the clamps and carefully pull the larger seawater hoses (C, **Figure 30**) from the cooler. Do not attempt to pry or cut the hoses off the fittings. Doing so will damage the thin fitting material. If necessary, use a blunt instrument to carefully push the hoses off the fittings. If the boat

is stored in the water, plug the disconnected hoses to prevent water from siphoning into the bilge.

NOTE
Always mark the hose connections before disconnecting the hoses from the cooler. The fluid hoses can be installed onto either fitting on the cooler. However, for maximum cooling efficiency, they must be connected to the fittings that will flow the fluid through the cooler in the opposite direction of the water flow.

4. Place a suitable container under the cooler to capture spilled power steering fluid. Loosen the clamps and carefully pull the fluid hoses (B, **Figure 30**) off the cooler. Drain the hoses and then plug the ends to prevent contamination.

5. Loosen the clamp bolt or nut (D, **Figure 30**) then spread the clamp enough to pull the cooler (A) out of the mounting bracket.

6. Drain all water and power steering fluid from the cooler.

7. Spread the clamp and slide the cooler into the mounting bracket. Rotate the cooler in the bracket to align the fittings with the fluid hoses. Then tighten the clamp bolt or nut to secure the cooler. Make sure the cooler is oriented properly and is not in contact with any moving components, electrical terminals and sharp or pointed surfaces.

8. Fit the clamps over the ends. Then push the power steering hoses (B, **Figure 30**) onto the cooler. Make sure the hoses are not kinked or in contact with sharp or pointed objects. Position the clamps over the cooler fittings then securely tighten the clamps.

9. Fit the clamps over the ends then push the seawater hoses (C, **Figure 30**) onto the cooler fittings. Position the clamps approximately 1/4 in. (6 mm) from the end of the hose. Then securely tighten the clamps. Make sure the

clamps are not in contact with moving components, wiring or wire terminals.

10. Check the power steering fluid level as described in Chapter Three.

11. Connect the battery cables.

WARNING
Stay clear of the propeller and propeller shaft while running an engine on a flush adapter.

CAUTION
Use a flush device or other means to supply the engine with cooling water if running the engine with the boat out of the water. The seawater pump is quickly damaged if operated without adequate cooling water.

12. Start the engine and immediately check for water or power steering fluid leakage from the cooler or hoses. Correct any leakage before continuing operation.

13. Stop the engine. Check the power steering fluid level.

14. Start the engine and allow it to reach normal operating temperature. To warm the fluid, rotate the steering wheel several times to the full port and starboard positions. Grasp each of the fluid hoses near the cooler and note which hose feels warmer to the touch. The cooler hose contains fluid that is exiting the cooler and flowing to the power steering pump. The warmer hose contains fluid that is exiting steering actuator and flowing to the cooler. Then trace the seawater hoses (D, **Figure 28**) to determine the direction water is flowing through the cooler. For maximum cooling efficiency, the cooler of the two hoses should be connected to the fitting nearest the water inlet end of the cooler. See **Figure 31**. Switch the hose connection points as needed.

Engine Oil Cooler Removal and Replacement

1. Disconnect the battery cables.

2. Mark all hoses and connections on the cooler to ensure proper assembly. Transfer marks to the replacement cooler.

3. Loosen the clamps and carefully pull the larger seawater hoses from the cooler. Do not attempt to pry or cut the hoses off the fittings. Doing so will damage the thin fitting material. If necessary, use a blunt instrument to carefully push the hoses off the fittings. If the boat is stored in the water, plug the disconnected hoses to prevent water from siphoning into the bilge.

NOTE
Always mark the hose connections before disconnecting the hoses from the cooler. The

oil hoses can be installed onto either fitting on the cooler. However, for maximum cooling efficiency, they must be connected to the fitting that will flow the fluid through the cooler in the opposite direction of the water flow.

4. Place a suitable container under the cooler to capture spilled oil. Hold the elbow fitting with a wrench and then use another wrench to loosen the oil hose fitting. Allow the oil to fully drain and then unthread the hose fitting. Using the same procedure, disconnect the other oil hose. Drain the hoses and then plug the ends to prevent contamination.

5. Loosen the clamp bolt and then spread the clamp enough to pull the cooler out of the mounting bracket.

6. Drain all water and oil from the cooler. If the cooler will be replaced, remove the elbow fittings and install them into the replacement cooler. Make sure the fittings are securely tightened and oriented properly to align with the hoses.

7. Spread the clamp and slide the cooler into the mounting bracket. Rotate the cooler in the bracket to align the fittings with the oil hoses. Then tighten the clamp bolt to secure the cooler. Make sure the cooler is oriented properly and is not in contact with any moving components, electrical terminals and sharp or pointed surfaces.

8. Thread the oil hose onto the cooler. Hold the elbow fittings with a wrench to prevent rotation. Then securely tighten the hose fittings. Make sure the hoses are not kinked or in contact with sharp or pointed objects.

9. Fit the clamps over the ends. Then push the seawater hoses onto the cooler. Position the clamps approximately 1/4 in. (6 mm) from the ends of the hose. Then securely tighten the clamps. Make sure the clamps are not in contact with moving components, wiring or wire terminals.

10. Check the engine oil level as described in Chapter Three.

11. Connect the battery cables.

WARNING
Stay clear of the propeller and propeller shaft while running an engine on a flush adapter.

CAUTION
Use a flush device or other means to supply the engine with cooling water if running the engine with the boat out of the water. The seawater pump is quickly damaged if operated without adequate cooling water.

8

12. Start the engine and immediately check for water or oil leakage from the cooler or hoses. Correct any leakage before continuing operation.

13. Stop the engine. Check the engine oil level.

14. Start the engine and allow it to reach normal operating temperature. Grasp each of the oil hoses and note which feels warmer to the touch. The cooler hose contains oil that is returning to the adapter after cooling. The warmer hose contains oil that is exiting the adapter and flowing into the cooler. Trace the seawater hoses to determine the direction water is flowing through the cooler. For maximum cooling efficiency, the cooler hose should be connected to the fitting nearest the water inlet end of the cooler. See **Figure 31**. Switch the hoses as needed.

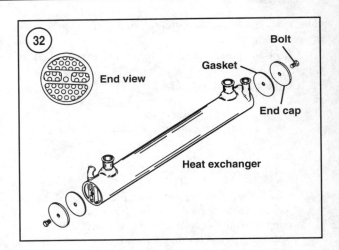

Heat Exchanger Removal, Cleaning and Installation

This section describes removal, cleaning and installation of the heat exchanger.

Contaminants and minerals collect in the copper tubes of the seawater section of the heat exchanger (**Figure 32**, typical). This material blocks seawater flow and reduces cooling system efficiency. Unless removed periodically, the blockage will cause engine overheating. It is a good practice to remove and clean the heat exchanger when changing the coolant. The seawater passages in the heat exchanger must be drained before exposing the engine to freezing temperatures. Freezing water will expand and rupture the heat exchanger body. In some instances, the end cap supports and baffles are pushed out of the body. If the body is not damaged, the end cap support and baffles can be reinstalled and soldered in place. However, they must be properly positioned. Otherwise, the seawater will not flow properly through the exchanger, and cooling efficiency is greatly reduced. For reference, note the mark left in the body from the original installation of the end supports. Someone who lacks the proper equipment or is unfamiliar with it should have a reputable radiator repair shop repair the heat exchanger.

1. Disconnect the battery cables.

2. Drain the seawater from the heat exchanger as described in Chapter Four. Refer to *Winterizing*.

3. Drain the coolant from the heat exchanger as described in Chapter Three.

4. Mark the hoses and corresponding fittings on the heat exchanger. Then loosen the hose clamps and carefully remove the hoses from the exchanger.

5. Remove the clamps and attaching bolts. Then carefully lift the exchanger off the mounting pad.

6. Remove the bolts (**Figure 32**, typical) and then carefully pry the end cap off each end of the heat exchanger.

Remove the gaskets from the end cap or exchanger surfaces.

7. Insert an appropriately sized wire brush into each passage in the heat exchanger. Work the brush back and forth in a vigorous motion, but work carefully to avoid damaging the soldered joints.

8. Remove the brush and then hold the exchanger vertically and use compressed air to blow loosened material from the passages.

9. Repeat Step 7 and Step 8 until no additional debris can be blown from the passages.

10. Apply a coat of Permatex Gasket Sealing Compound to both sides of the new end cap gaskets (**Figure 32**).

11. Fit the gasket and then the end cap onto the heat exchanger. Apply the sealing compound to the threads. Then install the bolt into the end cap, gasket and exchanger openings. Tighten the bolt to 120-144 in.-lb. (13.6-16.2 N•m). Repeat this step for the other end cap.

12. Carefully fit the heat exchanger onto the mounting pad. Rotate the heat exchanger to align the fittings with the corresponding hose. Install the heat exchanger clamps and attaching bolts and securely tighten.

13. Slide the clamps off the ends and then push the hoses fully onto the heat exchanger. Position the clamps approximately 1/4 in. (6 mm) from the ends of the hose. Then securely tighten the clamps. Make sure the clamps are not in contact with moving components, wiring or wire terminals.

14. Refill the engine with coolant as described in Chapter Three.

15. Connect the battery cables.

> *WARNING*
> *Stay clear of the propeller and propeller shaft while running an engine on a flush adapter.*

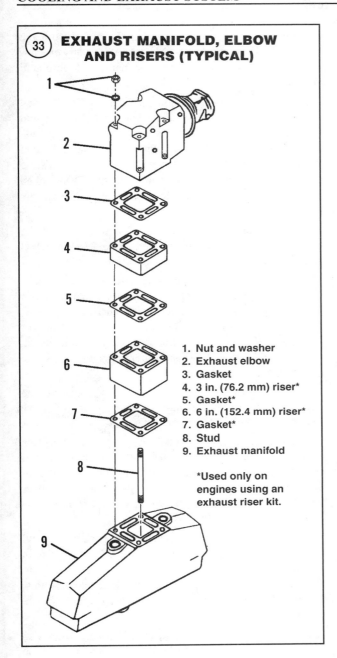

EXHAUST MANIFOLD, ELBOW AND RISERS (TYPICAL)

1. Nut and washer
2. Exhaust elbow
3. Gasket
4. 3 in. (76.2 mm) riser*
5. Gasket*
6. 6 in. (152.4 mm) riser*
7. Gasket*
8. Stud
9. Exhaust manifold

*Used only on engines using an exhaust riser kit.

CAUTION
Use a flush device or other means to supply the engine with cooling water if running the engine with the boat out of the water. The seawater pump is quickly damaged if operated without adequate cooling water.

16. Start the engine and immediately check for water or coolant leakage from the heat exchanger or hoses. Correct any leakage before continuing operation.

17. Stop the engine. Allow the engine to cool. Then check the coolant level.

EXHAUST ELBOW, RISER AND MANIFOLD

All models covered in this manual use an exhaust manifold and elbow for each cylinder bank. Rubber exhaust hoses connect each exhaust elbow and tube to the muffler or exhaust tube. Some models are equipped with risers (4 or 6, **Figure 33**, typical) to position the exhaust elbow at an adequate height above the outside water level. Inadequate height can allow water to enter the engine through the exhaust system.

The exhaust manifold(s), exhaust elbow, risers and exhaust hose can be replaced without removing the engine from the boat. However, the manifold requires clear access from the top and sides for removal. If the boat provides limited access due to seating or other boat structure, remove the engine before removing the manifold(s).

Exhaust Elbow and Riser
Removal and Installation

The exhaust elbows and the risers, if so equipped, can be replaced without removing the manifold from the engine provided that the boat allows adequate clearance. If clearance above the manifold is limited, remove the manifold before removing the elbow and risers.

Refer to **Figure 33** for this procedure.
1. Disconnect the battery cables.
2. Drain water from the exhaust manifold as described in Chapter Four. If the exhaust manifolds are cooled by a closed cooling system, drain the coolant as described in Chapter Three.
3. Loosen the two clamps (A, **Figure 34**) that secure the exhaust elbow outlet to the rubber exhaust hose.

8

4. On models with manifold drain hoses, loosen the clamp (B, **Figure 34**). Then carefully pull the hose off the manifold.

5. Note the orientation and then remove any clamps or brackets that attach to the exhaust elbow.

6. Insert a blunt awl or other suitable tool between the elbow outlet and the rubber exhaust hose. Carefully work the tool around the hose to break the bond between the rubber and metal. Work carefully to avoid damaging the hose.

7. If a water hose connects to the exhaust elbow, loosen the clamp and carefully pull the hose off the elbow.

8. Remove the four long bolts and washers or nuts and washers that secure the elbow to the manifold. Tap lightly on the elbow with a rubber mallet to break the bond. Then lift the elbow off the manifold or riser. *Do not* attempt to pry the elbow off the manifold or riser. Doing so will damage the mating surface and allow water and exhaust leakage.

9. Carefully pull the outlet end of the elbow out of the rubber exhaust hose. Work carefully to avoid dragging the elbow across the manifold mating surface.

10. Remove the gasket (3, **Figure 34**, typical) from the manifold, elbow or riser. Discard the gasket.

11. If equipped with risers (4 or 6, **Figure 33**), lift the riser(s) from the manifold. If seized, tap on the side of the riser(s) with a rubber mallet to break the gasket bond. *Do not* attempt to pry the riser off the manifold. Doing so will damage the mating surface and allow water and exhaust leakage.

12. Thoroughly clean all gasket material from the manifold, elbow and riser mating surfaces with a Scotch-Brite pad.

13. Inspect the mating surfaces of the manifold, exhaust elbow and riser for deep pitting, scratches, cracks or other defects. Have the mating surfaces machined to remedy surface defects. Do not remove more than 0.020 in. (0.5 mm) from the mating surfaces. Replace the manifold, elbow or riser if surface defects cannot be corrected by machining or if cracks are evident on either component.

14. Use an appropriate thread chaser to remove corrosion, old sealant or other foreign material from the bolt openings.

15. Inspect the rubber exhaust hose for cut, charred, cracked or hardened surfaces. Replace the tube if these or other defects are evident.

16. Inspect the exposed water passages in the manifold, elbow and riser for excessive salt, mineral or rust deposits. If heavy deposits are present, remove the manifold as described in this chapter and have it, the elbow and riser cleaned in an acid vat at a reputable machine shop. Deposits in the passages will cause the engine to overheat by re-

stricting water flow and insulating the water from the heat-producing components. Always remove any clamps, fittings or plugs from the elbow or manifold before acid cleaning.

17. If the elbow must be replaced, clamp the elbow in a vise with protective jaws and remove any fitting that might be present. Some models use a closed cooling system that flows coolant through the exhaust manifold, and the seawater exits the engine at the elbow through a fitting in the water jacket. Apply sealant to the threads and then install the fitting into the replacement elbow. Securely tighten the fitting.

18. If necessary, remove the elbow and risers from the other cylinder bank as described in Steps 3-17. Any defect affecting one elbow is probably affecting the other.

19. If the engine is equipped with exhaust risers (4 or 6, **Figure 33**, typical), apply a light coat of Permatex Gasket Sealing Compound to both surfaces. Then install a *new* gasket (5 or 7, **Figure 33**) onto the exhaust manifold. Install the riser onto the manifold and rest it on the gasket. Make sure all bolt, exhaust and water passages align in the manifold, gasket and riser.

20. Apply a light coat of gasket sealing compound to the gasket mating surfaces. Install the *new* gasket (3, **Figure 33**) onto the manifold or riser surface.

21. Apply a soap-and-water solution to the inner surfaces of the rubber exhaust hose. Install the two hose clamps over the rubber exhaust hose and then guide the outlet of the exhaust elbow into the exhaust hose. Carefully lower the elbow onto the manifold. Work carefully to avoid dislodging or damaging the gaskets.

22. Align the bolt openings in the elbow, gasket, riser and manifold. Install any bracket or clamp that attaches with the elbow mounting bolts. Then thread the four bolts into the elbow and manifold or nuts and washers into the studs. Tighten the bolts in a crossing pattern to 35-40 ft.-lb. (47-54 N•m).

23. Position the two hose clamps (A, **Figure 34**) approximately 1/4 in. (6.3 mm) and 1 1/4 in. (31.8 mm) from the end of the hose. Make sure the clamp surfaces are positioned directly over the clamping surfaces on the elbow. Then securely tighten the hose clamps.

24. On models equipped with manifold drain hoses, connect the drain hose to the manifold (B, **Figure 34**).

25. If a water hose connects to the exhaust elbow, push the hose fully onto the elbow. Position the hose clamps approximately 1/4 in. (6.2 mm) from the end of the hose and securely tighten.

26. If removed, install the remaining exhaust elbow as described in Steps 19-25.

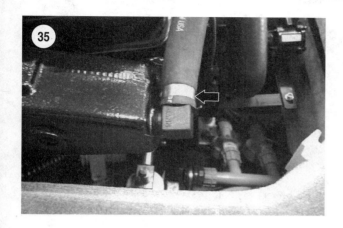

27. If the exhaust manifolds are cooled by the closed cooling system, refill the cooling system as described in Chapter Three.

28. Connect the battery cable.

WARNING
Stay clear of the propeller and propeller shaft while running an engine on a flush adapter.

CAUTION
Use a flush device or other means to supply the engine with cooling water if running the engine with the boat out of the water. The seawater pump is quickly damaged if operated without adequate cooling water.

29. Start the engine and immediately check for water, exhaust or coolant leakage at the hose fittings, rubber exhaust hose and elbow-to-riser-to-manifold mating surfaces. Tighten the hose clamps and check for damaged hoses if there is leakage from the fittings. If leaking from the mating surfaces, remove the elbow and riser. Then check for a damaged gasket or overlooked mating surface defects.

30. Allow the engine to cool completely and tighten the elbow attaching bolts or nuts as described in Step 22.

Exhaust Manifold Removal and Installation

1. Disconnect the battery cables.

2. Drain water from the exhaust manifold as described in Chapter Four. Refer to *Winterizing*. If the exhaust manifolds are cooled by a closed cooling system, drain the coolant as described in Chapter Three. Refer to *Changing the Coolant*.

3. Loosen the two clamps (A, **Figure 34**) that secure the exhaust elbow outlet to the rubber exhaust hose.

4. On models with manifold drain hoses, loosen the clamp (B, **Figure 34**) and then carefully pull the hose off the manifold.

5. Note the orientation and remove any clamps or brackets that attach to the exhaust elbow.

6. Insert a blunt awl or other suitable tool between the elbow outlet and the rubber exhaust hose. Carefully work the tool around the hose to break the bond between the rubber and metal. Work carefully to avoid damaging the hose.

7. If a water hose connects to the exhaust elbow, loosen the clamp and carefully pull the hose off the elbow.

8. Remove the water hose (**Figure 35**) from the end of the manifold.

9. Remove any bracket or clamp attached to the exhaust elbow or manifold.

10. Remove the spark plugs to prevent damage if the manifold should drop during the removal or installation process. Refer to *Tune-up* in Chapter Three.

11. Provide overhead support or have an assistant support the manifold before removing the mounting fasteners.

12. Remove the mounting fasteners. Then carefully pull the manifold forward until the elbow outlet is clear of the rubber exhaust tube. Then lift the manifold and elbow assembly out of the boat.

13. Remove the gasket from the manifold or cylinder block surfaces. Carefully scrape all gasket material from the surfaces.

CAUTION
Always thoroughly clean the manifold-to-cylinder head mating surfaces after removing the manifold. Debris or gasket material can allow exhaust leakage.

14. If necessary, remove the exhaust manifold from the other cylinder bank as described in Steps 2-12.

15. Inspect the manifold for cracks, corroded-through surfaces and other defects. Replace the manifold if these or other defects are evident.

16. Use a straightedge to check for warpage at the cylinder head mating surface. If a gap is visually apparent, measure it with a feeler gauge. Replace the manifold if the surface warpage exceeds 0.006 in. (0.15 mm) within any 12-in. (30.5 cm) span.

17. If replacing the manifold, remove the exhaust elbow and the riser, if so equipped, and install them onto the replacement manifold as described in this section. Remove any drain plugs, petcocks or hose fittings from the used manifold and install them into the replacement. Coat the threads of all plugs, petcocks and fittings with Permatex

8

Gasket Sealing Compound prior to installation. Securely tighten all plugs and fittings.

18. Fit the manifold onto the cylinder head as follows:

   a. Fit the *new* manifold-to-cylinder head gasket onto the manifold. Insert the mounting bolts into the manifold openings to help hold the gasket into position.

   b. Using overhead support or an assistant, carefully guide the exhaust elbow outlet into the rubber exhaust hose. Work carefully to avoid dislodging the gasket.

   c. Seat the manifold and gasket against the cylinder head. Thread the fasteners into the manifold and cylinder head.

   d. Starting from the center and working toward the ends, tighten the manifold fasteners to 30-35 ft.-lb. (41-47 N•m).

19. Connect the water hose to the fitting (**Figure 35**) on the end of the manifold.

20. On models with manifold drain hose, install the hose (B, **Figure 34**) onto the manifold. Position the clamp approximately 1/4 in. (6.2 mm) from the end of the hose. Then securely tighten the clamp.

21. Position the two hose clamps (A, **Figure 34**) approximately 1/4 in. (6.3 mm) and 1 1/4 in. (31.8 mm) from the end of the hose. Make sure the clamp surfaces are positioned directly over the clamping surface on the elbow. Then securely tighten the hose clamps.

22. If a water hose connects to the exhaust elbow, push the hose fully onto the elbow. Position the hose clamps approximately 1/4 in. (6.2 mm) from the end of the hose and securely tighten.

23. Reinstall any bracket, wire or hose clamp removed for manifold removal.

24. If removed, install the other exhaust manifold as described in Steps 17-23.

25. Install the spark plugs as described in Chapter Three. Refer to *Tune-up*.

26. If the exhaust manifolds are cooled by the closed cooling system, refill the cooling system as described in Chapter Three. Refer to *Changing the Coolant*.

27. Connect the battery cables.

> *WARNING*
> *Stay clear of the propeller and propeller shaft while running an engine on a flush adapter.*

> *CAUTION*
> *Use a flush device or other means to supply the engine with cooling water if running the engine with the boat out of the water. The seawater pump is quickly damaged if operated without adequate cooling water.*

28. Start the engine and immediately check for water, exhaust or coolant leakage at the hoses, rubber exhaust hose, elbow-to-riser-to-manifold and manifold-to-cylinder head mating surfaces. Tighten the hose clamps and check for damaged hoses if there is leakage from the fittings. If leaking from the mating surfaces, remove the elbow and riser or manifold. Then check for a damaged gasket or overlooked mating surface defects.

Table 1 COOLING AND EXHAUST SYSTEM TORQUE SPECIFICATIONS

Fastener	in.-lb.	ft.-lb.	N•m
Belt-driven seawater pump			
Mounting bolts	–	30	41
Crankshaft-driven seawater pump			
Pump body to crankshaft pulley	–	35-40	47-54
Pump body to support	–	20-25	27-34
Support to cylinder block	–	20-25	27-34
Exhaust elbow/riser to manifold	–	35-40	47-54
Exhaust manifold to cylinder head	–	30-35	41-47
Heat exchange end cap	120-144	10-12	13.6-16.2
Recirculation pump			
5.0L and 5.7L models	–	33	45
7.4L and 8.2L models	–	30	41
8.1L models	–	37	50
Thermostat housing to intake	240-300	20-25	27-34

Chapter Nine

Electrical System

BATTERY

Batteries used in marine applications endure far more rigorous duty than those used in automotive electrical systems. Marine batteries (**Figure 1**) have a thicker exterior case to cushion the plates during tight turns and rough water operation. Thicker plates are also used. Each one individually is fastened within the case to prevent premature failure. Spill-proof caps on the battery cells prevent electrolyte from spilling into the bilge.

Automotive batteries should be used in a boat *only* during an emergency situation when a suitable marine battery is not available.

Battery Rating Methods

The battery industry has developed specifications and performance standards to evaluate batteries and energy potential. Several rating methods are available to provide information on battery selection.

This chapter provides service procedures for the battery, charging, starting, ignition and warning systems. Wiring diagrams are located at the end of the manual. Torque specifications are listed in **Table 1**. Use the general tightening specifications listed in Chapter One for fasteners not listed in **Table 1**. Battery capacity, battery cable size recommendations, battery charge percentage and engine firing order specifications are listed in **Tables 2-5**. **Tables 1-5** are located at the end of this chapter.

Cold cranking amps (CCA)

Cold cranking amperage is the amperage the battery can deliver for 30 seconds at 0° F (-17° C) without dropping below 1.2 volts per cell (7.2 volts on a standard 12-volt battery). The higher the number, the more amps the battery can deliver to crank the engine. CCA × 1.3 = MCA.

Marine cranking amps (MCA)

Marine cranking amperage (MCA) is similar to the CCA rating. MCA, however, is based on operation at 32° F (0° C) instead of 0° F (-17° C). This is closer to actual boat operating environments. MCA × 0.77 = CCA.

Reserve capacity

Reserve capacity represents the time in minutes that a fully charged battery at 80° F (27° C) can deliver 25 amps without dropping below 1.75 volts per cell (10.5 volts on a standard 12-volt battery). The reserve capacity rating defines the length of time that a typical vehicle can operate after the charging system fails. The 25-amp figure takes into account the power required by the ignition system, lighting and other accessories. The higher the reserve capacity, the longer the vehicle could be operated after a charging system failure.

Ampere hour rating

The ampere hour rating is also called the 20-hour rating. This rating represents the steady current flow that the battery will deliver for 20 hours while at 80° F (27° C) without dropping below 1.75 volts per cell (10.5 volts on a standard 12-volt battery). The rating is actually the steady current flow multiplied by the 20 hours. Example: A 60 Ah battery will deliver 3 amps continuously for 20 hours. This rating method largely has been discontinued by the battery industry. Cold cranking amps or marine cranking amps and reserve capacity are now the most common battery rating methods.

Battery Recommendations

A battery with inadequate capacity can cause hard starting or an inability to start the engine. The minimum battery capacity for a carburetor-equipped model is 845 MCA and 975 MCA for a fuel-injected model.

A battery with a capacity exceeding the minimum requirement is acceptable and is highly recommended if the boat is equipped with numerous electrical accessories.

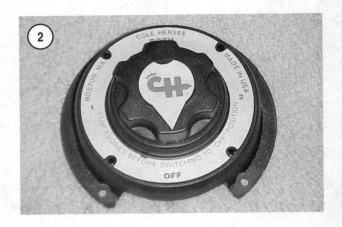

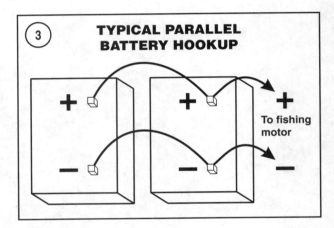

TYPICAL PARALLEL BATTERY HOOKUP

To fishing motor

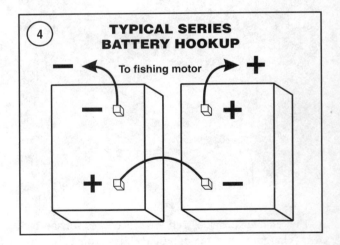

TYPICAL SERIES BATTERY HOOKUP

To fishing motor

Consider adding an additional battery and installing a battery switch (**Figure 2**) on such applications. The switch allows starting and charging operations to use one or both batteries. To prevent discharge caused by some on-board accessories, the switch may be turned off if the boat is at rest or in storage.

Battery Usage

Separate batteries may be used to provide power for accessories such as lighting, fish finders, depth finders and radios. To determine the required capacity of such batteries, calculate the accessory current amperage draw and refer to **Table 2**.

Two batteries may be connected in a parallel circuit to double the ampere hour capacity while maintaining the required 12 volts. See **Figure 3**. For accessories that require 24 volts, batteries may be connected in series (**Figure 4**), but only accessories specifically requiring 24 volts should be connected to the system. If charging becomes necessary, disconnect and charge the batteries individually connected in a parallel or series circuit.

Safe Battery Mounting

The battery must be fastened securely in the boat to prevent the battery from shifting or moving in the bilge area. The positive battery terminal or the entire top of the battery must be covered by a nonconductive shield or boot.

An improperly secured battery can contact the hull or metal fuel tank in rough water or while trailering the boat. If a battery terminal shorts against the metal hull or fuel

tank, it can create sparks and cause an electrical fire. An explosion can occur if the fuel tank or battery case is compromised.

If the battery is not properly grounded and the battery contacts the metal hull, the battery will seek a ground through the control cables or the boat wiring harness. Again, the short circuit can create sparks and an electrical fire. The control cables and boat wiring can be irreparably damaged.

Perform the following preventive steps when installing a battery in a boat, especially a metal boat or a boat with a metal fuel tank.

1. Choose a mounting location that provides good access to the battery for maintenance and is as far as practical from the fuel tank. If possible, choose a location that is close enough to the engine to use the original equipment battery cables. If longer cables are required, refer to the battery cable recommendations in **Table 3**. It is always preferable to use the shortest practical cable.

2. Secure the battery onto the hull with a plastic battery box and tie-down strap (**Figure 5**), or a battery tray (**Figure 6**) with a nonconductive shield or boot covering the positive battery terminal. Install an additional shield or boot onto the negative battery terminal for added protection against arcing between the terminals.

3. Make sure all battery cable connections (two at the battery and two at the engine) are clean and tight. *Do not* use wing nuts to secure battery cables. If wing nuts are present, discard them and replace them with corrosion-resistant hex nuts and lockwashers to ensure good electrical connections. Loose or dirty battery connections can cause engine malfunction and failure of expensive components.

4. Periodically inspect the installation to make sure the battery is physically secured to the hull and the battery cable connections are clean and tight.

Battery Care and Inspection

For reliable starting and maximum battery life, inspect the battery case and terminals on a frequent basis.

1. Remove the battery box cover or battery tray cover. See **Figure 5** or **Figure 6**.

2. Disconnect the negative battery cable and then the positive battery cable.

NOTE
*Some batteries have a built-in lifting strap (**Figure 1**).*

3. Attach a battery carry strap to the terminal posts. Remove the battery from the boat.

9

4. Inspect the entire battery case for cracks, holes, deep abrasion or other damage. Replace the battery if these or other defects are evident.

5. Inspect the battery box or battery tray for cracks, corrosion, deterioration or other damage. Replace the box or tray if these other defects are evident.

> *NOTE*
> *Do not allow the baking soda solution to enter the battery cells, or the electrolyte will severely weaken.*

6. Clean the top of the battery using a stiff bristle brush and a baking soda-and-water solution (**Figure 7**). Rinse the battery case with clear water and wipe it dry with a clean cloth or paper towel.

7. Clean the battery terminals with a stiff wire brush or battery terminal cleaning tool (**Figure 8**).

> *NOTE*
> *Do not overfill the battery cells. The electrolyte expands due to heat from the charging process and will overflow if the level is more than 3/16 in. (4.8 mm) above the battery plates.*

8. Remove the filler caps and check the electrolyte level. Add distilled water, if needed, to bring the level up to 3/16 in. (4.8 mm) above the plates in the battery case. See **Figure 9**.

9. Clean the battery cable clamps with a stiff wire brush (**Figure 10**).

10. Place the battery back into the boat and into the battery box or tray. When using a battery tray, install and secure the retaining bracket.

11. Connect the positive battery cable first. Then connect the negative cable.

12. Securely tighten the battery connections. Coat the connections with petroleum jelly or a light grease to minimize corrosion. When using a battery box, install the cover and secure the assembly with a tie-down strap.

Battery Test

Hydrometer test

On batteries with removable vent caps, the best way to check the battery state of charge is to check the specific gravity of the electrolyte using a hydrometer. Use a hydrometer with numbered graduations from 1.100-1.300 rather than one with color-coded bands. To use the hydrometer, squeeze the rubber bulb, insert the tip fully into the cell, then release the bulb to fill the hydrometer. See **Figure 11**.

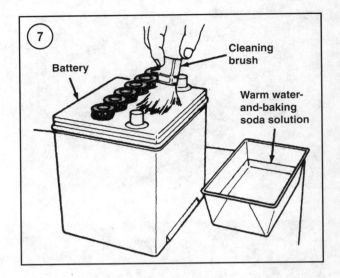

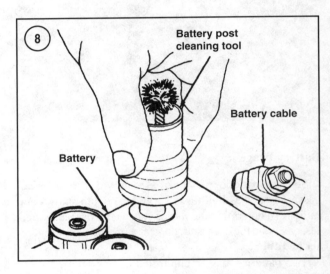

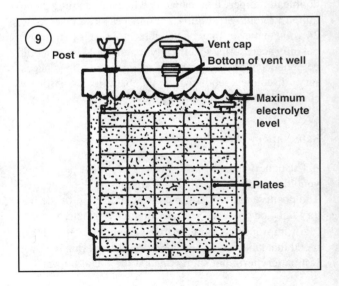

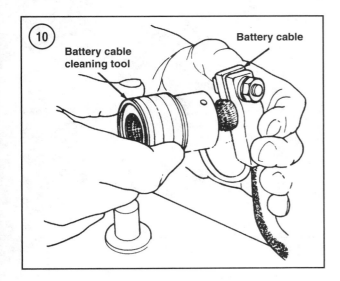

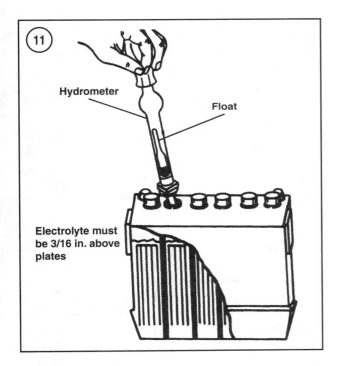

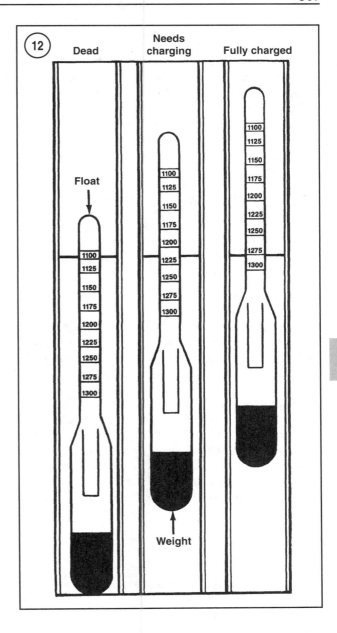

NOTE
Do not test specific gravity immediately after adding water to the battery cells because the water will dilute the electrolyte and lower the specific gravity. To obtain an accurate hydrometer reading, charge the battery after adding water and before testing with a hydrometer.

Draw enough electrolyte to raise the float inside the hydrometer. When using a temperature-compensated hydrometer, discharge the electrolyte back into the battery cell and repeat the process several times to adjust the temperature of the hydrometer to the electrolyte.

Hold the hydrometer upright and note the number on the float that is even with the surface of the electrolyte (**Figure 12**). This number is the specific gravity for the cell. Discharge the electrolyte into the cell from which it came.

The specific gravity of a cell indicates state of charge of the cell. A fully charged cell will read 1.260 or higher at 80° F (27° C). A cell that is 75 percent charged will read from 1.220-1.230. A cell with a 50 percent charge will read from 1.170-1.180. A cell reading 1.120 or lower is discharged. All cells should be within 30 points specific gravity of each other. If there is more than a 30-point variation, the battery condition is questionable. Charge the battery and recheck the specific gravity. If variation of 30 points or more remains between the cells after charging, the battery has failed and must be replaced. Refer to **Table 4** for battery charge level based on specific gravity readings.

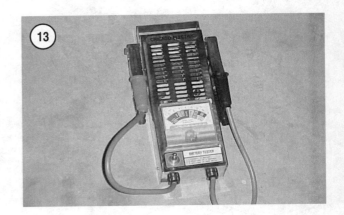

NOTE
*If a temperature-compensated hydrometer is **not** used, add 4 points specific gravity to the actual reading for every 10° above 80° F (27° C). Subtract 4 points specific gravity for every 10° below 80° F (27° C).*

Open-circuit voltage test

On sealed or maintenance-free batteries, check the state of charge by measuring the open-circuit (no load) voltage of the battery. For best results, use a digital voltmeter. For the most accurate results, allow the battery to rest and stabilize for at least 30 minutes. Then, observing the correct polarity, connect the meter to the battery terminals and note the meter reading. If the open-circuit voltage is 12.7 volts or higher, the battery is fully charged. A reading of 12.4 volts means the battery is approximately 75 percent charged, a reading of 12.2 volts means the battery is approximately 50 percent charged, and a reading of 12.1 volts means the battery is approximately 25 percent charged.

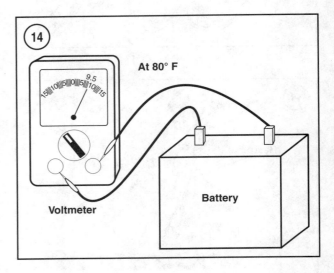

Load test

Two common methods are used to perform load tests on batteries. A load tester (**Figure 13**) measures the battery voltage as it applies a load across the terminals. If a load tester is not available, measure the cranking voltage by following the instructions in this section.

1. Attach a voltmeter to the battery terminals as shown in **Figure 14**.

2. To prevent accidental starting, disconnect and ground the spark plug leads.

3. Crank the engine for approximately 15 seconds while noting the meter reading. Note the voltage reading at the end of the 15-second period.

4. If the voltage is 9.5 volts or higher, the battery is sufficiently charged and has sufficient capacity for the engine.

5. If the voltage is below 9.5 volts, one of the following conditions is present:

a. The battery is discharged or defective. Charge the battery and retest.

b. The battery capacity is too small for the engine. Refer to *Battery Recommendations* in this chapter.

c. The starting system is drawing excessive current and causing the battery voltage to drop. Refer to Chapter Two for starting system troubleshooting procedures.

d. A mechanical defect is present in the engine or transmission/V-drive and is creating excessive load and current draw on the starting system. Inspect the engine and transmission/V-drive for mechanical defects.

6. Disconnect the voltmeter.

7. Reconnect the spark plug leads.

Battery Storage

Wet cell batteries slowly discharge when stored. Before storing a battery, clean the case with a solution of baking

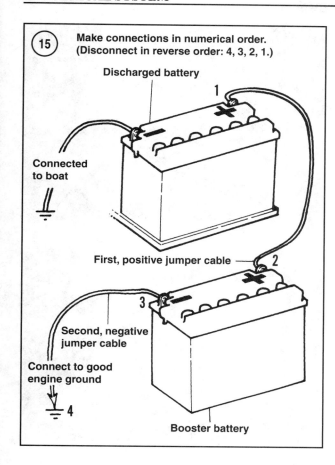

15 Make connections in numerical order.
(Disconnect in reverse order: 4, 3, 2, 1.)

Discharged battery

Connected
to boat

First, positive jumper cable

Second, negative
jumper cable

Connect to good
engine ground

Booster battery

1. Never smoke in close proximity to a battery.
2. Make sure all accessories are turned off before disconnecting the battery cables. Disconnecting a circuit that is electrically active will create a spark that can ignite explosive gas that might be present.
3. Always disconnect the battery negative cable first and then the positive cable.
4. On batteries with removable vent caps, always check the electrolyte level before charging the battery. Maintain the correct level throughout the charging process.
5. Never attempt to charge a battery that is frozen.

WARNING
Be extremely careful not to create any sparks around the battery when connecting the battery charger.

6. Connect the negative charger lead to the negative battery terminal and the positive charger lead to the positive terminal. If the charger output is variable, select a setting of approximately 4 amps. Slowly charge the battery at a low rate, rather than quickly at a high amp setting.
7. If the charger has a dual voltage setting, set the voltage to 12 volts. Then switch the charger ON.
8. If the battery is severely discharged, allow it to charge for at least 8 hours. Frequently check the charging progress with a hydrometer.

9

Jump-Starting

If the battery becomes severely discharged, the engine can be jump-started from another battery in or out of the boat. Jump-starting can be dangerous if the proper procedure is not followed. Always use caution when jump-starting.

Before attempting the jump start, check the electrolyte level of the discharged battery. If the electrolyte is not visible, or if it appears to be frozen, do not jump-start the discharged battery.

WARNING
*Use extreme caution when connecting the booster battery to the discharged battery to avoid personal injury or damage to the electrical system. **Make sure** the jumper cables are connected to the correct polarity.*

1. Connect the jumper cables in the order shown in **Figure 15**.

WARNING
An electrical arc can occur when the final connection is made. An electrical arc can cause an explosion if it occurs near the bat-

soda and water. Rinse it with clear water and wipe dry. Fully charge the battery. Then store it in a cool, dry location. Frequently check the electrolyte and state of charge during storage. If the specific gravity falls to 40 points or more below full charge (1.260), or if the open circuit voltage falls below 12.4 volts, recharge the battery.

Battery Charging

Check the state of charge with a hydrometer or digital voltmeter as described in the previous section.

Remove the battery from the boat for charging. A charging battery releases highly explosive hydrogen gas. In many boats, the area around the battery is not well-ventilated, unless the vessel is moving, and the gas can remain in the area for hours after the charging process has completed. Sparks or flames occurring near the battery can cause it to explode and spray battery acid over a wide area.

If the battery cannot be removed for charging, make sure the bilge access hatches, doors or vents are fully open to allow adequate ventilation. When charging batteries, take the following precautions:

tery. For this reason, make the final connection to a good engine ground away from the battery and not to the battery itself.

2. Make sure all jumper cables are out of the way of moving engine parts.

> *WARNING*
> *Stay clear of the propeller and propeller shaft while running an engine on a flush adapter.*

> *CAUTION*
> *Use a flush device or other means to supply the engine with cooling water if running the engine with the boat out of the water. The seawater pump is quickly damaged if operated without adequate cooling water.*

3. Start the engine. Once it starts, run it at a moderate speed (fast idle).

> *CAUTION*
> *Running the engine at high speed with a discharged battery can damage the charging system.*

4. Remove the jumper cables in the exact reverse of the order shown in **Figure 15**.

ALTERNATOR

This section describes alternator removal and installation. Alternator repair for the home mechanic is neither practical nor economical. In some cases, the necessary bushings, bearings or other components are not available at local marine parts stores. If testing indicates a defective alternator, install a new or rebuilt marine alternator. Make sure, however, that the new or rebuilt alternator is an exact replacement for the one removed.

Isolate the cause of failure before installing the replacement alternator. Alternator failure is usually caused by exposure to water or faulty wiring and connections. Dirty or corroded battery terminals are common causes of alternator failure. Another common cause is disconnecting the battery cables/wiring or turning the battery switch while the engine is operating. The alternator output and ground terminals must have a good circuit to the battery terminals. Wiring, fuses, switches and block ground connections are incorporated into the circuit. To prevent repeat failures, refer to the wiring diagrams at the end of the manual and check the entire circuit for faulty wiring, terminals, fuses or circuit breaker.

Drive belt removal, installation and tension adjustment are described in the alternator removal and installation procedure.

Alternator Removal

Early production engines have a common V-belt (A, **Figure 16**) drive system to drive the alternator and

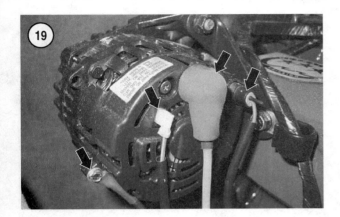

recirculation pump. Later production engines and all 8.1L models use a single serpentine multigroove belt (**Figure 17**) with a spring-loaded tensioner (A, **Figure 18**) to drive the alternator and all other engine-driven accessories. The instructions describe belt removal and installation for both types of belts.

1. Disconnect the battery cables.

2A. On models with a V-belt drive system, remove the drive belt as follows:

   a. Note the belt routing around all of the pulleys prior to removing the belt. Depending on the model, one or more of the other belts must also be removed. Refer to Chapter Eight for seawater pump belt removal. Refer to Chapter Eleven for power steering belt removal. If necessary, make a sketch of the belt routing around *all* of the pulleys.

   b. Loosen but *do not* remove the pivot (C, **Figure 16**) and adjusting bracket bolt (B). Carefully pivot the alternator toward the crankshaft and recirculation pump pulleys.

   c. Slip the belt off the alternator pulley.

2B. On models with a multigroove drive belt, remove the drive belt as follows:

   a. Note the belt routing around the pulleys prior to removing the belt. If necessary, make a sketch of the belt routing around *all* of the pulleys.

   b. Fit a 1/2-in. breaker bar into the square recess (B, **Figure 18**) with the handle facing right. Using the bar, have an assistant pivot the tensioner against the spring tension. Then slip the belt off the tensioner pulley. *Slowly* release the tensioner and remove the breaker bar.

3. Support the alternator and then remove the fasteners attaching the alternator to the mounting bracket. Carefully pull the alternator away from the bracket. Support the alternator until the wiring is disconnected in the next step.

4. Make a sketch of the wire terminal orientation and connections on the alternator (**Figure 19**, typical). Disconnect all engine wires from the alternator. Remove the alternator from the engine. If the alternator will be rebuilt, remove the jumper strap or wire (**Figure 20**) from the alternator terminals. The strap or wire is often lost during the rebuild. Clean rust or corrosion from the pulley surfaces. Rust or corrosion pitting on the belt contact surfaces will allow slippage and quickly wear a new belt. Clean, sand and repaint the pulley as necessary. Replace the pulley if a smooth belt surface cannot be achieved by sanding and painting.

5. Inspect the belt for wear, damage or deterioration and replace as needed. On the multigroove belt, small cracks are commonly found in the grooved side of the belt. These small cracks occur within the first few hours of operation and do not necessarily indicate a need to replace the belt. Replace the belt if the surfaces separate, if sections are missing and if other defects are evident.

Alternator Installation

1. Connect each wire to the corresponding terminals on the back of the alternator (**Figure 19**, typical). Rotate the terminals to prevent contact with other terminals or inadvertent contact with the alternator housing. Install and securely tighten the terminal nuts. If removed, install the jumper strap or wire (**Figure 20**) onto the alternator. To prevent terminal corrosion and possible repeat alternator failure, thoroughly coat the terminals with OMC Black Neoprene Dip. Purchase the neoprene dip (OMC part No. 909570) from an OMC dealership.

2. Carefully mount the alternator into the mounting bracket. Install and hand-tighten the mounting fasteners.

3A. On models with a V-groove drive belt, install and adjust the drive belt as follows:

9

a. Pivot the alternator toward the crankshaft and recirculation pump pulleys. Then slip the drive belt onto the crankshaft, recirculation pump and alternator pulleys. Make sure the belt is not twisted and fits into the groove in each pulley.

b. Pivot the alternator away from the crankshaft and recirculation pump pulleys to apply tension to the drive belt. When properly tensioned, the belt will deflect approximately 1/4-1/2 in. (6-13 mm) with thumb pressure applied at a point midway between the pulleys (**Figure 21**).

c. Hold the alternator in position to maintain belt tension while tightening the mounting bolts to 26-30 ft.-lb. (35-41 N•m).

3B. On models with a multigroove drive belt, install the drive belt as follows:

a. Tighten the alternator mounting fasteners to 26-30 ft.-lb. (35-41 N•m).

b. Slip the drive belt onto all pulleys (except the tensioner pulley). Make sure the belt is not twisted and the belt grooves fit into the pulley grooves.

c. Fit a 1/2-in. breaker bar into the square recess (B, **Figure 18**) with the handle facing right. Using the bar, have an assistant pivot the tensioner against the spring tension. Then slip the belt onto the tensioner pulley. *Slowly* release the tensioner and remove the breaker bar.

CAUTION
Never operate the engine without first providing cooling water. Use a flush device or operate the engine under actual conditions (boat in the water). Operating the engine without providing adequate cooling water will quickly damage the seawater pump and can result in serious engine damage.

NOTE
On carburetor-equipped models using an electric choke, the alternator might not supply charging output until the idle speed is raised to approximately 1500 rpm for a few seconds after starting. This allows the internal circuits to build enough field strength to switch on the alternator and begin charging. The alternator will provide charging output at normal idle speed after the initial rpm increase.

4. Connect the battery cables.

5. Start the engine and check the dash-mounted voltmeter for alternator output. The gauge should indicate 12.6-13.8 volts at idle speed. If the engine is equipped with a carburetor and choke heater, raise the NEUTRAL idle speed to

approximately 1500 rpm for a few seconds to switch on the alternator. Check for a slipping belt and faulty wiring or connections if the voltmeter does not indicate charging. If the belt is slipping, check for a faulty belt, incorrect belt routing, dirty or damaged pulleys, incorrect belt tension or seizure of the recirculation pump, water pump or alternator.

6. Stop the engine.

7. On models with a V-groove drive belt, seat the new belt and correct the tension as follows:

a. Start the engine and allow it to run for approximately 10 minutes at idle speed.

b. Stop the engine and disconnect the battery cables.

c. Apply thumb pressure at a point midway between the pulleys (**Figure 21**). The belt must deflect approximately 1/4-1/2 in. (6-13 mm). If necessary, loosen the mounting bolts (B and C, **Figure 16**) and pivot the alternator to correct the tension. Hold the alternator in position and tighten the mounting bolts to 26-30 ft.-lb. (35-41 N•m).

d. Connect the battery cables.

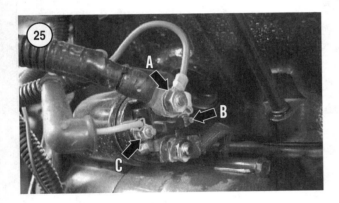

STARTER MOTOR AND SOLENOID

This section describes removal, repair and replacement of the starter motor and replacement of the starter solenoid. Although the starter solenoid can be replaced without removing the starter from the engine, it is usually easier to remove the starter first. Consider replacing the starter solenoid with the starter mounted only if you have clear access to the solenoid wire terminals and mounting screws.

Early models use the Delco starter (**Figure 22**) that is equipped with an electric coil frame and a straight armature shaft drive system.

Late models are equipped with a Delco permanent magnet gear reduction (PMGR) starter (**Figure 23**) that uses a permanent magnet frame and a planetary gear reduction drive assembly. The Delco PMGR drive system is much smaller and lighter than earlier starters. The starter solenoid is integrated into the starter housing, and the housing assembly must be replaced if the solenoid fails.

The latest production models use a Delco PG260 F1 starter motor (**Figure 24**), which is also equipped with a permanent magnet frame and a planetary gear reduction drive system. The PG260 F1 starter is slightly smaller than the Delco PMGR. Unlike the Delco PMGR starter, the starter solenoid can be replaced separately on the PG260 F1 starter motor.

The later-style starter motors may replace earlier-style starters used on some models. Always refer to **Figures 22-24** and identify the starter before performing any service procedure.

Starter motor removal and installation are simple operations provided that you have good access to the mounting bolts. In some instances, engine removal is required to gain access to the bolts. Engine removal and installation are described in Chapter Six. The manufacturer does not offer the individual internal starter components for the Delco PMGR and the Delco PG260 F1 starter motors. If internal components must be replaced, purchase a new or rebuilt marine starter or check with a reputable marine starter and alternator repair shop for a source of suitable aftermarket replacement parts. Be sure that the rebuilder is familiar with the required marine safety requirements for electrical devices installed on marine applications.

CAUTION
Some engines use a shim between the starter housing and the cylinder block. If so equipped, the shim must be reinstalled to provide adequate pinion gear-to-flywheel clearance. Otherwise, the starter will operate noisily, wear rapidly or fail. Inadequate clearance can cause rapid wear and eventual failure of the flywheel teeth as well as starter failure.

Removal

1. Disconnect the battery cables.
2. Disconnect all wires (A, B and C, **Figure 25**) and the terminal cap, if so equipped, from the starter solenoid.
3. On early models using the larger Delco starter, loosen the nut that secures the starter brace on the forward end of the starter to the engine block.
4. Support the starter while removing the two mounting bolts located near the flywheel. On models with a

9

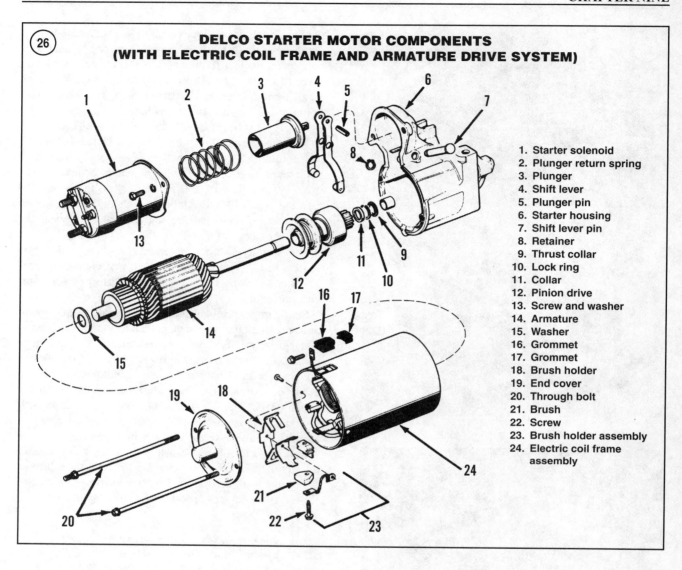

**DELCO STARTER MOTOR COMPONENTS
(WITH ELECTRIC COIL FRAME AND ARMATURE DRIVE SYSTEM)**

1. Starter solenoid
2. Plunger return spring
3. Plunger
4. Shift lever
5. Plunger pin
6. Starter housing
7. Shift lever pin
8. Retainer
9. Thrust collar
10. Lock ring
11. Collar
12. Pinion drive
13. Screw and washer
14. Armature
15. Washer
16. Grommet
17. Grommet
18. Brush holder
19. End cover
20. Through bolt
21. Brush
22. Screw
23. Brush holder assembly
24. Electric coil frame assembly

top-mounted starter, the bolts thread into the flywheel housing. Back the nose of the starter out of the flywheel housing. Then remove the starter. Retrieve the shim, if so equipped, from the starter or cylinder block mating surface.

5. Clean corrosion or debris from the starter mating surfaces. Use the proper thread chaser to clean and dress the mounting bolt holes.

Installation

1. Guide the nose of the starter into the flywheel housing. Align the starter with the cylinder block mounting holes. Insert the shim, if so equipped, between the starter and the cylinder block.

2. Thread the mounting bolts into the starter motor and cylinder block by hand. Do not tighten the bolts at this time.

3. Position the brace over the starter throughbolt stud at the forward end of the engine block. Do not tighten the nuts at this time.

4. Connect the yellow or yellow/red wire to the solenoid terminal (B, **Figure 25**) next to the *S* mark molded into the solenoid. Install and securely tighten the nut.

5A. On carburetor-equipped models, connect the ignition or fuel pump bypass circuit wire to the solenoid (C, **Figure 25**) next to the *I* mark molded into the solenoid. Install and securely tighten the terminal nut.

5B. On electronic fuel injection (EFI) models, install the terminal cap over the solenoid terminal (C, **Figure 25**) next to the *I* molded into the solenoid. If the cap is not

available, use another means to insulate the terminal completely. Use a heavy wrap of electrical tape if necessary.

6. Connect the battery cable to the large solenoid terminal (A, **Figure 25**). Thread the nut onto the terminal. Inspect the cable terminal to make sure it does not contact other terminals or the starter case. Reposition the cable terminals as needed. Then securely tighten the nut. Do not overtighten the nut. Overtightening can crack the solenoid housing.

7. Position the battery cable insulator over the cable end and terminal nut. To prevent terminal corrosion and possible starter failure, thoroughly coat the terminals with OMC Black Neoprene Dip. Purchase the neoprene dip (OMC part No. 909570) from an OMC dealership.

8. Tighten the two starter mounting bolts evenly to 30-36 ft.-lb. (41-49 N•m).

9. On early models equipped with the large Delco starter, install the starter brace and tighten the brace attaching bolt and nut securely.

10. Connect the battery cables.

Check for proper starter operation. Refer to *Starting System* in Chapter Two if the starter fails to operate or operates improperly.

Starter Solenoid Removal and Installation

Delco starter with electric coil frame

Refer to **Figure 26** for this procedure.

1. Remove the starter motor as described in this section.

2. Remove the screw from the solenoid terminal (A, **Figure 27**). Then pull the spacer (B, **Figure 27**) from between the solenoid terminal and brush holder terminal.

3. Remove the two screws and washers (13, **Figure 26**). Then, while pushing the solenoid toward the starter housing to collapse the spring, rotate the solenoid to disengage the solenoid flange from the slot in the starter motor housing.

4. Carefully relieve the pressure and remove the solenoid and spring from the starter (**Figure 28**). Inspect the spring for corrosion damage, bent loops or other damage, and replace as needed.

5. Inspect the plunger for corrosion pitting or other surface imperfections. Remove the pin and replace the plunger if surface imperfections cannot be removed by polishing with emory paper. Secure the replacement plunger to the shift lever with the pin. Replace the pin if it does not fit securely into the plunger and lever openings.

6. Guide the return spring into the solenoid opening.

7. Align the solenoid with the plunger and then rotate the solenoid to position the solenoid flange away from the slot in the starter motor housing. Guide the plunger into the spring and solenoid opening. Then seat the solenoid against the starter housing.

9

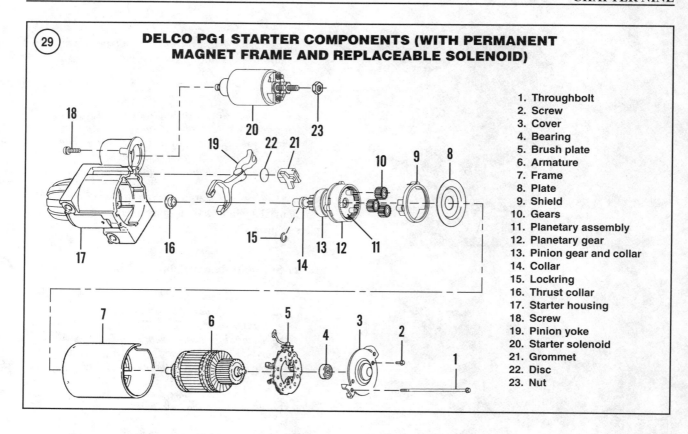

DELCO PG1 STARTER COMPONENTS (WITH PERMANENT MAGNET FRAME AND REPLACEABLE SOLENOID)

1. Throughbolt
2. Screw
3. Cover
4. Bearing
5. Brush plate
6. Armature
7. Frame
8. Plate
9. Shield
10. Gears
11. Planetary assembly
12. Planetary gear
13. Pinion gear and collar
14. Collar
15. Lockring
16. Thrust collar
17. Starter housing
18. Screw
19. Pinion yoke
20. Starter solenoid
21. Grommet
22. Disc
23. Nut

8. Maintain pressure to collapse the spring. Then rotate the solenoid until the flange enters the slot in the starter motor housing. Release the pressure. The flange engagement in the slot will hold the solenoid in place.

9. Install the two screws and washers (13, **Figure 26**) into the solenoid and starter motor housing. Securely tighten the screws.

10. Fit the spacer (B, **Figure 27**) between the solenoid terminal and brush holder terminal. Thread the screw into the brush holder terminal, spacer and starter solenoid terminal. Securely tighten.

11. Install the starter motor as described in this section.

Delco PG 1 starter

Refer to **Figure 29** for this procedure.

1. Remove the starter motor as described in this chapter.

2. Remove the nut (**Figure 30**). Then disconnect the brush plate lead (**Figure 31**) from the solenoid terminal.

3. Remove the three external inverted Torx screws (**Figure 32**) from the starter housing and solenoid.

4. Lift the plunger out of the slot in the pinion yoke (19, **Figure 29**). Then remove the starter solenoid (**Figure 33**).

5. Clean debris or corrosion from the solenoid mating surfaces.

6. Engage the plunger of the solenoid into the slot in the pinion yoke. Seat the body of the solenoid against the starter housing (17, **Figure 29**).

7. Rotate the solenoid to position the *R* terminal (B, **Figure 21**) toward the side of the starter that faces the cylinder block.

8. Install the three screws (**Figure 32**). Securely tighten the screws.

9. Attach the brush plate lead to the bottom terminal (**Figure 31**) of the solenoid. Install the nut (**Figure 30**) and tighten securely. Do not overtighten the nut. Overtightening can crack the solenoid housing.

10. Install the starter motor as described in this chapter.

Starter Motor Disassembly and Assembly

Delco starter with electric coil frame

Refer to **Figure 26** for this procedure.

1. Remove the starter motor and then the starter solenoid as described in this section.

2. Make match marks on the end cover, frame and starter housing (**Figure 34**).

3. Note the location of the throughbolt and stud bolt (**Figure 35**) prior to removal. To align with the starter brace, the stud bolt must be installed into the correct opening during assembly.

4. Remove the stud bolt and throughbolt. Then carefully pry the end cover off the starter frame (**Figure 36**).

5. Carefully pull the frame off the armature (**Figure 37**). Remove the washer (15, **Figure 26**) from the commutator end of the armature.

6. Tilt the armature in the housing to disengage it from the shift lever (4, **Figure 26**). Then pull the armature out of the starter housing (**Figure 38**).

7. Remove the thrust collar (9, **Figure 26**) from the armature drive shaft.

9

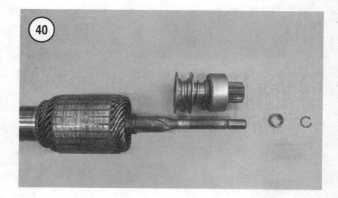

8. Using a punch, drive the collar toward the pinion gear until the lockring is exposed. Carefully pry the lockring out of the groove in the armature shaft (**Figure 39**). Then pull the lockring and collar off the armature shaft. Rotate the pinion drive counterclockwise to disengage it from the helical splines. Then pull the pinion drive off the armature (**Figure 40**).

9. Remove the grommets (16 and 17, **Figure 26**) from the brush holder terminal and armature slot. Replace the grommets if torn, deteriorated or in questionable condition.

10. Remove the pins (**Figure 41**) and then carefully pull the brush holders (18, **Figure 26**) out of the frame. Note the brush lead routing and connections. Then remove the screws (22, **Figure 26**) that hold the brush leads to the brushes (21).

11. Remove the retainer (8, **Figure 26**) and then pull the lever pin (7) and then the shift lever (4) out of the starter housing.

12. Remove the pin (5, **Figure 26**) and then pull the plunger (3) out of the shift lever.

13. Clean and inspect the starter motor components as described in this section.

14. Fit the plunger shaft into the slot in the shift lever (4, **Figure 26**). Align the openings. Then insert the pin (5, **Figure 26**) into the lever and plunger. Drive the pin until it reaches the same depth on each side of the lever.

15. Fit the shift lever (4, **Figure 26**) into the starter housing (7) as shown in **Figure 42**. Guide the shift lever pin (7, **Figure 26**) through the starter housing and shift lever yoke. Install the retainer (8, **Figure 26**) into the groove to retain the pin.

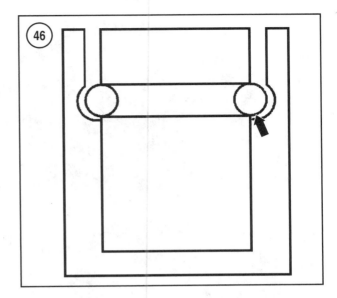

16. Apply grease onto the helical splines of the armature shaft. Then thread the pinion drive clockwise onto the splines.

17. Slide the collar over the shaft with the open end facing away from the pinion gear (**Figure 43**). Carefully fit the lockring onto end of the shaft (**Figure 39**). Work the ring down the shaft and into the groove (**Figure 44**). Use two pliers to pull the collar over the lockring (**Figure 45**). The ring must fully seat into the collar (**Figure 46**).

18. Fit the thrust collar (9, **Figure 26**) over the end of the shaft with the larger side facing away from the pinion gear. Seat the collar against the lockring and shaft collar.

19. Connect the brush leads to the brushes (21, **Figure 26**) and holder (18) with the screws (22). Securely tighten the screws.

20. Fit the brush holders and brushes into the frame assembly as shown in **Figure 41**. Insert the pins into the brush holders and open the frame brackets to secure the brush holders. Make sure the springs are installed behind the holders to press the brushes against the commutator when installed.

21. Fit the brush holder terminal into the frame. Fit the grommets (16 and 17, **Figure 26**) over the terminal and slide into the opening. Make sure the grooves in the grommets engage the opening. Otherwise, the grommets will not seal properly or will work out of the opening and short the lead against the frame.

22. Guide the armature and pinion drive assembly into the starter housing. Tilt the armature as needed to engage the shift lever yoke with the groove in the pinion drive (**Figure 47**). Then fit the end of the armature into the

9

bushing in the nose of the starter housing. Seat the armature shaft and pinion drive assembly into the housing.

23. Install the washer (15, **Figure 26**) over the end of the armature and seat against the commutator step.

24. Without disturbing the armature or starter housing, guide the frame assembly over the armature. Move the brush holders to compress the springs enough to fit the brushes over the commutator as shown in **Figure 48**. This will allow the frame to seat against the starter housing.

25. Apply a light coat of water-resistant marine grease to the bushing. Then install the end cover (19, **Figure 26**) onto the frame.

26. Rotate the armature and frame assembly and cover to align the match marks (**Figure 34**).

27. Insert the throughbolts (**Figure 35**) into the cover, frame and starter housing openings. Hand-tighten the throughbolts.

28. Verify proper alignment and seating of the housing, frame and cover. If necessary, disassemble the starter and correctly assemble.

29. Securely tighten the throughbolts. The starter housing and cover must fully seat onto the frame.

30. Install the starter solenoid and then the starter motor as described in this section.

Delco PMGR starter

NOTE
Except for the throughbolts and starter housing, the manufacturer does not offer individual starter motor components. Many of the components are available from starter and alternator repair shops that are experienced with marine starter repair. It is usually more economical to replace the starter if several components require replacement.

1. Remove the starter motor as described in this section.

2. Make match marks on the end cover, frame and starter housing (**Figure 49**).

3. Remove the nut (**Figure 50**) and then disconnect the braided brush wire from the solenoid terminal.

4. Remove the throughbolts (**Figure 51**) and pull the frame and cover assembly from the starter housing (**Figure 52**).

5. Remove the metal shield from the frame assembly or starter housing. Push in on the shaft to hold the armature in the rear cover and brush holder. Then pull the frame off the armature (**Figure 53**).

6. Carefully pull the armature out of the rear cover and brush holder.

7. Pull the planetary drive and pinion shaft assembly out of the starter housing bore enough to access the plastic pinion yoke shaft. Use a thin screwdriver to pry the pinion yoke arms off the pivots on the pinion shaft. Then pull the planetary drive and pinion shaft assembly out of the starter housing (**Figure 54**).

8. Remove the thrust collar from the pinion shaft (**Figure 55**).

9. Using a punch, drive the collar toward the pinion gear until the lockring is exposed. Carefully pry the lockring out of the groove in the pinion shaft (**Figure 39**). Then pull the lockring and collar off the armature shaft (**Figure 56**). Rotate the pinion drive counterclockwise to disengage it from the helical splines. Then pull the pinion drive and planetary ring gear off the pinion shaft (**Figure 57**).

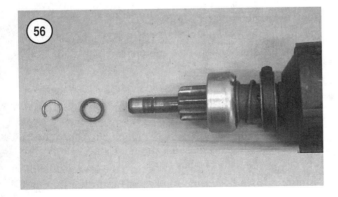

9

10. Clean and inspect the starter motor components as described in this section.

11. Apply a light coat of water-resistant marine grease to the roller bearing in the planetary ring gear. Then guide the ring gear (gear end first) over the pinion shaft. Align the planetary gear teeth with the ring gear teeth as shown in **Figure 58**. Then seat the ring gear onto the shaft.

12. Apply a light coat or marine grease to the helical splines of the pinion shaft. Then thread the pinion drive clockwise onto the splines.

13. Slide the lockring collar over the shaft with the open end facing away from the pinion gear (**Figure 43**). Carefully fit the lockring onto the end of the shaft (**Figure 39**). Work the ring down the shaft and into the groove (**Figure 44**). Use two pliers to pull the collar over the lockring (**Figure 45**). The ring must fully seat into the collar (**Figure 46**).

14. Fit the thrust collar over the end of the shaft with the larger side facing away from the pinion gear (**Figure 55**). Seat the collar against the lockring and shaft collar.

15. Align the planetary drive and pinion shaft with the opening in the starter housing (**Figure 54**). Hold the shaft toward the side opposite the starter solenoid. Then guide the shaft into the housing until the yoke arms align with the pivots on the shaft. Then hold the shaft parallel to the solenoid while moving it toward the solenoid. This will cause the pivots to spread the yoke arm shaft enough to snap the pivots into the yoke. The shaft will make two distinct snapping noises as the pivots enter the openings. Pull on the shaft to verify proper engagement.

16. Make sure the thrust collar was not dislodged from the shaft. Reposition the collar as needed.

17. Apply a light coat of water-resistant marine grease to the needle bearing in the nose of the starter housing. Then guide the pinion shaft into the bearing. Rotate the planetary ring to align the alignment bosses. Then seat the planetary and pinion shaft in the starter housing.

18. Apply a light coat of water-resistant marine grease to the armature shaft needle bearing and gears in the planetary assembly. Then install the metal shield onto the planetary assembly with the concave side toward the planetary assembly.

19. Collapse the brush springs and guide the commutator end of the armature into the rear cover and brush assembly. Release the brush springs. The brush surfaces must contact the commutator (**Figure 59**, typical).

20. Carefully guide the frame assembly over the armature, rear cover and brush assembly. Do not allow the magnets to inadvertently pull the armature out of the brushes. If necessary, insert a wooden dowel through the frame and use it to push the armature firmly into the cover while guiding the frame into position.

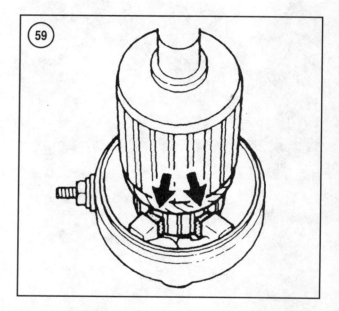

21. Apply a light coat of water-resistant marine grease to the gear teeth on the end of the armature shaft. Then guide the frame, armature and rear cover assembly into position on the starter housing. Rotate the frame to align the gear teeth. Then seat the assembly against the starter housing.

22. Rotate the armature and frame assembly and cover to align the match marks (**Figure 49**).

23. Insert the throughbolts (**Figure 51**) into the cover, frame and starter housing openings. Hand-tighten the throughbolts.

24. Verify proper alignment and seating of the housing, frame and cover. Disassemble the starter and correctly assemble if necessary.

25. Securely tighten the throughbolts. The starter housing and cover must fully seat onto the frame.

26. Connect the braided brush wire to the starter solenoid terminal. Thread the nut (**Figure 50**) onto the terminal.

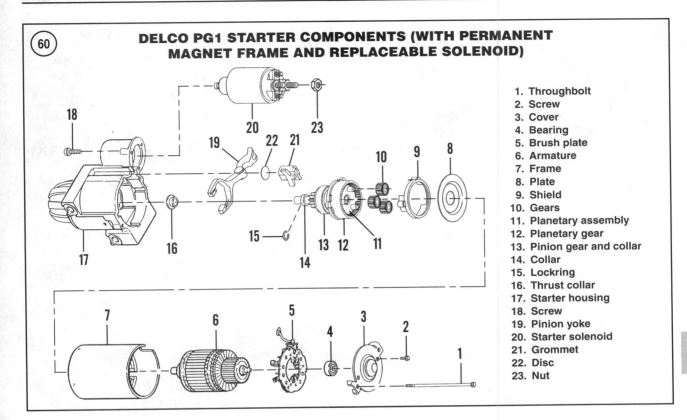

DELCO PG1 STARTER COMPONENTS (WITH PERMANENT MAGNET FRAME AND REPLACEABLE SOLENOID)

1. Throughbolt
2. Screw
3. Cover
4. Bearing
5. Brush plate
6. Armature
7. Frame
8. Plate
9. Shield
10. Gears
11. Planetary assembly
12. Planetary gear
13. Pinion gear and collar
14. Collar
15. Lockring
16. Thrust collar
17. Starter housing
18. Screw
19. Pinion yoke
20. Starter solenoid
21. Grommet
22. Disc
23. Nut

9

Verify that the brush terminal and wire are not contacting other terminals or the starter frame. Then securely tighten the nut.

27. Install the starter motor as described in this section.

Delco PG1 starter

> *NOTE*
> *Except for the starter solenoid, the manufacturer does not offer individual starter motor components. Many of the components are available from starter and alternator repair shops that are experienced with marine starter repair. It is usually more economical to replace the starter if several components require replacement.*

Refer to **Figure 60** for this procedure.

1. Remove the starter motor and starter solenoid as described in this section.

2. Make match marks on the end cover, frame and starter housing (**Figure 61**).

3. Remove the throughbolts (**Figure 62**) and pull the frame and cover assembly from the starter housing (**Figure 63**).

4. Push on the shaft to hold the armature in the cover. Then pull the frame off the armature (**Figure 64**).

5. Carefully pull the armature out of the cover (**Figure 65**). Remove the two inverted Torx screws (**Figure 66**). Then pull the brush plate out of the cover (**Figure 67**).

6. Remove the plate from the starter housing (**Figure 68**). Remove the grommet (**Figure 69**) and then pull the planetary shaft and related components from the starter housing (**Figure 70**).

7. Remove the thrust collar from the pinion shaft (**Figure 71**). Then lift the yoke and disc off the planetary assembly (**Figure 72**).

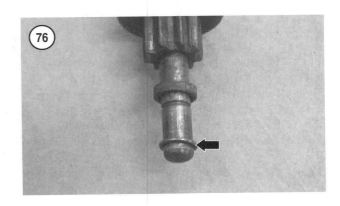

9

8. Push the ring gear toward the pinion gear to expose the planetary gears (**Figure 73**). Remove the three planetary gears from the pinion shaft (**Figure 74**).

9. Using a punch, drive the collar toward the pinion gear until the lockring is exposed (**Figure 75**). Carefully pry the lockring out of the groove in the pinion shaft (**Figure 76**). Then pull the lockring and collar off the armature shaft (**Figure 77**).

10. Rotate the pinion drive counterclockwise to disengage it from the helical splines. Then pull the pinion gear and planetary ring gear off the pinion shaft (**Figure 78**).

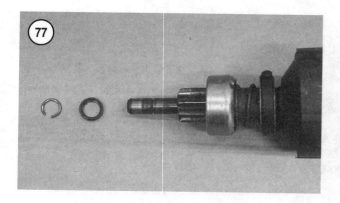

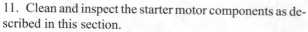

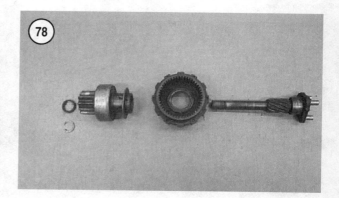

11. Clean and inspect the starter motor components as described in this section.

12. Carefully guide the frame assembly over the armature.

13. Collapse the brush springs and fit the brush plate over the commutator (**Figure 79**). Release the brush springs. The brushes must contact the commutator (**Figure 80**, typical).

14. Align the brush lead grommet with the notch and fit the cover onto the brush plate, armature and frame. Rotate the cover as needed to align the openings and then install and securely tighten the screws (**Figure 66**).

15. Guide the planetary ring gear over the helical spined end of the pinion shaft. The open side of the ring gear must face away from the helical splines when installed.

16. Apply a light coat of marine grease to the helical splines of the pinion shaft and then thread the pinion drive clockwise onto the splines.

17. Slide the lockring collar over the shaft with the open end facing away from the pinion gear (**Figure 81**). Carefully fit the lockring onto end of the shaft (**Figure 76**). Work the ring down the shaft and into the groove (**Figure 75**). Use two pliers to pull the collar over the lockring (**Figure 82**). The ring must fully seat into the collar (**Figure 83**).

18. Fit the thrust collar over the end of the shaft with the larger side facing away from the pinion gear (**Figure 71**). Seat the collar against the lockring and shaft collar.

19. Apply a light coat of water-resistant marine grease to the surfaces. Then install the gears onto the pinion shaft (**Figure 74**).

20. Align the planetary gear teeth with the ring gear teeth as shown in **Figure 84**. Then seat the ring gear onto the shaft.

21. Apply a light coat of water-resistant marine grease to the needle bearing in the nose of the starter housing.

22. Fit the yoke arm into the pinion gear spool (**Figure 85**). Align the yoke with the solenoid bore and then care-

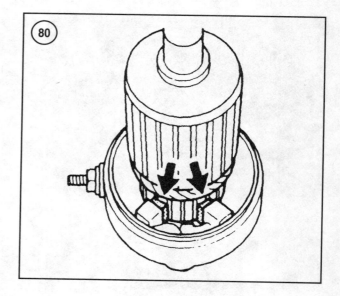

fully guide the planetary assembly into the starter housing (**Figure 70**). Align the end of the shaft with the needle bearing in the nose of the housing. Seat the planetary assembly into the housing.

23. Insert the disc (22, **Figure 60**) into the opening and then seat it against the pinion yoke (19). Insert the grom-

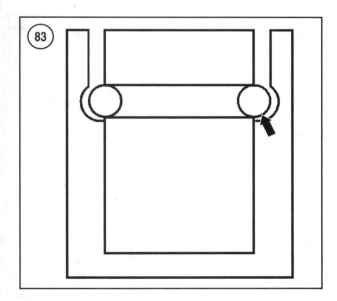

9

met into the starter housing (**Figure 69**). Make sure the lips on the side of the grommet fit over the slot in the starter housing.

24. Apply a coat of water-resistant marine grease to the planetary gear teeth, the needle bearing in the ring gear and the gear on the end of the armature shaft.

25. Install the plate into the starter housing with the open side facing outward (**Figure 68**). Seat the plate against the planetary ring gear.

26. Align the gear teeth on the armature shaft with the planetary gear teeth (**Figure 63**). Then guide the armature, frame and cover assembly into the planetary assembly. Rotate the armature to mesh with the gear teeth and then seat the frame assembly onto the starter housing. Rotate the armature and frame assembly to align the match marks (**Figure 61**).

27. Insert the throughbolts (**Figure 62**) into the cover, frame and starter housing openings. Hand-tighten the throughbolts.

28. Verify proper alignment and seating of the housing, frame and cover. Disassemble the starter and correctly assemble if necessary.

29. Securely tighten the throughbolts. The starter housing and cover must fully seat onto the frame.

30. Install the starter solenoid and then the starter motor as described in this section.

Starter Motor Component
Cleaning and Inspection

1. Clean all components in a mild solvent. Do not use solvents that damage plastic or rubber. Do not apply any solvent to the starter solenoid.

2. Inspect the pinion gear for chipped, cracked or worn teeth (**Figure 86**). Replace the gear if these or other defects are evident.

3. Inspect the helical splines at the pinion end of the planetary shaft for excessive wear or damaged splines. Replace as needed.

4. Inspect the armature for deep corrosion pitting on the commutator shaft or excessive wear on the bearing surfaces. Replace the armature if these or other defects are evident.

5. Carefully secure the armature in a vise with protective jaws (**Figure 87**). Tighten the vise just enough to secure the armature. Do not overtighten the vise. Using 600-grit Carborundum cloth, carefully polish away any corrosion deposits and glazing from the commutator. Avoid removing too much material. Rotate the armature often to polish the commutator evenly.

6. Calibrate an ohmmeter on the R × 1 scale. Connect the ohmmeter between any commutator segment and the armature laminations (**Figure 88**). Then connect the ohmmeter between any commutator segment and the armature shaft (**Figure 88**). The meter must indicate no continuity at both connections. If otherwise, the armature is shorted and must be replaced.

7. Connect the ohmmeter between commutator segments (**Figure 89**) and note the reading. Repeat this test with the meter connected to each commutator segment. The meter must indicate continuity between any pair of segments. If otherwise, the commutator has failed open and must be replaced.

8. On models using a Delco starter with an electric coil frame, have the frame coil tested at a reputable starter repair shop.

9. Using a small file, remove the mica particles from the undercut between the commutator segments (**Figure 90**).

10. Inspect the brushes for grooved, discolored or corroded surfaces. Inspect the brush springs for corrosion or weak tension. Replace the brush and lead or plate assembly if these or other defects are evident.

11. Measure the length of the four brushes (**Figure 91**).

    a. On the Delco starter with the electric coil frame, replace the brush plate assembly if any of the brushes are worn to less than 1/4 in. (6.0 mm).

    b. On the Delco PMGR or PG1 permanent magnet starter motor, replace the brush plate assembly if any of the brushes are worn to less than 0.30 in. (7.62 mm).

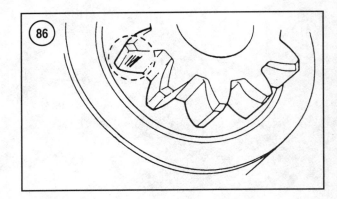

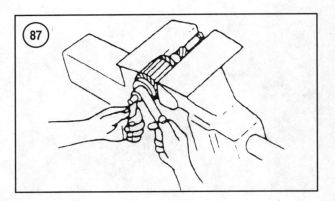

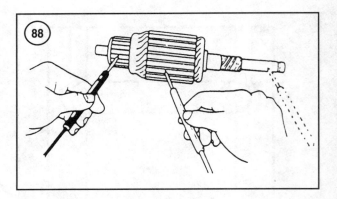

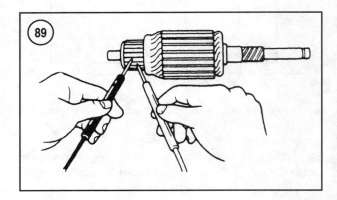

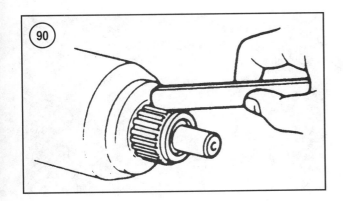

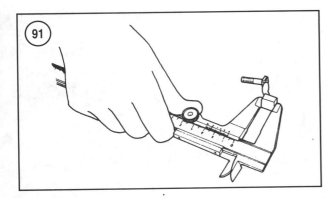

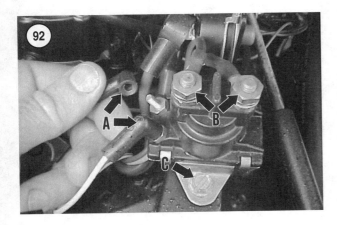

12. Inspect the bearing surfaces on the armature and planetary shaft for excessive or uneven wear. Inspect the planetary gears for worn, cracked or missing teeth. Inspect the needle bearing in the starter housing for wear, corrosion or discoloration. Replace all worn or damaged components.

Slave Solenoid Removal and Installation

The slave solenoid (**Figure 92**, typical) is located near the electrical terminal box on the upper rear or upper front

of the engine. Identify the slave solenoid by the yellow or yellow/red wires connecting to the terminals. The manufacturer has used different brands and types of solenoids, and the type used on later models can be installed on some of the earlier models. However, the standard slave solenoid used on later models with a transistorized ignition system cannot be used to replace the special switch solenoid used on some earlier models with a breaker-point ignition system. On other models with a breaker-point ignition system, a standard slave solenoid is used, and the bypass switch is incorporated into the starter solenoid. Refer to *Ignition System* in Chapter Two. Always identify the type of ignition system before ordering a replacement solenoid.

1. Disconnect the battery cables.
2. If so equipped, remove the terminal protector from the top of the solenoid.
3. Disconnect the yellow or yellow/red and black or tan wires from the small terminals (A, **Figure 92**, typical).
   a. Yellow or yellow/red and black wires are used on models with a transistorized ignition system or models with a breaker-point ignition system that use the bypass switch incorporated into the starter solenoid.
   b. Yellow or yellow/red and tan wires are used on models with a breaker-point ignition system with a switch slave solenoid.
4. Remove the terminal nuts and then disconnect the yellow or yellow/red and red or red/purple wires from the larger terminals (B, **Figure 92**, typical).
5. Remove the mounting screws or nuts (C, **Figure 92**, typical) and then lift the solenoid from the mount.
6. Clean all corrosion, belt material or oily deposits from the wire terminals and the solenoid mount.
7. Install the solenoid onto the mount. Install the mounting screws or nuts and tighten securely.
8. Connect the yellow or yellow/red and red or red purple wires to the larger terminals (B, **Figure 92**, typical). The larger wires can be installed onto either large terminal.
9. Connect the yellow or yellow/red and black or tan wires to the small terminals (A, **Figure 92**, typical).
   a. On models using a standard slave solenoid, the wires can be installed onto either small terminal.
   b. On models using a switch slave solenoid, the yellow or yellow/red wire must be attached to the terminal next to the *S* mark on the housing. The tan wire must be connected to the terminal next to the *I* mark on the housing.
10. Make sure the wire terminals do not contact other terminals or other components on the engine. Then securely tighten the terminals. To prevent terminal corrosion and possible repeat solenoid failure, thoroughly coat the ter-

minals with OMC Black Neoprene Dip. Purchase the neoprene dip (OMC part No. 909570) from an OMC dealership.

11. If so equipped, install the terminal protector onto the solenoid.

12. Connect the battery cables.

Starter Relay Removal and Installation

The starter relay (**Figure 93**, typical) mounts to a bracket or in an engine harness plug at the rear of the engine near the flywheel housing or at the front of the engine near the exhaust manifold. The starter relay is physically identical to the system and fuel pump relays used on electronic fuel injection (EFI) models and is usually mounted in the same general location. Identify the starter relay by the yellow or yellow/red wire leading to the harness connector. The system relay and fuel pump relay do not use a yellow or yellow/red wire.

1. Disconnect the battery cables.

2A. If the relay is mounted on a bracket, work the relay back and forth while carefully pulling it out of the mounting bracket.

2B. If the relay plugs into the engine harness, depress the locking tab and then pull the engine harness connector out of the bottom of the starter relay.

3A. If the relay is mounted in a bracket, align the spade terminals in the bottom of the relay with the corresponding terminal openings in the bracket. The relay will only fit one way. Carefully push the starter relay fully into the terminals.

3B. If the relay plugs into the engine harness connector, align the spade terminals in the bottom of the relay with the corresponding terminal openings in the harness plug. Depress the locking tab and then push the engine harness connector onto starter relay.

4. Connect the battery cables.

DISTRIBUTOR AND IGNITION SYSTEM COMPONENTS

Distributor Cap and Rotor Removal and Installation

Refer to *Ignition System* in Chapter Two and identify the ignition system used on the engine before beginning this procedure.

1. Disconnect the battery cables.

2. Use compressed air to blow loose material from the distributor and cap.

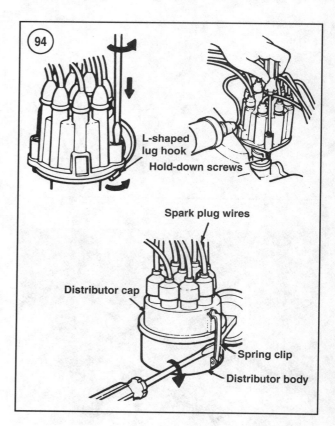

3. Mark the cylinder numbers on the plug wires and distributor cap. Carefully disconnect the spark plug wires and ignition coil secondary lead from the cap.

4. Make match marks on the side of the cap and distributor housing to aid in installation. Use two side-by-side marks on each component to avoid confusion with other alignment marks.

5. Fully loosen the screws, swing the L-shaped lugs away from the distributor or pry the spring clip off the cap. See **Figure 94**.

6. Lift the cap off the distributor.

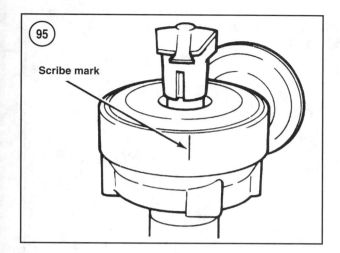

(95) Scribe mark

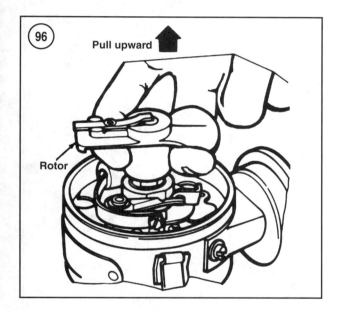

(96) Pull upward

Rotor

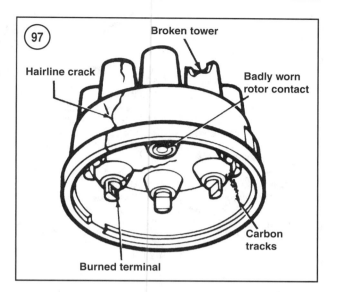

(97) Broken tower

Hairline crack

Badly worn rotor contact

Carbon tracks

Burned terminal

9

confuse the scribe mark with the distributor cap and housing match marks made in Step 3. Turn the rotor slightly to align the raised boss inside the rotor with the slot at the top of the distributor shaft. Then push down until the rotor fully seats on the shaft.

12A. On models using a breaker-point ignition system, align the match marks (Step 3) and fit the distributor cap onto the distributor housing. Fully tighten the screws or snap the clip onto the cap boss. See **Figure 94**.

12C. On models with a Prestolite BID (breakerless ignition distributor) ignition system, align the match marks (Step 3) and fit the distributor cap (1, **Figure 98**) over the distributor housing (20). Rotate the cap slightly to align the screw boss on the cap over the threaded boss on the housing. Then seat the cap onto the distributor. Thread the cap screws into the boss and tighten securely.

12C. On models using a Delco EST (electronic spark timing) ignition system, fit the slot in the cap (4, **Figure 99**) over the ridge on the ignition module (5). Rotate the cap slightly to align the screws with the openings in the housing. Then securely tighten the screws.

13. Starting with the No. 1 cylinder, plug the spark plug wire onto the corresponding cap. The cylinder number sequence working *clockwise* around the cap must match the firing order sequence listed in **Table 5**.

14. Connect the battery cables.

15. Adjust the ignition timing as described in Chapter Five.

Distributor Removal

1. Disconnect the battery cables.
2. Remove the spark plugs.

7. Again, use compressed air to blow loose material from the distributor and cap.

8. Scribe a *single* mark on the distributor housing that aligns with the rotor tip (**Figure 95**).

9. Lift the rotor straight up and off the distributor shaft (**Figure 96**). Do not twist the rotor on the shaft during removal.

10. Inspect the rotor for worn or burnt contacts. Inspect the cap (**Figure 97**) for hairline cracks, carbon tracking and worn, burned or corroded contacts. Replace the cap and rotor if these or other defects are evident. Transfer the mark made in Step 5 and the cylinder number marks to the replacement cap.

11. Fit the rotor onto the distributor shaft with the tip aligned with the *single* scribe mark (**Figure 95**). Do not

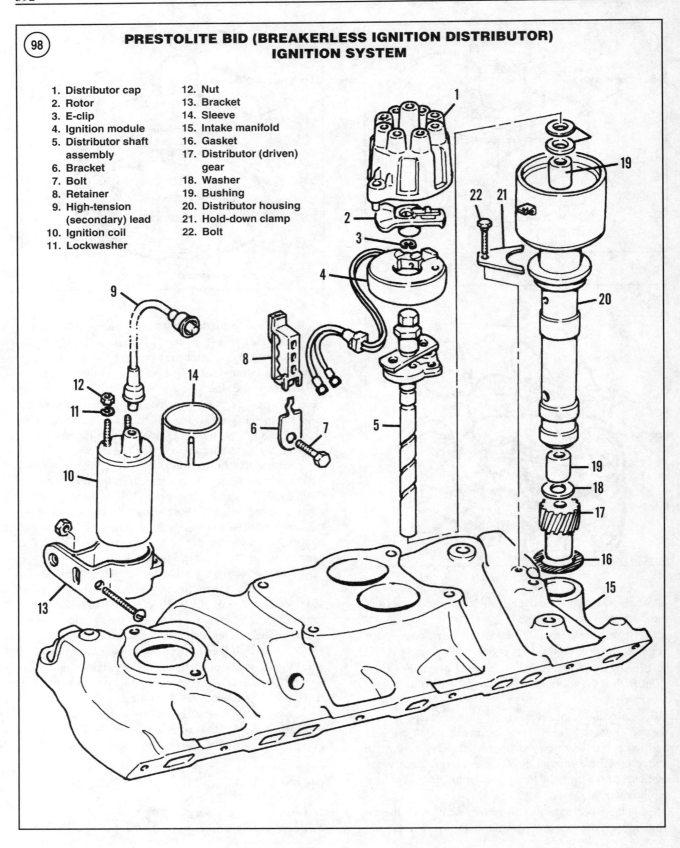

98 **PRESTOLITE BID (BREAKERLESS IGNITION DISTRIBUTOR) IGNITION SYSTEM**

1. Distributor cap
2. Rotor
3. E-clip
4. Ignition module
5. Distributor shaft assembly
6. Bracket
7. Bolt
8. Retainer
9. High-tension (secondary) lead
10. Ignition coil
11. Lockwasher
12. Nut
13. Bracket
14. Sleeve
15. Intake manifold
16. Gasket
17. Distributor (driven) gear
18. Washer
19. Bushing
20. Distributor housing
21. Hold-down clamp
22. Bolt

99 **DELCO EST (ELECTRONIC SPARK TIMING) DISTRIBUTOR**

1. Ignition coil
2. Distributor shaft
3. Rotor
4. Distributor cap
5. Ignition module
6. Retainer
7. Washer
8. Pickup coil
9. Pole piece
10. Locating pin
11. Housing
12. Bolt
13. Hold-down clamp
14. Washer
15. Washer
16. Distributor (driven) gear
17. Gasket
18. Intake manifold

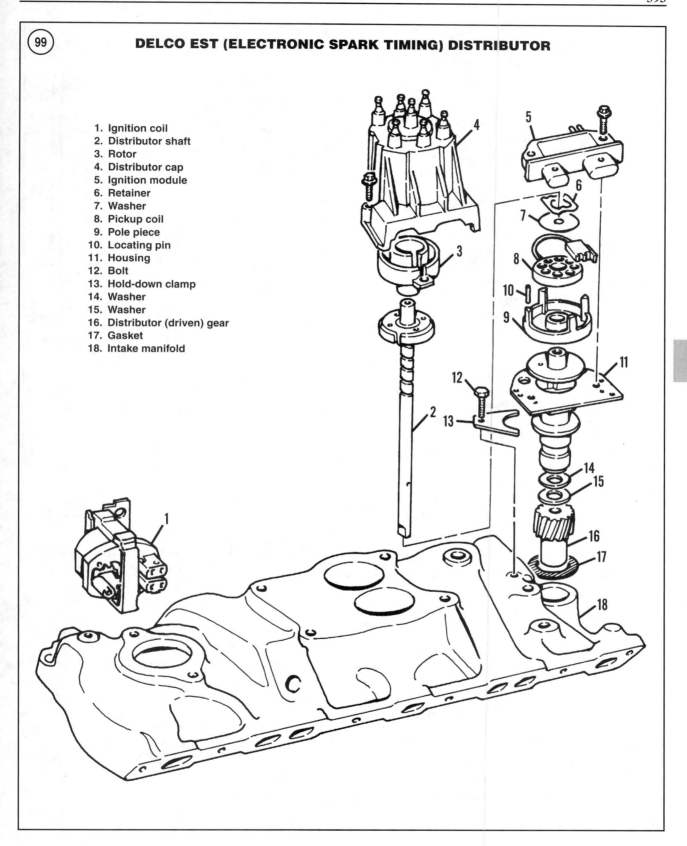

9

3. Place the No. 1 piston at TDC (firing position) as described in Chapter Six. Refer to *TDC (Firing Position)*.

4. Mark the cylinder numbers on the plug wires and distributor cap. Carefully disconnect the spark plug wires and ignition coil secondary lead from the cap.

5. Remove the distributor cap as described in this chapter. Verify that the tip of the rotor would align with the No. 1 cylinder terminal if the cap were installed onto the distributor. If it does not, refer to Step 3.

6. Scribe a *single* mark on the distributor housing that aligns with the rotor tip (**Figure 95**).

7. Note the wiring routing and connections. Then disconnect all wires from the distributor.

8. Scribe match marks on the intake manifold and the base of the distributor.

9. Use a special distributor wrench (**Figure 100**) to loosen the bolt. Then slide the hold-down clamp away from the base of the distributor. Lift the distributor from the engine.

10. Remove the gasket from the intake manifold, cylinder block or base of the distributor.

11. Inspect the driven gear teeth for excessive wear and cracked or missing teeth. Have a machine shop replace the driven gear if excessively worn or damaged. The replacement gear must be drilled to match the distributor shaft and requires special equipment and expertise. If gear teeth are missing, remove the oil pan and retrieve the remnants. Oil pan removal and installation are described in Chapter Six. Look into the distributor opening and check for damage to the camshaft teeth. If the camshaft gear teeth are damaged, replace the camshaft and lifters as described in Chapter Six.

Distributor Installation

Early Indmar marine engines were produced as both standard- and counter-rotation models. If in question, refer to *Engine Rotational Direction* in Chapter Six.

1. If the crankshaft was rotated with the distributor removed, place No. 1 piston at TDC (firing position as described in Chapter Six. Refer to *TDC (Firing Position)*.

2. If the distributor or intake manifold was replaced, transfer any mark made during the distributor removal to the replacement components.

3. Fit a new gasket over the driven gear and seat it onto the distributor base.

4. Turn the driven gear until the rotor tip aligns with the *single* scribe mark (**Figure 95**).

5. Carefully guide the distributor into the intake manifold and cylinder block. Do not insert the distributor into the opening enough to engage the driven gear teeth with the camshaft teeth at this time.

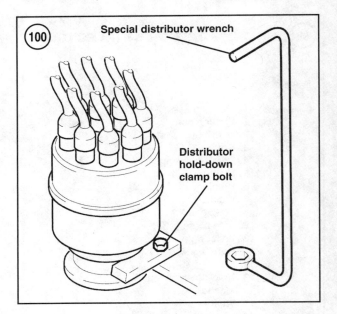

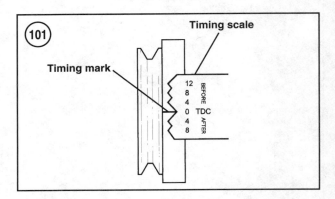

6. Rotate the distributor housing to align the distributor base and intake manifold match marks made during distributor removal (Step 8).

7. Verify that the rotor is aligned with the *single* scribe mark as describe in Step 4. Turn the rotor counterclockwise (as viewed from the top) approximately 45° (1/8 of a turn).

8. While installing the distributor, carefully guide the driven gear into the camshaft gear. The rotor will move toward alignment with the single scribe mark as the gear teeth mesh. The distributor base might not fully seat at this time because the oil pump drive shaft might not be aligned with the slot in the driven gear. Refer to the following:

   a. If the distributor is seated on the intake manifold, proceed to Step 10.

   b. If the distributor is not seated, proceed to Step 9.

9. Hold the distributor in position with the match marks aligned. Apply light downward pressure and count the

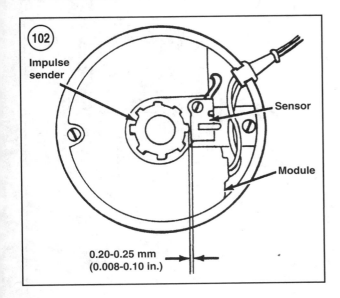

(102)

Impulse
sender

Sensor

Module

0.20-0.25 mm
(0.008-0.10 in.)

turns while an assistant *slowly* rotates the harmonic balancer clockwise on standard-rotation models or counterclockwise on counter-rotation models. The distributor base will drop onto the intake manifold when the oil pump drive shaft aligns with the slot in the gear. Have the assistant stop when the harmonic balancer has rotated *exactly* two revolutions and the timing mark aligns with the 0 (TDC) mark on the timing scale (**Figure 101**, typical). This should again place the No. 1 piston at TDC (firing position).

10. Turn the distributor to align the match marks as described in Step 6. The rotor tip should align with or be within a few degrees of the single scribe mark (**Figure 95**). Verify that the tip of the rotor would align with the No. 1 cylinder wire if the cap were installed on the distributor. If not, remove the distributor and repeat the installation procedures.

11. Hold the distributor in position while placing the hold-down clamp over the distributor base. Tighten the hold-down clamp bolt to 30 ft.-lb. (41 N•m).

12. Install the distributor cap as described in this section.

13. Starting with the No. 1 cylinder, plug the spark plug wires onto the distributor cap. The cylinder number sequence working clockwise around the cap must match the firing order sequence listed in **Table 5**.

14A. On 5.0L and 5.7L models, install the spark plugs and tighten to 22 ft.-lb. (30 N•m) if the cylinder head is new and 15 ft.-lb. (20 N•m) if the cylinder head is used.

14B. On 7.4L and 8.2L models, install the spark plugs and tighten to 15-20 ft.-lb. (20-28 N•m).

14C. On 8.1L models, install the spark plugs and tighten to 15 ft.-lb. (20 N•m).

15. Connect the spark plug wires.

16. Connect the engine wire harness to the distributor. To avoid electrical interference, route the wiring away from the ignition coil or spark plug secondary leads.

17. Connect the battery cables.

18. Adjust the ignition timing as described in Chapter Five.

Ignition Module Removal and Installation

The ignition module can be replaced without removing the distributor from the engine. On models using a Delco EST or Prestolite BID ignition system, the ignition module is located inside the distributor. On 5.7L LT-1 models, the ignition module is mounted on a bracket on the front of the engine. An ignition module is not used on 8.1L models.

Prestolite BID ignition system

The ignition module is located in the distributor housing. To prevent an ignition system malfunction, adjust the air gap between the sensor and the impulse sender (incorporated into the module and distributor shaft) during module installation.

Refer to **Figure 98** for this procedure.

1. Disconnect the battery cables.

2. Remove the distributor cap and rotor as described in this section.

3. Disconnect the ignition module leads coming out of the distributor housing from the engine wire harness.

4. Remove the two screws and lift the ignition module (4, **Figure 98**) out of the distributor.

5. Use compressed air to blow loose material off the module and distributor.

6. Wipe any oil film or debris from the sensor or mount in the distributor.

7. Guide the wiring through the opening. Then install the replacement module into the distributor. Seat the wire into the distributor opening.

8. Install the two screws into the module. Do not tighten the screws at this time.

9. Remove the spark plug. Rotate the harmonic balancer until the sensor in the module aligns with a finger on the impulse sender in the distributor shaft as shown in **Figure 102**.

10. Insert a 0.009 in. (0.22 mm) feeler gauge into the gap between the sensor and sender. Hold the module in light contact against the feeler gauge. Then securely tighten the module mounting screws. After tightening the screws, the gap must be 0.008-0.010 in. (0.20-0.25 mm). Reposition the module as needed.

9

11. Connect the ignition module leads to the engine wire harness. To avoid electrical interference, route the wiring away from the ignition coil or spark plug secondary leads.

12. Install the rotor and distributor cap as described in this section.

13A. On 5.0L and 5.7L models, install the spark plug and tighten to 22 ft.-lb. (30 N•m) if the cylinder head is new and 15 ft.-lb. (20 N•m) if the cylinder head is used.

13B. On 7.4L and 8.2L models, install the spark plugs and tighten to 15-20 ft.-lb. (20-28 N•m).

14. Connect the spark plug wires and then the battery cables.

15. Adjust the ignition timing as described in Chapter Five.

Delco EST ignition system

The ignition module is located in the distributor housing. To prevent overheating and module failure, apply heat transfer compound to the bottom of the module before installation. A small tube of compound is supplied with a new module. If the compound is removed and the module must be reused, purchase the compound from a GM automotive dealership.

Refer to **Figure 99** for this procedure.

1. Disconnect the battery cables.

2. Remove the distributor cap as described in this section.

3. Pull up on the locking tab and then disconnect the pickup coil connector (**Figure 103**) from the module.

4. Pull up on the locking tab and then disconnect the engine wire harness from the module. A single plug is used on carburetor-equipped models, and two plugs are used on electronic fuel injection (EFI) models.

5. Remove the two screws. Then lift the module off the distributor.

6. Use compressed air to blow loose material off the distributor.

7. Wipe the heat transfer compound from the distributor and the bottom of the module.

8. Apply an even film of the compound to the bottom of the module. The bottom of the module is metal.

9. Align the tabs on the bottom of the module with the openings in the distributor. Firmly seat the module on the distributor to spread the compound.

10. Install the module mounting screws and securely tighten them.

11. Plug the pickup coil connector (**Figure 103**) onto the module. The locking tab must engage the tab on the module.

12. Reconnect the engine wire harness to the ignition module. The locking tabs on the engine harness connectors must engage the tabs on the module. To avoid electri-

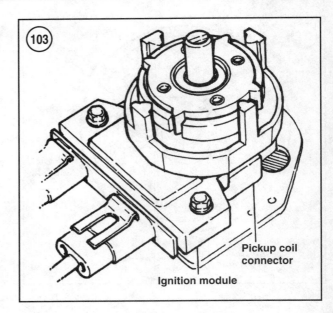

Pickup coil connector

Ignition module

cal interference, route the wiring away from the ignition coil or spark plug secondary leads.

13. Install the distributor cap as described in this chapter.

14. Connect the battery cables.

15. Adjust the ignition timing as described in Chapter Five.

5.7L LT-1 models

The ignition module mounts on a plate at the front of the engine.

Refer to **Figure 104** for this procedure.

1. Disconnect the battery cables.

2. Note the wire routing and connections. Then lift the locking tab and unplug each of the engine wire harness connectors from the module (4, **Figure 104**).

3. Disconnect each of the spark plug wires from the four ignition coils (5-8, **Figure 104**).

4. Support the module, ignition coils and mounting plate. Then remove the screws that secure the assembly to the cylinder head. Place the assembly on a clean work surface.

5. Remove the screws (17, **Figure 104**) that secure the ignition coils to the module. Then carefully unplug each of the ignition coils from the module. Do not bend the terminal blades (3, **Figure 104**) in the module during coil removal.

6. Remove the module from the mounting plate (1, **Figure 104**). Clean all corrosion, belt material or oily deposits from the mounting plate.

(104) IGNITION COILS AND IGNITION CONTROL MODULE (5.7L LT-1 MODELS)

1. Mounting plate
2. Ignition control (IC) module
3. Ignition coil terminals
4. Engine harness terminals
5. Ignition coil (cylinders No. 4 and No. 7)
6. Ignition coil (cylinders No. 1 and No. 6)
7. Ignition coil (cylinders No. 1 and No. 2)
8. Ignition coil (cylinders No. 5 and No. 8)
9. Spark plug wire terminal (cylinder No. 8)
10. Spark plug wire terminal (cylinder No. 5)
11. Spark plug wire terminal (cylinder No. 2)
12. Spark plug wire terminal (cylinder No. 3)
13. Spark plug wire terminal (cylinder No. 6)
14. Spark plug wire terminal (cylinder No. 1)
15. Spark plug wire terminal (cylinder No. 4)
16. Spark plug wire terminal (cylinder No. 7)
17. Mounting screw

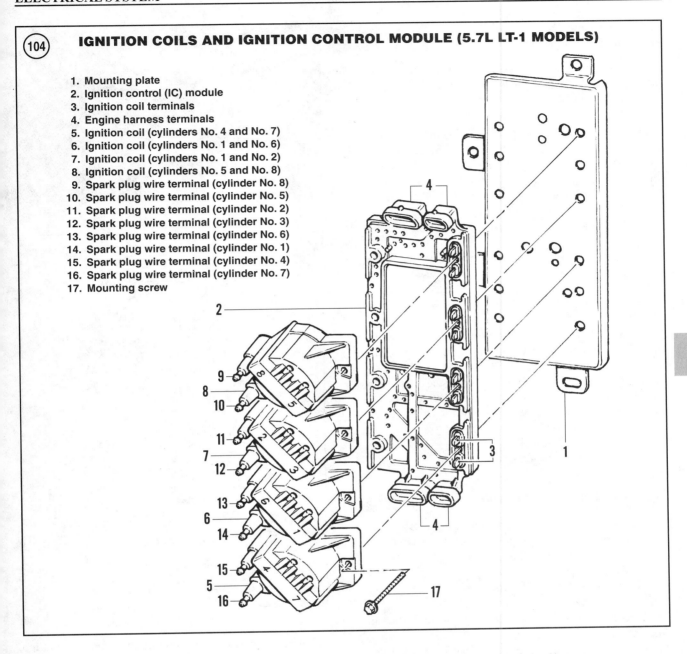

7. Align the terminal blades with the corresponding openings. Then carefully plug the ignition coils onto the ignition module. Make sure the coils are mounted in the order shown in **Figure 104**. The cylinder number is molded or stamped on the coil next to the corresponding high-tension lead terminals.

8. Insert the screws (17, **Figure 104**) into the module. Tighten the screws to 40 in.-lb. (4.5 N•m).

9. Fit the ignition module and coils onto the mounting plate. Then install the assembly onto the cylinder head. Install the screws into the module, mounting plate and cylin-

der head. Tighten the screws in a crossing pattern to 106 in.-lb. (12 N•m).

10. Lift the locking tab. Then connect each of the engine wire harness connectors (4, **Figure 104**) to the ignition module. Route the wiring to prevent entanglement with belts, pulleys and other moving components. Secure the wiring with clamps as needed.

11. Connect the spark plug wires to the ignition coil. The cylinders are numbered from front to rear (1-3-5-7 on the port side and 2-4-6-8 on the starboard side).

12. Connect the battery cables.

Camshaft Position Sensor
Removal and Installation

The camshaft position sensor is used only on 8.1L models. The sensor is located on the front of the timing chain cover (**Figure 105**).

1. Disconnect the battery cables.

2. Pull up on the locking tab. Then unplug the engine harness from the camshaft position sensor (**Figure 105**).

3. Use compressed air to blow loose debris or deposits from the timing chain cover and sensor.

4. Remove the screw and then carefully pull the sensor out of the timing chain cover. Remove the O-ring from the sensor. Discard the O-ring. Wipe all debris from the sensor opening.

5. Lubricate with engine oil and then install a *new* O-ring onto the sensor.

6. Guide the sensor into the timing chain cover. To prevent O-ring damage, rotate the sensor *slightly* during installation.

7. When seated, rotate the sensor to align the screw openings. Thread the screw into the sensor and timing chain cover and tighten to 106 in.-lb. (12 N•m).

8. Pull up on the locking tab and then plug the engine harness onto the camshaft position sensor. The locking tab must engage the tab on the sensor. Route the wiring to prevent contact with drive belts or other moving components. Clamp the wiring as needed.

9. Connect the battery cables.

Pickup Coil Removal and Installation

The pickup coil is used on all models using a Delco EST (electronic spark timing) ignition system. The pickup coil is located inside the distributor. The coil can be replaced without removing the distributor.

Refer to **Figure 99** for this procedure.

1. Disconnect the battery cables.

2. Remove the distributor cap and rotor as described in this section.

3. Pull up on the locking tab and then disconnect the pickup coil connector (**Figure 103**) from the module.

4. Grip two opposing corners of the retainer (6, **Figure 99**) with needlenose pliers. Pull up on the corners until the retainer slips off the distributor bushing. Discard the retainer.

5. Lift the copper shield off the pole piece (9, **Figure 99**). Remove the washer (7, **Figure 99**) from the pickup coil (8).

6. Lift the pickup coil out of the distributor. Use compressed air to blow debris and loose material from the distributor.

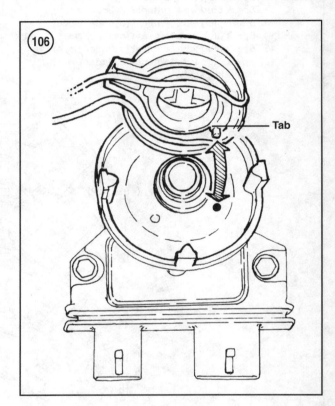

7. Guide the tab on the pickup coil into the opening (**Figure 106**) and seat the pickup coil into the pole piece.

8. Align the notch over the pickup coil wiring and insert the copper shield onto the pole piece (9, **Figure 99**). Install the washer (7, **Figure 99**) over the distributor shaft and seat or rest on the pickup coil (8).

9. Fit a *new* retainer over the distributor bushing with the teeth side facing outward. Position a deep 5/8-in. socket over the bushing and seat against the retainer. Tap on the socket until the teeth on the retainer fit into the groove in the bushing. The retainer must hold the shield and pickup coil firmly onto the distributor body.

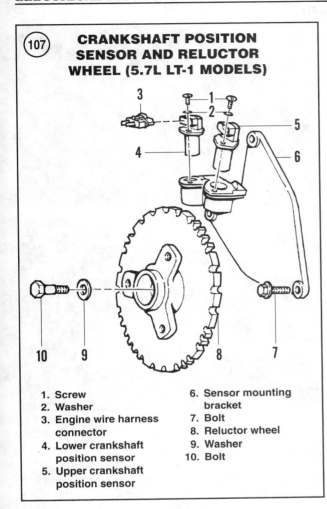

CRANKSHAFT POSITION SENSOR AND RELUCTOR WHEEL (5.7L LT-1 MODELS)

1. Screw
2. Washer
3. Engine wire harness connector
4. Lower crankshaft position sensor
5. Upper crankshaft position sensor
6. Sensor mounting bracket
7. Bolt
8. Reluctor wheel
9. Washer
10. Bolt

5.7L LT-1 models

Refer to **Figure 107** for this procedure.

1. Disconnect the battery cables.

2. Note the wire routing and connections on the crankshaft position sensors.

3. Lift the locking tabs and then unplug the engine harness (3, **Figure 107**) from each of the crankshaft position sensors (4 and 5).

4. Remove the screws (1, **Figure 107**) and washers (2). Then carefully lift the sensor out of the mounting pockets.

5. Use compressed air and mild solvent to remove all corrosion, debris or oily deposits from the mounting bracket and sensor pockets.

6. Install the sensors into the respective openings in the bracket. Rotate the sensors to align the openings and then thread the screw and washers (1 and 2, **Figure 107**) into the sensors and mounting bracket. Tighten the screws evenly to 90 in.-lb. (10 N•m).

7. Lift the locking clip and then plug each of the engine wire harness connectors (3, **Figure 107**) to the sensor. Route the wiring to prevent entanglement with belts, pulleys and other moving components. Secure the wiring with clamps as needed.

8. Connect the battery cables.

8.1L models

The crankshaft position sensor is located on the upper rear of the cylinder block. The sensor extends vertically into an opening that reaches the crankshaft. A screw threaded into the back of the block (just below the intake manifold mating surface) secures the sensor. Depending on surrounding boat structure, it might be difficult to access the sensor plug and mounting screw. Remove engine components as needed to provide clear access.

1. Disconnect the battery cables.

2. Pull up on the locking tab and then unplug the engine harness connector from the sensor.

3. Use compressed air to blow debris and loose material away from the sensor and cylinder block.

4. Remove the screw that secures the sensor arm to the rear of the cylinder block.

5. Carefully pull the sensor up and out of the cylinder block. If necessary, twist the sensor *slightly* to break the bond. If the connector breaks free from the sensor (common occurrence), grip the aluminum terminals with pliers and pull the sensor out.

6. Remove the O-rings from the sensor shaft. Discard the O-rings.

9

10. Plug the pickup coil connector (**Figure 103**) onto the module. The locking tab must engage the tab on the module.

11. Install the rotor and distributor cap as described in this chapter.

12. Connect the battery cables. Adjust the ignition timing as described in Chapter Five.

Crankshaft Position Sensor Removal and Installation

The crankshaft position sensor is used on 5.7L LT-1 and 8.1L models.

On 5.7L LT-1 models, the two sensors fit onto a bracket on the front of the engine. The tips of the sensors align with the reluctor ring mounted on the harmonic balancer.

On 8.1L models, the sensor fits into an opening at the rear of the cylinder block with the tip positioned next to the sensor ring on the crankshaft.

7. Wipe any debris from the cylinder block opening. Debris can damage the crankshaft or sensor upon startup or possibly interfere with sensor operation.

8. Coat with engine oil and then fit the *new* O-rings into the sensor grooves.

9. Carefully guide the sensor into the opening. To prevent O-ring damage, rotate the sensor *slightly* while feeding it into the bore.

10. When seated, rotate the sensor to position the opening in the connector over the mounting screw opening. Thread the screw into the opening and tighten to 106 in.-lb. (12 N•m).

11. Pull up on the locking tab and then plug the engine harness connector onto the crankshaft position sensor. The locking tab must engage the tab on the sensor. Route the wiring to prevent entanglement with belts, pulleys and other moving components. Secure the wiring with clamps as needed.

12. Connect the battery cables.

Ignition Coil Removal and Installation

On models equipped with a breaker-point ignition system or Prestolite BID ignition, the ignition coil (**Figure 108**, typical) is located on the intake manifold.

On models with Delco EST ignition, the ignition coil (**Figure 109**) is located on the rear of the cylinder head or the intake manifold.

On 5.7L LT-1 models, the four ignition coils are mounted on a plate on the front of the engine.

On 8.1L models, the eight ignition coils (**Figure 110**) mount on the rocker arm covers (four on each bank).

Breaker-point or Prestolite BID ignition system

1. Disconnect the battery cables.

2. Grip the rubber boot and then carefully pull the secondary wire off the coil tower. Do not tug on the wire.

3. Remove the terminal nuts and then lift the tan, white and black or gray and purple wires off the coil.

4. Loosen the screw and nut that secures the coil to the mounting bracket. If the screw is not accessible, remove the bolt that secures the coil and bracket to the cylinder head.

5. Pull the coil out of the mounting bracket. Remove the sleeve from the coil or mounting bracket. Replace the sleeve if it is torn or has deteriorated surfaces.

6. Wipe all material off the coil tower. Inspect the coil tower for hairline cracks or carbon tracking. Replace the coil if either of these defects is evident.

7. Apply a soap-and-water solution to the sleeve and then slide it over the ignition coil.

8. Insert the coil into the mounting bracket and carefully slide into position. Securely tighten the screw and nut that secure the coil into the bracket. If removed for access, install the coil and bracket assembly onto the cylinder head. Install the bolt into the bracket and cylinder head openings and tighten securely.

9. Plug the coil secondary lead onto the coil tower.

10. Attach the black or gray wire to the negative coil terminal and the tan and white or purple wires to the positive coil terminal. Install and securely tighten the terminal nuts.

11. To prevent terminal corrosion and reduce arcing, thoroughly coat the terminals with OMC Black Neoprene Dip. Purchase the neoprene dip (OMC part No. 909570) from an OMC dealership.

12. Connect the battery cables.

Delco EST ignition system

1. Disconnect the battery cables.

2. Pull up on the locking tabs and disconnect the black and gray wire harness connectors as an assembly. Separate the connectors after removal.

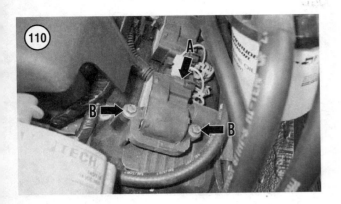

3. Grip the rubber boot and then carefully pull the secondary wire off the coil tower. Do not tug on the wire.

4. Remove the two mounting bolts and lift the coil off the engine.

5. Use compressed air to blow debris and loose material off the coil mounting surface. Remove rust or other contaminants from the mating surface. To operate at full efficiency, the coil must have a good contact to engine ground.

6. Wipe all material off the coil tower. Inspect the coil tower for hairline cracks or carbon tracking. Replace the coil if either of these defects is evident.

7. Install the coil onto the engine and secure with the two bolts. Tighten the bolts evenly to 20-25 ft.-lb. (27-34 N•m).

8. Plug the coil secondary lead onto the coil tower.

9. Fit the gray wire harness connector into the black harness connector. Match the shape of the openings with the shape of the coil terminal. Carefully plug both connectors as an assembly onto the coil. Make sure the locking tab engages the tab on the coil.

10. Connect the battery cables.

8.1L models (with distributorless ignition system)

The eight ignition coils (**Figure 110**) mount on the rocker arm covers (four on each bank).

1. Disconnect the battery cables.

2. If multiple coils will be removed, mark the cylinder number on the ignition coil, engine wire harness connector and spark plug lead. The ignition coil is located above the respective cylinder. Odd-numbered cylinders are located on the port bank with the No. 1 cylinder at the front followed by No. 3, 5 and 7. Even-numbered cylinders are located on the starboard bank with the No. 2 cylinders at the front followed by No. 4, 6 and 8.

3. Lift the locking tab and then unplug the engine wire harness connector (A, **Figure 110**).

4. Grip the boot and then pull the spark plug secondary lead out of the coil tower. Do not tug on the lead.

5. Remove the two screws (B, **Figure 110**) and then lift the coil off the rocker arm cover.

6. Use compressed air to blow debris or loose material from the coil and rocker arm covers. Clean all corrosion deposits or other contaminants from the coil mounting post. To operate at full efficiency, the ignition coil must have a good contact to engine ground.

7. Inspect the coil tower for hairline cracks or carbon tracking. Replace the coil if either of these defects is evident.

8. If necessary, remove and inspect the other ignition coils as described in Steps 2-4.

9. Install the ignition coil onto the rocker arm mounting post. Thread the two screws (B, **Figure 110**) into the coil and rocker arm cover. Tighten the screws evenly to 12 N•m (106 in.-lb.).

10. Lift the locking tab and then plug the engine harness connector onto the ignition coil. Make sure the locking tab engages the tab on the coil. Plug the secondary coil lead onto the coil tower.

11. If removed, install any remaining ignition coils as described in Step 9 and Step 10.

12. Connect the battery cables.

SENDERS, SWITCHES AND WARNING SYSTEM COMPONENTS

Oil Pressure Sender Removal and Installation

NOTE
The oil pressure sender and oil pressure switch are similar in appearance and mount in the same area on the engine. An orange or light blue wire connects to the oil pressure sender. A tan/blue wire connects to the oil pressure switch.

An oil pressure sender is used on all models. The sender operates the oil pressure gauge. It is not part of the ignition or fuel injection system. The sender is usually on the top rear of the cylinder block next to the distributor (**Figure 111**), or it is on the rear and port side of the cylinder block (A, **Figure 112**).

1. Disconnect the battery cables.

2. Remove the nut and then disconnect the orange or light blue wire from the sender terminal.

3. Place a shop towel under the sender to capture spilled oil.

4. Attach a wrench to the brass fitting to prevent rotation and then use another wrench to remove the sender from the fitting.

9

5. Clean all sealant from the brass fitting and sender threads.

6. Apply a light coat of Loctite Pipe Sealant with Teflon onto the sender threads. Purchase the sealant from an automotive parts store or GM automobile dealership (GM part No. 12346004).

7. Thread the sender into the fitting by hand. Attach a wrench to the brass fitting to prevent rotation and then tighten the sender to 124-168 in.-lb. (14-19 N•m).

8. Connect the orange or light blue wire to the sender terminal. Install the brass terminal nut and tighten securely.

9. To prevent corrosion and loosening, thoroughly coat the terminal with OMC Black Neoprene Dip. Purchase the neoprene dip (OMC part No. 909570) from an OMC dealership.

10. Connect the battery cables.

> *WARNING*
> *Stay clear of the propeller and propeller shaft while running an engine on a flush adapter.*

> *CAUTION*
> *Use a flush device or other means to supply the engine with cooling water if running the engine with the boat out of the water. The seawater pump is quickly damaged if operated without adequate cooling water.*

11. Start the engine and immediately check for oil leakage. Make sure the oil pressure gauge operates properly. If the gauge is not operating, the sender might not have a good connection to engine ground. Temporarily attach a jumper wire to the sender body and a good ground. If the gauge now operates, remove the sender, clean the threads, and reinstall as described in this procedure.

Oil Pressure Switch Replacement

> *NOTE*
> *The oil pressure switch and oil pressure sender are similar in appearance and mount in the same area on the engine. Refer to the wiring diagrams at the end of the manual to identify the wires for the sender. A tan/blue wire connects to the oil pressure switch. An orange or light blue wire connects to the oil pressure sender.*

Two different types of oil pressure switches are used. The one-wire switch (B, **Figure 112**) is located on the port side of the cylinder block and is used to activate the low oil pressure warning system.

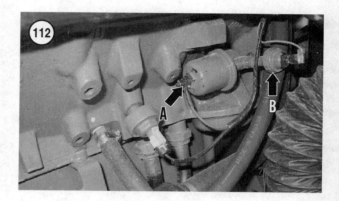

The two-wire oil pressure switch (**Figure 113**) threads into the top of the engine near the distributor. The oil pressure switch provides battery voltage to the electric fuel pump used on later carburetor-equipped models.

One-wire pressure switch

1. Disconnect the battery cables.

2. Pull the tan/blue wire off the switch terminal.

3. Place a shop towel under the switch to capture spilled oil.

4. Attach a wrench to the brass fitting to prevent rotation and then use another wrench to remove the switch from the fitting.

5. Clean all sealant from the brass fitting and switch threads.

6. Apply a light coat of Loctite Pipe Sealant with Teflon to the switch threads. Purchase the sealant from an automotive parts store or GM automobile dealership (GM part No. 12346004).

7. Thread the replacement switch into the fitting by hand. Attach a wrench to the brass fitting to prevent rotation and then securely tighten the switch.

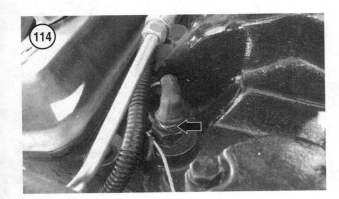

8. Connect the tan/blue wire to the switch. The terminal must fit snugly. If necessary, remove the wire and pinch the connector to achieve a snug fit.

9. Calibrate an ohmmeter on the R × 1 scale. Touch one ohmmeter lead to the metal body of the switch. Touch the other lead to a known engine ground. The meter must indicate continuity. If not, remove the switch, clean the threads and reinstall the switch as described in this procedure. The switch cannot operate properly with a faulty ground connection.

10. Connect the battery cables.

WARNING
Stay clear of the propeller and propeller shaft while running an engine on a flush adapter.

CAUTION
Use a flush device or other means to supply the engine with cooling water if running the engine with the boat out of the water. The seawater pump is quickly damaged if operated without adequate cooling water.

11. Start the engine and immediately check for oil leakage. If oil is leaking, remove the switch, clean the threads, and reinstall the switch as described in this procedure.

Two-wire oil pressure switch

1. Disconnect the battery cables.

2. Pull the wire terminals off the switch.

3. Place a shop towel under the switch to capture spilled oil.

4. Attach a wrench to the brass fitting to prevent rotation. Then use another wrench to remove the switch from the fitting.

5. Clean all sealant from the brass fitting and switch threads.

6. Apply a light coat of Loctite Pipe Sealant with Teflon to the switch threads. Purchase the sealant from an automotive parts store or GM automobile dealership (GM part No. 12346004).

7. Thread the replacement switch into the fitting by hand. Attach a wrench to the brass fitting to prevent rotation. Then securely tighten the switch.

8. Connect the wires to the switch. The terminal must fit snugly. If necessary, remove the wire and pinch the connector to achieve a snug fit. Wire polarity does not affect switch operation.

9. Connect the battery cables.

WARNING
Stay clear of the propeller and propeller shaft while running an engine on a flush adapter.

CAUTION
Use a flush device or other means to supply the engine with cooling water if running the engine with the boat out of the water. The seawater pump is quickly damaged if operated without adequate cooling water.

10. Start the engine and immediately check for oil leakage. If oil is leaking, remove the switch, clean the threads, and reinstall the switch as described in this procedure.

Engine Temperature Sender
Removal and Installation

An engine temperature sender (**Figure 114**, typical) is used on all models. The sender operates the engine temperature gauge and is not part of the ignition or fuel injection system.

On 5.0L, 5.7L, 7.4L and 8.2L models, the sender threads into the front starboard side of the intake manifold or thermostat housing.

On 8.1L models, the sender threads into the crossover tube portion of the thermostat housing that connects to the

9

front of each cylinder head. The sender is just under the hose that connects to the port side of the thermostat cover.

NOTE
The engine temperature sender, engine temperature sensor and engine overheat switches are very similar in appearance and mount in the same area on the engine. A green or tan wire connects to the engine temperature sender.

1. Disconnect the battery cables.

2A. On models with an open cooling system, drain all water from the cylinder block.

2B. On models with a closed cooling system, drain coolant from the cylinder block as described in Chapter Three.

3. Reinstall the drain plugs after draining the water or coolant.

4. If so equipped, move the insulating boot away from the terminal. Remove the terminal nut and then disconnect the green or tan wire from the sender.

5. Use a deep socket to remove the sender. Thoroughly clean the threads on the sender and in the thermostat housing or intake manifold.

6. Apply a light coat of Loctite Pipe Sealant with Teflon to the sender threads. Purchase the sealant from an automotive parts store or GM automobile dealership (GM part No. 12346004).

7. Thread the sender into the thermostat housing or intake manifold by hand. Then use a deep socket to securely tighten the sender.

8. Connect the green or tan wire to the sender. Install the brass terminal nut and tighten securely. To prevent corrosion and loosening, thoroughly coat the terminal nut with OMC Black Neoprene Dip. Purchase the neoprene dip (OMC part No. 909570) from an OMC dealership. If so equipped, slide the insulating boot fully over the terminal and sender body.

9. On models with a closed cooling system, refill the engine with coolant as described in Chapter Three. Refer to *Changing the Engine Coolant*.

10. Connect the battery cables.

WARNING
Stay clear of the propeller and propeller shaft while running an engine on a flush adapter.

CAUTION
Use a flush device or other means to supply the engine with cooling water if running the engine with the boat out of the water. The seawater pump is quickly damaged if operated without adequate cooling water.

11. Start the engine and immediately check for water or coolant leakage at the sender threads. Allow the engine to operate long enough to make sure the temperature gauge is operating properly. If the gauge is not operating, the sender might not have a good connection to the engine ground. Temporarily attach a jumper wire to the sender body and a known good ground. If the gauge now operates, remove the sender, clean the threads, and reinstall as described in this procedure.

Engine Overheat Switch
Removal and Installation

An engine overheat switch (**Figure 115**, typical) is used on some carburetor-equipped models. The switch controls operation of the warning horn by completing the ground circuit if the engine temperature exceeds a preset limit. The switch threads into the thermostat housing, intake manifold or cylinder head.

1. Disconnect the battery cables.

2A. On models with an open cooling system, drain all water from the cylinder block as described in Chapter Four. Refer to *Winterizing*.

2B. On models with a closed cooling system, drain coolant from the cylinder block as described in Chapter Three. Refer to *Changing the Engine Coolant*.

3. Reinstall the drain plugs after draining the water or coolant.

4. Disconnect the tan/blue wire terminal from the switch.

5. Use a deep socket to remove the switch. Thoroughly clean the threads on the switch and in the thermostat housing.

6. Apply a light coat of Loctite Pipe Sealant with Teflon to the switch threads. Purchase the sealant from an automotive parts store or GM automobile dealership (GM part No. 12346004).

tion varies by the brand and type of transmission used on the engine. Trace the yellow or yellow/red wires to the switch.

1. Disconnect the battery cables.

2. If so equipped, move the insulating boot away from the switch.

3. Remove the terminal screws or disconnect the plugs for the two yellow or yellow/red wires.

4. Use a deep socket to unthread the switch from the transmission.

5. Clean all sealant from the transmission opening and switch threads.

6. Apply a light coat of Loctite Pipe Sealant with Teflon to the switch threads. Purchase the sealant from an automotive parts store or GM automobile dealership (GM part No. 12346004).

7. Thread the switch into the transmission opening by hand. Use a deep socket to securely tighten the switch.

8. Connect the two yellow or yellow/red wires onto the switch. Securely tighten the terminal screws. If push-on terminals are used, they must fit snugly. If necessary, remove the wires and pinch the connector to achieve a snug fit. Wire polarity does not affect switch operation. If so equipped, slide the insulating boot fully over the switch terminals and switch body.

9. Connect the battery cables.

10. Test the neutral start switch operation as described in Chapter Two.

WARNING
Stay clear of the propeller and propeller shaft while running an engine on a flush adapter.

CAUTION
Use a flush device or other means to supply the engine with cooling water if running the engine with the boat out of the water. The seawater pump is quickly damaged if operated without adequate cooling water.

11. Start the engine and immediately check for fluid leakage. If fluid is leaking, remove the switch, clean the threads and reinstall the switch as described in this procedure.

Transmission Overheat Switch
Removal and Installation

The transmission overheat switch (B, **Figure 116**, typical) threads into the transmission housing and is exposed to the fluid in the transmission. The mounting location varies by the brand and type of transmission used on the

7. Thread the replacement switch into the opening by hand. Then use a deep socket to securely tighten the switch.

8. Plug the tan/blue wire terminal onto the switch. The terminal must fit securely. If not, disconnect the wire and squeeze the terminal to provide a secure fit.

9. Calibrate an ohmmeter on the R × 1 scale. Touch one ohmmeter lead to the metal body of the switch. Touch the other lead to a known engine ground. The meter must indicate continuity. If not, remove the switch, clean the threads, and reinstall the switch as described in this procedure. The switch cannot operate properly with a faulty ground connection.

10. On models with a closed cooling system, refill the engine with coolant as described in Chapter Three. Refer to *Changing the Engine Coolant*.

11. Connect the battery cables.

WARNING
Stay clear of the propeller and propeller shaft while running an engine on a flush adapter.

CAUTION
Use a flush device or other means to supply the engine with cooling water if running the engine with the boat out of the water. The seawater pump is quickly damaged if operated without adequate cooling water.

12. Start the engine and immediately check for water or coolant leakage at the switch threads. If coolant is leaking, remove the switch, clean the threads, and reinstall the switch as described in this procedure.

Neutral Start Switch (Transmission-Mounted)

The neutral start switch (A, **Figure 116**, typical) threads into the transmission housing and is operated by a cam on the control valve/shift lever assembly. The mounting loca-

9

engine. Trace the tan/blue and black wires to the switch. Some models use individual wires secured to the switch with terminal screws. Other models use a plug connector to connect the wire harness to the switch.

1. Disconnect the battery cables.

2. Remove the terminal screws to disconnect the individual wires or lift the locking tab and unplug the harness from the switch.

3. Use a deep socket to unthread the switch from the transmission.

4. Clean all sealant from the transmission opening and switch threads.

5. Apply a light coat of Loctite Pipe Sealant with Teflon to the switch threads. Purchase the sealant from an automotive parts store or GM automobile dealership (GM part No. 12346004).

6. Thread the replacement switch into the transmission opening by hand. Use a deep socket to securely tighten the switch.

7. Connect the individual wires to the switch and secure with the terminal screws. Wire polarity does not affect switch operation. Make sure the terminals do not touch other terminals, cables or other engine components. Securely tighten the terminal screws. If a plug connector is used, lift the locking tab and plug the harness onto the switch.

8. Connect the battery cables.

WARNING
Stay clear of the propeller and propeller shaft while running an engine on a flush adapter.

CAUTION
Use a flush device or other means to supply the engine with cooling water if running the engine with the boat out of the water. The seawater pump is quickly damaged if operated without adequate cooling water.

9. Start the engine and immediately check for fluid leakage. If fluid is leaking, remove the switch, clean the threads, and reinstall the switch as described in this procedure.

Low Fluid Pressure Switch Removal and Installation (Walters V-Drive Unit)

The low fluid pressure switch (**Figure 117**) threads into the side of the V-drive unit and is exposed to the pressure developed by the internal oil pump system. The switch controls operation of the warning horn by completing the

ground circuit if the operating pressure drops below a preset limit.

1. Disconnect the battery cables.

2. Move the insulating boot away from the switch.

3. Remove the terminal screws or lift the locking tab and disconnect the harness plug.

4. Use a deep socket to unthread the switch from the V-drive unit.

5. Clean all sealant from the V-drive unit opening and switch threads.

6. Apply a light coat of Loctite Pipe Sealant with Teflon to the switch threads. Purchase the sealant from an automotive parts store or GM automobile dealership (GM part No. 12346004).

7. Thread the switch into the V-drive unit opening by hand. Use a deep socket to securely tighten the switch.

8. Connect the wires and securely tighten the screws or lift the locking tab and plug the harness plug onto the switch.

9. Slide the insulating boot fully over the switch body.

10. Connect the battery cables.

WARNING
Stay clear of the propeller and propeller shaft while running an engine on a flush adapter.

CAUTION
Use a flush device or other means to supply the engine with cooling water if running the engine with the boat out of the water. The seawater pump is quickly damaged if operated without adequate cooling water.

11. Start the engine and immediately check for oil leakage. If oil is leaking, remove the switch, clean the threads and reinstall the switch as described in this procedure.

Warning Horn Removal and Installation

1. Disconnect the battery cables.

2. Trace the tan/blue wire to the dash-mounted warning horn.

3. Unplug the purple and tan/blue wires from the warning horn.

4. Cut the plastic locking clamp that secures the horn to the instrument wiring. Remove the horn.

5. Use a plastic locking clamp to secure the warning horn to the instrument wiring.

6. Plug the purple and tan/blue wires onto the warning horn. Route the wires to prevent interference with the control cables or other moving components. Secure loose wiring with plastic locking clamps.

7. Connect the battery cables.

ELECTRONIC FUEL INJECTION (EFI) COMPONENTS

Engine Temperature Sensor (ETS) Removal and Installation

An ETS (**Figure 118**, typical) is used on all electronic fuel injection (EFI) models. The sensor provides a varying resistance value to the engine control unit (ECU) to indicate the water or coolant temperature in the cooling system. The ECU adjusts the fuel delivery and ignition timing to the optimum setting for the given temperature. The ECU also uses the input to operate the warning horn if the engine overheats. The ETS is not part of the circuit that operates the engine temperature gauge.

On 5.0L, 5.7L, 7.4L and 8.2L models, the sensor threads into the intake manifold or thermostat housing. On 8.1L models, the sensor threads into the crossover tube portion of the thermostat housing.

NOTE
The engine temperature sender, engine temperature sensor and engine overheat switches are very similar in appearance and mount in the same area on the engine. A harness connector plug containing a yellow and black wire connects to the engine temperature sensor.

1. Disconnect the battery cables.

2A. On models with an open cooling system, drain all water from the cylinder block as described in Chapter Four. Refer to *Winterizing*.

2B. On models with a closed cooling system, drain coolant from the cylinder block as described in Chapter Three. Refer to *Changing the Engine Coolant*.

3. Reinstall the drain plugs after draining the water or coolant.

4. Lift the locking tab and then unplug the engine wire harness from the sensor. The engine temperature *sensor* wires use a locking plug on the harness connector. Do not confuse the engine temperature sensor with the engine temperature sender or engine overheat switch, which use a push-on or ring terminal connector.

5. Use a deep socket to remove the sensor. Thoroughly clean the threads on the sensor and in the thermostat housing or intake manifold.

6. Apply a light coat of Loctite Pipe Sealant with Teflon to the sender threads. Purchase the sealant from an automotive parts store or GM automobile dealership (GM part No. 12346004).

7. Thread the sensor into the opening by hand and then use a deep socket to tighten the sensor to 108 in.-lb. (12 N•m).

8. Lift the tab and then plug the engine harness connector fully onto the sensor. The tab must engage the tab on the sensor.

9. On models with a closed cooling system, refill the cooling system as described in Chapter Three. Refer to *Changing the Engine Coolant*.

10. Connect the battery cables.

WARNING
Stay clear of the propeller and propeller shaft while running an engine on a flush adapter.

CAUTION
Use a flush device or other means to supply the engine with cooling water if running the engine with the boat out of the water. The seawater pump is quickly damaged if operated without adequate cooling water.

9

11. Start the engine and immediately check for water or coolant leakage at the sensor threads. If coolant is leaking, remove the sensor, clean the threads, and reinstall the sensor as described in this procedure.

EFI System Relay Removal and Installation

The EFI system relay (**Figure 93**, typical) mounts in a bracket or in an engine harness plug on the rear of the engine near the flywheel housing or at the front of the engine near the exhaust manifold. The EFI system relay is physically identical to the starter relay and fuel pump relay and is usually mounted in the same general location. Identify the starter relay by the purple wire leading to the harness connector. The starter relay and fuel pump relay do not use a purple wire.

1. Disconnect the battery cables.

2A. If the relay is mounted in a bracket, work the relay back and forth while carefully pulling it out of the mounting bracket.

2B. If the relay plugs into the engine harness, depress the locking tab and then pull the engine harness connector out of the bottom of the starter relay.

3A. If the relay is mounted into a bracket, align the spade terminals in the bottom of the relay with the openings in the bracket. The relay will only fit one way. Carefully push the starter relay fully into the terminals.

3B. If the relay plugs into the engine harness connector, align the spade terminals in the bottom of the relay with the corresponding terminal openings in the harness plug. Depress the locking tab and then push the engine harness connector onto the starter relay.

4. Connect the battery cables.

Fuel Pump Relay Removal and Installation

The fuel pump relay (**Figure 93**, typical) mounts in a bracket or in an engine harness plug on the rear of the engine near the flywheel housing or at the front of the engine near the exhaust manifold. The fuel pump relay is physically identical to the starter relay and EFI system relay and is usually mounted in the same general location. Identify the starter relay by the gray or green wire leading to the harness connector. The starter relay and fuel pump relay do not use a gray or green wire.

1. Disconnect the battery cables.

2A. If the relay is mounted in a bracket, work the relay back and forth while carefully pulling it out of the mounting bracket.

2B. If the relay plugs into the engine harness, depress the locking tab and then pull the engine harness connector out of the bottom of the starter relay.

3A. If the relay is mounted into a bracket, align the spade terminals in the bottom of the relay with the terminal openings in the bracket. The relay will only fit one way. Carefully push the starter relay fully into the terminals.

3B. If the relay plugs into the engine harness connector, align the spade terminals in the bottom of the relay with the openings in the harness plug. Depress the locking tab and then push the engine harness connector onto starter relay.

4. Connect the battery cables.

Manifold Air Pressure (MAP) Sensor Removal and Installation

On models with throttle body injection (TBI) or multiport injection (MPI) with a center-mounted throttle body, the MAP sensor mounts on a bracket near the throttle body, mounts on the throttle body-to-intake manifold adapter (**Figure 119**) or, on some models, is simply plugged onto a hose leading to the back of the throttle body (**Figure 120**).

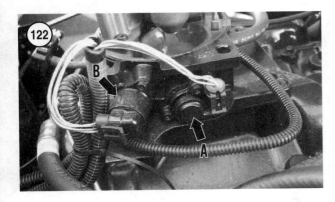

dishwashing soap and water. Then guide the sensor tube (with seal attached) into the adapter or intake plenum opening. Seat the sensor and then rotate to align the mounting screw(s) opening(s). Install the mounting screws and tighten evenly to 44-62 in.-lb. (5-7 N•m).

7B. On models with the sensor mounted onto a bracket near the throttle body, fit the sensor onto the mounting bracket and align the mounting screw openings. Install the screws and tighten to 44-62 in.-lb. (5-7 N•m). Push the hose fully over the sensor tube and secure with a plastic locking clamp.

7C. On models with the sensor attached onto a hose at the rear of the throttle body, push the hose fully over the sensor tube and secure with a plastic locking clamp. Route the hose to prevent hose or sensor interference with moving engine components. Secure the hose and/or sensor with clamps as needed.

8. Lift the locking tab and plug the engine harness connector fully onto the sensor. The locking tab must engage the tab on the sensor.

9. Connect the battery cables.

Intake Air Temperature (IAT) Sensor Removal and Installation

The IAT sensor (**Figure 121**) threads into the intake plenum. Refer to Chapter Seven to locate the intake plenum. Refer to *Fuel Rail and Injectors (Removal and Installation)*.

1. Disconnect the battery cables.

2. Lift the locking tab and then disconnect the engine wire harness connector from the sensor.

3. Use a deep socket to unthread the sensor from the plenum. Clean the threads on the sensor and in the plenum opening.

4. Use compressed air to remove debris or loose material from the sensor. Do not apply solvent to the sensor. Wipe oily deposits from the sensor with a clean shop towel.

5. Thread the replacement sensor into the plenum opening and securely tighten.

6. Lift the locking tab and then connect the engine harness connector to the sensor.

7. Connect the battery cables.

Throttle Position Sensor (TPS) Removal and Installation

Two screws secure the TPS (A, **Figure 122**, typical) to the throttle body. Refer to Chapter Seven to locate the throttle body assembly. Refer to *Throttle Body*.

On models with MPI with a front-mounted throttle body, the MAP sensor mounts on the intake plenum. The tip of the sensor fits into a manifold opening to expose the sensor to the air pressure.

1. Disconnect the battery cables.

2. If so equipped, disconnect the hose from the sensor.

3. Lift the locking tab and then unplug the engine harness connector from the sensor.

4. If the sensor is mounted on the throttle body, adapter, bracket or intake plenum, remove the screw(s) and lift the sensor off the adapter, bracket or plenum. If the sensor is mounted on a bracket, disconnect the hose from the sensor tube.

5. Clean all debris, oil deposits or other contamination from the bracket, adapter opening, plenum opening or connecting hose.

6A. On models with the sensor mounted onto the throttle body adapter or intake plenum, inspect the soft rubber seal on the sensor tube for tears, distortion or other damage. Replace the seal unless found in excellent condition.

6B. On models with the sensor connected to a hose, inspect the hose for torn, pinched or deteriorated surfaces. Replace the hose if these or other defects are evident.

7A. On models with the sensor mounted onto the throttle body adapter or intake plenum, lubricate the seal with

1. Disconnect the battery cables. Verify that the throttle valve is completely closed.

2. Pull up on the locking tab and then unplug the engine wire harness from the sensor.

3. Use compressed air to blow debris or loose material off the sensor and throttle body.

4. Remove the two screws and then pull the sensor off the throttle body.

5. Retrieve the seal from the sensor shaft or throttle body. Replace the seal if deteriorated or damaged.

6. Rotate the sensor to align the flat surfaces on the sensor and throttle shaft. Then fit the replacement sensor onto the throttle body.

7. Verify that the throttle valve is completely closed.

8. Slightly rotate the sensor counterclockwise on the throttle shaft to align the mounting screw openings. Then seat the sensor on the throttle body.

9. Thread the two screws into the sensor and throttle body. If *new* screws are supplied with the replacement sensor, use them during the installation. Tighten the two screws evenly to 18 in.-lb. (2.0 N•m).

10. Pull up on the locking tab. Then plug the engine wire harness connector onto the throttle position sensor. The tab on the harness connector must engage the tab on the sensor.

11. Connect the battery cables.

Idle Air Control Motor (IAC)
Removal and Installation

Two screws secure the IAC (B, **Figure 122**, typical) to the throttle body. Refer to Chapter Seven to locate the throttle body assembly. Refer to *Throttle Body.*

1. Disconnect the battery cables.

2. Pull up on the locking tab and then unplug the engine wire harness from the IAC.

3. Use compressed air to blow debris or loose material off the motor and throttle body.

4. Remove the two screws and then pull the motor off the throttle body. If the IAC will be reused, *do not* remove the threadlocking compound from the screws.

5. Retrieve the O-ring from the motor housing or throttle body opening. Discard the O-ring.

> *CAUTION*
> *Do not use carburetor cleaner containing methyl ethyl ketone to clean the IAC. This type of cleaner removes the protective coating and can dam- age the carburetor.*

6. If the IAC will be reused, wipe debris or contaminants from the motor body, spring and pintle shaft. Use aerosol

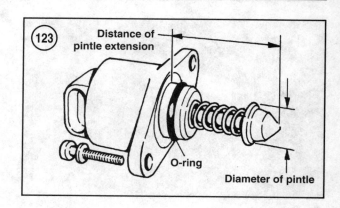

carburetor cleaner to remove stubborn deposits from the pintle shaft and spring. Work carefully to avoid moving the pintle shaft in or out. Moving the pintle will disturb the computer-controlled setting, and moving the pintle shaft with excessive force will damage the internal components.

7. If a new IAC will be installed, *carefully* remove the wire retaine. Then measure the distance from the tip of the pintle to the mating surface (**Figure 123**). The distance must be 1.10 in. (28 mm). If necessary, use light finger pressure and push on the pintle tip to achieve the desired distance. Light pressure will not damage the internal components. Measure the pintle diameter and compare with the diameter of the original IAC. The diameter must be the same. If not, the part is not correct for the model. Install the correct part.

8. Lubricate with engine oil and then fit a *new* O-ring onto the IAC body and seat against the mating surface.

9. *Carefully* guide the pintle shaft into the throttle body and seat the motor onto the throttle body. Work carefully to avoid contact and inadvertently moving the pintle shaft.

10. Rotate the motor on the throttle body to align the screw openings. Install the two screws and tighten evenly to 28 in.-lb. (3.2 N•m).

11. Lift the locking tab and then plug the engine wire harness connector onto the motor. The tab on the harness connector must engage the tab on the motor.

12. Connect the battery cables.

> *WARNING*
> *Stay clear of the propeller and propeller shaft while running an engine on a flush adapter.*

> *CAUTION*
> *Use a flush device or other means to supply the engine with cooling water if running the engine with the boat out of the water. The seawater pump is quickly damaged if operated without adequate cooling water.*

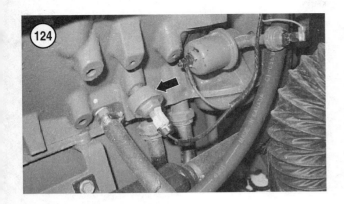

13. Start the engine. Then put the engine into service mode as described under the ignition timing adjustment in Chapter Five. Take the engine out of service mode after operating at idle speed for a few minutes. Operating the engine in service mode calibrates the idle air control motor (IAC) position to the engine control unit (ECU) setting. Improper calibration can cause hard starting (particularly when cold), too fast or too slow idle speed or stalling when returned to the idle position.

Knock Sensor Removal and Installation

A knock sensor (**Figure 124**, typical) is used on all electronic fuel injection (EFI) models. On 5.0L and 5.7L models, the sensor threads into the starboard side of the cylinder block. On all 8.1L models and some 7.4L models, a sensor threads into both the starboard and port sides of the cylinder block.

1. Disconnect the battery cables.

2A. On models with an open cooling system, drain all water from the cylinder block as described in Chapter Four. Refer to *Winterizing*.

2B. On models with a closed cooling system, drain coolant from the cylinder block as described in Chapter Three. Refer to *Changing the Engine Coolant*.

3. Pinch the longer side of the connector and then pull the engine harness connector off the knock sensor.

4. Use a deep socket to remove the sensor from the cylinder block. Thoroughly clean the threads on the sensor and in the cylinder block.

5. Apply a light coat of Loctite Pipe Sealant with Teflon to the sensor threads. Purchase the sealant from an automotive parts store or GM automobile dealership (GM part No. 12346004). Thread the sensor into the block by hand. Then use a deep socket to tighten the sensor to 168 in.-lb. (19 N•m).

6. Calibrate an ohmmeter on the R × 1 scale. Touch one ohmmeter lead to the metal body of the sensor. Touch the

other lead to a known engine ground. The meter must indicate continuity. If not, remove the sensor, clean the threads, and reinstall the sensor as described in this procedure. The sensor cannot operate properly with a faulty ground connection.

7. On models with a closed cooling system, refill the cooling system as described in Chapter Three. Refer to *Changing the Engine Coolant*.

8. Pinch the longer side of the connector and then plug the engine harness connector onto the sensor. Release the grip. Then tug *lightly* on the wire to verify a secure connection.

9. Connect the battery cables.

> *WARNING*
> *Stay clear of the propeller and propeller shaft while running an engine on a flush adapter.*

> *CAUTION*
> *Use a flush device or other means to supply the engine with cooling water if running the engine with the boat out of the water. The seawater pump is quickly damaged if operated without adequate cooling water.*

10. Start the engine and immediately check for water or coolant leakage at the sensor threads. If leaking, remove the sensor, clean the threads and reinstall the sensor as described in this procedure.

Knock Sensor Module Removal and Installation

A knock sensor module is used on models with an MEFI 1 or MEFI 2 ECU. Refer to *Electronic Fuel Injection* in Chapter Two to identify the ECU. If spark knock is detected, the knock sensor module amplifies the knock sensor signal and signals the ECU. On models using an MEFI 3 or MEFI 4 ECU, the knock sensor module circuitry is incorporated into the engine control unit.

The knock sensor module is a small component with a black plastic housing mounted on the circuit breaker housing, exhaust elbow or mounting bracket on the rear of the engine. Refer to the wiring diagrams at the end of the manual to identify the wire colors connecting onto the knock control module.

1. Disconnect the battery cables.

2. Lift the locking tab and then unplug the engine harness connector from the module.

3. Remove the two mounting screws and then lift the module off the bracket.

9

4. Use compressed air to blow debris and loose material off the module and mounting bracket. Wipe oily deposits or other contaminants from the mating surfaces.

5. Fit the module onto the bracket and install the mounting screws. Make sure to fit the ground wire onto the mounting screw. Tighten the screws securely.

6. Lift the locking tab and then plug the engine harness connector onto the module. The harness locking tab must engage the tab on the module.

7. Connect the battery cables.

Engine Control Unit (ECU) Removal and Installation

Either three or four screws secure the ECU (**Figure 125**, typical) to the exhaust elbow, flywheel hosing or intake manifold mounting bracket.

1. Disconnect the battery cables.

2. Mark the two harness connectors and engine control unit to identify the J1 and J2 harness connectors. The connectors are similar in appearance.

3. Depress the locking tab (**Figure 125**) and then pull the J1 and J2 harness connectors off the engine control unit.

4. Remove the three screws and then lift the engine control unit off the mounting bracket.

5. Use compressed air to blow debris and loose material off the engine control unit and mounting bracket. Wipe

oily deposits or other contaminants from the mating surfaces.

6. Fit the ECU onto the bracket and install the mounting screws. Make sure to fit the ground wire onto the mounting screw. Tighten the mounting screws to 89-124 in.-lb. (10-14 N•m).

7. Depress the locking tabs and then carefully plug the J1 and J2 harness connectors onto the ECU. Do not force the connectors into the openings. The connectors are similar in appearance, but the shape is different. Check to make sure the connector is installed into the proper opening before installation. Forcing the connector into the wrong opening can damage the connector, engine control unit or both components.

8. Connect the battery cables.

Table 1 ELECTRICAL SYSTEM TORQUE SPECIFICATIONS

Fastener location	in.-lb.	ft.-lb.	N•m
Manifold air pressure (MAP) sensor	44-62	–	5-7
Alternator mounting bolts	–	26-30	35-41
Camshaft position sensor			
8.1L models	106	–	12
Crankshaft position sensor			
5.7L LT-1 models	90	–	10
8.1L models	106	–	12
Distributor hold down clamp bolt	–	30	41
Engine control unit (ECU)	89-124	–	10-14
Engine temperature sensor (EFI system)	108	–	12
Idle air control motor (IAC)	28	–	3.2
Ignition coil			
Models with Delco EST ignition	–	20-25	27-34
8.1 L models	106	–	12
5.7L LT-1 models	40	–	4.5
Ignition module			
5.7L LT-1	106	–	12
Knock sensor	168	–	19
Oil pressure sender	124-168	–	14-19

(continued)

Table 1 ELECTRICAL SYSTEM TORQUE SPECIFICATIONS (continued)

Fastener location	in.-lb.	ft.-lb.	N•m
Spark plug			
5.0L and 5.7L models			
With used cylinder head	–	15	20
With new cylinder head	–	22	30
7.4L and 8.2L models	–	15-20	20-28
8.1L models	–	15	20
Throttle position sensor (TPS)	18	–	2.0

Table 2 BATTERY CAPACITY (HOURS)

Accessory draw	Provides continuous power for:	Approximate recharge time
80 amp-hour battery		
5 amps	13.5 hours	16 hours
15 amps	3.5 hours	13 hours
25 amps	1.6 hours	12 hours
105 amp-hour battery		
5 amps	15.8 hours	16 hours
15 amps	4.2 hours	13 hours
25 amps	2.4 hours	12 hours

9

Table 3 BATTERY CABLE RECOMMENDATIONS

Cable length	Minimum cable gauge size (AWG)
0-10 ft.	0
10-15 ft.	00
15-20 ft.	0000

Table 4 BATTERY STATE OF CHARGE

Specific gravity reading	Percentage of charge remaining
1.120-1.140	0
1.135-1.155	10
1.150-1.170	20
1.160-1.180	30
1.175-1.195	40
1.190-1.210	50
1.205-1.225	60
1.215-1.235	70
1.230-1.250	80
1.245-1.265	90
1.260-1.280	100

Table 5 ENGINE FIRING ORDER

Model	Firing order
5.0L, 5.7L, 7.4L and 8.2L models	
Standard-rotation models	1-8-4-3-6-5-7-2
Counter-rotation models	1-2-7-5-6-3-4-8
8.1L models	1-8-7-2-6-5-4-3

Chapter Ten

Drive System

This chapter describes transmission identification and removal/installation of the transmission, Walters V-drive unit, propeller and propeller shaft.

Transmission repair requires numerous costly special tools in addition to experience repairing hydraulically controlled transmissions. Having the transmission professionally repaired usually costs less than the special tools and equipment. Most marine transmission shops stock rebuilt units that can be shipped immediately to avoid unnecessary downtime. The failed transmission is typically sent to the shop for rebuilding.

Table 1 lists tightening specifications for most transmission mounting fasteners. Use the general tightening specifications provided in Chapter One for fasteners not listed in **Table 1**. **Table 1** is located at the end of this chapter.

> *WARNING*
> *Stay clear of the propeller and propeller shaft while running an engine on a flush adapter.*

> *CAUTION*
> *Use a flush device or other means to supply the engine with cooling water if running the engine with the boat out of the water. The seawater pump is quickly damaged if operated without adequate cooling water.*

TRANSMISSION

Identification

Indmar inboard marine engines are equipped with a number of different types of transmissions.

Most models use a Borg-Warner, Regal Beloit (Velvet-Drive) or ZF Hurth inline transmission that positions the front of the engine (pulley side) toward the front of the boat. See **Figure 1**.

Some models are equipped with a Walters V-drive unit attached to the end of a Borg-Warner or Regal Beloit (Velvet-Drive) transmission. See **Figure 2**. This arrangement positions the front of the engine (pulley side) toward the rear of the boat.

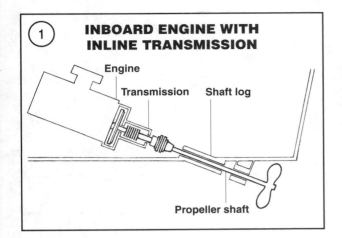

INBOARD ENGINE WITH INLINE TRANSMISSION

Engine
Transmission
Shaft log
Propeller shaft

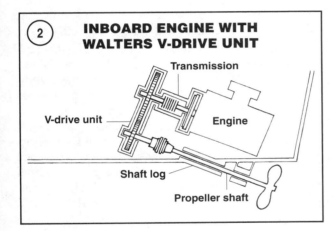

INBOARD ENGINE WITH WALTERS V-DRIVE UNIT

Transmission
V-drive unit
Engine
Shaft log
Propeller shaft

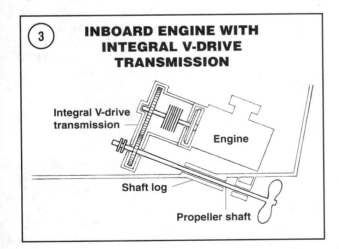

INBOARD ENGINE WITH INTEGRAL V-DRIVE TRANSMISSION

Integral V-drive transmission
Engine
Shaft log
Propeller shaft

Other models use a Borg-Warner/Regal Beloit (Velvet-Drive) or ZF Hurth integral V-drive transmission. See **Figure 3**. This arrangement also positions the front of the engine facing the rear of the boat.

10

Identify the transmission brand, model, ratio and serial number by the identification tag attached to the top of the housing (**Figure 4**, typical). The Walters V-drive can be identified by the large rectangular cover (A, **Figure 5**) on the top of the unit.

Rotation

Marine transmissions are divided into two basic types: unirotational and birotational. Refer to the following descriptions to identify the propeller rotational directions relative to the engine flywheel rotation.

Unirotational transmissions

Unirotational transmissions are designed to accept full power only in FORWARD. The unirotational transmission provides REVERSE by using a planetary gear set to reverse the propeller shaft direction. The planetary gear set in the transmissions cannot withstand continuous REVERSE operation at higher throttle settings.

The unirotational transmissions, used on the models covered in this manual, are produced by Borg-Warner/Regal Beloit (Velvet-Drive). Refer to the identification tag and locate the transmission gear ratio and model number. Inline transmissions that are unirotational have a model number starting with 10-17 or 10-18. V-drive transmissions that are unirotational have a model number starting with 10-04 or 10-05. The gear ratio and type of transmission are required to determine the output shaft and propeller shaft rotation.

On vessels with twin engines (**Figure 6**) that use unirotational transmissions, a standard-rotation engine is used alongside a counter-rotation engine. The standard-rotation engine rotates the flywheel counterclockwise when viewed from the flywheel end. The transmission used on the standard-rotation engine has the fluid pump *indexed* in the standard position. This allows the pump to develop fluid pressure with the input shaft turning in the same direction as the flywheel.

The counter-rotation engine rotates the flywheel clockwise when viewed from the flywheel end. The transmission used on the counter-rotation engine has the fluid pump *indexed* in the nonstandard position. This allows the pump to develop fluid pressure with the input shaft turning in the same direction as the flywheel.

On engines using an inline transmission (**Figure 1**) with a 1:1, 1.5:1, 2.5:1 or 3:1 gear ratio, the output shaft and propeller shaft rotate in the same direction as the flywheel when in forward gear. If a standard-rotation engine is used, a left-hand propeller must be used to provide forward thrust in FORWARD. If a counter-rotation engine is used, a right-hand propeller must be used to provide forward thrust in FORWARD.

On engines using an inline transmission (**Figure 1**) with a 1.91:1 or 2:1 gear ratio, the output shaft and propeller shaft rotate in the opposite direction as the flywheel when in FORWARD. If a standard-rotation engine is used, a right-hand propeller must be used to provide forward thrust in FORWARD. If a counter-rotation engine is used, a left-hand propeller must be used to provide forward thrust in FORWARD.

On engines using a Walters V-drive unit attached to an inline transmission (**Figure 2**) or an integral V-drive transmission (**Figure 3**), the output shaft and propeller shaft rotate in the same direction as the flywheel due to the engine mounting arrangement (flywheel end forward). If a standard-rotation engine is used, a right-hand propeller must be used to provide forward thrust in FORWARD. If a counter-rotation engine is used, a left-hand propeller must be used to provide forward thrust in FORWARD.

Birotational transmissions

Birotational transmissions are designed to accept full power when operated in FORWARD or REVERSE. This

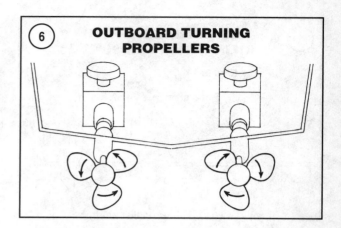

allows counter-rotating propellers without the need for a special engine or transmission. Birotational transmissions are available in both inline and V-drive configurations.

The birotational transmissions used on the models covered in this manual, are produced by Borg-Warner/Regal Beloit (Velvet-Drive) and ZF Hurth. Refer to the identification tag (**Figure 4**) and locate the transmission gear ratio and model number. Borg-Warner/Regal Beloit (Velvet-Drive) models that are birotational have a model number starting with 20-01 or 20-02. All ZF Hurth transmissions used on the models covered in this manual are birotational. A standard-rotation engine is used with all birotational transmissions. The flywheel of the standard-rotation engine rotates counterclockwise as viewed from the flywheel end.

On vessels with twin engines (**Figure 6**) that use birotational transmissions, a right-hand propeller is used on one side and a left-hand propeller is used on the other. The remote control cables are arranged to shift one transmission into FORWARD and the other into REVERSE for forward thrust. The propellers used must correspond to the propeller shaft direction in FORWARD.

Removal

The transmission can be removed without removing the engine from the boat. However, it is usually easier to remove the engine and transmission as an assembly and then remove the transmission from the engine.

Refer to **Figure 7** for this procedure.

1. Disconnect the battery cables.

2. Remove the engine and transmission as described in Chapter Six. Place wooden blocks under the side engine mounts and the flywheel housing. Rest the engine and transmission assembly on a stable surface. Do not support the engine on the oil pan.

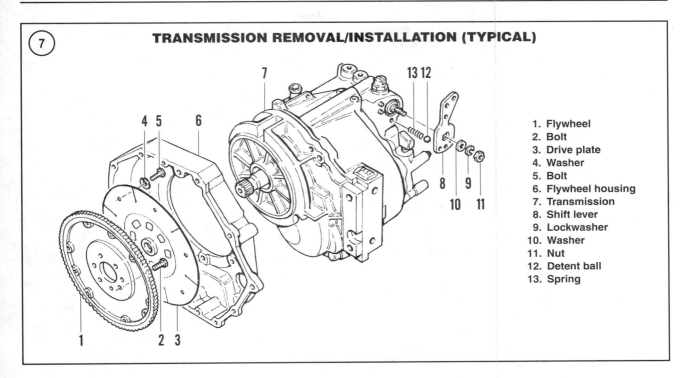

TRANSMISSION REMOVAL/INSTALLATION (TYPICAL)

1. Flywheel
2. Bolt
3. Drive plate
4. Washer
5. Bolt
6. Flywheel housing
7. Transmission
8. Shift lever
9. Lockwasher
10. Washer
11. Nut
12. Detent ball
13. Spring

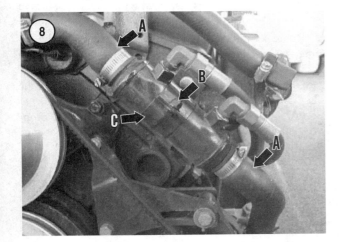

3. Drain the transmission fluid as described in Chapter Three.

NOTE
Always mark the hose connections before disconnecting the hoses from the cooler. The fluid hoses can be installed onto either fitting on the cooler. However, for maximum cooling efficiency, they must be connected to the fittings that will flow the fluid through the cooler in the opposite direction of the water flow.

4. Loosen the clamps and then carefully pull the larger seawater hoses (A, **Figure 8**) from the transmission fluid cooler. Do not attempt to pry or cut the hoses off the fittings. Doing so will damage the thin fitting material. If necessary, use a blunt tool to carefully push the hoses off the fittings. If the boat is stored in the water, plug the disconnected hoses to prevent water from siphoning into the bilge.

5. If the transmission will be replaced, remove the transmission overheat switch (A, **Figure 9**, typical) and neutral start switch (B) as described in Chapter Nine.

6A. If the transmission will be replaced, remove the power steering fluid cooler as described in Chapter Eight. Drain all fluid from the hoses and plug the ends to prevent leakage and contamination.

6B. If the transmission will only be removed from the engine, loosen the clamp bolt (B, **Figure 8**) and then spread

10

the clamp enough to pull the cooler out of the mounting bracket (C). Loosen any clamps and route the cooler away from the engine. Secure the cooler and hoses to the transmission housing in preparation for removal.

7. If a Walters V-drive unit is installed on the transmission, loosen the clamps and then carefully pull the cooling water hoses (B, **Figure 5**) off the V-drive. Disconnect the engine wire harness from the low fluid pressure switch.

8. Support the transmission housing with an overhead cable. Then remove the bolts and washers that secure the transmission to the flywheel housing.

9. Provide continual overhead support while carefully sliding the transmission output shaft out of the drive plate splines. Place the transmission on a suitable work surface.

10. If the transmission will be replaced, perform the following procedure:

    a. Remove the plugs from the hoses and drain any all transmission fluid. Note the fluid hose routing and connections before removing the hoses. Loosen and then unthread the fluid hoses from the transmission. Direct solvent through the hoses to remove contaminants. Dry the hoses with compressed air. Cover the hoses to prevent contamination.

    b. Remove the fluid hose fittings from the transmission. Clean all sealant from the fitting threads.

    c. Remove the rear mount bracket from each side of the transmission.

11. If the transmission is equipped with a Walters V-drive unit, remove the V-drive unit as described in this chapter.

12. If the transmission will be replaced or rebuilt, remove the transmission fluid cooler and connecting hoses as described in Chapter Eight. Thoroughly flush all contaminants from the fluid cooler passages and hoses.

Installation

CAUTION
Failure of the transmission will deposit clutch material and other debris into the transmission fluid cooler and hoses connecting the cooler to the transmission. To avoid repeat transmission failure, thoroughly flush all debris from the fluid cooler and hoses prior to installation.

Refer to **Figure 7** for this procedure.

1. Apply a coat of water-resistant grease to the splines of the transmission input shaft and the splined opening in the drive plate (3, **Figure 7**).

2. Use an overhead cable and lift to support the weight of the transmission during installation.

3. Carefully guide the transmission input shaft into the drive plate (3, **Figure 7**). Rotate the transmission housing to align the splines. When aligned, the transmission will seat against the flywheel housing (6, **Figure 7**).

4. Rotate the transmission housing enough to align the bolt openings. Then thread the bolts and washers (7-9, **Figure 7**) into the transmission and flywheel housing. Tighten the transmission bolts in a crossing pattern to 50 ft.-lb. (68 N•m).

5. If removed, install the rear mount brackets onto the transmission housing. Install and tighten the bolts to 45 ft.-lb. (61 N•m).

6. If removed, apply Loctite Pipe Sealant with Teflon to the threads of the transmission fittings. Do *not* allow any sealant to enter the fitting. Remove any plugs from the transmission and then thread the fittings into the transmission. Securely tighten the fittings.

7. Remove any covers from the fluid hose and then attach the hoses onto the transmission fittings. Hold the transmission fitting with a wrench to prevent rotation. Then use another wrench to tighten the hose fitting to 25 ft.-lb. (34 N•m).

8. If the transmission is equipped with a Walters V-drive unit, install the V-drive unit as described in this chapter.

9. Route the transmission fluid cooler hoses over the engine. Then spread the clamp and slide the transmission fluid cooler into the mounting bracket (C, **Figure 8**). Rotate the cooler in the bracket to align the fittings with the fluid hoses. Then tighten the clamp bolt (B, **Figure 8**) to secure the cooler. Make sure the cooler is oriented properly and is not in contact with any moving components, wires and sharp or pointed surfaces.

10. Remove any covers and then fit the clamps over the ends. Then push the seawater hoses (A, **Figure 8**) onto the cooler. Position the clamps approximately 1/4 in. (6 mm) from the ends of the hose and then securely tighten the clamps. Make sure the clamps are not in contact with moving components, wiring or wire terminals.

11. If a Walters V-drive unit is installed on the transmission, fit the clamps over the ends and then push the cooling water hoses (B, **Figure 5**) onto the V-drive. Position the clamps approximately 1/4 in. (6 mm) from the ends of the hose and then securely tighten the clamps. Connect the engine wire harness to the low fluid pressure switch.

12. If removed for transmission replacement, install the transmission overheat switch and neutral start switch as described in Chapter Nine.

13. Install the engine and transmission as described in Chapter Six. Make sure to align the engine as described in Chapter Six.

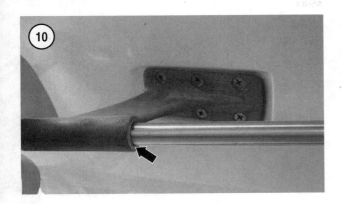

14. Fill the transmission with the recommended fluid as described in Chapter Three. Refer to *Transmission Fluid Change*.

15. Adjust the shift cable as described in Chapter Five.

16. Connect the battery cables.

> **WARNING**
> *Stay clear of the propeller and propeller shaft while running an engine on a flush adapter.*

> **CAUTION**
> *Use a flush device or other means to supply the engine with cooling water if running the engine with the boat out of the water. The seawater pump is quickly damaged if operated without adequate cooling water.*

> **CAUTION**
> *If the engine must be shifted into gear with the boat stored on a trailer, have an assistant spray water onto the propeller shaft surface where it passes through the support strut (Figure 10). The water spray is required to lubricate the cutlass bearing in the support strut.*

17. Start the engine and immediately check for water or transmission fluid leakage from the cooler or hoses. Correct any leakage before continuing operation. Do *not* shift the transmission into gear at this time.

18. Stop the engine. Check and correct the transmission fluid level.

19. Start the engine and operate at fast idle (1200-1500 rpm) in NEUTRAL until it reaches normal operating temperature. Return the engine to idle.

20. With the engine running at idle, shift the engine repeatedly into FORWARD and REVERSE. Repeat the shift cable adjustment if improper or delayed shifting is noted while shifting.

21. Make sure the propeller rotates in the proper direction to move the boat forward in FORWARD and reverse in REVERSE. If otherwise, the cable is attached onto the wrong shift arm, the wrong rotation propeller is installed, or the transmission is malfunctioning. If the cable orientation in the remote control and propeller rotational direction is correct, refer to *Drive System* in Chapter Two. Do *not* operate the engine if any shifting malfunction is evident.

22. Stop the engine.

WALTERS V-DRIVE UNIT

Removal

Six nuts and washers or six bolts and washers secure the Walters V-drive unit mounts to the transmission output housing. The Walters V-drive unit can be replaced without removing the engine from the boat provided that the engine compartment provides good access to the output flange and V-drive-to-transmission fasteners. It is usually easier to remove the engine and transmission as an assembly and then remove the V-drive unit from the transmission. It is not necessary to remove the transmission from the engine when replacing the V-drive unit.

1. Disconnect the battery cables.

2. Remove the engine and transmission as an assembly as described in Chapter Six. Place suitable wooden blocks under the side engine mounts and the flywheel housing. Rest the engine and transmission assembly on a stable surface. Do not support the engine on the oil pan.

3. Drain the V-drive unit as described in Chapter Three.

4. Loosen the clamps and then carefully pull the cooling water hoses (B, **Figure 5**) off the V-drive.

5. Disconnect the engine wire harness from the low fluid pressure switch.

6. Remove the six fasteners that secure the V-drive unit to the transmission output flange. Then carefully pull the V-drive unit off the transmission. Place the V-drive unit on a stable work surface.

7. If the V-drive unit will be replaced, perform the following procedure.

  a. Note the hose routing and connections. Then remove the fluid hoses from the pump and drive unit body. Drain all fluid into a suitable container.

  b. Remove the hose fittings from the V-drive unit and plug the openings to prevent fluid leakage and contamination. Remove sealant from the fitting threads.

  c. Direct solvent through the fluid hoses to remove contaminants. Then dry the hoses with compressed

10

air. Cover the hose fittings to prevent contamination.

   d. Remove the low fluid pressure switch as described in Chapter Nine.

Installation

1. If the hose fittings are removed, apply Loctite Pipe Sealant with Teflon to the threads of the hose fittings. Do *not* allow any sealant to enter the fitting openings. Remove any plugs from the V-drive unit openings and then thread the fittings into the drive unit. Securely tighten the fittings.

2. Remove any covers from the fluid hoses and then attach the fluid hose fittings onto the V-drive unit. Hold the V-drive unit fittings with a wrench to prevent rotation. Then use another wrench to tighten the hose fittings to 25 ft.-lb. (34 N•m).

3. If removed, install the low fluid pressure switch as described in Chapter Nine.

4. Thread a bolt with a lifting hook into the V-drive unit (C, **Figure 5**). Connect an overhead cable to the lifting hook. Using a hoist, lift the V-drive unit off the work surface.

5. Lower the V-drive unit until the V-drive input flange is aligned with the transmission output flange.

6. Guide the transmission output shaft into the V-drive unit input flange. Rotate the output shaft on the V-drive unit to align the transmission and V-drive splines. When aligned, the V-drive unit will seat against the transmission output flange.

7. Rotate the V-drive unit enough to align the openings. Then thread the six bolts into the V-drive unit and transmission output flange. Tighten the bolts in a crossing pattern to 55 ft.-lb. (75 N•m).

8. Fill the V-drive unit with the recommended fluid as described in Chapter Three.

9. Fit the clamps over the ends and then push the cooling water hoses (B, **Figure 5**) onto the V-drive. Position the clamps approximately 1/4 in. (6 mm) from the ends of the hose and then securely tighten the clamps.

10. Connect the engine wire harness to the low fluid pressure switch.

11. Install the engine and transmission as described in Chapter Six. Make sure to align the engine as described in Chapter Six.

12. Adjust the shift cable as described in Chapter Five.

13. Connect the battery cables.

WARNING
Stay clear of the propeller and propeller shaft while running an engine on a flush adapter.

CAUTION
Use a flush device or other means to supply the engine with cooling water if running the engine with the boat out of the water. The seawater pump is quickly damaged if operated without adequate cooling water.

CAUTION
*If the engine must be shifted into gear with the boat stored on a trailer, have an assistant spray water onto the propeller shaft surface where it passes through the support strut (**Figure 10**). The water spray is required to lubricate the cutlass bearing in the support strut.*

14. Start the engine and immediately check for water or fluid leakage. Correct any leakage before continuing operation. *Do not* shift the transmission into gear at this time.

15. Stop the engine. Check and correct the V-drive fluid level.

16. Start the engine and operate at fast idle (1200-1500 rpm) in NEUTRAL until it reaches normal operating temperature. Return the engine to idle.

17. With the engine running at idle, shift the engine repeatedly into FORWARD and REVERSE. Repeat the shift cable adjustment if improper or delayed shifting is noted while shifting.

18. Make sure the propeller rotates in the proper direction to move the boat forward in FORWARD and reverse in REVERSE. If otherwise, the cable is attached to the wrong shift arm, the wrong rotation propeller is installed, or the transmission is malfunctioning. If the cable orientation in the remote control and propeller rotational direction is correct, refer to *Drive System* in Chapter Two. Do

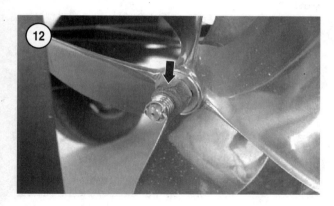

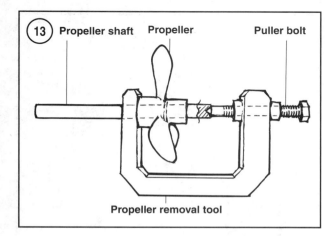

(13) Propeller shaft   Propeller   Puller bolt

Propeller removal tool

not operate the engine if any shifting malfunction is evident.

19. Stop the engine.

PROPELLER

Removal and Installation

The propeller and propeller shafts used with Indmar inboard marine engines are produced by numerous manufacturers. However, propeller removal and installation are similar for most models. A propeller removal tool is required to remove the propeller from the shaft. Purchase or rent the tool from a marine dealership before beginning this procedure.

1. Disconnect the battery cables.

2. Remove any seating or other boat structure necessary to access the transmission output and propeller shaft flange.

3. Remove the cotter pin from the propeller nut and propeller shaft. Discard the cotter pin.

4. Have an assistant insert a pry bar or other suitable tool onto the output shaft flange bolts (**Figure 11**, typical) to prevent propeller shaft rotation. Shifting the transmission into gear will not prevent propeller shaft rotation. Remove the propeller nut (**Figure 12**, typical).

5. Fit the slot in the removal tool over the propeller shaft and rest against the forward edge of the propeller hub. Align the puller bolt with the end of the propeller shaft. Then tighten the bolt until it contacts the propeller shaft. Make sure the tip in the puller bolt fits into the depression in the propeller shaft. See **Figure 13**.

6. Hold the removal tool to prevent rotation. Then tighten the puller bolt until the propeller is free from the propeller shaft.

7. If the propeller shaft and propeller have a key slot, inspect the key for bending, corrosion or other damage. Replace the key if these or other defects are evident.

8. Clean all corrosion, marine growth or other material from the propeller shaft surfaces. Apply a light coat of water-resistant grease onto the propeller contact surface on the propeller shaft.

9. Align the key slot or splines in the propeller bore with the key slot or splines on the propeller shaft and then slide the propeller onto the propeller shaft. Seat the propeller against the step or taper on the propeller shaft.

10. Have an assistant insert a pry bar or other suitable tool onto the output shaft flange bolts (**Figure 11**, typical) to prevent propeller shaft rotation. Shifting the transmission into gear will not prevent propeller shaft rotation. Thread the propeller nut (**Figure 12**, typical) onto the propeller shaft. Contact the boat manufacturer to determine the propeller nut torque for the propeller shaft and propeller used on the boat. Then tighten the nut to the specification.

11. If the propeller nut uses a cotter pin, tighten the nut as needed to align the slots in the nut with the opening in the propeller shaft. Never loosen the nut to align the slots and opening. Install a *new* stainless steel cotter pin and bend over both prongs.

12. Connect the battery cables.

Shaft Removal and Installation

The propeller shaft, shaft log and support strut are produced by numerous manufacturers and are selected and installed by the boat builder. Except for the shaft log seal arrangement, propeller shaft removal and installation procedures are similar. These procedures describe removal and installation for the typical propeller shaft arrangement. Contact the boat manufacturer for specific instructions.

Refer to **Figure 14** for this procedure.

10

1. Disconnect the battery cables.

2. Remove any seating or other boat structure necessary to access the transmission output and propeller shaft flange.

3. Remove the propeller as described in this chapter.

4. Have an assistant rotate the propeller shaft flange while observing the end of the propeller shaft. If bending is apparent, the propeller shaft must be replaced.

5. Remove the four bolts, washers and nuts (**Figure 11**) securing the output flange to the propeller shaft flange. Tap on the side of the propeller shaft flange to separate the flanges. Use a rubber mallet with light force to prevent damage to the flanges.

6A. If the propeller shaft flange is equipped with square set screws (**Figure 15**), cut the safety wire and then remove the setscrews.

6B. If the propeller shaft flange is equipped with recessed Allen setscrews, remove the setscrews. If necessary, heat the flange near the setscrews to soften the threadlocking compound.

7. Slide the propeller shaft flange down the propeller shaft enough to access the mating surfaces. Clean any corrosion or debris from the surfaces with solvent and dry with compressed air.

8A. If the shaft log uses a packing seal, remove the large nut that surrounds the propeller shaft and threads into the shaft log.

8B. If the shaft log uses a carbon rubbing seal, remove the rubbing plate from the propeller shaft following the boat manufacturer's instructions.

8C. If the shaft log uses standard lip seals, contact the boat manufacturer to determine steps that must be performed before removing the propeller shaft.

9. Pull the propeller end of the shaft out of the support strut (**Figure 14**) enough to remove the flange (**Figure 15**) off the propeller shaft.

10. Carefully pull the propeller shaft out of the shaft log and support strut.

11. If the shaft log uses a packing seal, remove the packing material from the shaft log.

12. Inspect the cutlass bearing in the support strut for excessive wear, discoloration or other defects. Replace the cutlass bearing in the strut following the manufacturer's instructions.

13. Clean all corrosion, marine growth or other material from the propeller shaft.

14. Inspect the propeller shaft for wear, corrosion pits, discoloration or roughness. Replace the propeller shaft if these or other defects are evident.

15. Support the propeller shaft on V-blocks. Position a dial indicator at a point between the V-blocks with the stem in contact with the shaft (**Figure 16**). Observe the

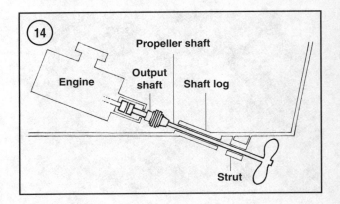

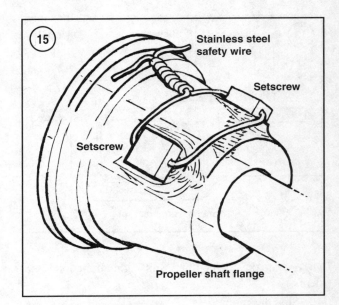

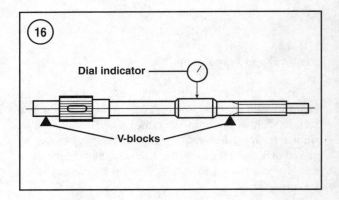

dial indicator while *slowly* rotating the shaft. The amount of needle movement indicates the shaft runout. Contact the boat manufacturer to determine the maximum allowable runout. Replace the shaft if the runout exceeds the specification.

16. Carefully guide the propeller shaft into the support strut and shaft log. Fit the packing seal nut, carbon rubbing seal plate or other shaft seal components over the end of the shaft. Then fit the propeller shaft flange (**Figure 15**) over the shaft. Make sure the propeller shaft fully engages the flange.

17. Inspect the clearance between the cutlass bearing in the support strut and the propeller shaft. The clearance should be even around the perimeter of the shaft. Uneven clearance usually indicates a bent or improperly shimmed support strut. If the clearance is uneven, follow the boat manufacturer's instructions and install shims between the strut and the boat hull to achieve even clearance. Replace the strut if the clearance cannot be corrected with shims.

18A. If the shaft log uses a packing seal, install *new* packing material and install the large nut by following the boat manufacturer's instructions.

18B. If the shaft log uses a carbon rubbing seal, install the rubbing plate onto the propeller shaft by following the boat manufacturer's instructions.

18C. If the shaft log uses standard lip seals, contact the boat manufacturer to determine steps that must be performed when installing the propeller shaft.

19. Align the engine and connect the propeller shaft flange to the propeller shaft as described in Chapter Six. Refer to *Engine Alignment*.

20. Install the propeller as described in this chapter.

21. Connect the battery cables.

Table 1 DRIVE SYSTEM TORQUE SPECIFICATIONS

Fastener	in.-lb.	ft.-lb.	N•m
Fluid drain plug	–	25	34
Fluid hose fittings	–	25	34
Rear mount brackets	–	45	61
Transmission to flywheel housing	–	50	68
V-drive unit to transmission	–	55	75

10

Chapter Eleven

Steering System

Indmar inboard marine engines can be equipped with a mechanical (not power-assisted) or power steering system. Proper operation of the steering system is essential for safe boating. The steering system should be rigged *only* by an experienced marine technician and serviced (whenever possible) by one who is equally qualified. This chapter covers steering safety precautions and repair of the steering system pump. Replacement of the power steering fluid cooler is described in Chapter Eight. The power steering actuator is located near the steering arm for the rudder. Actuators are produced by numerous manufacturers and are selected and installed by the boat builder. Contact the boat manufacturer for maintenance and repair instructions for the brand and type of actuator used on the boat.

Table 1 lists torque specifications for the power steering pump fasteners. Use the general tightening specifications in Chapter One for fasteners not listed in **Table 1**. **Table 1** is at the end of this chapter.

SAFETY PRECAUTIONS

The steering system connects the rudder to the steering wheel. When properly installed and maintained, the steering system gives the boater control over the vessel. A steering system that hesitates or jams prevents the operator from avoiding obstacles, such as other boats. If the steering system is loose, the boat will weave regardless of attempts to maintain a straight course. A steering system failure can cause complete loss of control that can result in a serious accident and possible loss of life.

The most important safety precaution to observe is proper lubrication and maintenance of the steering system. It is especially important to check the steering system if the rudder receives a severe blow, such as hitting a piling or other underwater object. Damaged or weak components can fail at a later time while you are on the water. Know what to look for and have any problems corrected before operating the boat.

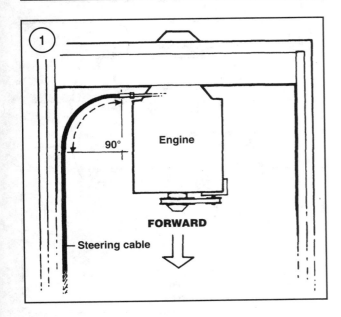

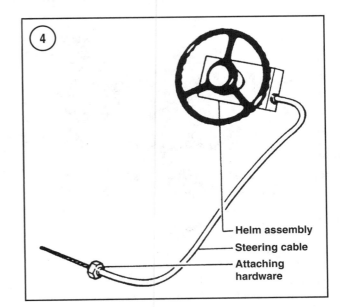

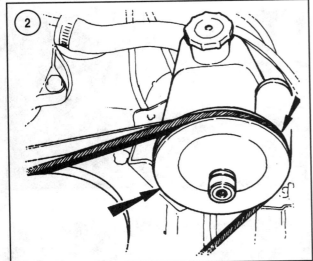

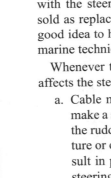

11

If you choose to make adjustments or repairs yourself, make them carefully and use only the fasteners supplied with the steering attachment kit or equivalent fasteners sold as replacement items by marine dealers. It is also a good idea to have your work checked by an experienced marine technician to make sure no safety hazards exist.

Whenever the engine is removed or other service that affects the steering system is performed, make sure that:

a. Cable movement is not restricted. The cable must make a smooth bend (**Figure 1**) from the steering to the rudder and must not bind against the boat structure or other components. Cable restrictions can result in possible jamming of the system. On power steering models, a cable restriction can prevent the power steering from operating or cause the rudder to unexpectedly go into a full turn without turning the wheel.

b. Boat structure or other components do not contact the power steering pump or pulley (**Figure 2**).

c. The power steering cable moves freely and operates the power steering actuator (**Figure 3**, typical) only when turning the steering wheel.

MECHANICAL (MANUAL) STEERING SYSTEM

A mechanical steering system is used primarily on smaller inboard ski or water sport boats. Many larger boats use a power steering system. A mechanical system (**Figure 4**, typical) consists of the helm and steering wheel assembly, the steering cable and hardware connecting the

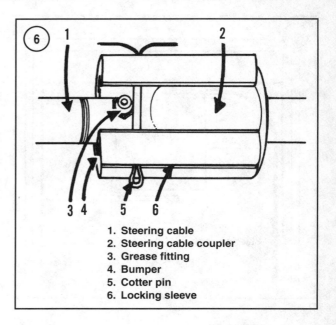

1. Steering cable
2. Steering cable coupler
3. Grease fitting
4. Bumper
5. Cotter pin
6. Locking sleeve

cable to the rudder lever located inside the boat directly above the rudder.

If faulty, replace the steering cable and helm as an assembly. Both components are subject to wear and the effects of corrosion, and failure of one usually precedes the other. Purchase the helm and cable from a marine dealership or marine supply business. Follow the manufacturer's instructions to install the helm into the boat.

> *WARNING*
> *Failure of the steering system can cause a serious accident. Do not operate a boat with loose or binding steering.*

> *WARNING*
> *The steering cable must have a self-locking coupler nut (Figure 5, typical) or coupler-locking mechanism (Figure 6, typical) to prevent the cable from loosening. A loose cable results in excessive steering play and eventual lack of steering control. Do not operate the boat if this important safety feature is lacking.*

POWER STEERING SYSTEM

The power steering system consists of the same components used on the mechanical steering system in addition to the belt-driven power steering pump (**Figure 7**), power steering fluid cooler (**Figure 8**) and steering actuator (**Figure 3**). The power steering pump is mounted on the front of the engine and is belt-driven by the crankshaft pulley. The steering actuator assembly mounts on the boat hull and connects to the steering lever for the rudder and steering cable ram.

Figure 9 shows the fluid flow diagram for a typical power steering system. The pump moves the fluid through the system under pressure. The relief valve functions to limit the maximum pressure developed by the pump while it is working and lowers the pressure when the system is

static (no steering cable movement). Special passages in the relief valve hydraulically sense when the system is loaded, and the valve reacts accordingly. Lowering the pressure when the system is static reduces parasitic power

TYPICAL POWER STEERNG SYSTEM

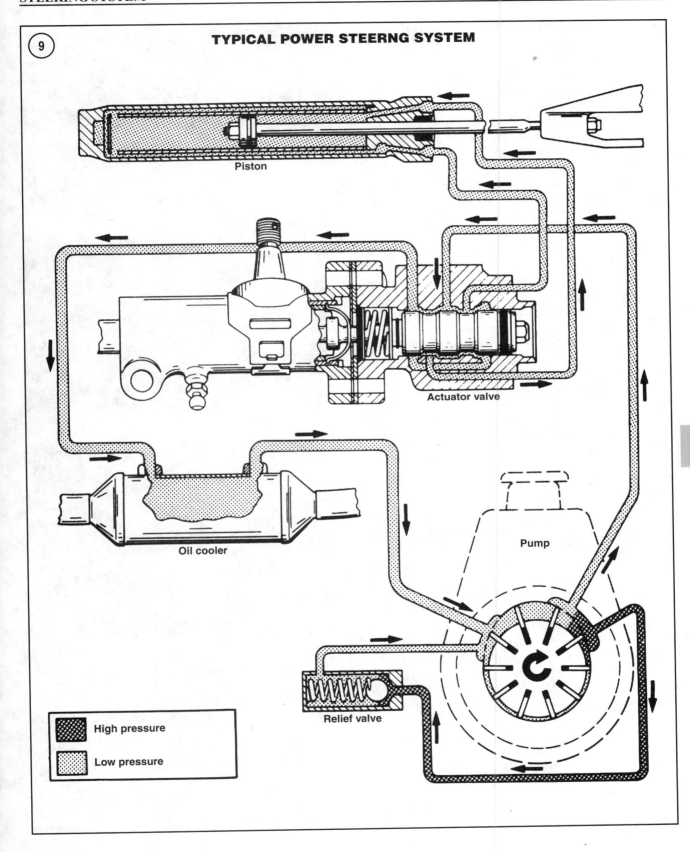

Piston

Actuator valve

Oil cooler

Pump

Relief valve

High pressure

Low pressure

11

loss, reduces fluid temperature and reduces wear on the power steering system components. The spool valve in the actuator moves in response to movement of the steering cable. Although the spool valve movement is small (approximately 0.125 in. [3.2 mm]), it is enough to open the valve and direct pressurized fluid to one side or the other of the piston. This provides the power assist. The spring portion of the control valve pushes the spool valve to the static position as the cable movement ceases. If the cable movement is restricted by clamps, excessively tight bends or boat structure, the spool valve might not react properly to steering cable movement and cause hard steering in one or both directions. The wire harness and other cables must not be attached to the steering cable.

This section describes removal, installation and repair of the power steering pump. If faulty, replace the steering cable and helm as an assembly. Both components are subject to wear and the effects of corrosion, and failure of one usually precedes the other. Purchase the helm and cable from a marine dealership or marine supply business. Follow the manufacturer's instructions to install the helm into the boat. Steering actuators are produced by numerous manufacturers. The brand and model are selected and installed by the boat builder. Contact the boat builder for maintenance and repair instructions for the brand and model of actuator used on the boat. Power steering system troubleshooting is described in Chapter Two.

Power Steering Pump

This section describes power steering pump removal, pulley removal and installation, pump disassembly and assembly, and pump installation. Replacement and adjustment of the power steering belt is described in the pump removal and installation procedure. Early models use a conventional V-groove drive belt (**Figure 10**). The power steering pump pivots in the mounting bracket to adjust the belt tension. Later models and all 8.1L models use a single serpentine multigroove belt (**Figure 11**, typical) to drive the power steering pump and the other belt-driven components. The multigroove belt uses a spring-loaded tensioner (A, **Figure 12**, typical) to maintain the proper belt tension. The procedure describes belt removal and installation for both types of belts.

> *CAUTION*
> *The power steering pump hose fittings and mounting fasteners have metric threads and bolt head size. To prevent rounding of the fittings and fasteners, use only metric wrenches.*

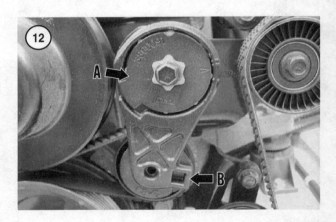

Power steering pump removal

1. Disconnect the battery cables.
2A. On models with a V-groove drive belt, remove the drive belt as follows:
   a. Note the belt routing around all of the pulleys prior to removing the belt. Depending on the model, one or more of the other belts must also be removed. If the alternator belt must be removed to remove the power steering pump belt, refer to Chapter Nine for the procedure. Refer to Chapter Eight if the seawa-

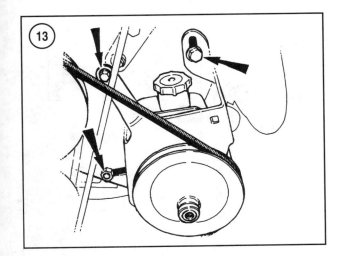

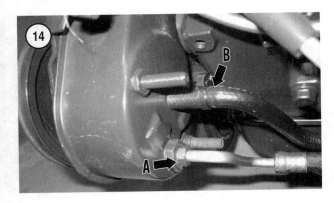

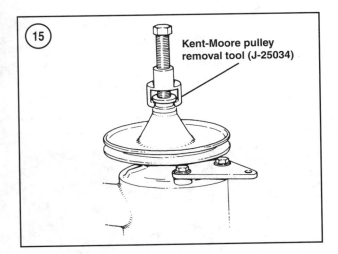

Kent-Moore pulley removal tool (J-25034)

ter pump belt must be removed to remove the power steering pump belt. If necessary, make a sketch indicating the belt routing around *all* of the pulleys.

   b. Loosen but *do not* remove the pivot and bracket clamping bolts (**Figure 13**, typical). Carefully pivot

the pump toward the crankshaft and recirculation pump pulleys. *Do not* push against the filler neck portion of the pump. The weld at the pump body can break and allow fluid to leak. If so equipped, use a breaker bar inserted into the 1/2-in. square opening in the bracket to pivot the pump.

   c. Slip the belt off the power steering pulley. Inspect the belt for worn, damaged or deteriorated surfaces and replace as needed.

2B. On models with a multigroove drive belt, remove the drive belt as follows:

   a. Note the belt routing around the pulleys prior to removing the belt. If necessary, make a sketch of the belt routing around *all* of the pulleys.

   b. Fit a 1/2-in. breaker bar into the square recess (B, **Figure 12**, typical) with the handle facing port. Using the bar, have an assistant pivot the tensioner against the spring tension. Then slip the belt off the tensioner pulley. *Slowly* release the tensioner and remove the breaker bar.

   c. Inspect the belt for wear, damage or deterioration and replace as needed.

3. Place a suitable container or shop towels under the pump hose fittings (A and B, **Figure 14**) to capture spilled fluid. Loosen the clamp on the return hose. Push the hose off the return fitting (B, **Figure 14**). Discard the clamp. Drain all fluid from the hose. Use a metric flare nut wrench to loosen the pressure hose fitting (A, **Figure 14**). Do not loosen the larger fitting that threads into the pump body. Allow all fluid to drain from the loosened fitting for a few minutes. Then disconnect the hose from the pump. Drain residual fluid from the hose.

4. Remove the nut and washers from the stud at the rear bottom of the pump. This nut retains the pump into the lower support bracket. Support the pump while removing the two bolts and washers that hold the pump to the front support bracket. The bolts are located behind the pulley, and a thin profile wrench might be required.

5. Lift the pump out of the mounting brackets. Position the pump over a suitable container and drain all fluid from the pump.

6. Clean rust or corrosion from the pulley surfaces. Rust or corrosion pitting on the belt contact surfaces will allow slippage and quickly wear out a new belt. Clean, sand and repaint the pulley as necessary. Replace the pulley if a smooth belt surface cannot be achieved by sanding and painting.

Pulley removal

   The power steering pump pulley can be removed with the pump on or off the engine. Use a power steering pulley removal tool (**Figure 15**) to pull the pulley from the pump

11

shaft. The pulley removal and installation tools are commonly used in automotive applications. Purchase the tools from a tool supplier or rent them from an automotive part store. Use a pulley installation tool and a long straightedge to install the pulley. Install the pulley with the pump installed on the engine. This is necessary to properly align the belts and pulleys. Improper alignment results in noisy operation, increased wear on the pulley(s) and premature drive belt failure.

The pulley must fit tightly onto the pump shaft. If the fit is loose, the pulley bore, pump shaft or both are excessively worn. To correct a loose fit, first install a new pulley. If the new pulley fits loosely, replace the power steering pump. The pump shaft is not available separately.

1. Disconnect the battery cables.

2. If the pump is mounted on the engine, remove the drive belt from the pulley as described in the pump removal procedure in this section.

3. Slide the pulley removal tool onto the hub of the pulley as shown in **Figure 15**. Thread the puller bolt by hand into the puller until it contacts the pump shaft. Hold the body of the tool with a suitable wrench and tighten the bolt to remove the pulley.

4. Clean grease from the pulley with warm soapy water. Sand surface corrosion from the steel pulleys with Carborundum paper. Thoroughly clean all abrasive material from the pulley. Apply paint to the pulley to help prevent corrosion. Inspect the pulley and pump shaft for cracks or wear. Replace as needed.

Pulley installation

The pump must be mounted onto the engine to install the pulley.

Refer to **Figure 16** for this procedure.

1. Position the pulley on the pump shaft. Fit the drive belt around the pulleys. Do not adjust the belt tension or fit the belt onto the tensioner at this time.

2. Thread the stud (2, **Figure 16**) from the pulley installation tool as far as possible into the pump shaft.

3. Position the bearing from the tool assembly over the stud. Do not use the spacer (3, **Figure 16**) included in the tool kit.

4. Thread the nut (5, **Figure 16**) onto the shaft (6). Thread the shaft and nut as far as possible into the stud.

5. Position the straightedge against the crankshaft and power steering pulleys as shown in **Figure 16**. Tighten the nut (5, **Figure 16**) until the drive belt surfaces are parallel to the straightedge.

6. Remove the straightedge and installation tool components.

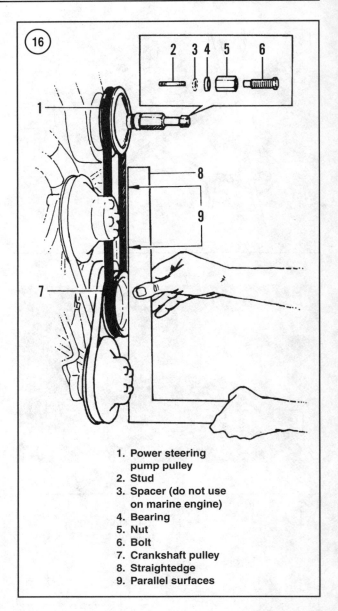

1. **Power steering pump pulley**
2. **Stud**
3. **Spacer (do not use on marine engine)**
4. **Bearing**
5. **Nut**
6. **Bolt**
7. **Crankshaft pulley**
8. **Straightedge**
9. **Parallel surfaces**

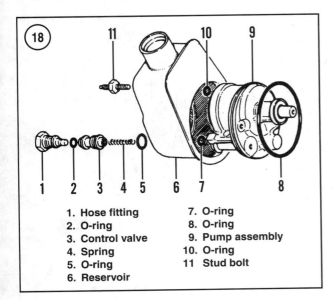

1. Hose fitting
2. O-ring
3. Control valve
4. Spring
5. O-ring
6. Reservoir
7. O-ring
8. O-ring
9. Pump assembly
10. O-ring
11 Stud bolt

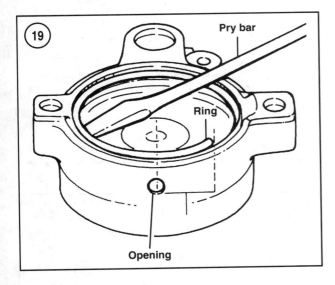

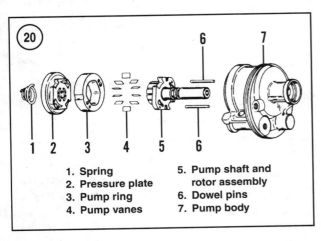

1. Spring
2. Pressure plate
3. Pump ring
4. Pump vanes
5. Pump shaft and rotor assembly
6. Dowel pins
7. Pump body

7. Install the belt and adjust the belt tension as described in the pump installation procedure in this section.

8. Connect the battery cables.

Power steering pump disassembly

The power steering pump can be disassembled, but internal components (except for seals and O-rings) are not available separately. Replace the pump if an inspection reveals faulty components. This procedure is primarily of value if the engine has been submerged and water has entered the pump. If done promptly, this procedure can prevent corrosion of the internal components and the need to replace the entire pump.

Replace all seals and O-rings if removed from the pump. Purchase a seal kit from a local GM dealership (part No. 5688044).

1. Remove the power steering pump as described in this chapter.

2. Remove the front pump mounting bracket from the engine. Clamp the bracket into a vise. Then temporarily attach the pump to the bracket using the original fasteners.

3. Remove the power steering pump pulley as described in this chapter. Remove the pump from the bracket and reinstall the bracket onto the engine. Securely tighten the fastener bracket.

4. Remove the fill cap (**Figure 17**). Invert the pump and pour any remaining fluid into a suitable container.

5. Remove the fitting (1, **Figure 18**). Pull the control valve (3, **Figure 18**) and spring (4) from the pump. Remove and discard the O-rings (2 and 5, **Figure 18**).

6. Remove the stud(s) (11, **Figure 18**) from the reservoir and pump body. Carefully tap the reservoir (6, **Figure 18**) from the pump body (9). Remove and discard the O-rings (7, 8, and 10, **Figure 18**).

7. Place the pump body (shaft side down) onto a vise with open jaws. Do not clamp the body with the jaws.

8. Insert an awl into the opening on the side of the body (**Figure 19**) and push the ring from the groove. Then pry the ring from the body. Lift the end plate and spring (1, **Figure 20**) from the pump.

9. Lift the pressure plate (2, **Figure 20**) and pump ring (3) from the pump. Push on the exposed end of the pump shaft to remove the rotor and shaft assembly (5, **Figure 20**). Remove the two O-rings and dowels (6, **Figure 20**). Discard the O-rings.

10. Slide the pump vanes (4, **Figure 20**) from the rotor. Remove the retaining ring (1, **Figure 21**) and then slide the rotor and thrust plate (2 and 3) from the pump shaft (4).

11

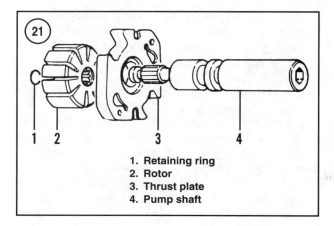

1. Retaining ring
2. Rotor
3. Thrust plate
4. Pump shaft

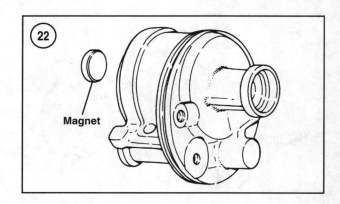

Magnet

11. Remove the magnet from the pump body (**Figure 22**). Carefully pry the oil seal from the pump shaft bore. Work carefully to avoid damaging the seal bore.

12. Clean all components with clean solvent and dry them with compressed air.

13. Inspect the pump body for cracks or damage.

14. Slide each vane (rounded side out) into each of the slots in the rotor. The vanes must slide freely in the slots.

15. Inspect the pump shaft, pressure plate and rotor for wear, discoloration or roughness.

16. Replace the pump assembly if the pump body is cracked; if the pump shaft, pressure plate or rotor is worn, damaged or discolored; or if the vanes bind or stick in the rotor slots. Internal components are not available separately.

17. Use crocus cloth to polish burrs or minor imperfections from the control valve surfaces. The valve must slide freely within the pump bore. Replace the pump if the valve surfaces are damaged or if the spring is corroded. The parts are not available separately.

Power steering pump assembly

Replace all seals and O-rings if removed from the pump. Purchase a seal kit from a local GM dealership (part No. 5688044). Prior to assembly, lubricate all O-rings with Dexron III automatic transmission fluid (ATF).

1. Install the pump shaft seal as follows:

    a. Clean the seal bore in the pump body with a quick-drying solvent such as carburetor cleaner.

    b. Place the pump body on the base of a press as shown in **Figure 23**. The body must be well-supported. Otherwise, the body might distort while installing the seal.

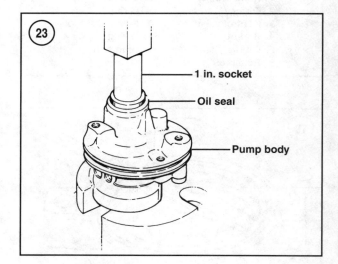

1 in. socket

Oil seal

Pump body

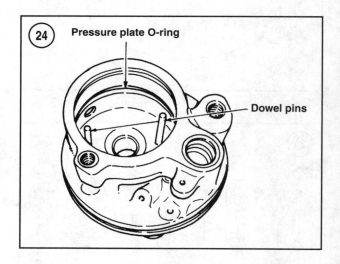

Pressure plate O-ring

Dowel pins

    c. Place the oil seal (lip side down) into the bore. Use a 1-in. socket to press the seal fully into the bore.

2. Lubricate all metal components and the seal lip with Dexron III ATF. Install a new pressure plate O-ring into

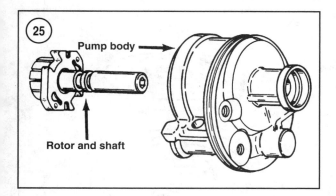

25

Pump body →

Rotor and shaft

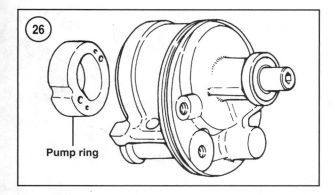

26

Pump ring

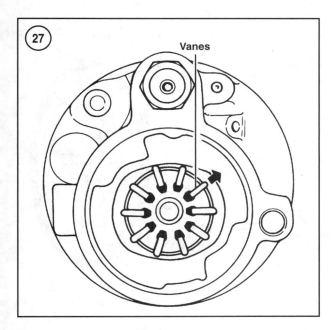

27

Vanes

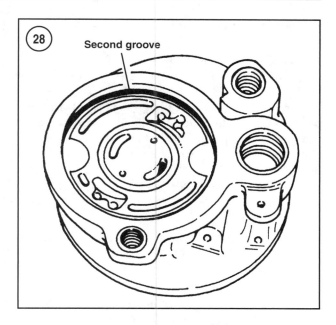

28

Second groove

shaft groove. Slide the rotor and shaft assembly into the pump body (**Figure 25**).

4. Fit the two smaller holes over the dowel pins while installing the pump ring into the body (**Figure 26**).

5. Insert the rotor vanes into the rotor slots with the rounded edges facing the ring (**Figure 27**).

6. Install the pressure plate (2, **Figure 20**) with the spring groove facing outward. Install a new end plate O-ring into the second groove in the pump body (**Figure 28**). Install the spring (1, **Figure 20**) and align it with the groove in the pressure plate. Place the end plate onto the spring (**Figure 29**).

7. Press down on the end plate just enough to expose the groove for the ring (**Figure 19**). Carefully work the ring into the groove. The ring must fit fully into the groove around the entire perimeter of the body. Do not align the ring gap with the opening.

8. Install new O-rings onto the pump body (**Figure 30**). Slide the body into the reservoir. Insert the stud bolt (11, **Figure 18**) through the reservoir and hand-thread them into the pump body. Tighten the stud bolt to 25 ft.-lb. (34 N•m).

9. Lubricate the spring and control valve with Dexron III ATF and slide the spring and control valve into the pump.

10. Lubricate the O-rings (2 and 5, **Figure 18**) with ATF. Install the O-rings onto the control valve fitting and then install and tighten the fitting to 15-26 ft.-lb. (20-35 N•m).

11. Install the power steering pump as described in this chapter.

12. Install the power steering pulley as described in this chapter.

the third groove of the housing. Install the two dowel pins (**Figure 24**).

3. Slide the thrust plate and rotor (2 and 3, **Figure 21**) onto the pump shaft (4). Install the retaining ring into the

11

Power steering pump installation

1. Place the pump into the mounting bracket. Install the mounting fasteners (**Figure 13**, typical). Do not tighten the fasteners at this time.

2. Thread the pressure hose fitting (A, **Figure 14**) into the control valve fitting. Rotate the fitting to prevent contact with the pump mounting bracket and other components. Hold the position and then tighten the fitting to 177-204 in.-lb. (20-23 N•m).

3. Fit a *new* clamp over the return hose. Install the return hose fully into the pump (B, **Figure 14**). Securely tighten the hose clamp.

4. If removed, install the pulley as described in this chapter.

5A. On models using a single V-groove drive belt, install and adjust the drive belt as follows:

   a. Pivot the pump toward the crankshaft pulley and then slip the drive belt onto the pulleys. Make sure the belt is not twisted and fits into the groove in each pulley.

   b. Pivot the pump away from the crankshaft pulley to apply tension to the drive belt. If so equipped, use a breaker bar inserted into the 1/2-in. square opening in the bracket to pivot the pump. When properly tensioned, the belt will deflect 1/4-1/2 in. (6-13 mm) with thumb pressure applied at a point midway between the pulleys (**Figure 31**).

   c. Hold the pump in position to maintain belt tension while tightening the mounting bolts to 25 ft.-lb. (34 N•m).

5B. On models using a multigroove drive belt, install the drive belt as follows:

   a. Tighten the pump mounting fasteners to 25 ft.-lb. (34 N•m).

   b. Slip the drive belt onto all pulleys. Make sure the belt is not twisted and the belt grooves fit into the pulley grooves.

   c. Fit a 1/2-in. breaker bar into the square recess (B, **Figure 12**, typical) with the handle facing port. Using the bar, have an assistant pivot the tensioner against the spring tension. Then slip the belt onto the tensioner pulley. *Slowly* release the tensioner and remove the breaker bar.

6. Fill and bleed the system as described in this section.

> *WARNING*
> *Stay clear of the propeller and propeller shaft while running an engine on a flush adapter.*

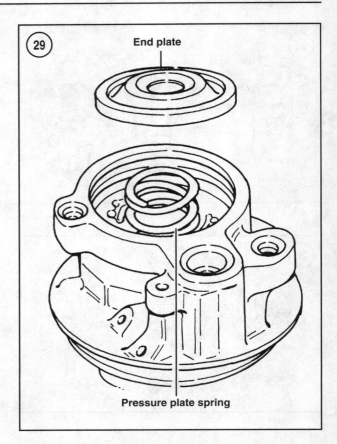

End plate

Pressure plate spring

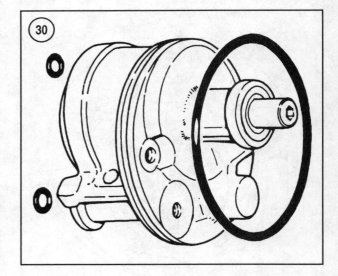

> *CAUTION*
> *Use a flush device or other means to supply the engine with cooling water if running the engine with the boat out of the water. The seawater pump is quickly damaged if operated without adequate cooling water.*

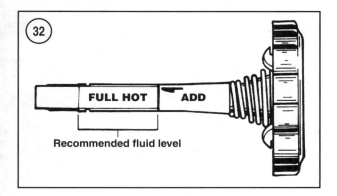

7. Connect the battery cables.

8. Start the engine and immediately check for fluid leakage. Have an assistant rotate the steering through several lock-to-lock cycles while checking for fluid leakage or unusual noises. Correct fluid leakage before proceeding.

9. Correct the fluid level as described in this chapter.

10. On models using a single V-groove drive belt, seat the new belt and correct the tension as follows:

    a. Start the engine and allow it to run at idle speed for approximately 10 minutes.

    b. Stop the engine and disconnect the battery cables.

    c. Apply thumb pressure at a point midway between the pulleys (**Figure 31**). The belt must deflect 1/4-1/2 in. (6-13 mm). If necessary, loosen the mounting bolts (**Figure 13**, typical) and pivot the pump to correct the tension. Hold the pump in position and tighten the mounting bolts to 25 ft.-lb. (34 N•m).

    d. Connect the battery cables.

Filling and Bleeding the Steering System

Perform this operation if the system was operated with a low fluid level and after repairing or replacing any steering system component. To fill the power steering system,

use only Dexron III automatic transmission or a power steering fluid designed for use in inboard marine engine applications.

CAUTION
Never operate the power steering system with a low or high fluid level. Operating the system while low on fluid causes foaming of the fluid, increased steering effort and damage to the hydraulic pump components. Operating the system with a high fluid level causes fluid overflow.

1. Place the rudder and steering wheel in straight-ahead position. Disconnect the battery cables. Remove the fill cap (**Figure 17**).

2. Wipe the dipstick on the fill cap with a shop towel and reinstall it into the pump reservoir.

3. Remove the cap and note the fluid level on the dipstick (**Figure 32**). Correct the fluid level as follows:

    a. If the engine is warm, add fluid into the cap opening until the fluid level just reaches the upper end of the range (**Figure 32**).

    b. If the engine is cold, add fluid into the cap opening until the fluid level just reaches the groove below the *add* mark.

4. Bleed air from the system as follows:

    a. Without starting the engine, rotate the steering wheel in the port and starboard directions while stopping frequently and checking the fluid level and for foam in the reservoir. Immediately stop rotating the wheel and add fluid if the level drops below the tip of the dipstick. Otherwise, foam can appear in the fluid. If foam appears, stop turning the steering wheel and allow the foam in the reservoir to dissipate.

    b. Continue until the wheel reaches a minimum of five turns lock to lock and bubbles stop appearing in the reservoir.

    c. Position the steering wheel in the straight-ahead position. Correct the fluid level as described in Step 3.

WARNING
Stay clear of the propeller and propeller shaft while running an engine on a flush adapter.

CAUTION
Use a flush device or other means to supply the engine with cooling water if running the engine with the boat out of the water. The seawater pump is quickly damaged if operated without adequate cooling water.

5. Connect the battery cables.

11

6. Start the engine and cycle the steering wheel through several turns lock to lock while checking the fluid level and for foam or bubbles in the reservoir. Immediately stop the engine if foam appears in the reservoir. Allow a few minutes for the foam to dissipate and then repeat Step 4. The bleeding procedure is complete when neither bubbles nor foam appear in the reservoir.

7. Install the fill cap.

Table 1 STEERING SYSTEM TORQUE SPECIFICATIONS

Fastener	in.-lb.	ft.-lb.	N•m
Control valve fitting	–	15-26	20-35
Pressure hose fitting at pump	177-204	–	20-23
Power steering pump mounting bolts	–	25	34
Reservoir stud bolt	–	25	34

Chapter Twelve

Remote Control

The remote control provides a means to control throttle, shifting and other engine operations from a location well beyond reach of the engine. It links the boat operator to the engine. There are numerous models and brands of remote controls, and the boat may be equipped with any of them. This chapter provides remote control operating instructions, shift/throttle cable replacement procedures and remote control disassembly/assembly instructions for the commonly used Teleflex/Morse MV2 panel-mount remote control. Contact a reputable marine dealership for parts and repair instructions for other brands and models of controls.

Use the general tightening specifications listed in Chapter One for remote control fasteners. Unless specified otherwise, apply a threadlocking compound to all remote control fasteners.

CAUTION
Always refer to the owner's manual for specific operating instructions of the remote control. Become familiar with all control functions before operating the engine.

Operation

This section describes remote control operation for the Teleflex/Morse MV2 remote control that is commonly used on inboard marine engines.

To operate the neutral throttle advancement, place the control handle in NEUTRAL. Then pull out on the neutral throttle button (A, **Figure 1**). The throttle can then be advanced without shifting the engine into gear. This feature allows easier starting and quicker engine warm-up. On models with electronic fuel injection (EFI), the throttle must be in idle for starting; however, the throttle can be advanced after starting for quicker warm-up. To return to normal operation, place the handle into NEUTRAL and push in on the neutral throttle button.

To shift the remote control into gear, make sure the control handle is in NEUTRAL and the neutral throttle button is disengaged (pushed in). Grasp the ball end of the control handle. Then with two fingers, pull up on the neutral lock pull (B, **Figure 1**). Carefully move the remote control handle toward the front (bow) of the boat for FORWARD or toward the rear (stern) of the boat for reverse. Release the neutral lock pull after moving the remote control enough to engage the desired gear.

To shift the remote control to NEUTRAL, simply move the control handle to NEUTRAL. It is not necessary to lift the neutral pull when shifting into NEUTRAL. The neutral lock should automatically engage when the control reaches NEUTRAL.

Refer to the owner's manual for neutral throttle operation if using a different brand or model of control.

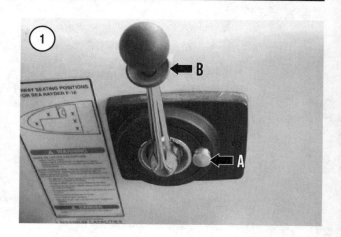

WARNING
A malfunction in the remote control can lead to a lack of shift and throttle control. Never operate the engine if any malfunction is noted with the remote control. Damage to property, serious bodily injury or death can result if the engine is operated without proper control. Check for proper remote control operation before operating the engine or after performing any service or repair.

Throttle/Shift Cable Removal and Installation

Replacement is required if the cables become hard to move or if excessive play occurs due to cable wear. Replace both the throttle and shift cables at the same time. The conditions that caused one cable to require replacement probably are present in the other cable. Mark the cables prior to removal to make sure that the cables are installed to the proper attaching points. To avoid confusion, remove and attach one cable at a time.

1. Disconnect the battery cables.

2. Remove the four screws (5, **Figure 2**) attaching the remote control to the boat structure.

3. Carefully guide the remote control assembly with cables attached out of the opening in the boat structure. If more cable slack is needed, disconnect the cables from the throttle and shift linkage on the engine as described in Chapter Five. Refer to *Throttle Cable Adjustment* and *Shift Cable Adjustment*. If the wiring does not provide enough slack to remove the control, disconnect the yellow/red neutral start switch leads from the key switch and instrument harness.

4. Identify the shift cable by the attachment to the shift arm (15, **Figure 2**) on the back of the control assembly.

5. Note which cable/pivot opening is used in the shift arm. The opening closest to the square shaft opening provides less shift cable movement than the opening farther from the shaft opening. Use the alternate opening only if

the shift cable adjustment procedure indicates a need for more or less cable movement.

6. Remove the cotter pin or locking clip (20, **Figure 2**) from the cable anchor/pivot (19). Then pull the cable anchor and shift cable out of the shift arm. If so equipped, loosen the jam nut on the threaded cable end and then count the number of turns while unthreading the cable anchor/pivot from the shift cable.

7. Note which two screw openings in the cable attaching plate (7, **Figure 2**) are used to secure the cable clamp (29, **Figure 2**).

8. Remove the screws (30, **Figure 2**) and then lift the cable clamp (29) and cable off the attaching plate (7). Note which groove in the cable is engaging the cable clamp. Most cables have two grooves. Lift the clamp off the cable.

9. Fit the cable clamp (29, **Figure 2**) into the correct groove in the cable. Refer to Step 8. Fit the cable and clamp onto the cable attaching plate (7, **Figure 2**). Align the screw opening in the cable clamp with the correct pair of screw openings in the attaching plate. Refer to Step 7. Apply Loctite 242 to the threads. Then install the two screws (30, **Figure 2**) into the cable clamp and attaching plate. Make sure the raised step in the clamp fits into the corresponding groove in the cable. Then securely tighten the clamp screws.

10. Thread the cable anchor/pivot onto the threaded end of the shift cable the number of turns noted in Step 6. The threaded section of the cable must pass completely through the anchor with enough threads extending past the anchor to secure the jam nut.

11. Fit the cotter pin/locking clip end of the cable anchor/pivot into the correct opening in the shift lever. Refer to Step 5. Rotate the cable anchor/pivot on the shift cable as needed to align the pivot with the opening in the shift arm. Make sure the threads on the shift cable extend past the anchor/pivot as described in Step 10. If the threads do

REMOTE CONTROL COMPONENTS
(TYPICAL TELEFLEX/MORSE MV2 CONTROL)

1. Control handle grip
2. Control handle assembly
3. Allen set screw
4. Neutral lock cam
5. Screw
6. Control module
7. Cable attaching plate
8. Lockwasher
9. Screw
10. Cotter pin or locking clip
11. Throttle arm
12. Cable anchor/pivot
13. Washer
14. Screw
15. Shift arm
16. Neutral start cam
17. Washer
18. Screw
19. Cable anchor/pivot
20. Cotter pin or locking clip
21. Washer
22. Nuts
23. Screws
24. Bracket
25. Washer
26. Screws
27. Bracket
28. Nut
29. Cable clamp
30. Screw
31. Pivot bracket
32. Screw
33. Cable clamp
34. Screw
35. Neutral start switch

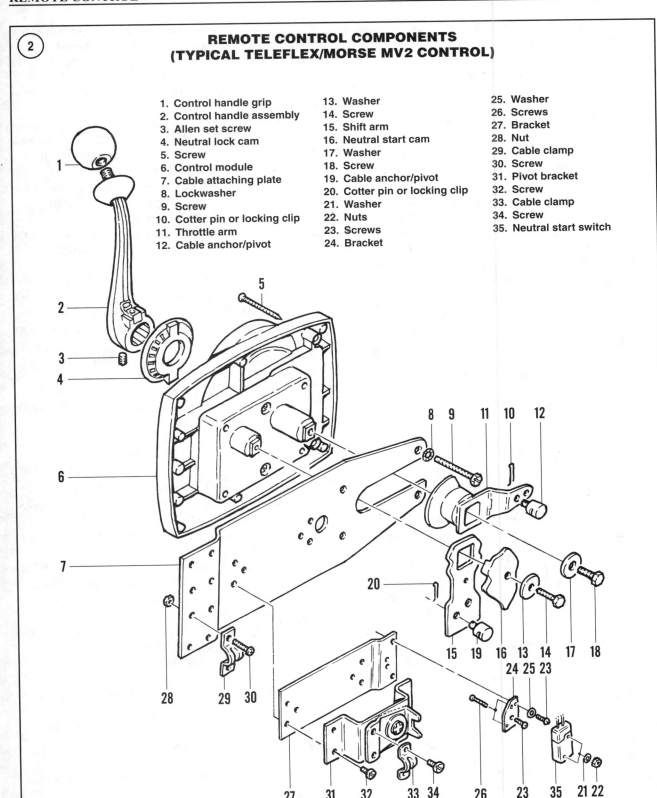

12

not extend far enough, use the alternate set of screw openings in the attaching plate. Refer to Step 9.

12. With the anchor/pivot in the shift arm opening, install the cotter pin or locking clip (20, **Figure 2**) into the small opening in the anchor/pivot. Tug on the anchor/pivot to verify a secure connection. If using a cotter pin, bend over both cotter pin prongs. Securely tighten the jam nut if so equipped.

13. Identify the throttle cable by the attachment onto the throttle arm (11, **Figure 2**) on the back of the control assembly.

14. Note which cable anchor/pivot opening is used in the throttle arm. The opening closest to the square shaft opening provides less throttle cable movement than the opening farther from the shaft opening. Use the alternate opening only if the throttle cable adjustment procedure indicates a need for more or less cable movement.

15. Remove the cotter pin or locking clip (10, **Figure 2**) from the cable anchor/pivot (12). Then pull the cable anchor/pivot and throttle cable out of the throttle arm. If so equipped, loosen the jam nut on the threaded cable end and then count the number of turns while unthreading the cable anchor/pivot from the throttle cable.

16. Note which groove in the cable fits into the slot in the pivot bracket (31, **Figure 2**). Most cables have two grooves.

17. Remove the screws (34, **Figure 2**) and then lift the cable clamp (33) off the pivot bracket (31). Pull the cable out of the slot in the pivot bracket.

18. Align the correct groove in the replacement cable (Step 16) with the slot in the cable pivot bracket (31, **Figure 2**). Guide the cable groove into the slot. Hold the cable in position and then fit the cable clamp (33, **Figure 2**) onto the cable and pivot bracket. Apply Loctite 242 to the threads. Then install the two screws (34, **Figure 2**) into the cable clamp and pivot bracket. Make sure the raised step in the clamp fits into the corresponding groove in the cable anchor. Then securely tighten the clamp screws.

19. Thread the cable anchor/pivot (12, **Figure 2**) onto the threaded end of the throttle cable the number of turns noted in Step 15. The threaded section of the cable must pass completely through the anchor with enough threads extending past the anchor to secure the jam nut.

20. Fit the cotter pin/locking clip end of the cable anchor/pivot into the selected opening in the throttle lever. Refer to Step 14. Rotate the cable anchor/pivot on the shift cable as needed to align the pivot with the opening in the shift arm. Make sure the threads on the shift cable extend past the anchor/pivot as described in Step 19. If the threads do not extend far enough, use the alternate groove in the throttle cable anchor. Refer to Step 16.

21. With the anchor/pivot in the shift arm opening, install the cotter pin or locking clip (10, **Figure 2**) into the small opening in the anchor pivot. Tug on the anchor/pivot to verify a secure connection. If using a cotter pin, bend over both cotter pin prongs. Securely tighten the jam nut if so equipped.

22. Carefully guide the control and cables into the opening in the boat structure. Work carefully to avoid pinching the yellow/red neutral start switch wires between the remote control and the boat structure.

23. Seat the remote control onto the boat structure. Thread the four screws (5, **Figure 2**) into the remote control and boat structure. Securely tighten the screws.

24. If disconnected, reconnect the yellow/red neutral start switch wires to the key switch and instrument harness leads.

25. Route the neutral start switch wiring to prevent contact with any moving remote control components. Secure the wiring with plastic locking clamps as needed.

26. If disconnected, reconnect the throttle and shift cables to the engine.

27. Adjust the shift and throttle cables as described in Chapter Five.

28. Connect the battery cables.

29. Check for proper shift and throttle operation before operating the engine.

Remote Control Removal

1. Disconnect the battery cables.

2. Remove the four screws (5, **Figure 2**) attaching the remote control to the boat structure.

3. Carefully guide the remote control assembly with cables attached out of the opening in the boat structure. If more cable slack is needed, disconnect the cables from the shift and throttle linkage on the engine as described in Chapter Five. Refer to *Throttle Cable Adjustment* and *Shift Cable Adjustment*.

4. Disconnect the yellow/red neutral start switch leads from the key switch and instrument harness.

5. Remove the shift and throttle cables as described in this chapter.

6. Disassemble the remote control to replace faulty components as described in this chapter.

Remote Control Installation

1. Assemble the remote control as described in this chapter.

2. Install the shift and throttle cables as described in this chapter.

3. Carefully guide the control and cables into the opening in the boat structure. Work carefully to avoid pinching the yellow/red neutral start switch wires between the remote control and the boat structure.

4. Seat the remote control onto the boat structure. Thread the four screws (5, **Figure 2**) into the remote control and boat structure. Securely tighten the screws.

5. Reconnect the yellow/red neutral start switch wires to the key switch and instrument harness leads.

6. Route the neutral start switch wiring to prevent contact with any moving remote control components. Secure the wiring with plastic locking clamps as needed.

7. If disconnected, reconnect the shift and throttle cables to the engine.

8. Adjust the shift and throttle cables as described in Chapter Five.

9. Connect the battery cables.

10. Check for proper shift and throttle operation before operating the engine.

Remote Control Disassembly and Assembly

If complete disassembly is not required to access the faulty component(s), perform the disassembly until the desired component is accessible. Reverse the disassembly steps to assemble the remote control.

To save a great deal of time and to ensure proper assembly, make notes, marks or drawings prior to removing any component from the remote control. Improper assembly can cause internal binding, reversed cable movement or improper control operation.

Clean all components, except the neutral start switch, in a suitable solvent. Use compressed air to blow debris from the components. Inspect all components for damage or wear. Replace any defective components. Apply a good quality water-resistant grease to all pivot points or sliding surfaces upon assembly. Test the neutral start switch as described in Chapter Two before installing the switch. Apply Loctite 242 to the threads of all fasteners during the assembly procedure.

Refer to **Figure 2** for this procedure.

1. Disconnect the battery cables.

2. Remove the remote control as described in this chapter.

3. Remove the shift and throttle cables from the remote control as described in this chapter.

4. Place the remote control on a clean work surface.

5. Make marks on the control module (6, **Figure 2**) that align with the sides of the control handle. This is necessary to make sure the handle is in the same neutral position after assembly.

6. Loosen the Allen setscrew (3, **Figure 2**). Then carefully pull the control handle off the splined shaft of the control module.

7. Make match marks on the neutral lock cam (4, **Figure 2**) and the control module. This is necessary to make sure the locking mechanism operates only with the control in NEUTRAL. Carefully pull the cam off the control module.

8. Remove the screw (14, **Figure 2**) and washer (13) and then pull the throttle arm (11) off the control module shaft.

9. Note the orientation of the shift arm (15, **Figure 2**) relative to the top of the control module. On most standard applications with the remote control mounted on the starboard side of the boat, the control arm is installed with the cable anchor/pivot opening facing downward. On applications with the remote control mounted on the port side of the boat or applications requiring reversed shift cable movement, the anchor/pivot opening faces upward. Remove the screw (18, **Figure 2**) and washer (17) and then pull the shift arm (15) off the control module shaft.

10. Remove the neutral start cam (16, **Figure 2**) from the shift arm.

11. Remove the screws (23, **Figure 2**) and washer (25) and then lift the neutral start switch (35) and the switch mounting bracket (24) from the cable bracket (27).

12. Remove the nuts (22, **Figure 2**) and washers (21). Then pull the neutral start switch off the switch bracket. Remove the screw (26, **Figure 2**) from the bracket.

13. Remove the screws (32, **Figure 2**) that secure the cable pivot bracket (31) and cable mounting bracket (27) to the cable attaching plate (7). Pull both brackets off the attaching plate.

14. Remove the screws (9, **Figure 2**) and washers (8). Then lift the cable attaching plate off the control module.

15. Unthread the control handle grip (1, **Figure 2**) from the control handle (2).

16. Inspect all components for excessive wear, corrosion damage or other defects. Replace the control module if it was malfunctioning and no fault is found with any of the removed components.

17. Thread the control handle grip onto the control handle threads and securely tighten.

18. Fit the cable attaching plate (7, **Figure 2**) onto the control module (6). Make sure the shafts extending from the control module pass through the opening and slot in the plate. Align the openings and then thread the screws (9, **Figure 2**) with washers (8) into the plate and control module. Securely tighten the screws.

19. Fit the neutral start switch (35, **Figure 2**) onto the switch bracket (24). Align the screw openings in the switch and bracket and then insert the screws (26, **Figure 2**) through the switch bracket and switch. Install the wash-

12

ers (21, **Figure 2**) and then thread the nuts (22) onto the screws. Hold the screws and securely tighten the nuts.

20. Fit the cable bracket (27, **Figure 2**) onto the cable attaching plate with the offset end toward the shafts extending through the cable attaching plate. The offset end must face away from the attaching plate.

21. Fit the cable pivot bracket (31, **Figure 2**) onto the cable bracket with the cable slot facing toward the shafts extending through the cable attaching plate.

22. Align the screw openings in the cable pivot bracket, cable bracket and cable attaching plate. Thread the screws (32, **Figure 2**) into the openings and securely tighten.

23. Fit the neutral start switch and bracket assembly onto the cable bracket. Install the screws (23, **Figure 2**) with the washers (25) into the switch bracket and cable bracket. Securely tighten the screws.

24. Align the square opening in the arm with the square boss on the shaft. Then fit the shift arm (15, **Figure 2**) onto the shaft closest to the pivot bracket. If the control module was replaced, make sure the replacement is in NEUTRAL. Make sure the shift arm is positioned as noted prior to disassembly. Refer to Step 9.

25. Install the neutral start cam (16, **Figure 2**) onto the shift arm. Make sure the roller on the end of the switch lever contacts the cam surface. Then install the screw (18, **Figure 2**) with the washer (17) into the shift arm. Securely tighten the screw.

26. Align the square opening in the arm with the square boss on the shaft. Then fit the throttle arm (11, **Figure 2**) onto the shaft extending from the plate. Make sure the arm is positioned with the cable anchor/pivot end extending

forward or away from the shafts. If the control module was replaced, make sure the replacement is in NEUTRAL.

27. Thread the screw (14, **Figure 2**) with the washer (13) into the arm and shaft. Securely tighten the screw.

28. Install the neutral lock cam (4, **Figure 2**) onto the control module. Make sure the cam fits into the depressions in the module that allow alignment of the marks made prior to removal. Refer to Step 7.

29. Install the control handle onto the module as follows:

   a. Without dislodging the lock cam, fit the control handle onto the splined shaft of the module. Make sure the sides of the handle align with the marks on the module made prior to removal. Refer to Step 5.

   b. Lift the neutral lock pull (B, **Figure 1**). Then seat the control handle onto the splined shaft.

   c. Hold the handle firmly seated onto the splined shaft and then securely tighten the Allen setscrew (3, **Figure 2**).

30. Install the shift and throttle cables as described in this chapter.

31. Install the remote control as described in this chapter.

32. Adjust the shift and throttle cables as described in Chapter Five.

33. Connect the battery cables.

34. Check the neutral start switch operation as described in Chapter Two.

35. Check for proper shift and throttle operation before operating the engine. Do *not* operate the engine if any control system malfunction is evident.

Index

13

W

Wiring Diagrams

CHARGING SYSTEM WITH DASH-MOUNTED AMMETER
(EARLIER BIA WIRE COLORS)

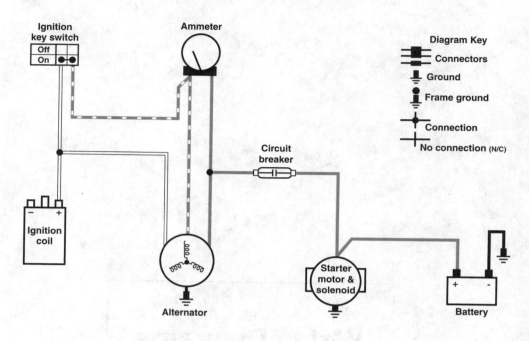

CHARGING SYSTEM WITH DASH-MOUNTED AMMETER
(LATER BIA WIRE COLORS)

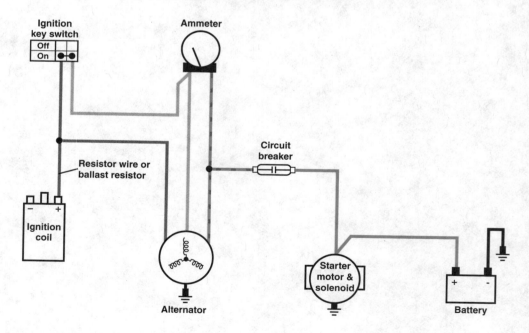

CHARGING SYSTEM WITH DASH-MOUNTED VOLTMETER

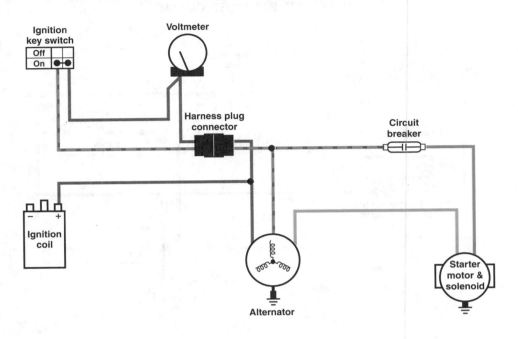

STARTING SYSTEM WITH SWITCH-TYPE SLAVE SOLENOID

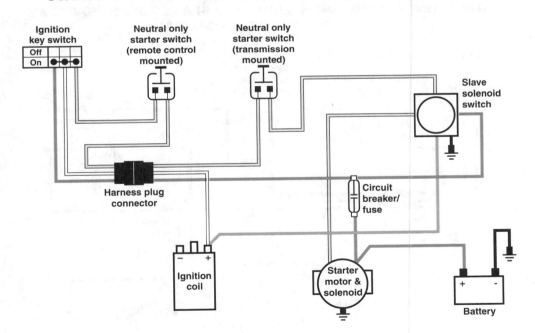

14

STARTING SYSTEM WITH STANDARD SLAVE SOLENOID RELAY
(EARLIER BIA WIRE COLORS)

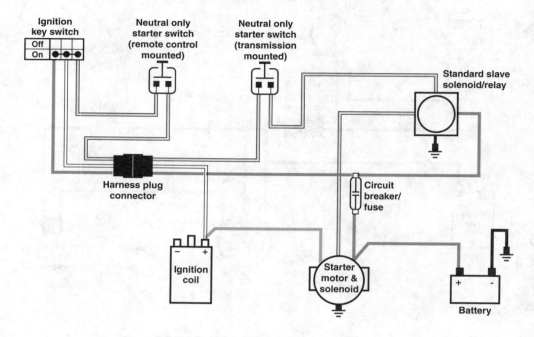

STARTING SYSTEM WITH STANDARD SLAVE SOLENOID RELAY
(LATER BIA WIRE COLORS)

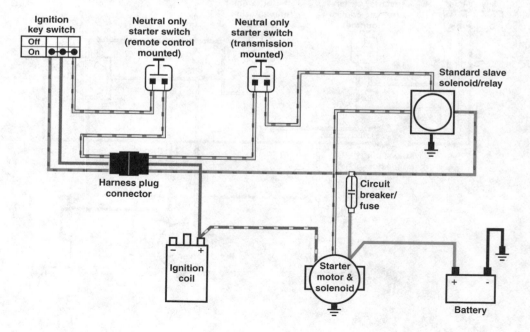

STANDARD BREAKER-POINT IGNITION SYSTEM
(EARLIER BIA WIRE COLORS)

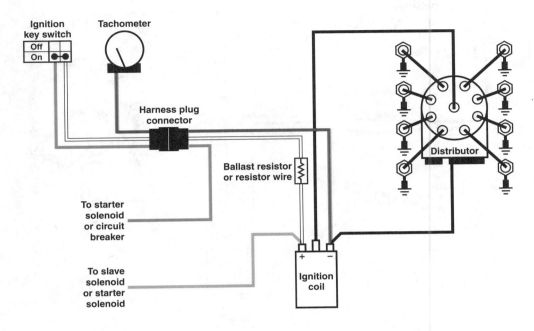

STANDARD BREAKER-POINT IGNITION SYSTEM
(LATER BIA WIRE COLORS)

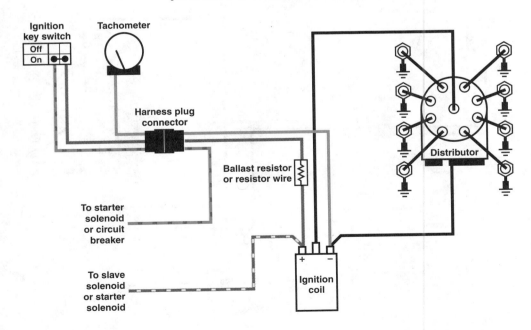

14

PRESTOLITE BID IGNITION SYSTEM (CARBURETOR-EQUIPPED MODELS)

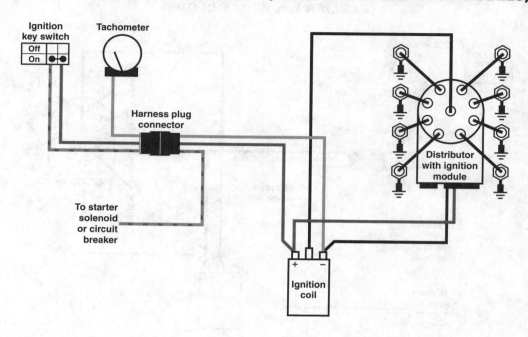

DELCO EST IGNITION SYSTEM (CARBURETOR-EQUIPPED MODELS)

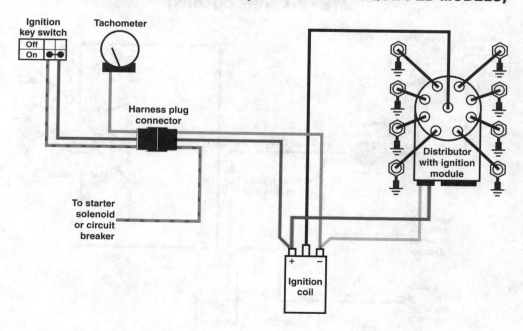

DELCO EST IGNITION SYSTEM (EFI, EXCEPT LT-1 ENGINE)

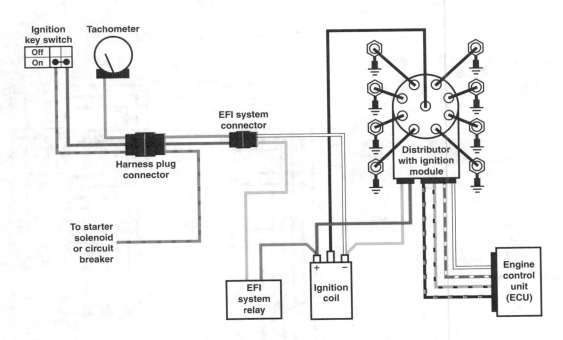

ELECTRONIC IGNITION (EI) SYSTEM
(DISTRIBUTORLESS IGNITION SYSTEM, LT-1 ENGINE)

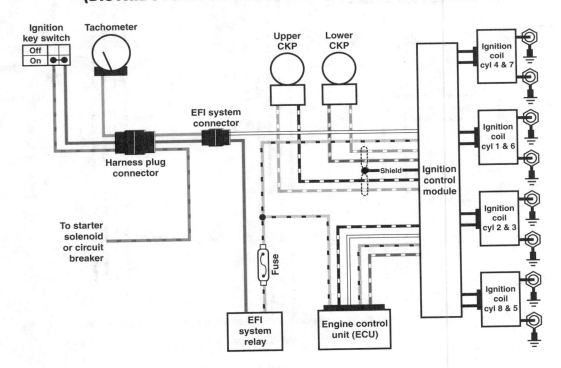

14

DISTRIBUTORLESS IGNITION SYSTEM (8.1L MODELS)

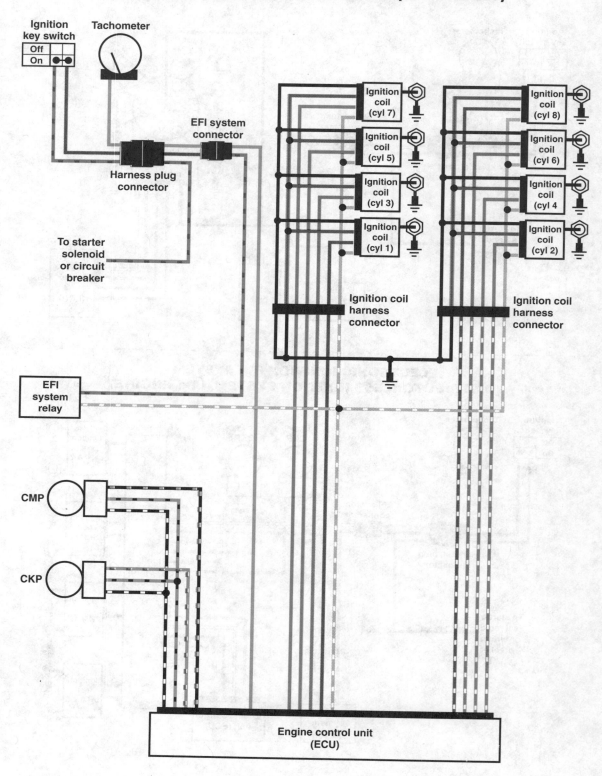

TBI WITH MEFI 1 OR MEFI 2 ECU

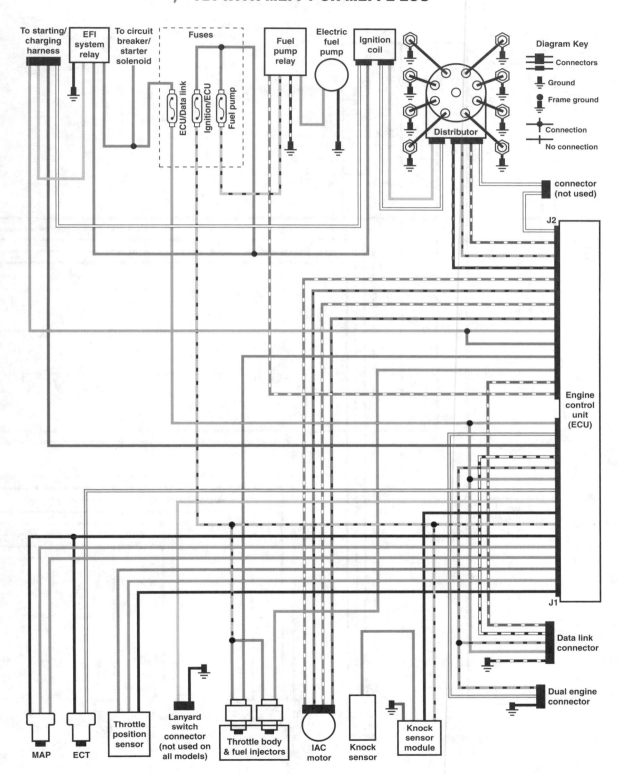

14

MPI WITH MEFI 1 OR MEFI 2 ECU

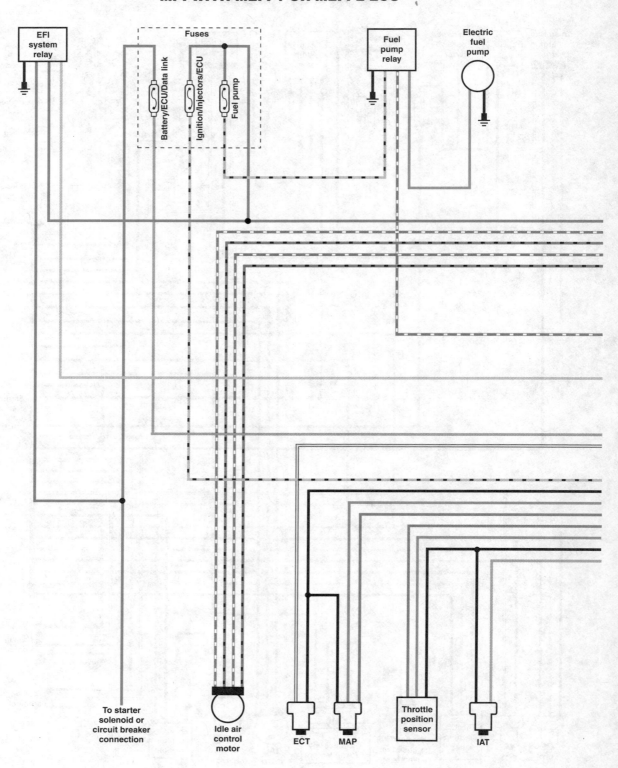

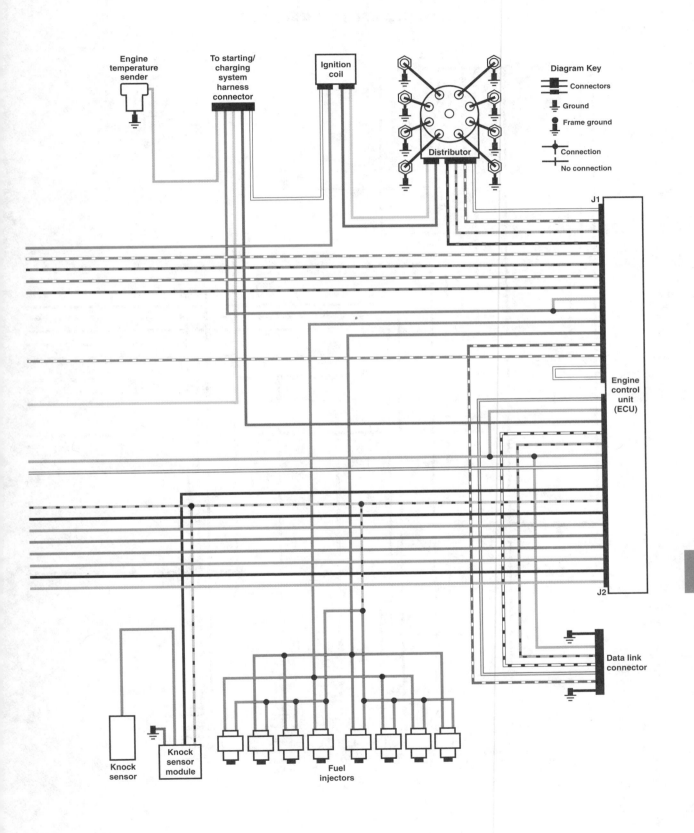

Engine temperature sender

To starting/ charging system harness connector

Ignition coil

Distributor

Diagram Key

Connectors

Ground

Frame ground

Connection

No connection

J1

Engine control unit (ECU)

J2

Data link connector

Knock sensor

Knock sensor module

Fuel injectors

14

TBI WITH MEFI 3 OR MEFI 4 ECU

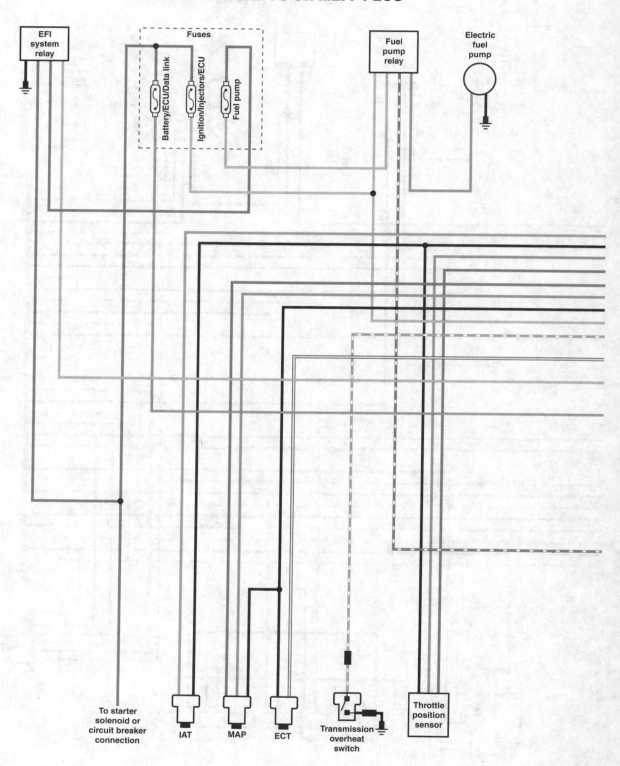

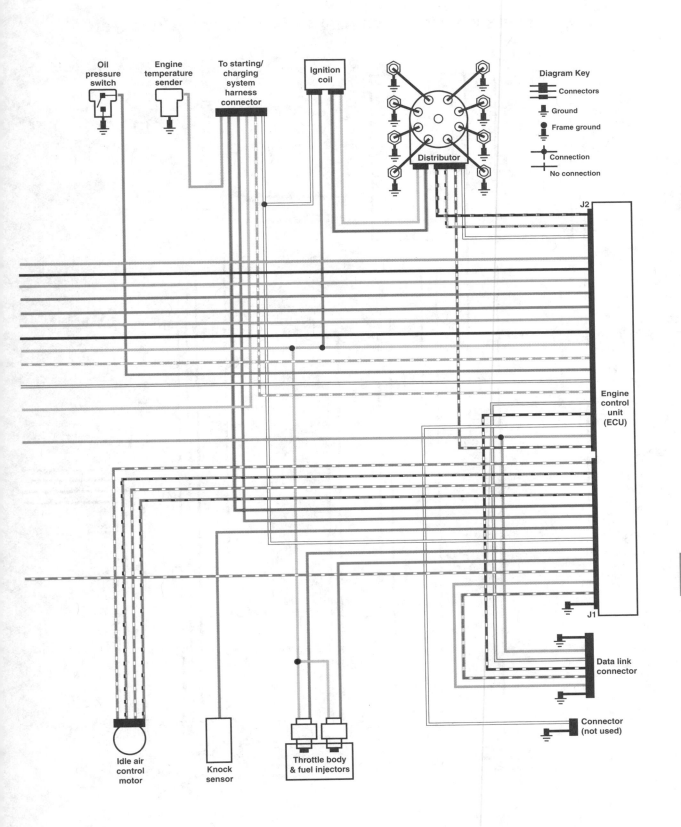

MPI MODELS WITH MEFI 3 OR MEFI 4 ECU (EXCEPT 8.1L MODELS)

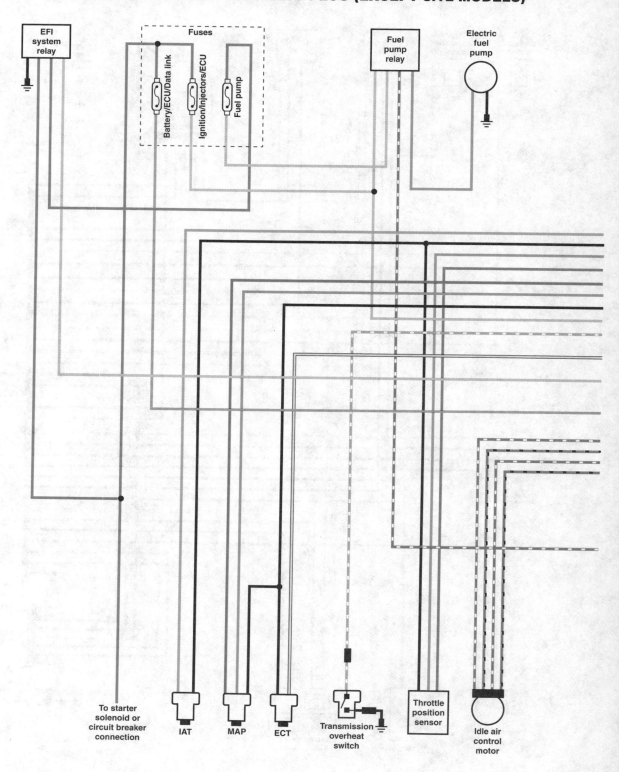

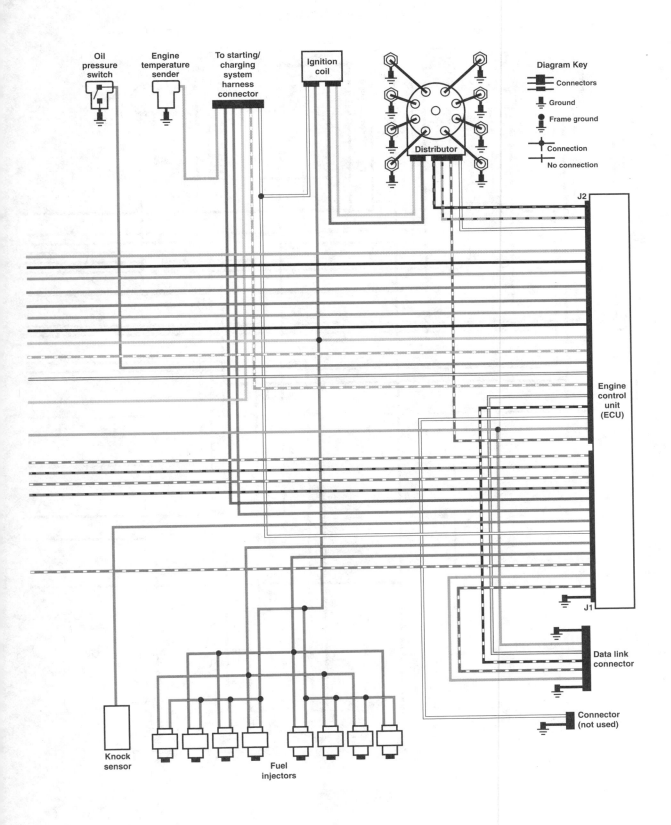

MPI 8.1L MODELS

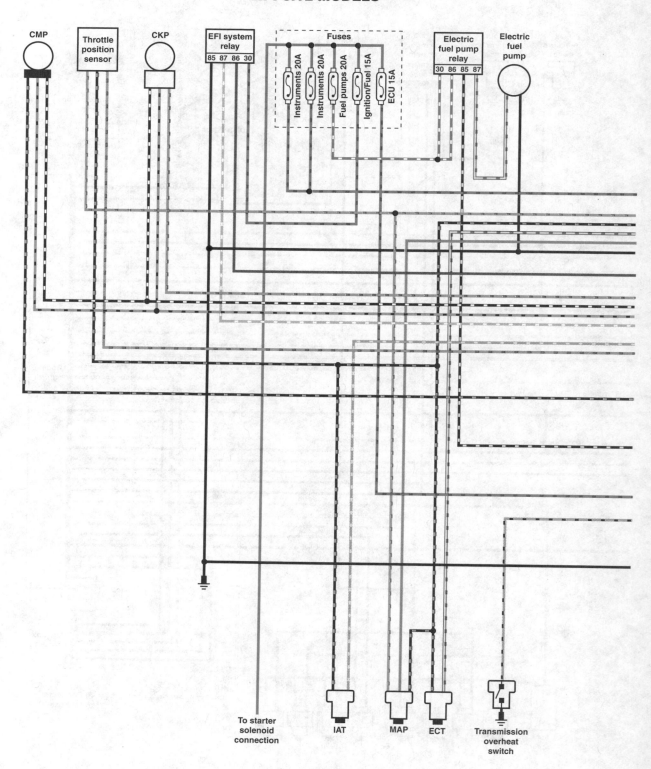

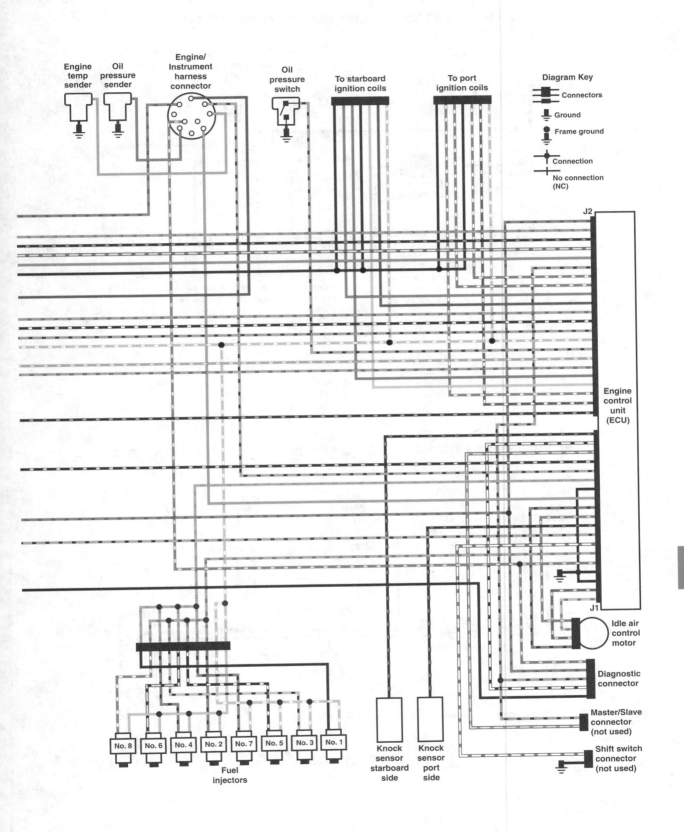

14

WARNING SYSTEM (CARBURETOR-EQUIPPED MODELS)

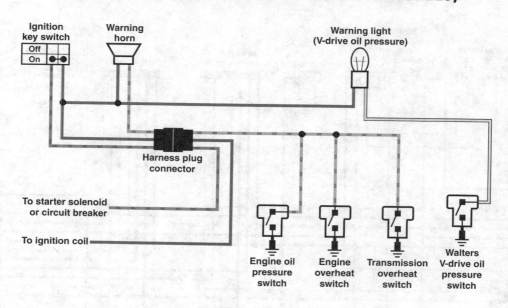

ELECTRIC FUEL PUMP CIRCUIT (CARBURETOR-EQUIPPED MODELS)

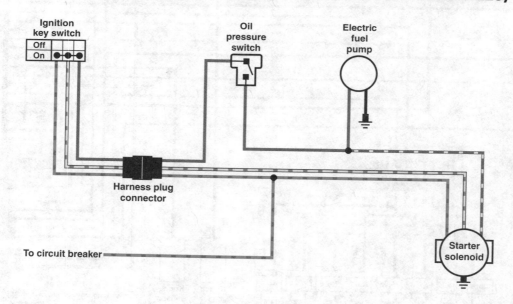

WARNING SYSTEM (EFI MODELS)

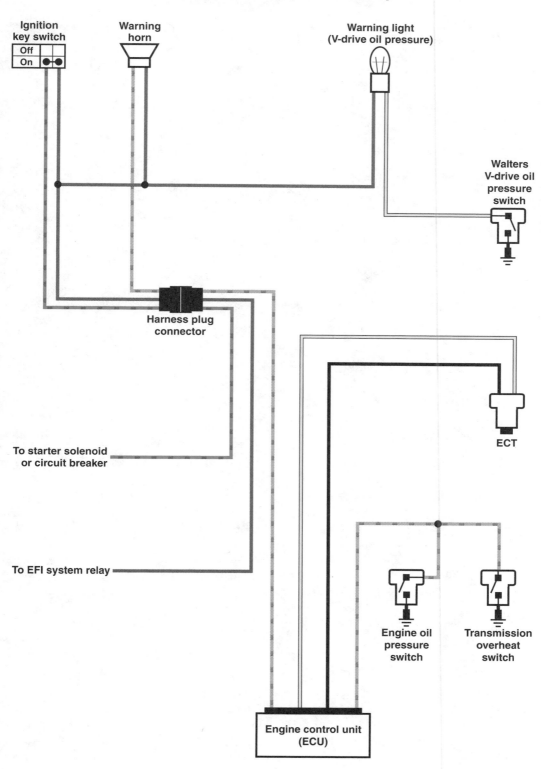

Ignition key switch

Off		
On	●	●

Warning horn

Warning light (V-drive oil pressure)

Walters V-drive oil pressure switch

Harness plug connector

ECT

To starter solenoid or circuit breaker

To EFI system relay

Engine oil pressure switch

Transmission overheat switch

Engine control unit (ECU)

14

NOTES

MAINTENANCE LOG

Date	Engine Hours	Type of Service